THE WORLD'S MOST EXPENSIVE WATCHES

ARIEL ADAMS

ACC ART BOOKS

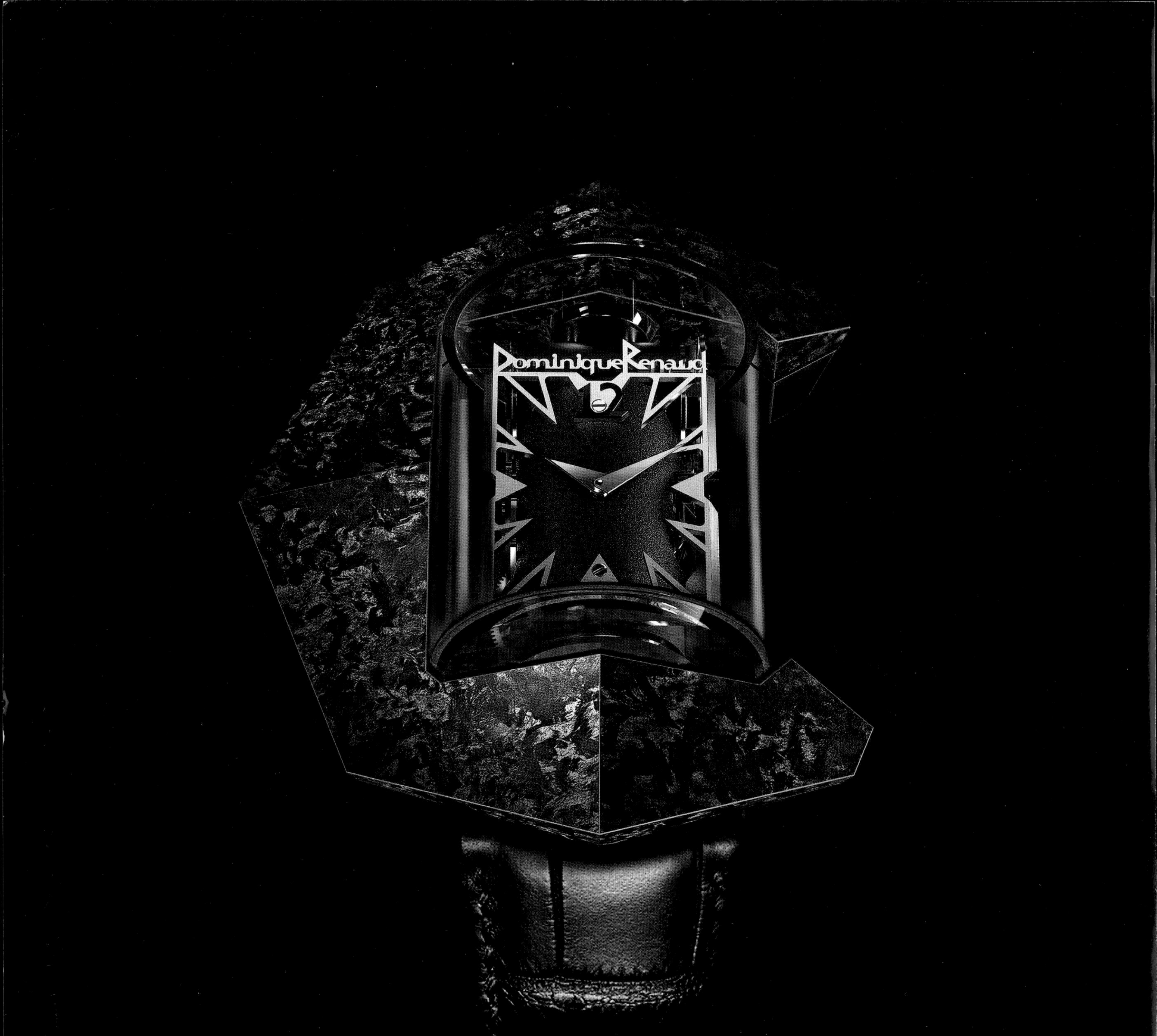
DominiqueRenaud
12

In dedication of my father Richard Adams (1945 – 2014)
who was the biggest fan and friend a son could ever hope for.

He was proud and took interest in my fascination for watches and encouraged
above all else a passion for understanding and learning about the world.

This book was made to be good enough for him.

CONTENTS

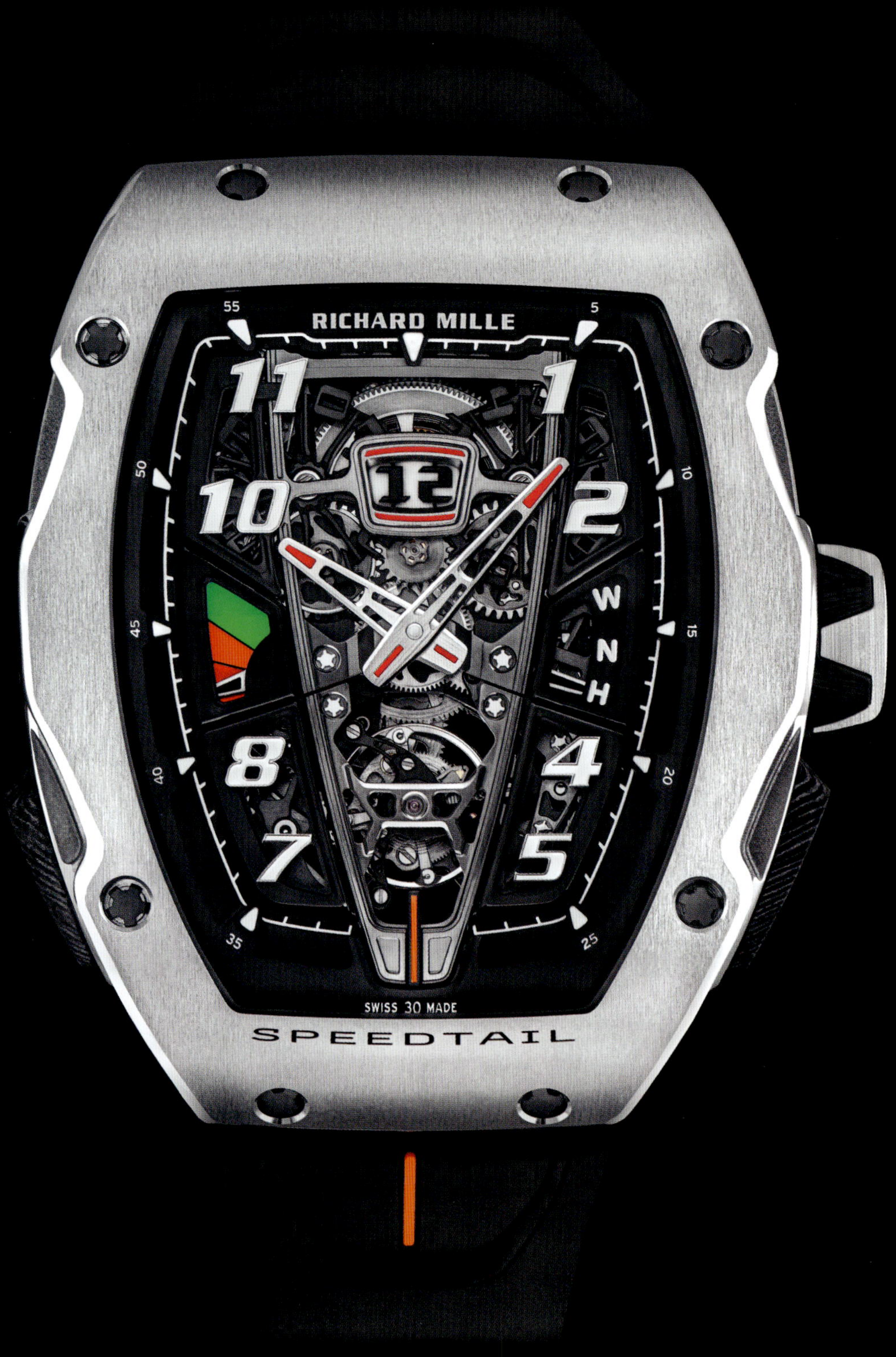
RICHARD MILLE
SWISS 30 MADE
SPEEDTAIL

FOREWORD
JEAN-CLAUDE BIVER

In my business, among the many ways to consider an object, I have always favoured the analysis of the quality of the workmanship. It is, of course, not the only criteria to take into consideration but it is certainly, in my opinion and the way of the watch industry in general, one of the main and most important criteria.

A second criterion, which also plays an important role, is the material used to make the product. It goes without saying that the cost of a watch will vary depending on whether a bezel is set with diamonds or not. The same watch in steel will naturally cost less than the one in 18-karat gold. A third criterion, that is quite often underestimated, is the quantity produced. In the industrial process, the more you produce, the more the production costs go down.

While there are many criteria to take into consideration, by looking at just these three elements, it already becomes easier to assess if a product is expensive or not. However, for me, the most important factor is the first one, the workmanship involved, for which I have the deepest understanding and respect. The miracles created by the hands of our master watchmakers can only be described as 'invisible visibility'. In other words, they will not only finish, decorate and polish what people can see, but they also give equal attention and devotion to every detail that is not visible to our eyes.

History tells us that this is essential if one wants to give birth to the 'soul of a watch', as well as to prepare it for 'eternity', by which I mean that each piece is for life. That is the unmatched value of such a masterpiece, considering that eternity has no competition.

Just consider that to create a single black polished-and-angled screw, the watchmaker will spend at least one hour. Given that in a standard movement you will find 100 screws, this adds up to 100 additional hours of work for the screws alone – that nobody will ever see! This is the inestimable price that is paid in order to give birth to a watch's soul.

For this reason alone, with my passion and dedication to the business, I can only analyse the price of a masterpiece through its 'invisible visibility', because eternity and soul have no competitors, and are therefore priceless.

THE WORLD'S MOST EXPENSIVE WATCHES: INTRODUCTION

ARIEL ADAMS

In 2014, when *The World's Most Expensive Watches* was originally released, I wrote the book to help showcase the typically hidden world of extremely high-end wristwatches priced at $200,000 and over. Like rare exotic birds, many of these watches are elusive rarities that few people ever actually see with their own eyes. Nevertheless, once in a while, lucky collectors or wealthy buyers get to experience these finely made objects in reality.

In 2014, the logic behind making or owning an extremely high-end luxury wristwatch was a perplexing value proposition to the vast majority of people. Since the first edition of this book, the visibility of expensive wristwatches in both pop culture and the mainstream media (for better or worse) has, surprisingly, increased. Many casual investors now consider wristwatches to be among a litany of alternative financial asset classes, and the idea that successful, flashy people wear high-end watches is a popular concept with youth culture. In all, despite near-cataclysmic challenges since the start of the pandemic in 2019, the luxury watch industry has again beat the odds to be well-positioned as a market power.

Reasons for the popularity of very high-end watches can often intersect with politically charged issues. While the watches themselves might be innocent, their famous wearers aren't always successful for morally-sound exploits. To some people (and of course depending on the context), the idea of brazenly showing off a luxury watch corresponds with the undesirable effects of adjacent cronyism, corruption and inequality. Wristwatches are not alone. On occasion, publicity-interested segments of society's elite have been known to openly compete with one another by demonstrating who among them owns the most exclusive of otherwise exclusive items. In this respect, watches are among cars, real estate, wine, clothing, jewellery, and just about any other expensive item you can think of. All these things have probably reached an oversaturation point with middle-range consumer segments that cannot foreseeably afford most of the products dangled in front of them.

This book is decidedly not about things the middle class or even most rich classes can afford. For what it's worth, watchmakers aren't trying to make their timepieces any more expensive than they need to be. The high cost of engineering and industrialisation development, plus ultra-low production numbers, means that much of the high-end wristwatch industry is a demonstration in the opposite of an economy of scale. Those who purchase such watches do so as true patrons of the arts. Some buyers may claim they are buying for value, but most end up admitting they are buying for a far more cherished reason: beauty. The resulting wisdom in that generalisation is the suggestion that high-end watches are purchased not because they serve some utilitarian purpose in life (though the heritage of wristwatches is very much about functional, purposeful products), but rather they are sought-after for the emotions they evoke when they are worn.

Consumer envy among those who regrettably cannot obtain these fancy accessories, is perhaps a small price to pay for a thriving luxury watch industry that today dazzles the minds of consumers, just as it has for many generations. Mechanical watches continue to serve as remarkably practical timekeepers in a world dominated by connected digital devices. In fact, the world's most popular modern smartwatches are still heavily inspired by the world of traditional watches in their look and feel: with each new generation of smartwatch released, their design and character feel closer to that of traditional watches, not further away from the classics.

The expressive and status-signalling value of a smartwatch is no match for pretty much all the products in this book. Most of the items in *The World's Most Expensive Watches* are designed to impress and evoke awe, as well as to delight and sooth. This is art and emotion masquerading as a tool to measure our trajectory throughout the day. Many traditional watch lovers are opting to wear smartwatches during working and activity hours, while choosing to wear a traditional watch during leisure and social hours. Contrary to the fears of some reactionary managers in the traditional watch industry, classic watches and smartwatches can coexist and brands do not need to fear usurpation from the now market-dominant junior smartwatch industry. New and heritage industries in the wristwatch space can both enjoy market interest – and probably tend to feed off one another more than they disrupt one another. With that said, competition at even the highest levels of the mechanical watch industry is fierce. For the most part, people who survey today's product landscape see a market full of exceptional products. What sways consumers to trust their money with one brand versus another comes down to difficult-to-measure, non-tangible factors, such as how it feels to shop at a brand or whether or not their friends are familiar with it. Therefore, the most value a high-end watch brand can have today is wide general-public awareness. It is no longer enough to merely make good watches.

The World's Most Expensive Watches opens with a series of chapters where I explain why many of these watches cost what they do. While there are a few notable auction lot results included in these pages, the vast majority of price tags given to these wristwatches are retail prices. With prices into the millions of dollars each, the goal of these chapters is to explain the sources of values – and why particular forms of rarity or craftsmanship are desirable. Often high prices are not a result of mere material costs, but rather a calculation of professional human working hours all dedicated to the task.

Having said all that, more people now than ever are accustomed to the notion that luxury wristwatches can come with extremely high prices, some with a price tag of more than $200,000. An adjacent question I have asked myself is whether or not monetary inflation has prompted a moving of the book's target – perhaps to an opening price of $235,000 or so. I decided against it. It turns out that while inflation has hit the watch industry, so has increased competition. It was not a particular challenge therefore to update *The World's Most Expensive Watches* with products that have become commercially released since the publication of the first edition. Volume 2 has around 50% more watches than the original book and, like the original, it will also be published in a variety of languages. This is not surprising given that a fondness for high-end watches is common among sophisticated members of all societies – making this hobby among the few truly cross-cultural intellectual and pleasure pursuits.

So, have watches costing $200,000 and up, that have been released since 2014, changed the game technically or with regards to their design? Indeed, there have been a number of new trends that have emerged over the last several years which demonstrate that the luxury maisons and most brilliant watchmakers have novel concepts on their minds. Size is important in new watches again, with smaller, lighter, and thinner watches being a new area of demand alongside larger and heavier watches. Not only are lighter watches more comfortable to wear, but they are also more suitable for daily life and activities. The shift in popularity from heavy, showy and complicated watches to lightweight, lean and legible watches is, in reality, a reflection on how many people are wearing luxury watches. It was once believed that people wearing ultra-luxury wristwatches would be in formal attire and in environments where they could show off precious stones. Today, even the most expensive luxury watches are expected to be comfortable and attractive enough to jet-set in, exercise in, shop in and socialise in. While there will always be a place for delicate spectacle watches, the most popular status watches today are those which can be conveniently worn on a daily basis.

Synthetic sapphire crystal has proven to be the most popular contemporary material in today's most expensive watches. Once a material used as mere circular sheets over watch dials, now entire cases are made of the hard stuff using sophisticated computer-controlled milling techniques with diamond-tipped cutting tools. Sapphire crystal can be made to be transparent or in a host of colour shades and opacities – a variety of which can be found in this book.

The current popularity of luxury watches has made purchasing many of these products as arduous as being able to afford them in the first place. At the time of writing, a number of small-production watchmakers have order books full for the next several years. Prices for pre-owned pieces are sometimes higher than the original retail price, and at times the market value of rarer lower-priced watches is higher than that of less-rare costlier watches. Tracking the economics around the watch industry can be dizzying, but it's clear that a lot of hard-earned money is going to wards the production and purchase of these treasures.

As always, it is my enduring desire to avoid the world of shameless glitz in favour of true artistry and good taste. Effort is expensive, but in a world where luxury dollars need to be spent somewhere, I believe it most prudent for me to celebrate those products with the most inherent value. It would be impossible for any one book to take into account all the watches priced at $200,000 and above, but it is my experienced belief that this book is the best possible variety that faithfully introduces you to the best of breed items when it comes to today's most expensive watches.

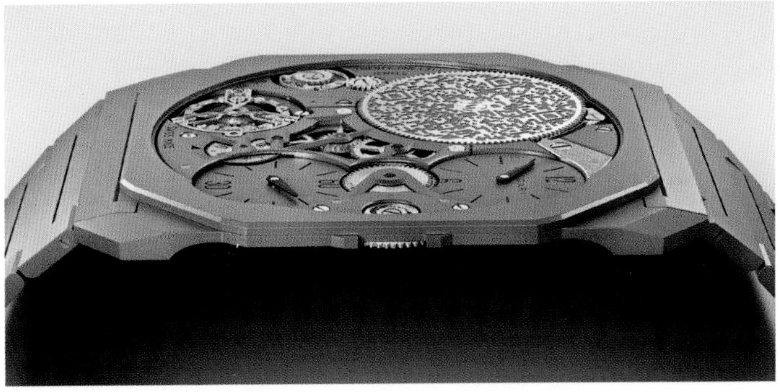

Bulgari – Octo Finissimo Ultra

EXPENSIVE WATCHES EXPLAINED: COMPLICATIONS & MECHANICAL FEATURES

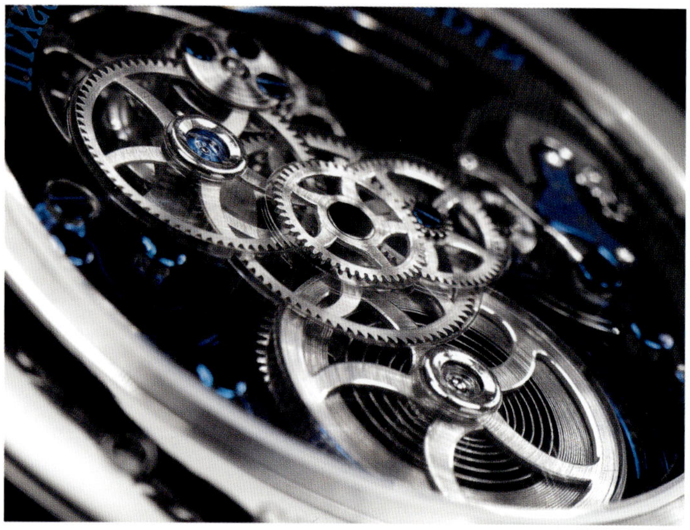

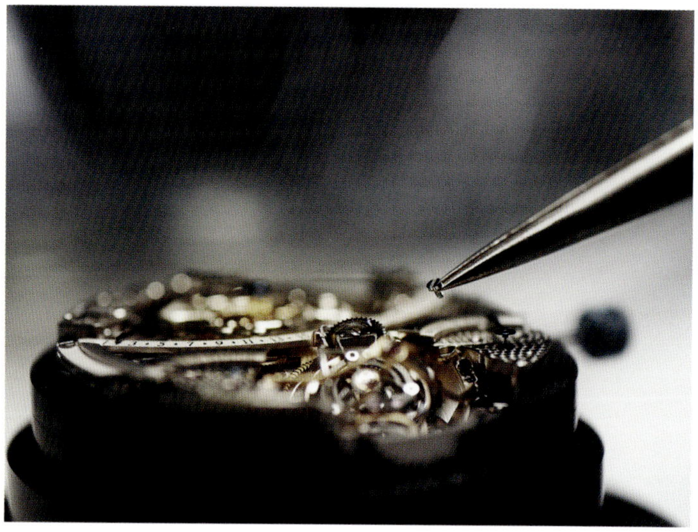

Most of the value in a watch is often said or perceived to be in the movement. "Movement" is the term given to the mechanical engine inside the case that is responsible for its operation. The watches in this book each have a mechanical movement, which means that they are powered by a spring, and have no electronic, components. Compared to mechanical movements, electronic ones are much more common these days and happen to have a lot of important benefits over mechanical movements – such as accuracy. Nevertheless, connoisseurs prefer mechanical watches, which more or less exclusively populate luxury men's timepieces. This fact may seem confusing at first but begins to make sense once you've explored the reasons more intently.

Mechanical movements are visually appealing, and they represent mechanisms that one can appreciate with one's own eyes. Electronic watches are mass produced and employ technology that can only be appreciated in theory, given the microscopic nature of electricity. It is also a fact that even inexpensive mechanical movements are often assembled – at least in part – by hand. A hallmark of most luxury items is a large degree of human attention. The movements in most luxury timepieces are to a great extent assembled and decorated by hand. Some of them even contain components that are produced by hand.

It is important to understand the time required to build a mechanical movement. Luxury is also about effort, and a complicated mechanical movement can sometimes take up to a year to produce. Simple movements indicate just the time, but there are also some highly complex movements that only indicate the hours and minutes. Complexity is a key factor in the value of a movement, and the features or indicators a mechanical watch has are referred to as "complications."

The more complications a watch has, the more difficult it is to design, produce, and assemble. It is actually rare for "new" complications to show up in timepieces. In fact, most watch technology was developed over 100 years ago, if not much longer. Many of today's complex, exclusive timepieces simple reinterpret past inventions, though often they do so by the miniaturisation of mechanisms that already existed in larger forms, such as in clocks or pocket watches. An interesting modern example is Jaquet Droz's The Charming Bird with a small singing automaton reduced in size from items built in the 18th century.

Movement of Ulysse Nardin – Royal Blue Tourbillon

Assembly of a Jaeger-LeCoultre movement

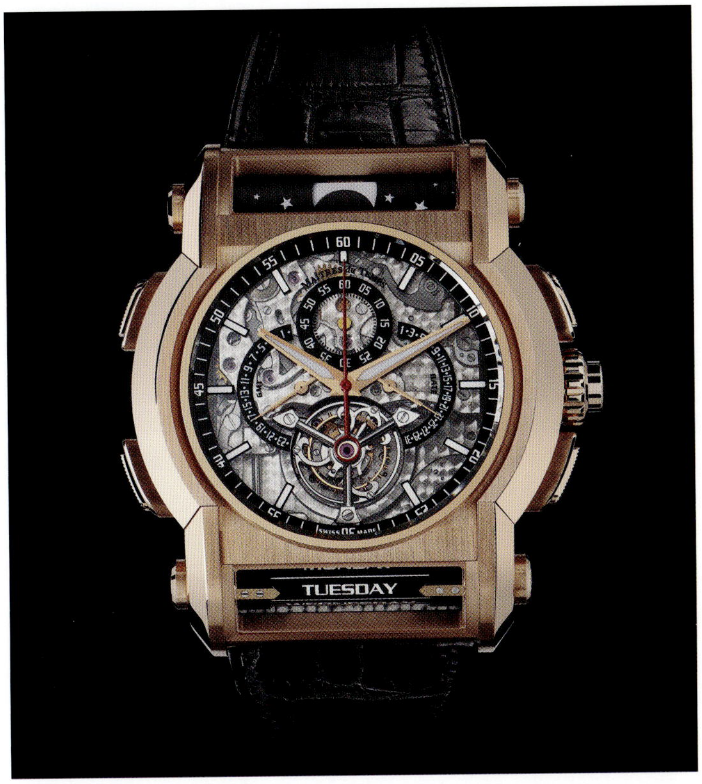

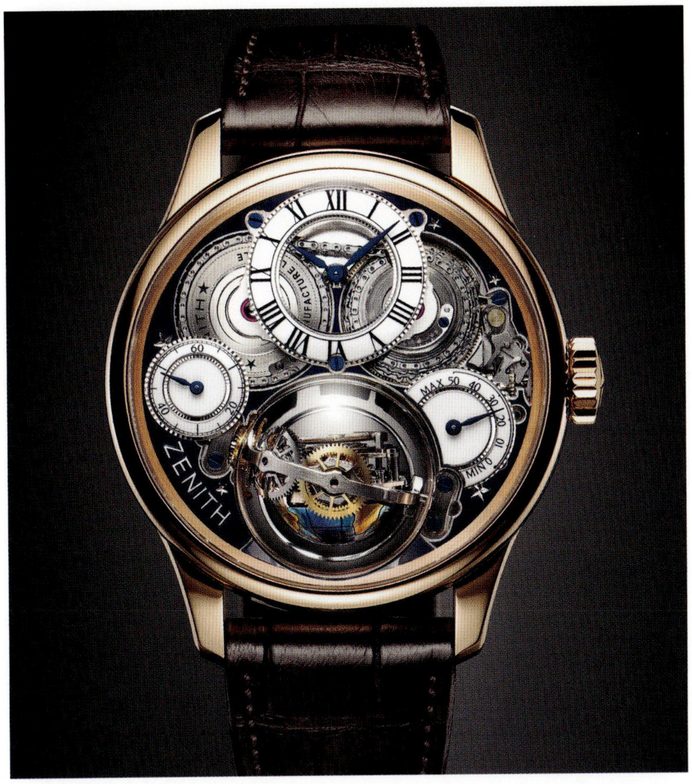

The most complex watch complications to assemble include chronographs, perpetual calendars, tourbillons, and minute repeaters. What makes them complex is the number of parts and the levels of individual regulation and attention the watchmaker must give each specific watch. Very few mechanical watch movements can be assembled without any human intervention to regulate and adjust them in order to ensure that they work. If an unskilled person were somehow able to simply put all the parts of a watch movement together (in some instances there can be upwards of 1,000 parts) it is highly likely not to work – or at least not to work very well. That is because each movement requires assembly in a particular way, with particular tools, points of lubrication, and areas of adjustment.

It is important to consider a watch movement like any other engine: it has a power source, a transmission system, and an output. What makes a watch movement unlike most other engines is that it needs to operate consistently (typically for years on end), and perform with over 99.99% precision in order to reliably indicate the time. Imagine a car engine that needed to operate at exactly 6,000 RPMs for years on end.? It would take perhaps a few days for it to break down. One of the genius elements of the simple mechanical watch movement is that, in addition to its ability to operate without any maintenance for years, it is also able to resist shock and constant movement.

Taking mechanical watch movements for granted is simple, because of their relative availability, but it is difficult to deny the beauty inherent in precision engineering, and the decorative arts that can accompany many of the world's most exclusive movements. Even simple movements that only indicate the time can hide features such as a tourbillon-style escapement, constant force escapement, or fusee and chain transmission. These historical features existed to increase precision and reliability, and are placed in select luxury watches such as the Zenith Academy Christophe Claret Hurricane or Cabestan Winch Tourbillon Vertical.

In the last decade or so, particular attention has been given to the tourbillon. Invented in the late 18th century, the tourbillon was one of many systems designed to increase the accuracy of clocks and pocket watches. The idea was that by rotating a spinning escapement around its own axis there would never be a "top" or "bottom" and thus the pull of gravity would be averaged out because the entire assembly kept rotating. The tourbillon was first placed inside a wristwatch in the 1950s, but it was as an experiment for a timepiece produced by Omega to compete in a chronometry competition. It was not until later that the tourbillon found its way into a commercial wristwatch as a luxury feature to entice collectors. Ironically, as a feature designed to increase accuracy, it often led to even lower accuracy in wristwatches. The best tourbillon-based timepieces are merely as accurate as those without one.

Maîtres du Temps – Chapter One Round Transparence

Zenith – Academy Christophe Colomb Hurricane

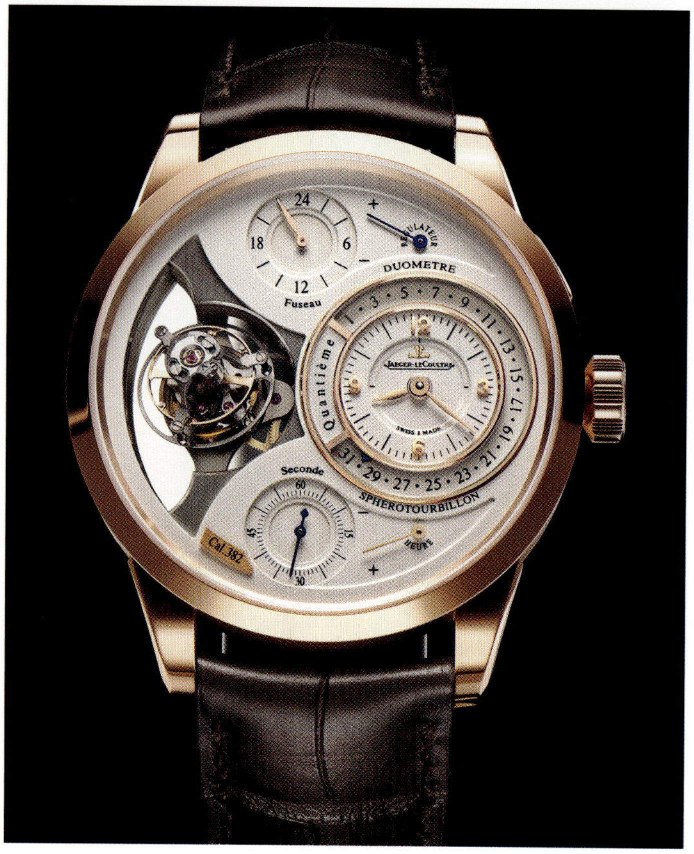

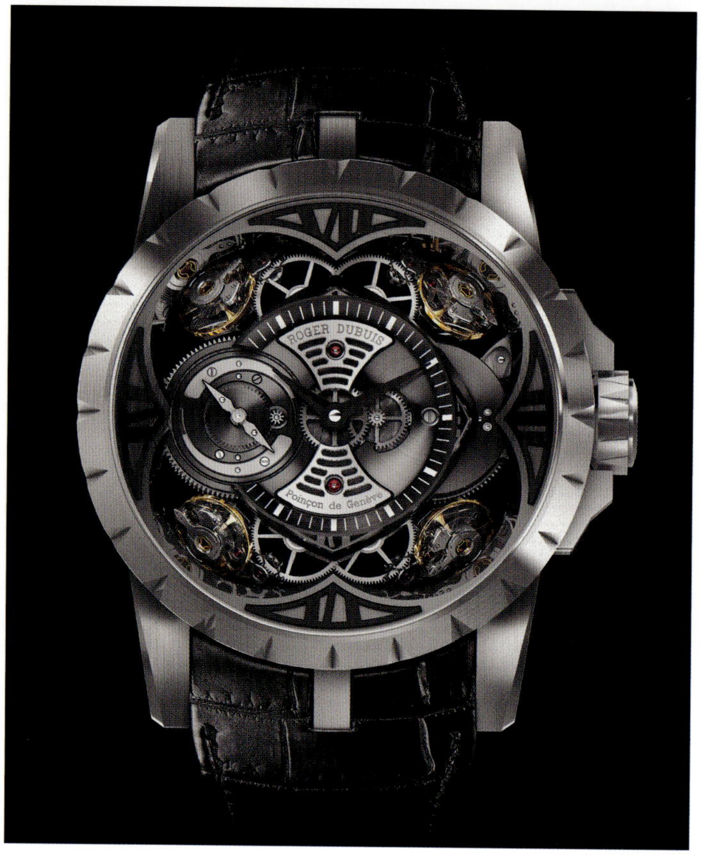

Jaeger-LeCoultre – Duomètre Sphérotourbillon

Roger Dubuis – Excalibur Quatuor Silicon

Nevertheless, the tourbillon remains a popular status symbol among high-end watch lovers. The real appeal of a tourbillon is the perception that it is difficult to assemble (which is more or less true), and the visual appeal of watching it in action. Most (though not all) tourbillon escapement watches feature the mechanism operating on the dial through a hole or cut-out section of the dial. The tourbillon began an era of showing the movement on the dial in a way that was probably unprecedented. The variety of tourbillons is staggering and can lead to exotic interpretations such as the Jaeger-LeCoultre Duomètre Sphérotourbillon and the Thomas Prescher Triple Axis Tourbillon.

The resulting fascination with mechanics led to an era of mechanical visual voyeurism. Not only were watchmakers pressured to show off their movements, but they were likewise pressured to produce beautiful movements. Many of today's luxury watches have movements that are designed as much to be visually appealing as they are to be functional.

This new way of thinking about the appeal of a movement was not radically different from the past, because watch movements had been decorated for generations, though it did expose the movement to the front of a dial as well to the rear of a watch. Aside from the tourbillon, perhaps the most interesting-to-view complication when it comes to operation is the minute repeater, or related sonnerie. These are what are known as musical complications, because they actually involve the watch playing a small tune that signals the time. The extremely complicated Bulgari Magsonic Sonnerie Tourbillon actually combines a few of these musical complications in one watch.

Minute repeaters remain an enduring complication because of their auditory and visual appeal. Most provide a view of the gears moving while small hammers strike against gongs that produce the chimes. As this occurs one can place one's ear close to the watch, to count out the chimes in order to decipher the time. Most minute repeaters play at least two notes. The first set of chimes counts out the hours, followed by the quarter hours, and ending with chimes for the remaining minutes. Operating and listening to minute repeaters is often a great source of satisfaction for collectors, and the very best models such as the Christophe Claret Soprano are celebrated for the clarity and complexity of their notes.

Minute repeaters were originally designed as a rather complex way to know the time in the dark. Inspired by chiming

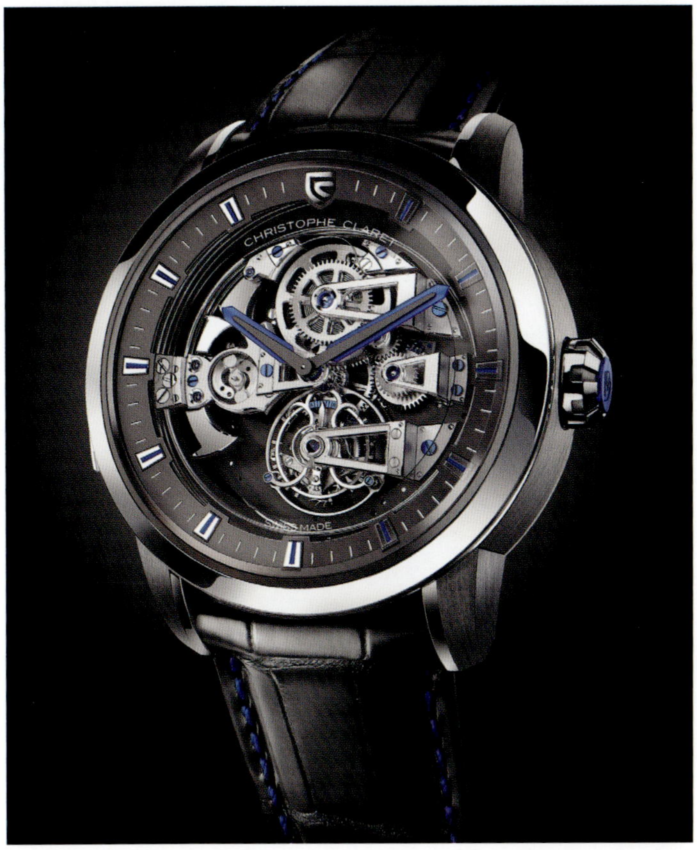

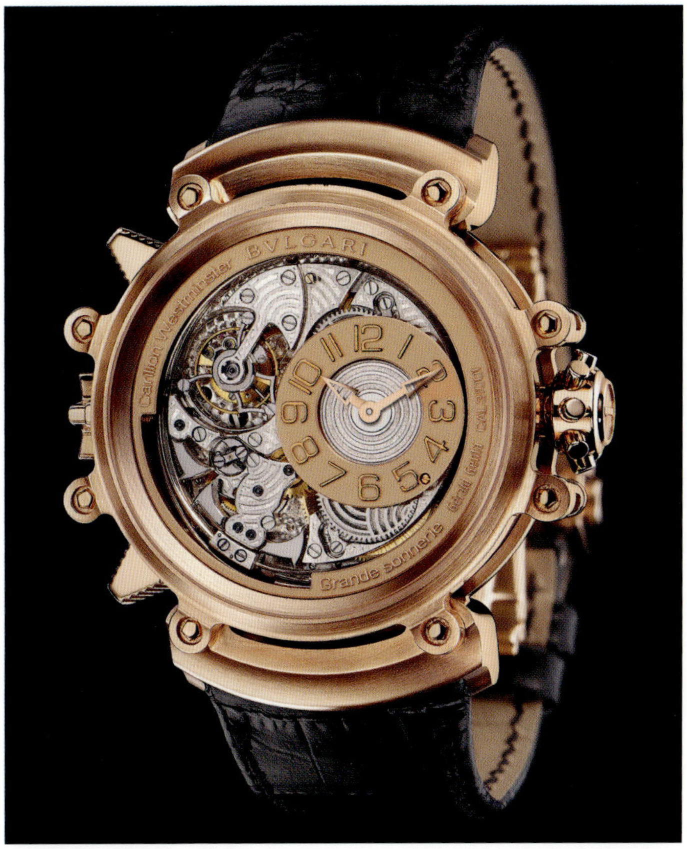

clocks and ringing bell towers, it was an ultimate luxury to have a portable chiming timepiece that could indicate the time without candle or daylight. The ironic end of the minute repeater's practicality was an extremely simple feature – luminous paint (though luminous paint was radioactive and thus rather toxic to begin with).

Most complications began with admirable utilitarian goals in mind, no matter how difficult they were to produce. Today many of the most complicated timepieces are practically obsolete, though highly desirable given their relative rarity. Often the simplest complications, such as a date indicator or a second time zone, prove the most useful. Nevertheless, aficionados seeking ultimate high-end watches are looking for models that beautifully combine more than one complication.

The loose term "Grand Complication" is often applied to timepieces that feature a multitude of complications in a single movement. The most complicated wristwatches in existence have over 20, and in rare instances over 30 complications. For a long time the Blancpain 1735 Grande Complication was the most complicated wristwatch in the world. Later its record was broken without surprise, by the same person who designed it, with the Loiseau 1f4. Watches with these movements are so complex that very few people in existence are able to design them, let alone physically produce them. A "typical" grand complication watch will at the least include the time, perpetual calendar, chronograph, and minute repeater – all in the same timepiece.

In more recent times, watchmakers have proposed a new type of complication style that, rather than adding a new indicator to the watch, exists to display the time in a novel fashion. The traditional means of indicating the time is via hands that revolve around a circular dial, in a clockwise manner, to indicate the hours, minutes, and often seconds. It is true that even centuries ago watchmakers toyed with innovative means of indicating the time, but, more recently, entire brands have developed with that notion in mind. Mechanical watches exist that offer the time digitally, on moving belts, via flipping cubes, with hands that extend and contract, or on spinning drums. Novel approaches to indicate the time can be more or less legible than the traditional way, but creativity is always valued. What collectors look for is mechanical intrigue and refinement as well as a preservation of mechanical tradition. When it comes down to it, the most valuable mechanical watches are not only well made, but also thoughtfully made with discernible passion.

Christophe Claret – Soprano

Bulgari – Magsonic Sonnerie Tourbillon

EXPENSIVE WATCHES EXPLAINED: PRECIOUS MATERIALS & ARTISTIC TECHNIQUE

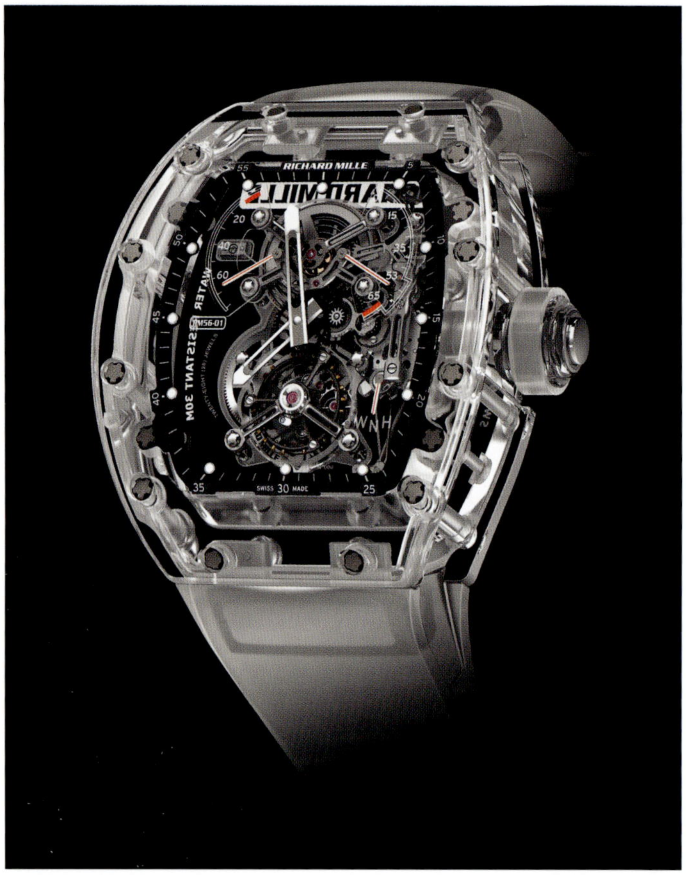

The most common luxury items in the world are gold and diamonds – which is somewhat ironic given that they are afforded a high value due to their rarity. Compared to many other metals or gems, gold and diamonds are far less common, but what makes them so important is their inherent beauty. Gold polishes up really nicely, and, when properly cut, diamonds sparkle wondrously. Rare and precious materials have been a cornerstone of luxury items for eons as they are able to make the ordinary extraordinary, or offer a bold sense of decorative value where there may have been none before.

While a diamond might be a naturally occurring rarity, a skilled artistic technique is a social rarity. For thousands of years artists and artisans have been producing or embellishing items, ranging from jewellery to furniture, that are valuable because of the skill involved in producing them – even if they are made from ordinary materials. Of course the best luxuries combine the use precious materials with honed artistic techniques.

Richard Mille – RM 56-01 Sapphire

Many of the earliest timepieces were produced and decorated with precious materials, therefore the luxury timepiece is as old as the timepiece itself. The main reason for this is that only the wealthiest people could afford the skill necessary to produce a clock or pocket watch. Naturally, the people who created these items wanted to impress their discerning clients by including both mechanical and artistic skill in their hand-made products. As timepieces evolved, so did the notions of how luxury materials might enhance the design or ownership experience of items meant for utilitarian purposes. Today, the variety of precious or artistic techniques exhibited in luxury watches is staggeringly diverse.

The most common luxury metals used to produce wristwatch cases are 18k gold or platinum. 18k gold is a safe blend, given that gold is inherently very soft. Most gold watches are either 18k rose or white gold, but yellow gold is also common in certain parts of the world. As platinum is among the most expensive metals, it still enjoys a high degree of popularity for high-end watches. Sterling silver is however a very uncommon watch case material due to its softness and tendency to tarnish.

In modern times, watchmakers have looked to many alternative precious metals, as well as other materials, from which to make watches. It is not uncommon to find a luxury watch produced from a high-grade titanium, or a more exotic platinum alloy, such as palladium. Some watchmakers have even developed their own alloys such as Harry Winston's Zalium. Borrowing from the aerospace, boating, and racing worlds, watch brands have also incorporated a range of other materials into the design of watch cases and dials. Carbon fibre has frequently been used in high-end sports watches, and even the synthetic sapphire crystal used to produce watch crystals is sometimes used as a case or dial material.

Richard Mille has produced at least a handful of million dollar plus watches in complex all-sapphire cases, and

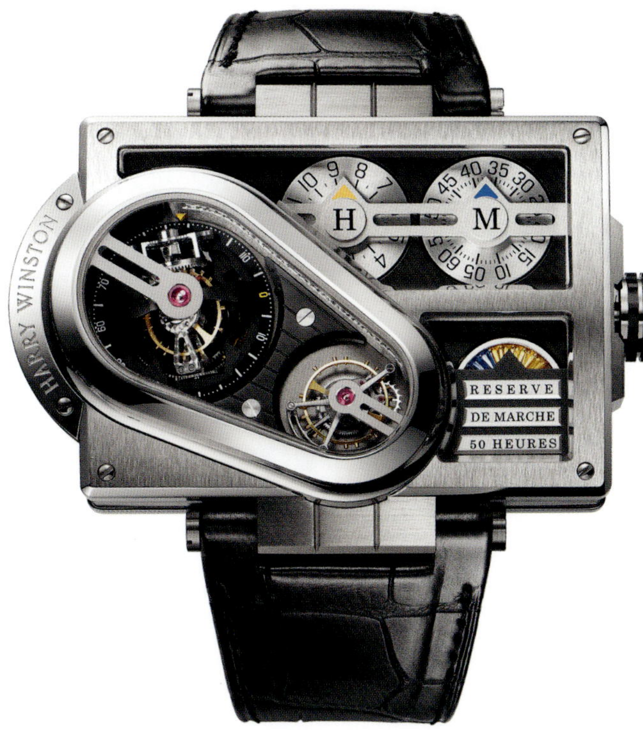

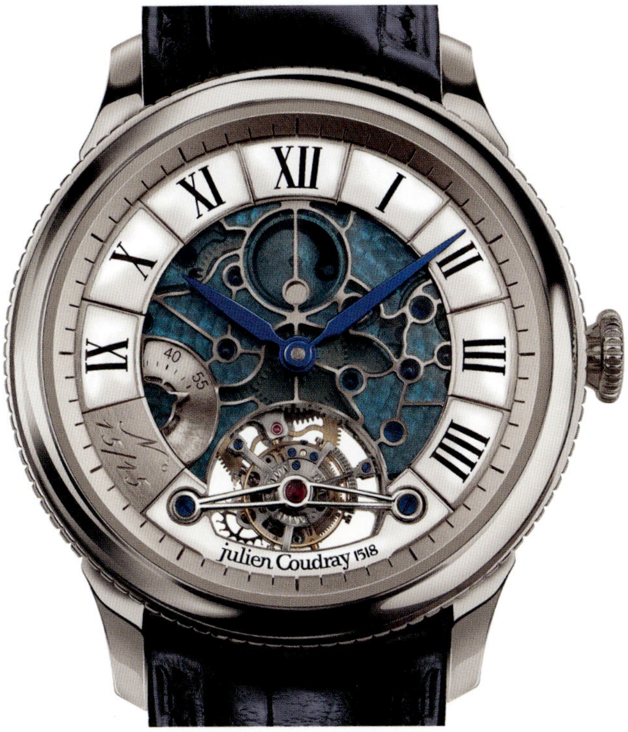

Roger Dubuis has produced a watch with a case made out of silicon. Perhaps the most surprising material to become popular in luxury watches is industrial ceramic. Often as zirconium dioxide, ceramic is used in many applications because of its incredible level of scratch resistance and inability to lose colour over time. Even though many of these newer alternative materials are not inherently precious, what makes them exclusive is the difficultly of producing and precision machining them. Sapphire crystal for example has a tendency to break when not cut into perfectly round sheets, so there is a high failure rate, which leads to very slow production times.

Watchmakers enjoy using rare materials that may have limited availability, as well as the many precious and semi-precious stones that are more commonly available. Frequently these take the form of meteorite slivers for use in decorative dials, but can also include fossils, or stones from space, such as from Mars or from asteroids. These materials can help increase the value of a watch, and are often used in a visible location such as the case or dial. Watchmakers sometimes like to use materials from historic events in the production of limited edition timepieces. This can be metal from an important vintage car, or wood from an historic ship. The idea is not only to imbue a timepiece with extra precious elements, but also to allow the wearer to connect emotionally with the theme of the timepiece. Louis Moinet's Magistralis watch, for example, includes a series of extra-terrestrial stones and is meant to appeal to astronomy enthusiasts. Romain Jerome's Titanic DNA collection of watches is said to contain metal harvested from the *Titanic* deep in the ocean.

The setting or arrangement of precious stones on a timepiece is a time consuming and difficult task, which is often overlooked by watch collectors who may admire a finely made movement with more appreciation. Nevertheless, a timepiece completely covered in diamonds is still a valuable luxury. What the best diamond-covered watches also include is an artistic arrangement of the stones, which results in discernible patterns and motifs among the gems. This is an artistic skill, and is a valued feature among the world's top timepieces, such as the Piaget Emperador Temple or Hublot Big Bang $5 Million.

Precious materials are best joined with artistic techniques that provide for stunning miniature decorative works on or inside timepieces. The most traditional decorative techniques, aside from gem setting, are engraving and miniature painted-in enamel. Engraving is a time-honoured practice on high-end watches, that can be done entirely by hand or with the help of special hand-operated machines. Grieb & Benzinger's Blue Whirlwind combines a range of engraving styles for a stunning result as most surfaces of the movement and case are decorated.

Engraving or painting can also produce miniature scenes in addition to decorative patterns and motifs. Often, under a microscope, the dials or movements of some bespoke watches have pictures of people or places that can take months

Harry Winston – Histoire de Tourbillon 3

julien Coudray 1518 – Competentia 1515

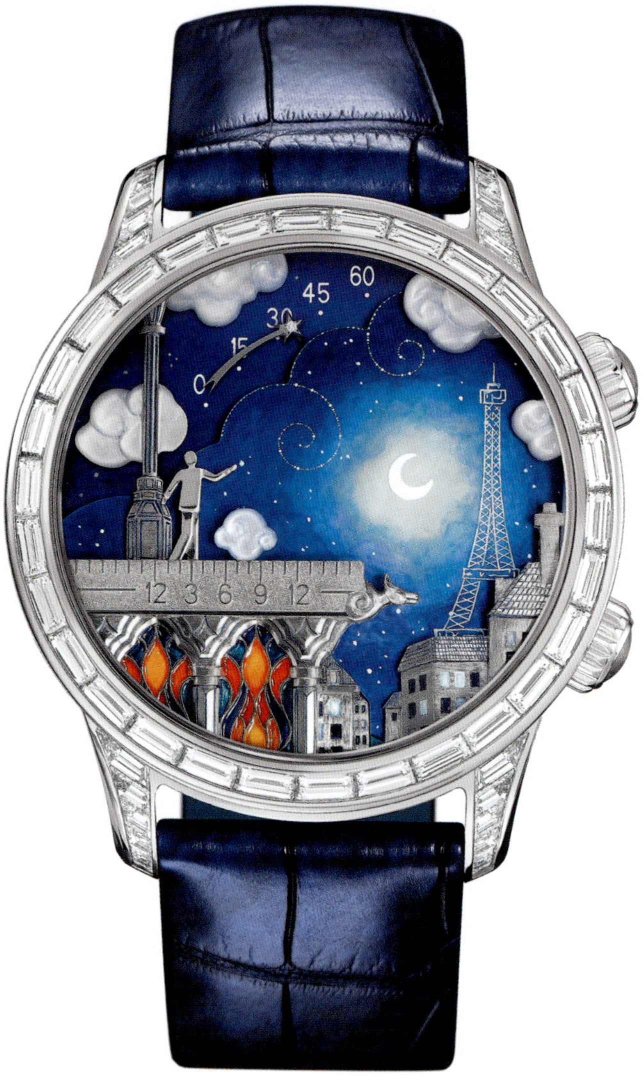

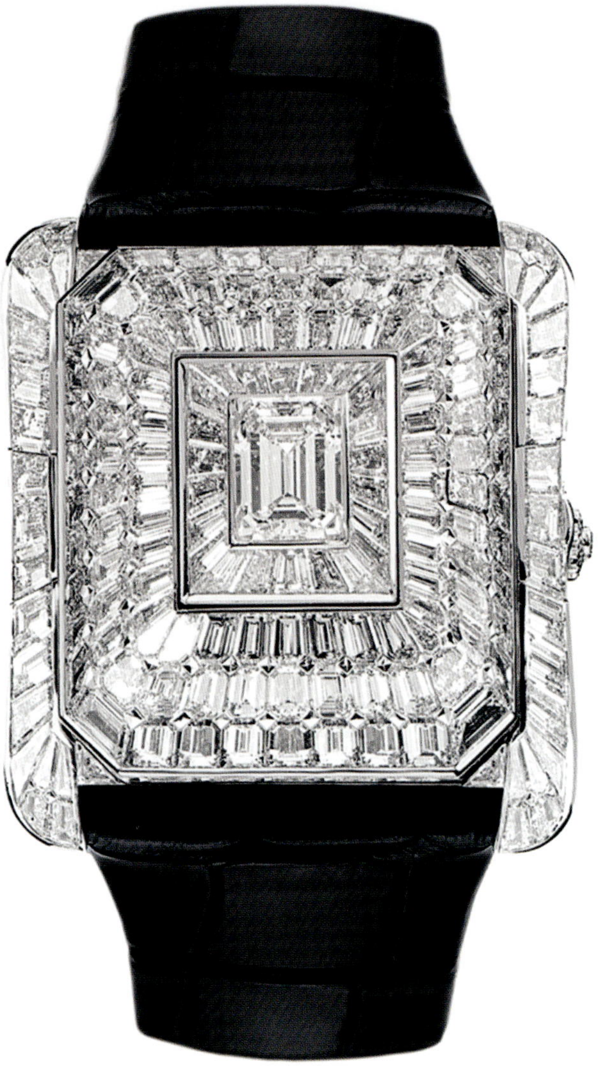

to complete. It is often the case that luxury watch clients prefer to have unique decorations produced exclusively for them. Many of the world's most impressive one-of-a-kind timepieces are unknown save by the owner and the people by who produced them.

Many watches with hand-applied art borrow styles and themes from other areas of luxury, such as jewellery. However, certain forms of decorative techniques on watches are exclusively a watchmaker's skill. These include the ability to skeletonise a watch movement as well as to finish the surface of metal.

"Finishing" is a relatively broad term in the watch industry; it applies to the visual quality of a component. Today, most watch parts are produced by machine, but what separates a high-end watch from something more ordinary, aside from the materials, is the finishing. Luxury watch cases are typically hand polished, and in many instances so are the movements and even elements such as the hands – yes, traditional watchmakers such as George Daniels, Roger Smith, and Philippe Dufour hand-polish even the hands that go on the dials of their timepieces.

More common however is the hand-polishing and finishing of watch movements. In the best watches the majority of parts in a movement are individually hand-finished, under magnification, using a series of delicate tools. In and around Switzerland, local woods or specially-made sandpaper are used to polish tiny gears, rods, or wheels that are held with a pair of tweezers. Masters in their field are known for their skilled ability to apply mirror perfect polishes.

Some watch movements are given a skeletonisation treatment, which deconstructs the mechanism to its most important

Van Cleef & Arpels – Poetic Wish Mens

Piaget – Emperador Temple

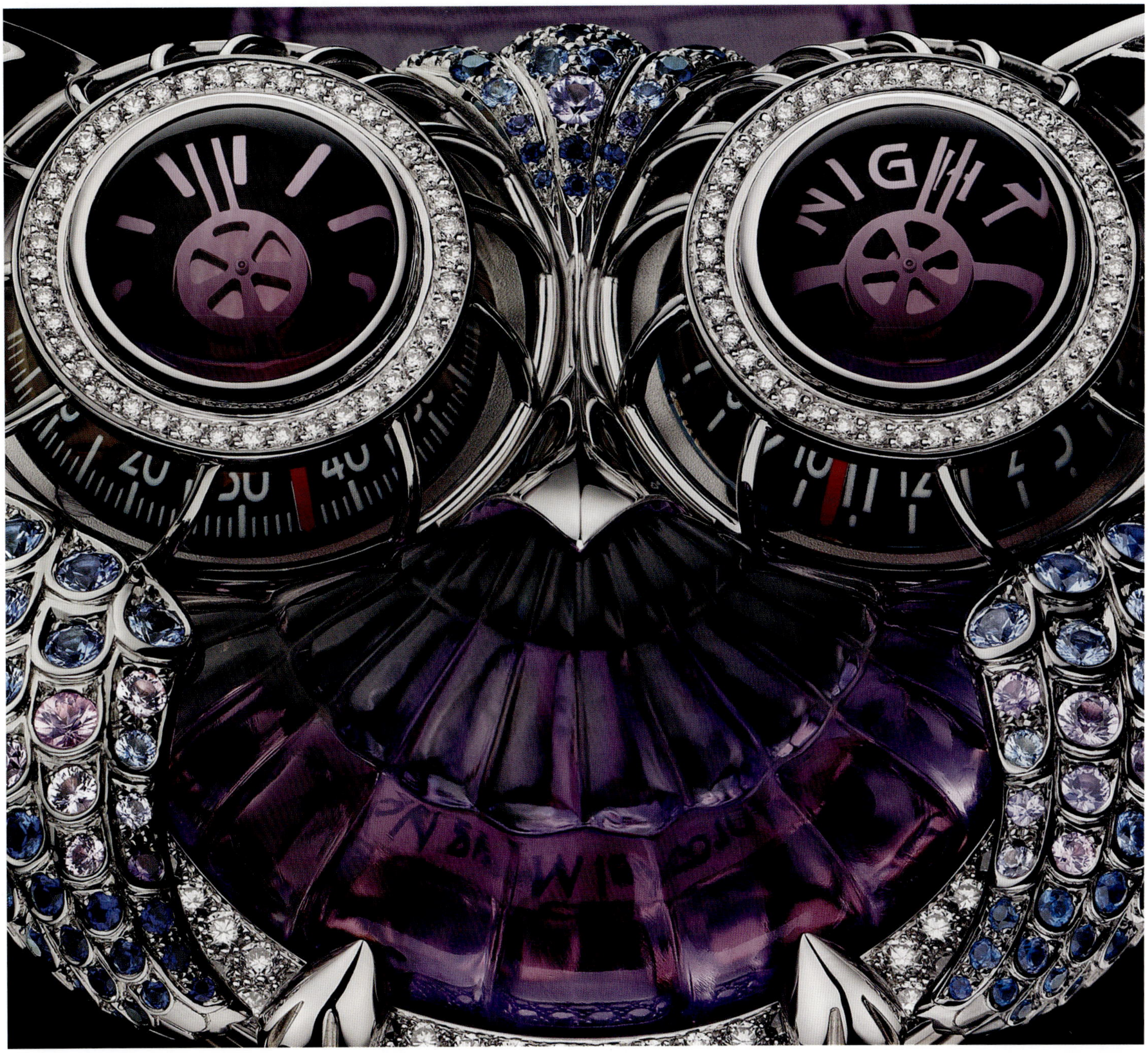

Detail of MB&F – HM3 JwlryMachine Watch

support structures to offer a deep view of how a movement operates. Skeletonisation can be a complex process and in the most high-end pieces involves careful finishing of each angle and component for an owner's voyeuristic pleasure. Skeletonised watches have movements that are specifically meant to be viewed, but in many watches the parts that the watchmakers so carefully polish are invisible to the owner, as they buried within a movement. It is often said that the only other people who will see most of the decoration in a finely made luxury watch are other watchmakers who may later service it.

The majority of watch collectors primarily seek out timepieces for their mechanical virtues: they are looking for complex and beautiful movements, which require both scientific and artistic skills to create. However, the allure of a hand-made item that requires special and incredible effort to produce, is appealing emotionally – as well as being inherently valuable – only to the most sophisticated of watch lovers. Not everyone has the interest to delve deep into the mechanism of a timepiece, and because watches are noticeable items that people wear, a great number of ultra-high-end watch buyers seek out pieces with detailed decorative arts and a wealth of precious stones and other materials in order to satisfy their tastes and lifestyle choices.

EXPENSIVE WATCHES EXPLAINED: HISTORICAL IMPORTANCE & PROVENANCE

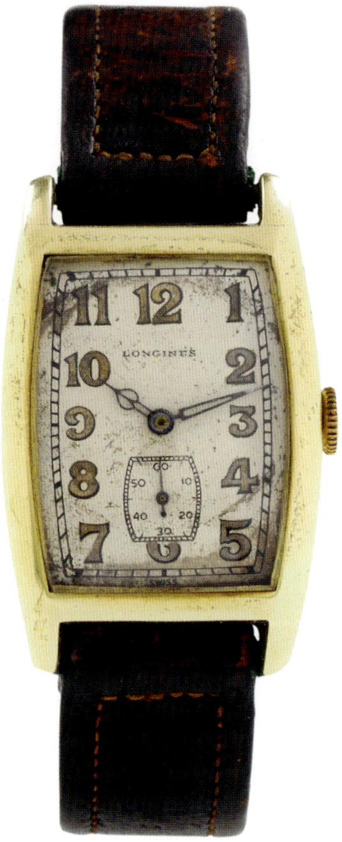

A rational way to understand the motivation behind acquiring rare or expensive items is the desire to own an important story. With a watch, one can actually carry that story around on one's wrist: the story of how and why it was made; and the story of who has worn it. Nothing is more inherent in an element of luxury than the concept of exclusivity. The fact that something is rare automatically affords it value; that it is rare and important is the ultimate combination of value creation for luxury items.

Popular rare items that can be included in timepieces to create value, are precious stones, metals, and other materials. These will be the topic of a different discussion. An alternative focus is on rarity created by the historical significance of a particular object because a famous or important person wore or owned it. A pen is just a pen until it is used to sign a famous document; in the same way, a vintage watch may be relatively ordinary until one discovers who has owned it. It is common in the sphere of collecting that celebrity ownership of an object increases its value. Often that value is a function not only of the popularity of the celebrity, but of how important a part the object may have had in identifying and shaping their personality. If the celebrity has died, and society has summed up their existence and their contribution as being truly significant, then the value of the object they owned – however intrinsically simple it is – may become astronomical.

Albert Einstein's personal Longines

Watches are a unique type of celebrity possession because they can be so inherently personal. Watches are physically worn by someone, relied on by them as a tool, are a measure and indication of their taste, as well as an important style cue that helps people understand their personality and how they wanted to communicate with the people around them. The more interested society is in a particular celebrity, the more important their watches will become. Therefore, celebrity-owned timepieces have enormous potential to become valuable due to social interest in their owners. The Longines watch that Albert Einstein wore would ordinarily have been a simple antique gold watch, but, because of its owner, it achieved a price of many hundreds of thousands of dollars at auction.

The most valuable of history's celebrity timepieces have come from the 20th century. One reason for this is provenance and the ability to prove that a celebrity actually owned it – which is often done through photographs and witness accounts. There are exceptions of course, especially when a pocket watch includes a personalised engraving for the owner. Another important reason is that it was not until the 20th century that the wristwatch was commercialised and that people other than the very wealthy even owned pocket watches.

There are three primary types of people whose ownership of a timepiece can increase its value: first, the celebrities such as actors, athletes, musicians and artists; secondly, the powerful social figures or politicians; and, thirdly, there are innovative scientists or people who have somehow changed the world through invention or achievement. It should also be mentioned that the mere fact that a celebrity is known to have owned or chosen a specific model or style of watch can increase the desirability and value of all such pieces even years later. This certainly helped Rolex with the now highly valuable "Paul Newman" Daytona watches.

Establishing provenance is an important element in asserting the value of a timepiece that is primarily associated with a particular owner. The better proof a seller offers, the more likely it is that an item will achieve a high price. History, and even some of today's auction houses, are full of timepieces that provide dubious claims of important ownership. Just as many fear purchasing a replica or inauthentic timepiece, collectors are often cautious of sellers who aren't able to adequately prove actual ownership. This is often tricky because during most people's lives they aren't specifically interested in ensuring that photographs exist of them in all their wearable finery.

Whist ownership by important historical figures and celebrities can be significant in adding value to a timepiece, other areas of historical importance can also increase the value: Who made the watch? How innovative or complicated is its design? Is there something about its manufacture that makes it unique?

Collectors are often interested in items that are "the first, the most, or the best". In the watch world this is applied to timepieces in a number of ways. As the art world has its famous artists, so the watch world has its famous watchmakers. A few dozen such individuals lived throughout history and there is particular attention given to seminal watchmakers from the 17th and 18th centuries who pioneered much of the technology that goes into the timepieces of today. Timepieces produced by these famous names (such as "the father of modern watchmaking" Abraham-Louis Breguet who worked mostly during the late 18th century) are valuable not only because they are often extremely beautiful, but also because of the importance of their creators to the timepiece collectors of today.

Timepieces with unique mechanisms or those that were the very first to include a piece of technology or feature, are also often very valuable. A lot of interest is given to first or early generation models that offer movements unlike those of their contemporaries. In today's watch world the same is often true; new watches with innovative mechanics can command a premium. Having said that, it is incredibly rare to locate specific historic timepieces that were the first to feature new technology. Typically, collectors settle for a "very early example" of a particular item.

While many of these concepts, when related to vintage or historical timepieces, may be common knowledge, it is more difficult to predict the value of new watches with novel features. The problem with new things is that the market has not yet been able to test them and thus assign a value based on demand. Watchmakers today are increasingly focused on proving themselves with unique, independent designs. This has a net benefit for the industry at large, but many of these watches do not necessarily achieve commercial success merely because they are new and interesting.

A less common way of thinking about significant watches is to consider the case of the "*piece unique*". This is a term applied to any timepiece that is a one-of-a-kind creation. *Piece unique* watches can have a unique dial, or even a totally unique movement. For generations, private collectors have requested that watchmakers produce special timepieces exclusively for them. Most of the "uniqueness" is merely cosmetic, but once in a while a collector is able (and can afford) to convince a watchmaker to produce a completely unique case or movement. Due to their limited nature, watches such as this can be of particular interest to collectors. Their real value depends mostly on who produced the watch and why. One of the most famous brands to have auction success with *piece unique* models is Patek Philippe. The allure of an item that only exists as a single object is particularly attractive in the world of watches, where exclusivity is so valued.

In rare instances, a watch can become highly valuable not only because of celebrity ownership, but also because of its inherent technical qualities and features. For some collectors this is the holy grail of watch collecting – to find a famous watch lover with a famous watch made especially for them.

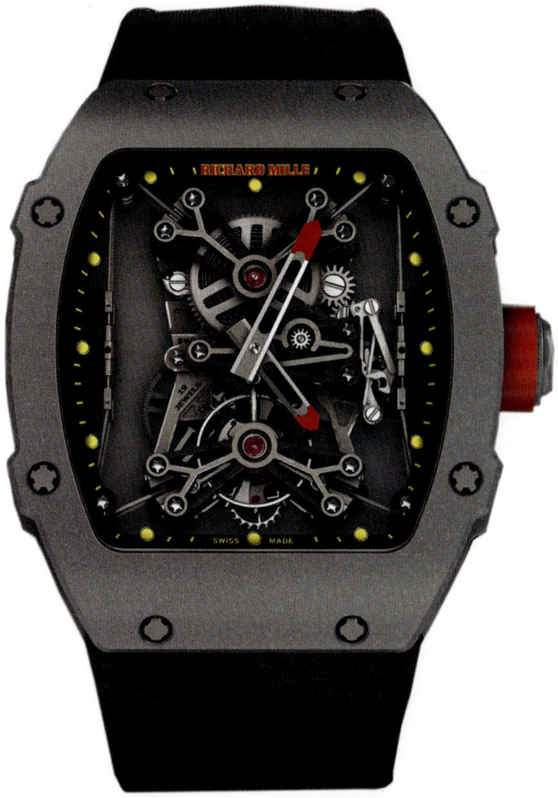

Richard Mille – RM 27-01 Tourbillon Rafael Nadal

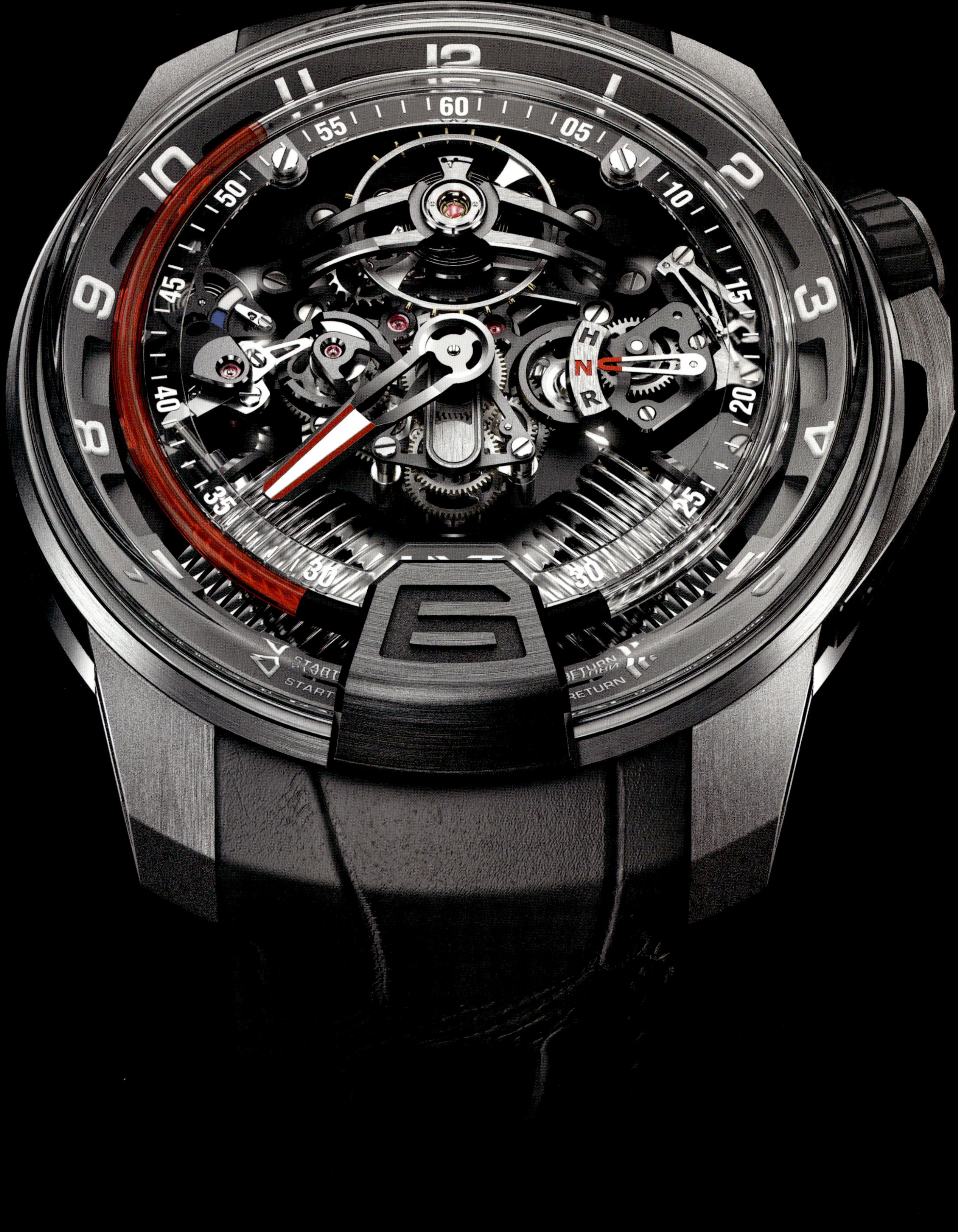
START
RETURN

HYT – H2 IN PLATINUM

$ 200 000

A VIEW ON THE REAR OF THE WATCH COMPLETES THE ATTRACTIVE MODERN DESIGN, WHICH SEEMS TO MIX SCIENCE FICTION WITH THE AESTHETIC OF AUTOMOTIVE ENGINES.

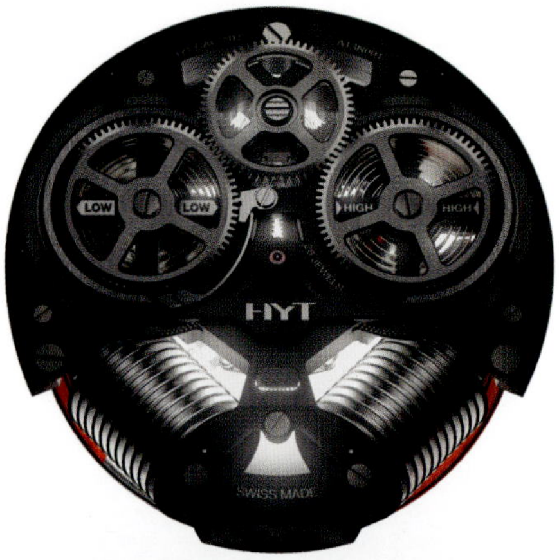

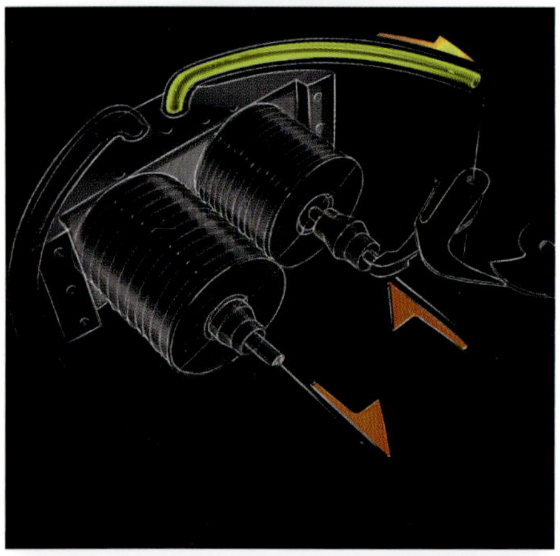

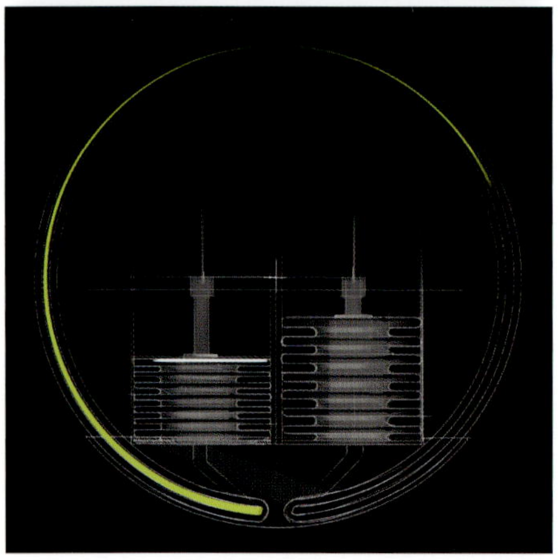

HYT, a boutique Swiss watch brand, refers to themselves as the "Hydro Mechanical Horologists". The company represents the finality of founder Vincent Perriard's ultimate vision of marrying mechanical watches with liquid indictors. He broached the concept while previously working at the watch company Concord, but only at HYT was he able to realize the concept in a truly satisfactory manner. The H2 watch, like the H1 model before it, uses a tube filled with liquid to indicate the hours.

In colours such as green, blue, and red, the liquid level in the circular tube travels along an hour marker scale on the periphery of the dial as it indicates the time. Two billow-style reservoirs are mechanically controlled to alter the liquid level so that the glow-in-the-dark liquid travels across the scale in a manner similar to how a traditional hour hand might. A more traditional hand, tipped in red, is used to indicate the minutes.

While HYT succeeded in presenting their hydro-mechanical watch concept in their debut H1 watch model in 2012, the H2 timepiece extended the concept deeper into the world of high-horology when it was presented in 2013 as a limited edition. HYT worked with the industry-honoured firm APRP (Audemars Piguet Renaud Papi) to develop a magnificent mechanical engine designed to be fully displayed on the dial for a higher-end product. Ironically enough, the H2 watch has fewer features than its lower-priced H1 model (as the H2 does not indicate the running seconds), but the H2's manually wound mechanical movement does make up for it with a much more impressive design and 192 hours (eight days) of power reserve. The movement functions include a liquid indicator for the hours, a minute hand, crown function selector, and a movement temperature gauge. The latter feature is useful because high or low temperatures can affect the operation of the liquid chambers.

A view on the rear of the watch completes the attractive modern design, which seems to mix science fiction with the aesthetic of automotive engines. A curved sapphire crystal sits over the dial offering an expansive view into the intricate movement, framed by the highly innovative liquid hour indicator system. At 48.8mm wide, the H2 makes an imposing, yet surprisingly comfortable fit on the wrist. Initially offered in titanium, the HYT H2 watch was also produced in titanium mixed with 18k white gold parts, as well as titanium with platinum. The former H2 white gold model was matched with blue liquid and limited to 20, while the H2 platinum model was matched with red liquid and limited to just 14 pieces.

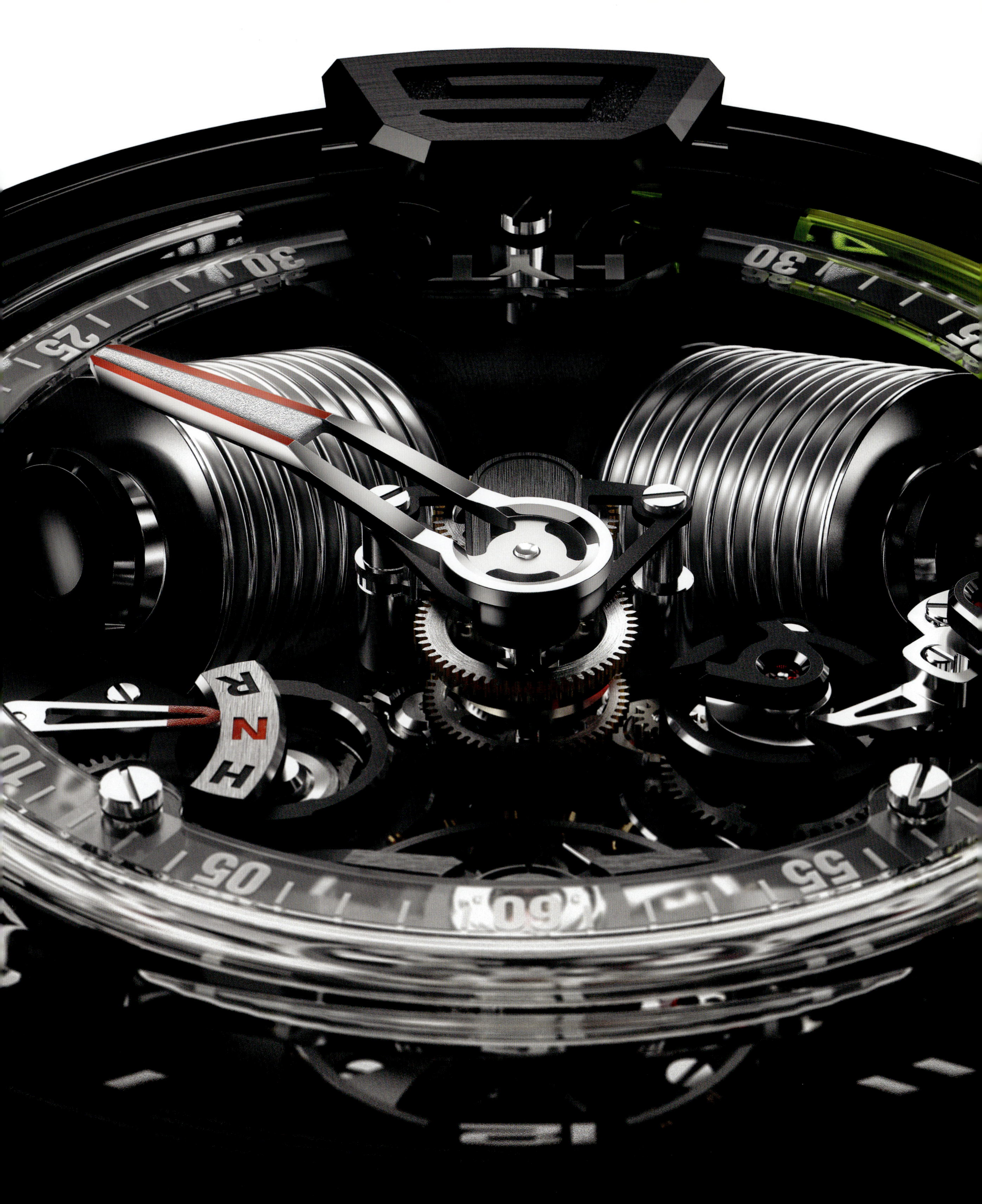

KERBEDANZ – MAXIMUS TOURBILLON

$ 200 000

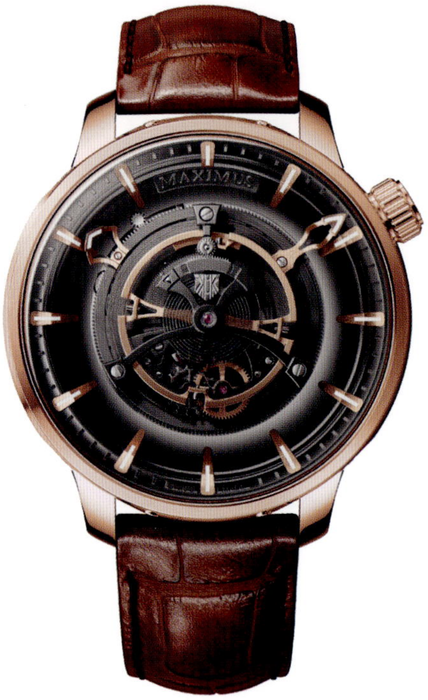

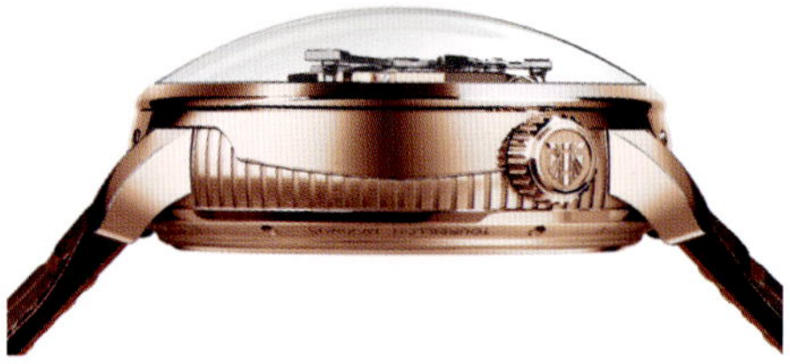

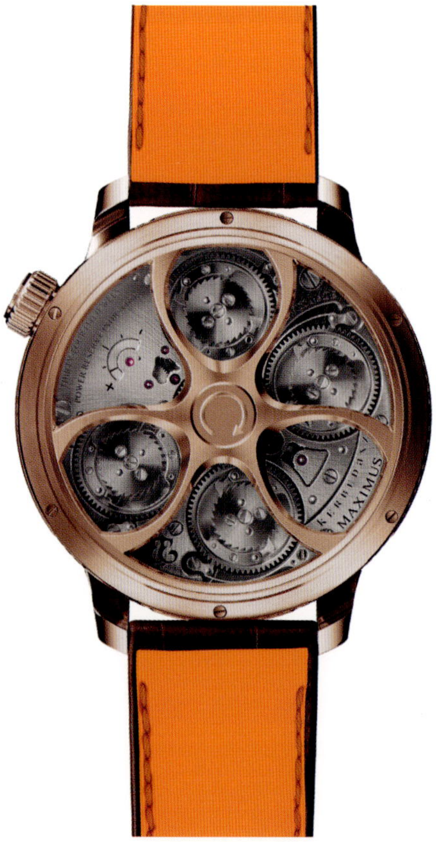

Size is everything in the realm of horology. In the watch world of micro-architecture, designers often like to play with superlatives – though not always those that collectors expect. Timepieces are often known to boast "the smallest", "the most efficient", "the most discreet", "the thinnest", or "the most complex" of features. Each of these efforts makes sense when the goal is to put as much as possible into a package designed to be worn on the wrist. At other times, a watchmaker's goal is to boast, impress or simply attract attention. In those instances, the engineering efforts at play may be the exact opposite to the above. Case in point is the Swiss Kerbedanz Maximus, with a tourbillon so large it requires specially designed hands that sit underneath it.

At 27mm wide, the diameter of the "giant" flying tourbillon takes centre stage on the Kerbedanz Maximus watch dial. Most tourbillons rotate once per minute, but the Maximus' tourbillon makes a full rotation once every six minutes. With this slower rotation and a 2.5Hz operational frequency, simply gazing at the persistently animated dial of the Maximus is, for many, a mesmerising experience.

With 415 parts required for assembly, the complicated movement requires an enormous level of consistent torque to power the large tourbillon-based regulation system. Winding the watch is actually performed by turning the case back, which offers a view of the four mainspring barrels along with a power-reserve indicator. Few watch movements indicating only the time with an hour and minute hand are this intensely complicated. Kerbedanz needed to develop a unique system of hands that exist around the tourbillon, as opposed to cutting through it, in order to maintain the aesthetic quality of the dial and further offer the technically sophisticated experience that collectors at this level demand.

How "maximum" is the Maximus on the wrist? The case (available in titanium or 18k gold) is a hefty 49mm wide and appreciably thick thanks to the steeply domed sapphire crystal. The intention behind the doming is to allow visibility of the large tourbillon through the sapphire crystal when viewed from the side, offering yet another visual perspective to this massive tourbillon-based piece of wearable timepiece art.

BREVA – GENIE 01 IN PLATINUM

$ 205 000

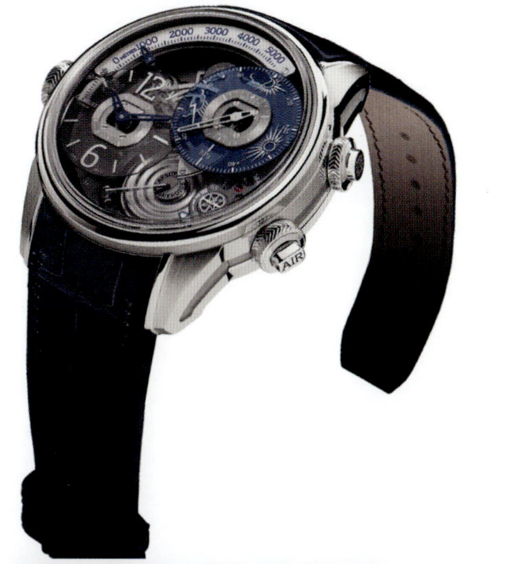

Sometimes a luxury watch is really about celebrating the art of the instrument. Launched in 2013, Swiss Breva's debut product was the Genie 01, the world's first timepiece with a mechanical altimeter, barometer, and weather prediction complication. In many instances today the luxury world mimics or conforms to what is popular in consumer electronics. When mobile phones became ubiquitous, luxury brands responded in kind to produce very high-end mobile phones. Later, environmental and fitness sensors on gadgets began to attract consumer attention. A watch like the Genie 01 is in actuality an environmental sensor, developed and curated for the luxury watch buyer.

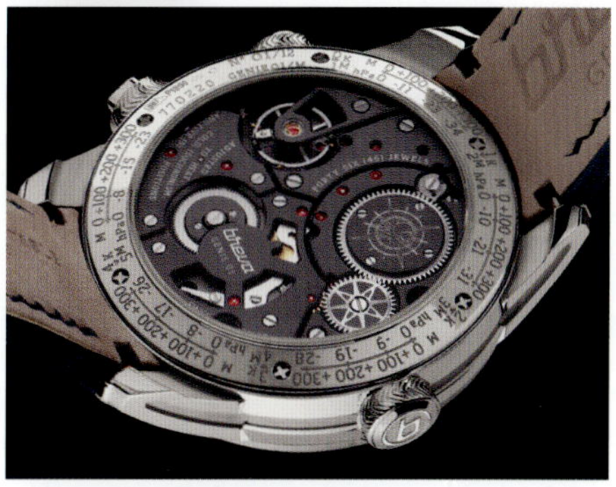

There is a legitimate argument to be made that Breva's Genie 01 watch has limited utility in a world dominated by ultra-precise digital instruments. Nevertheless, few can argue that most electronic environmental sensors are as elegant or beautiful to behold as the Genie 01. More importantly, it has technology that can be understand with the naked eye, a principle element that allows for many instrument lovers to have an emotional connection with an object. The dial of the Genie 01 is masterfully open-worked with overlapping dials produced from semi-transparent crystal to allow for a legible, albeit open view into the mechanism.

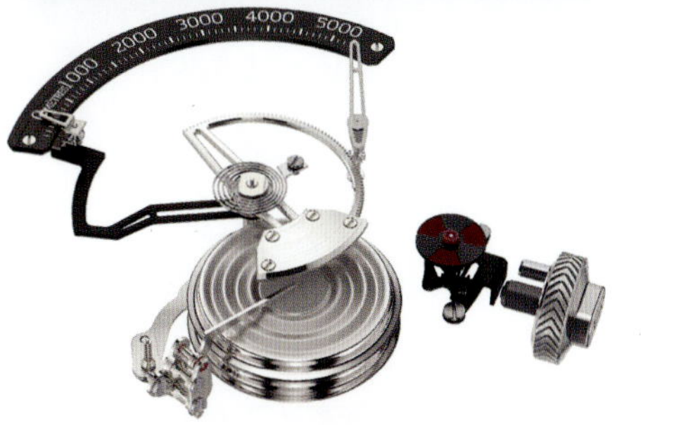

Breva worked with the well-regarded movement designer Jean-François Mojon and his company Chronode on the development of this innovative movement. On the left of the Genie 01's face is a subsidiary dial for the time, and to the right is the barometric pressure scale, which is also used to predict the weather based on the increase or decrease of atmospheric pressure over time. To the top of the face is an altitude scale, while the dial also contains indicators for the running seconds as well as the power reserve of the mechanical movement. At the bottom of the dial is the most important element of the altimeter and barometer system: a specially produced aneroid capsule.

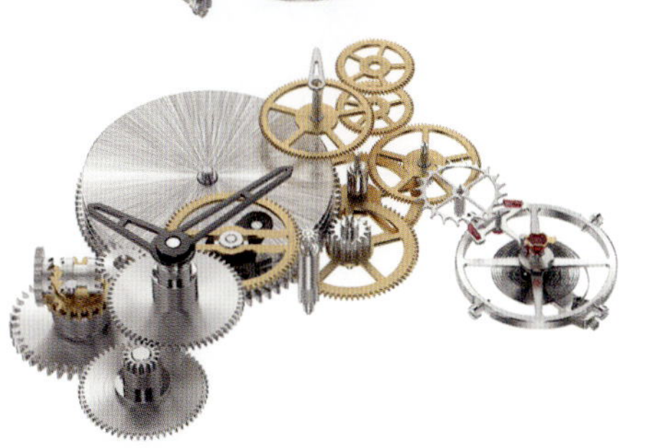

Over the capsule is a small arm that measures the expansion of the capsule, which occurs naturally in a predictable manner with a change in barometric pressure. Using the Breva Genie 01 watch to predict the weather is a bit less straight forward than electronic tools. One must first take the altitude into consideration, and must also equalize the pressure in the case – by opening a small air valve – while taking different readings over time.

Breva imagines the Genie 01 to be used by well-funded skiing enthusiasts and other such adventurers interested in how the weather may affect their treks. The watch is, nevertheless, produced exclusively from precious materials and makes a bold statement at 44.70mm wide and 15.60mm high. Initially produced in 18k rose or white gold, the Breva Genie 01 was also produced in platinum, which was limited to just 12 pieces.

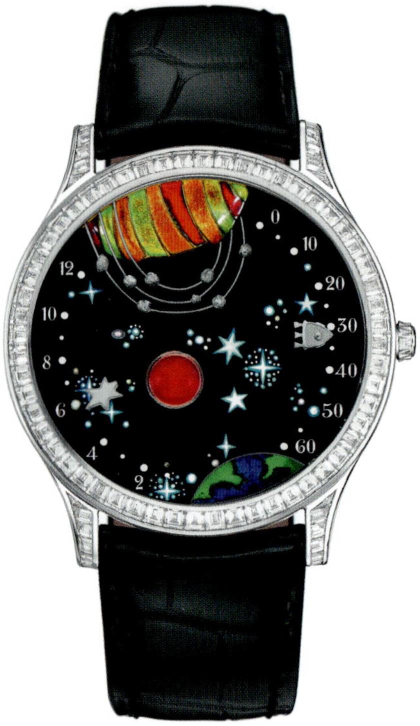

VAN CLEEF & ARPELS — LES VOYAGES EXTRAORDINAIRES "FROM THE EARTH TO THE MOON"

$ 205 000

Some of the most exclusive items of whimsy and beauty produced on the planet come from the house of Van Cleef & Arpels in Paris. A producer of fine jewellery and luxuries of emotion, the brand also produces a select collection of timepieces. Rather than exhibit expertise producing timepieces with traditional mechanical complications, Van Cleef & Arpels prefers instead to focus on what it calls "Poetic Complications." That is their way of saying that the goal of most Van Cleef & Arpels watches is to make people feel something.

Each year Van Cleef & Arpels chooses at least a few themes to build on. These have included focus areas such as fairies, butterflies, California nature, ocean creatures, gardens, and the fantasy travels of Jules Verne. The latter was a theme that Van Cleef & Arpels built upon heavily in 2011 into a collection known as Les Voyages Extraordinaires.

The collection includes a range of "high jewellery" pieces and watches, meant to celebrate a sense of wonder and exploration by visualising the world of Jules Verne in a manner only Van Cleef & Arpels could accomplish. An exemplary model is a watch based on Jules Verne's book From the Earth to the Moon.

Completely decorated by hand under a microscope, the dial of "From the Earth to the Moon" depicts a small space craft carved from gold flying through a hand-painted scene of space. The view contains an enamel painted Earth, Mars, and Jupiter. The Earth's moon is conspicuously absent from the view, despite the timepiece's name.

Time is indicated via two retrograde hands on the dial. The left side of the face has a small golden star that moves across a scale to indicate the hours, and to the right is the spaceship, which is used to indicate the minutes. This system is unique, being designed to maintain an unobstructed view of the celestial dial, while also being able to indicate the time. The mechanical movement inside the watch was produced for Van Cleef & Arpels by the well-regarded Swiss watchmaker Jaeger-LeCoultre.

BADOLLET – IVRESSE

$ 205 500

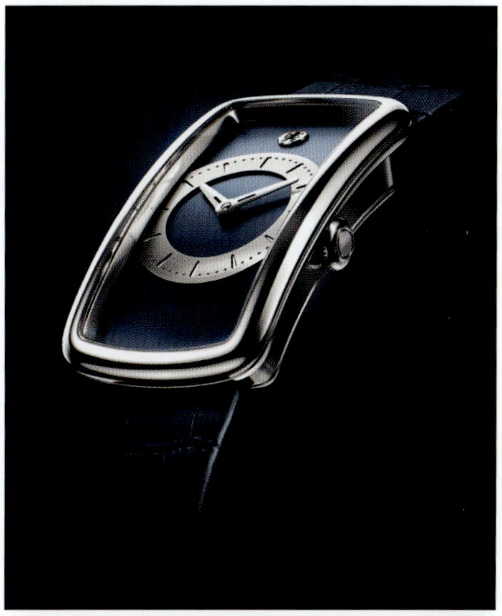

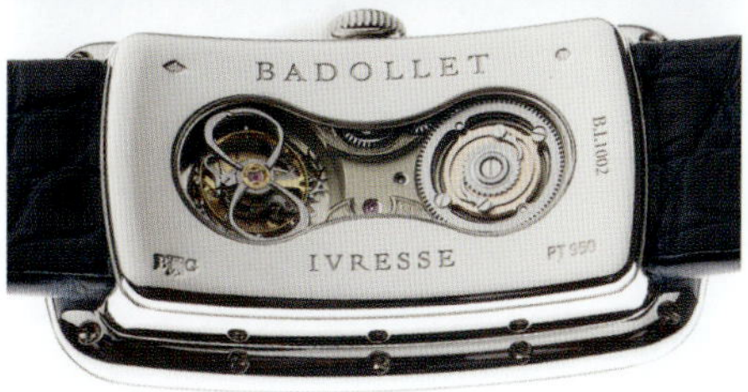

When Badollet approached the well-regarded watch designer Eric Giroud, they asked him to design a unique luxury watch that would be as simple as possible. In the watch industry, simplicity is often tantamount to derivative design; however, Giroud wanted to design something that would be visually simple, but also distinct. Uniqueness is among the most important elements of interest when it comes to boutique high-end timepieces.

The resulting watch was the Ivresse, a modern timepiece born from a brand with history going back to 1655. According to the company, the Badollet family name experienced an unbroken line of watchmakers, from Jean Badollet in the 17th century all the way to 1924, when the company was closed due to poor economic factors relating to the aftermath of the First World War. In 2006, Badollet was revived and c.2012 the Ivresse was released.

According to Badollet, their signature complication is the tourbillon – a popular mechanical feature – that puts the oscillator assembly on a rotating cage that revolves around its own axis. Typically displayed on the dial-side of watches, the Ivresse opted for a more discreet presentation of the tourbillon. The mechanism was originally invented in the 18th century as a means of improving the accuracy of clocks and pocket watches, but in its modern interpretation it is more akin to a display of luxury mechanical art.

"Hiding" a tourbillon on the rear of a watch means that only the owner can see it in operation. This stealthier placement of the tourbillon appeals to those collectors who want to own a high-end watch but do not want to be overt about its value. Often referred to as "stealth wealth", luxuries of a more discreet nature are considered to be a direct response to the general public's tendency to reject "showy" wealth.

The tourbillon is large in diameter, with an infinity symbol on the cage, as a tribute to the persistent ongoing passage of time, which is the driving force of the universe. The movement inside the Ivresse is unique because, like the case, it is curved. Most movements are flat, given the nature of their flat components such as gears and springs, so the design and production of a curved movement is difficult. The Ivresse offers just the time, with hours and minutes, which are displayed in a minimalist yet legible fashion, in a round dial on an otherwise rectangular face.

With the Ivresse watch, Badollet succeeded in creating a complicated yet outwardly simple design. The original Ivresse debuted with a deep blue face and matching alligator strap, while later models offered additional colours. Each piece has a solid platinum case. Badollet claims that no more than 50 Ivresse watches can be produced per year.

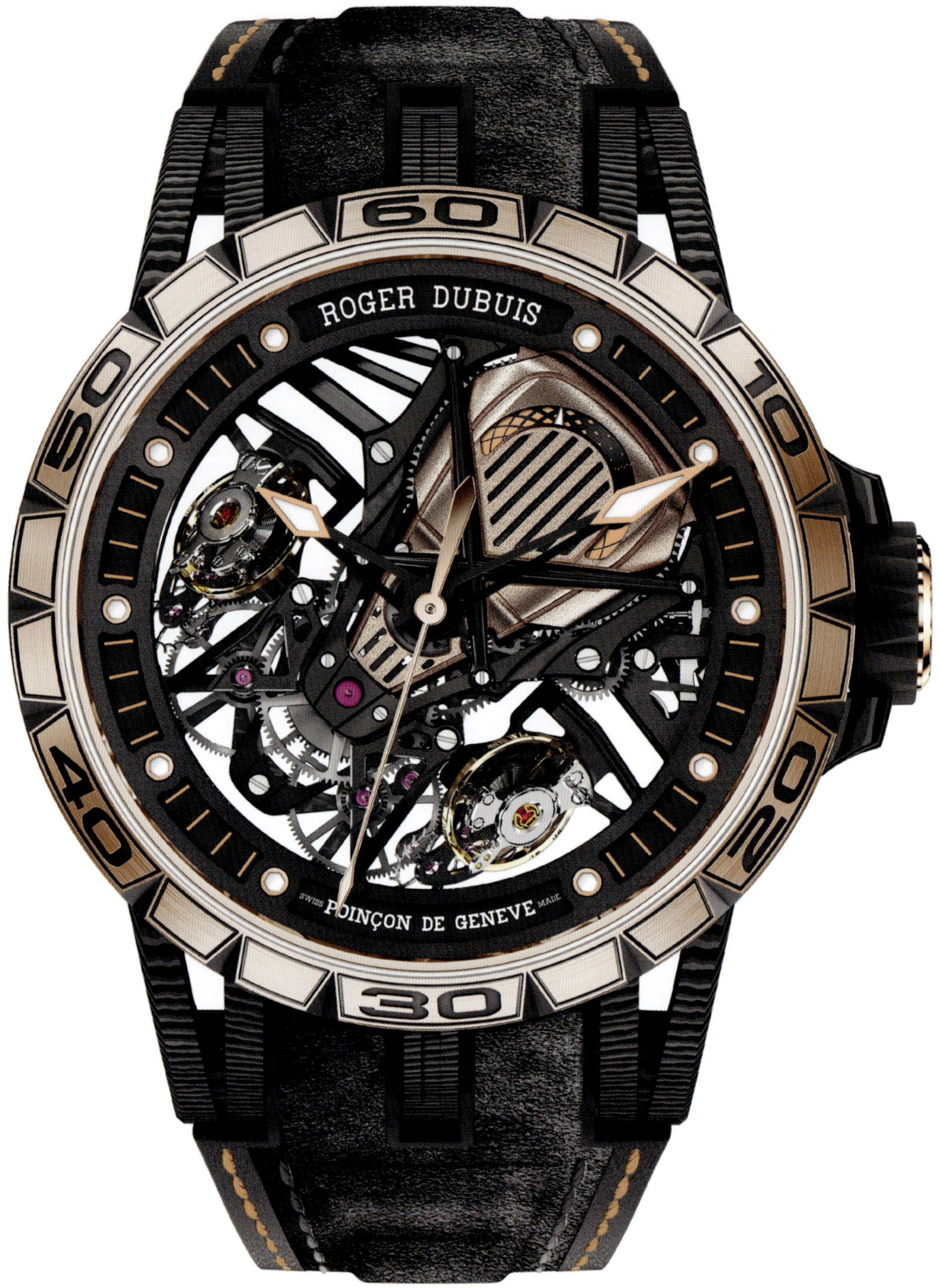

ROGER DUBUIS — EXCALIBUR AVENTADOR S

$ 210 000

With a mechanical movement co-developed with partner Squadra Corse – the motorsport division of Italian manufacturer of luxury sports cars Lamborghini – the Excalibur Aventador S is Swiss Roger Dubuis's affectionate homage to the acclaimed Lamborghini Aventador street-legal and luxurious racing machine. The calibre RD103SQ mechanism powering the watch is fitted with a transaxle support bridge and generally has a shape that is intended to suggest a powerful combustion engine sitting in an automobile's engine bay. Skeletonised for visual pleasure, like many of Roger Dubuis's in-house made products, this exotic movement combines the allure of traditional watchmaking with an ultra-modern design intended to be married with a passion for driving contemporary supercars.

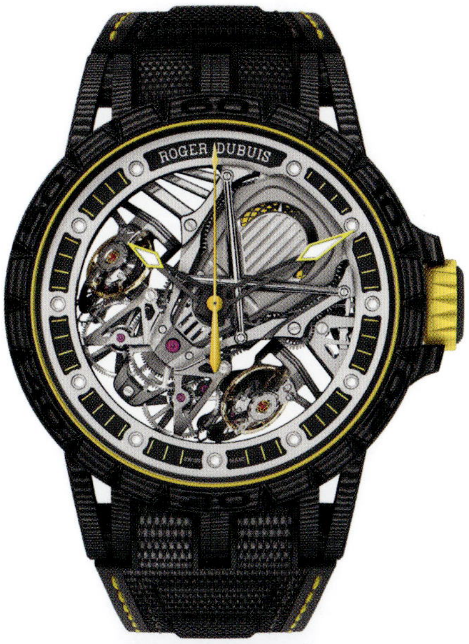

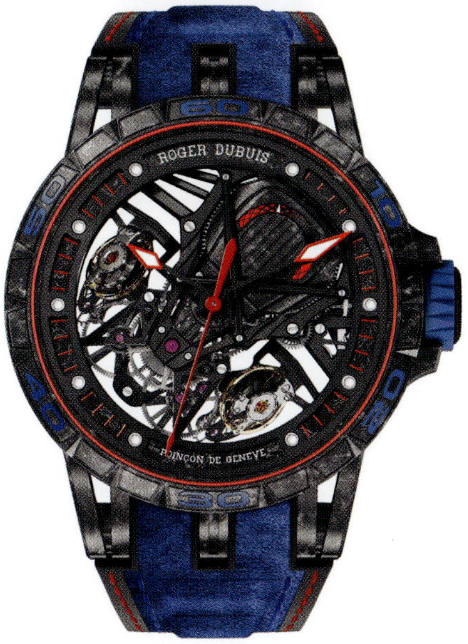

Tradition is not only found in the movement's receipt of the acclaimed Geneva Seal (which is a mark of both quality and beauty, as well as provenance), but also in its approach to ensuring horological excellence. Accuracy is the goal of this uncommonly exotic movement and, thus, Roger Dubuis uses dual regulation systems, which are oriented at opposing ends of the movement. Not only are they mounted diagonally (which helps reduce the accuracy-hampering effects of gravity), but the entire movement is seemingly mounted diagonally which brings a playful asymmetry to the overall composition of the dial. The dual balance wheel systems are connected via a differential, the results of which are averaged out offering a powerful "timing error elimination" system to the timepiece package.

A power-reserve indicator is located between 1 and 2 o'clock on the dial which allows the wearer to know when to manually wind the 312-part movement. With precision in mind, Roger Dubuis designed the movement to have a "jumping seconds" hand, which ticks rather than sweeps as is common on most mechanical movements. This allows the wearer to more easily count out the seconds for the purposes of timing an event.

Using light-weight C-SMS-forged carbon for this 45mm-wide Excalibur-style case, Roger Dubuis was further inspired by the world of Lamborghini racing in designing the bright, rich colours available for the various Excalibur Aventador S watch models. Each is part of a limited edition of just 88 pieces.

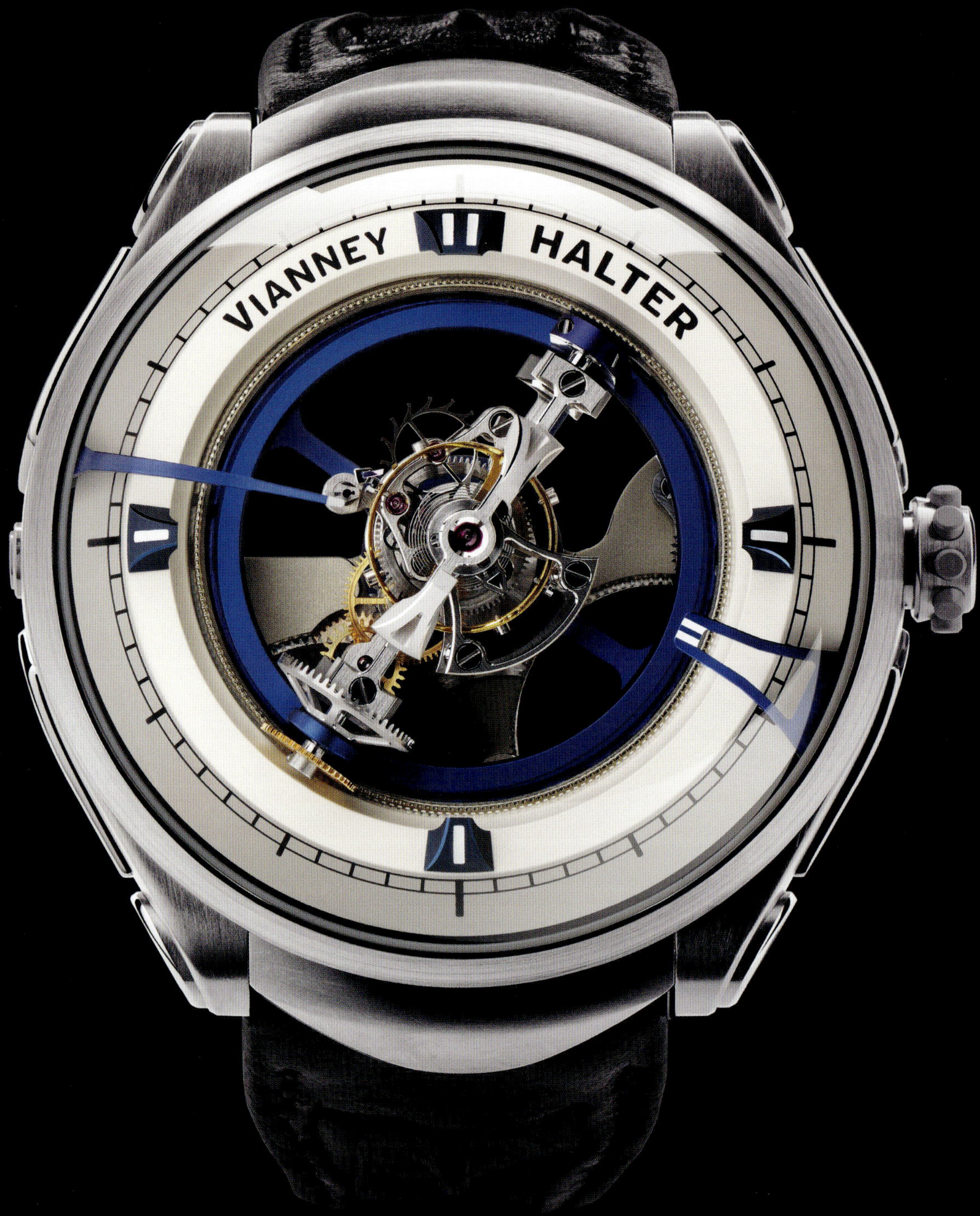

VIANNEY HALTER — DEEP SPACE TOURBILLON

$ 210 000

Avant Garde watchmaker and designer Vianney Halter is at heart his own biggest fan. His work is a testament to producing items that he personally wants to wear. A taste for science fiction in many forms has deeply influenced his work, and in the high-end watch industry he has a unique reputation for being strange, unpredictable, and a genius.

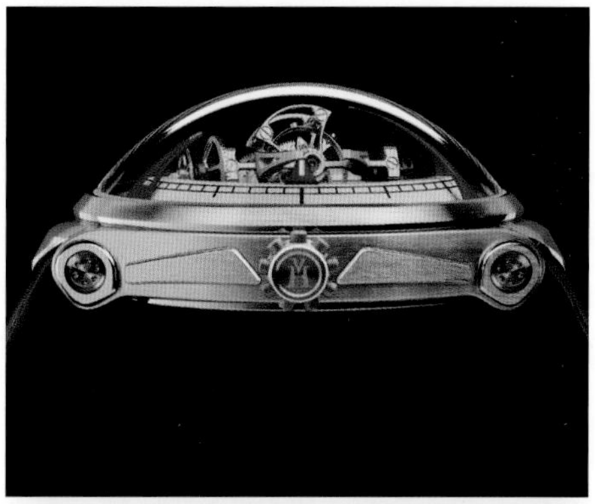

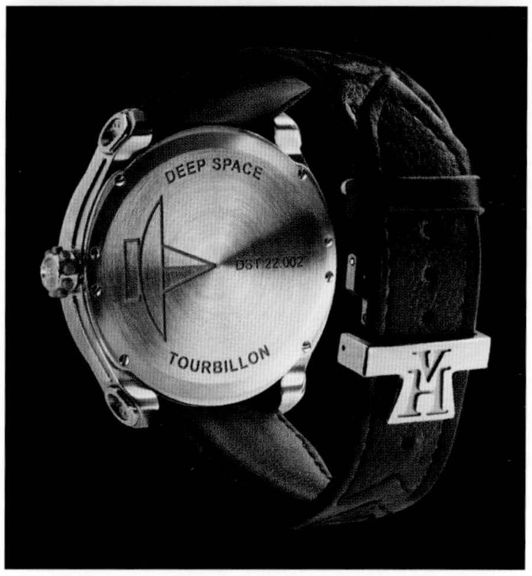

One of the things credited to Vianney Halter is the introduction, and perhaps legitimisation, of the Steampunk aesthetic into the worlds of both luxury, and high-end watches. His very first watch was the "19th-century science-fiction themed" Antiqua, which, in its own subtle way, was a nod to the world of Jules Verne. More recently, the style has become known as steampunk, but in the late 1990s almost no one in the watch industry had heard of it. The Antiqua put Halter on the map, setting a high degree of industry expectation for him. The next few years included a series of highs and lows for the often reclusive watchmaker, and after 2007, when he released a piece known as the Classic Janvier Sun & Moon, he conceded that he would probably never make another watch.

Halter's reason for wanting to "quit watches", was what he perceived as a lack of creative inspiration. Then, after a few years, he rediscovered a childhood passion, Star Trek. Halter claims that watching original Star Trek episodes, while in his native France as a youth, helped him learn English. In the late 2000s he began to watch reruns of the Star Trek series, Deep Space Nine.

Almost seven years after his "last watch", Vianney Halter released a new model known as the Deep Space Tourbillon. A not-so-subtle homage to the Star Trek: Deep Space Nine series, the watch received an award, and helped justify Halter's position as one of today's most interesting and creative watchmakers. The Deep Space Tourbillon watch begins with a spacecraft-style case that, in his own marketing materials, Halter depicts flying through space in an armada.

From a design perspective, the Deep Space Tourbillon appears little like Halter's previous creations, though small details, such as riveting on the lug screws, offer a helping of brand DNA. All the action is in the dial of the watch, which contains a suspended tourbillon-style escapement that rotates on three distinct axis points. The shape of the dial interior is highly inspired by "Deep Space Nine," which in the television show was a space station.

Hour and minute hands rotate around the periphery of the dial and are inspired by the fantasy space station's vertical spires. The interior tourbillon structure is unique, not only for being centrally-mounted, but also for its multi-axis rotating. The entire tourbillon suspension structure revolves around the dial, while it also rotates on its own axis, making for striking and complicated display. Born from fantasy, the Deep Space Tourbillon is Vianney Halter's ultimate homage to the sources that inspire him.

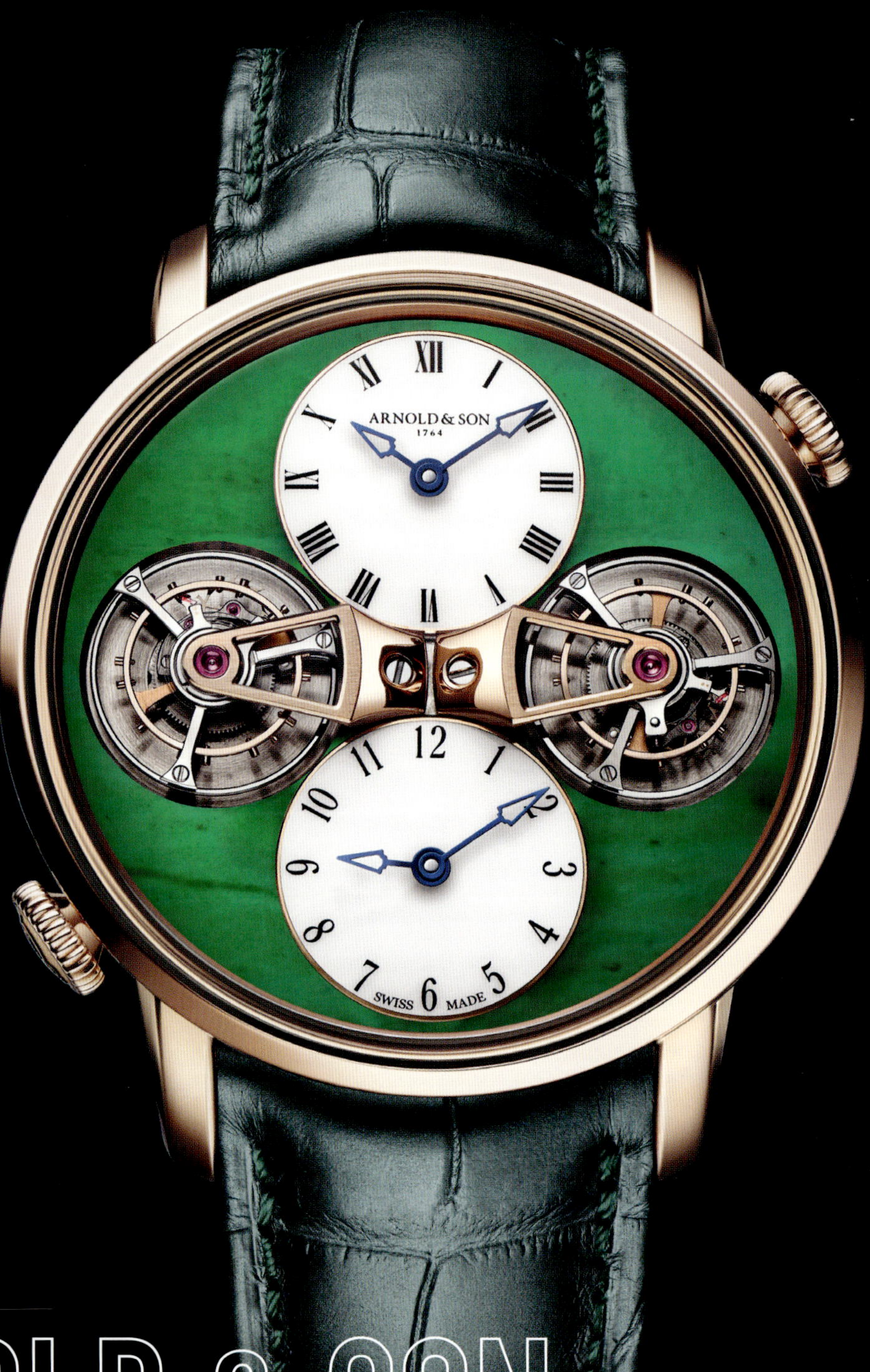

ARNOLD & SON — DOUBLE TOURBILLON ESCAPEMENT (DTE)

$ 215 850

For the 250th anniversary of the brand's namesake, watchmaker Arnold & Son released their most ambitious mechanical creation to date – the Double Tourbillon Escapement. In 1764, British watchmaker, John Arnold, was awarded a timepiece commission by King George III, which truly launched the promising master of horology's career. More than two centuries later, his ethos and work resumed in Switzerland under the direction of the celebrated watch designer and movement engineer Sébastien Chaulmontet. Inspired by an actual John Arnold pocket watch with a dial-mounted escapement system, the DTE's dial has both double tourbillons as well as double indicators for the time (which naturally can be independently adjusted).

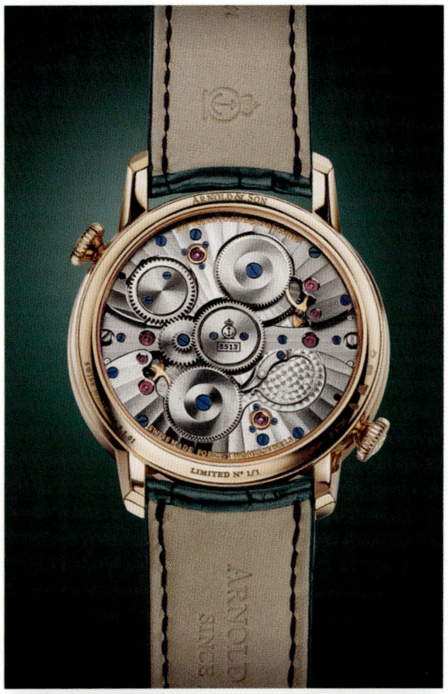

Timepieces with more than one tourbillon (many would argue, with any tourbillon) are not intended to increase the accuracy of a watch, despite the fact that traditionally that was exactly what tourbillons were invented to do. *Tourbillon* is French for "whirlwind", and is a mechanical system which places the regulation organ of a watch on a spinning "cage", intended to help average out the negative effects of gravity to make the watch more accurate. Tourbillons were invented at the end of the 18th century for use in clocks and pocket watches which, despite having a tendency to be carried around, typically had their regulation-systems position in the same vertical orientation all the time.

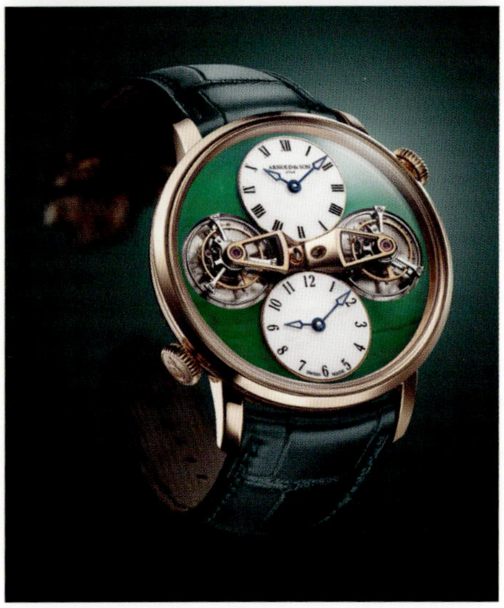

Today, tourbillons exist to excite collectors and aficionados not with their horological performance, but rather with their mechanical and decorative beauty. Watchmakers lovingly hand-polish each of the many tiny elements of tourbillons, which alone can be close to 100 parts not counting the rest of the mechanical movement. For the DTE watch, Arnold & Son produced two distinct tourbillon mechanisms on the dial that receive power from the same mainspring. Rather than be joined by a differential, the tourbillons each have their own running train, which means the two time-dials on the face of the DTE watch have their own tourbillon-regulation system. Such engineering is extremely uncommon, made even more uncommon by the symmetrical layout of both the items on the dial-side of the watch, as well as for the bridges and elements of the movement itself.

Unique to the traditional styling of the Arnold & Son brand, the dress-style DTE timepiece is designed for a subtle (classy) execution of wealth-on-the-wrist. It favours the refined execution of technique versus a blatant expression of excess, which typify many comparable watches at this $200,000 and upwards price-point.

PANERAI – LUMINOR 1950 EQUATION OF TIME TOURBILLON TITANIO PAM00365

$ 220 000

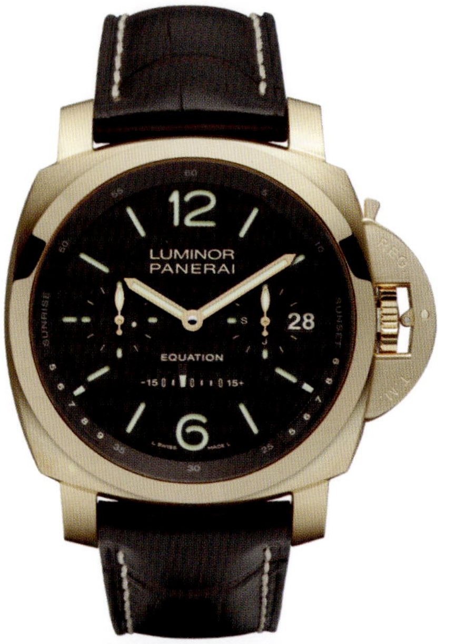

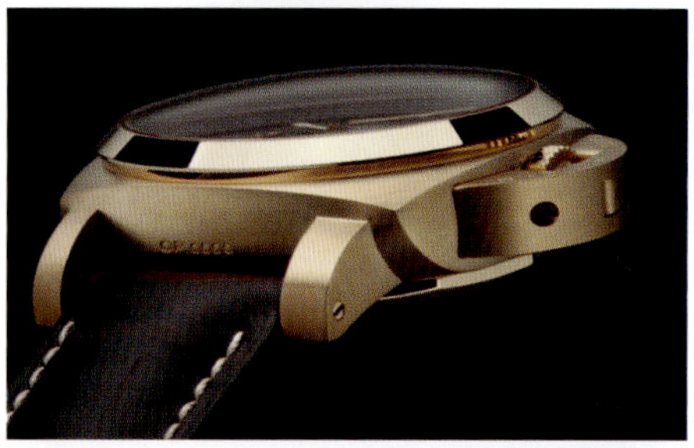

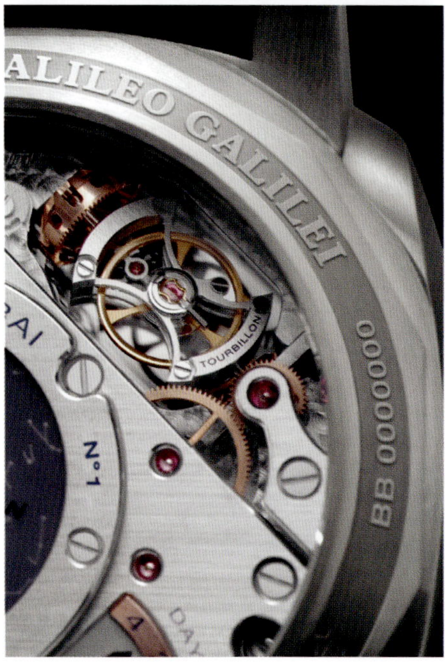

Originally Italian, the watchmaker Panerai enjoys a "cult-like" following among collectors today; it currently operates in Switzerland. Panerai timepieces are mostly based on historical designs going back to the 1930s. It was Rolex who helped Panerai – a Florence-based instrument maker who had a contract with the Italian Navy – to produce their first water-resistant dive watch. Panerai's core product designs were developed between the 1930s and '50s, but it wasn't until the late 1990s that the brand gained wide recognition.

While all Panerai products are luxury-priced, the brand rarely produces ultra-high-end creations. In 2010, Panerai released their most complicated timepiece ever, with the limited edition 1950 Equation of Time Tourbillon Titanio reference PAM00365 (PAM365). With indications on both the front and back of the case, the PAM365 arrived in an unusually large 50mm wide case produced from titanium. Panerai would also offer the piece in 18k rose gold on special request from customers.

The 1950 Equation of Time Tourbillon at heart was an astronomical watch – something highly unusual for the brand that focuses on mostly diving-style timepieces. The charm of Panerai design for many people is the simple, yet functional dials. The Equation of Time Tourbillon, nevertheless, contained a range of indicators on the dial, including: the time, linear equation of time, month, date, and sunrise and sunset times placed on the sloped flange ring on the outside periphery of the dial. The latter times aligned with a single city chosen by the owner of the watch upon ordering it.

The Equation of Time is an exotic complication, which shows the difference between the solar time and "civil" time, which is arguably most useful for those who own sundials. Nevertheless, its complexity having to take into account data that varies over the entire year, makes it desirable for collectors. The rear of the watch contains a star chart. This is linked to sky over a city and hemisphere of the owner's choosing, when they purchase the watch.

Changing each day, the star chart displays the view of the night sky from that reference city location. Also on the rear of the case, is an indicator for the movement's four days of power, allowing the wearer to know when to wind the mechanism. The movement also includes a tourbillon-style escapement, which is a unique interpretation of the complication. Panerai designed the tourbillon to rotate on a horizontal, rather than a vertical axis, and to turn every 30 seconds, rather than every minute, as most tourbillons do. Extremely rare, and available only to special order, Panerai only produced 30 pieces of the 1950 Equation of Time Tourbillon Titanio.

CARTIER – ROTONDE DE CARTIER ASTROTOURBILLON CARBON CRYSTAL

$ 221 000

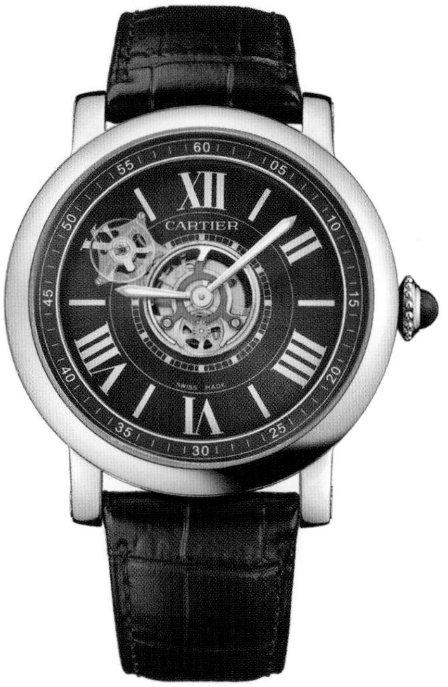

When Cartier chose to produce ultra-high-end "haute horlogerie" watches in addition to its more mainstream and jewellery-based luxury watches, a decision had to be made. The problem was that the luxury watch market can be both crowded and contradictory. Collectors want modern interpretations of historic concepts. Keeping tradition alive is a fundamental part of most good watches, but at the same time, buyers are always looking for something new.

When going even higher upmarket, Cartier was tasked with the responsibility of offering something new, that looked familiar, and that also spoke to where the brand was going. They succeeded, when they released a timepiece called the ID One in 2010, which was followed by the ID Two in 2012. Each of these spectacular watches succeeded in using brand new materials or techniques to build traditional watches.

Practically speaking, in the ID One and Two timepieces, Cartier found ways of using exotic sounding materials, such as ceramyst, niobium, and carbon crystal, to build movements that eliminated mechanical annoyances such as friction, air resistance, need for lubrication, and sensitivity to temperature and magnetism. The problem was that neither the ID One nor the ID Two watches were ever planned for commercial production.

Cartier did, however, release the limited edition Astrotourbillon Carbon Crystal, as a way of incorporating some of the ID series technology into a production timepiece, and they couldn't have picked a better model. Cartier originally released the Astrotourbillon in 2010, to much fanfare. The name of the watch stemmed from a unique feature that incorporated the balance wheel and escapement into the second hands on the dial. Cartier effectively turned the most important part of a mechanical movement into one of the hands, and it was deemed to be brilliant.

Given that the escapement orbits around the dial, which arguably allows it to perform like a tourbillon (though it isn't a true tourbillon), "astrotourbillon" was a fitting name. This special version of the Astrotourbillon uses a material called carbon crystal for some of the movement parts, and has a case produced from an exotic metal alloy similar to titanium, but with a bit more lustre, called niobium.

Carbon crystal is actually a form of diamond-coated silicon, and is used in the mechanical movement because, unlike metal, it require zero lubrication and lasts much longer. The diamond coating makes the parts very strong. They also happen to be almost perfectly transparent, which means they are beautiful to look at. Modern, and considerably important to Cartier's most high-end horological achievements, the Astrotourbillon Carbon Crystal was limited to 50 pieces.

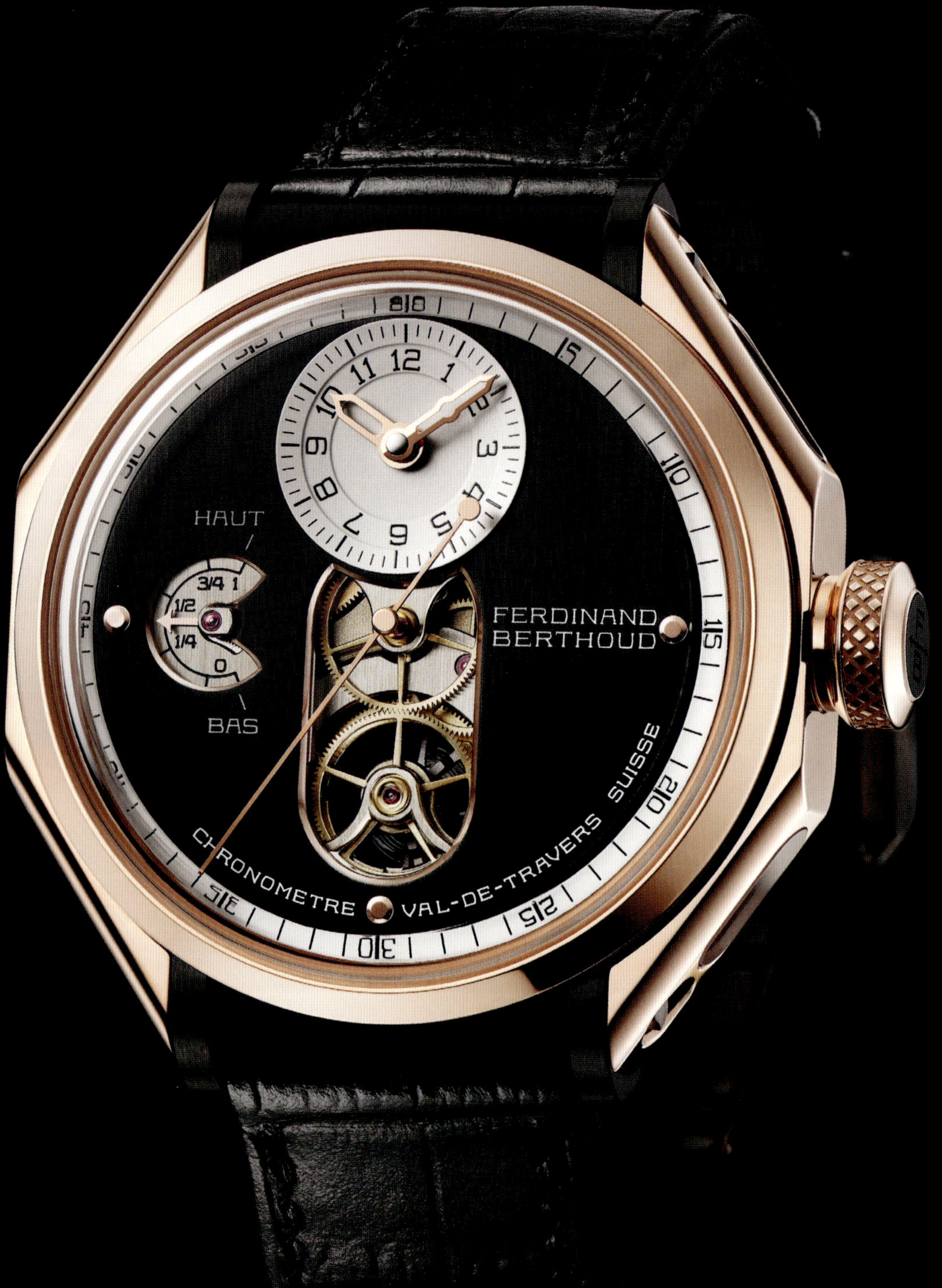

FERDINAND BERTHOUD — CHRONOMÈTRE FB 1.2

$ 222 890

Recently resurrected as a modern brand under the larger aegis of Swiss Chopard, boutique ultra-high-end watchmaker Ferdinand Berthoud exists almost exclusively to satisfy tastes of the most seasoned timepiece collectors. Ferdinand Berthoud himself was a historic watchmaker from the 18th century whose accomplishments include producing a series of marine chronometers as well as producing accurate timepieces for both royal and naval official use. This technical and aesthetic legacy are integral, not only in the visual design of the Chronomètre FB 1.2 case, but also in understanding the goal of its ambitiously difficult-to-produce mechanical movement.

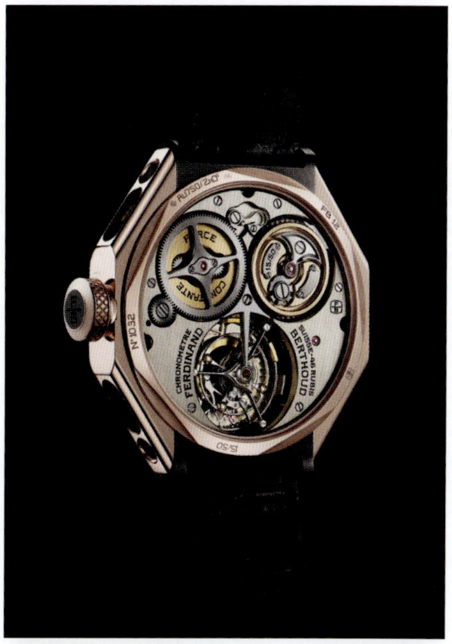

The Chronomètre FB 1.2 begins with a distinctive angular case inspired by the containers that held ship-based marine chronometer clocks. These timing mechanisms were designed to be impeccably accurate, even when bobbing and weaving with the motion of a boat hull. The Chronomètre FB 1.2 is designed to be worn on a wrist as opposed to serving duty on a naval ship, but both this contemporary timepiece creation and the historic machines it was inspired by are obsessed with precision. The time in hours and minutes is shown as a subsidiary dial, with a larger track for the seconds hand. The dial also features a useful power-reserve indicator that is connected to an unusual conical-shaped system that sits below the dial. What makes the in-house made and designed caliber FB-T.FC movement compelling are the number of features in its design, intended to promote accuracy and high performance over time. Only the most educated timepiece collectors, literate in horology, will fully understand the philosophy behind how the various systems in this exclusive movement work together. Anyone, however, can appreciate its hand-decorated beauty and the majesty of the large spinning tourbillon visible through the rear of the case.

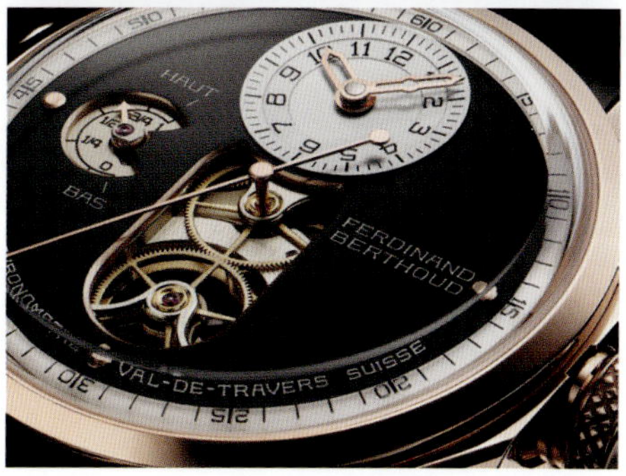

One of the most uncommon mechanical features in the Ferdinand Berthoud Chronomètre FB 1.2 is a fusee-and-chain transmission system. This moves power from the mainspring barrels to the regulation system in a highly consistent manner which ensures not only temporary accuracy, but accuracy over time as the tension in the mainspring winds down. The system works using an extremely tiny chain produced from a total of 474 steel links that together are 28cm long. Integration of a constant-force system, fusee-and-chain transmission, and the tourbillon-style escapement, combine to create a beautiful package that is also uncommonly focused on precision and timekeeping accuracy in watches at this price point and pedigree, and is officially certified as a Swiss Chronometer.

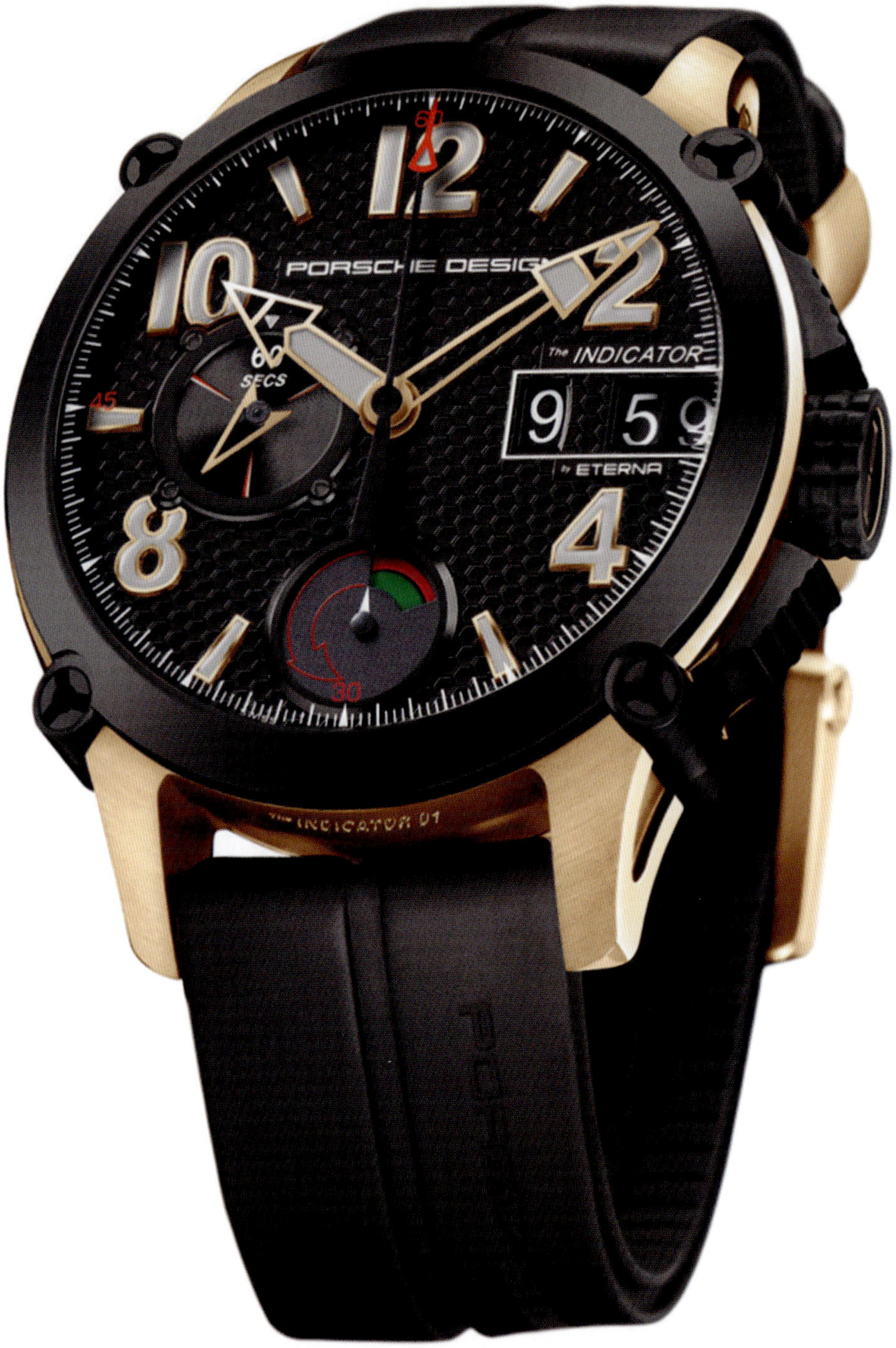

PORSCHE DESIGN — P'6910 INDICATOR

$ 225 000

The elegance and aesthetic attractiveness of an analogue watch dial is something collectors have come to admire and prefer, even when faced with the legibility of a digital one. Beauty tends to beat functionality when it comes to an item people are going to wear on their wrist. Having said that, functionality can be beautiful when it is designed to be simple and effective. In other words, a perfectly operating machine is a beautiful one. This latter design ethos is a governing rule behind creative firms such as Porsche Design.

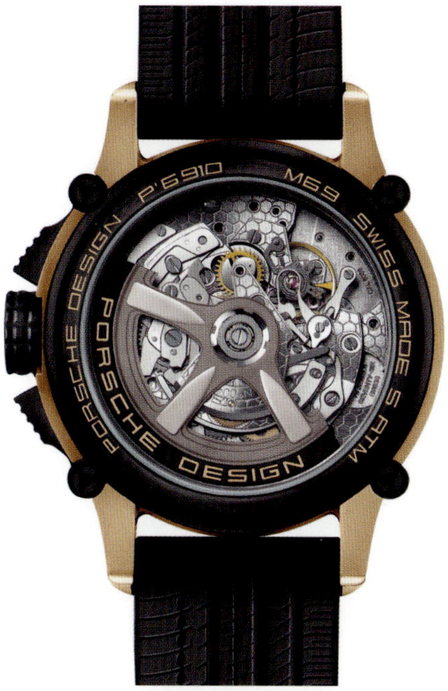

Porsche Design timepieces have helped epitomise beautiful "tool watches" since the 1970s, but Porsche Design themselves have never built a watch. Rather, they have teamed up with various Swiss watchmaking partners, over the years, to manufacture their products. Companies such as Orfina and IWC have produced watches for Porsche Design in the past and, as of 2013, the official watchmaker for Porsche Design is the historic Swiss brand Eterna.

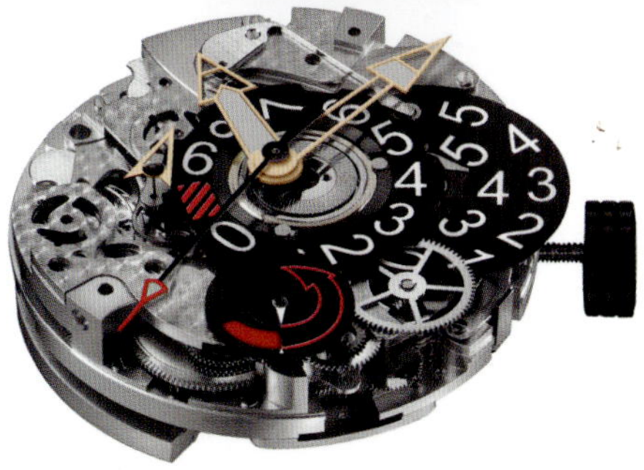

In the mid 2000s, Porsche Design wanted to create an impressive and technologically unprecedented timepiece, to sit at the top of its product line. Together with Eterna, they imagined what the ultimate Porsche Design timepiece could be, staying within the function-first DNA of the brand. In 2008, they released the incredibly unique (and expensive) P'6910 Indicator watch. A leader in sports chronographs, it was Porsche Design's goal to combine their relationship with mechanical watches and the simple legibility of digital timepieces.

The P'6910 Indicator was the first watch to display a digital counter for the elapsed hours and minutes counted by the chronograph. The numerals are displayed on discs that jump each passing minute and hour, while the chronograph seconds are displayed on a traditional hand that travels around the dial. In addition to the time and chronograph, the P'6910 also has a power reserve indicator for the automatic movement. Porsche Design claim that each P'6910 watch movement requires 40 days for their watchmakers to assemble.

At 49mm wide and rather thick, the Indicator is, nevertheless, an extremely wearable watch. A honeycomb pattern on the design is a unique visual trait for Porsche Design watches, and the motif is mimicked on the surface of the mechanical movement. Porsche Design watches rarely reference Porsche automobiles, but the automatic rotors on their movements are meant to appear like Porsche wheels. Produced in titanium as well as 18k pink gold, in the latter precious metal, the Porsche Design P'6910 Indicator watch was limited to just 10 pieces.

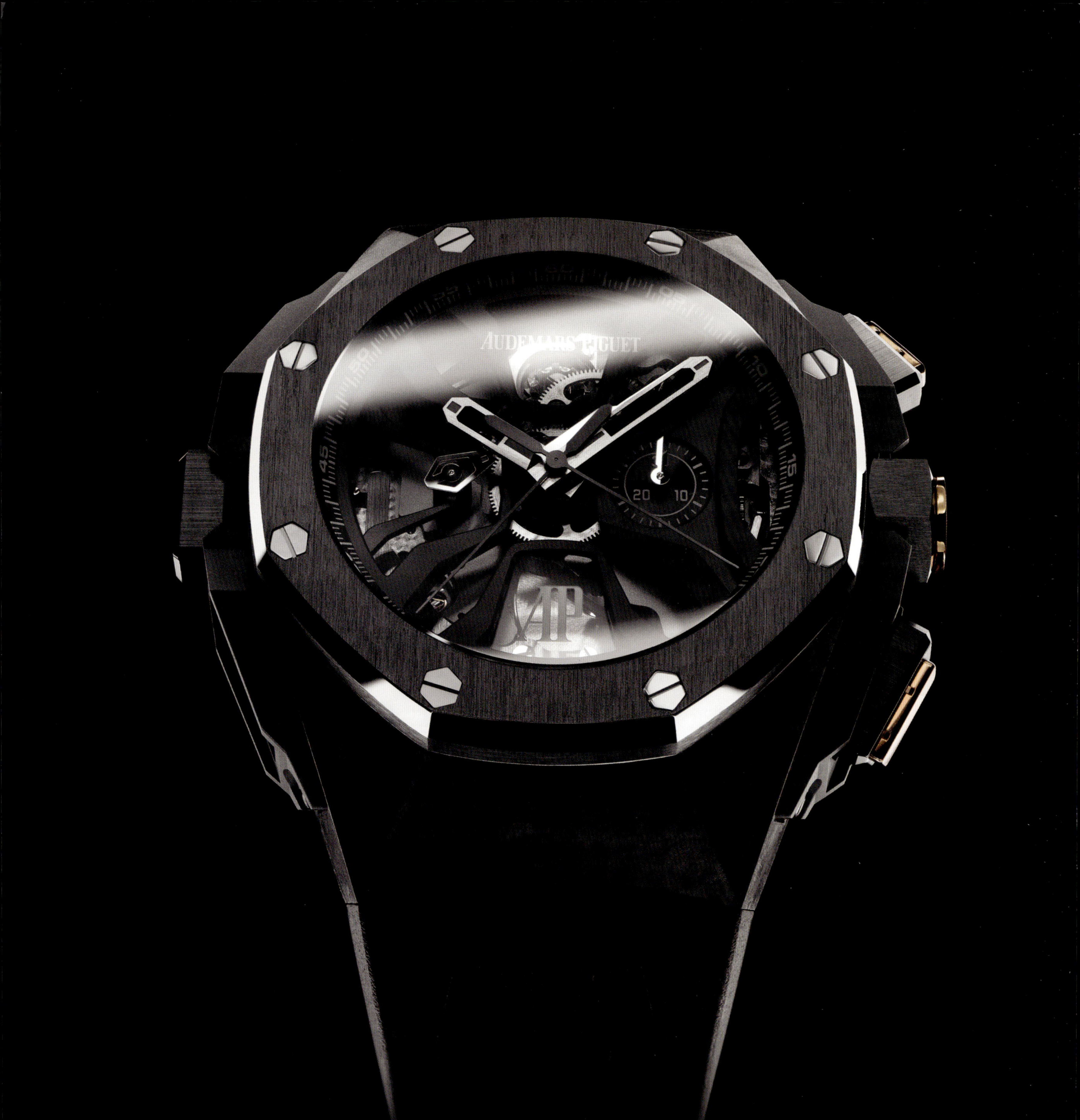
AUDEMARS PIGUET
AP

AUDEMARS PIGUET — ROYAL OAK CONCEPT LAPTIMER MICHAEL SCHUMACHER

$ 229 500

THE IMMEDIATE BENEFIT OF THE NEW TIMING FEATURES IN THE ROYAL OAK CONCEPT LAPTIMER MICHAEL SCHUMACHER IS THAT THE WEARER IS ACTUALLY ABLE TO SAVE TIME.

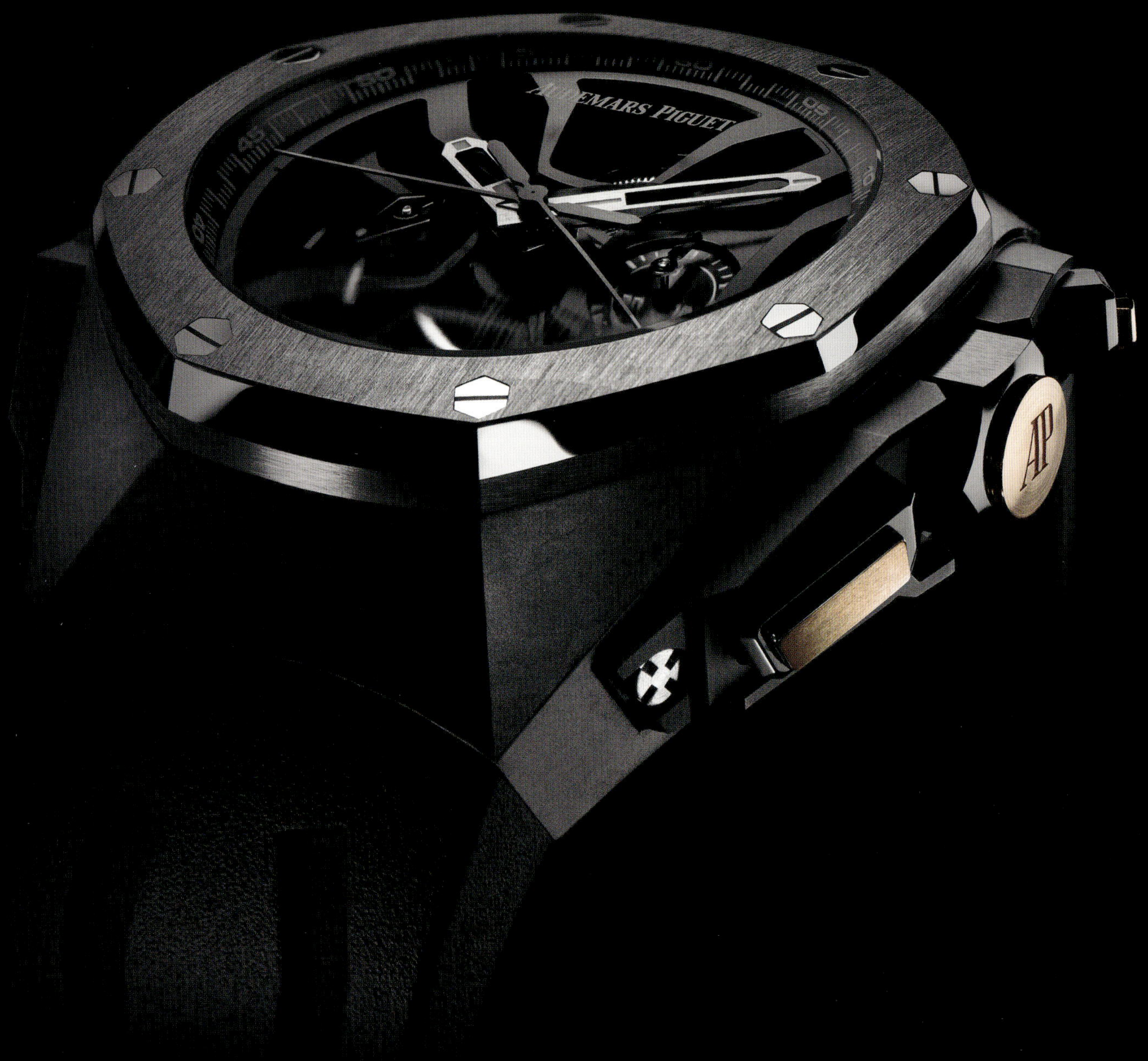
PIGUET
AP

In 2012, Audemars Piguet introduced its first limited-edition timepiece in honour of the famed Formula One racing-car driver, Michael Schumacher. Tragically, the following year in 2013, the world champion suffered a debilitating skiing accident. In 2015, following up the success of the first model, Audemars Piguet released the Royal Oak Concept Laptimer Michael Schumacher, once again in honour of the man who inspired the ambitious chronograph – although with some regret that he might never have a chance to actually use it in the field. Both a timepiece aficionado and a popular personality, German-born Schumacher had his name on multiple timepieces, across multiple brands (Audemars Piguet being the most exclusive).

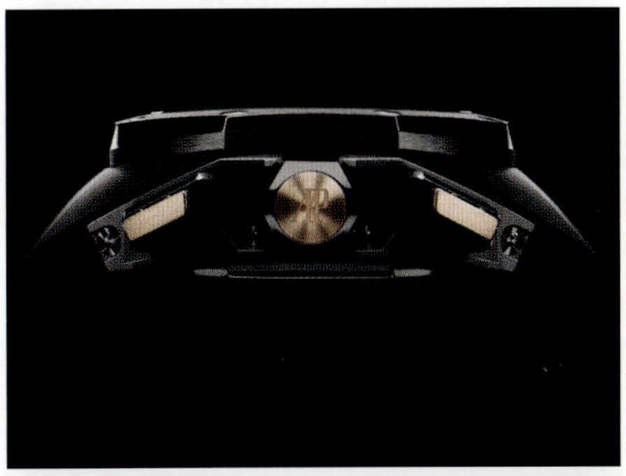

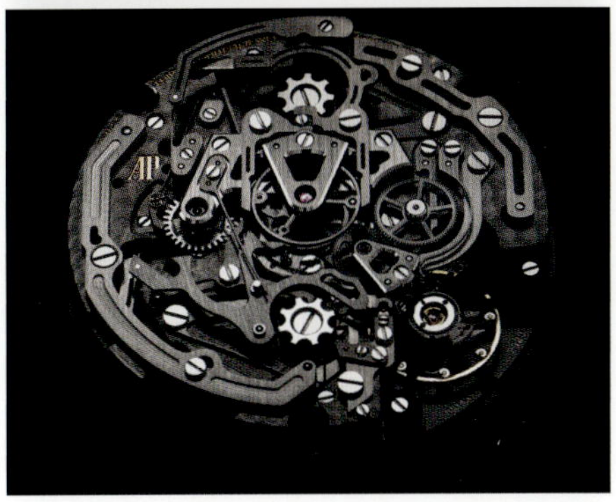

Most watches that are designed to be used in conjunction with motor sports have the ability to measure intervals of time, such as the duration of a lap. What distinguishes this chronograph from other chronographs is a small yet difficult-to-engineer feature that allows users to either recall the last lap time, or measure two laps concurrently. In essence, Audemars Piguet evolved the historic and collector-prized "rattrapante" (split-second) into something slightly more purpose-built for track observation, as well as for actual racing. The immediate benefit of the new timing features in the Royal Oak Concept Laptimer Michael Schumacher is that the wearer is actually able to save time. After all, in sports every moment counts. The new hand on the dial – whose functions are controlled via a pusher on the case – can be stopped while the rest of the chronograph is still running. At the same time, the user can know the exact time of the last lap while trying to beat their time in the current lap. The utility of such a chronograph complication is similarly useful to an observer tracking the performance – a role envisioned by Schumacher for the mechanical watch he always wanted to wear.

Visually, the Royal Oak Concept Laptimer Michael Schumacher is boldly intimidating with its many strong, architectural lines. Based on the iconic Royal Oak case design from the early 1970s, with its distinctive eight-sided bezel, this watch sits imposingly on the wrist. Its 44mm-wide case is made from forged carbon; the bezel, case edges and case back are made from titanium, and the push-pieces are made from ceramic and 18k pink gold. Audemars Piguet succeeded in pleasing both lovers of traditional horology and admirers of contemporary design with the aesthetic and technical appeal of the in-house made, manually wound movement. The novelty of the two second hands is the most obvious innovation, but the watch's mechanical movement also makes use of uncommon parts, such as difficult-to-manufacture conical gears and long-lasting solid lubricants. The collection was limited to 221 pieces – the number of F1 World Championship races in which Schumacher scored points; along with seven stars etched into the side of the watch, to mark each of his F1 World Championship titles.

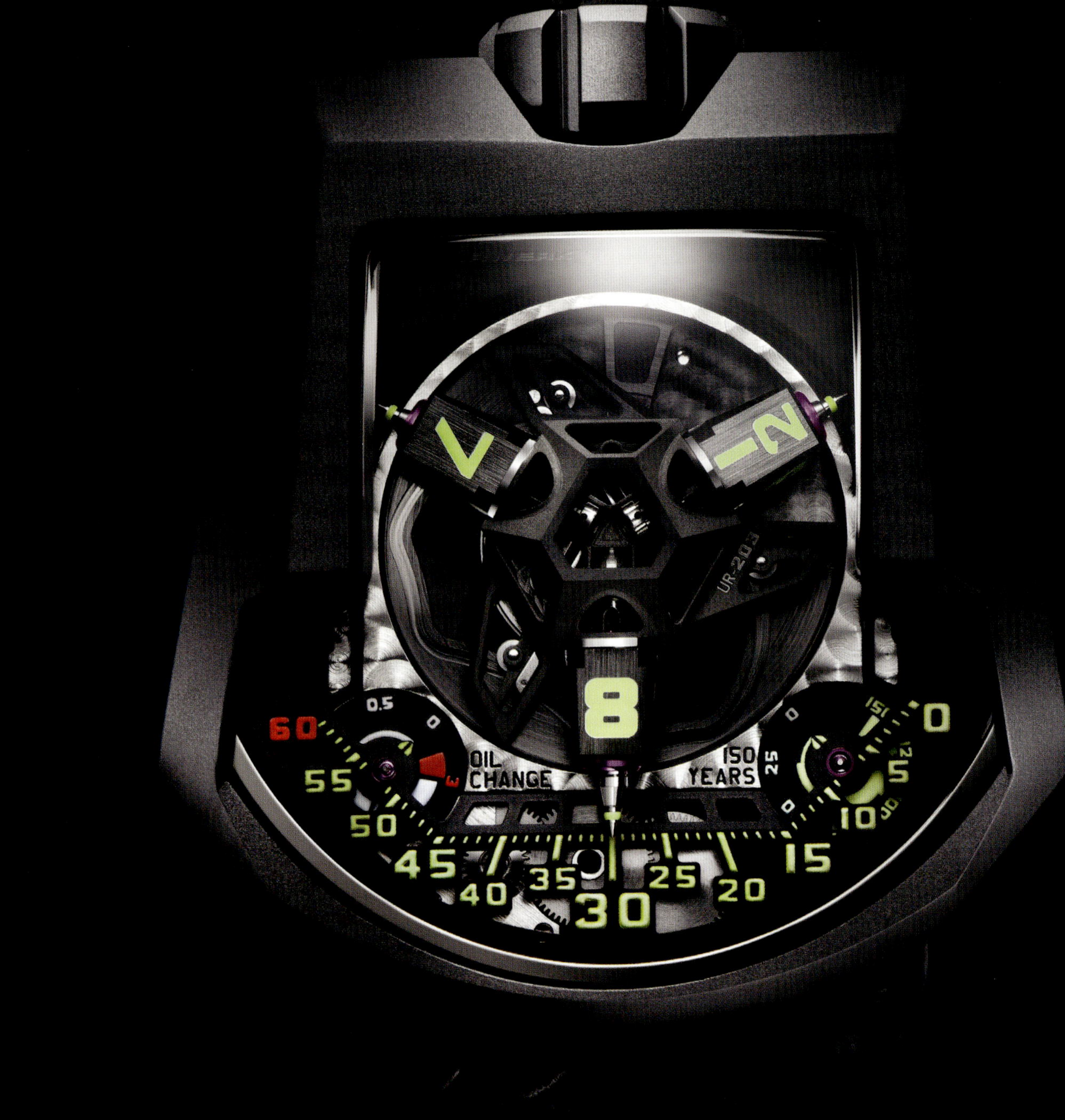

URWERK — UR-203

$ 230 000

When the boutique Geneva-based watchmaker URWERK first came to market, it made a name for itself by telling the time in a unique fashion. Indeed, as a manner of distinguishing themselves, it is common for small, high-end watchmakers to attract collectors by offering new ways to do old things. A great deal of intellectual energy in the horological world is put into developing ways of telling the time that are different from the standard 12-hour round dial. It isn't that anything is wrong with society's circular clocks, but rather that finding alternatives is stimulating, possibly artistic and, of course, challenging.

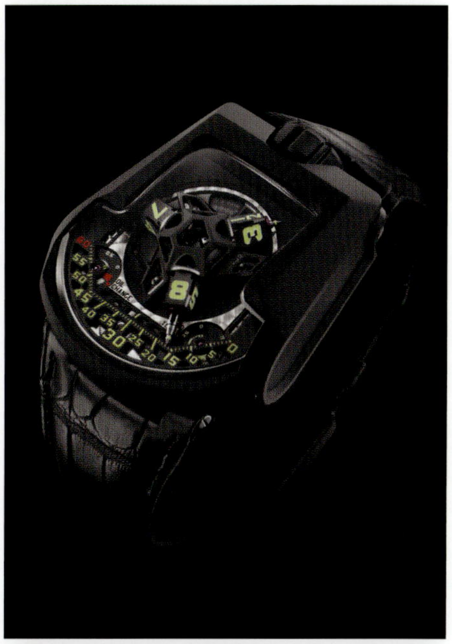

While URWERK did not invent the "satellite" approach to displaying the time, they've certainly taken a sense of modern ownership of the theme, given how well they interpret it. The idea is that revolving satellites move around a dial to display the hour along a scale that indicates the minutes. In this case, three cubes rotate to display the correct hour along the minute scale at the lower part of the dial. Each of the cubes has four sides, and the correct hour turns into position as the last one moves aside. What is also interesting is that a small telescopic hand extends from the hour indicators when it is their turn to move across the minute scale.

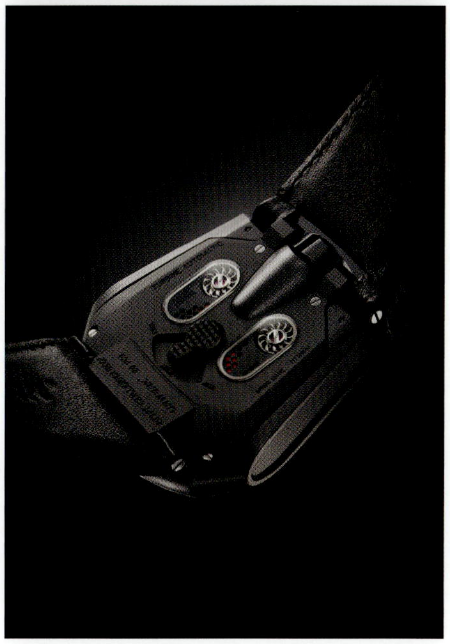

The UR-203 is a follow-up model to the UR-202, which URWERK nicknamed the "Hammerhead" due to the shape of the case. This particular model was offered in all black, being released in 2010 as a limited edition. Typical of URWERK's presentation of luxury, the black coating hides a fully platinum case. The conventional logic would be to expose a luxury case made of platinum (with a titanium back) in order to show off the material, but at URWERK it was decided to mask it in black.

Inside the UR-203 is an interesting movement that shows off the playful nature of the brand. As an automatic mechanism, URWERK designed it with a small switch to slow or completely stop the automatic rotor from spinning. Why? Well in order to protect the movement during periods of "extreme wear," the user can block or slow the rotor from spinning.

In addition to telling the time, the UR-203 has two interesting indicators on the dial. To the left is an "Oil Change" indicator meant to suggest when the watch should be returned for servicing, and to the right is a sort of odometer. It runs constantly with the movement tracking its total running time for up to 150 years. URWERK produced just 20 pieces in total.

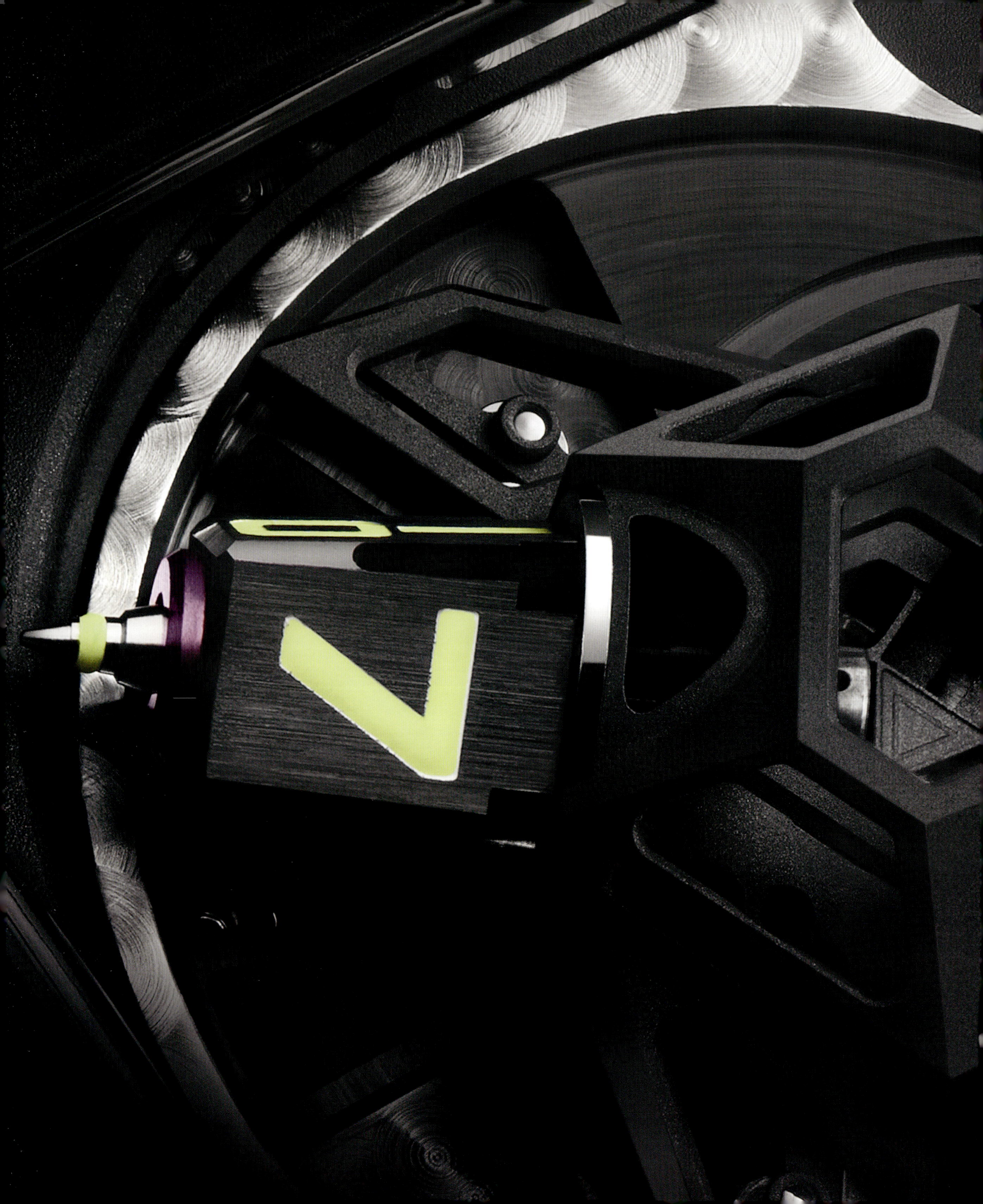

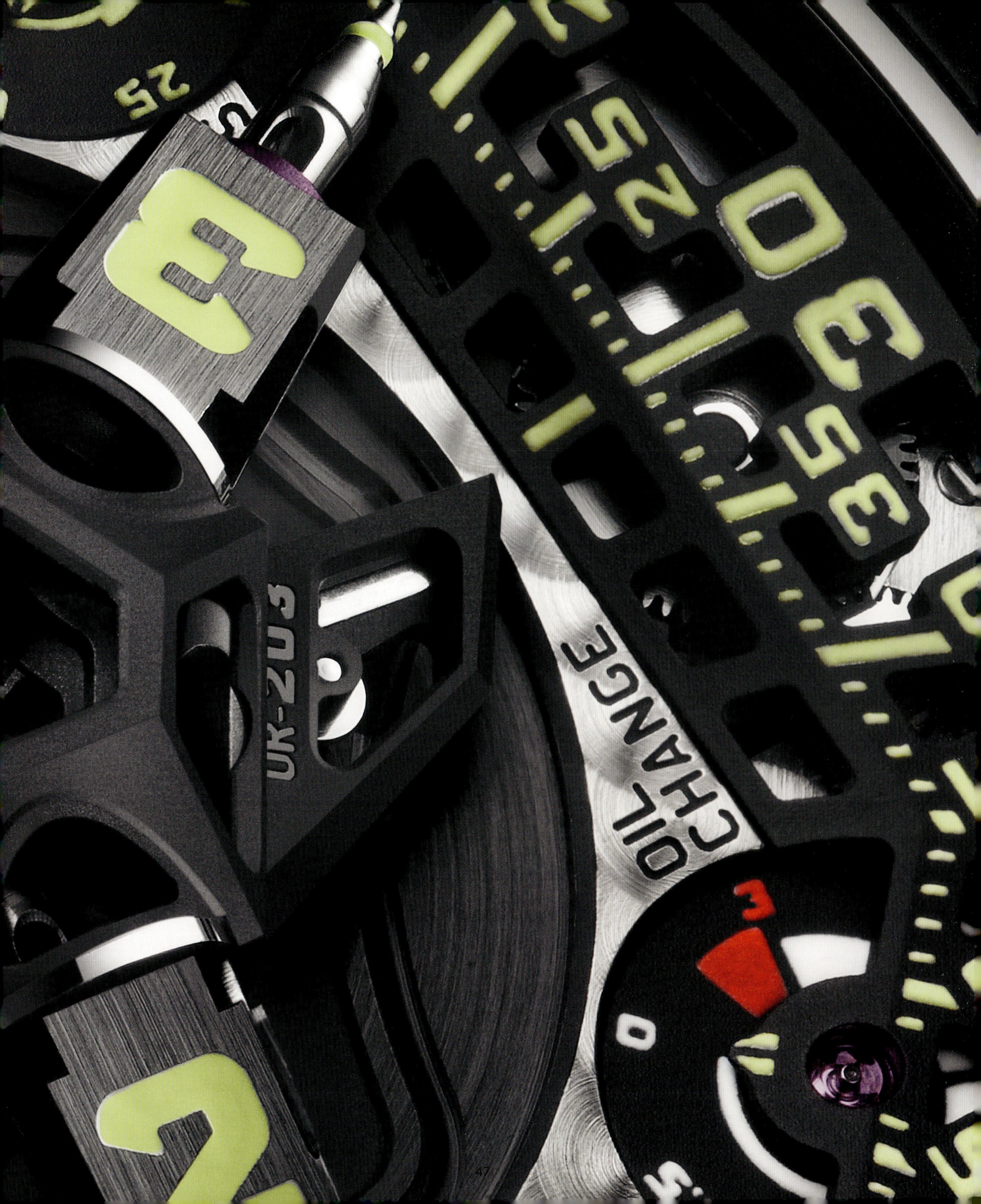
OIL
CHANGE

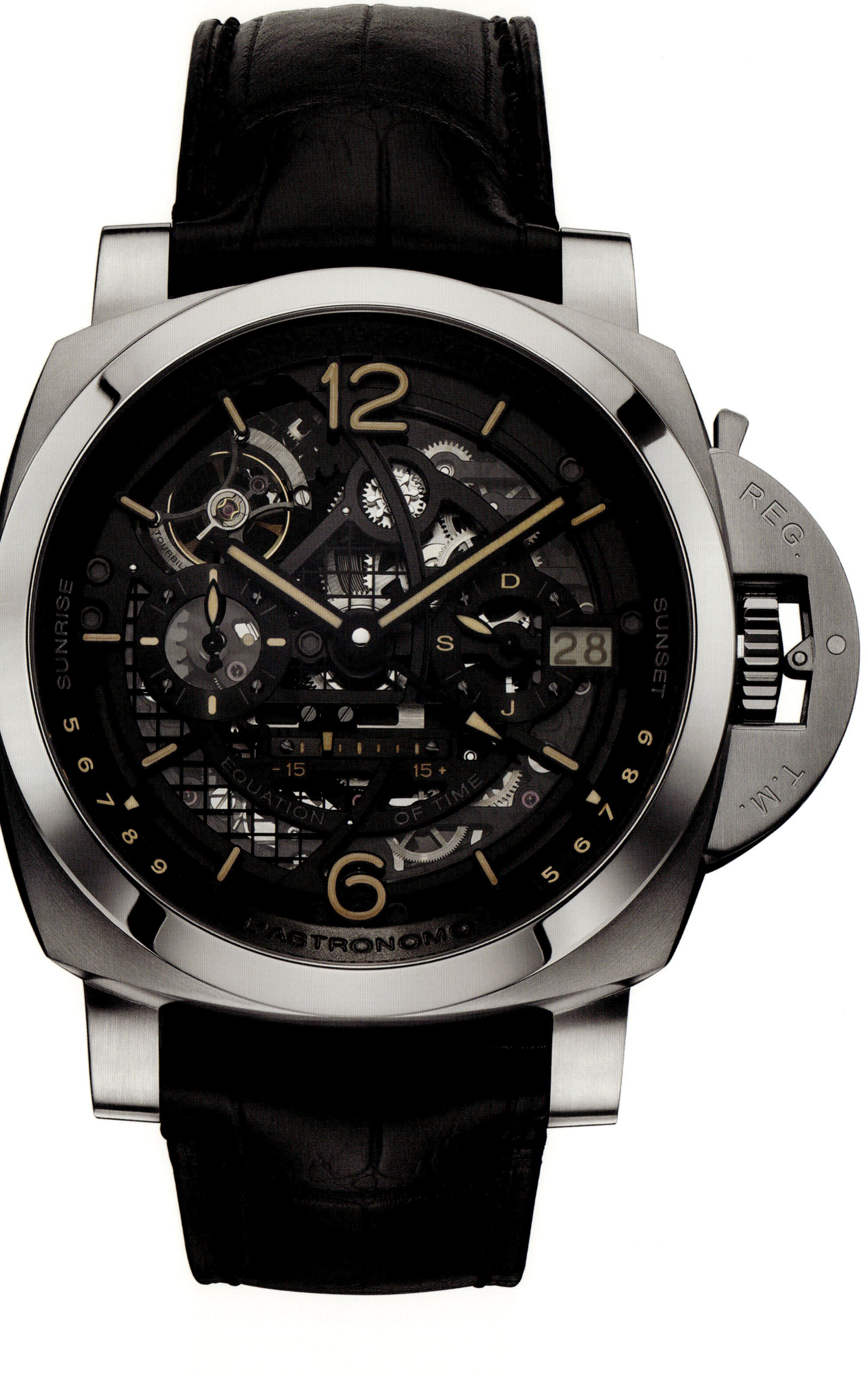
SUNRISE
SUNSET
EQUATION OF TIME
-15
15+
28
L'ASTRONOMO
REG. T.M.

PANERAI — L'ASTRONOMO LUMINOR 1950 TOURBILLON MOON PHASES EQUATION OF TIME GMT

$ 230 000

THE FRONT DIAL'S OPEN-WORKED FACE IS A DELICATE EXERCISE IN PRECISION MANUFACTURING AND FOR THE FIRST TIME USES STACKED PIECES OF POLARIZED BOROSILICATE GLASS FOR THE DATE DISPLAY.

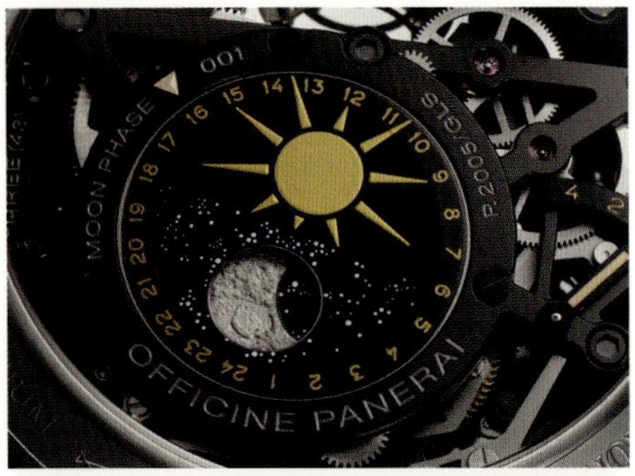

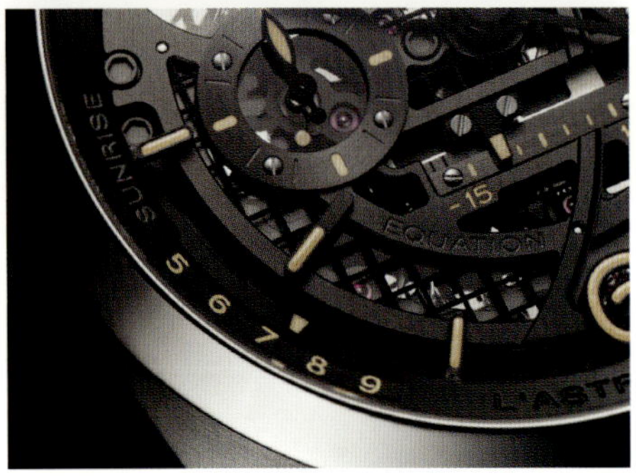

Known as the Panerai "PAM920" to collectors, the aptly named L'Astronomo watch is markedly different from your average Panerai luxury sports watch, which was typically defined by aesthetic simplicity. The PAM920 is the second variant of the L'Astronomo timepiece collection and adds a few important technical features that help round out this astronomically themed timepiece that the Italian/Swiss brand says is dedicated to famed historic astronomer, Galileo Galilei.

Sized at 50mm wide and initially presented in a titanium case, Panerai makes it clear that the majority of L'Astronomo PAM920 watches will be produced on special order by the client. Buyers can choose from various case materials and aesthetic options, but their most important decision is what part of the Earth should be the basis for the astronomical complications – notably the sunrise and sunset times that are indicated on the timepiece's front dial. Turn the watch over and the rear of the case presents a secondary face with a power-reserve indicator and an additional view of the complicated in-house made movement, as well as an attractive integrated display which indicates the current phase of the Moon as the entire mechanism spins once every 24 hours.

Core design elements make the PAM920's case and dial very much a Panerai creation, but the complicated, skeletonised dial offers a view unlike more "pedestrian" Panerai timepieces. The front dial's open-worked face is a delicate exercise in precision manufacturing and for the first time uses stacked pieces of polarized borosilicate glass for the date display. This ensures that the date is readable at its 3 o'clock window, but that the rest of the otherwise visible date disc appears transparent. At the 10 to 11 o'clock position is a view of the tourbillon-regulation system – which is patented and unique to Panerai. In addition to spinning once each 30 seconds (as opposed to the more customary 60 seconds), the tourbillon rotates on a horizontal versus vertical axis.

Other functions not mentioned above in the impressive L'Astronomo's P.2005/GLS movement include the equation of time, GMT second time zone, and of course the time as part of the manually wound mechanical movement that has 96 hours of power reserve. As a result, the Panerai PAM920 is the ideal combination of intensive Swiss mechanical engineering and Italian design sophistication.

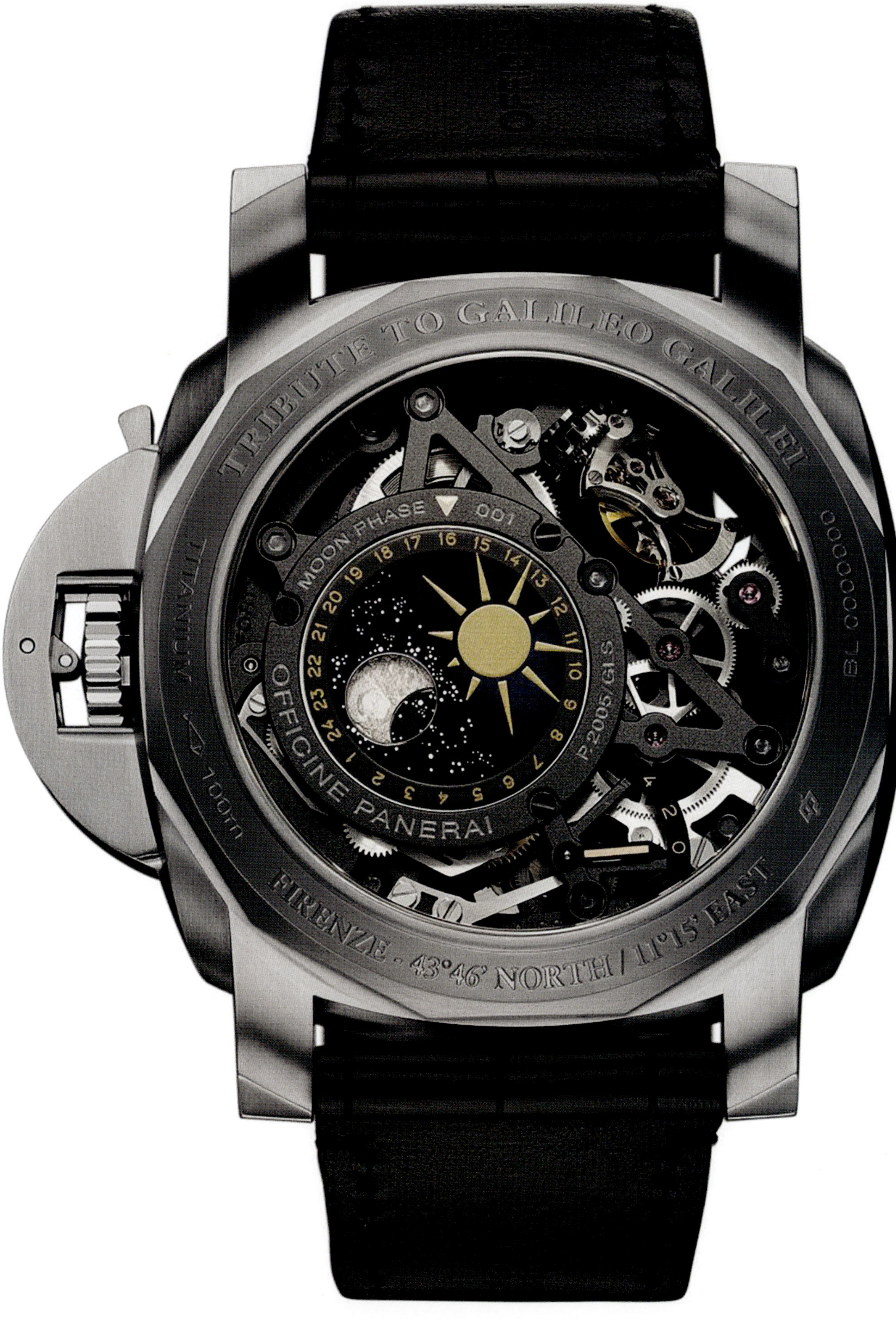
TRIBUTE TO GALILEO GALILEI
FIRENZE - 43°46' NORTH / 11°15' EAST
TITANIUM
100m
MOON PHASE
001
OFFICINE PANERAI
P.2005/GLS
BL 0000000

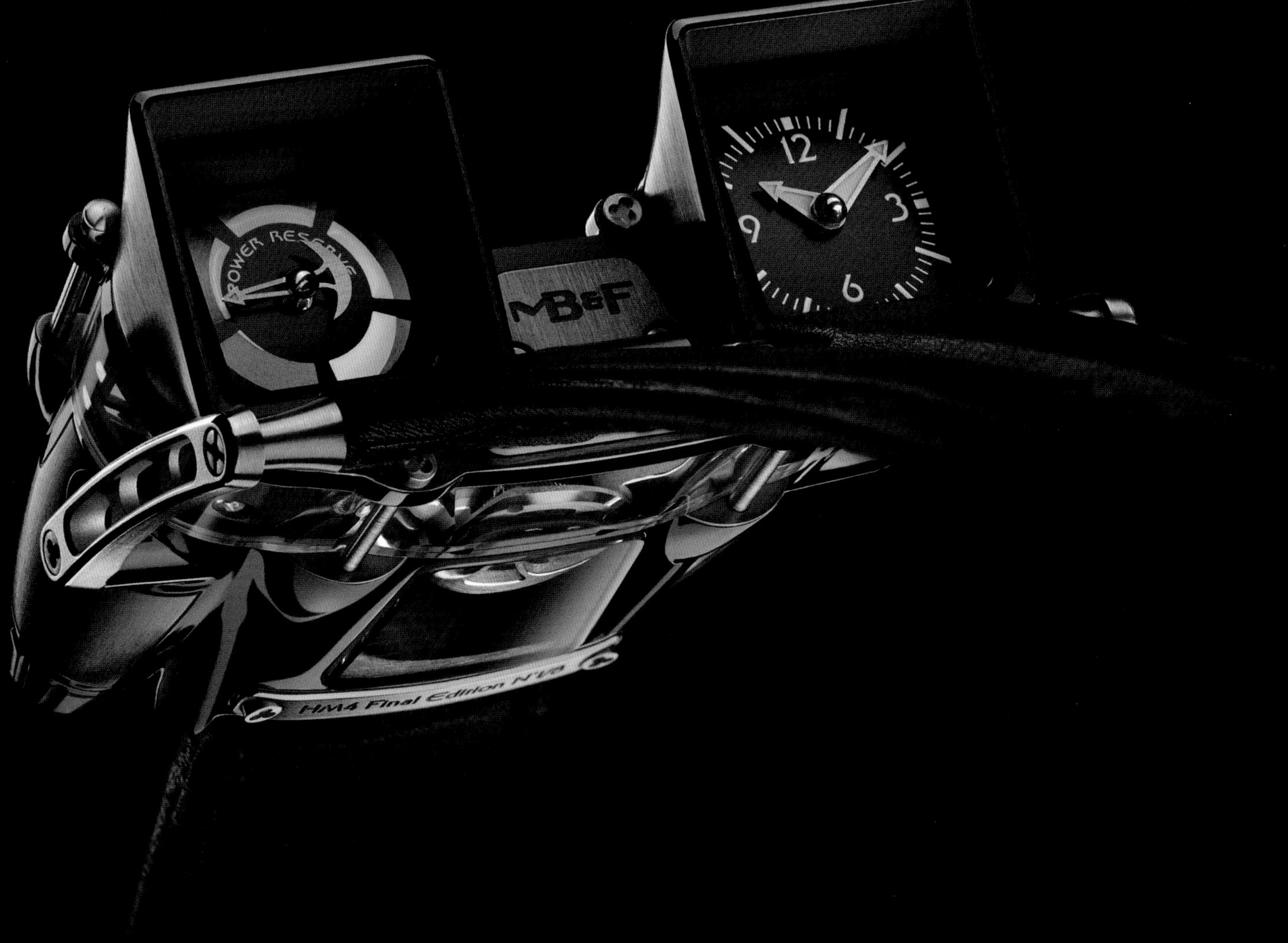

MB&F — HOROLOGICAL MACHINE NO. 4 FINAL EDITION

$ 230 000

Horological Machines are wearable pieces of mechanical art produced by Max Busser and friends (MB&F). Each piece combines Busser's love of mechanical timepieces – machines that inspired him as a youth – with his appreciation for visual art. As a boutique brand that focuses on exclusively avant-garde luxury watches, MB&F has been an envied success among its peers.

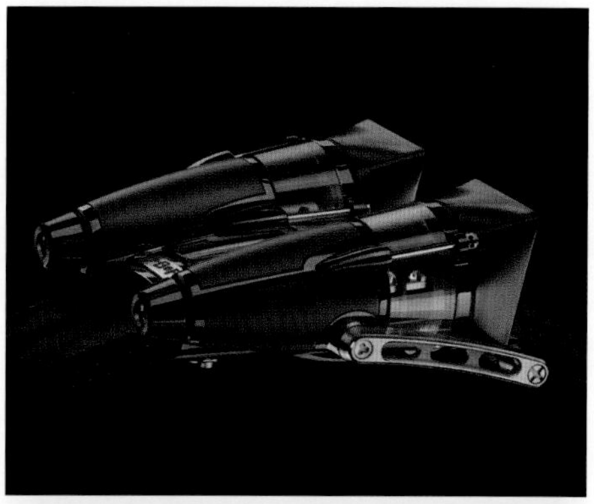

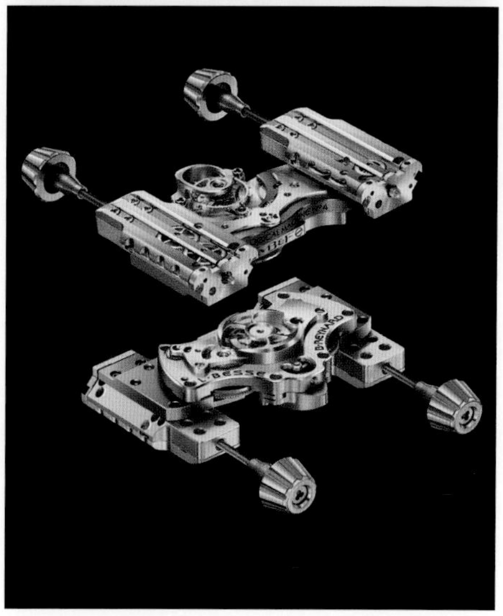

Like the world-class artists who fill gallery exhibitions with people eager to see their latest work, Busser has nurtured a fervent following of collectors and media across the globe, eager to experience his latest creations. A master storyteller, it can be said that anyone buying an MB&F watch is also purchasing a bit of Busser's personality.

The fourth instalment of the Horological Machine (HM4) was nicknamed "Thunderbolt" when the first version was released in 2010. Inspired by military aircraft, the HM4's case consists of two fuselage-style segments, which collectors sometimes refer to as the "engines". One dial indicates the power reserve for the movement, while the other displays the time with hours and minutes. Inside is a unique movement, inspired by science fiction spacecraft. Produced mostly from titanium, a middle section of the case has been produced from precision-milled synthetic sapphire crystal, to allow for a view of the movement.

Appearing like no other wristwatch that has ever existed, the HM4 has a movable lug system, design to conform to the wearer's wrist for better comfort. Like driving watches of old, the time is told from the side rather than from the top. This is actually a theme that MB&F has explored before in their timepieces.

As with anything so unique, the Horological Machine No. 4 was controversial. It was extremely complicated to produce, and, given the highly bespoke parts, MB&F promised to produce just two HM4 watches per a month, with a total of only 100 pieces overall.

The Thunderbolt was only the first model, and a few different versions of the HM4 followed until the "Final Edition" was released in 2013. Released as a limited edition of just eight pieces (to complete the 100 total), the HM4 Final Edition was themed after stealth aircraft. The titanium case is coated black and square hoods have been placed over the two dials, making it more difficult for onlookers to tell the time.

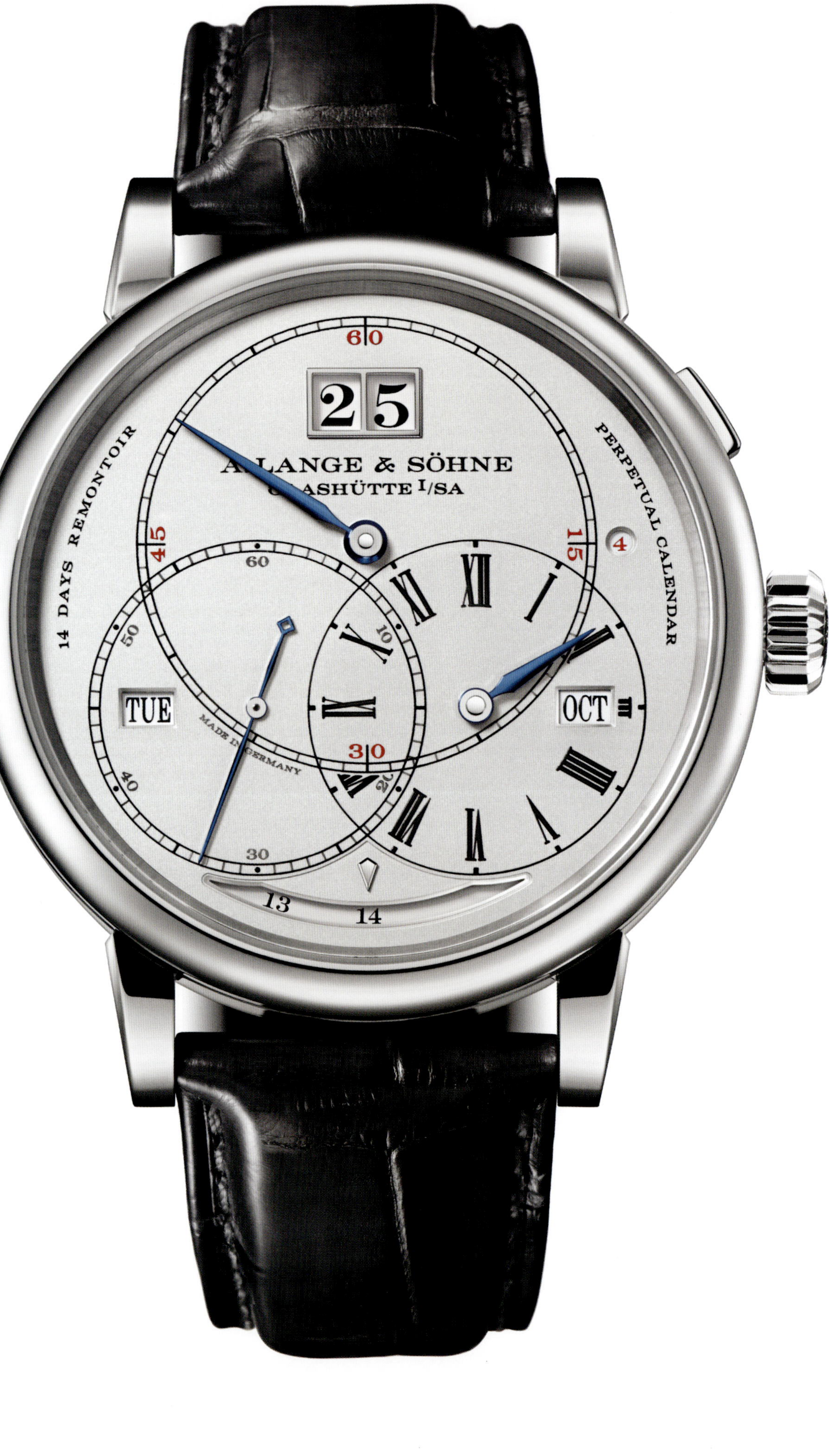

25
LANGE & SÖHNE
14 DAYS REMONTOIR
PERPETUAL CALENDAR
TUE
OCT
13
14

A. LANGE & SÖHNE — RICHARD LANGE PERPETUAL CALENDAR "TERRALUNA"

$ 231 500

THIS WATCH HAS AN EXTREMELY COMPLICATED MOVEMENT, ASSEMBLED FROM CLOSE TO 800 HAND-FINISHED AND DECORATED PARTS.

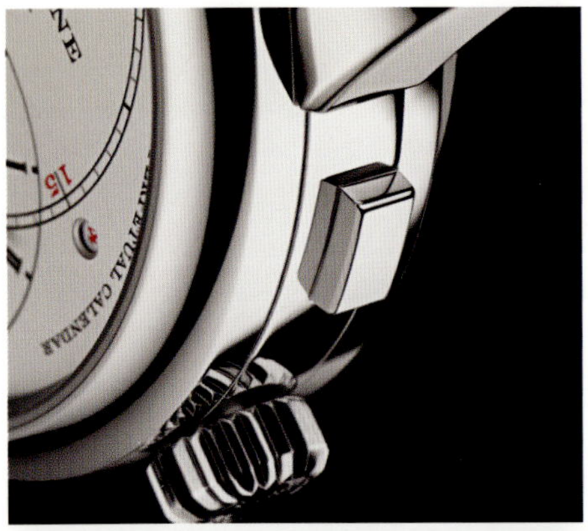

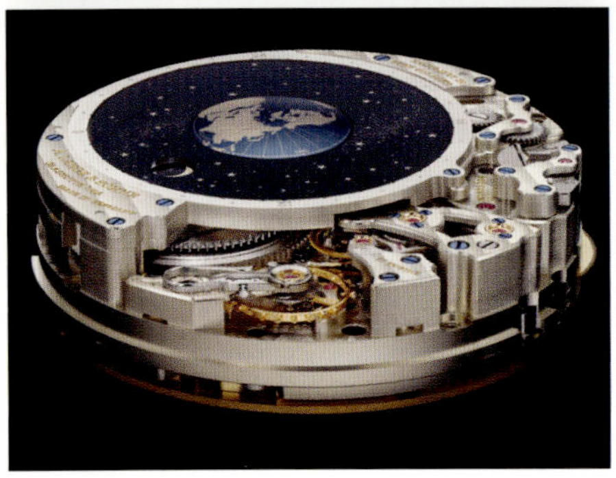

A. Lange & Söhne is known for practicality as well as luxury. Those qualities translate themselves into a deep dedication to functional and ergonomic considerations in their products, as much as their vaunted timepieces are designed to wow and impress some of the world's most discriminating collectors. One of the most complicated timepieces ever produced by the brand's manufacturer, located in the small town of Glashütte, Germany, is the Richard Lange Perpetual Calendar "Terraluna".

This watch has an extremely complicated movement, assembled from close to 800 hand-finished and decorated parts. A. Lange & Söhne famously "builds each of their watches twice", meaning that, after assembling the movements, they disassemble them, sometimes tweak them, and then reassemble them piece by piece. While such a process is no doubt time-consuming, it is part of the company's commitment to the consumer that their machines not only look fantastic but perform in a likewise manner.

Richard Lange watches are part of a small collection of models, with the "Terraluna" sitting at the apex of the product collection in terms of complexity and value. The main dial of the watch has a regulator-style display with three overlapping subdials – a design which was inspired by an antique pocket watch produced by a celebrated German clock-and-instrument maker at the beginning of the 19th century. In addition to the time, the watch's dial has a series of windows for the perpetual calendar feature, which display the correct date up to the current leap-year cycle.

On the rear of the large 45.5mm-wide timepiece is a gloriously detailed visual display depicting the Moon's phase and orbit around the Earth. Three carefully styled rotating gold discs are used to display this information which is at the heart of the name of the "Terraluna" (which literally means "Earth Moon"). Such astronomical calendar watches have been celebrated for literally hundreds of years, with new ones pushing the limits of both accuracy and aesthetic appeal. For example, the Moon-phase indication system in the watch (assuming the timepiece remains in operation) would not need a manual correction for over 1,000 years.

Additional decorative and mechanical secrets exist with the movement. A. Lange & Söhne designed the manually wound movement of the "Terraluna" to have a full two weeks of power reserve. An additional system, known as a constant force escapement, is relied upon in the movement to ensure consistent accuracy as the power from the slowly unwinding mainspring changes when the spring winds down. That is just one more way in which A. Lange & Söhne celebrates both the artistry and functionality of their precious little "engines" that power their celebrated watches.

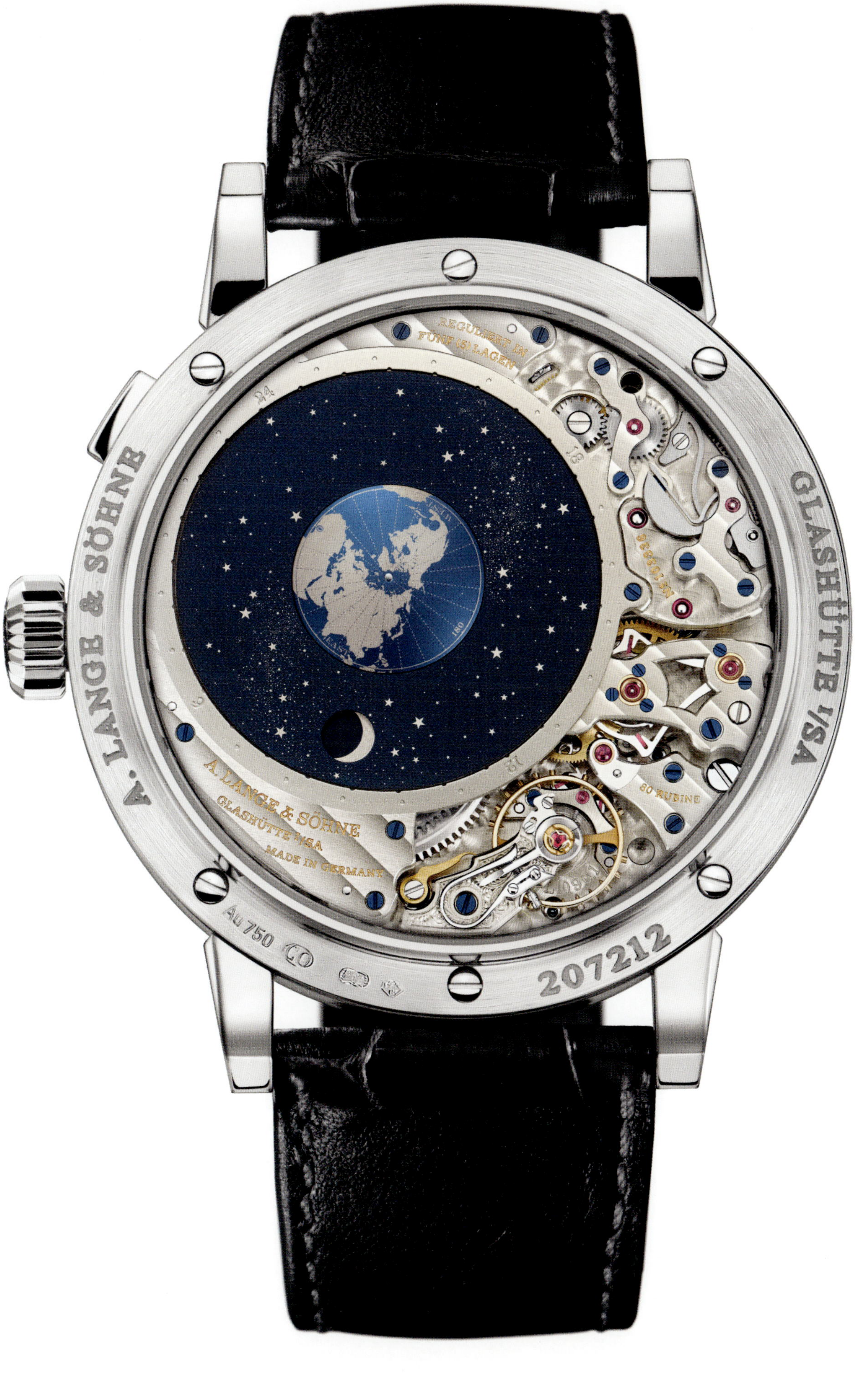
A. LANGE & SÖHNE
GLASHÜTTE I/SA
REGULIERT IN
FÜNF (5) LAGEN
A. LANGE & SÖHNE
GLASHÜTTE I/SA
MADE IN GERMANY
Au 750
207212

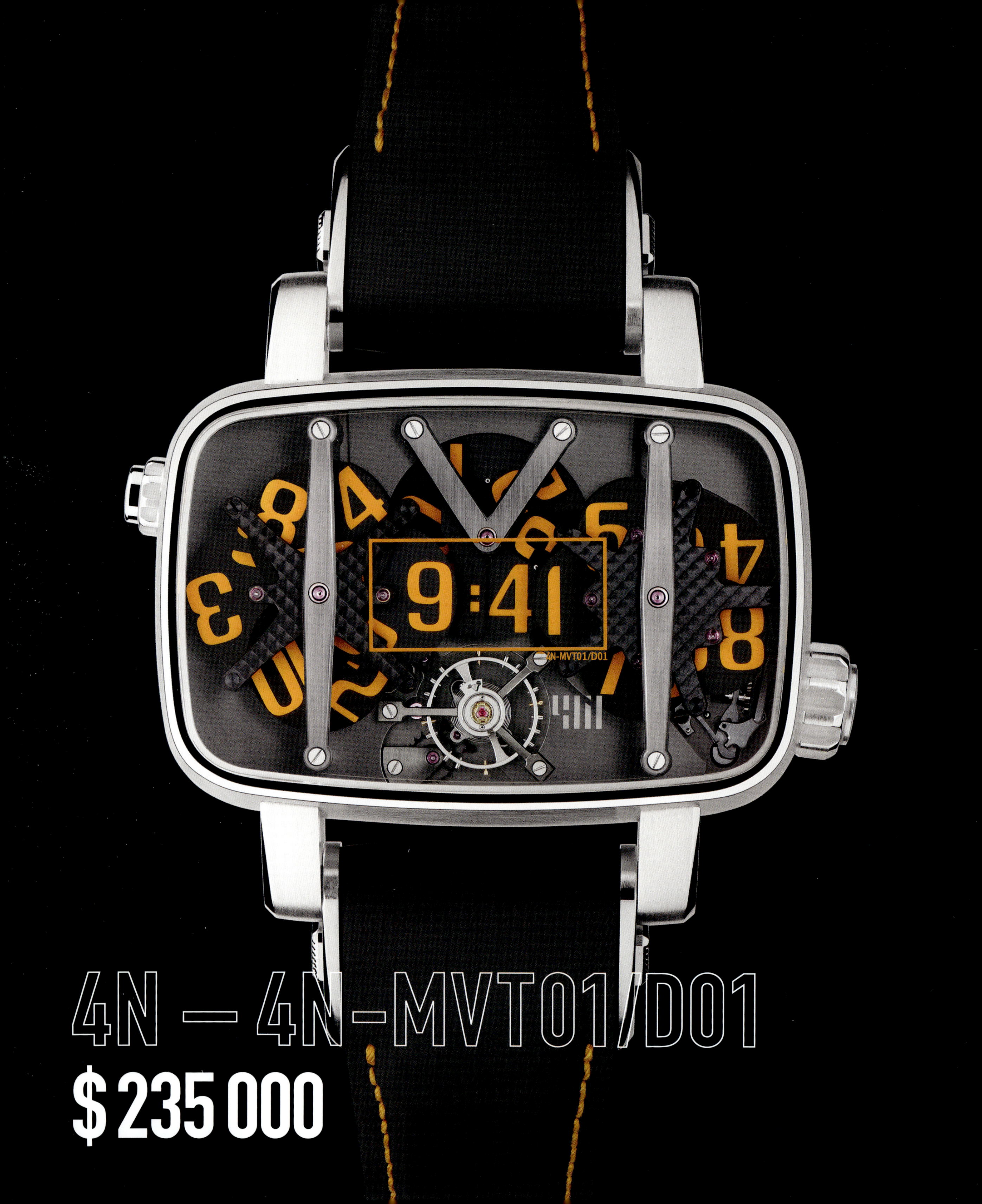

4N — 4N-MVT01/D01

$ 235 000

The first, and currently only watch by 4N is the cryptically named 4N-MVT01/D01. The purpose of this timepiece was to display the time digitally, using a mechanical movement. This has been accomplished in other timepieces using different techniques, but 4N's execution of the idea, in the 4N-MVT01/D01, is unique. An assortment of almost a dozen discs, is used to display the time in the very middle of the dial. The rest of the watch is an open view into the movement and its parts.

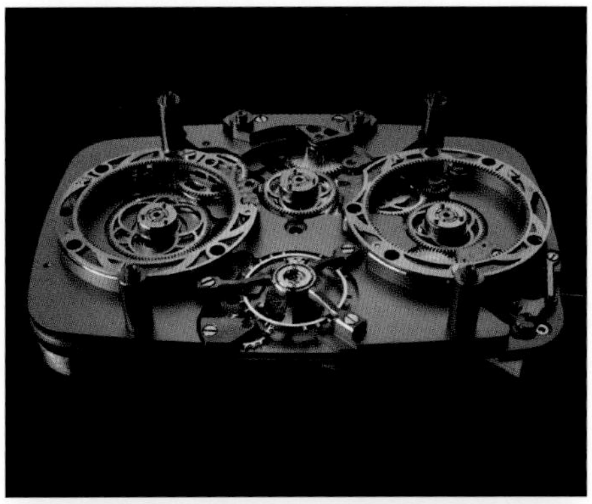

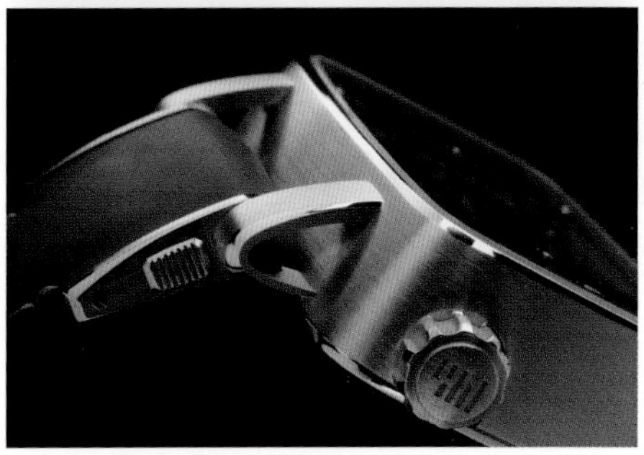

4N spent years trying to prefect the movement for production. A major issue in timepieces such as this is that, unlike traditional analogue watches with hands that are constantly moving (even at a slow rate), the discs on the 4N-MVT01/D01 must "jump" each time they move. For a range of technical reasons, this presents a problem for mechanical movements, when it comes to maintaining their accuracy. 4N eventually needed to consult the master watch design firm APRP to complete the 4N-MVT01/D01.

Only 16 4N-MVT01/D01 pieces were produced; the final one being released in 2013. The wide "TV screen" style was produced in a range of optional materials, such as 18k white gold, platinum, or titanium. It features a spring-powered movement that is able to go 10 days between winding.

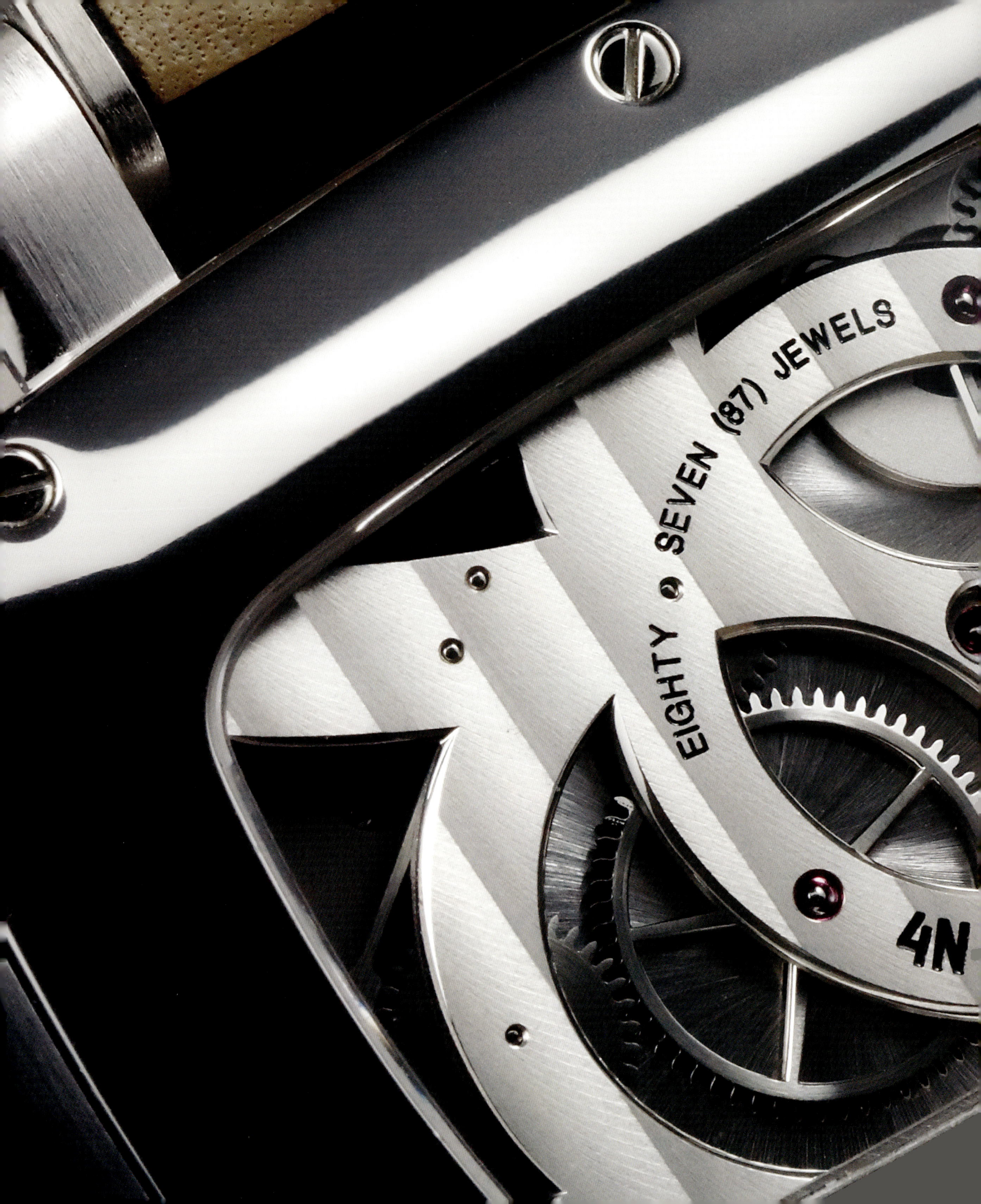
EIGHTY SEVEN (87) JEWELS
4N

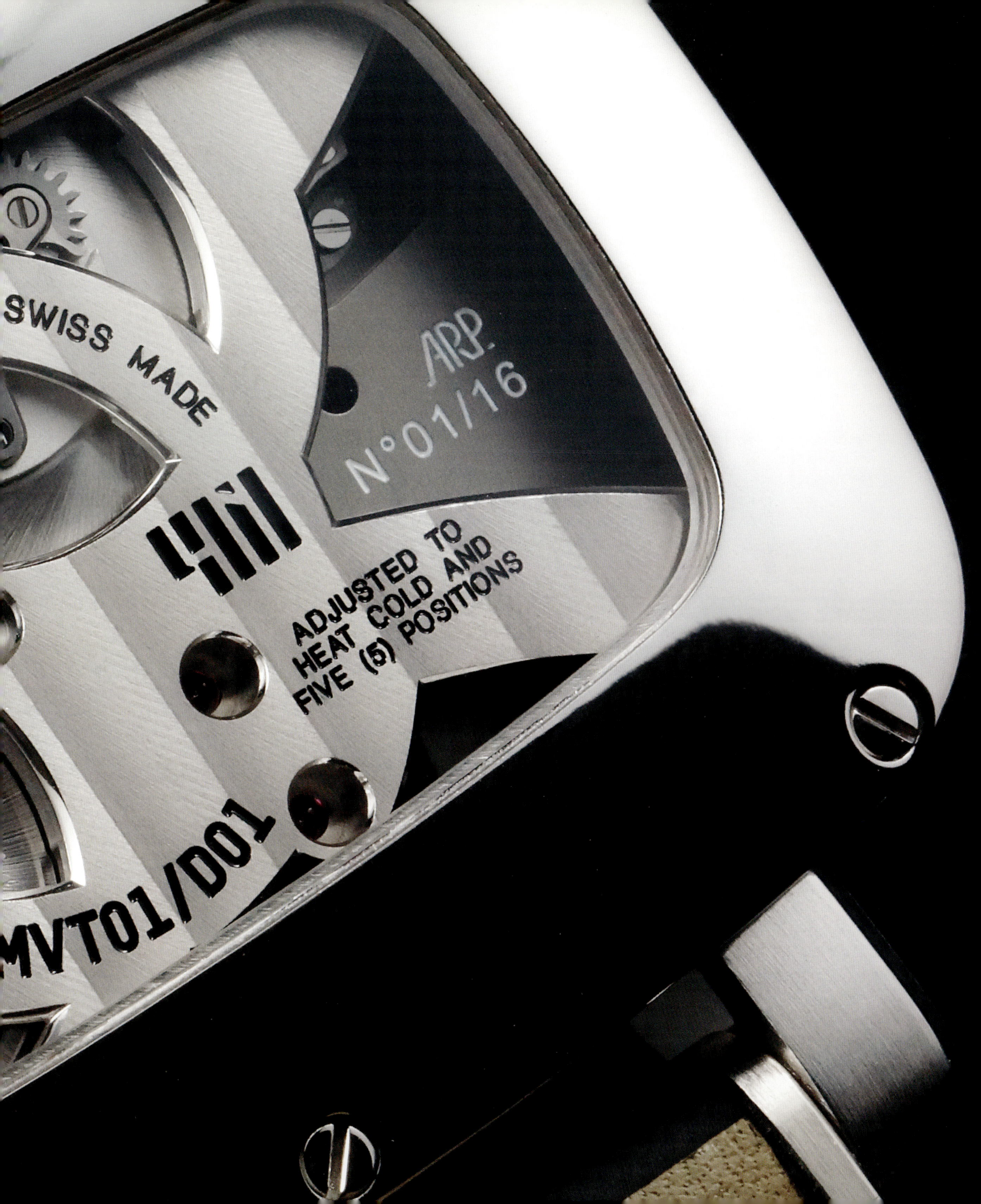
SWISS MADE
ARP.
N°01/16
ADJUSTED TO
HEAT COLD AND
FIVE (5) POSITIONS
MVT01/D01

HAUTLENCE – HL2.2

$ 240 000

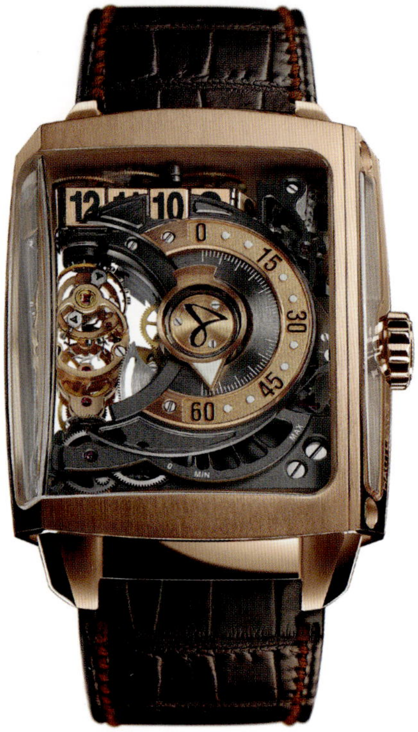

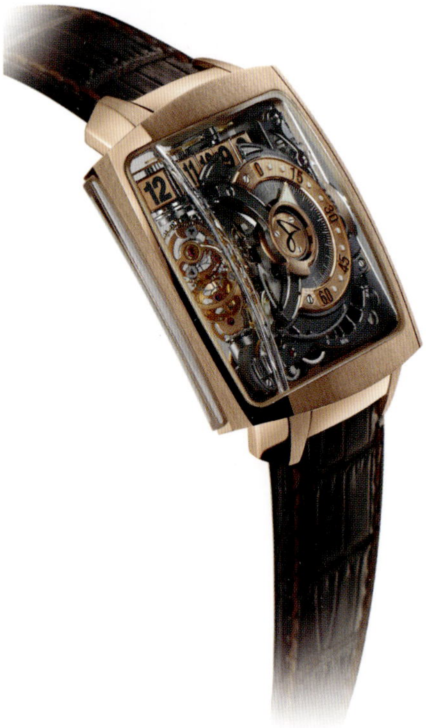

In 2005, Hautlence debuted its first working prototype. Two years later the quirky brand produced its first pieces and the world was welcomed with a case shaped like a television screen and retro-futuristic dial, with a lot of character and an obvious disdain for telling the time in a normal analogue format. Instead, hours were displayed via a disc in a window and minutes shown on a retrograde display. True to their brand, this is a theme Hautlence has, for the most part, maintained in their later models.

In 2010, Hautlence released an extremely ambitious prototype timepiece with the HL2.0. The rectangular case is almost entirely wrapped with a sapphire crystal, and the watch contains an innovative movement. This combines the brand's trademark way of displaying the time, with a complex mechanism incorporating a tank-tread style hour indicator, and an escapement stack that spins slowly like a barber's pole.

It took over a year for the HL2.0 watch finally to be released, eventually being offered in HL2.1 and HL2.2 forms. The watch is protected by several patents, and acts as a halo product to the already high-end Hautlence brand, with a novel movement that is both aesthetically pleasing and functional. It benefits from having appeal to collectors and causal enthusiasts (each ideally well-funded), which is rare for such an experimental watch.

Viewing the movement inside the HL2.2, reveals that as the hour indicators change, they are connected to the column with the escapement and, in turn, rotate it. This acts in a manner similar to a tourbillon and provides a constantly changing view of the dial. The movement also happens to be an automatic, with a small micro-rotor hidden on the rear of the case.

A product of the modern age of mechanical watchmaking, the HL2.2 represents the type of design that comes from balancing computer-assisted design and the confines of traditional spring-powered mechanics. The HL2.2 version was produced as a limited edition of 28 pieces.

CHOPARD — L.U.C TOURBILLON BAGUETTE

$ 240 000

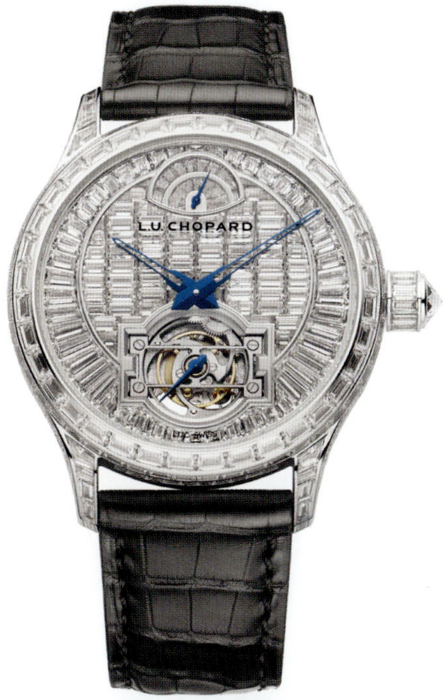

It is often thought, in the watch industry, that timepieces priced high due to complexity, and pieces priced high due to the presence of precious stones and materials, should not co-mingle. The presumption being that if a customer is merely looking to show wealth then placing diamonds on a relatively simple watch (mechanically speaking) will prove sufficient. It is further believed that consumers interested in watches with complicated movements aren't interested in items with many precious stones.

These stereotypes may be true often enough, but they don't represent the entirety of the watch market, as there are plenty of high-end consumers looking for both. Chopard is as much a jewellery maker as it is a watchmaker, and a timepiece like the L.U.C Tourbillon Baguette is certainly an intersection of both worlds.

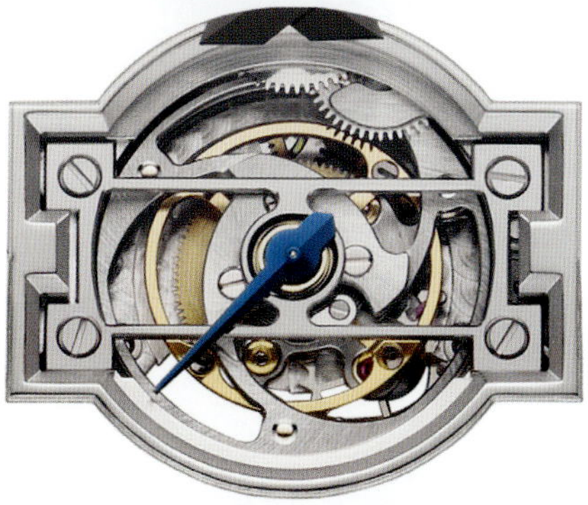

Chopard's most high-end creations often have the title "L.U.C" in their name. L.U.C stands for "Louis-Ulysse Chopard," who was the founder of the brand. The L.U.C designation means that the watch contains a movement made in-house by Chopard; it started appearing on select Chopard watches in 1996.

The L.U.C Tourbillon is Chopard's take on a classic tourbillon-based dress watch, but throws in a few extra features that help set it apart from the crowd. For one thing, the movement has a power reserve of 216 hours (with an indicator under 12 o'clock). That means the watch can go for over a week between being wound. This Chopard tourbillon is also extremely accurate. To prove this, Chopard offers a COSC Chronometer certificate with the watch (given individually to watches after passing accuracy tests).

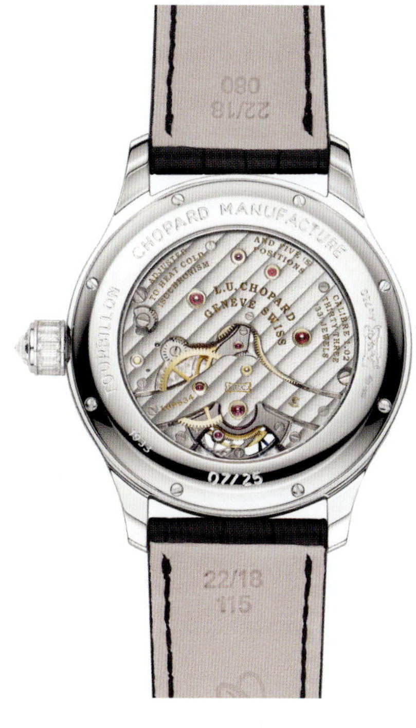

Even though the L.U.C Tourbillon is attractive enough as it is, Chopard decided to produce a limited edition version of the watch completely covered in diamonds. Very little of the 18k white gold case is visible under the more than 300 baguette-cut diamonds placed all over the watch case, dial, and crown. Chopard managed to include over 27 carats of stones in the watch, and still retain a sense of elegance (as well as legibility). The L.U.C Tourbillon was produced as a limited edition of 25 pieces only.

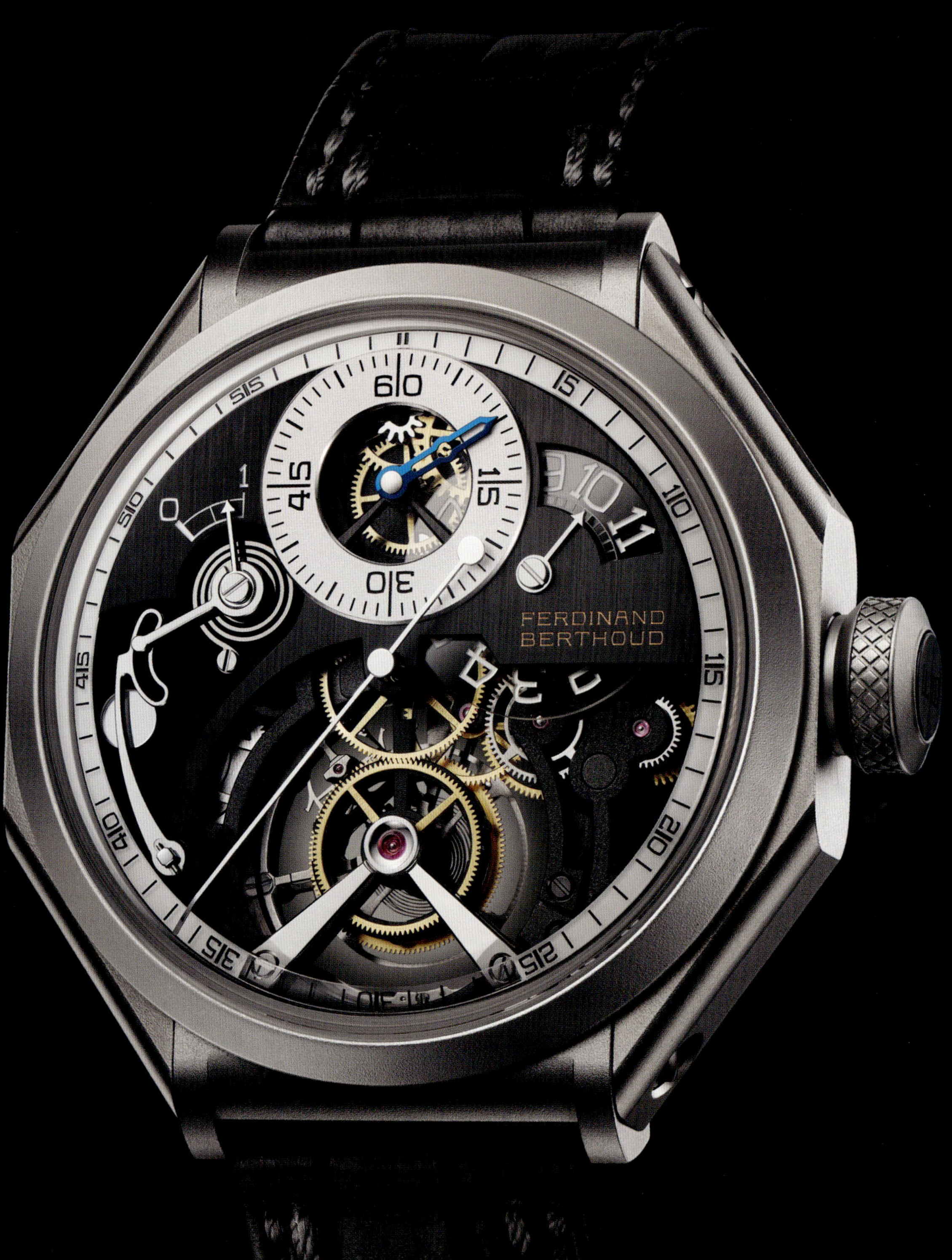

FERDINAND BERTHOUD — CHRONOMÈTRE FB 1.RS

$ 247 000

One of the most challenging feats of watchmaking is to engineer a novel timepiece movement that works well. Watch movements are essentially miniature mechanical engines with moving parts, power-transmission systems are subject to wear and tear and capable of varying degrees of performance. To be accurate in telling the time, a watch movement must be over 99.9% stable in its performance while operating constantly and being jostled around. Watch movements can operate for literally years on end while receiving minimal-to-no maintenance. Creating a new engine from scratch and to have it perform with racing-car-like accuracy is no small effort.

For that reason, many of the most exotic, complicated mechanical watchmakers out there do not put much stock into how accurate their timepieces are – although that is not universally true. Serious horological afficionados are a sub-genre of the larger collector community, and often desire exceptional hand-made designs that also offer superlative chronometric performance. In this rarified realm of high-end, accurate luxury timepieces are a small number of players, including the Ferdinand Berthoud Chronomètre.

Sitting at the top of the Chopard Group of brands, Ferdinand Berthoud is a revived name based on a historic watchmaker, whose classic work has inspired a contemporary ultra-luxury wristwatch brand. The "Chronomètre" term in the name refers to the lauded "chronometer" rating which is awarded to wristwatch movements that have been tested for accuracy. Chronometer certificates are not commonly awarded to timepieces priced at a quarter of a million dollars; the theory being that, at this price point, few consumers particularly care about being on time. For those that do, Ferdinand Berthoud as a company produces exclusively chronometer-certified products.

The Chronomètre FB 1.RS is a skeletonised version of the brand's most popular platform, the original FB series – which houses an elaborate movement consisting of both a tourbillon and a fusee-and-chain transmission system. The hand-assembled and decorated FB-T.FC-RS manually wound movement is just 10mm thick and has 1,158 components in it. Nearly 800 of these components are directly part of the tiny hand-made bicycle-chain-style transmission that wraps around a conical gear. The open-work watch dial has separate dials for the hours, minutes and seconds, along with a power-reserve indicator. Only 20 of the movements will ever be produced.

What Ferdinand Berthoud is adept at doing is borrowing traditional concepts from mechanical watchmaking that go back hundreds of years, and engineering them into a modern, wearable system. It also happens to be quite accurate and perform as well as most daily-wear mainstream mechanical watches.

Ferdinand Berthoud offers the Chronomètre FB 1.RS in 18k rose gold (for a bit more), but also in carburised steel – which is a special metal surface-strengthening process. The resulting surface is smooth and extremely scratch resistant, with an almost sandblasted finish. It suits Ferdinand Berthoud's distinctive, and imminently wearable, 44mm-wide case perfectly.

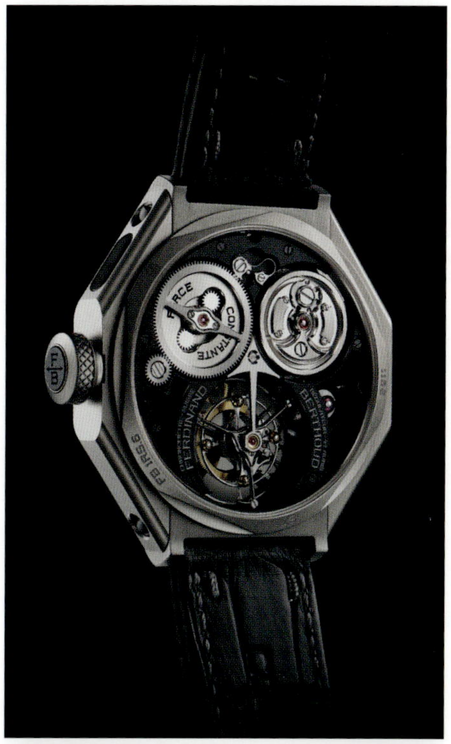

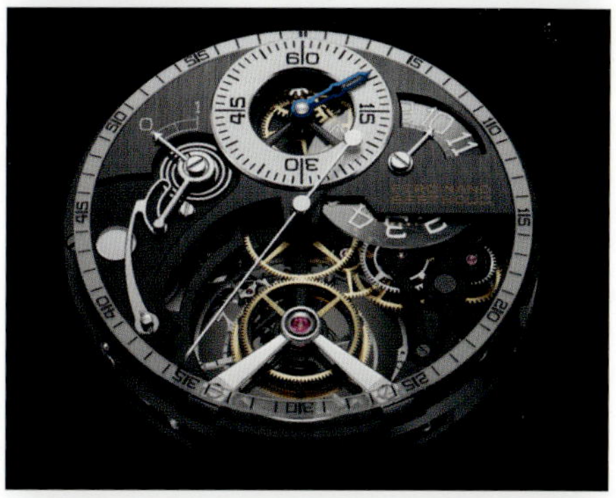

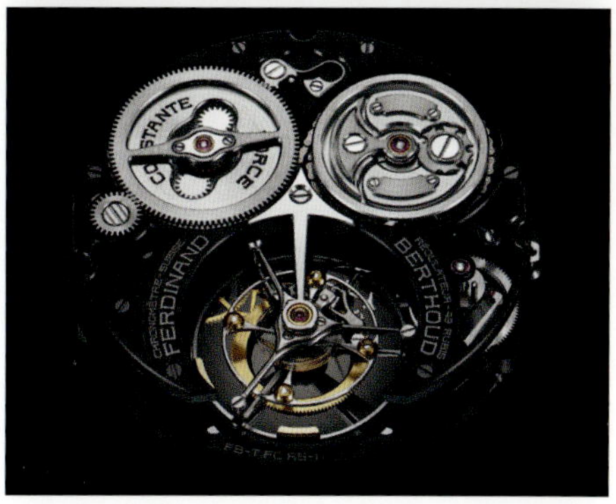

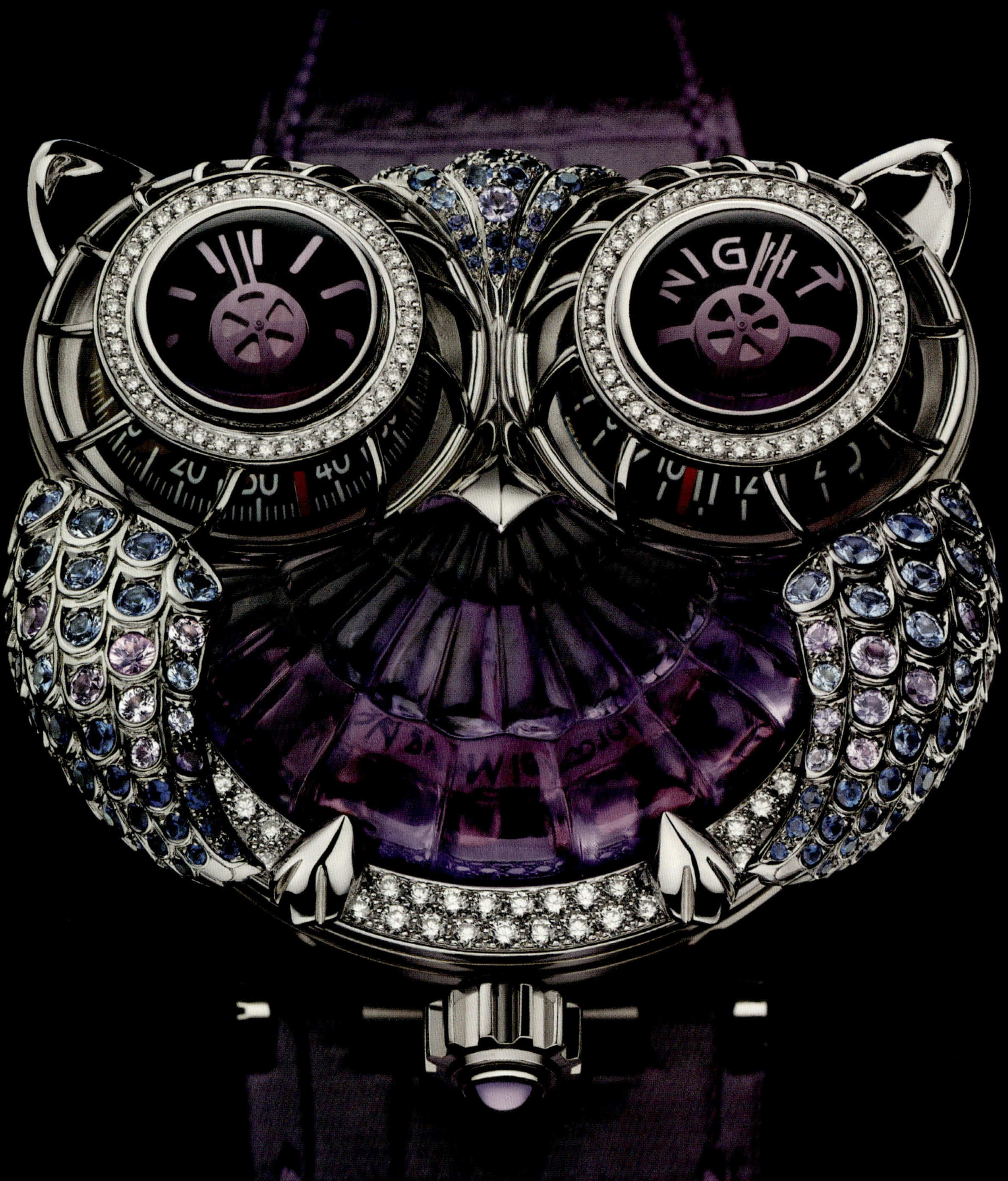

MB&F — HM3 JWLRYMACHINE WATCH

$ 250 000

For much of its short existence since being founded in 2004, Geneva-based MB&F has claimed not to make watches, but, rather, "horological machines". Producing only a few hundred pieces each year, MB&F products are as much art as they are timepieces. A defining element of the brand is collaboration with others. The name "MB&F" actually stands for "Max Busser (the founder) and friends."

MB&F engaged in a unique collaboration with Parisian watch and jewellery maker Boucheron in 2010. Boucheron adapted MB&F's well-regarded Horological Machine No. 3 (HM3) into a highly limited jewellery-style watch in the shape of an owl. Boucheron frequently takes inspiration from the animal world, and two versions of the JwlryMachine were produced. One version in purple used amethyst with an 18k white gold and titanium case, while a second version in pink used quartz with an 18k pink gold and titanium case. Additional precious gems such as diamonds were used for decoration.

The watch contains a unique automatic mechanical movement that indicates the time via two cylinders, representing the eyes of the owl. The left eye indicated the minutes, while the right eye indicated the hours. As recently as 2013, the JwlryMachine was the only women's watch ever produced by MB&F.

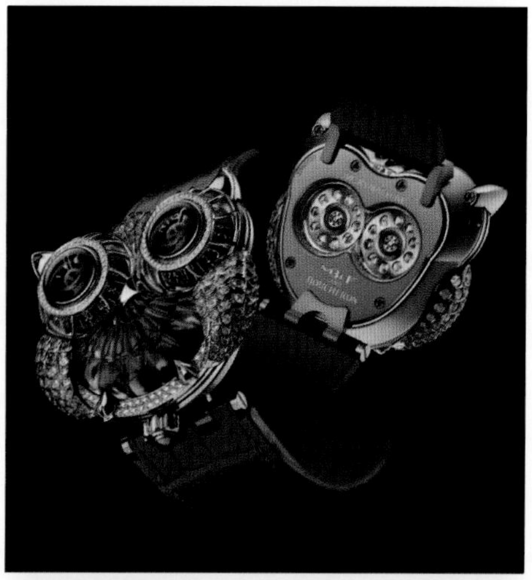

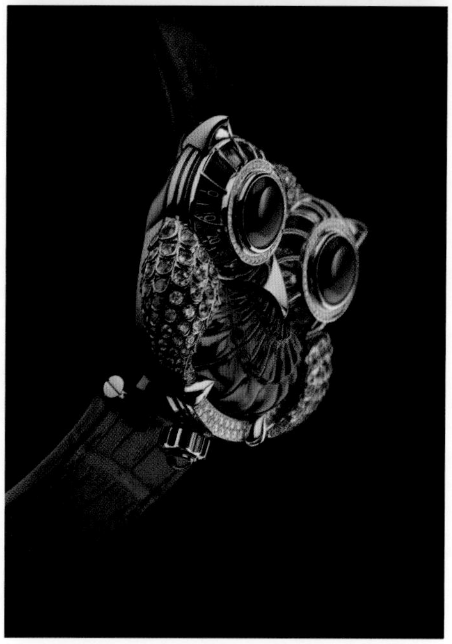

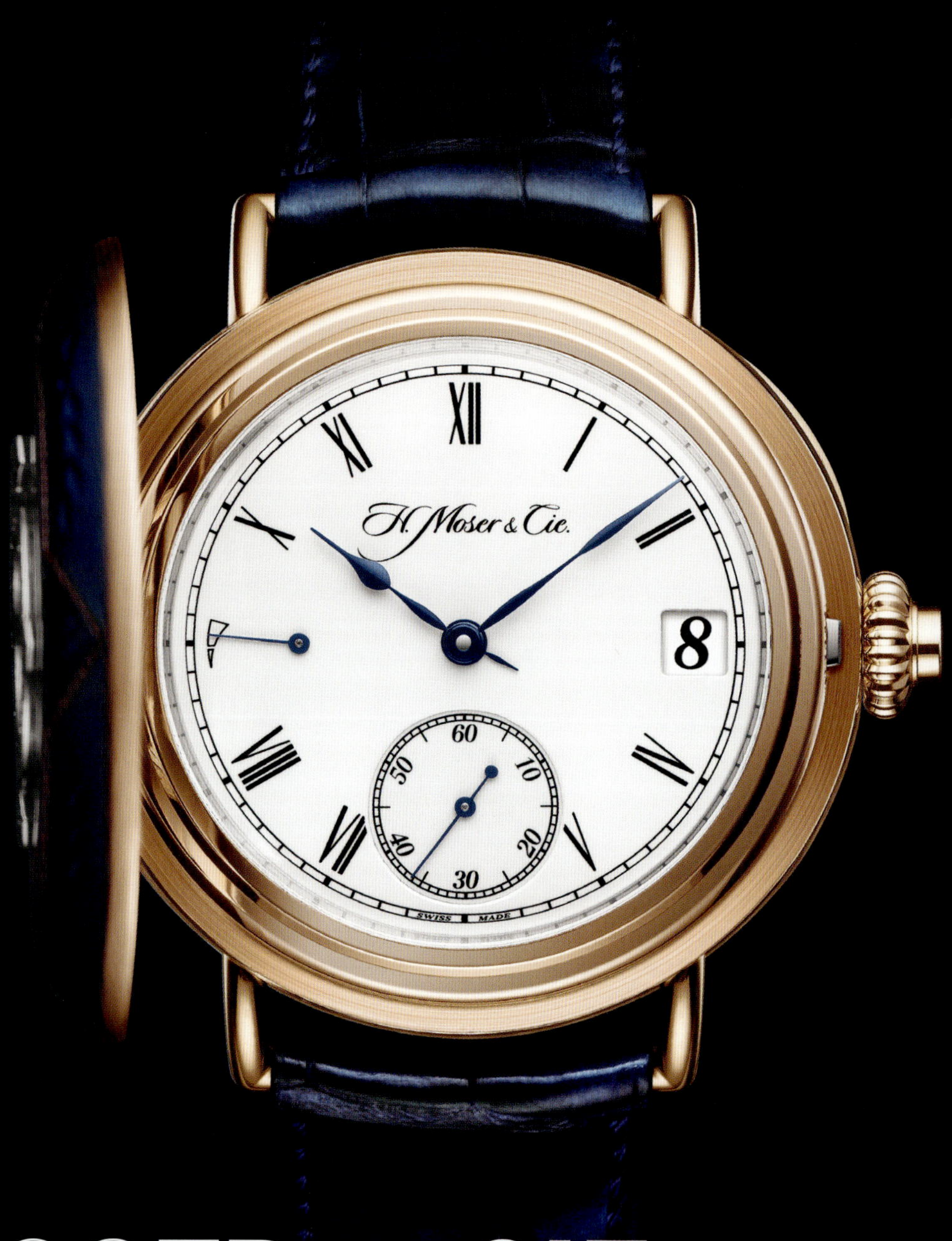

H. MOSER & CIE — HERITAGE PERPETUAL CALENDAR

$ 250 000

Many of today's watchmakers tend to feel as though they are giving their clientele added value by reminding them how long their brand name has been associated with watchmaking. The tactic works, and it also helps to usher in unique timepiece creations that merge contemporary timepiece products with old-world artisanship and design ethos. An excellent example is the Heritage Perpetual Calendar by Swiss H. Moser & Cie. It was launched in honour of the 10th anniversary of the in-house developed perpetual calendar-based movement inside of it, with a distinctive hinged watch case that is directly inspired by a historic pocket watch produced in the same region during the 19th century.

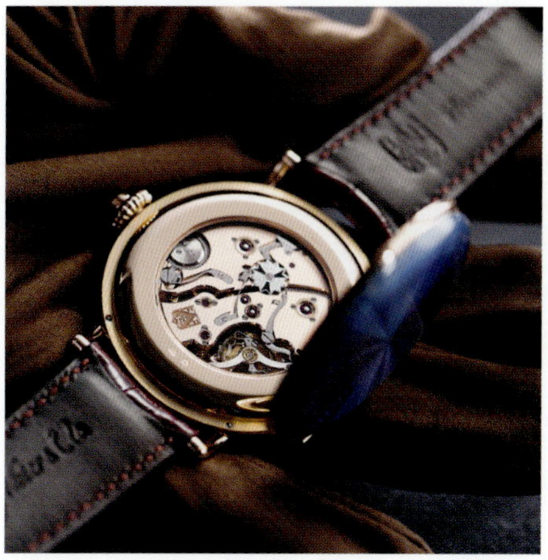

For H. Moser & Cie., development of the Heritage Perpetual Calendar depended on their ability to recreate the ornate decoration of the 19th-century watch. This included gem-setting and enamelling, including the Champlevé enamel technique that begins with an engraved metal substrate that is then painted with enamel and backed for permanency. This particular composition, featuring blue-coloured semi-translucent enamel and diamonds, is set atop a symmetrical floral-style motif, which itself must be hand-engraved. Both the hinged case lid and side of the 18k gold case are fitted with these engraved and enamel-painted sky-blue sections. Continuing the "Heritage" part of the timepiece's theme, H. Moser & Cie. mimics the look of the original pocket watch with a high-contrast white face with black-print enamel dial.

A pusher on the side of the case opens the hinged lid, while another cover over the rear of the watch opens to reveal a view of the mechanical movement (that is nevertheless protected behind sapphire crystal). What makes the movement special for H. Moser & Cie. (in addition to the time required to develop it) is how elegantly the perpetual calendar is able to indicate all the necessary calendar dates in such a minimalised form. The dial features a small central hand that is actually used to indicate the month (each hour marker can double as a month indicator), while the only other piece of calendar data on the dial is the large aperture date window. In addition to the time, the dial also features a handy power-reserve indicator. A crucial part of all perpetual calendars is a leap-year indicator – though being aware of this information all the time is hardly critical for most users. As such, H. Moser & Cie.'s perpetual-calendar movement places this indicator on the rear of the movement, further freeing up space on the dial. Few products in existence combine such ergonomic and modern mechanisms with traditional artistry style and design as the Heritage Perpetual Calendar by H. Moser & Cie.

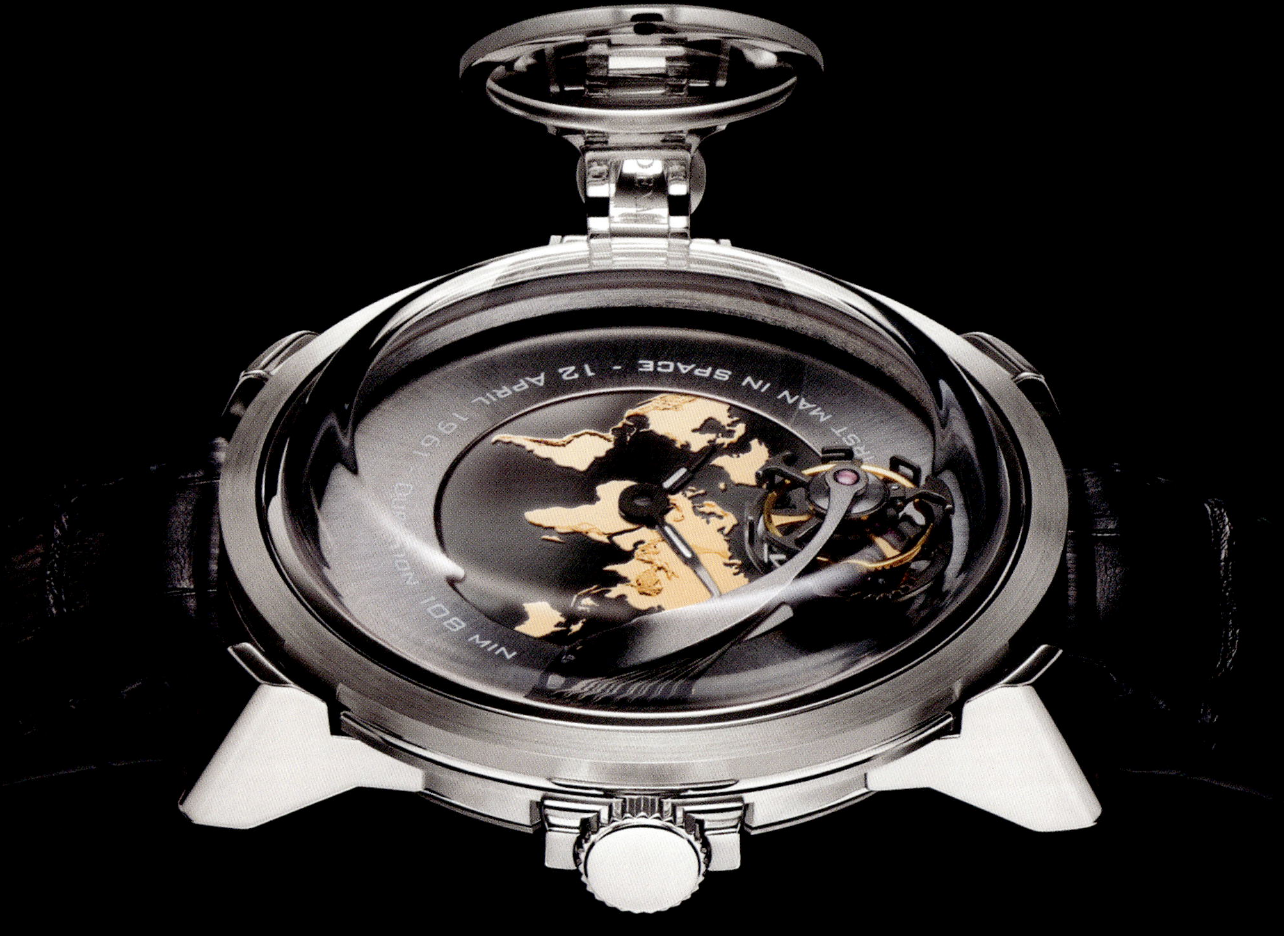
MAN IN SPACE - 12 APRIL 1961
108 MIN

BERNHARD LEDERER — THE GAGARIN TOURBILLON

$ 260 000

THE GAGARIN TOURBILLON IS A DECIDEDLY HIGH-END WAY TO CELEBRATE THE COSMONAUT, AS WELL AS THE RUSSIAN SPACE PROGRAMME.

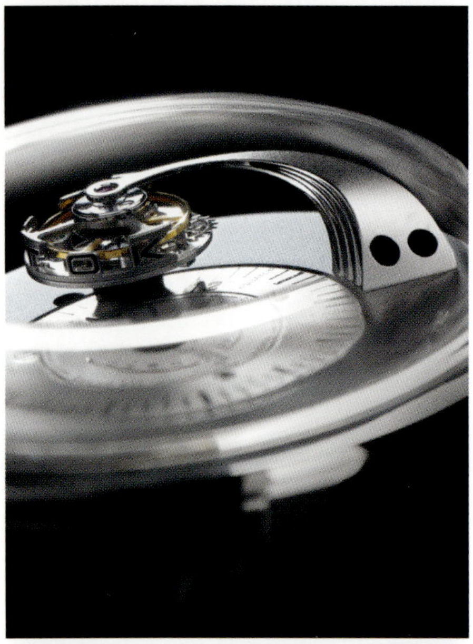

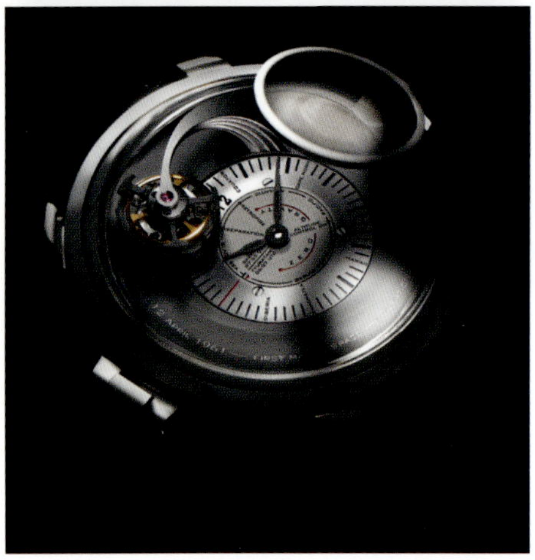

In 2011 esteemed watchmaker Bernhard Lederer debuted a new collection of high-end watches aimed at honouring the historic space flight of Yuri Gagarin. The release date was not coincidental, being exactly 50 years after Gagarin rode into space, and became the first man to orbit the Earth in 1961. The Gagarin Tourbillon is a decidedly high-end way to celebrate the cosmonaut, as well as the Russian space programme.

The watch has been produced in several versions over the years, with the debut piece being in a platinum case. The case design has a unique folding magnifying glass over the dial, which enables the wearer to view the detail of the tourbillon complication.

The main feature of the watch is a tourbillon mounted on a small arm that rotates around the entire dial in a counterclockwise direction once every 108 minutes. That is the amount of time Gagarin spent in space while orbiting the Earth. The famous Russian rocket Vostok took Gagarin into orbit, and its name is written on the tourbillon cage.

Designed like a historic navigation instrument, the dial of The Gagarin Tourbillon tracks the major places on Earth that Gagarin passed over while riding in the Vostok capsule. Commemorative text on the dial explains additional details about Gagarin's historic flight.

Many watchmakers have produced timepieces that honour achievements in all forms of flight, both in space and closer to Earth. The Gagarin Tourbillon is one of the most high-end watches of this ilk, and is further distinctive because it is not itself a pilot's or astronaut's watch.

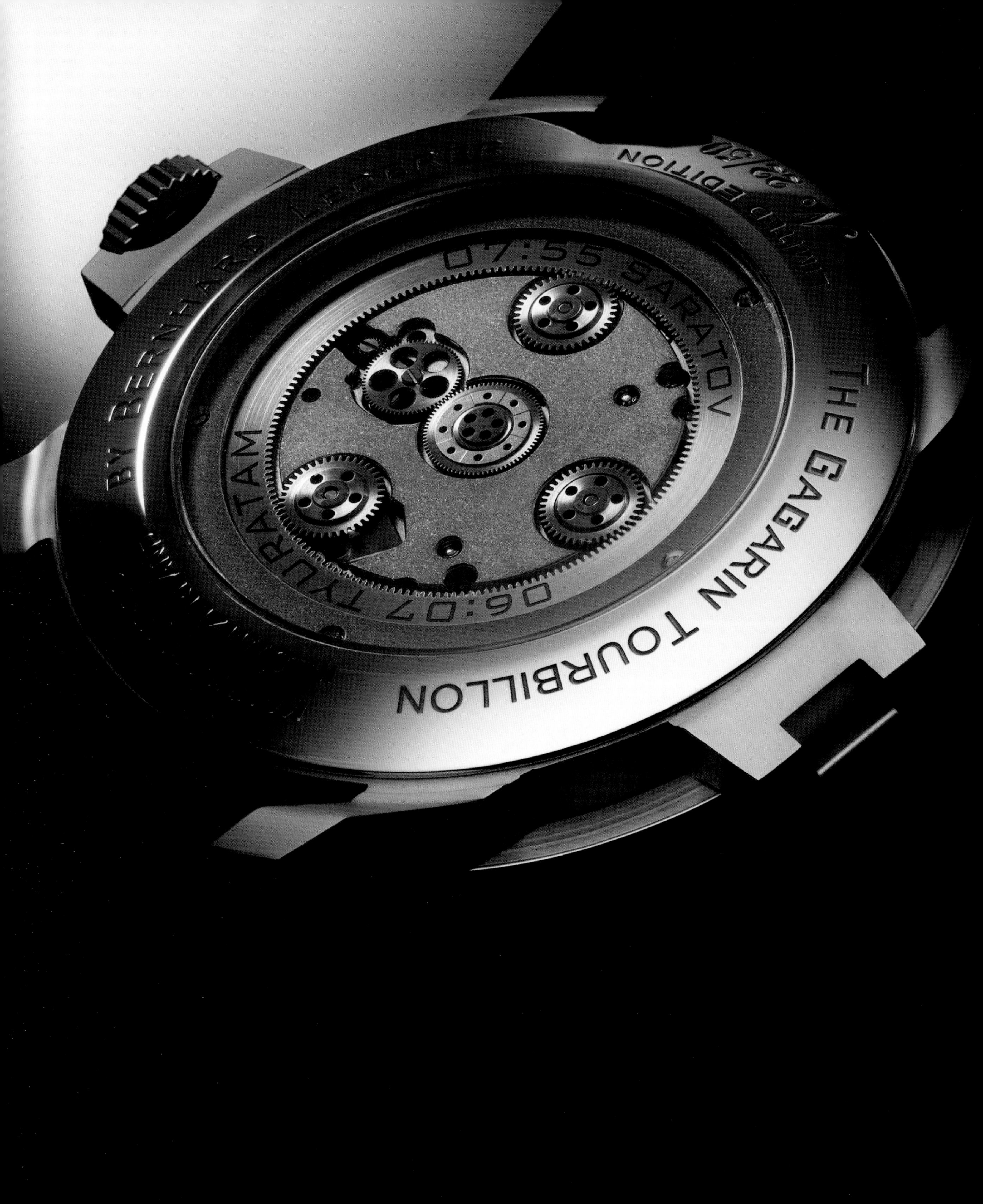
THE GAGARIN TOURBILLON
LIMITED EDITION
07:55 SARATOV
06:07 TYURATAM
BY BERNHARD

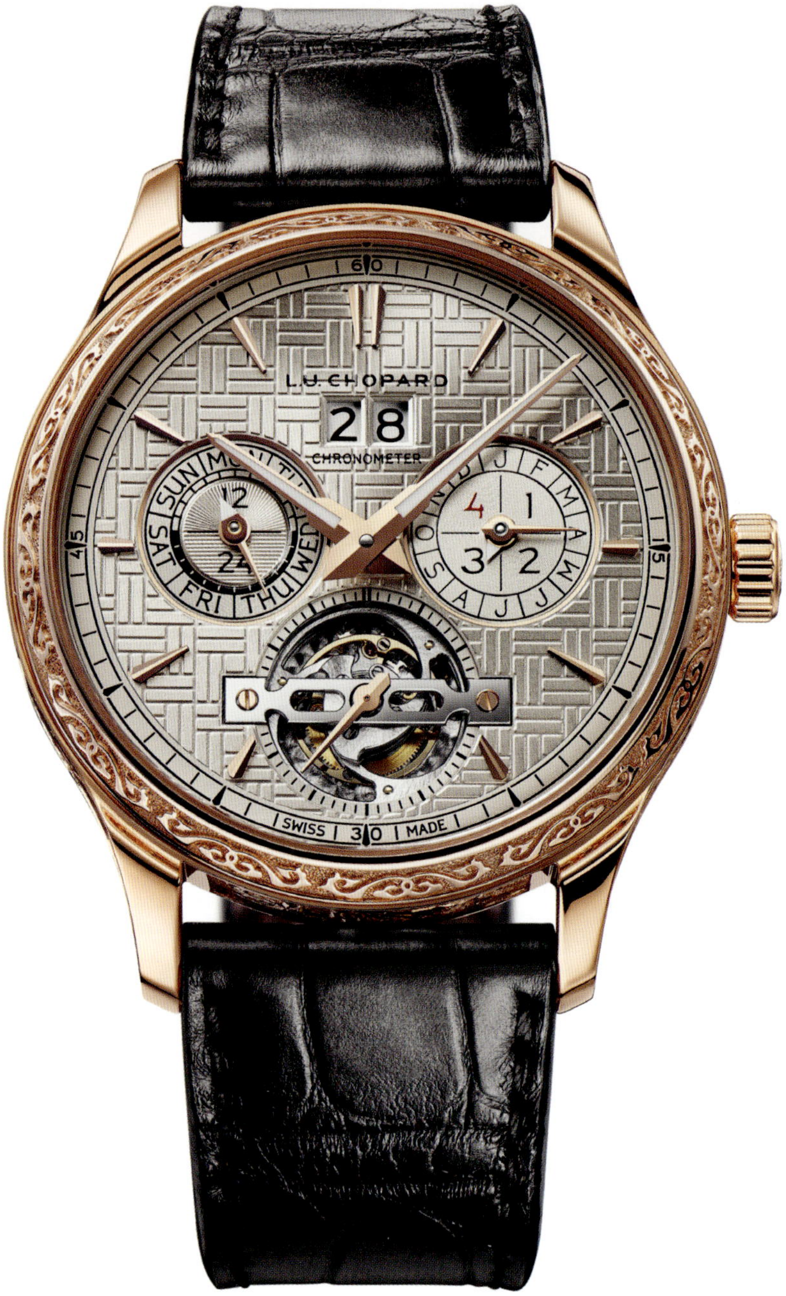

CHOPARD — L.U.C PERPETUAL T — SPIRIT OF THE CHINESE ZODIAC

$ 262 000

Survey many of the more exclusive wristwatches produced by European brands for the Chinese market and you'll notice that Chinese timepiece collectors are particularly interested in products specifically related to Chinese culture. Case in point is this "piece unique" (watch-industry terminology for "one-of-a-kind") version of the Chopard L.U.C Perpetual T, with the telling name of "Spirit of the Chinese Zodiac".

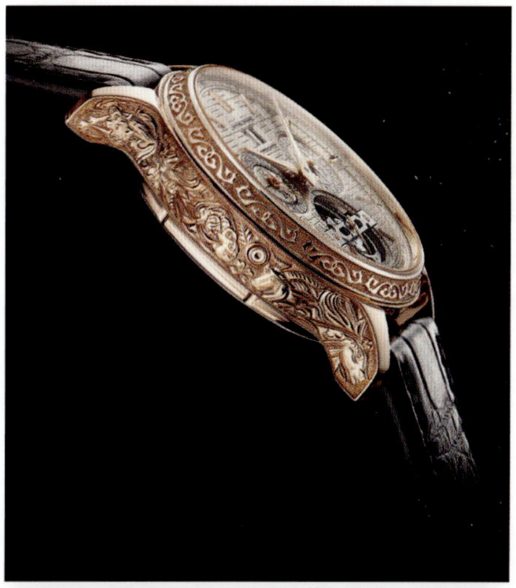

The "spirit" is in the detailed hand-engraved decoration all over the 43mm-wide, 18k rose-gold case on which Chopard has included a motif of each of the 12 Chinese zodiac symbols. The Fleurier, Switzerland-based and family-owned company chose to use a champlevé-engraving technique which fills in engraved sections with black ink in order to allow the designs to pop, creating a more detailed visual experience.

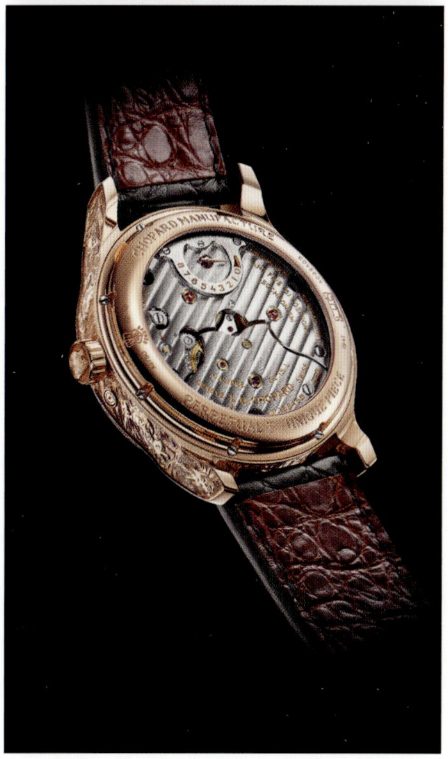

All 12 Chinese zodiac animals are arranged chronologically according to the Chinese calendar. Additional hand-engraved decoration on the bezel is inspired by Chinese iconography, which continues on the dial of the L.U.C Perpetual T face. According to Chopard, a total of approximately 200 hours were needed to complete just the engraved elements of the watch. That does not take into consideration the time required to produce, decorate and assemble the 353-part in-house made tourbillon-based mechanical movement featuring a perpetual calendar, that powers the watch and is visible through the sapphire-crystal exhibition window on the rear of the case.

Chopard produces their L.U.C collection timepieces in a dedicated facility with master watchmakers specially trained to assemble and decorate such highly complicated movements (many of which are awarded the prestigious Geneva Seal). Enthusiasts agree that few companies produce better polished movements than Chopard – who also focus on practicality and utility as much as they do visual splendour. The movement inside of the Perpetual T has a power reserve of eight days when fully wound (with an indicator placed on the rear of the watch), along with an uncluttered display for the time, date, day of the week, month, leap year, AM/PM indicator and of course an open window for the tourbillon.

At least once a year, Chopard attempts to dazzle its most valued clients by artistically enhancing models such as the L.U.C Perpetual T. Many, but not all, are one-of-a-kind creations such as the Spirit of the Chinese Zodiac.

LOUIS VUITTON – TAMBOUR MYSTÉRIEUSE

$265 000

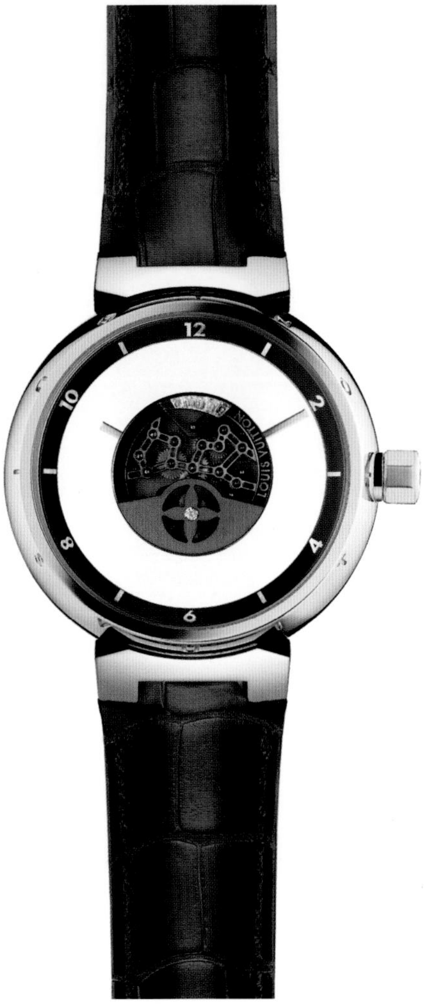

The Tambour Mystérieuse was Louis Vuitton's very first foray into extremely high-end watchmaking, even though the brand already quietly sold more accessibly priced luxury watches through a limited number of its brand boutiques. Released in 2009, the Tambour Mystérieuse combined Swiss watchmaking know-how and a long legacy of French watch and clockmaking.

Completely produced in-house by Louis Vuitton-employed specialists, the Tambour Mystérieuse represents a historically honoured form of indicating the time, using a 'mystery display'. Another Paris-based luxury brand, Cartier, found fame with mystery style clocks in the early 20th century, but the concept predates them. The idea of a mystery clock is that some element of the dial's construction isn't readily apparent. For most mystery clocks, the mystery was in how the hands were attached, as they seemed to float in mid air.

With the Tambour Mystérieuse, Louis Vuitton took this concept to another dimension by having not only the hands as part of the mystery dial, but also the entire movement. A view of the dial shows a relatively small movement with hands extending from its sides, seemingly suspended in the centre of the case. Nothing like it had ever been done before. The trick was to use transparent sapphire crystal plates, that not only hold the movement in place, but stealthily rotate to allow for the movement to be wound and adjusted.

The movement was designed like a sandwich, as various discs penetrate it and the hands extend from it, moving in the empty space between the movement and the case. Louis Vuitton designed the mechanical mechanism to have a long power reserve. In honour of the brand's loyal customer base to the East, the power reserve of the Tambour Mystérieuse is said to be eight days and eight hours – eight being a number that represents good fortune in certain Eastern cultures.

Would it be true Louis Vuitton without custom luggage? Louis Vuitton wanted to connect this ultra-timepiece with its more popular products, so it designed a customer trunk as the presentation box for the Tambour Mystérieuse. An additional service, inherent in this and later high-end luxury watches from Louis Vuitton, is a degree of customisation for customers. Each Tambour Mystérieuse can be produced from various materials and in a range of decorative styles for either men or women to enjoy.

JAEGER-LECOULTRE – DUOMÈTRE SPHÉROTOURBILLON

$ 270 000

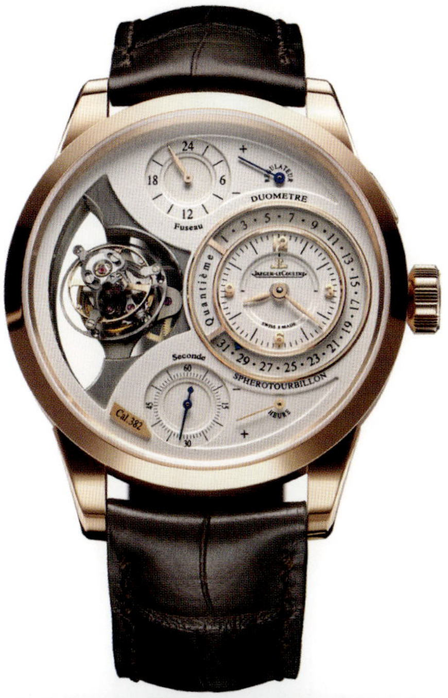

What happens when you have a luxury watch company, run by engineers who have the power to create anything they like? Probably something like the Duomètre Sphérotourbillon, by Swiss firm Jaeger-LeCoultre. A combination of exclusive mechanical prowess, and a deep understanding of what gets high-end watch enthusiasts excited, went into to the creation of this highly complicated wristwatch, aimed at promoting visual interest and a sense of awe. When Jaeger-LeCoultre released the watch in 2012, it was unlike anything that had been created before it.

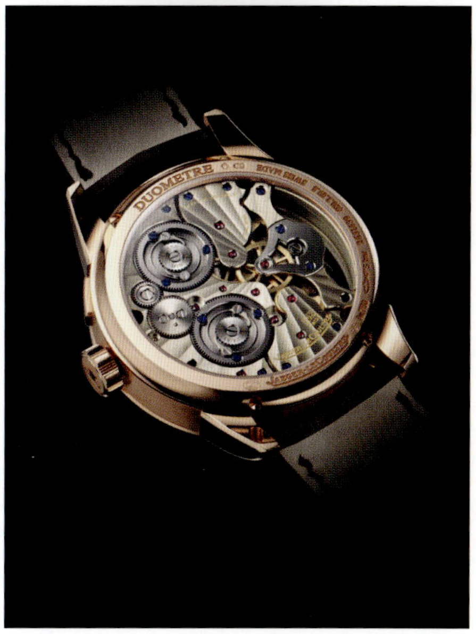

Explaining what happens visually on the dial of the Duomètre Sphérotourbillon, is a challenge. Even Jaeger-LeCoultre seem to be at a loss for specific adjectives when officially describing the functionality of the 'sphérotourbillon.' A normal tourbillon is an oscillator, mounted inside a tiny cage, which rotates on its own axis – usually once per a minute. Invented long ago to promote accuracy, tourbillon mostly serve as visual marvels on those of today's luxury watches that contain them. Jaeger-LeCoultre's strong points include, not only creating tourbillons that are animated to provide strong visual appeal, but also engineering them to be as accurate (if not more so) than standard mechanical watches.

Situated in a large open window on the dial of this Jaeger-LeCoultre, the sphérotourbillon complication is a tourbillon that not only rotates once each minute, but does so while tilted at a 20 degree angle. On top of that, the escapement does not contain a typically flat hairspring spiral, rather, the hairspring inside the balance wheel is shaped like a cylinder.

To understand why Jaeger-LeCoultre designed these exotic complications, it is important to understand the role of the tourbillon itself in the modern luxury watch landscape. In addition to being difficult to produce, and being prized for its visual appeal, it is also a status symbol of wealth and prestige. For Jaeger-LeCoultre to offer the sphérotourbillon, along with other exotic tourbillons, it is able to place itself at the high-end, even on the pecking order of 'super-watch' makers.

The watch is built on Jaeger-LeCoultre's Duomètre movement concept, which includes separate mainsprings for the time and for the other of the watch features. They claim this helps preserve accuracy, as the timing function isn't being interfered with by the rest of what the watch is doing. A power reserve for each of the barrels is placed on the dial, along with other functions that include the time, 24 hour indicator, jumping date, and subsidiary seconds with a "stop seconds" function, that resets it instantly, using a pusher on the dial of the case to allow for more precision setting of the time

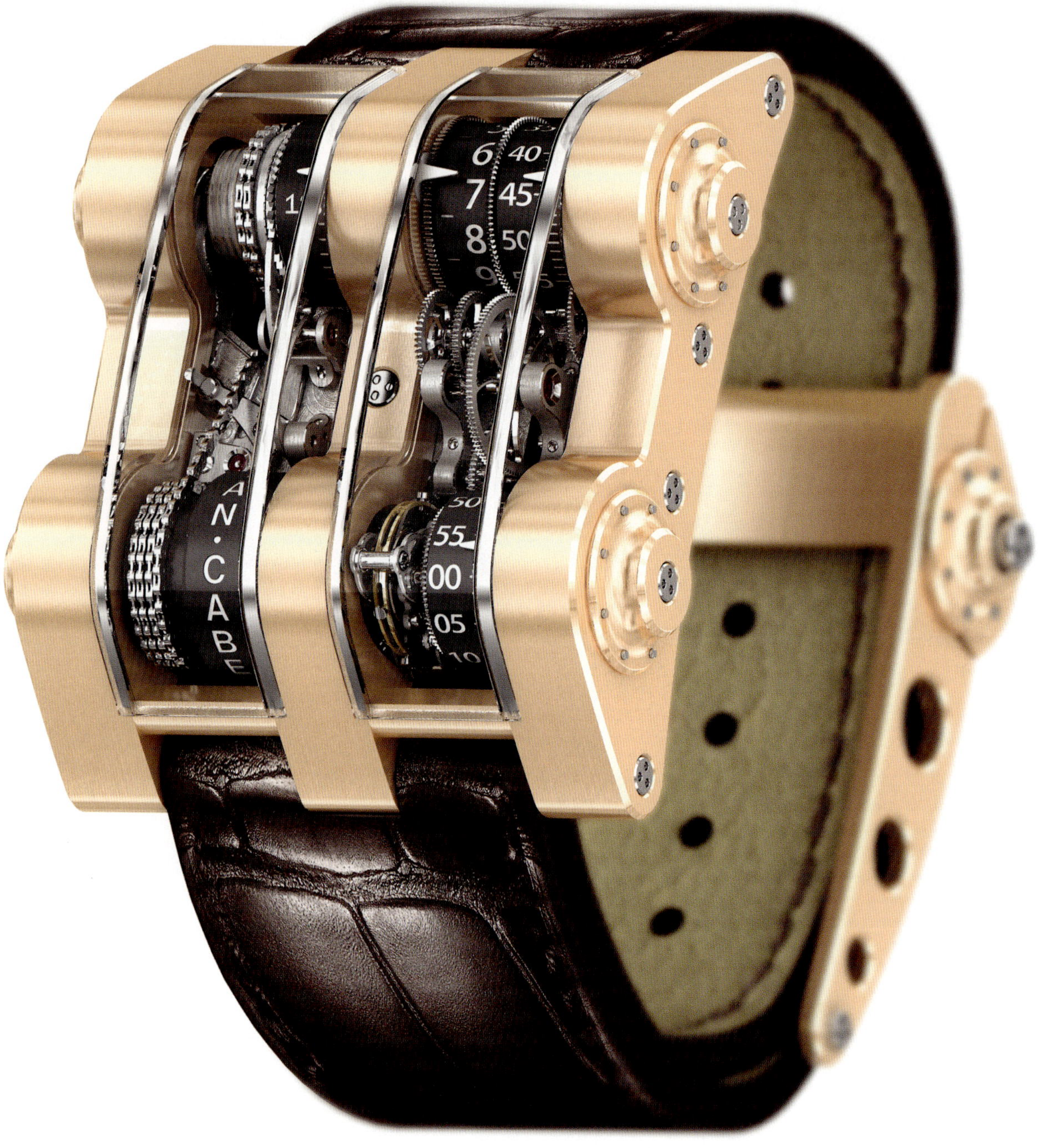

CABESTAN — WINCH TOURBILLON VERTICAL

$ 275 000

It turns out that a ship's capstan was the inspiration for one of the world's most innovative luxury watches. On a boat a capstan is a form of winch, developed for use on sailing ships, to apply force when pulling ropes and cables. Sailors would often insert pegs into the capstan and rotate it in one direction, as a means of pulling something that required a lot of effort.

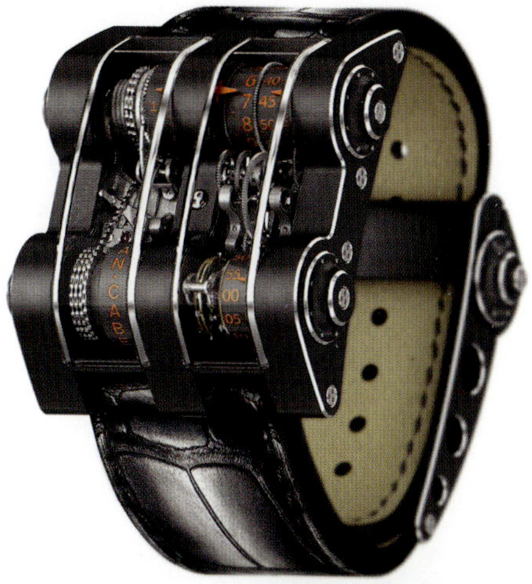

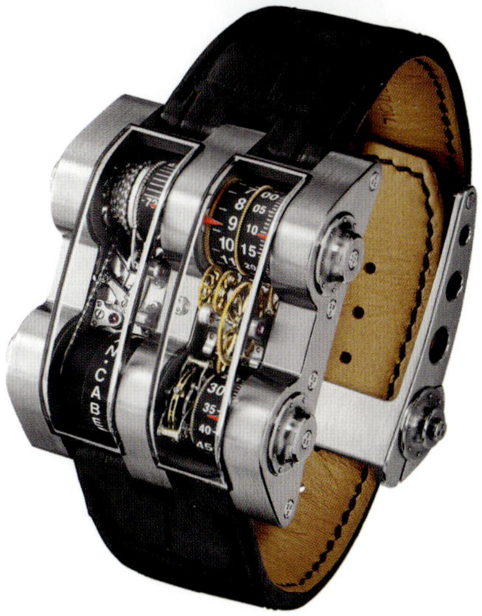

"Cabestan" is simply the French translation of capstan, and the brand birthed a unique timepiece known as the Winch Tourbillon Vertical. The watch was originally designed in 2006, by a pair of men who are as well known in the watch industry as they are quirky. They are responsible for some of the most disruptive designs the luxury watch industry has seen in the last decade. First of the pair is watchmaker and designer Vianney Halter, who, among other things, is often credited for introducing the aesthetic of "steampunk" to the luxury world, with his Antiqua. The second is Jean-François Ruchonnet, a charismatic and easily distractible designer who designed the well-regarded Monaco V4 watch for TAG Heuer with a movement inspired by a car engine.

The Winch Tourbillon Vertical reimagined the layout of a watch movement and the way one interacts with it. Time is told on a series of spinning drums, and almost all the components are laid out in a vertical, rather than horizontal fashion. It also contains a tourbillon, as well as a fusee and chain transmission, each beautifully visible through the dual sapphire crystal windows.

The movement proved incredibly tricky to produce, and its production was arguably only possible thanks to a watchmaker named Eric Coudray, who developed the famous Gyrotourbillon for watchmaker Jaeger-LeCoultre. Coudray produced most of each of the Winch Tourbillon Vertical watches personally, by hand.

Containing no crown or setting mechanism, the Winch Tourbillon Vertical requires a separate, smaller, capstan-style device, to wind it and set the time. This device comprises over 40 parts. Cabestan later redesigned a simpler watch that didn't include this separate winding component – which owners kept losing.

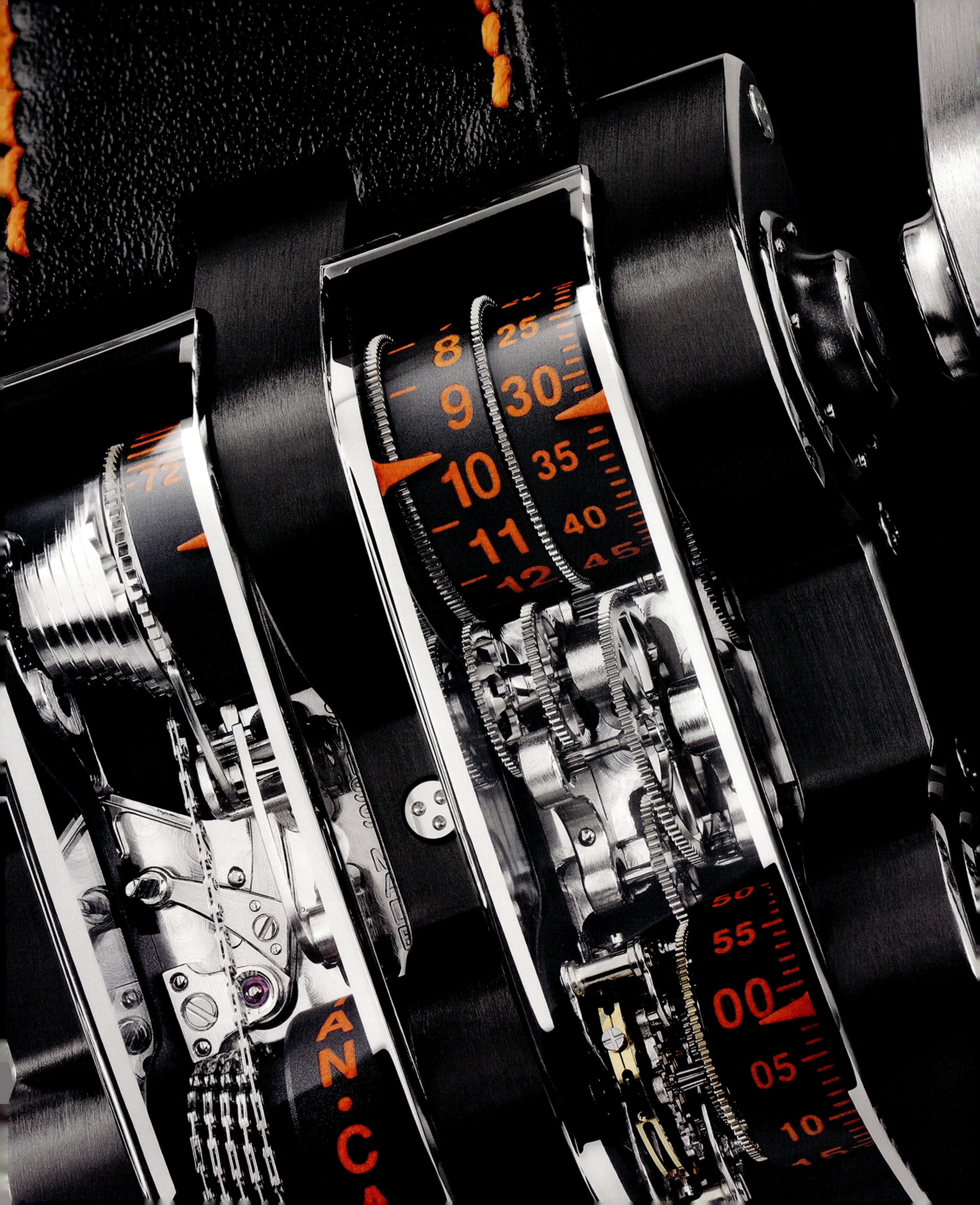

8
9
10
11
12
25
30
35
40
45
50
55
00
05
10
72

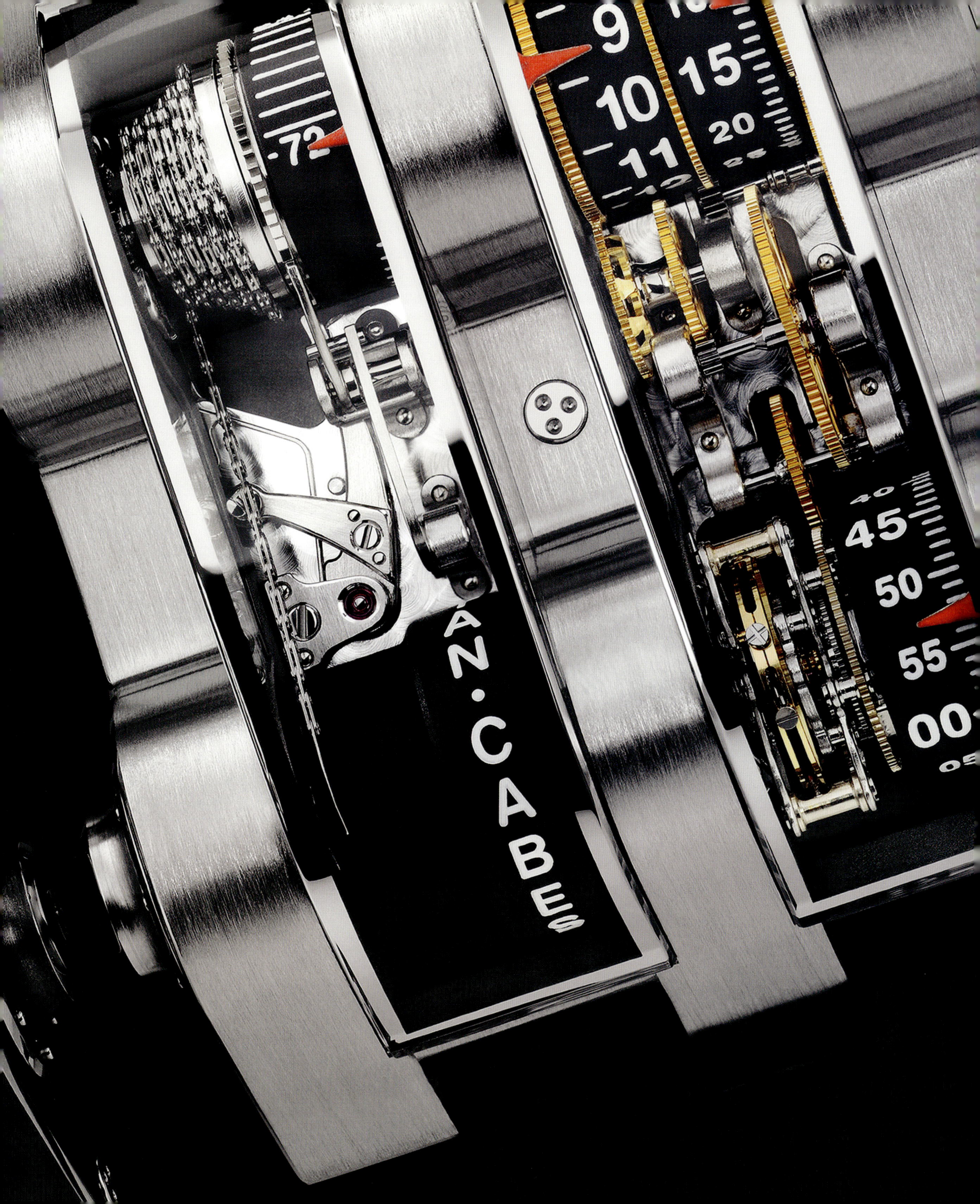

72
9
10
11
15
20
45
50
55
00
AN·CABES

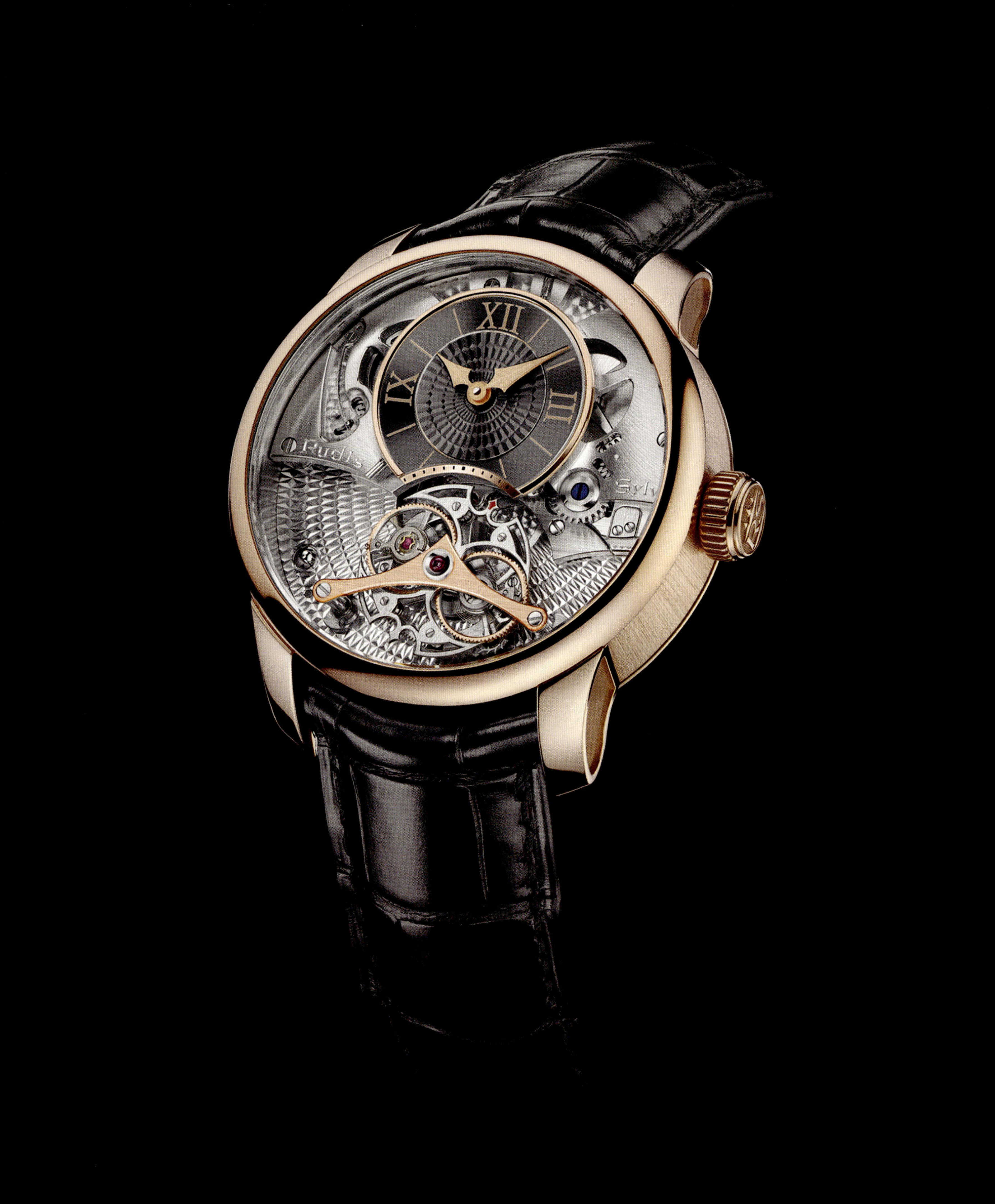
XII
IX
III
Rudis

RUDIS SYLVA — RS12 GRAND ART HORLOGER HARMONIOUS OSCILLATOR

$ 276 000

RUDIS SYLVA INVENTED A UNIQUE SYSTEM THAT TAKES THE TRADITIONAL TOURBILLON IN A TOTALLY NEW DIRECTION.

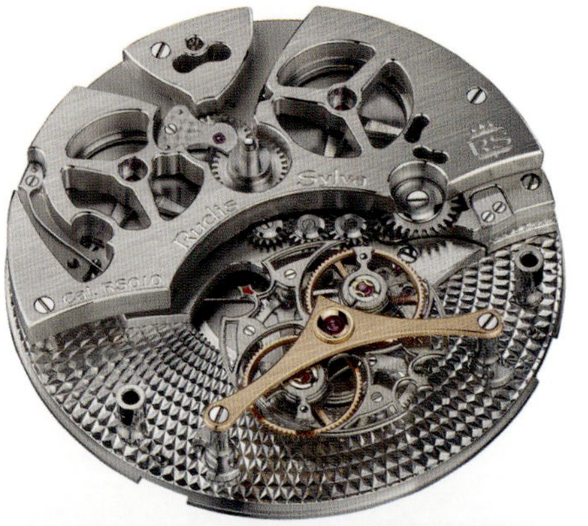

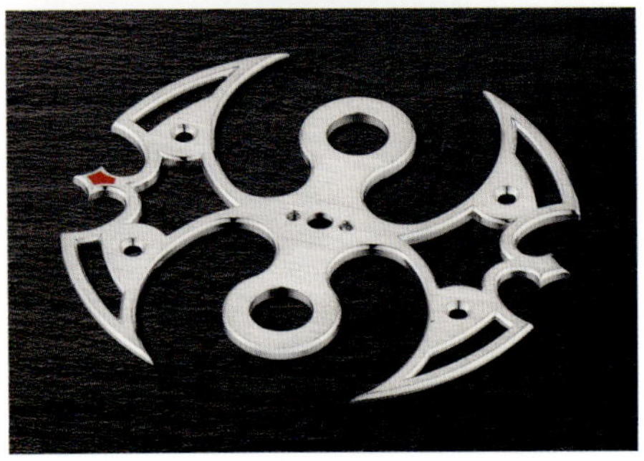

Only the fringes of the mechanical watchmaking world are focused on improving the accuracy of timepieces. Of course that wasn't always the case by any means. Most of the effort in the world of watches, over its long history, has almost exclusively focused on improving accuracy and reliability. In the 1980s that all changed with the introduction of cheap, highly accurate electronic quartz movements. Mechanical watches became art, status symbols, and collectables – with accuracy more often than not becoming less than important.

There are, however, purists who find the pursuit of means to improve the accuracy of mechanical watches to be a worthy endeavour. Boutique Swiss watch brand Rudis Sylva is one of them, and the allure probably comes from the unique challenge of unraveling issues faced by watchmakers for literally hundreds of years.

Over the course of history there have been many successful – and many less successful – techniques designed to improve the accuracy of mechanical watches. The balance wheel and hairspring (together, making the oscillator) are perhaps the most famous, as they are included in virtually all mechanical watches made. The most noteworthy means of improving the standard oscillator, was the invention of the tourbillon by Abraham-Louis Breguet in the late 18th century. Tourbillons are popular today in very high-end watches, but the irony is that their application in a wristwatch, while upgrading its prestige and aesthetics, doesn't really increase accuracy.

Rudis Sylva invented a unique system that takes the traditional tourbillon in a totally new direction. It is called the Harmonious Oscillator (debuted in 2009) and incorporates at least once principle that would be considered heresy by most watchmakers. In most watches, balance wheels are design to oscillate freely with as little resistance as possible. Even tiny things like air resistance can affect accuracy. However, in the Harmonious Oscillator, which contains two balance wheels, each is connected to the other via a set of geared teeth on the edges. How is that possible?

A unique system forces one balance wheel to move when the other does as they are geared together, yet they still operate at a frequency of 21,600 beats per hour. Then, the entire assembly spins on its own axis like a tourbillon. Rudis Sylva claims that it creates an entirely consistent rate, which offers vastly improved accuracy over most other mechanical watches.

Each Rudis Sylva watch and movement is hand-made and decorated, while the RS12 Grand Art Horloger model adds two other hand-applied artistic techniques. The open dial of the watch offers a view of the movement, as well as a guilloché machine-engraved dial and baseplate. The Harmonious Oscillator doubles as the seconds indicator, with the hours and minutes being indicated above, on the dial.

On the rear of the watch case is an engraved and enamel painted sundial. Even though the mechanism in the RS12 movement is thoroughly modern, the overall composition is meant to remind the wearer of watchmaking history, apparently beginning with telling the time by light from the sun.

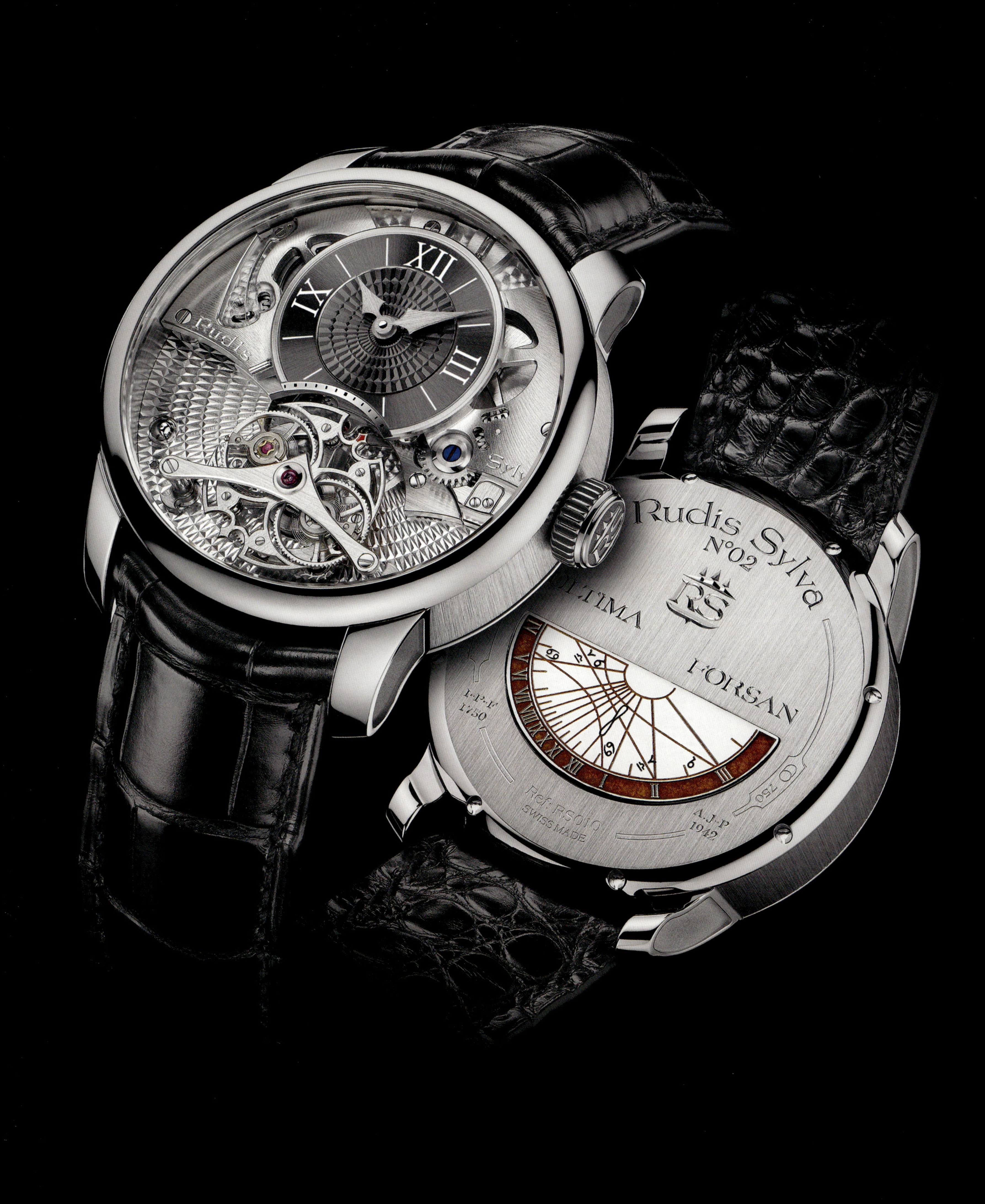
XII
IX
III
Rudis Sylva
N°02
FORSAN
I·P·F
1730
Ref. RS010
SWISS MADE
A.J.P
1942
750

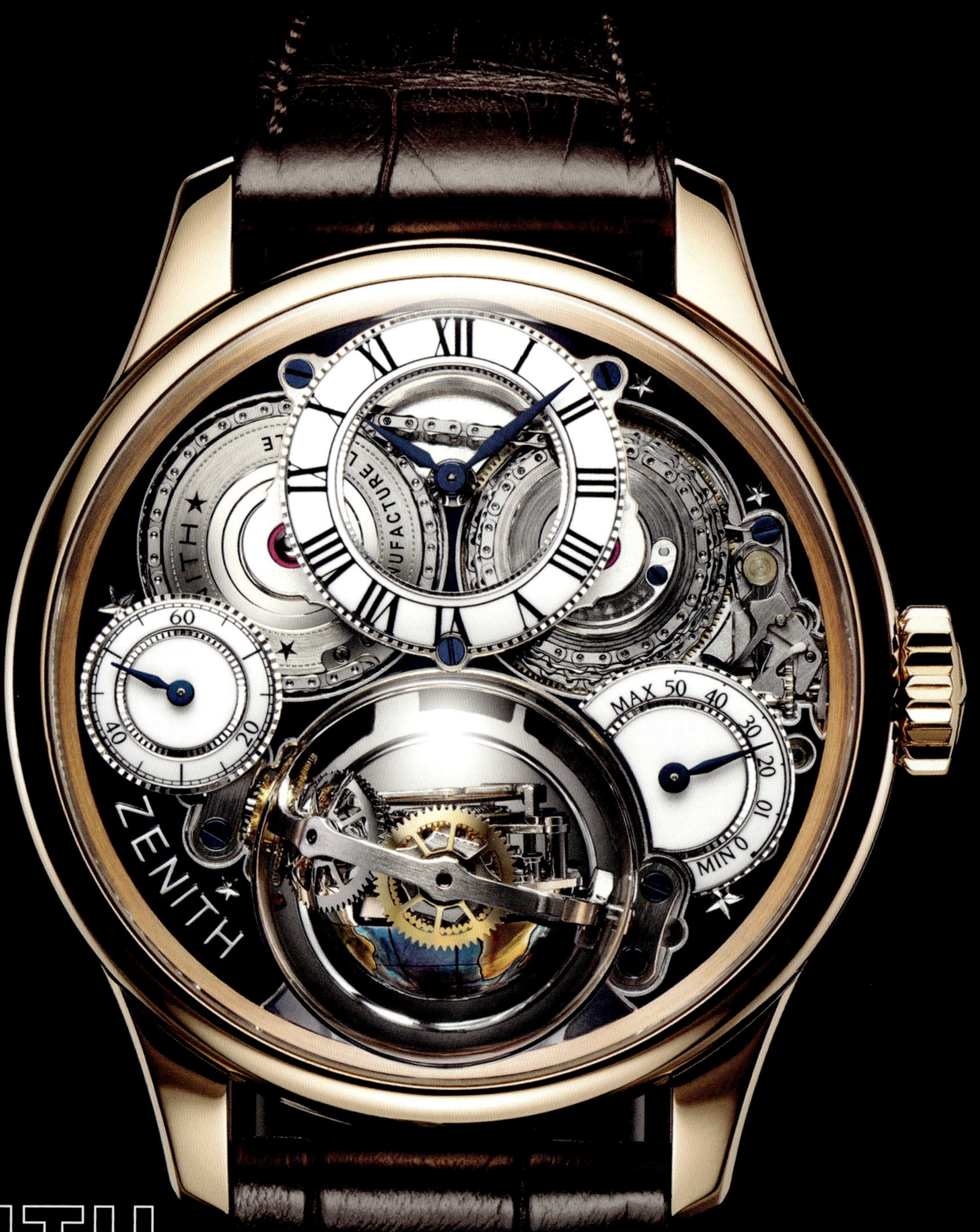

ZENITH — ACADEMY CHRISTOPHE COLOMB HURRICANE

$ 280 000

In the mid-2000s the high-end watch complication known as the tourbillon began to go from being rare to common-place among luxury watches. At one time the tourbillon was seen as a pinnacle of visual and technical achievement in mechanical timepieces. This caused so many brands to release their own tourbillons, that it resulted in a need for variations on the tourbillon theme to help brands distinguish themselves.

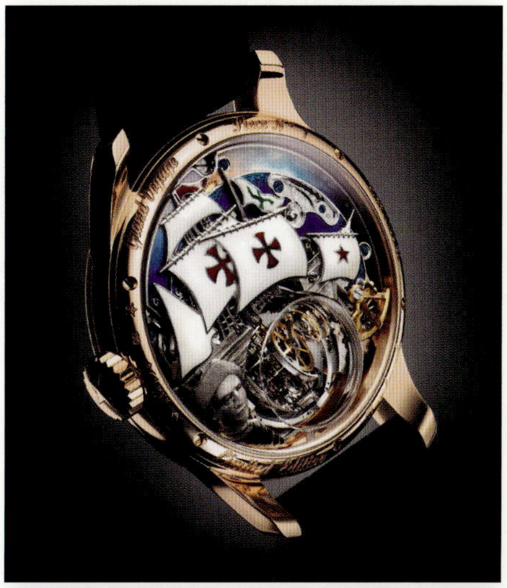

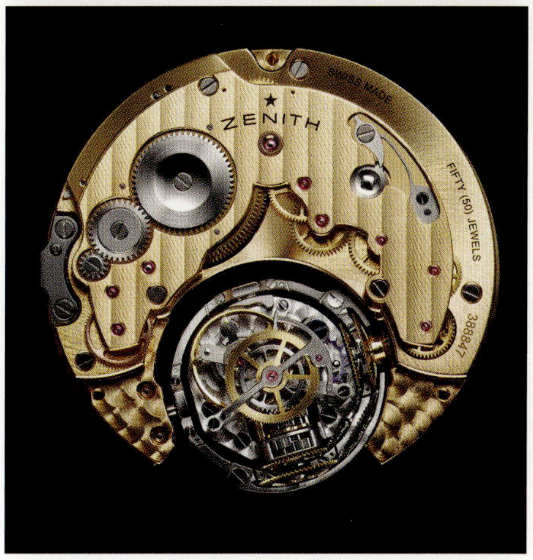

Swiss watchmaker Zenith offered a unique alternative, that was originally called a "zero gravity tourbillon", even though it was not a tourbillon at all. While a tourbillon is an escapement and balance wheel that revolves on its own axis, Zenith's invention is an escapement and balance wheel that exists in a gimbal with a weight so that it remains upright, no matter what position the watch is in.

In many ways their new "zero gravity" mount for the balance wheel is just as (if not more) interesting to look at compared with a tourbillon. The system is shaped like a ball and exists in a pronounced bubble on the watch. The most distinguishing thing on all Zenith watches with this feature is the large dome that extends from the sapphire crystal over the dial.

Zenith eventually put this unique complication to work as the base of their Christophe Colomb watch collection. The most technically challenging version of the Academy Christophe Colomb collection is the Hurricane. Set in an imposing yet graceful 45mm wide 18k rose gold case, the dial offers a clear view into the movement.

Added to the unique gyroscopic-style escapement system is another complex mechanism known as a fusee and chain. This historic invention from several hundred years ago, uses what is essentially a tiny bicycle chain to act as a transmission of power from the mainspring barrel to the rest of the movement. The chain itself is hand-made and uses over 580 parts. The entire movement in the watch has almost 1,000 individual parts, and is based on the famous Zenith "El Primero" family of movements, that tend to offer more accuracy over time.

The Academy Christophe Colomb Hurricane is favoured by collectors not only for its technical marvels, but also for offering such a handsome design. Zenith produced only 25 pieces in total.

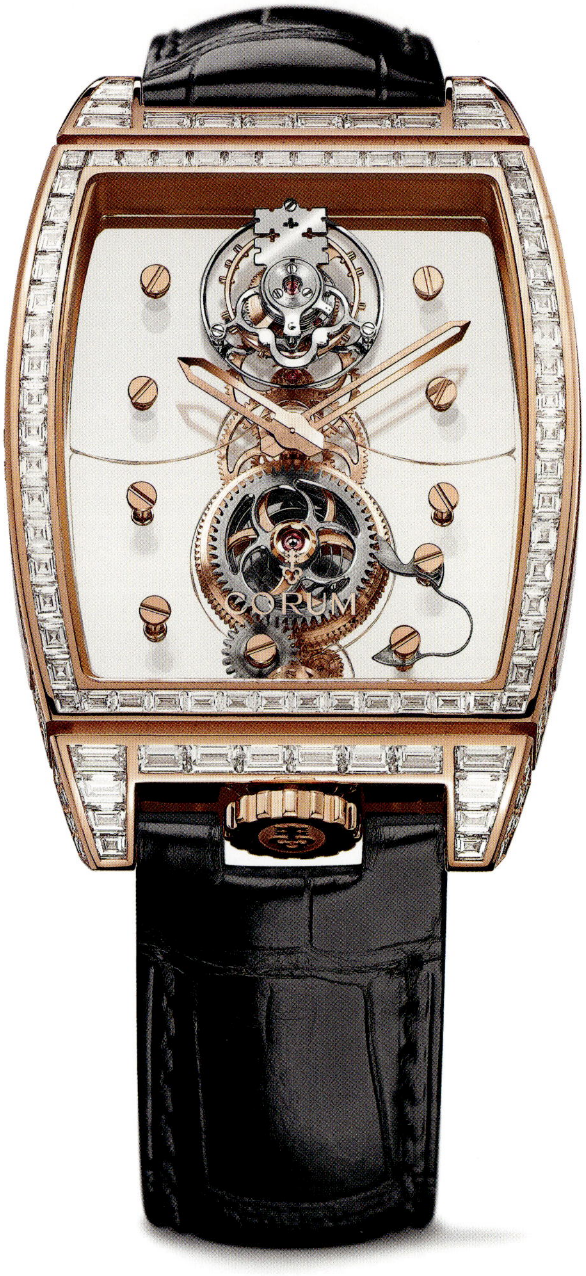

CORUM — GOLDEN BRIDGE TOURBILLON PANORAMIQUE

$ 283 200*

When Corum released the original Golden Bridge watch in the 1980s, it was yet another inventive watch from the brand that was known for refusing to release anything with a design that may be confused for another watchmaker's product. To this day one of the defining elements of a Corum watch is that you know one when you see it.

The Golden Bridge began as a beautiful concept, which entailed a thin, vertically linear movement, that was enjoyable to look at, because its mechanics were simple to see and understand. Golden Bridge movements proved so useful in helping people to realize how a mechanical watch movement works, that Corum claims some watchmaking schools in Switzerland currently use the movements for educational purposes.

"Golden Bridge", as a name, refers to the fact that the mainplate running down the centre of the movement, which holds it all together, is typically in gold. This Panoramique version of the watch, however, does not have any easily visible bridges or mainplate at all. Corum designed the Tourbillon Panoramique to use transparent sapphire crystals as the bridges, which was unique for the Golden Bridge collection. However, like most other Golden Bridge watches, this one has the entire gear train in one vertical stack, and also happens to throw in a tourbillon-style escapement that shoots up the value even more.

Synthetic sapphire bridges may be strong, but they can also be brittle. Merely assembling the movement inside the Golden Bridge Tourbillon Panoramique can risk breaking the bridges. The most dangerous thing a watchmaker can do is merely tighten screws. Though once these movements are assembled they should prove rather durable. Corum produced only 20 pieces of the limited edition Golden Bridge Tourbillon Panoramique and 10 of them were decorated with diamonds.

* Price based on watch pavé-set with diamonds

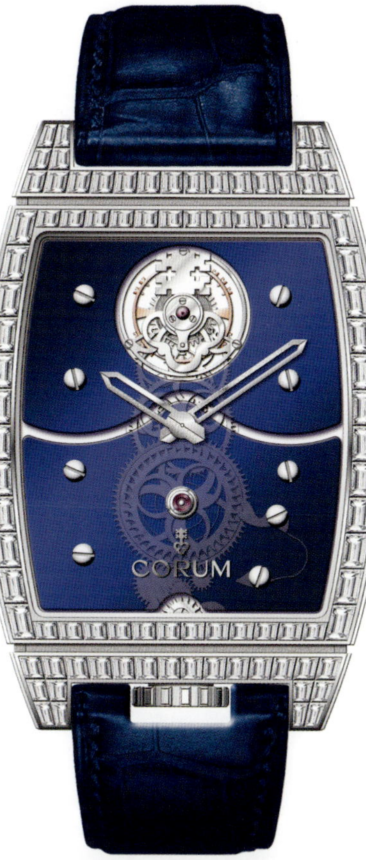

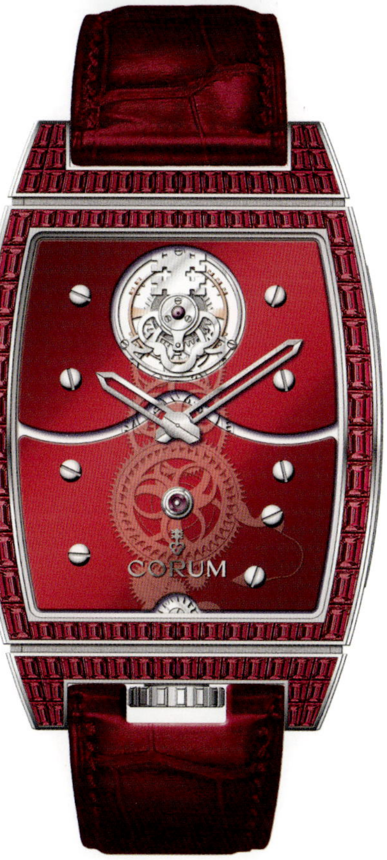

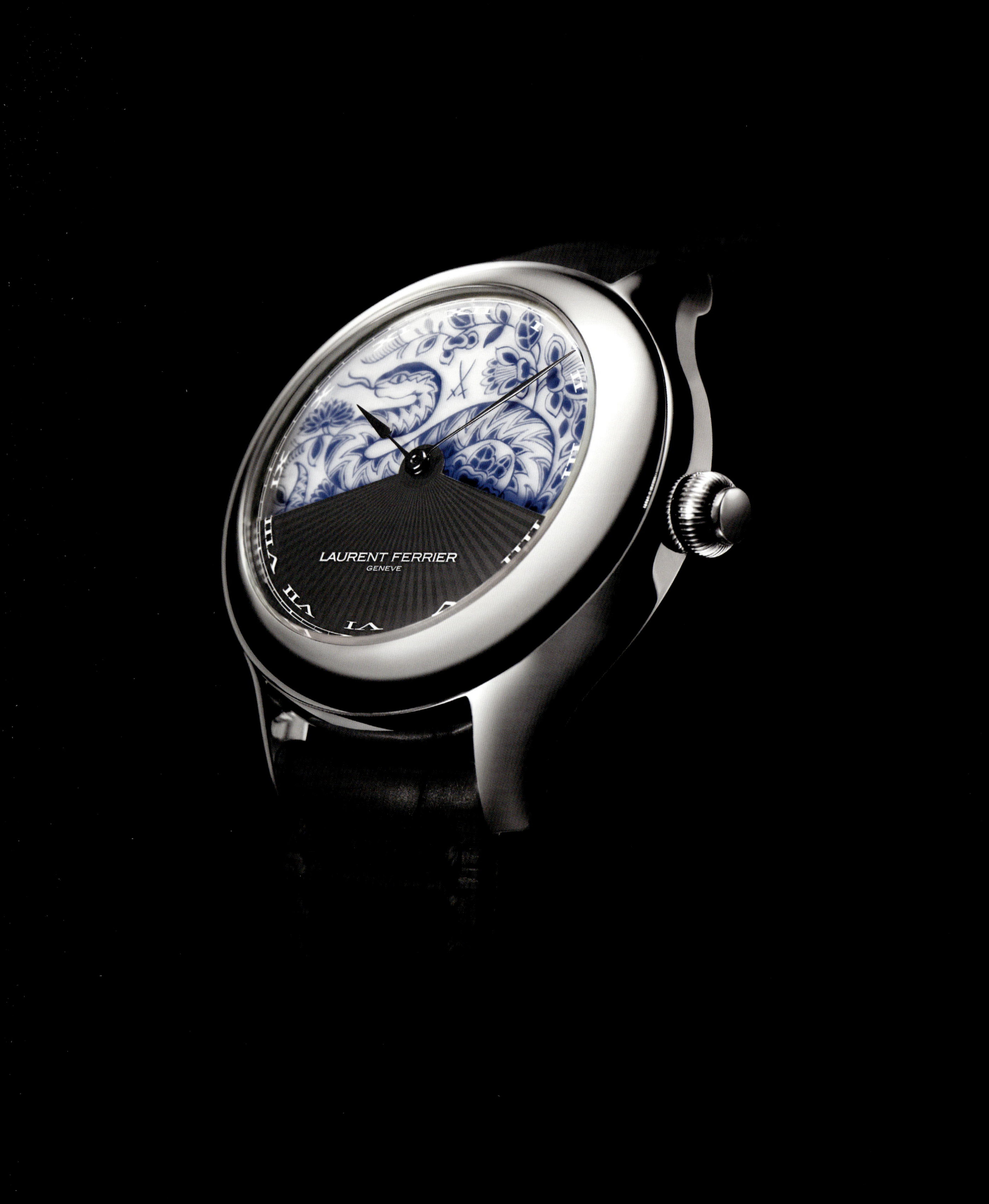
LAURENT FERRIER
GENEVE

LAURENT FERRIER — GALET SECRET TOURBILLON DOUBLE SPIRAL MEISSEN

$ 284 000

WHILE SOME COLLECTORS SEEK DISTINCTIVE OR AVANT-GARDE WATCHES, LAURENT FERRIER INSTEAD APPEALS TO THOSE SEEKING REFINEMENT.

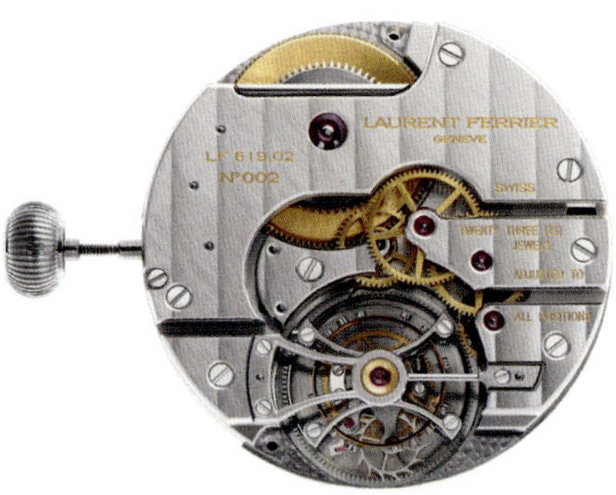

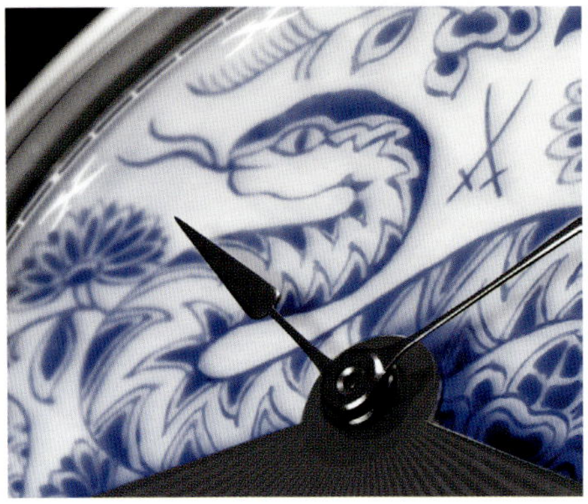

After spending time as a watchmaker and designer for the leading firm Patek Philippe, Laurent Ferrier – like many others in similar circumstances – decided to begin his own eponymous watch brand in 2010. The rise of the independent high-end watchmaker in modern times is a novel concept. Twenty years earlier, this practice would have been impossible. Many attribute the ability to produce small watch parts, using modern computer-aided technology as well as the internet, as making it possible for small watchmakers to thrive.

Laurent Ferrier did not make his mark by being that different, but rather by being supremely traditional in design. His first timepiece, known as the Galet Classic Tourbillon Double Balance Spring, bears a familiar looking design with an incredible level of fit, finish, and attention to detail. For many collectors it is the epitome of a classically-themed luxury watch.

"Galet" actually translates to "pebble," which refers to the graceful curves of the case, and fine polishing of the gold, that result in a design both elegant and comfortable to wear. Traditionally proportional dials, often produced from enamel, allude to a vintage style, but in the form of a modern package. While some collectors seek distinctive or avant-garde watches, Laurent Ferrier instead appeals to those seeking refinement.

The "Double Balance Spring" refers to a system in the watch that uses not one but two hair (or balance) springs, connected to the balance wheel. The balance wheel is further connected to a tourbillon, that rotates the entire oscillator assembly around itself on its own axis. Visible through the rear of the watch, these mechanical mechanisms, with their technical complexity and aesthetic beauty, provide a high level of appeal for collectors. Laurent Ferrier is not without its mechanical tricks or appeals to whimsy. Building on the style of the Galet Classic Tourbillon Double Balance Spring, the brand released a novel concept with the Galet Classic Secret. The watch features a dial with a fan-like partition, that opens and closes to reveal a secondary display. The dial may open on command by pressing a pusher in the crown, but also gradually opens automatically for one hour each day. The specific hour is chosen by the customer and then set by a watchmaker.

Laurent Ferrier uses the special space behind the dial for a range of "secret" images that include hand-painted enamel art. This Meissen Edition set of Galet Classic Secret watches involved a partnership with the well-known, almost 300-year-old, German porcelain maker Meissen. Known by their crossed swords logo, Meissen was the first European "China" porcelain maker to emulate the ancient techniques of the Chinese.

Laurent Ferrier produced a limited number of Galet Secret Tourbillon Double Balance Spring watches with Meissen offering symbols of the Chinese Zodiac, such dragons or snakes. Produced as one-of-a-kind pieces, the dials of the watches open up to reveal hand-painted porcelain inner dials produced using traditional artistic techniques. Often, timepieces with zodiac symbols are sold to Chinese customers; perhaps slightly ironic, because, regardless of the immense prestige of Meissen work, it was originally meant to copy Chinese crafts.

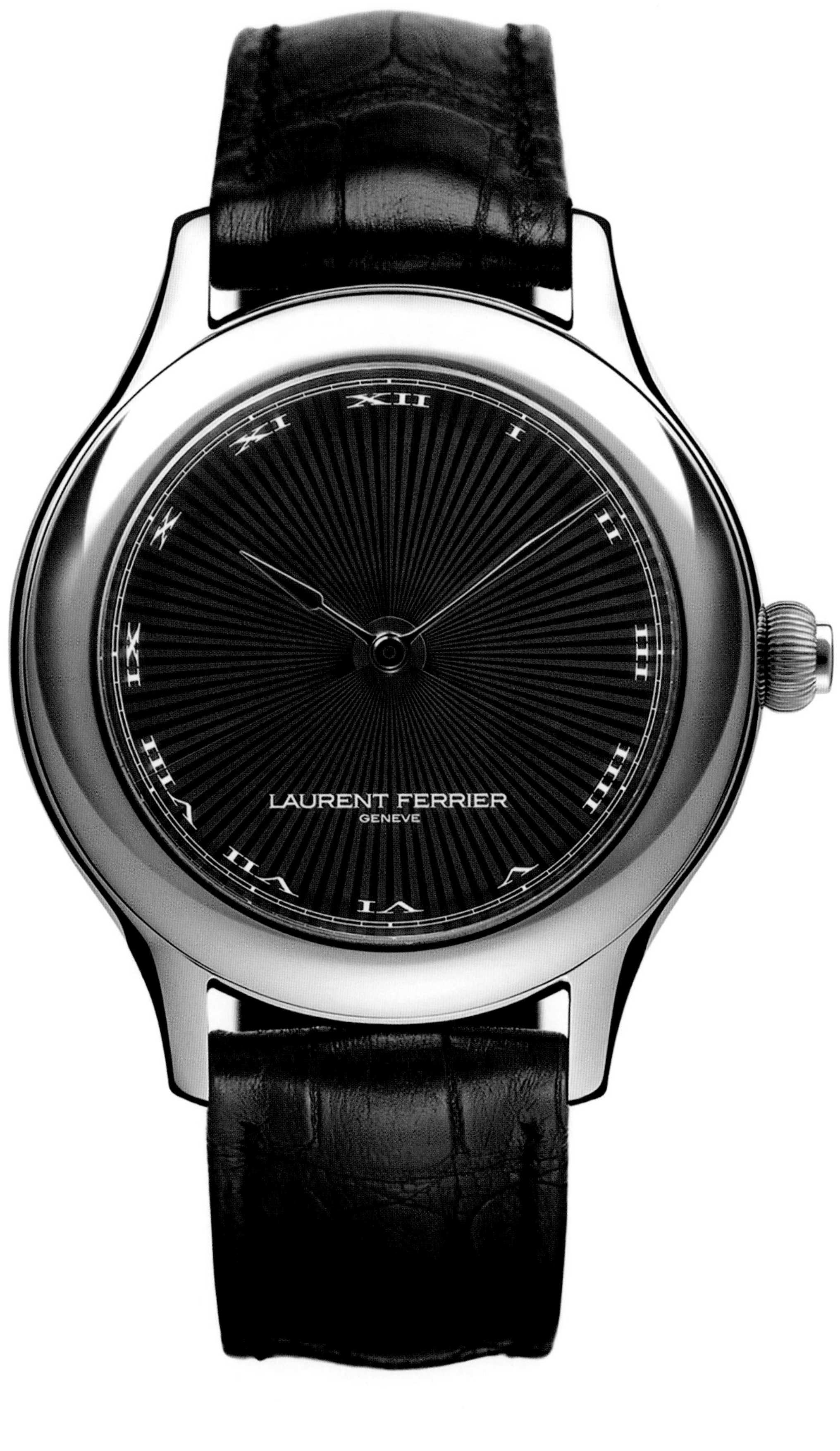

LAURENT FERRIER
GENEVE

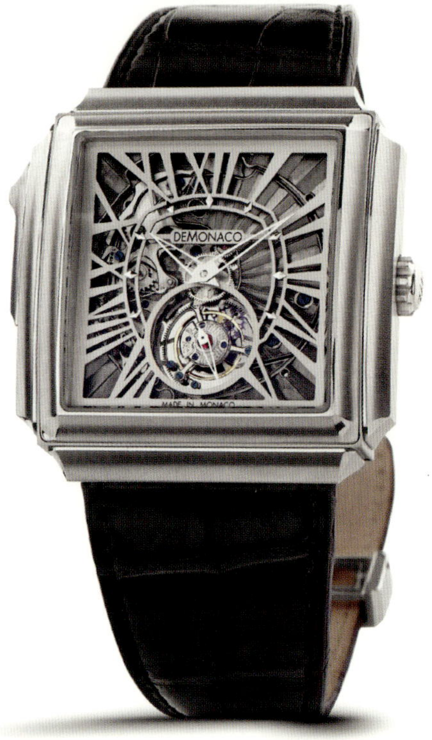

ATELIERS DEMONACO – GRAND TOURBILLON MINUTE REPEATER

$ 290 000*

Ateliers DeMonaco watches are assembled and decorated in the principality of Monaco. The watchmaker Ateliers DeMonaco is peopled by a unique blend of European personalities. The components of the brand's watches are produced in Switzerland, while the brand is run by Dutch people (living in Switzerland). This unique mix injects an original flair to Ateliers DeMonaco timepieces, which lie at the ultra-high end of the timepiece market.

Available in both round ("Ronde") or square ("Carré") cases, Grande Tourbillon Minute Repeaters sum up the strengths and the personality of the brand, and were originally released in 2010. In the square-shaped case, the pictured model technically bears the illustrious sounding name of "Carré d'Or Squelette Grand Tourbillon Répétition Minute TB-RM1." The name merely explains the features of the watch, and that it comes in a gold case and contains tourbillon and minute repeater complications as part of the skeletonised movement.

Perhaps the most crowd-pleasing element of the watch is the hand-engraved movement, which is made entirely in-house by Ateliers DeMonaco. While this movement is manually wound, some of the brand's other watches, with automatic-winding movements, feature beautifully decorated rotors bearing intricate designs that celebrate Monaco.

Watch collectors appreciate Ateliers DeMonaco movements for their emphasis on modern reliability, as well as on detail. Minute repeater complications, which chime the time back to the wearer on command using a series of hammers and gongs, can often have a humming sound, due to a necessary air regulator mechanism. Ateliers DeMonaco "quiets" their minute repeater using a special system of 18k gold weights. The movement also features silicon – versus metal – for internal components such as the escape wheel and lever. Silicon is considered more reliable because it does not require oil for lubrication and is not affected by magnetism or temperature.

In order to protect the movement, the core of the Grand Tourbillon Minute Repeater case is in titanium, while the outside of the 46mm-wide case comes in 18k gold. The skeletonised dial has precision cut Roman numeral hour indicators that sit over a view of the movement. While not limited in production, this, and other Ateliers DeMonaco watches, are extremely rare.

HYT — H3

$290 000

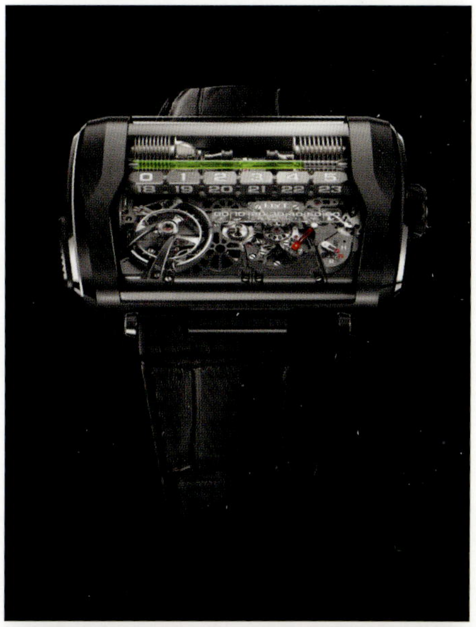

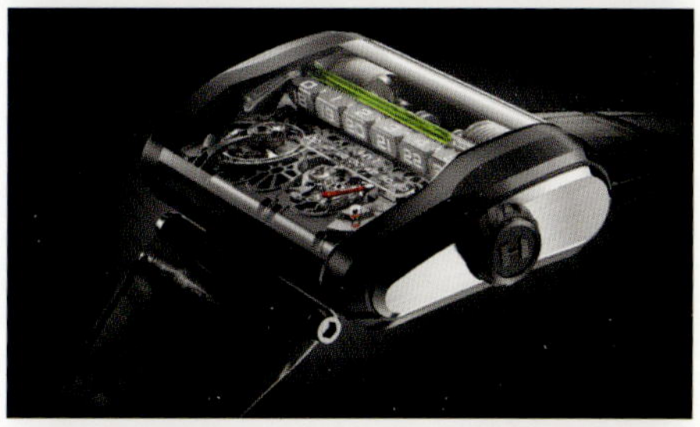

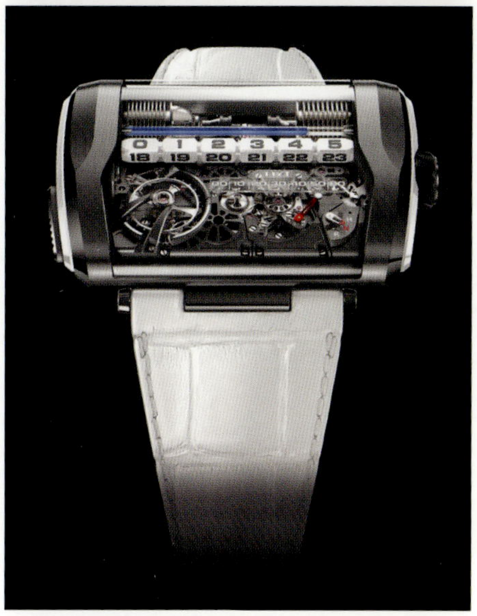

Originally conceived as a purely "linear portrayal of time", the H3 is probably the most uncommon and exclusive creation by Swiss watchmaker HYT, the Hydro Mechanical Horologists. The H3 is an uncanny item, even at first glance, thanks to the sideways-long, almost rectangular case. The finely polished case is a beefy 62mm wide and is made from mixed components of both titanium and platinum.

Shaped much like a synthesiser keyboard for the wrist, the H3 wears impressively well, assuming one isn't sporting tight sleeves. Timepiece enthusiasts may choose to brave this inspired case design in order to appreciate the bespoke mechanical movement contained within. Given that this is an HYT-brand product, the H3 would not be complete without a liquid-filled indicator for the time. At the top of the dial is a linear "capillary" tube produced from sapphire crystal. This contains a green liquid that indicates the current hour in conjunction with the row of six rotating cubes that contain the hour markers. Using a 24-hour format, the complete set of hour-indicators is displayed once per day with the row of cubes rotating four times before starting the cycle over again.

What powers the liquid to move in the thin tubes is a metal bellows system, which is connected to the rest of the mechanical movement. Minutes are indicated on their own linear scale as a platform-style hand tracks a horizontal path underneath it in order to indicate the current minute (to within 2–3 minutes of reading precision). A selection indicator on the dial is used to inform the user of the crown's current mode – whether it is set to manual winding, to set the time, or to simply spin freely in neutral mode. When fully wound, the movement's power reserve lasts for 170 hours. Only 25 pieces of each version of the HYT H3 watch will ever be produced.

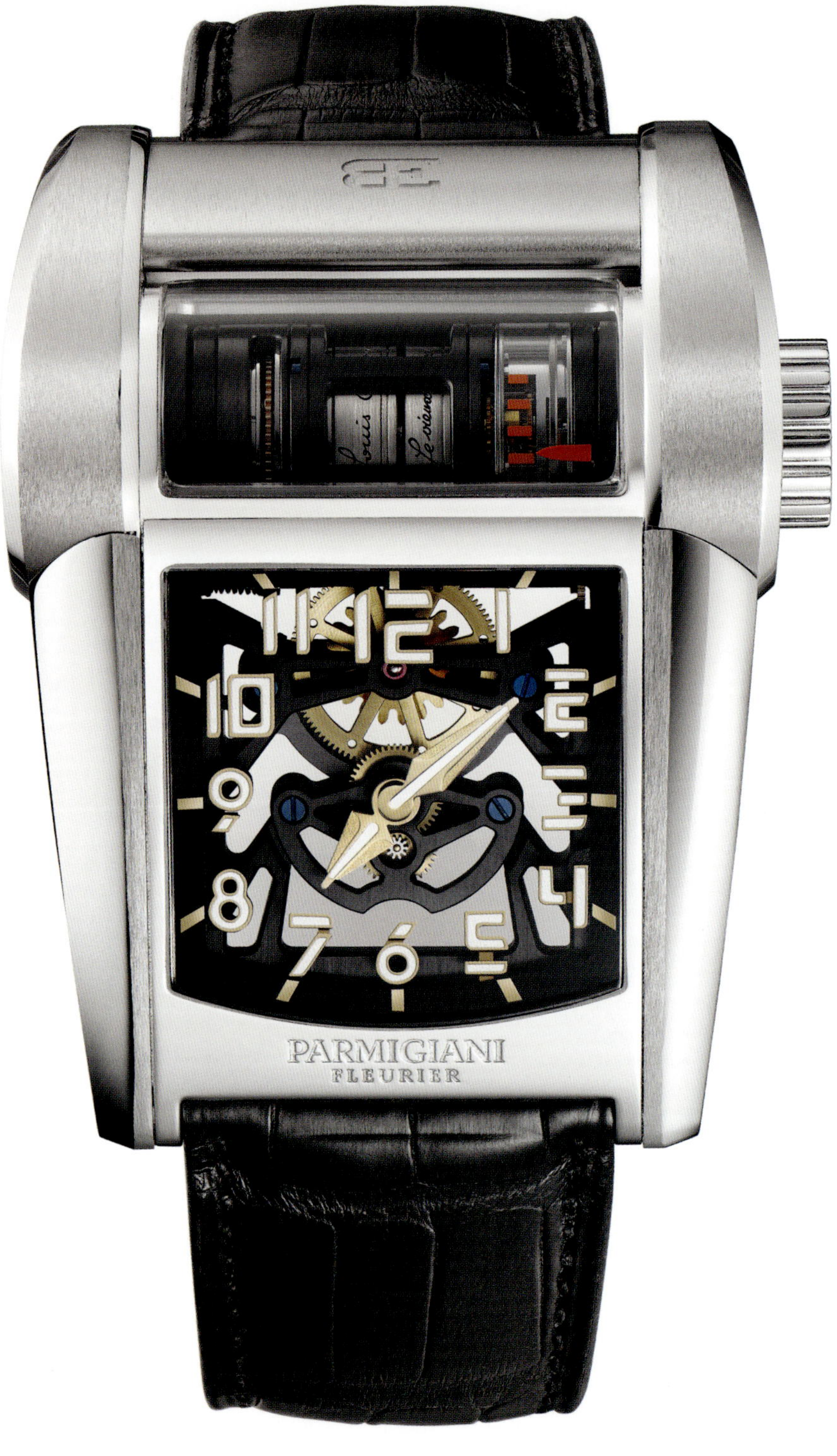

PARMIGIANI FLEURIER — BUGATTI TYPE 390

$ 295 000

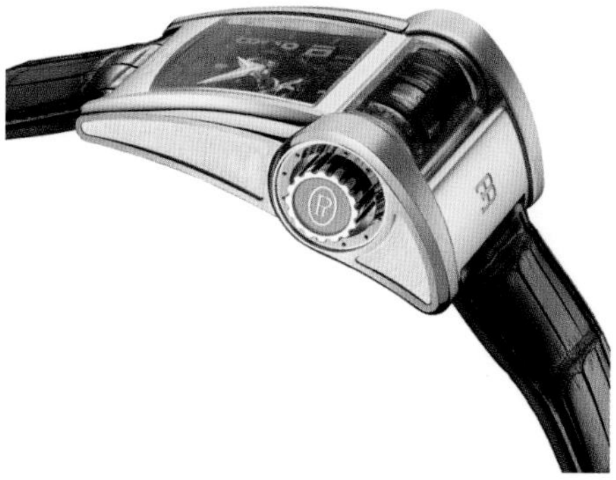

Founder Michel Parmigiani, of the eponymous Swiss Parmigiani Fleurier brand, calls the Bugatti Type 390 both a court jester and their most technical watch ever created. Neither silly nor simple, clearly Mr Parmigiani's description of this complicated, automotive-inspired timepiece is meant to evoke a thoughtful question. So, too, is the intellectual intrigue of this uncommonly conceived machine designed to delight by evoking polarised opinion.

The Type 390's case is meant to be read at a side-angle in the spirit of historic drivers' watches. Specifically, Parmigiani had the Bugatti Chiron car in mind when designing the aesthetic elements of the watch's case and dial. At the time of writing, the Bugatti Type 390 watch collection is the most complicated product to come out of Parmigiani's status as the official watchmaking partner of Bugatti. Reading the time is simple and legible, with an interesting dial inspired by the interior of the Chiron. The neo art-deco style Arabic hour numerals contrast nicely with the open-worked movement, as seen through the skeletonised dial.

One of the most complicated elements of the Type 390's movement is the separation of the mainsprings and regulation organ systems from the running gear train that moves the hands. The two sections of the 80-hour power-reserve movement are connected with a worm gear. Stacked mainspring barrels offer a visual power-reserve indicator and the tubular column-style assembly ends with a horizontally mounted tourbillon. This position for the tourbillon (which is visible through a window in the case) is probably more logical for overall timing performance accuracy than a vertical orientation – a tactic employed by only a small number of watchmakers, including Parmigiani.

The 302-part mechanical movement is housed within a case of respective complexity. Comfort for the wearer of the Bugatti Type 390 is enhanced by the prominent top lug structure, which pivots a few degrees to better fit around different wrist sizes. In accordance with Parmigiani aesthetic brand codes, the two parts of the case form signature teardrop-style shapes featuring lines that follow the geometry of the Fibonacci Sequence.

Parmigiani claims that over five years of research and development went into crafting the Bugatti Type 390 timepiece. The reason that the brand asserts the highly technical nature of the watch is not related to its list of mechanical features, but more generally how many of its parts required specialised manufacturing as well as micro-engineering developments. An entirely new mechanical system, along with hundreds of bespoke parts, must work together with the harmony of the parts powering a racing (or timing) machine – and that comes at a price that only a select few get to enjoy.

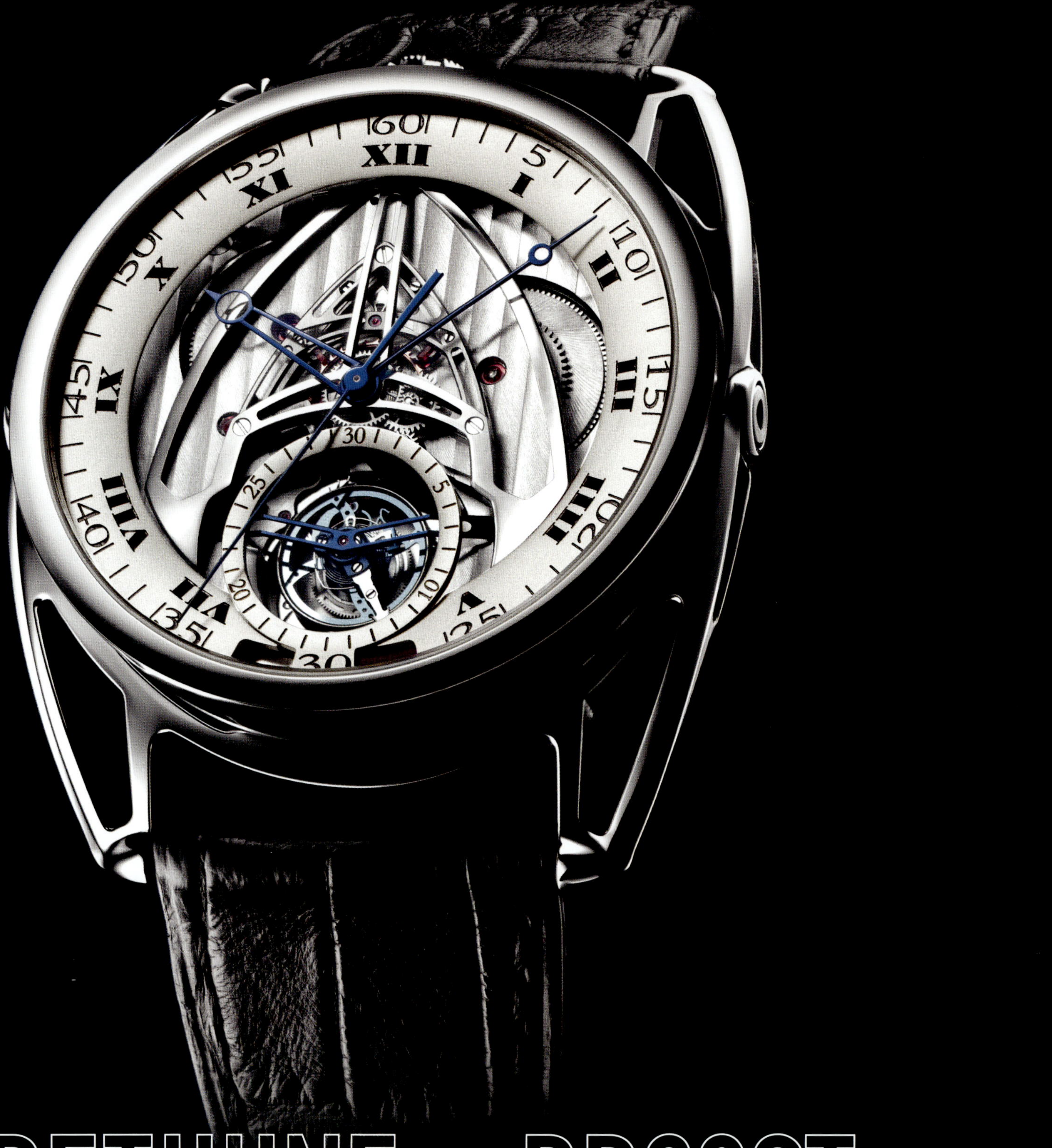

DE BETHUNE — DB28ST

$ 299 000

The universe of luxury watches is layered with ironies and obscure references to the past. To be a true timepiece collector often means that you freely admit to defying your own rules from time to time, in order to fully appreciate the larger world of what is available. A great example is the ubiquitous "sweeping versus ticking" preference on watch dials. Ask most people what the hallmark of a mechanical watch is and they will quickly point to the existence of a constantly sweeping, versus "tick tocking", seconds hand.

Ticking seconds hands, that move from one indicator to the next each second, are the sign of an electronic quartz watch, something few collectors would want to be seen wearing. Having said that, there is a class of exotic mechanical watches, that contain "dead" or "jumping" seconds hands, that do precisely that. In fact, if you want to count the passing of each second more precisely, a ticking hand is much more useful than one which sweeps. Scientists long ago knew this and mechanical dead second hands were a useful feature present on many historic instrument-style clocks. Flash-forward to today and a small breed of extremely high-end, certainly non-quartz, watches such as this DB28ST (and other De Bethune watches), contain precisely that.

With a richly skeletonised dial, that exposes the movement, few would mistake the DB28ST as anything but lusciously mechanical. Also, adding further irony to the presence of a jumping seconds hand, is the fact that the movement operates at a higher frequency than most movements. Why is this ironic? Because faster movements allow for sweeping seconds hands to move even more smoothly.

The quirky machine inside this De Bethune timepiece, once again presents their mastery of modern traditional movements, with a focus on their silicon balance wheel-based tourbillon, right above 6 o'clock, which rotates once each 30 (versus the average 60) seconds, due to the speed of the movement. Seconds on the dial jump each second, precisely from marker to marker, on a traditional looking scale that lines the periphery of an otherwise extremely modern dial. The case of the DB28ST is produced in a rare, highly polished titanium and contains a unique ergonomic lug system designed to increase wearing comfort. The lug structures (which attach the strap to the case) are hinged from the middle of the case and offer a bit of give, allowing the watch to conform to the wearer's wrist.

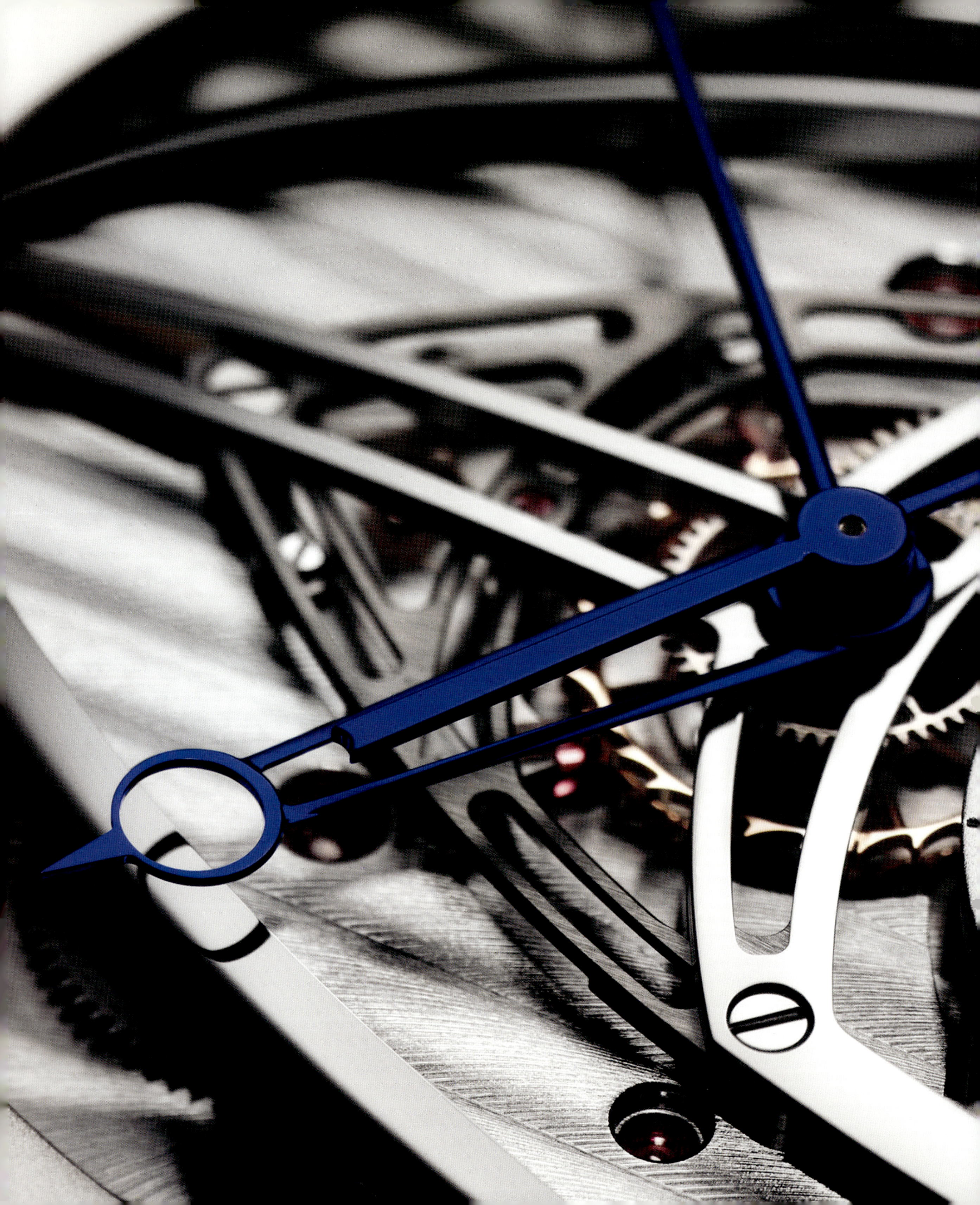

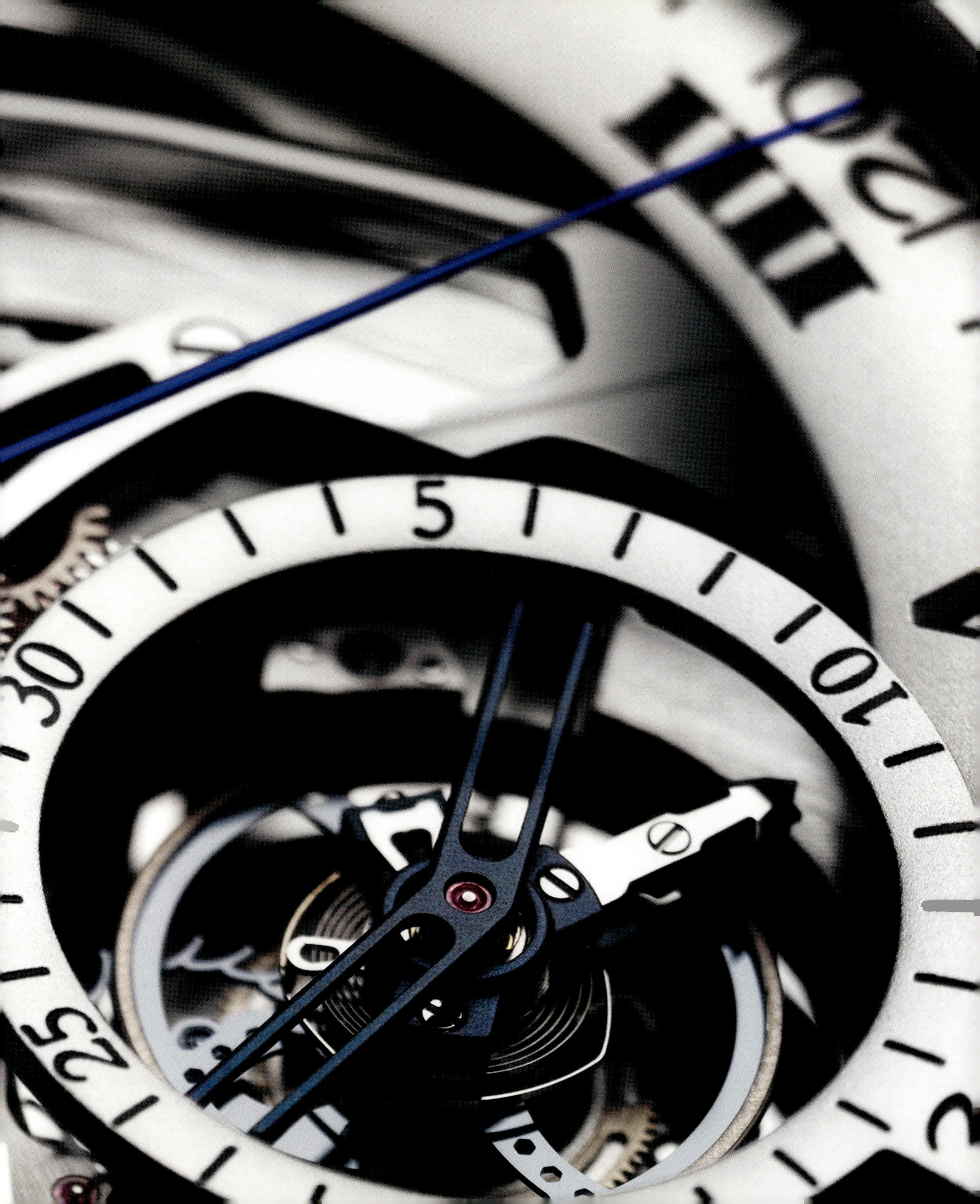

5
10
30
25

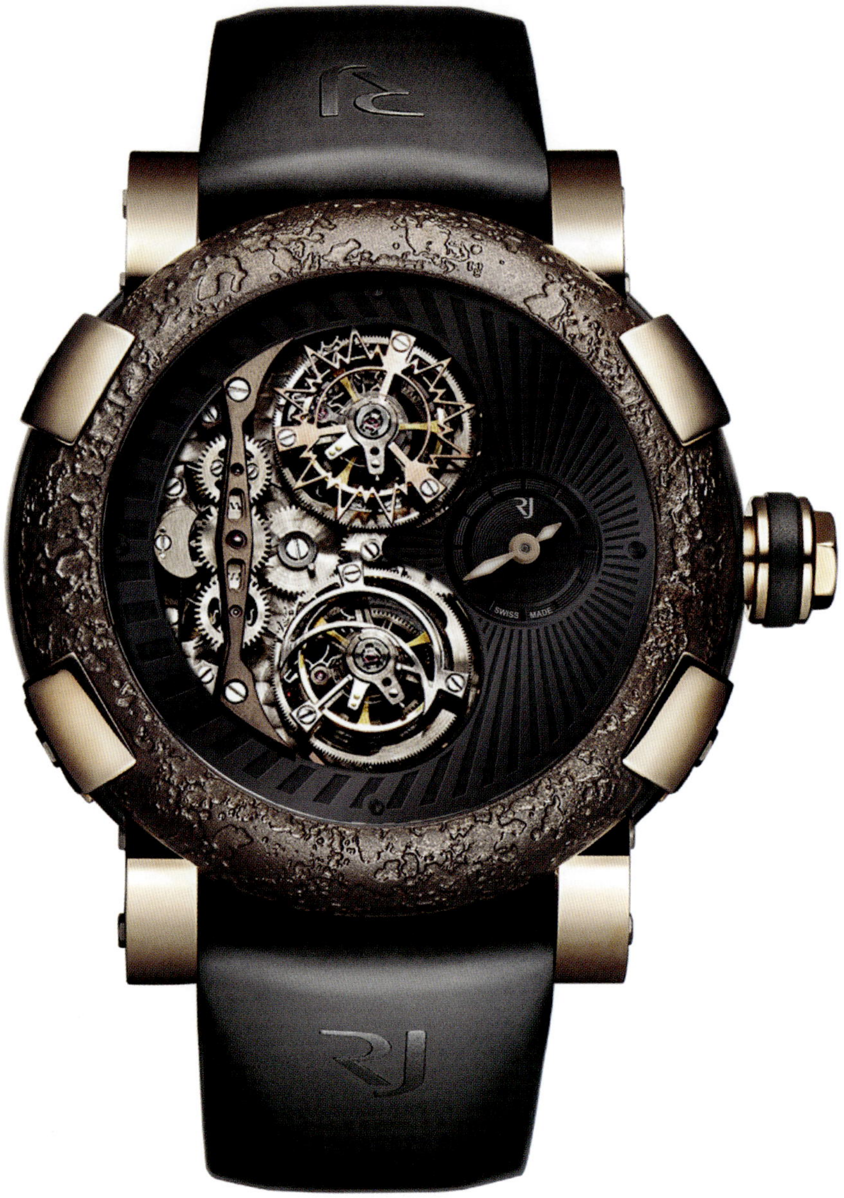

ROMAIN JEROME – TITANIC DNA DAY & NIGHT DOUBLE TOURBILLON

$ 300 300

People in the watch industry often throw around the arguably counter-intuitive notion that "people don't buy watches to tell the time". What they mean is that, in today's world of mobile phones with integral clocks and inexpensive digital watches, people don't purchase high-end timepieces just in order to know the time. Instead, watches are purchased because of status, appreciation for the art of horology, and as style or fashion items.

Having said that, a brief look at today's most successful luxury watches will reveal a series of models with easy-to-read dials. One could take it as proof that, while people don't buy high-end watches merely to tell the time, there is at least a cursory expectation that they do so. For many watch lovers, timepieces represent a unique, expressive tool, and function is an important part of the ownership experience.

What if – for argument's sake – the watch industry were to take its own suggestion more seriously? Would it produce a mechanical watch with no indication of the time? In 2008, it did just that, and the resulting timepiece, unsurprisingly, came from the avant-garde Swiss watchmaker Romain Jerome (RJ).

The Titanic DNA Day & Night Double Tourbillon is an extremely strange creation on multiple fronts. The bezel, for example, is produced from artificially rusted metal, and contains trace amounts of actual metal recovered from the sunken wreck of the Titanic. The former Romain Jerome CEO, Yvan Arpa wanted to introduce a material that was luxurious because it was both incredibly rare but also well known. The use of metal from the famed Titanic, provided a unique, albeit controversial decision for the brand.

Often referred to as a "Steampunk" style design, the Titanic DNA case and dial theme is really a unique take on a practice many brands participate in, to produce new watches that appear old. Even though the watch does not tell the time, it still indicates something, via the manually wound mechanical movement.

The dial features a skeletonised view into the movement as well as two flying tourbillons. One tourbillon represents the sun, and the other the Moon. They function as AM/PM indicators, given that one tourbillon operates during AM hours, while the second operates during PM hours. As one tourbillon stops operating the other one begins to spin after each 12 hour shift.

Only nine pieces of the watch were ever produced. Romain Jerome eventually produced a similar version of the Titanic DNA Day and Night Double Tourbillon known as the "Day and Night II" that actually did indicate the time.

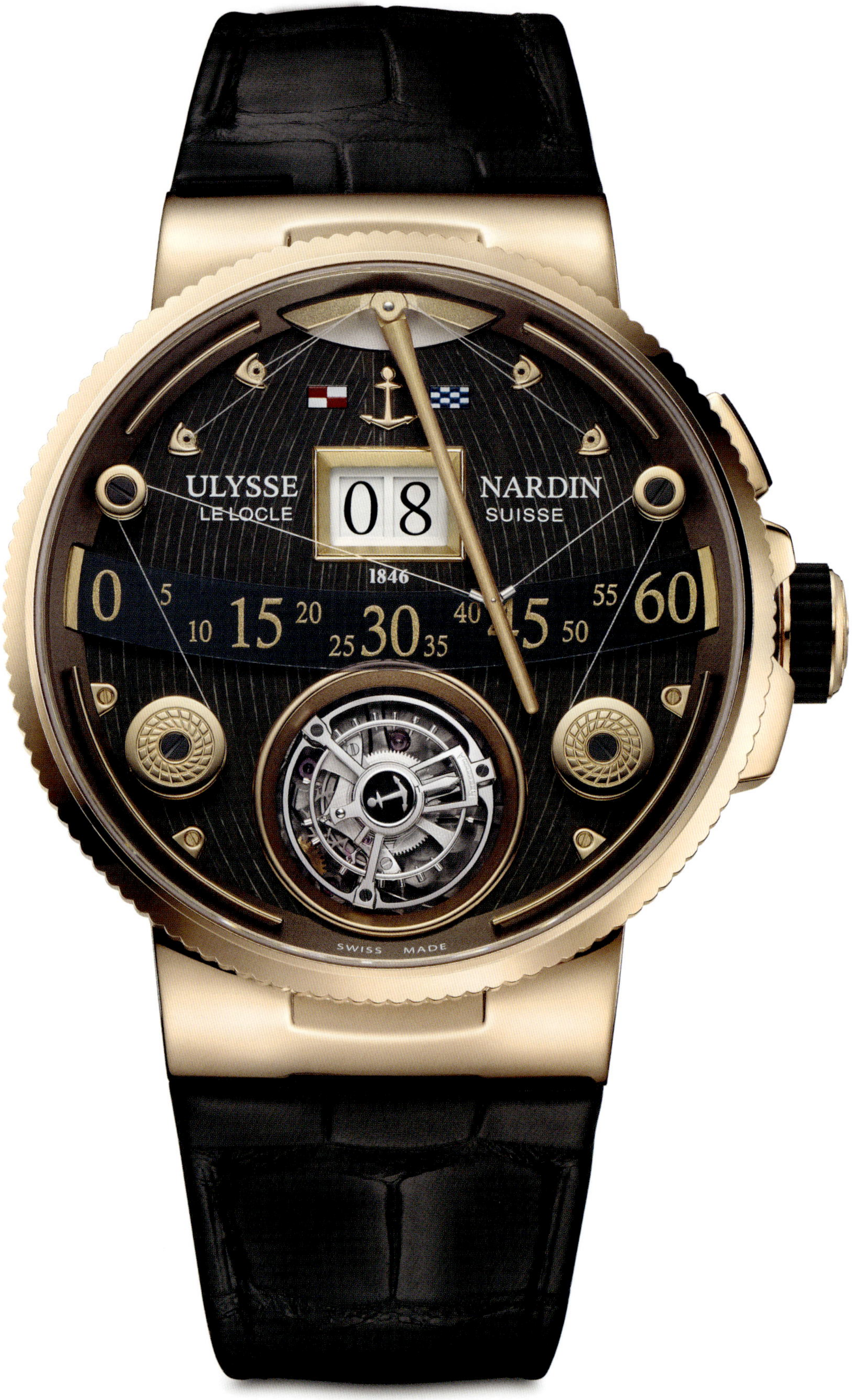

ULYSSE
LE LOCLE
08
NARDIN
SUISSE
1846
0 5 10 15 20 25 30 35 40 45 50 55 60
SWISS MADE

ULYSSE NARDIN — GRAND DECK MARINE TOURBILLON

$ 310 000

THE ENGINEERING REQUIRED TO POWER THIS UNIQUE TIME-INDICATION SYSTEM IS A BEAUTIFUL EXAMPLE OF THE TYPE THAT NOVELTY-SEEKING WATCHES AT THIS PRICE LEVEL REQUIRE TO STAND OUT.

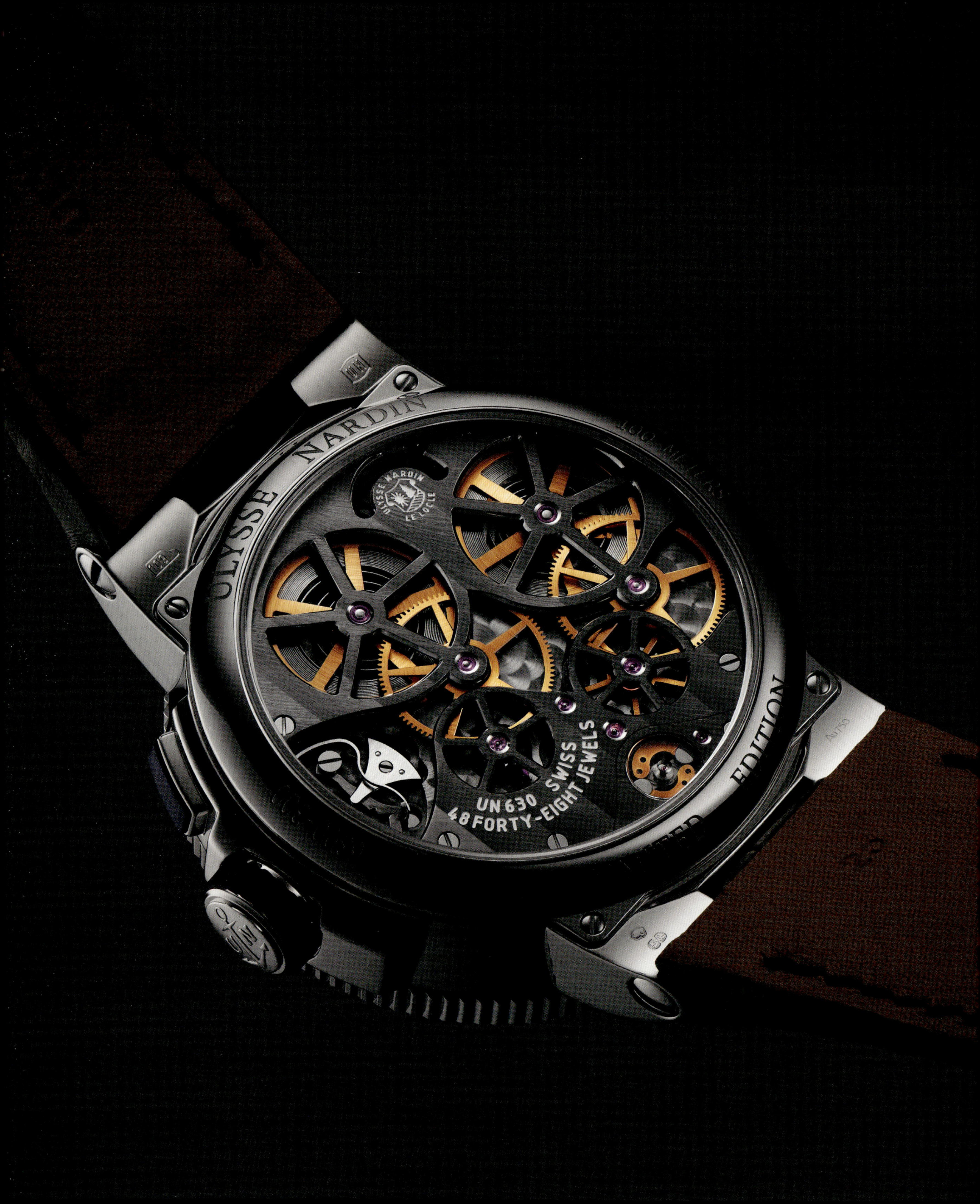
ULYSSE NARDIN
ULYSSE NARDIN
LE LOCLE
UN 630
SWISS
48 FORTY-EIGHT JEWELS
EDITION

The Grand Deck Marine Tourbillon is Swiss watchmaker Ulysse Nardin's most ambitious nod to their nautical history. For many years the company produced marine chronometers, which are ship clocks designed to be highly accurate and which were crucial for navigation. Today, companies like Ulysse Nardin continue to celebrate this fact with their well-articulated "Marine" timepiece collection. The Grand Deck Marine Tourbillon is less a tool than a mechanical homage to the romance of both mechanical timekeeping and sailing. Nothing else like it exists and, in addition to its dial playfully suggesting elements of ship decks, it also happens to indicate the time with remarkable clarity.

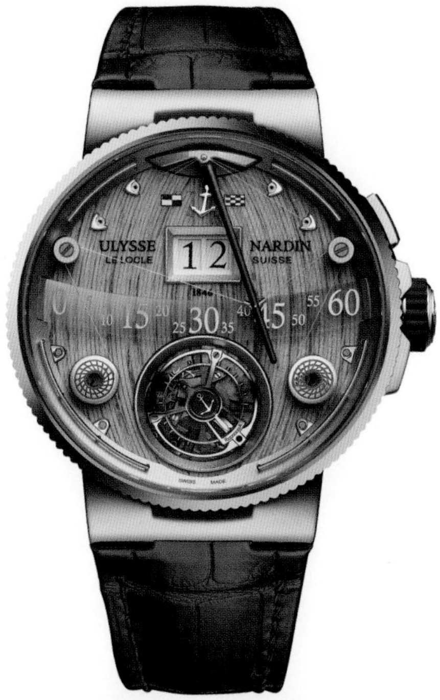

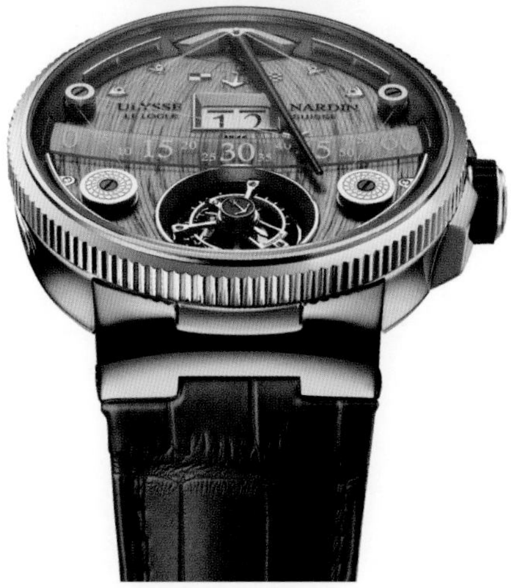

The Ulysse Nardin Grand Deck Marine Tourbillon's dial strives to suggest common design features found on most high-end sailing ships. This includes an actual wood dial created using micro-marquetry to mimic the look of a teak-wood deck. The time is indicated using a jumping-hour window located near 12 o'clock, as well as a retrograde minute indicator with a hand inspired by a boom and related rigging. The boom-style minute hand is moved, not by a series of hidden gears under the dial, but rather by tiny threads that act like ropes to pull and push the hand across the arching minute-indicator scale. The elegant fluidity of the minute hand in motion (such as when setting the time) is something anyone handling the Grand Deck Marine Tourbillon will both immediately notice and appreciate. The engineering required to power this unique time-indication system is a beautiful example of the type that novelty-seeking watches at this price level require to stand out.

At 6 o'clock on the dial is an open window with a view to the flying tourbillon which also doubles as a seconds indicator. The movement inside the watch is entirely produced and developed by Ulysse Nardin, who have a well-deserved reputation for relishing in the avant-garde yet somehow still practical horological creations like the Grand Deck Marine Tourbillon. Turn the watch over and the large gears on display suggest the aesthetic appeal of traditional pocket watches. The timepiece is also quite wearable, being presented in a 44mm-wide case offered in either gold or platinum, the latter of which is part of a limited edition of just 18 pieces.

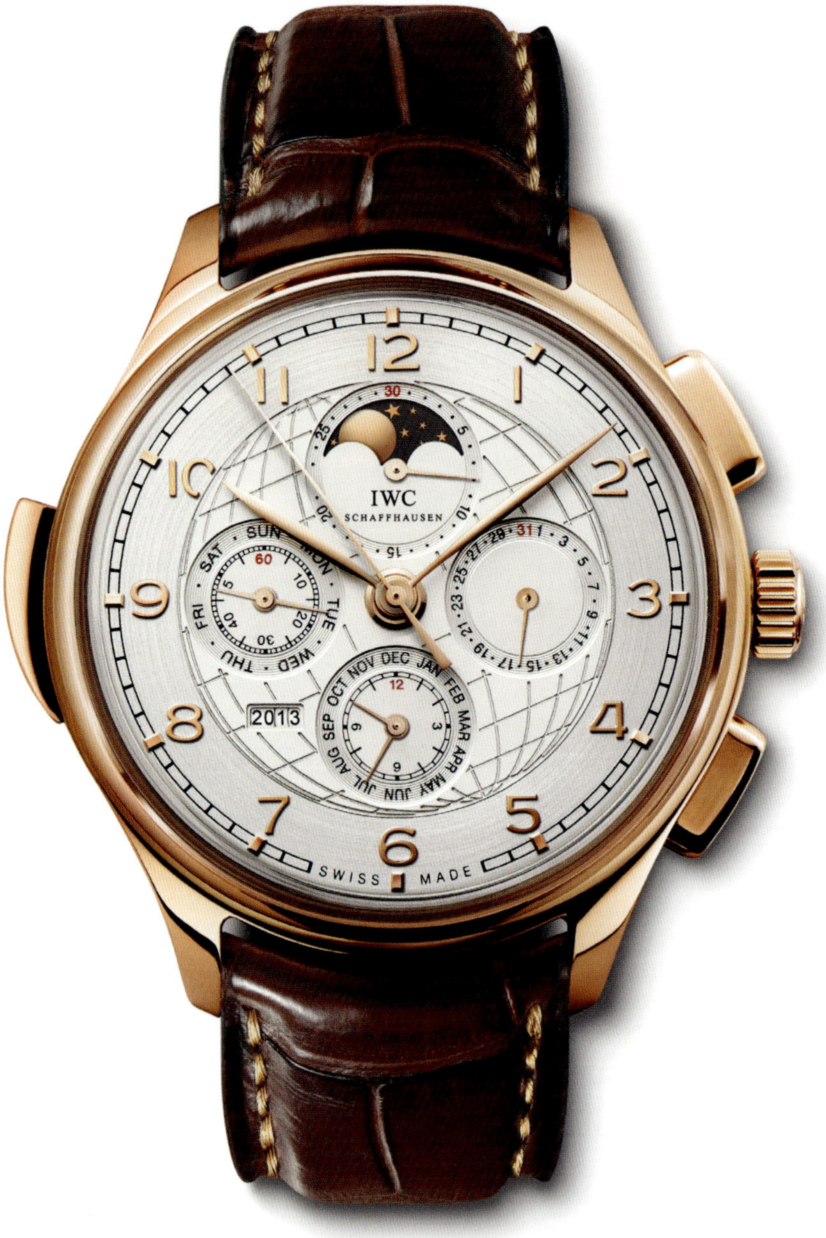

IWC — GRANDE COMPLICATION PLATINUM (REF. 9270-20)

$ 318 000

The opinion of many men is that a luxury watch should be both valuable and complicated, while also being timeless and stylistically versatile. If you think about it, that is a tall order for any product. First, an item has not only to be expensive in price but also actually valuable in terms of the materials used to make it. Next, it has to be difficult to produce as well as inherently impressive in its design. On top of that, it needs not only to be wearable, but something that goes with a lot of outfits.

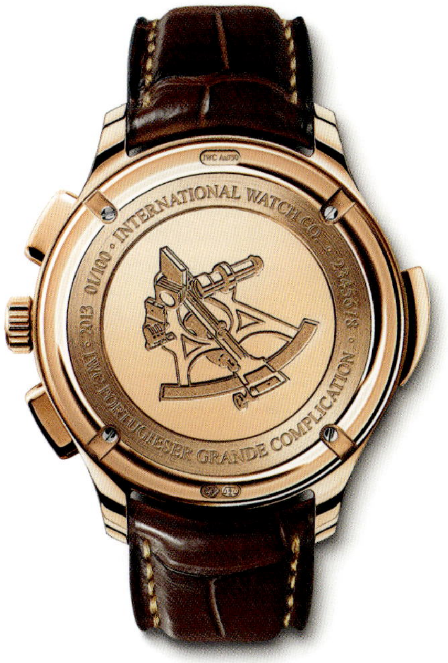

There are only a few timepieces that truly meet these criteria, often because, at the highest-end of the market, brands succeed through specialisation rather than through mass appeal. There simply isn't a huge demand for a mainstream $300,000 timepiece. Assuming there were, a strong case could be made for the IWC Grande Complication. Handsomely traditional, it is a watch that helped begin an era of enthusiasts casually wearing some of the most complicated watches in the world.

This original Grande Complication model was later followed with versions that fit into other IWC family products, such as those in the Portuguese collection, though these seminal models offer a rare purist design, outside IWC's more established model families. IWC was aiming to create the perfect complicated men's dress watch without making it too formal or delicate in appearance. At just over 42mm wide, it was suitable and comfortable for daily wear, while the available bracelet added a welcome sheen of class (and extra precious metal).

Available on an alligator strap, or a bracelet, this completely platinum model topped out the collection, offering a heavy, masculine timepiece rich with intricate utility. The almost generic name of the watch explains that the movement offers a large assortment of complications. In this case, the major features are a chronograph, perpetual calendar, and minute repeater.

Built on a robust Swiss-based movement, for reliability, the movement is produced in small quantities at IWC's headquarters in Schaffhausen, in Switzerland, near the German border. Designed for ease of use and longevity, the movement is nevertheless extremely complicated, being made up of 659 parts. IWC claims to produce only 50 of them a year. The perpetual calendar mechanism is unique because, in addition to offering the date, month, day of the week, leap year indicator, and Moon-phase indicator, it also indicates the year. The calendar is in fact perpetually accurate for 500 years.

The automatic-winding mechanical movement, also contains a minute repeater complication, that sounds the time back to the user on demand, and is activated by the lever to the left of the date. Despite having over 10 indicators of information on the dial, it bears a design that is surprisingly legible, making for a truly "everyday high-luxury watch."

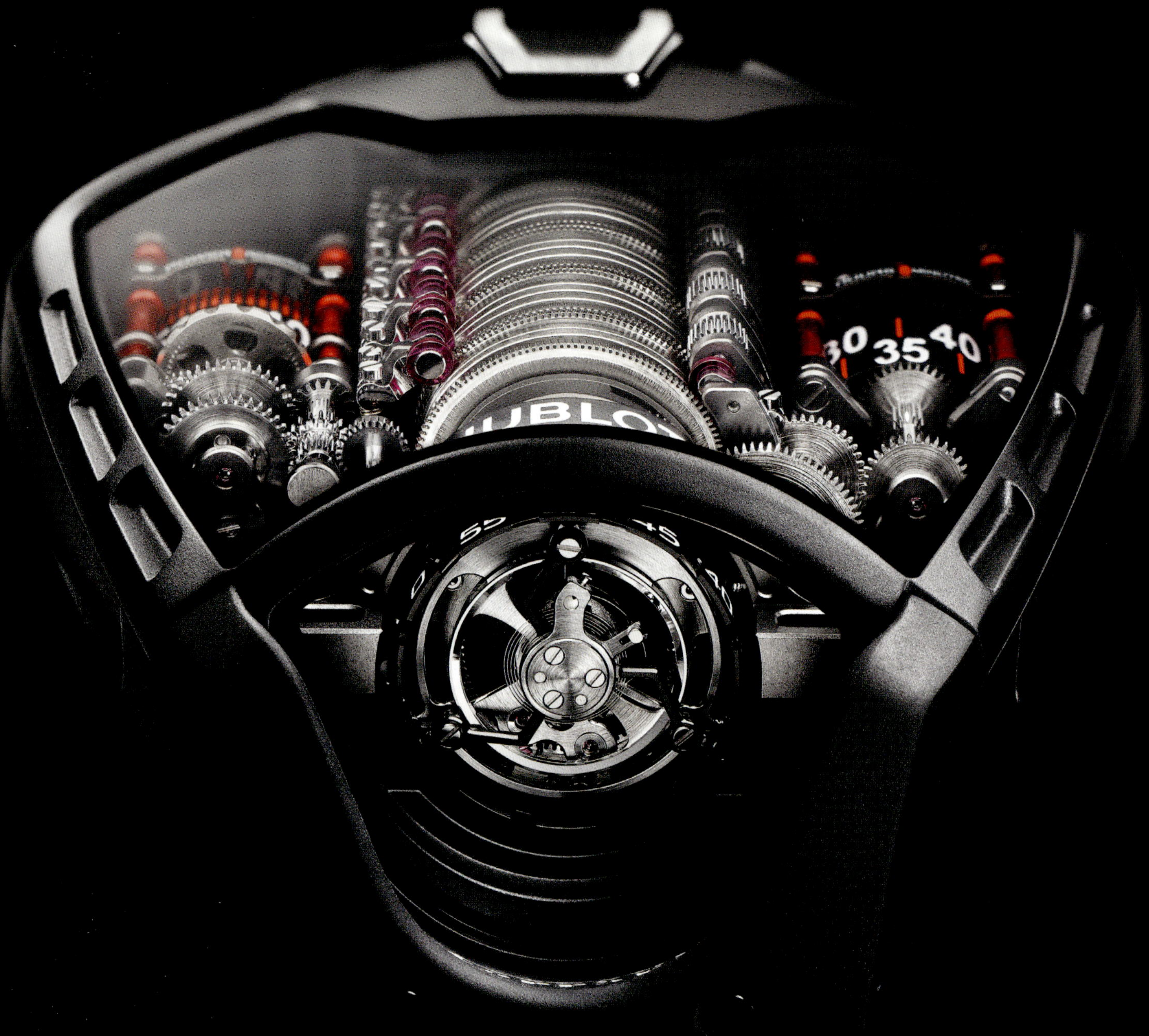

HUBLOT —
MP-05 LAFERRARI

$ 318 000

In 2012 Hublot partnered with the Italian automobile maker Ferrari, as their official luxury watchmaker and event sponsor. In the watch industry, Ferrari is known for being the source of several failed high-profile partnerships, that never quite resulted in highly-demanded timepieces, despite the great value and world-wide appreciation of the brand. Hublot was intent on making the relationship work, and they did.

According to Hublot Chairman, Jean-Claude Biver, the key to producing a successful Ferrari watch was in making a totally unique creation, that combined Hublot and Ferrari DNA. Others, before Hublot, simply tried to adapt existing designs and then include the Ferrari logo on them. Hublot would not make this same mistake, which ended up being the correct decision. Hublot released the Big Bang Ferrari collection, and it became an instant hit with watch lovers. As a showpiece to embody the spirit of the relationship, as well the technical might of both brands, a high complication piece needed to be produced.

Existing as part of Hublot's Masterpiece (MP) collection, the MP-05 LaFerrari coincided with the release of the automobile of the same name. To car lovers it would be a timepiece inspired by a Ferrari engine bay, and to watch lovers it would be important for containing a movement with the world's longest power reserve.

Most mechanical watches have enough power for about two days of operation. Mechanical watches are powered by a tightly wound spring that slowly unwinds over time. Watches with power reserves between three to 10 days are available, and beyond that there are perhaps three or so watches with a power reserve of around one month. Hublot's goal was to do even better. After a great deal of development, the movement for the LaFerrari watch was capable of storing enough power for a total of 50 days worth of power reserve.

That much power required Hublot to stack 11 mainspring barrels on top of one another. The tricky part was in designing a system that allowed them to unwind slowly and consistently, so that the watch would remain accurate. Time is indicated on moving drums on the right of the dial, and to the left is a power reserve indicator that allows the wearer to know when to wind the movement. Hublot could not resist placing a tourbillon in the watch – which is horizontally displayed through the lower part of the case at the bottom of the stack of springs.

Winding the watch is no doubt a chore and the LaFerrari contains no crown. Instead, Hublot includes a special drill with the piece, that is used to wind it up when necessary. The MP-05 LaFerrari will be produced as a limited edition of only 50 pieces.

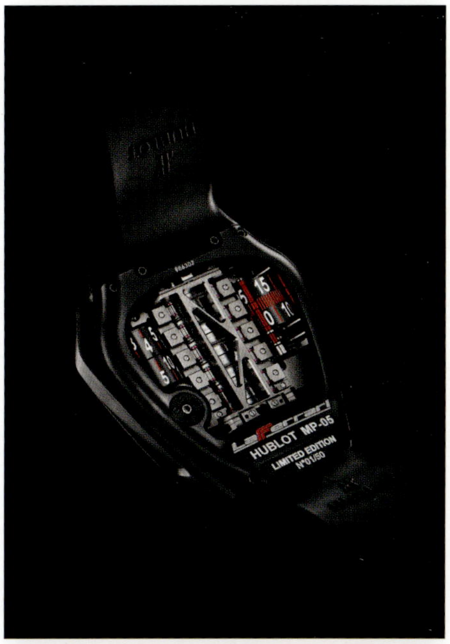

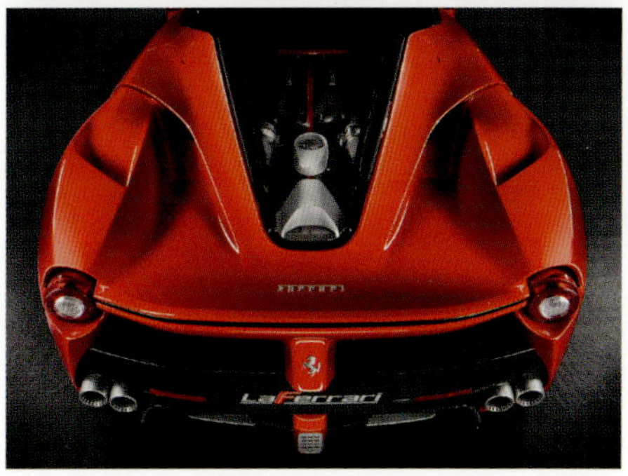

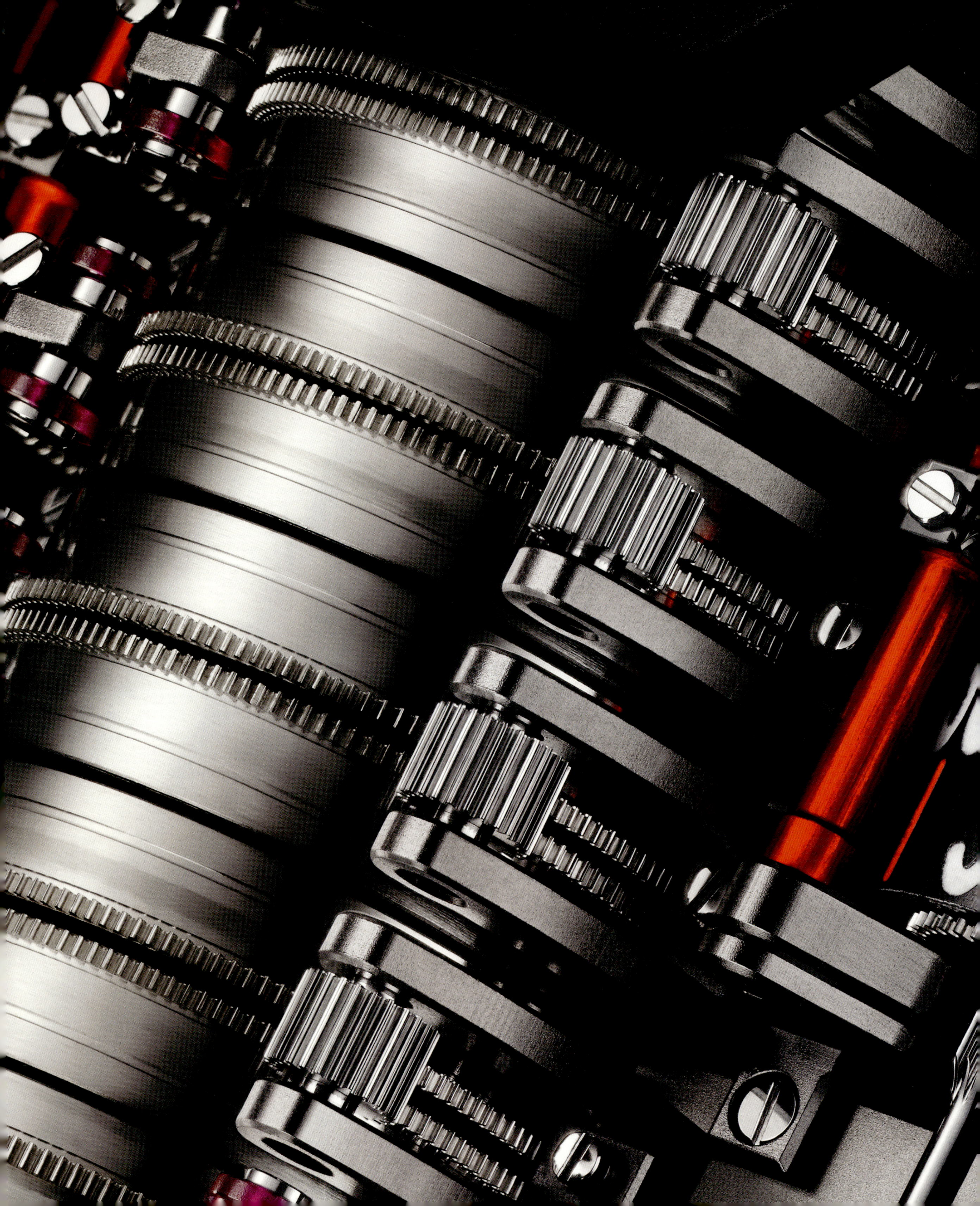

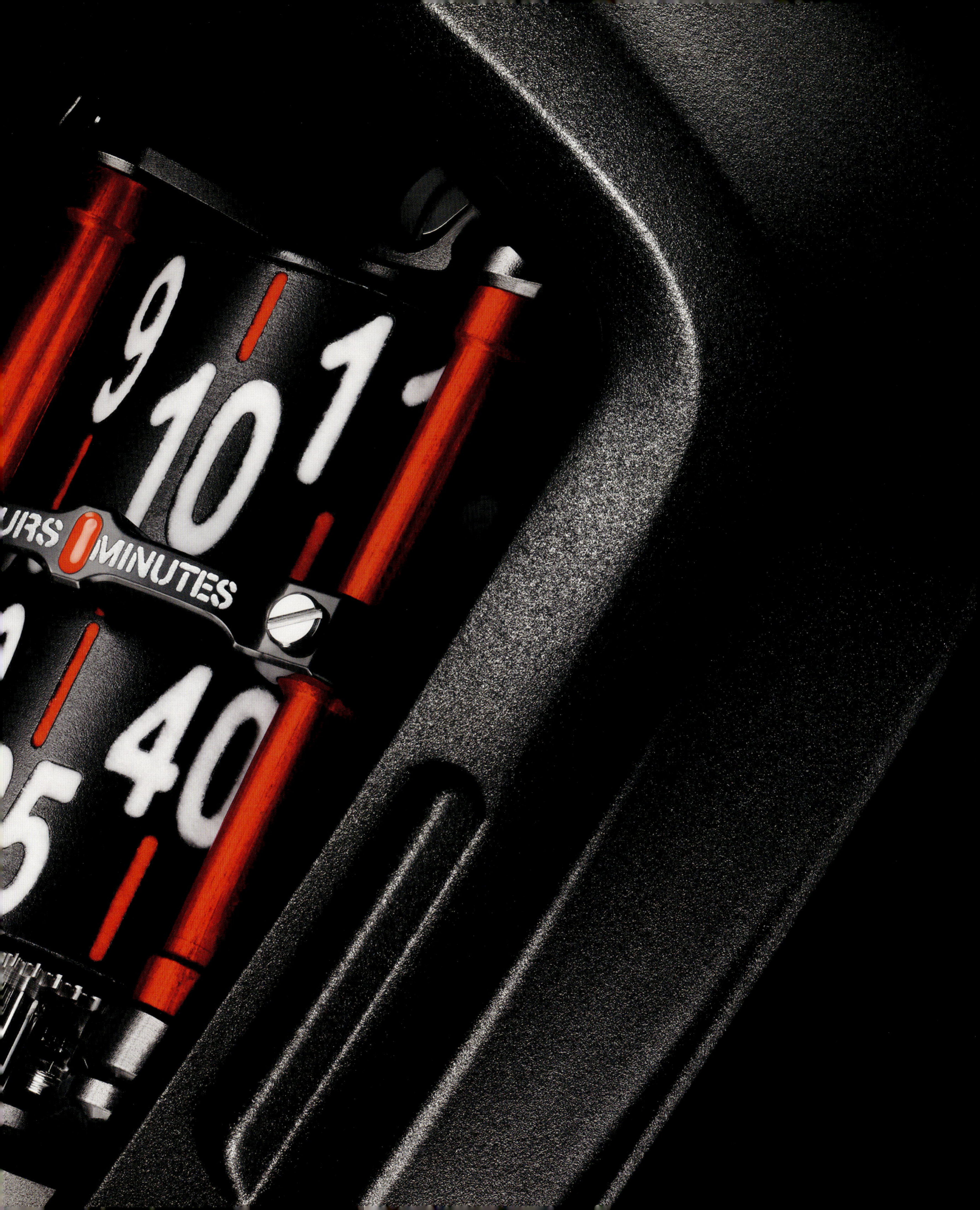
MINUTES

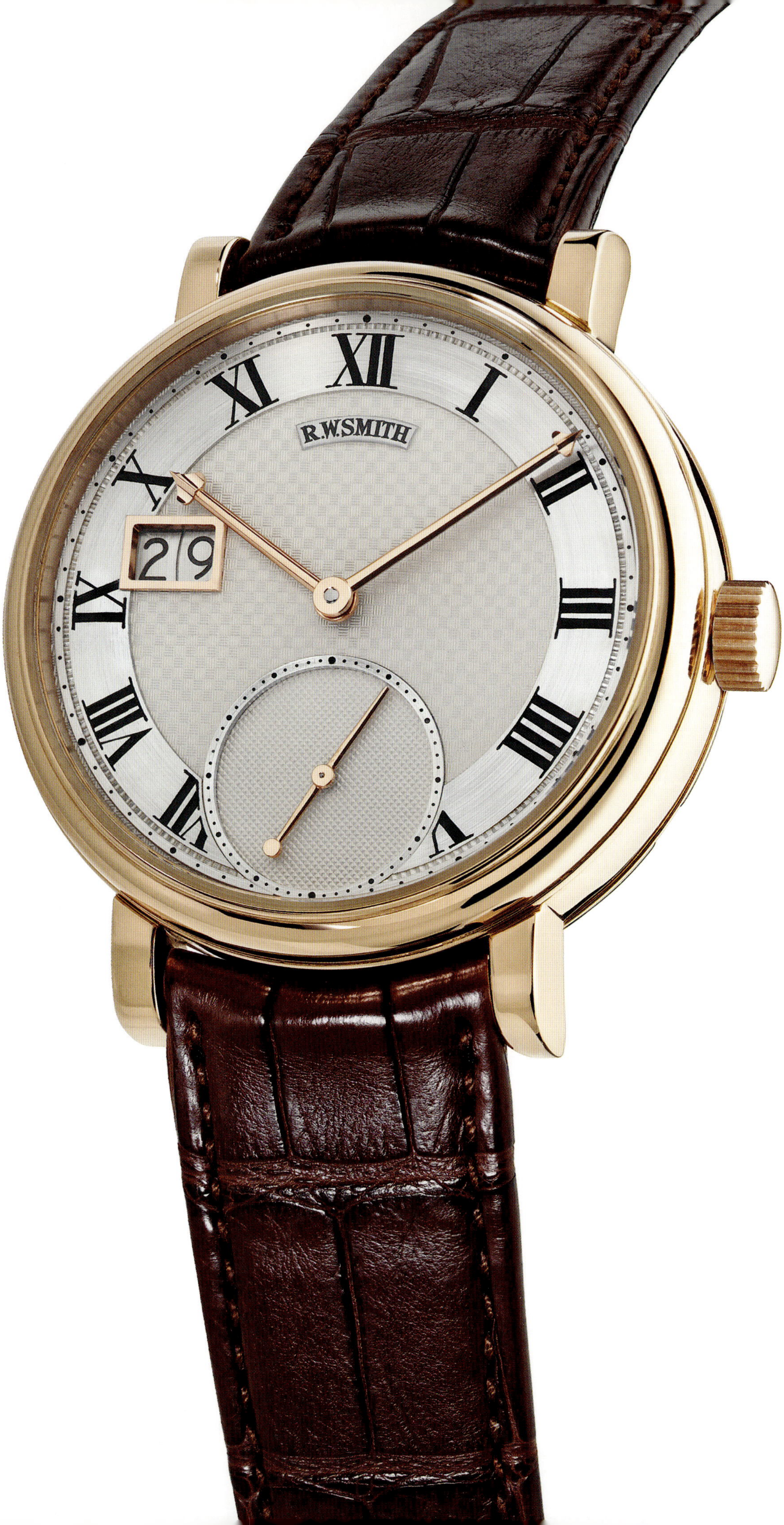
R.W.SMITH
29

ROGER W. SMITH — UNIQUE TOURBILLON NO. 4

$ 324 000

BEAUTIFULLY SIMPLE, IN ROGER SMITH'S OWN WORDS THE TOURBILLON NO. 4 IS "UNDERSTATED".

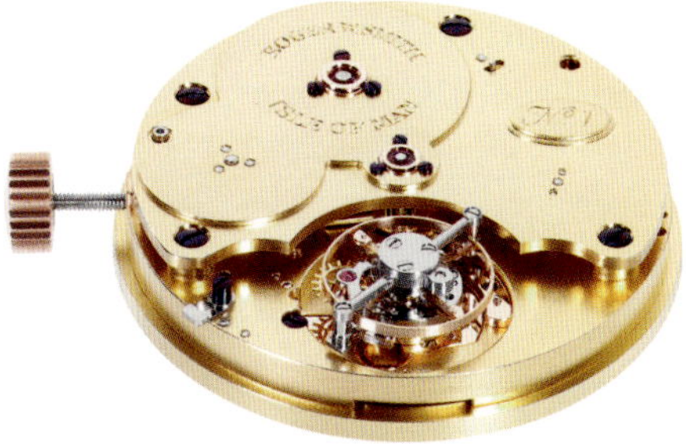

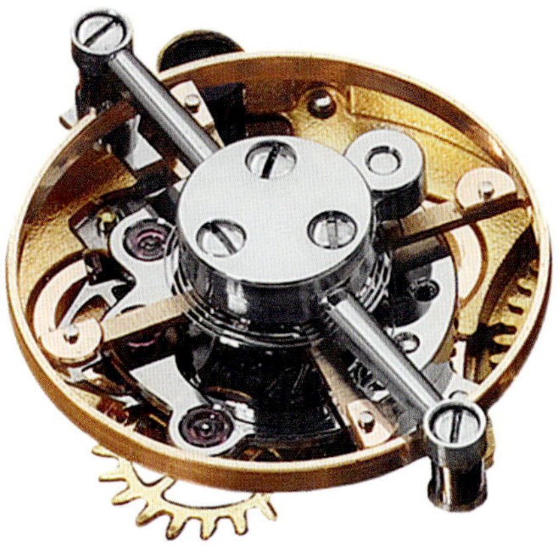

On the Isle of Man, in the Irish Sea between the United Kingdom and Ireland, lives watchmaker Roger Smith. While not the only one, he is often considered by collectors as the greatest living man to keep traditional English watchmaking alive. A common theme among watchmakers is that they reside in relative isolation. In Switzerland, for example, most live in small mountain towns far away from bustling city life. When the Japanese wanted to recreate a "European style" watchmaking environment they set up shop far away from cities, often up in the mountains. Peace and quiet seem to be the ultimate recipe for making traditional mechanical watches the old-fashioned way.

It is entirely possible that watchmaking benefits from a more relaxed, slower pace of life, because the process itself is so time consuming. For example, the Tourbillon No. 4 made by Roger Smith required two years to complete, and Roger Smith produced it himself, by hand. In fact, Roger Smith produces a maximum of just 12 watches per year. He doesn't have a large staff, with his wife doing most of the administrative work while Roger focuses on his passion and art.

Roger answered the call of horology after reading a book called Watchmaking by famed fellow English watchmaker George Daniels. It was Roger's intent to become Daniels' apprentice, though Daniels shunned the idea at first, having a policy of not accepting anyone under his wing.

Smith proved to Daniels that he was worthy by displaying a mastery of the techniques Daniels had laid out in his book. Realising that someone needed to maintain his work and efforts to enliven traditional English watchmaking, Daniels eventually took Smith on and the two formed a tight bond.

Daniels was a meticulous and often strict teacher, but the result was a pupil who could faithfully carry on the work of a master. Today, Smith is highly respected in his own right and has developed a style all his own, though his work does intentionally resemble that of George Daniels (who, over his entire life, produced fewer than 40 watches).

Daniels died in 2011, and in that same year Roger Smith released one his most important watches, a bespoke creation for a private client. Simply titled the Tourbillon No. 4, the 18k red gold watch contained a tourbillon, power reserve indicator, and the date. Entirely produced by hand, each part was carefully formed and decorated using traditional techniques, and hand-operated machinery.

Beautifully simple, in Roger Smith's own words the Tourbillon No. 4 is "understated". He added that "English watchmaking is all about understated designs". Timepieces such as this can have the greatest appeal to collectors, because they combine absolute exclusivity, an important story, and a timeless, elegant design that strongly recalls the values inherent in all things hand-made.

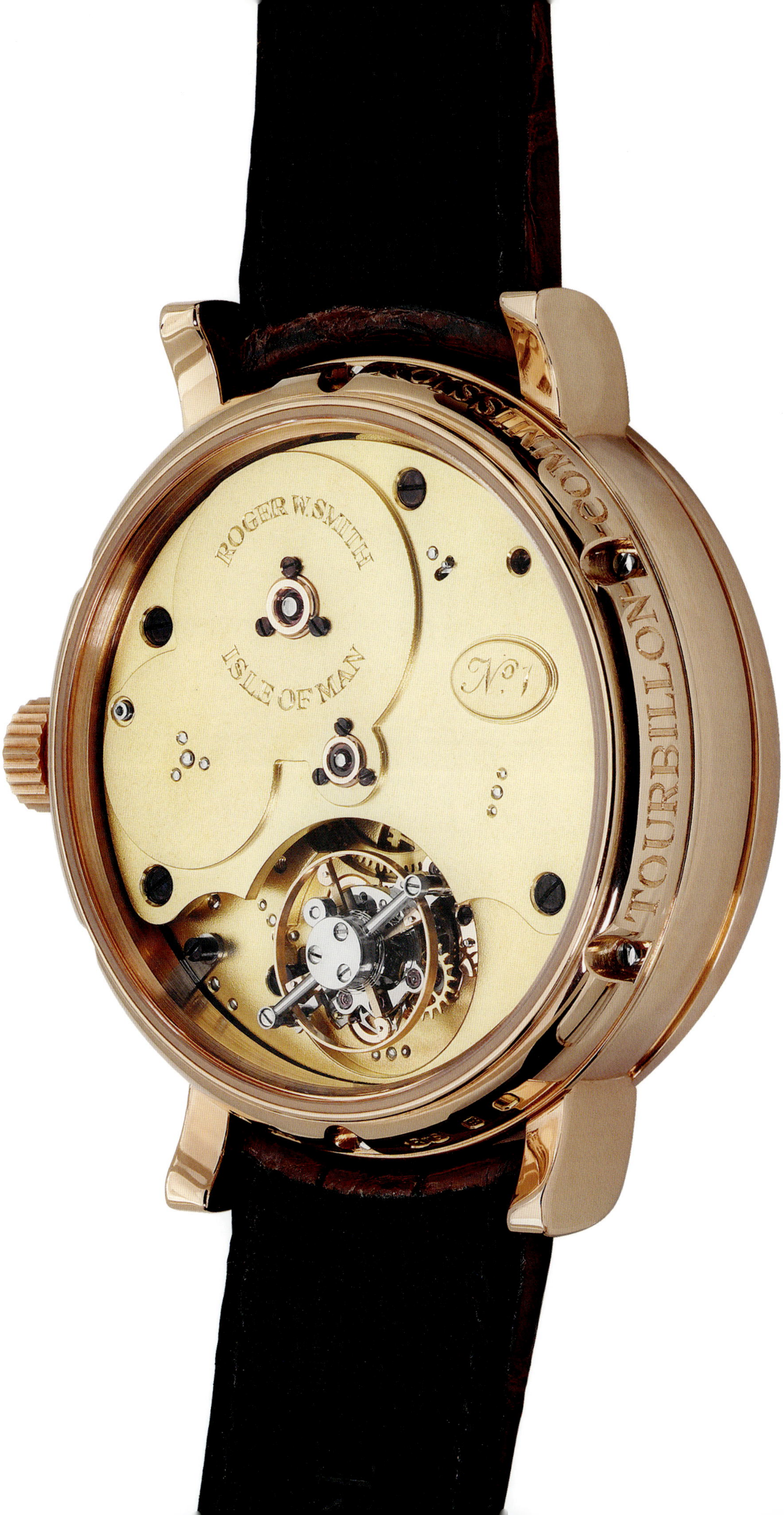
ROGER W. SMITH
ISLE OF MAN
No. 1
TOURBILLON-COMMISSION

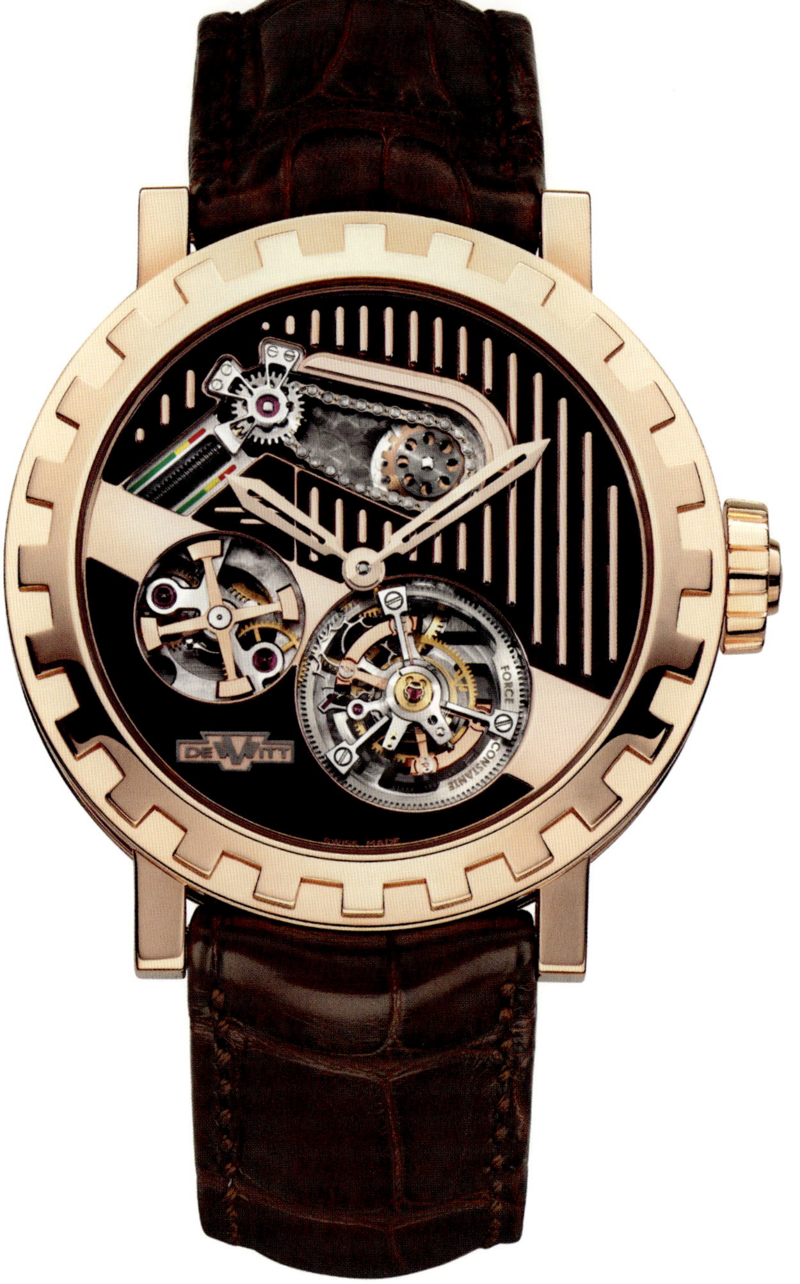

DE WITT —
ACADEMIA TOURBILLON FORCE CONSTANTE

$ 324 300*

It would not be shocking to hear a watch aficionado describe timepieces in the same manner as a man might describe the stereotypical male outlook on the opposite sex. Just as many men may comment about the female psyche that when one feels confident that they fully understand the ins and out of how one operates, new wrinkles come about only adding further questions. In this case, one of the most important, and frequently overlooked issues in the world of horology is the matter of "constant force."

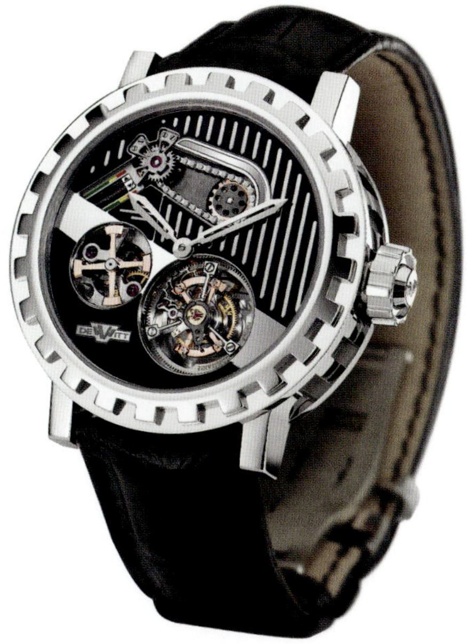

The issue revolves around the idea of a watch not only being accurate, but also staying accurate over the course of a mainspring winding down. It is easy to conceive that when a spring is fully wound, the power (torque) it releases is greater than when it is almost totally unwound. This concept is simple, but what is challenging, is how to ensure that a mechanical timepiece remains accurate as its power reserve goes down.

Most mechanical timepieces have no mechanism to ensure a consistent flow of force from the mainspring to the escapement (which is the regulating heart of the watch). Thus, most watches should operate, at all times, with the movement somewhere between fully wound and almost empty. It would be tantamount to suggesting that, when putting fuel in a car, you should never completely fill the tank, and when topping it up again, you should do so when it is around three quarters empty.

Those who can follow the implications of this mechanical dilemma, should be able to appreciate that a feature in a watch movement able to deliver "constant force" to the escapement from the mainspring, would be quite useful. That is precisely what De Witt designed in the Academia Tourbillon Force Constante.

Ironically, the display of time is totally de-emphasised on the dial of this watch, as it sits off-centre towards the top of the dial. Instead, wearers are given a view of the constant force mechanism, right on the dial, sitting next to the exposed tourbillon-style escapement. What the watch does, is move power from the mainspring to an intermediary system, rather than directly to the escapement. This intermediary system collects power and moves it to the escapement in a consistent manner, no matter how much torque is coming from the mainspring.

In the scheme of precision and accuracy over time, constant force mechanisms are beloved by collectors, and have been an area of vast horological experimentation over the centuries. The Academia Tourbillon Force Constante, is just one interpretation of these systems; it is unmistakably De Witt, with its castle-crenellation-style bezel around the case.

* Price based on watch in rose gold

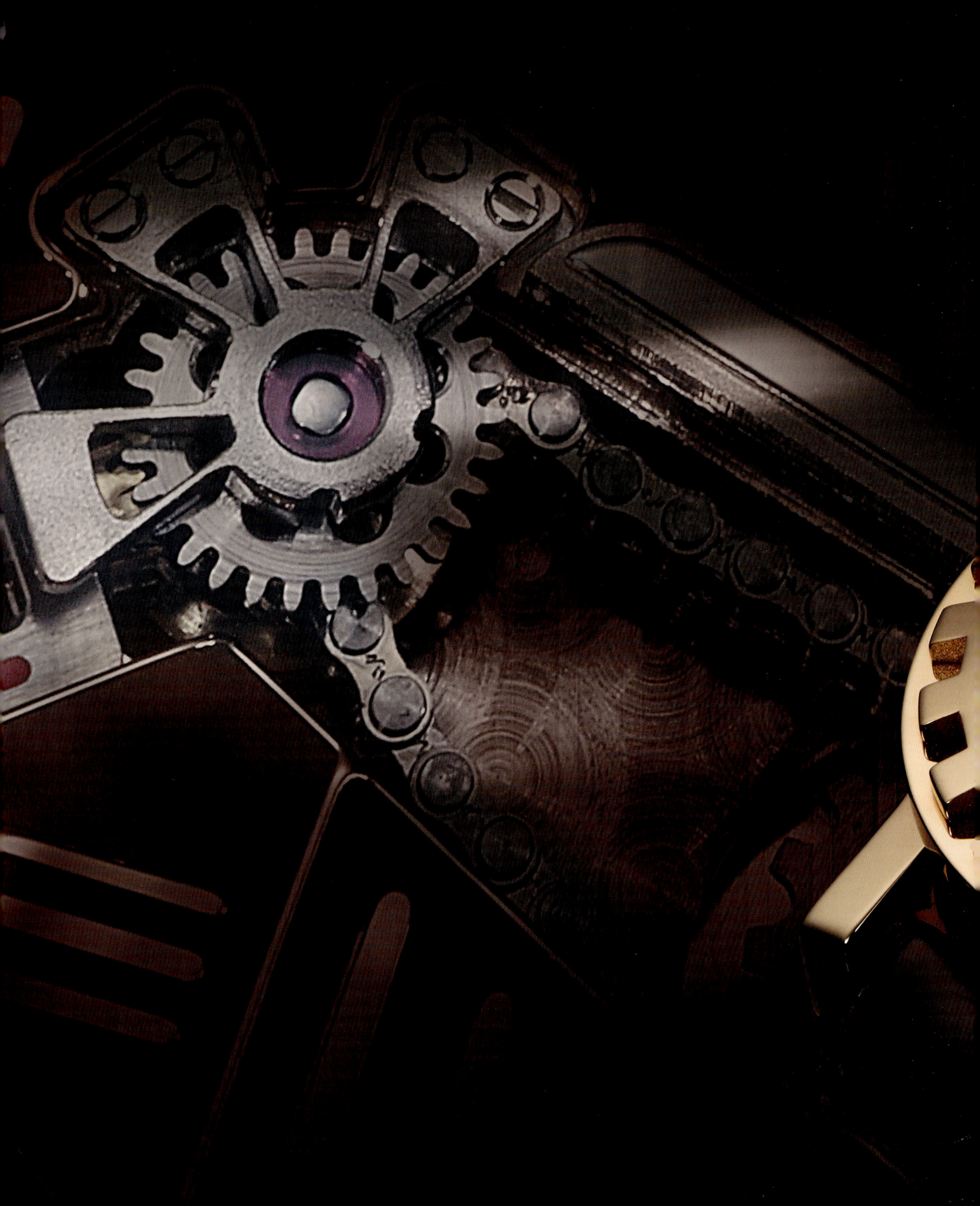

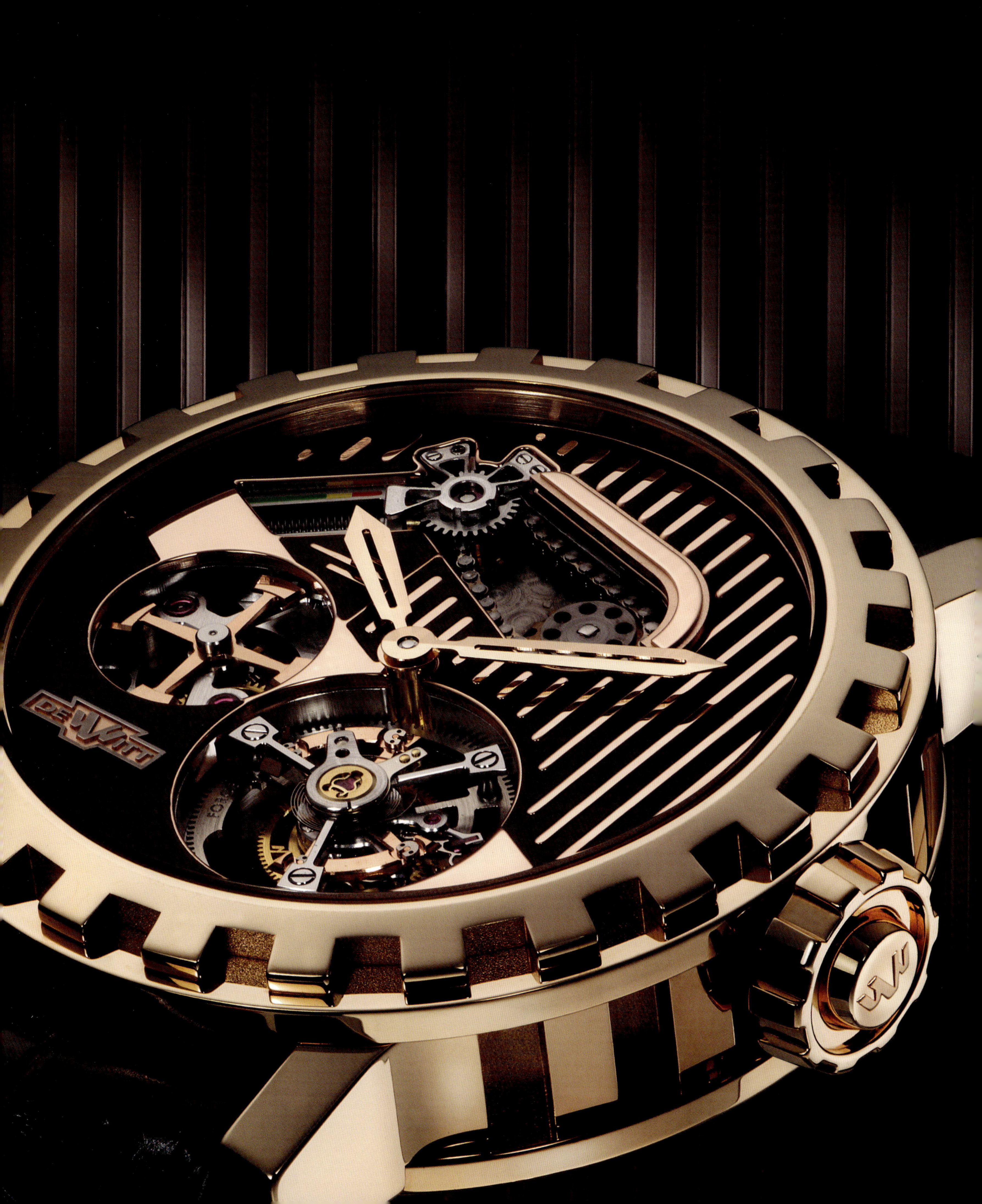
DeWITT

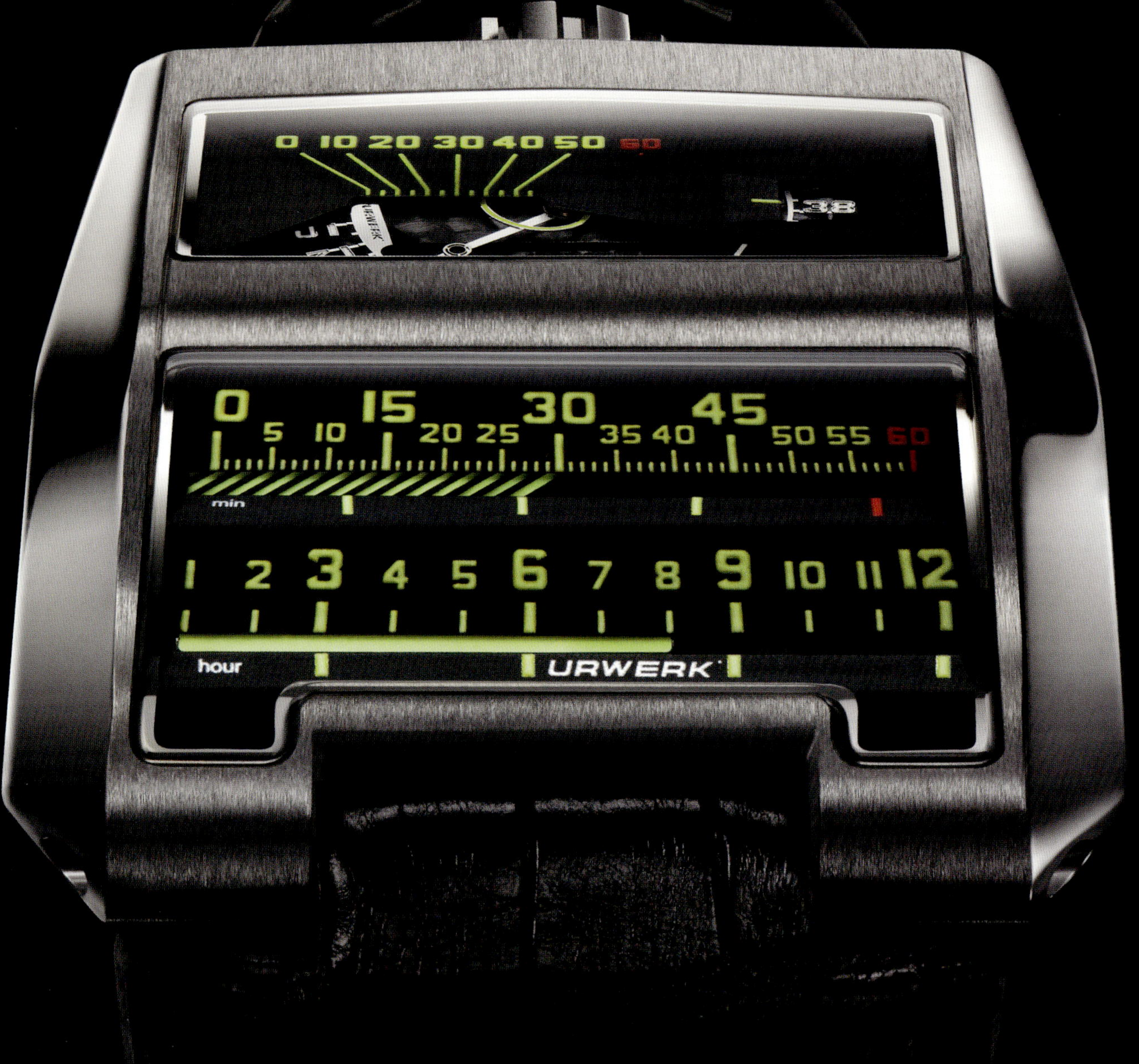

URWERK —
UR-CC1 KING COBRA

$ 328 000

The genius of boutique Swiss watchmakers such as URWERK is in how insane they are. The genesis of the UR-CC1 watch comes neither logically as an evolution of timekeeping instruments, nor as a predictable work of art combing traditional artisanal decorative practices within fine watchmaking. No, the "King Cobra" watch, as it is nicknamed, is inspired by relatively mundane old automobiles, obscure horological experimentation that was never commercialised, and a watchmaker's penchant for simply being different.

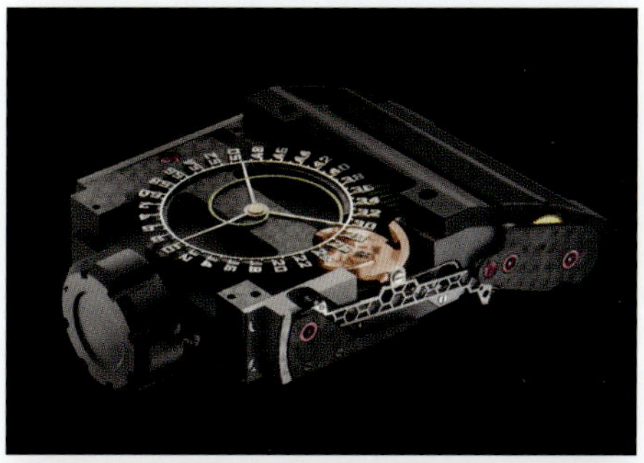

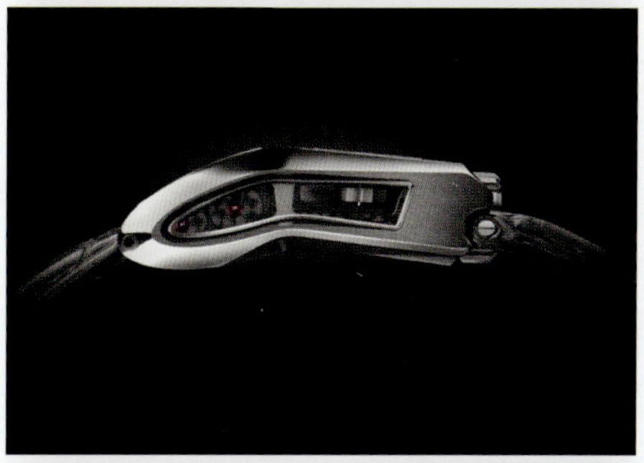

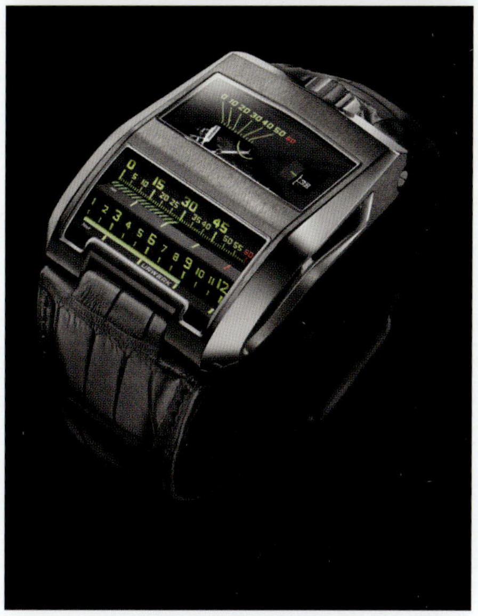

The UR-CC1 watch has the alternative name "King Cobra" for no other reason than URWERK enjoys adding the name of a fearsome natural predator (often a reptile or arachnid) to each of their new creations. A better way of thinking about this wild watch is to understand that the goal was to display the hours, minutes, and seconds, each on a linear – versus circular – display.

URWERK, as a brand, is interested in reimagining not only how watch movements are typically built, but also how time is displayed. It is a provocative concept given that the majority of analogue watch or clock dials on the planet are round. URWERK wanted to make them linear, and in so doing, comment on how time goes continuously in one direction, rather than round and round in repetitive circles.

Pointing to the speedometers of certain mid-20th century automobiles, such as Dodge and Volvo, URWERK imagined how to incorporate such a display on a timepiece. Despite being wearable on a wrist, the UR-CC1 case and dial barely resemble most other timepieces. Neon green displays contrast with an 18k white gold case. One version of the King Cobra watch even places a black coating over the white gold entirely hiding it from view, and allowing only the wearer to know the true case material.

From the bottom of the case to the top, three distinct dials offer the hours, minutes, and seconds – the latter display being both linear and digital. Flip the watch over and the time is displayed even more elegantly on the back of the watch.

Inside the UR-CC1 is a mechanical movement completely developed from the ground up for this application, and the watch is designed to offer glimpses of it through a series of sapphire crystal windows all over the case. Originally released in 2009, URWERK produced just 50 pieces of the UR-CC1 King Cobra.

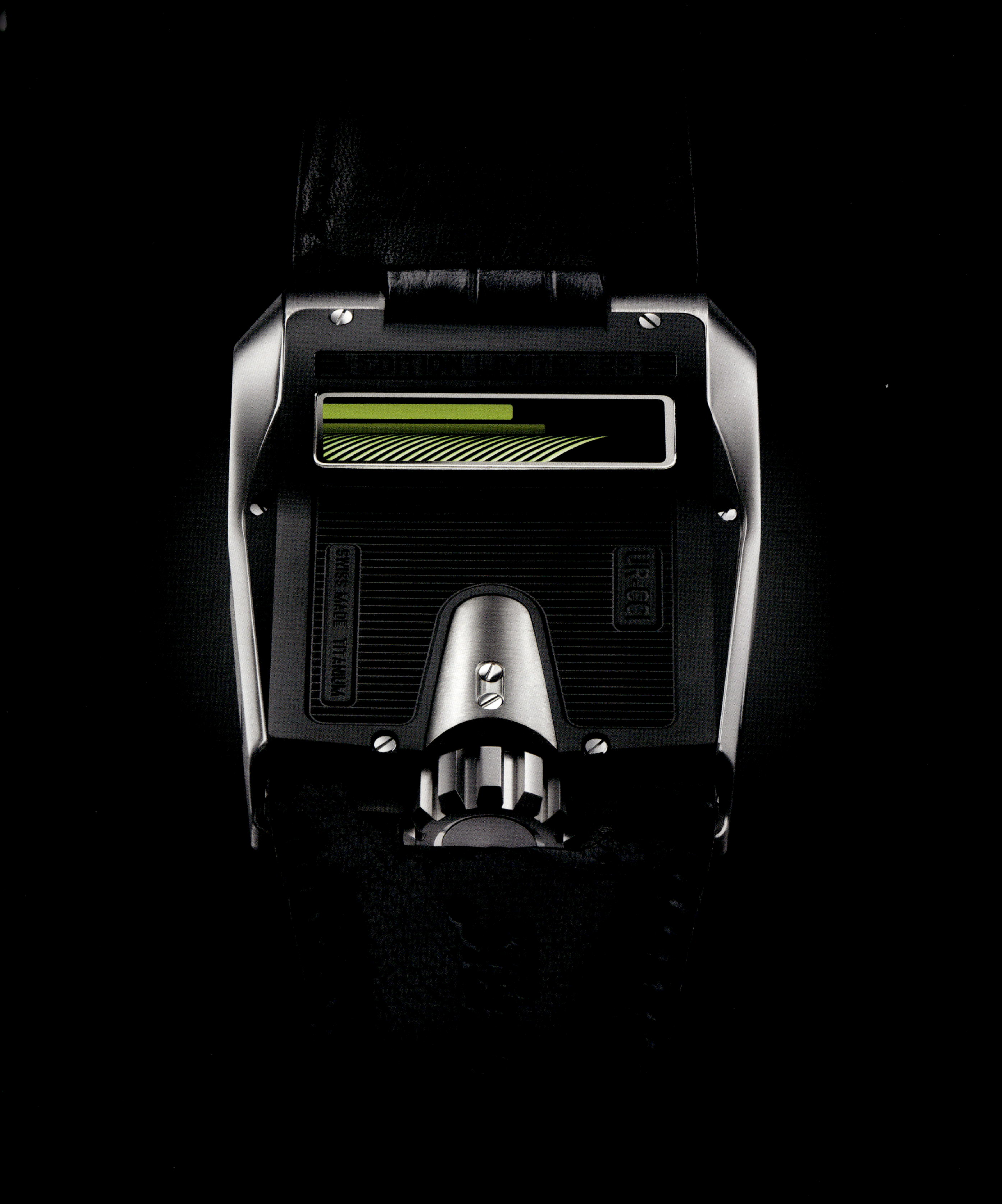
SWISS MADE TITANIUM
UR-CC1

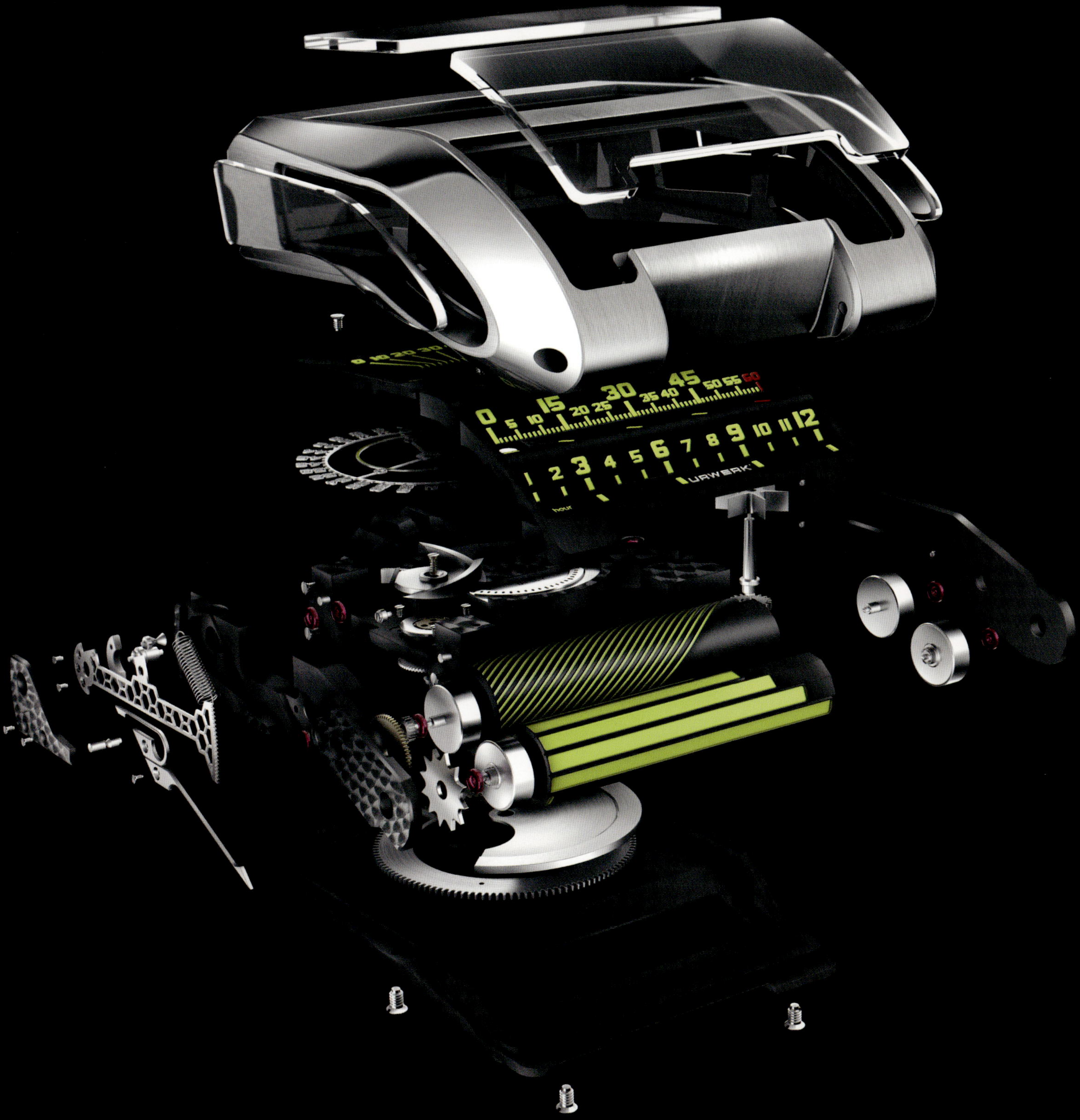
0 5 10 15 20 25 30 35 40 45 50 55 60
1 2 3 4 5 6 7 8 9 10 11 12
URWERK
hour

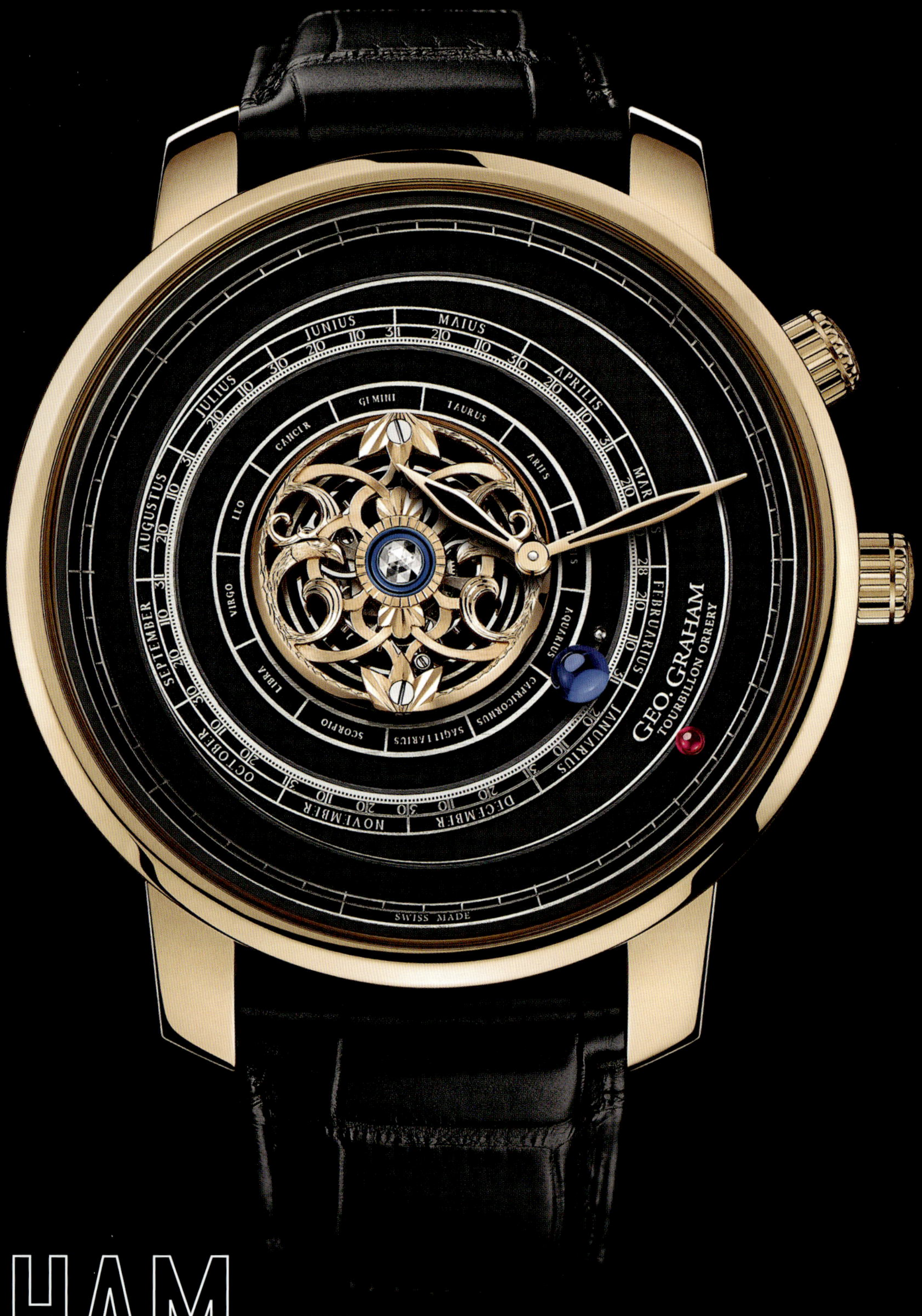

GRAHAM — TOURBILLON ORRERY

$ 330 000

The watch industry is often a good place to learn obscure terminology. Orrery, if one is not familiar with the term, is the proper name for an apparatus that uses rotating spheres on small rods, to indicate the relative positions of the planets in the solar system. The name is derived from a mechanism that was presented to the 4th Earl of Orrery at the beginning of the 18th century, and since then has been applied to similar devices that many people today have seen at least once in their lives.

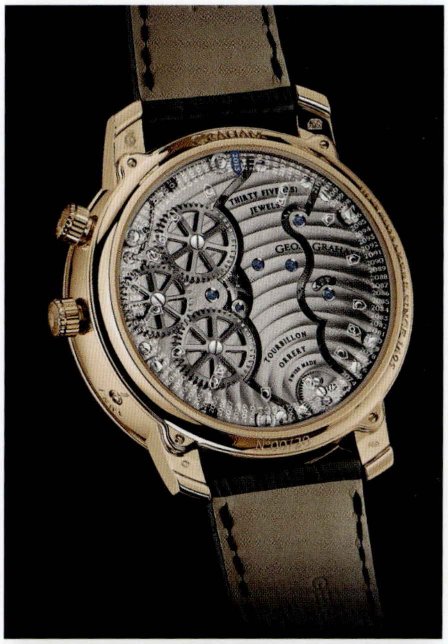

While the Early of Orrery had the pleasure of having his title attached to the apparatus, it was famed English clockmaker George Graham who, with the help of some other talented contemporaries, designed and built the first Orrery machine. Its purpose was to present a realistic view of the movements of the planets around the sun.

In 2013, the watch brand Graham, based on the legacy of George Graham, released a wristwatch version of the Orrery, in the Tourbillon Orrery timepiece. Taking design cues from the original contraption, as well as from pocket watches of Mr. Graham's era, the Tourbillon Orrery was produced in collaboration with famed Swiss watchmaker and designer Christophe Claret.

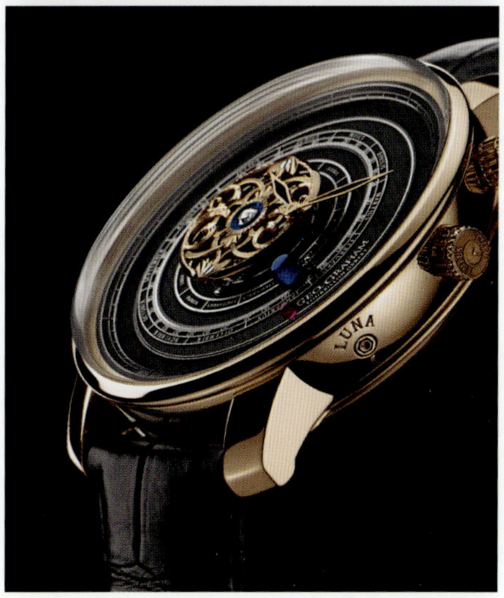

Impressively large, the timepiece is a unique blend of historic design and modern mechanics. The dial features a tourbillon hidden under a cage, with a design inspired by early pocket watch movements. It also thematically serves as the sun. Around it are the rotations of three heavenly bodies; the Earth, its Moon, and Mars. The former is represented as a blue sapphire orb, while Mars is a ruby. A large diamond sits in the centre of the tourbillon cage.

Nothing is centred on the watch face, with the time being eccentrically placed to the right. Track the movement of the Earth and one will notice a calendar scale that indicates the date and month. The small Moon orb is seen constantly moving around the Earth, as each day passes. On the rear of the watch, through the sapphire crystal case back, is a year indicator that displays up to 100 years into the future. Those passing the Tourbillon Orrery watch down to their heirs will be thankful that Graham supplies two extra year indicator discs along with the pieces, thus enabling it to indicate the correct figure for up to 300 years. Only 20 Graham Tourbillon Orrery timepieces will ever be produced.

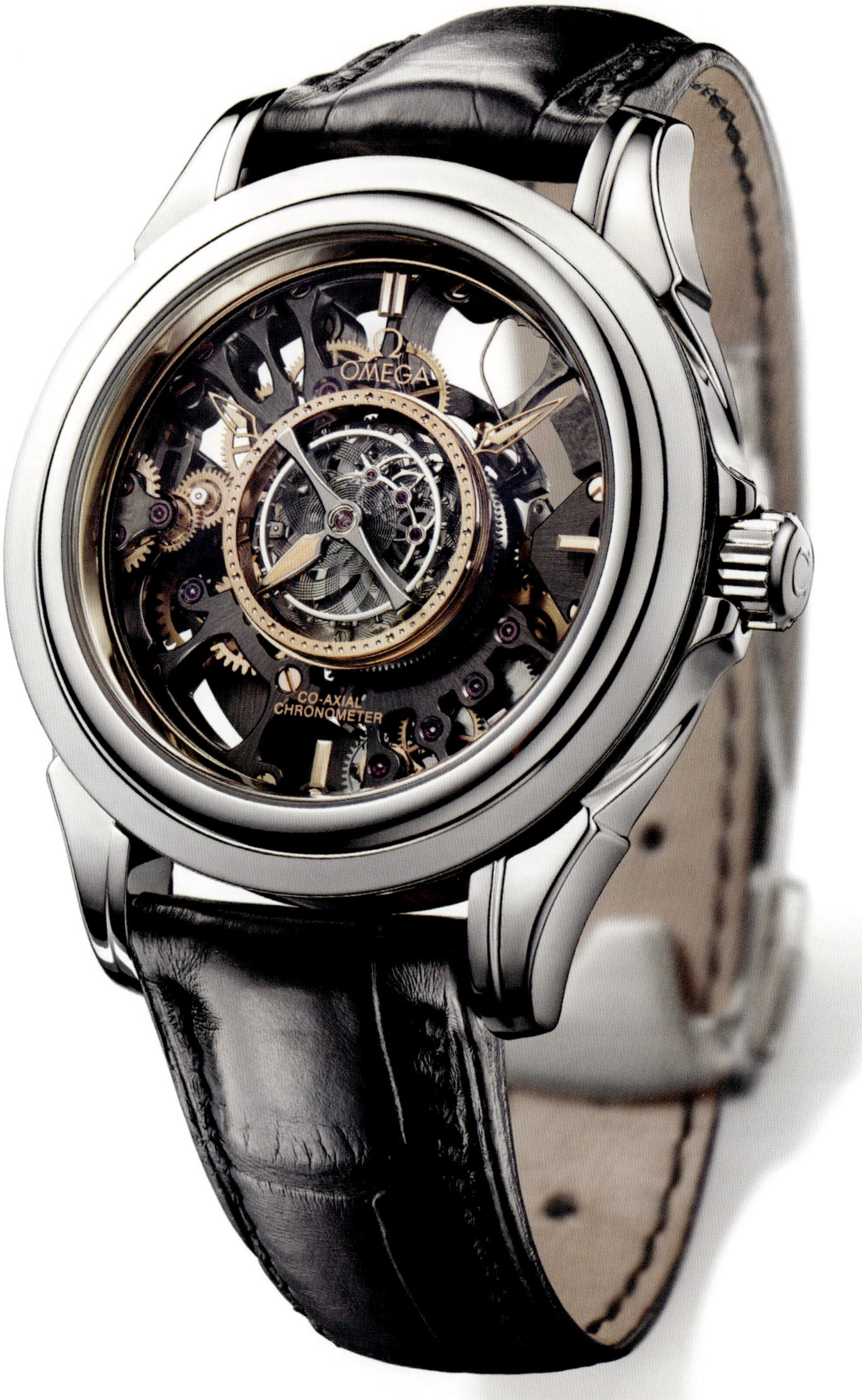

OMEGA — DE VILLE CENTRAL TOURBILLON

$ 333 000

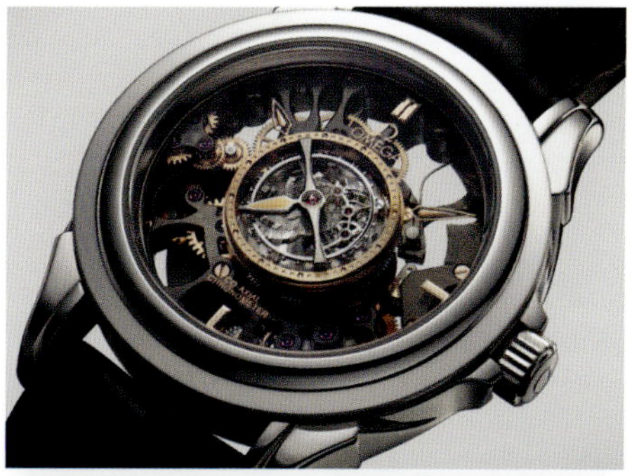

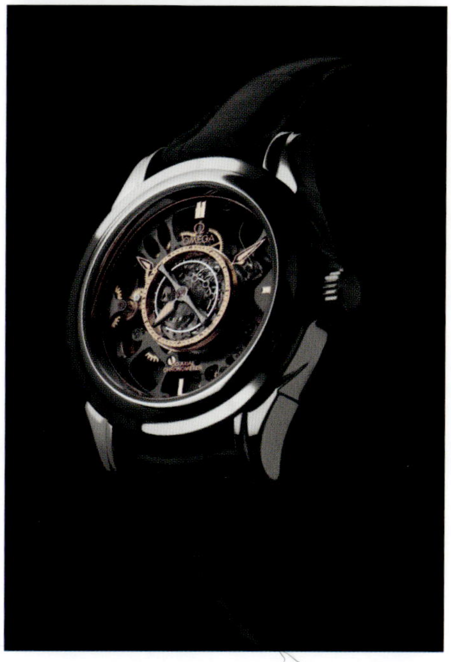

In the high-end luxury watch arena, the tourbillon has dominated the last decade or so. It has become both a sign of status and a rite of passage. Brands interested in proving their position as a brand of prestige, are almost required to release at least one timepiece with a tourbillon inside it. Luxury consumers are drawn to watches with tourbillon-based movements, not only because they are beautiful to look at, but also because they communicate, with incredible ease, that their watches must have cost a great deal of money.

The tourbillon is an artistic treat for the eyes, and a way to prove a timepiece was more difficult to assemble than most. Its origins, however, are more performance-related. Originally conceived in the late 18th century to improve the accuracy of clocks, it was not until the mid 20th century that a tourbillon was included in a wristwatch. The very first brand to do it was Omega in 1947, with a small collection of "competition" watches, made during a time when brands competed for who could produce the most accurate movement.

When most consumers think of Omega, they probably think of popular mainstream luxury watches such as the Seamaster or the Speedmaster, rather than of highly complicated limited edition pieces. However, Omega does produce modern tourbillon timepieces in extremely limited numbers, and they have been doing so since 1994.

The Omega tourbillon isn't like others, because it places the tourbillon in the absolute centre of the dial. Mechanically, this is incredibly difficult, because, normally, hands would be placed in the centre of the watch. Most tourbillon-based timepieces have a tourbillon either at the top or bottom of a dial. Omega was able to produce a central tourbillon by placing the hands around the tourbillon using a "mystery setting". At first glance it does not appear as if the hands are at all connected to the movement. Omega etches the hands on transparent sapphire crystal discs that rotate around the dial as the time passes. The tourbillon in the centre of the dial bears an Omega logo and is used as a seconds indicator.

Since the debut of the De Ville Central Tourbillon, Omega has steadily improved the mechanisms. Omega also began to offer fully skeletonised Central Tourbillon movements, with fully decorated views of their operation. Two of the most important improvements Omega made to the Central Tourbillon movement family, were the inclusion of their famed Co-Axial Escapement technology, and the inclusion of COSC Chronometer certifications, designating a degree of high accuracy. A rare and exclusive offering, available with diamond decoration, the Omega De Ville Central Tourbillon still shares the basic tenets of dependability and performance that are a given for the rest of the Omega watch family.

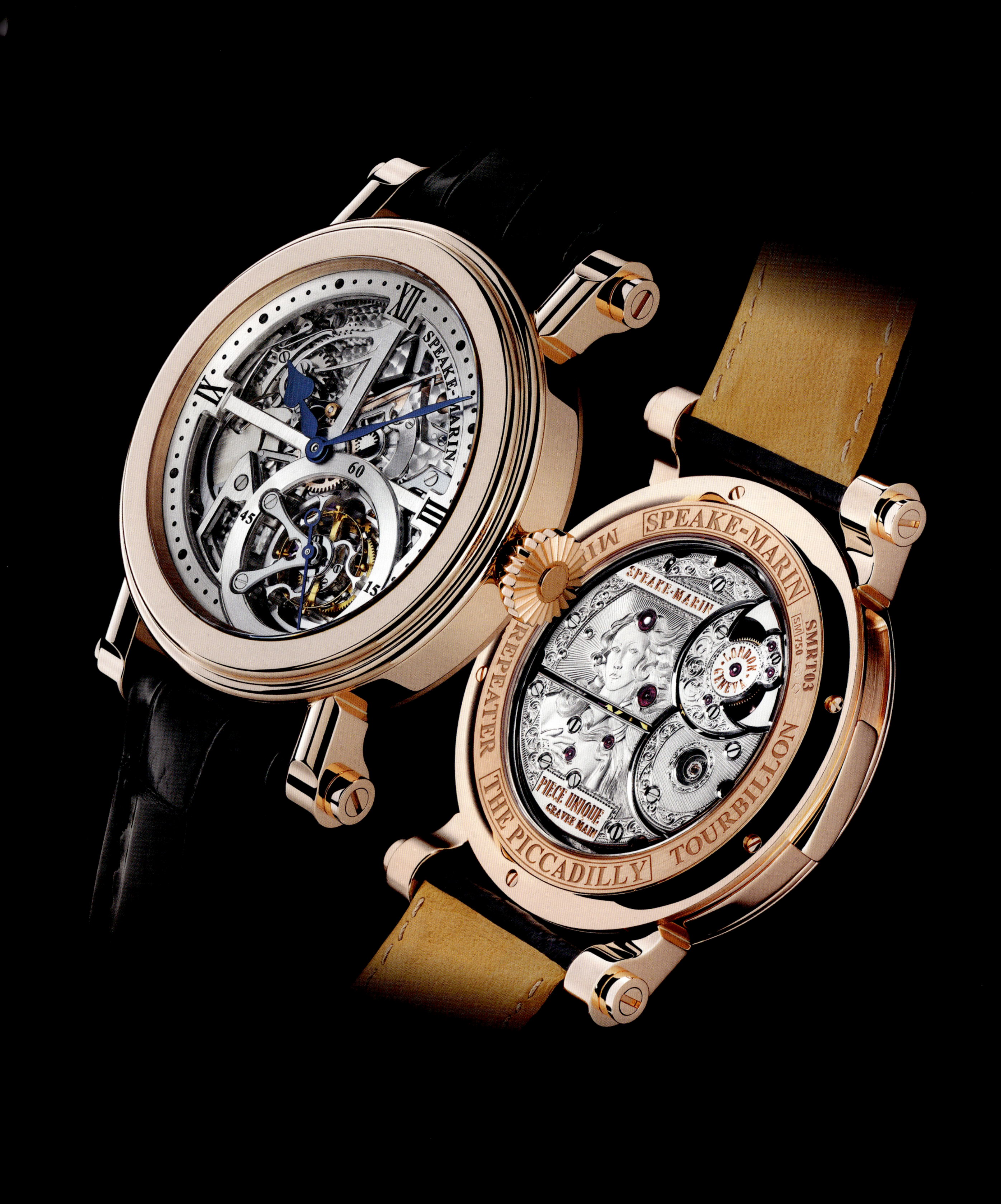
SPEAKE-MARIN
SPEAKE-MARIN
REPEATER
THE PICCADILLY
TOURBILLON
SMRT03
SPEAKE-MARIN
PIECE UNIQUE
GRAVEE MAIN
LONDON GENEVA

SPEAKE-MARIN — RENAISSANCE TOURBILLON MINUTE REPEATER

$ 337 000

WHAT SPEAKE-MARIN UNDERSTOOD EARLY IN HIS CAREER IS THAT EMOTION WAS THE LEADING REASON COLLECTORS PURCHASED TIMEPIECES.

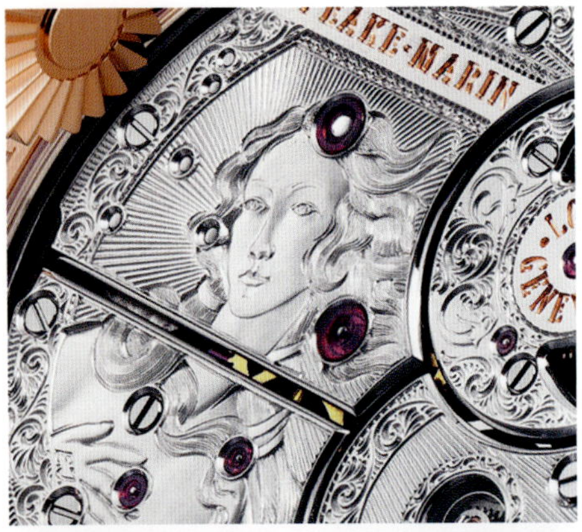

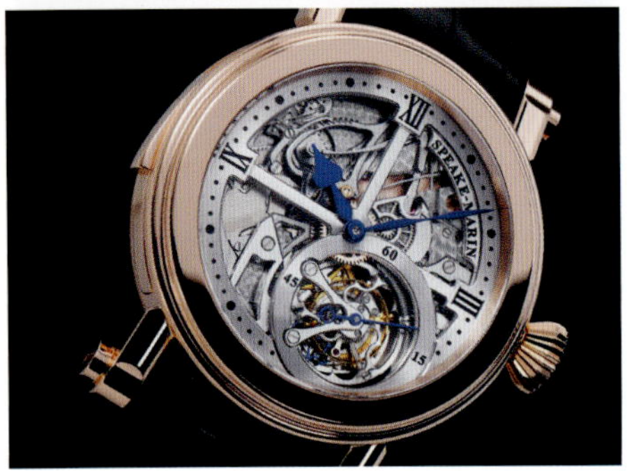

Most British watchmakers remain in England but Peter Speake-Marin moved to Switzerland in order to succeed in the watch industry. Before beginning his own eponymous brand in the year 2000, his laurels included a range of intense horological work such as the restoration of antique minute repeater-based timepieces in London, and working at the extremely well-regarded movement design and production firm Renaud & Papi.

What Speake-Marin understood early in his career is that emotion was the leading reason collectors purchased timepieces. Logically, no-one requires a traditional watch, but rather a range of factors cause mechanically-mind people to want them (often quite badly). Speake-Marin watches are known for smoothly combining classical aesthetics and a modern sense of wearability.

Inseparable from Speake-Marin himself is the brand's "Piccadilly" case, which refers to a unique design the majority of his timepieces bear. The term "Piccadilly" was used by him as a reminder of his time working in London. Speake-Marin's most impressive timepiece is yet another homage to his past. Called the Renaissance, the highly limited edition piece was produced in honour of the pocket watch that began his career as the type of watchmaker whom others took seriously.

Legitimacy is an important part of being a watchmaker, especially if one puts their name on a dial and expects others to pay for it. When Speak-Marin produced the "Foundation Watch", it afforded him a sense of respect as it contained both a tourbillon and minute repeater. He gave it that name because, in his opinion, it was the foundation of his career.

Like the Foundation, the Renaissance contains both a tourbillon as well as a minute repeater. The former being a complication designed for beauty, that spins the balance wheel on its own axis, and the latter being a mechanism that sounds the time back to the wearer via chimes, on command, as controlled by a lever on the side of the case.

For Speak-Marin a highly limited, complex-to-produce timepiece was not enough. He decided that the rear of the watch movement should provide an artistic ground to serve as a base for engravings. Thus each of the six pieces of the Renaissance watch would bare a unique hand-engraved display visible through the rear of the case.

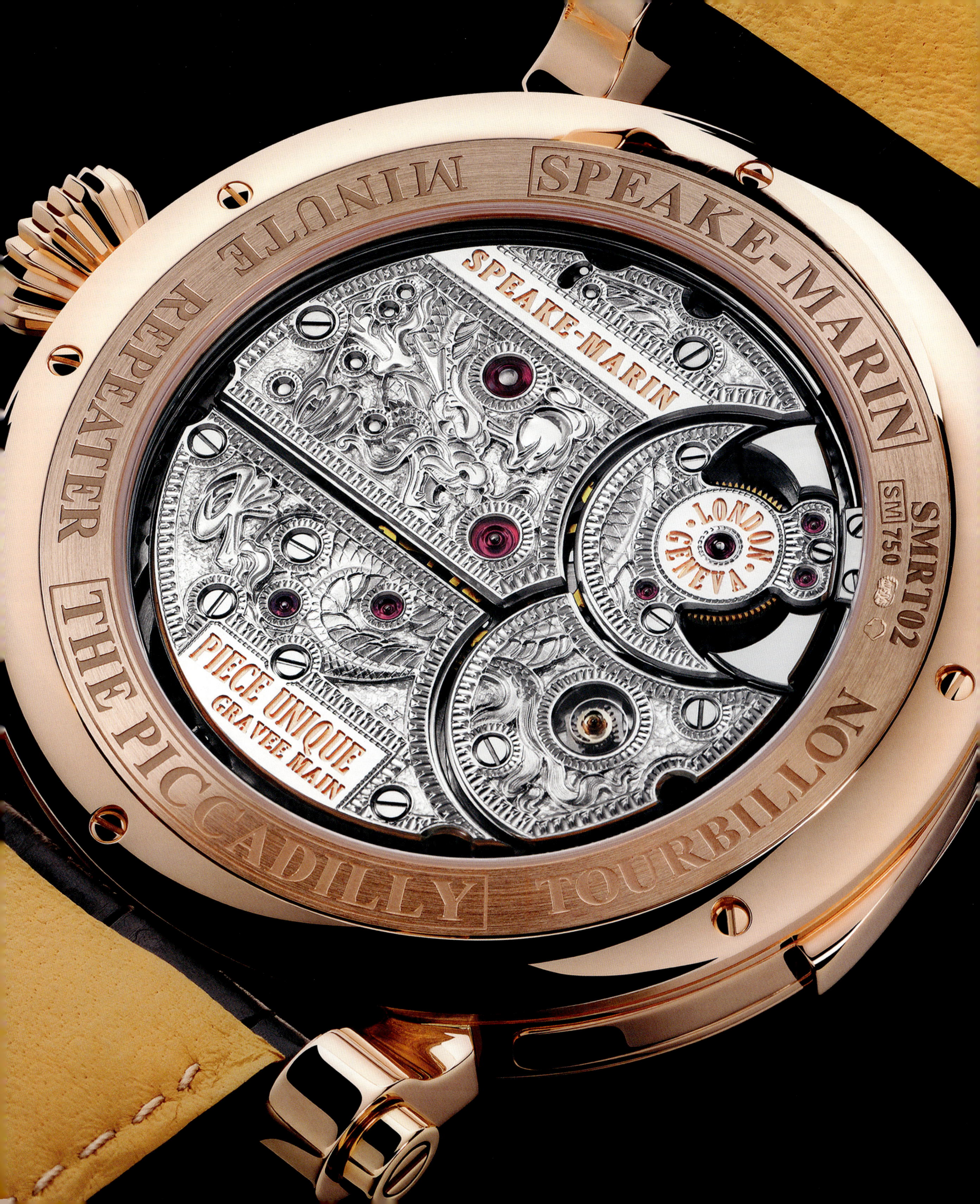
SPEAKE-MARIN
MINUTE REPEATER
THE PICCADILLY
TOURBILLON
SMRT02
SM 750
SPEAKE-MARIN
LONDON GENEVA
PIECE UNIQUE
GRAVEE MAIN

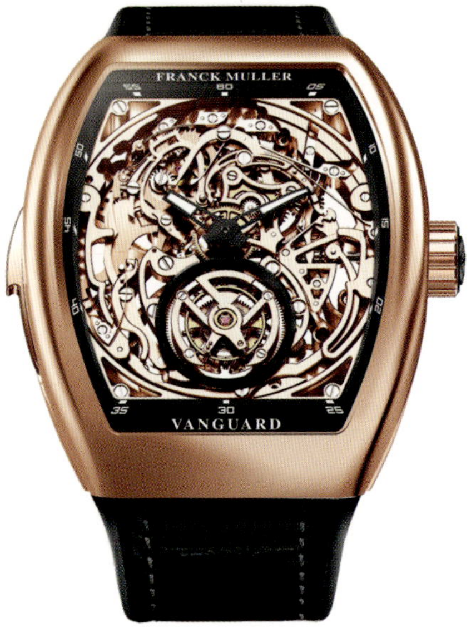

FRANCK MULLER – VANGUARD TOURBILLON MINUTE REPEATER SKELETON

$ 340 000

Vanguard is the lofty title Swiss watchmaker Franck Muller bestowed upon the most contemporary watch case in their collection. The name is a not-so-subtle proclamation that Franck Muller considers themselves at the forefront of what makes traditional watchmaking great. This heritage of timepiece-making also includes a great viewing experience with the marvellous mechanical movement brazenly displayed through the Vanguard Tourbillon Minute Repeater Skeleton's "naked" dial.

The movement contains almost 400 components and, with its many hand-finished parts, features the time with seconds displayed via the tourbillon, as well as a minute-repeater complication. The latter is activated by a sliding lever on the left side of the tonneau-shaped case. Franck Muller has produced one-of-a-kind versions of the Vanguard Tourbillon Minute Repeater Skeleton in precious metals such as gold and platinum, but only one example in steel. Known as the Caliber V 50, this normally round mechanical movement needed to be slightly restructured to fit within the barrel-shaped Vanguard case. Franck Muller uses the modern aesthetic of the case, along with the hands (Franck Muller actually designed them a tad too short) and hour markers, as a frame to display what is in actuality a rather traditional-style mechanical movement. The lack of dial over the movement is both a testament to the core reason collectors appreciate mechanical watches to begin with, as well as a bold assertion of the watch's prestigious guts. More so, visual juxtaposition of modern and historic visual cues makes for a compelling artistic statement timepiece, which few brands but Franck Muller might attempt (and subsequently pull off).

Even though other versions of the V 50 mechanical movement are present in a select number of other Franck Muller timepieces, the Vanguard Tourbillon Minute Repeater Skeleton is reported as a "piece unique" creation, meaning that only a single example per case material will ever be produced.

ANTOINE PREZIUSO – MEGA TOURBILLON

$ 340 000

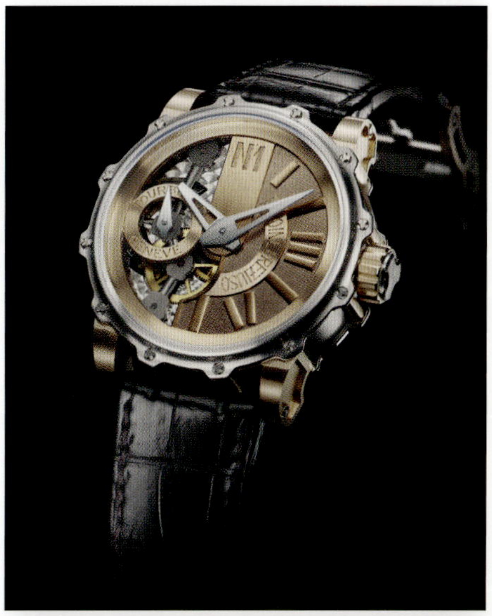

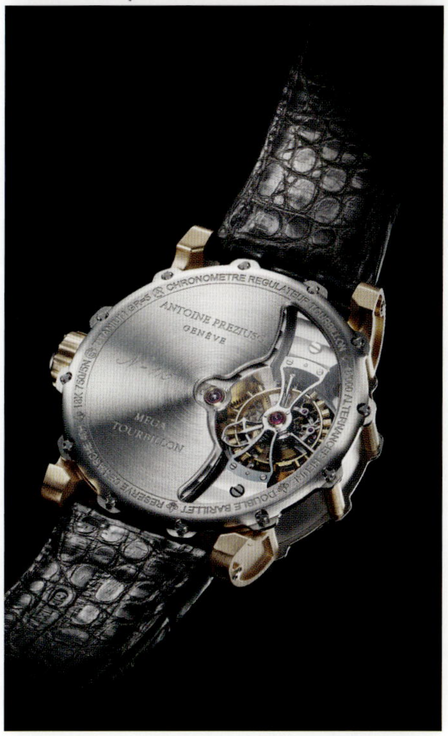

In 2010 watchmaker Antoine Preziuso released what they claimed to be the "world's largest tourbillon watch". At the time, this claim referred not only to the diameter of the tourbillon itself (a mechanism inside the mechanical movement), but also to the watch. Most would agree that the Mega Tourbillon timepiece is barely wearable, but it does speak to the superlative character with which luxury watch brands often assert themselves.

The Mega Tourbillon was sometimes called the "Monumental Tourbillon" by Antoine Preziuso, and it certainly was. The most important detail is that the uniquely designed watch case is 65mm wide. Compare that with the fact that most men's watches are about 42mm wide. At about 50% larger than "normal" watches, the Mega Tourbillon is often described as a showpiece, rather than a wristwatch intended for actual wearing.

The movement inside the Mega Tourbillon watch is based on a Swiss pocket watch movement from 1928, which Antoine Preziuso adapted for the manually wound movement inside this massive case. An interesting element of the design is that, despite the tourbillon being 25mm wide and perhaps still the largest tourbillon in the world, it is not visible on the dial side of the timepiece. The Mega Tourbillon was produced at a time when, as well as "showing off" through avant-garde design, it was important to show a tourbillon on its dial side, in order to assert the luxurious nature of the piece. This "record-breaking" tourbillon is only visible through the rear of the watch.

Antoine Preziuso designed the large case from a mix of 18k pink gold and titanium parts. The dial however is solid 18k pink gold, engraved with hour markers and partially skeletonised to display some of the movement. Arguably, the Mega Tourbillon is more a pocket watch on straps than a wristwatch, and Antoine Preziuso produced only five pieces in total.

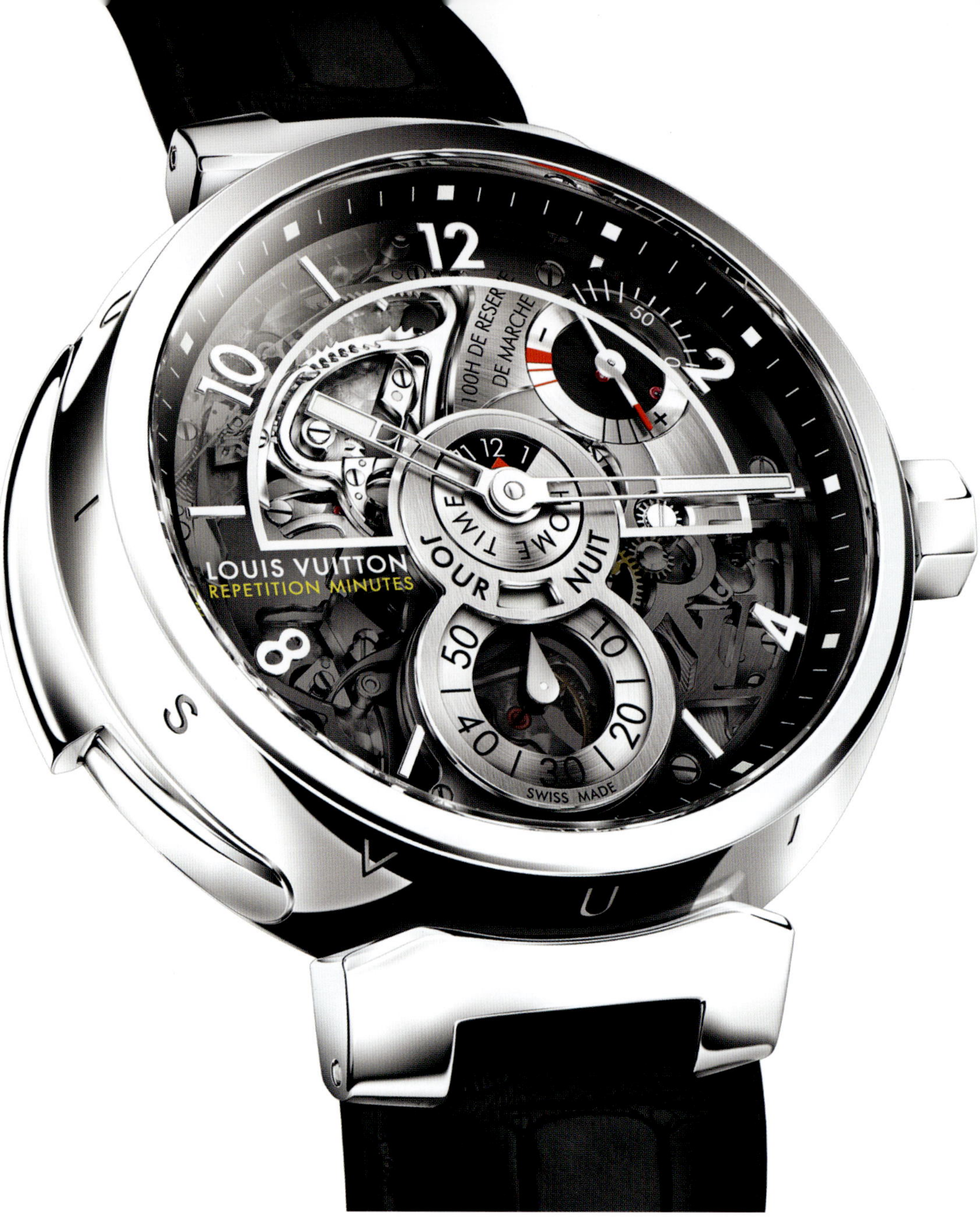

LOUIS VUITTON – TAMBOUR MINUTE REPEATER

$ 343 750

Easily one of the best-known luxury brands in the world, Louis Vuitton is not regularly thought of as a watchmaker. Indeed, when people consider items produced by Louis Vuitton, they may imagine everything from iconic women's handbags to stylish shoes. Nevertheless, Louis Vuitton does produce wristwatches, and many models are exceedingly rare.

Given the large global footprint Louis Vuitton enjoys from the standpoint of retail presence, only select boutiques actually carry their watches. The cornerstone of the Louis Vuitton watch collection is the Tambour-style case. Wider at the base than at the bezel, the unique design has been a successful foundation for many interesting watches.

While Louis Vuitton watches are luxury goods, very few of them have reached the level of mega luxury. In 2011 they released a highly complicated, classically conceived model into the Tambour Family. This model reached new heights, putting Louis Vuitton firmly into a new category of watchmaker.

Louis Vuitton belongs to the LVMH luxury group (Louis Vuitton Moët Hennessy), which also includes other fine watchmakers such as TAG Heuer, Zenith, Hublot, and Bulgari. This talented team of brands no doubt helped Louis Vuitton design and produce a watch like the Tambour Minute Repeater. However, this new level of prestige for Louis Vuitton proper, was largely based on Louis Vuitton's purchase of the esteemed mechanical watch movement design La Fabrique du Temps.

In a nutshell, this version of the Tambour is a GMT-style travel watch with a minute repeater and dazzling three-dimensional dial. Much of the dial is produced from smoked sapphire crystal, offering the legibility of actual markers and bold hands, matched with a view of the complicated movement below. Louis Vuitton designed the movement in a unique manner, allowing many of the highly animated functional elements for the minute repeater (an on-demand mechanism that sounds the time out in a series of musical chimes) to be visible through the dial (as opposed to through the rear of the watch).

The centre of the dial contains a disc that indicates the home time as the GMT indicator. Adjacent to it is an AM/PM indicator for the second time zone. The dial also features a subsidiary seconds dial, as well as a power reserve indicator for the movement. Designed from the ground up for aesthetics and beauty, the mechanical movement is framed by the slick presentation of the Tambour case and Louis Vuitton style. The Tambour Minute Repeater watch is highly limited in production and most pieces are customised for each buyer.

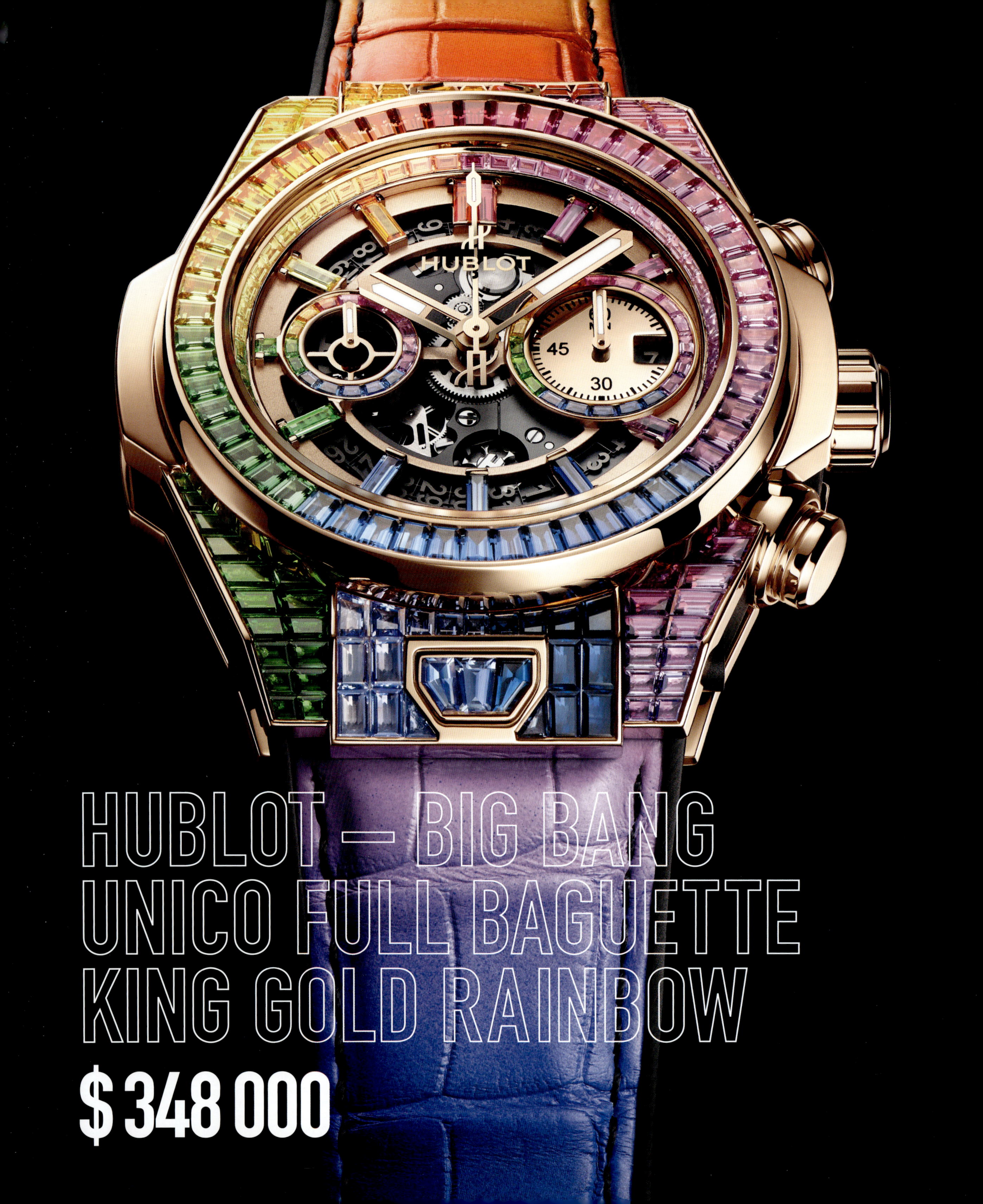

HUBLOT — BIG BANG UNICO FULL BAGUETTE KING GOLD RAINBOW

$ 348 000

Among the most interesting trends in men's fashion circa 2021, is the re-democratisation of the rainbow. From men's basic clothing items all the way up to elaborate luxury timepieces, the rainbow is once again entering the domain of universal fashion acceptance. In contrast, just a few years ago, almost any item emblazoned with a rainbow would have been frequently understood as representing LGBTQ+ pride. However, today, given the popularity of the rainbow flag, it has since become a favourite among all gender denominations.

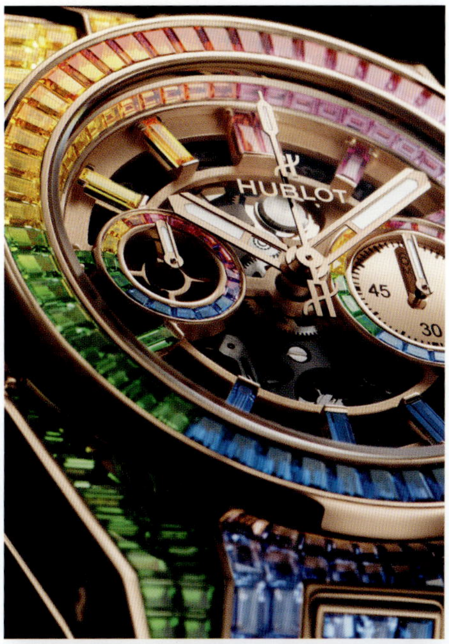

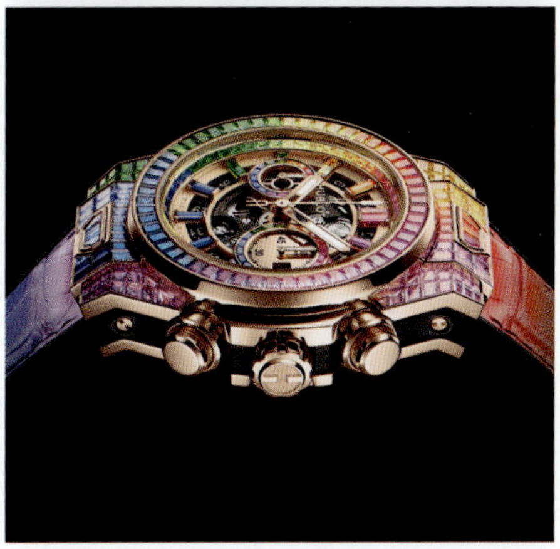

In the world of fashion today, rainbows show up just about everywhere, including men's timepieces worn by rap and popular music artists. The design of this spectacularly dazzling Hublot Big Bang Unico Full Baguette King Gold Rainbow was so appealing for Hublot, they even produced a less expensive version costing just under $100,000, with less baguette-cut precious stones. Hublot took the rainbow colour theme to its logical end by pairing the watch with a rainbow-hued alligator strap, set into a comfortably moulded rubber liner.

The 45mm-wide case is produced in Hublot's warm-toned "King Gold" (akin to 18k red gold), which is part of the larger and highly popular Big Bang Unico sport lifestyle watch collection. The watch contains Hublot's in-house made automatic chronograph Unico movement and a modern case with a refined push-button strap release system.

What takes this timepiece from the roughly $20,000 average price of the Big Bang Unico, to nearly $400,000 is the gold case, not to mention the lavish assortment of large, baguette-cut stones in a stunning variety of colours. Baguette-cut stones decorate the watch case, strap buckle, and even the dial, including rainbow-array baguette-cut stones placed in each of the hour markers. This entire Hublot creation uses 290 precious and semi-precious stones.

Gemologically speaking, the Big Bang Unico Full Baguette King Gold Rainbow watch's organic-style rainbow motif uses rubies, amethysts, blue topaz, tsavorites, and pink, blue, yellow and orange sapphires. The technical challenge in each piece is not only in setting the stones correctly but, more importantly, in carefully selecting the right harmony of stones to set in the first place. The most impressive thing about Hublot's accomplishment is the emotional magnitude that the final result conveys on the eyes. It's a rainbow of joy for all.

ROGER DUBUIS – EXCALIBUR SKELETON DOUBLE FLYING TOURBILLON

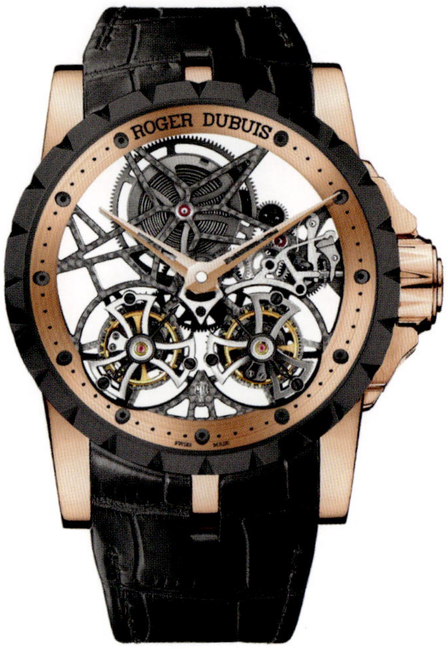

$ 350 000

For a time, in the late 1990s and early 2000s, Roger Dubuis was the hot modern "haute horlogerie" watch brand. The latter term is generally used to reference timepieces and brands that represent a high calibre of both original design and traditional watchmaking techniques. In other words, it is applied to the very best and often most expensive timepieces.

What helped separate Roger Dubuis from the rest of the pack was its less-than-subtle approach to design and mechanics. It helped start a new era of glitzy "show me" dial and case aesthetics that was a sharp departure from the much more conservative fare offered by most comparable brands. In fact, what really connected it to its peers was its focus on the production of perhaps unique, albeit traditionally made, mechanical movements.

Roger Dubuis, as a brand, tells the interesting story of how modern watch companies take form. It was begun by a watchmaker named Roger Dubuis, who later sold the company, along with the name, to a third party who was a controversial character, but who helped put the name on the map. The brand was later sold to the large luxury Richemont Group, which, as serendipity would have it, eventually hired back Roger Dubuis himself.

Their successful Excalibur collection is perhaps the brand's most popular watch style. Its trademark design features include a triple lug structure, and a bezel with an almost serrated edge. Excalibur watches are also often very complicated, and are most perfectly exemplified by the Skeleton Double Flying Tourbillon collection.

At the heart of the watch is a movement that perfectly represents the values of the company. The mechanism contains two adjacent tourbillons. They are in a highly skeletonised architecture, which looks something between a spider's web and a crystalline structure that has been decorated with a perlage-style polish. It is among the most highly skeletonised movements in the world.

One reason Roger Dubuis found success, was its base of clients who sought wrist-worn prestige; they were a much younger generation, often with new money, when compared to the traditional luxury watch buyer. A timepiece is a visually obvious and rather portable means of showing one's lifestyle and wealth. Donning a more traditional timepiece perhaps communicates taste and success, but it does not communicate a youthful or active lifestyle as does a timepiece in the "modern luxury watch" category. Roger Dubuis helped define this segment, and – with a distinctive case, available diamond decoration, and visually engaging, complex, mechanical movement – set a high bar for all those coming after it. In 18k white gold with a diamond-set inner bezel, the Excalibur Skeleton Double Flying Tourbillon was limited to 28 pieces.

JAEGER-LECOULTRE – REVERSO GYRO-TOURBILLON 2

$ 350 000

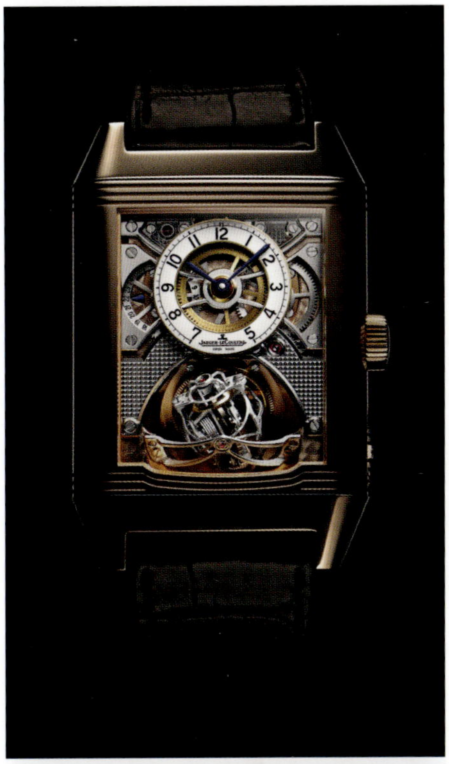

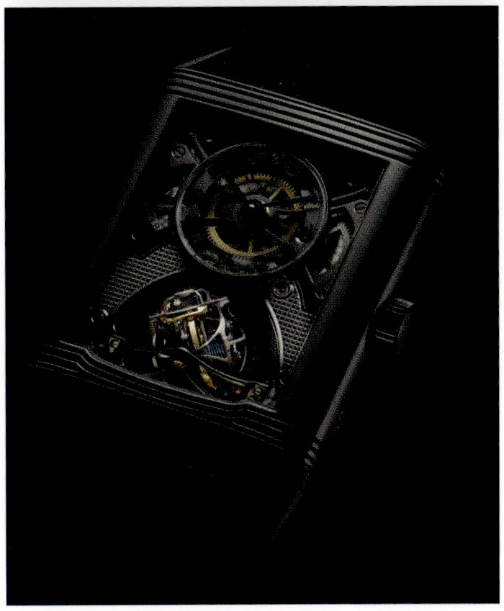

It is mesmerising to view the operation of Jaeger-LeCoultre's Gyrotourbillon. Originally released in 2004, this novel creation places a typically horizontally flat tourbillon complication into a spherical cage, that spins on two axis points, looking like a spinning gyroscope. Inside the tourbillon of the second Gyrotourbillon watch is a cylindrical (as opposed to flat) hairspring. Beating like a metal heart as the balance wheel oscillates, the three-dimensional hairspring sits in the centre of this very life-like mechanical complication.

Jaeger-LeCoultre does not hide the fact that only a few highly-trained watchmakers are able to produce a Gyrotourbillon tourbillon, principally, French watchmaker Eric Coudray. The titanium cage is so small and fragile that simply holding it incorrectly will damage it. While tourbillons aren't nearly as exotic and exclusive as they once were, unique varieties such as the Gyrotourbillon have once again helped the tourbillon's status as a highly regarded luxury treat and symbol of incredible prestige.

In 2008, Jaeger-LeCoultre followed-up the original Gyrotourbillon with a sequel. Dressed in an extra-large Reverso-style case, the Gyrotourbillon 2 took the now world-famous complication into a new direction visually. The complex movement was opened up and decorated, revealing a beautiful skeletonised creation inside Jaeger-LeCoultre's iconic art-deco style housing, that was originally born in the 1930s.

Patents protect Jaeger-LeCoultre's inventions in the movement, which is a beautifully satisfying combination of traditional horological design and decoration, and the virtues of modern design. While an object like the gyrotourbillon builds upon a legacy of watchmaking started over 200 years ago with the original invention of the tourbillon, today's version would not be possible without modern computer-aided design, and precision manufacturing techniques.

Compared to the original Gyrotourbillon, the Reverso Gyrotourbillon 2 is arguably simpler, offering fewer features. The original contained both a perpetual calendar and long power reserve, of over a week, in the movement. The point of the follow-up Gyrotourbillon 2 model, was to focus on the introduction of artistic and decorative allure, at which it was highly successful. Only 75 pieces of the Reverso Gyrotourbillon 2 were produced. In 2013 Jaeger-LeCoultre released the Gyrotourbillon 3.

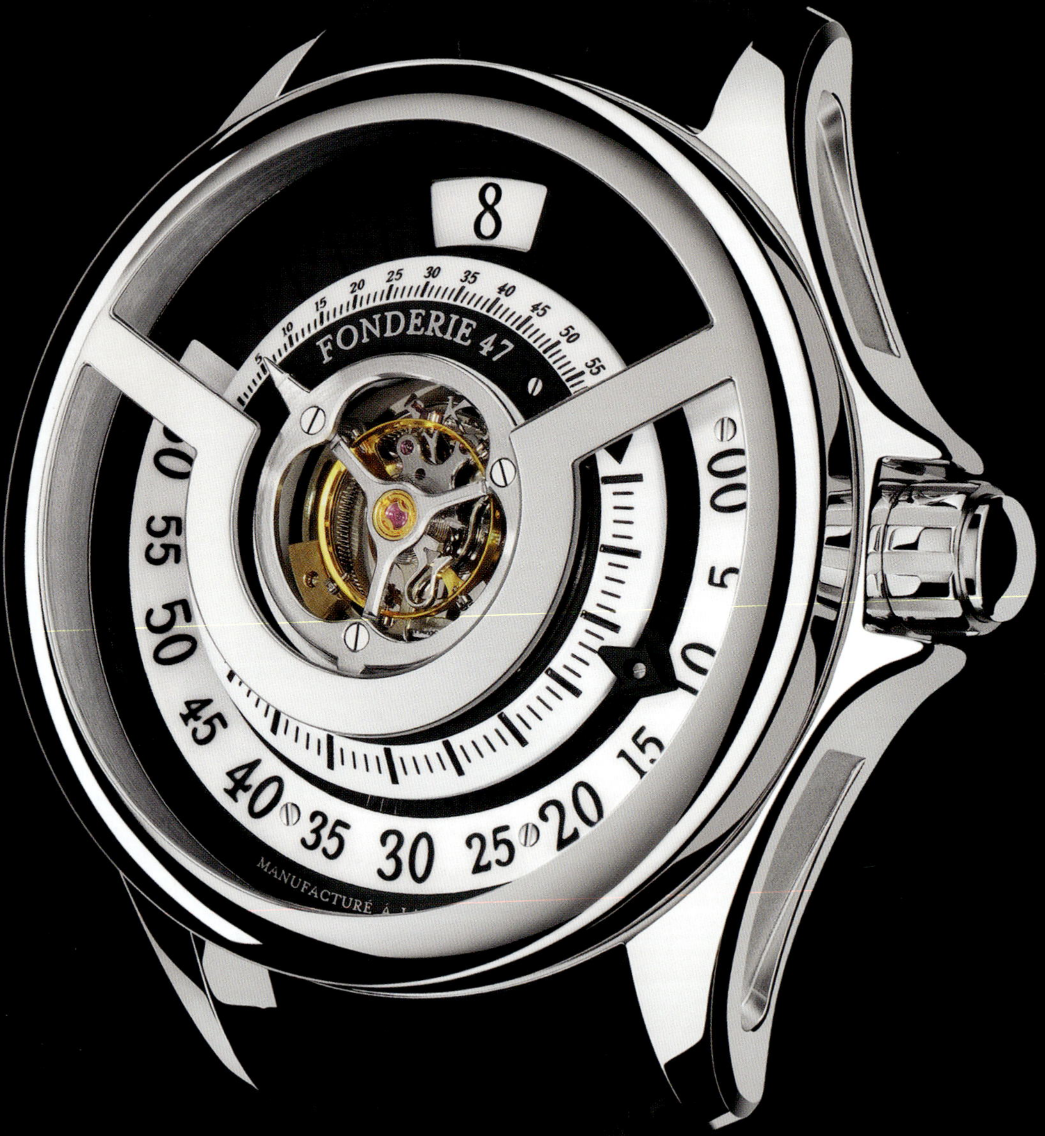

FONDERIE 47 — INVERSION PRINCIPLE TOURBILLON

$ 350 000

A brilliant marketing plan conceived the Fonderie 47 brand. Two entrepreneurs, from New York and San Francisco, developed the idea of producing ultra-luxury products sold to the ultra-wealthy at special events, parties and benefits, which would ultimately be used to prevent violence in Africa. "Feel good", socially-conscious luxury products are rare, and Fonderie 47 was intent on producing unique products that would pull on the charitably intentions of its customers.

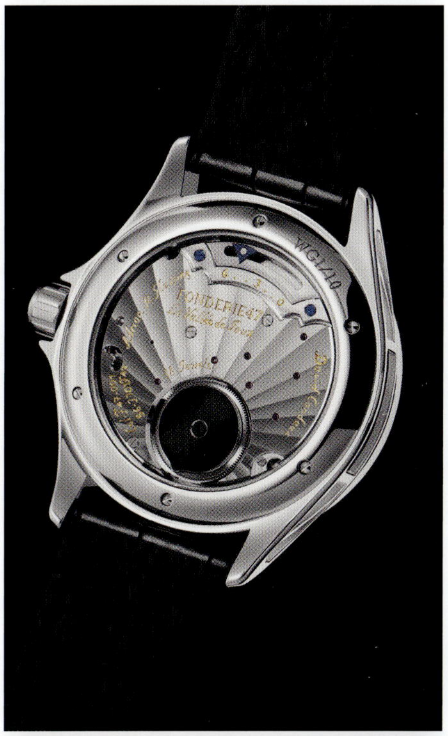

Here is how it worked. Fonderie 47 would purchase AK-47 assault rifles from people in Africa. These would be sold to Fonderie 47's agents because, according to the brand, guns are often used as currency, given their value and relative availability. The sellers would be motivated by the cash, which would help them live much better than the guns would. Fonderie 47 would then take those guns and destroy them, thus reducing the overall availability of rifles. The hoped net benefit of fewer guns would be less violence.

It didn't end with the destruction of the guns. Parts of those guns would be melted down and used in the items themselves. In addition to watches, Fonderie 47 also creates jewellery, and each of its products has metal in it from a destroyed assault rifle purchased in Africa. Revenue from the sale of the products is put towards buying more guns from African people.

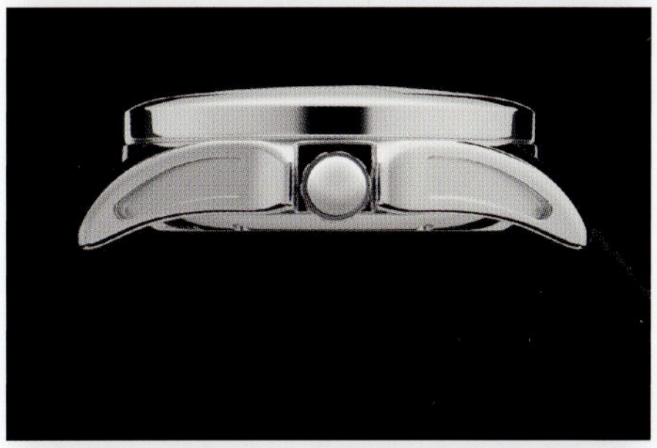

In 2013, Fonderie 47 finally released their first timepiece, called the Inversion Principle Tourbillon. Swiss watch designer Adrian Glessing came up with the concept, which is based on a centrally-mounted tourbillon escapement that requires three minutes to rotate. In mostly black and white, in either an 18k white or red gold case, the "tuxedo style" timepiece has an aesthetic that is very far removed from the larger theme of the brand.

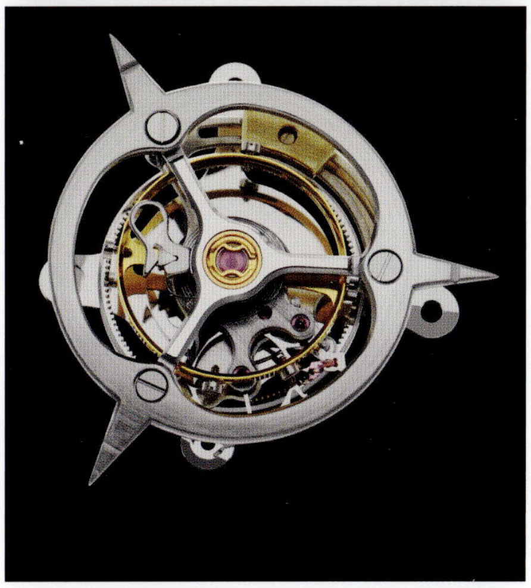

The dial of the watch is simple to read once the wearer knows what they are looking at. Hours are indicated through a digital window, located at 12 o'clock, that jumps to the next digit each time an hour passes. Minutes are indicated by a retrograde counter at the lower part of the watch. The tourbillon doubles as a seconds indicator (using one of three hands since it takes 180 seconds to fully rotate).

The manually wound movement has a power reserve of six days, and the watch has two power reserve indicators. One is located on the rear of the watch, on the movement, and the other is uniquely visible through the left side of the case. Only 30 pieces of the Inversion Principle Tourbillon limited edition watch were produced.

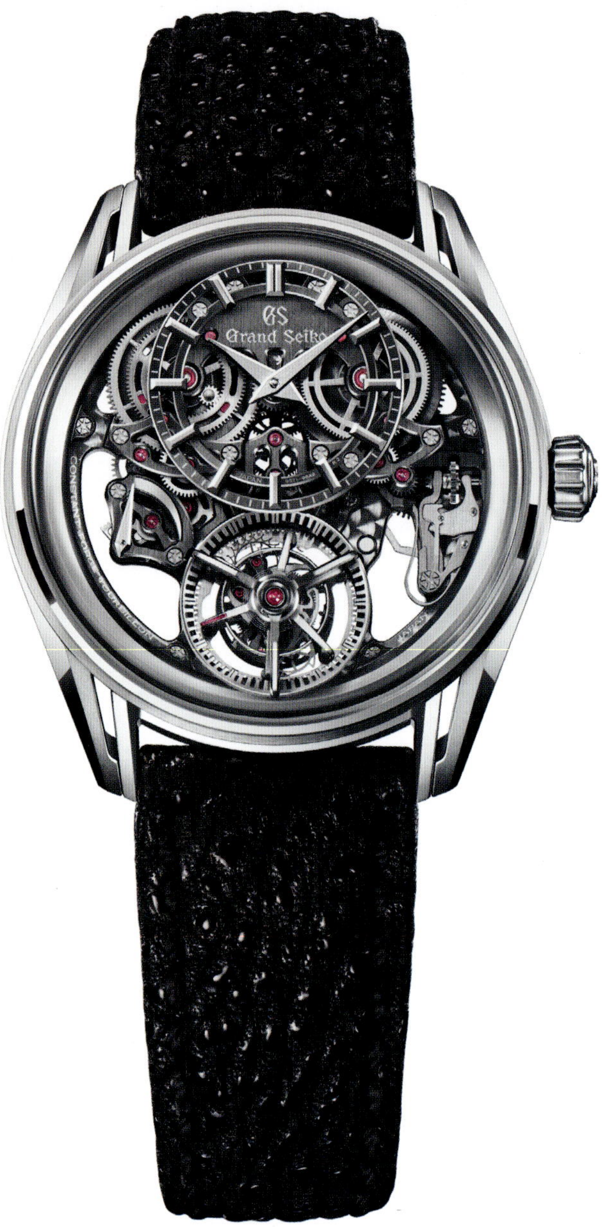

GRAND SEIKO — KODO CONSTANT-FORCE TOURBILLON

$ 350 000

Grand Seiko is the most prestigious name in Japanese watchmaking when it comes to following traditional horological arts. The Kodo Constant-force Tourbillon timepiece is arguably the company's most ambitious effort yet to put a high-performance, high-design miniature machine on the wrist. Grand Seiko teased the enthusiast community in 2020 by releasing a prototype of just the movement (an early version, that is) to great fanfare. Two years later in 2022, during a fair in Switzerland, Grand Seiko finally unveiled the Kodo with its innovative Constant-force Tourbillon movement and mega-luxury pricing.

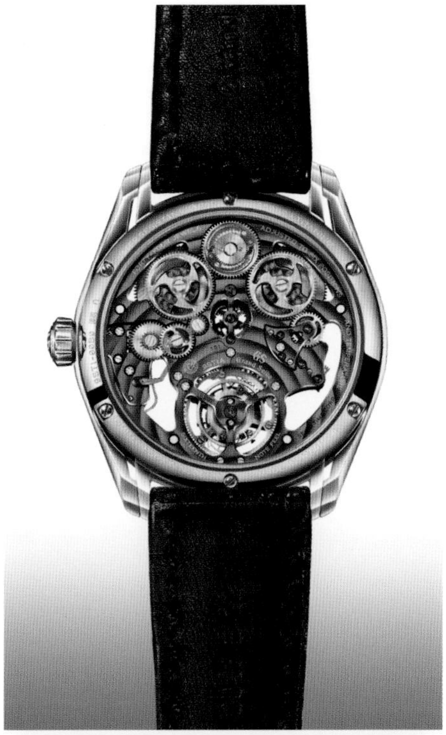

Unlike some other leaders of watchmaking in Japan, Grand Seiko prefers a more European approach to luxury timepieces, which prompts a grand fascination with mechanical ingenuity and precision engineering. From a philosophical perspective, the Kodo Constant-force Tourbillon is a potent message to Europe's major watchmakers that Japanese horological culture can meet – and even beat – the old-world masters anytime they put their minds to it.

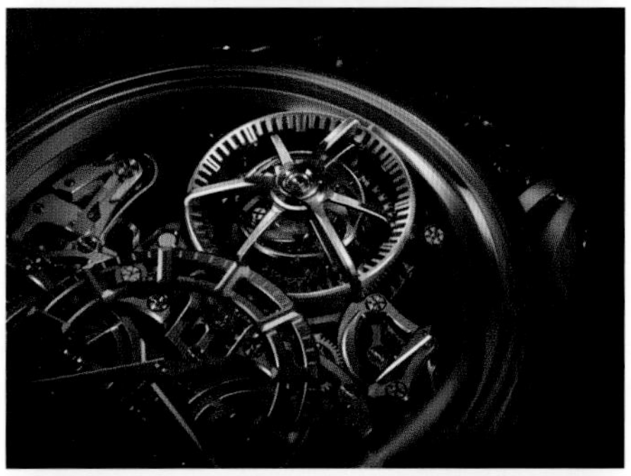

With the Kodo, Grand Seiko invented a brand-new way to imagine a mechanical watch with both a tourbillon and a constant-force mechanism by engineering the latter component to sit around the former. The manually wound movement at the heart of the watch features a 4Hz frequency tourbillon that makes a full rotation every 60 seconds. Around the tourbillon is a ring-style constant-force mechanism that releases a pulse of power each second. The melodious motions of these two ticking components are carefully tuned to an attractive sounding 16th note – an added delight to experience.

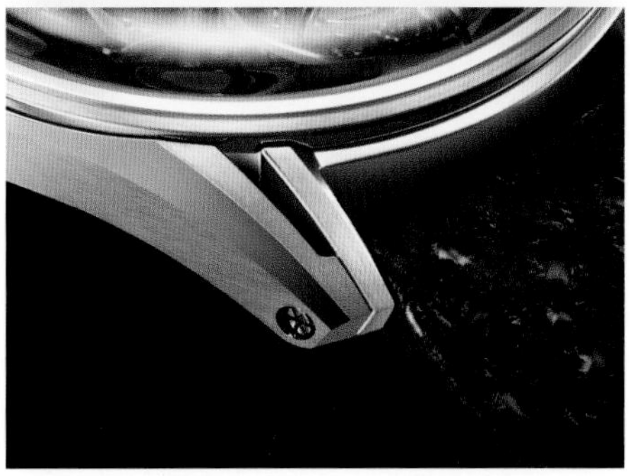

Created from extremely detailed parts, with a skeletonised bridge design, the three-day power-reserve movement inside of the Kodo also doubles as the face of the watch; a built-in subsidiary dial to indicate the time is placed above the large, constant-force tourbillon system. For decorative purposes, Grand Seiko intentionally played with colour in the form of the red synthetic ruby palettes used in parts of the movement that experience friction. Seiko introduced one purely illustrative ruby in the form of a narrow piece on the constant-force system that is used to indicate the running seconds.

Mostly symmetrical in design and crafted in shades of finely polished grey, the complex movement inside of the Kodo Constant-force Tourbillon watch is produced from both platinum-950 and hardened-titanium components . The case is nearly 44mm wide and offers a sporty 100 metres of water resistance. Attached to the case is a highly avant-garde strap made from calfskin leather which has been specially painted using Japanese Urushi lacquer. Grand Seiko only produced 20 of the Kodo Constant-Force Tourbillon pieces, as the reference SLGT003.

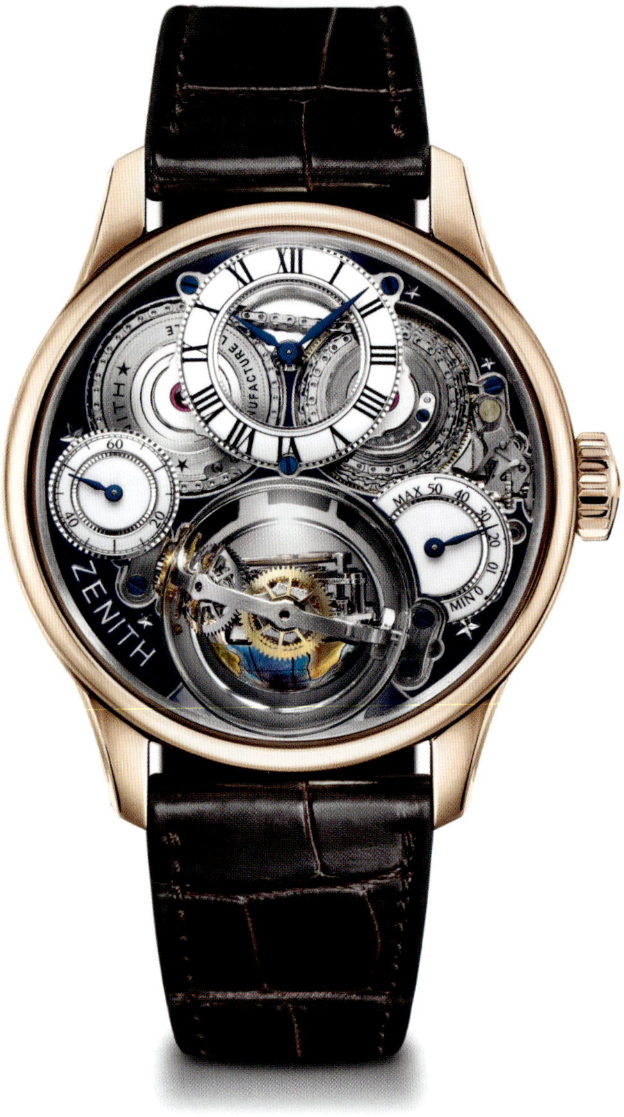

ZENITH — ACADEMY CHRISTOPHE COLOMB HURRICANE GRAND VOYAGE II

$ 353 000

Remarkably ambitious – and some would argue, controversial – one of many "I didn't see that coming" high-horology creations from Swiss Zenith watches is the Academy Christophe Colomb Hurricane Grand Voyage II watch. For some collectors, this super luxury wearable has it all: from proud bare-chested hand-engraved motifs of a native man and woman, to an industry-only gyroscopically mounted regulation system.

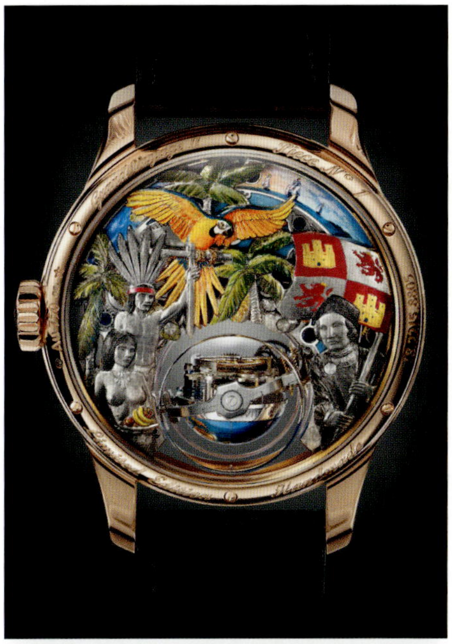

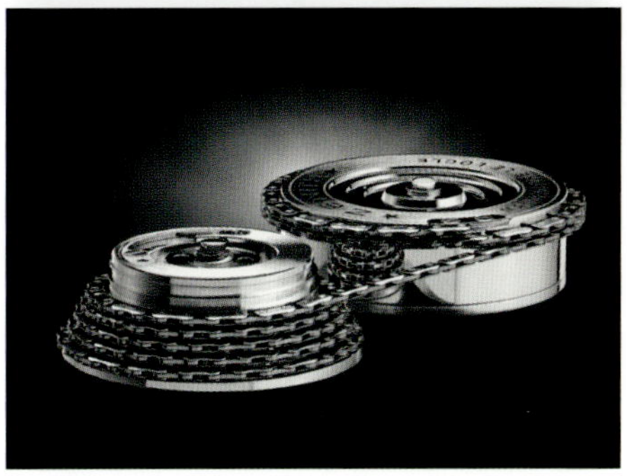

This watch was not the first time Zenith has celebrated the historically morally nebulous explorer Christopher Columbus in a timepiece. The rear of the viewable movement is ornately decorated with a hand-carved and painted miniature mural depicting an "effigy" of Christopher Columbus holding the Spanish flag (with his famed three ships in the background), as he looks on to the native people and their lands, which he and his contemporaries eventually take by force. Critics and fans alike of this remarkably pain-staking-to-create artistic timepiece agree that its theme is "conquering and commanding"; a message Zenith hoped would appeal to at least 10 (the number of pieces produced in this limited-edition set) well-funded watch collectors around the world.

Truly appreciating the rationale behind the exotic El Primero caliber 8805 movement powering the 45mm-wide, 18k rose-gold watch can require some lengthy watch collector education. In short, the engineers at Zenith attempted to combine – in one watch movement – both modern and historic mechanisms meant to promote accuracy. Borrowing from 200 years in the past, the Academy Christophe Colomb Hurricane uses a fusee-and-chain power transmission system designed to wrap a tiny bicycle-style chain around a conical gear which is hand-assembled from almost 600 parts by itself. This system is designed to ensure that a constant level of force is delivered from the mainspring to the gear train in the pursuit of long-term accuracy.

The modern analog to the fusee-and-chain assembly also in the watch is a system Zenith created which they call "Gravity Control". Based on the principle that a balance wheel operates most consistently when in a horizontal position, the Gravity Control system uses a weighted gyroscopic mounting for the movement's 36,000 beats per hour speed-regulation system to make sure that it is "always pointed up". Zenith later miniaturised this system in future watches, but in the Academy Christophe Colomb, the Gravity Control system was so large that it required the case to have a "bubble" in the sapphire crystal to help accommodate its size.

JACOB & CO. – QUENTTIN

$ 360 000

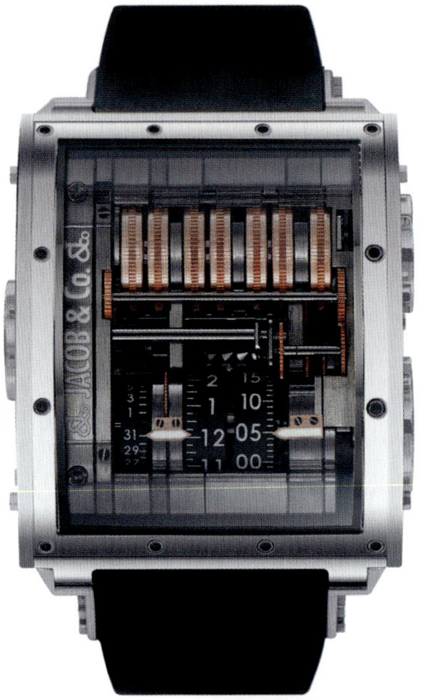

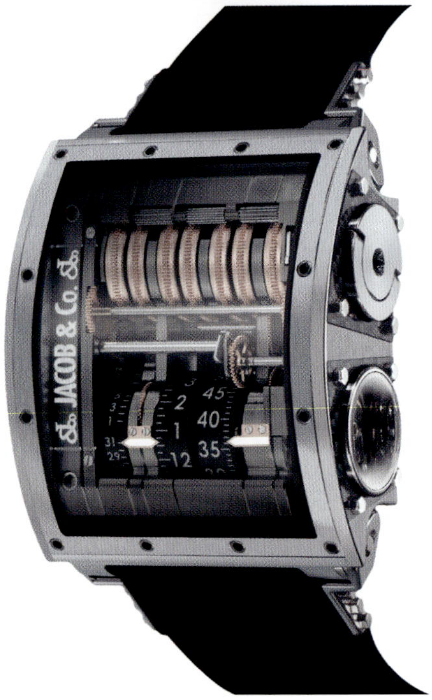

Easily one of the most colourful figures in the luxury watch industry in the 2000s, was Jacob Arabo, otherwise known as "Jacob the Jeweller". A focus on diamond-decorated timepieces, for pop stars and urban culture icons, propelled Jacob into the personal company of an extremely diverse range of individuals. Known for a while as the modern jeweller to the stars, Jacob & Co practically penned the term "bling" before it was part of the popular lexicon.

Arabo even met with serious legal trouble, due to his client relationships, but retained a sense of credibility for never giving up the trust of his closest customers. In addition to offering creatively be-jewelled watches, Jacob & Co. was also interested in pushing the boundaries of modern mechanical watchmaking technology.

In 2006, Jacob & Co. released what would forever change the face of the timepiece industry, with a watch called the Quenttin. Produced in collaboration with a Swiss firm known as BNB Concept, it was Jacob & Co.'s goal to produce the most complicated modern timepiece anyone had seen. During this time the "modern" high-luxury watch was a mere avant-garde oddity, as most ultra-high-priced timepieces represented renderings of classic designs.

Jacob & Co. was intent on mixing modern design with mechanical luxury in a watch that influenced countless others models, and entire brands, after the release of the Quenttin. The almost industrial rectangular-shaped case, was offered in a range of luxury materials and included a movement with what was, at the time, the worlds' longest power reserve of 31 days. This was achieved by stacking a series of mainspring barrels on top of one another, and aligning them horizontally on the dial. The movement required a full 200 turns, using a fold-out crown to fully wind it. The good news is that the Quenttin arrived with a motion-sensing box that contained an electronic winder that clamped on to the crown.

Time is indicated on the Quenttin without traditional hands: towards the bottom of the watch face, two vertically aligned drums turn to indicate the hours and minutes. To their right is a vertical tourbillon-style escapement, which is visible through the right side of the case.

Mechanically complex and artistically contemporary, the Quenttin opened up luxury timepieces for a new era of consumers, who would not necessarily have interest in traditionally designed timepieces. Jacob & Co.'s movement partner, BNB Concept, went bankrupt in 2010, perhaps a reason why fewer than 150 Quenttin watches were ever produced.

REBELLION – WEAP-ONE

$ 360 000

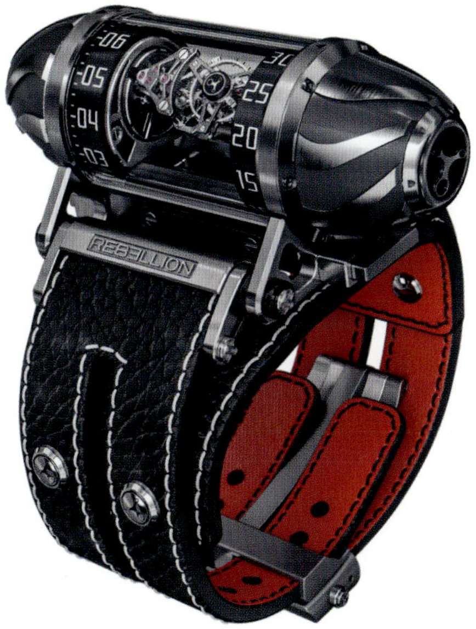

Aggressively named and aggressively styled, the otherwise ultra-masculine Rebellion WEAP-ONE watch is also an achievement in the horological arts. Produced as a scant limited edition of just 10 pieces, the WEAP-ONE is wholly original, from its bespoke mechanical movement to the innovative cylinder-style case design produced entirely from sapphire crystal and titanium. It's worn wide on the wrist with a complicated double-band style strap and intricate lug hardware system. Rebellion – as the brand name implies – sees itself as producing luxury timepieces not for the many, but rather for a select few who identify with such a unique design and product ethos.

The movement itself uses two rotating drums to indicate the hours to the left and the minutes to the right. Between them is the Asymmetric Flying Tourbillon, which Rebellion boasts as the most compelling technical feature of the WEAP-ONE. It is a multi-axis mechanism designed to spin the regulation system in two directions – sometimes known as a bi-axial tourbillon. The tourbillon itself sits slightly off-centre which accounts for the "asymmetric" aspect of the name. It first spins once every 60 seconds on its own axis, and then rotates once every 120 seconds within the axis of the tube it sits in. Such complexity is mainly artistic, as the entire regulation assembly provides an attractive visual animation for the wearer to enjoy. Exotic tourbillons are a favourite of collectors because of their rarity and difficulty in engineering, as well as the fact that only the most skilled watchmakers can assemble them.

Capping each end of the cylindrical case are crowns used for winding the movement's 50 hours of power reserve or for setting the time. In contrast to the headline "Asymmetric Flying Tourbillon" feature of the timepiece, Rebellion cleverly designed the watch itself to be remarkably symmetrical overall. Significant engineering effort is always required when mechanical watch movements do not fit the standard "round watch" design. Much of the expense associated with such high-end machines is related to low-volume production of the many original parts used to put them together, not to mention the careful science required to not only make the watch work, but also to tell the time with any level of accuracy.

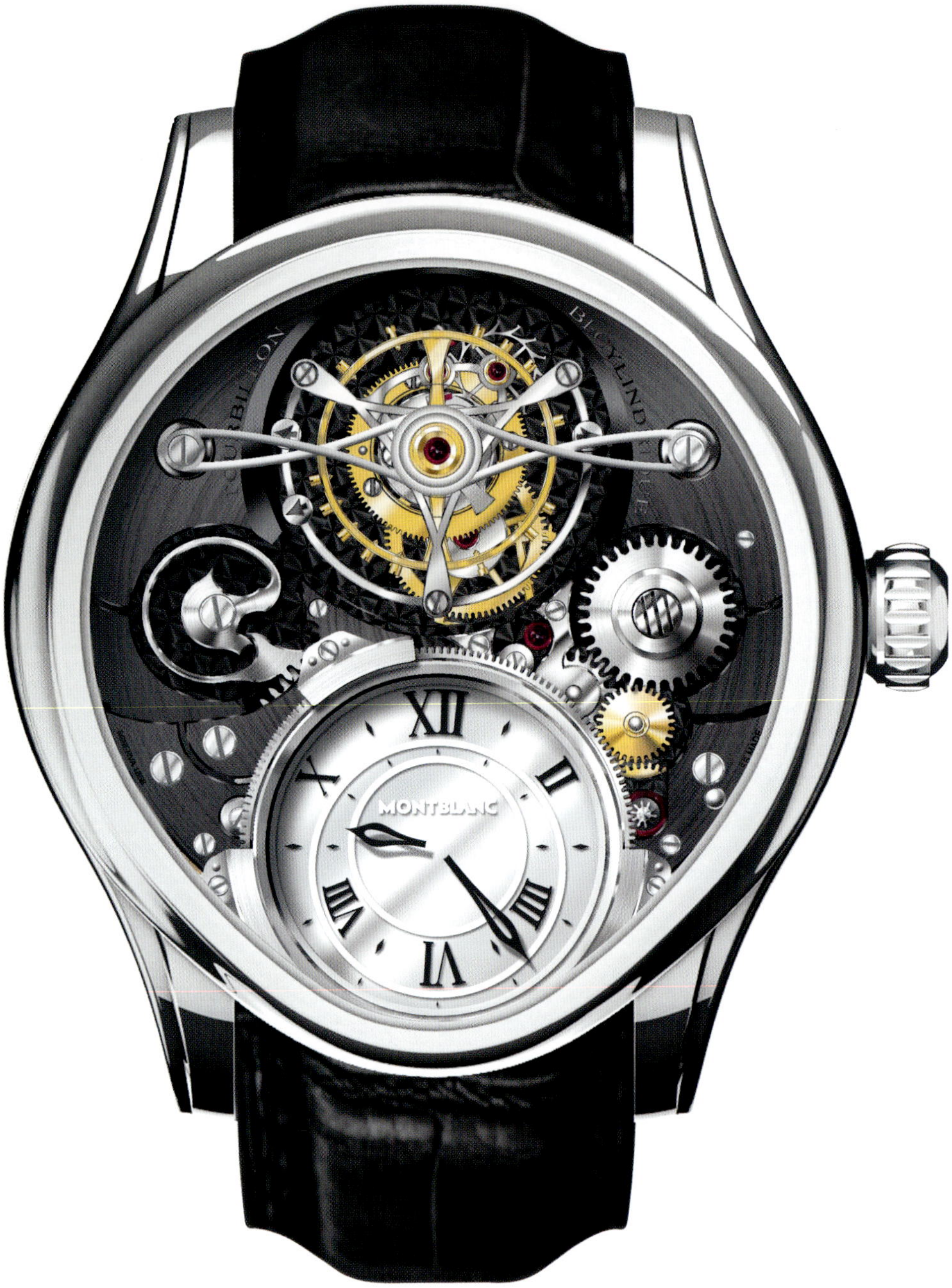

MONTBLANC — VILLERET 1858 TOURBILLON BI-CYLINDRIQUE

$ 360 300

One of the oldest continuously operating watchmakers exists in the small Swiss town of Villeret. In 1858, Minerva opened its doors and, in some manner, has been producing timepieces ever since. In 2004, Minerva watch was purchased by the Richemont Group, a large luxury firm responsible for some of the world's most important high-end watch brands. Richemont's intent was to allow Minerva to continue to operate much as it had done for so long under the aegis of one of their brands.

It was decided that Montblanc would take the Minerva facility under its wing. Montblanc, traditionally a producer of writing instruments, was becoming increasingly involved in the watch business. The Minerva facility would allow for an ultra-exclusive collection of Montblanc timepieces, with a uniquely historic character. Under the larger Montblanc umbrella, the new facility and its watches were given the "Montblanc Villeret 1858" name.

Debuting the Montblanc Villeret 1858 collection in 2009 was the Grand Tourbillon Heures Mystérieuses, a timepiece whose character helped strongly influence the future of the sub-brand that sat at the top of the Montblanc pyramid.

In a case like a teardrop, the Grand Tourbillon Heures Mystérieuses represented a new side to the German brand, which now sold everything from affordable luxury pens to $300,000 plus watches. The Villeret facility produces fewer than 300 watches a year.

The dial displaying the hours and minutes seems to have "mystery" floating hands, but they are actually placed on transparent sapphire crystals connected to a series of gears. Mystery displays, while rare, are a celebrated form of artistic expression in timepieces. Two years later the Grand Tourbillon Heures Mystérieuses was followed by a similar model that removed much of the dial. This revealed the hidden "mystery" mechanisms, exposing the carefully hand-made movement and a new feature to the tourbillon.

For perhaps the first time ever, Montblanc fitted a tourbillon-style escapement with two cylindrical hairsprings. To most people this detail is of little importance, but for watch lovers who find interest in even the most obscure technical differences from watch to watch, this fact has great value. There are two elements to the unique oscillator (escapement plus balance wheel plus hairspring) that are rare. First is the use of not one, but two hairsprings (tiny beating springs named as such for being as thin, or thinner than hair). This rare and complicated feature is designed to maintain timing accuracy. Second is the use of a cylindrical, rather than horizontally flat, hairspring. Visually distinct from traditional hairsprings, cylindrical springs were used in the 18th century by those racing to create ultra-precise ship's chronometers for marine navigation.

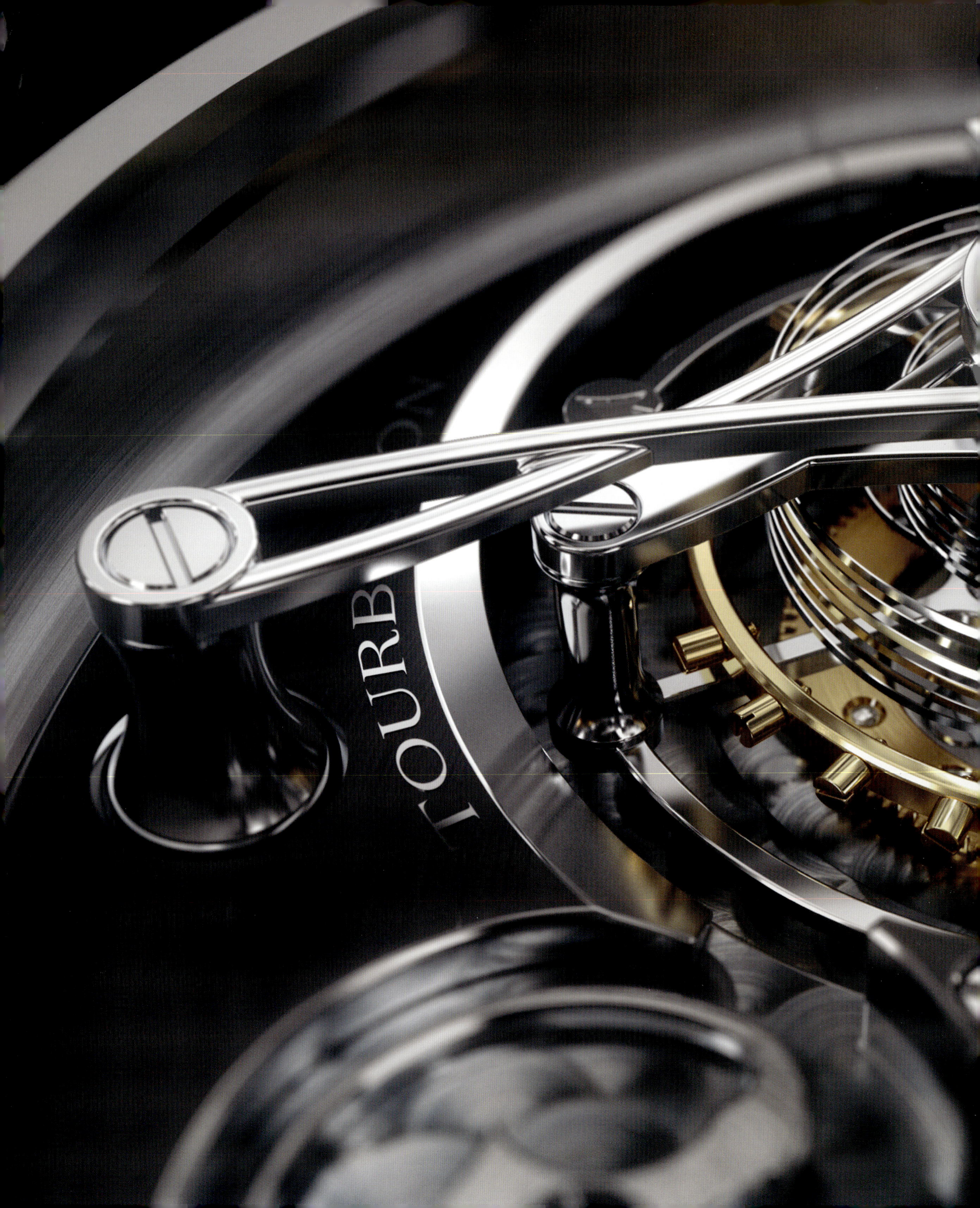
TOURB

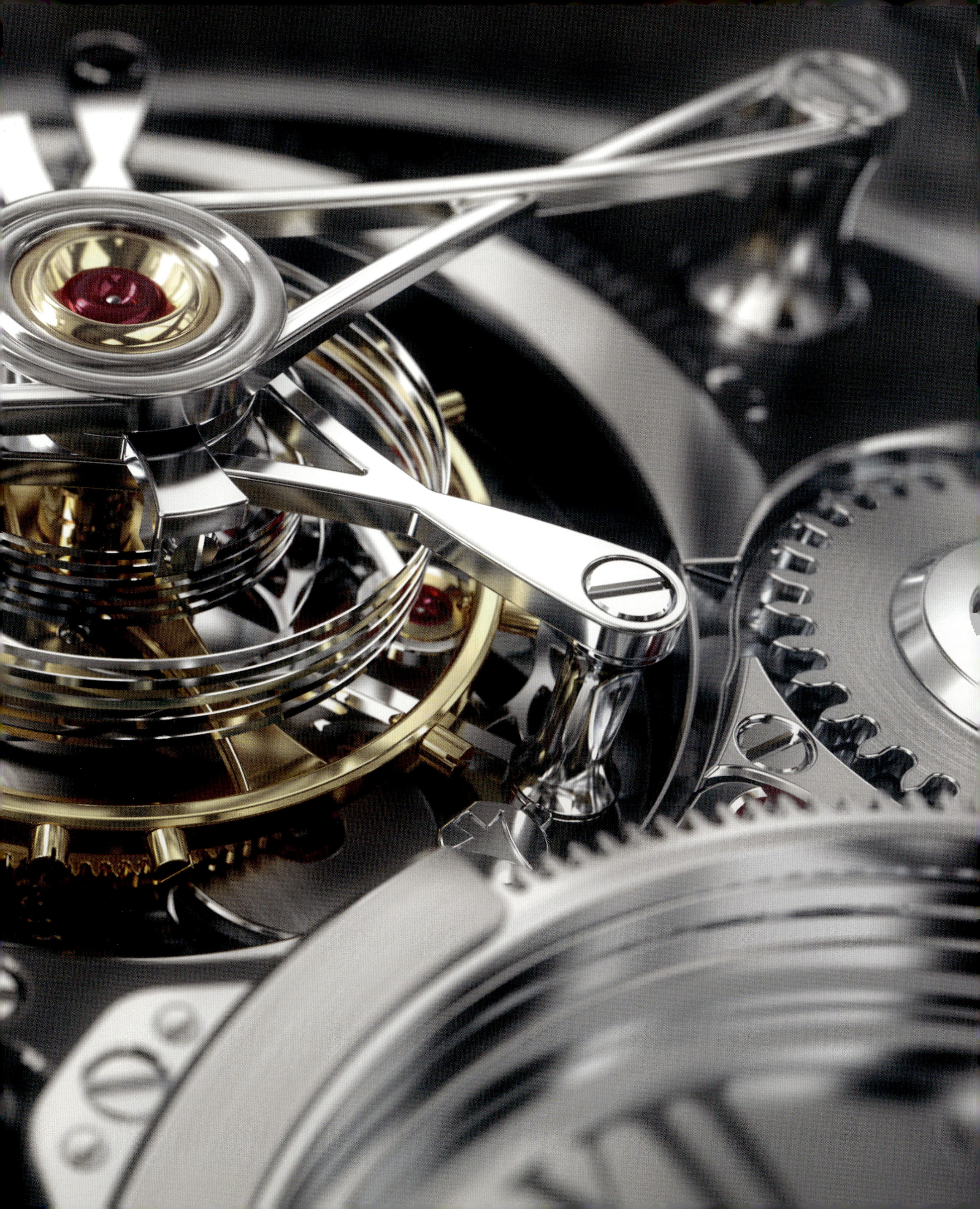

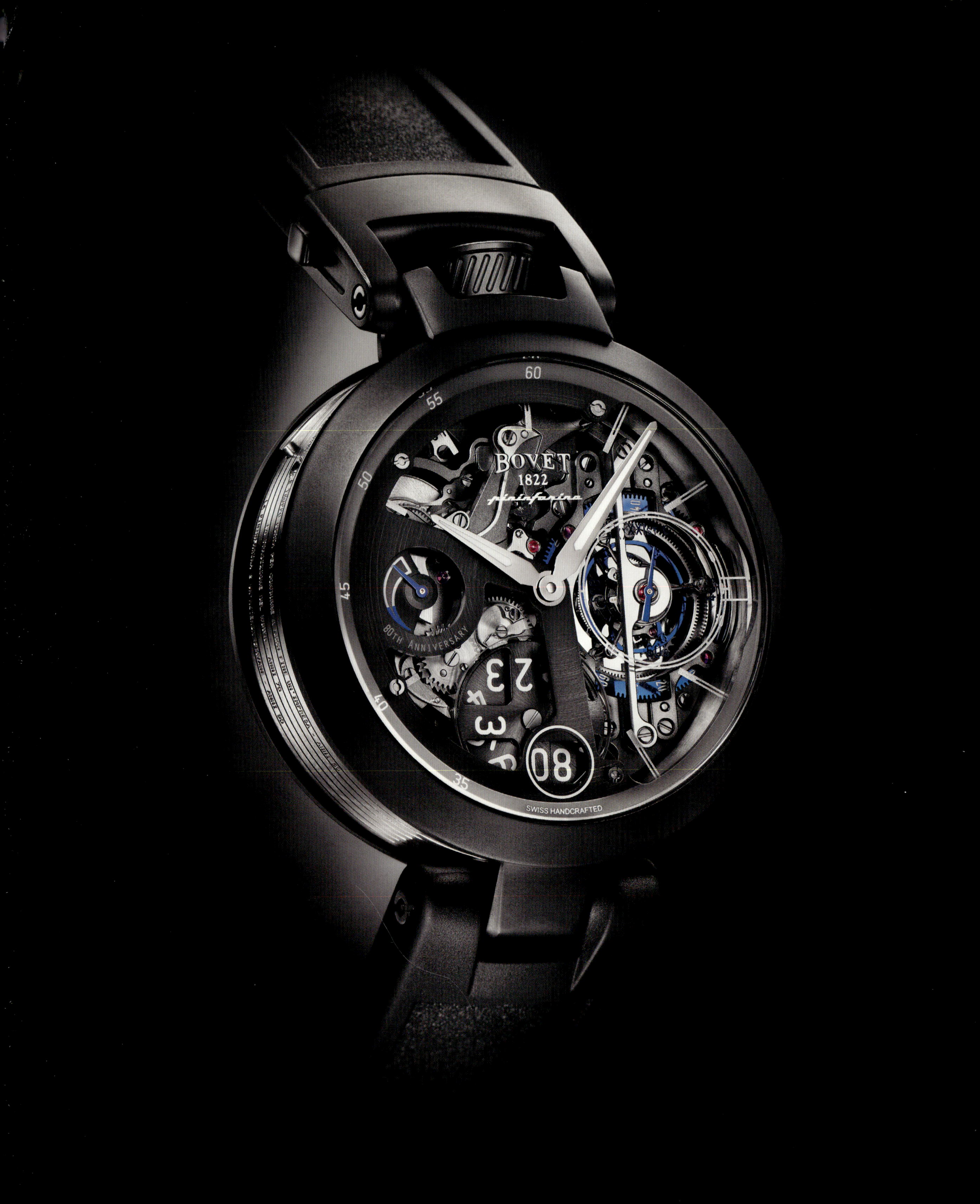
BOVET
1822
pininfarina
80TH ANNIVERSARY
SWISS HANDCRAFTED

BOVET 1822 — PININFARINA TOURBILLON OTTANTA

$ 364 000

UNLIKE MANY OF BOVET'S MORE CLASSICAL TIMEPIECES, THE TOURBILLON OTTANTA IS EXTREMELY MODERN IN DESIGN.

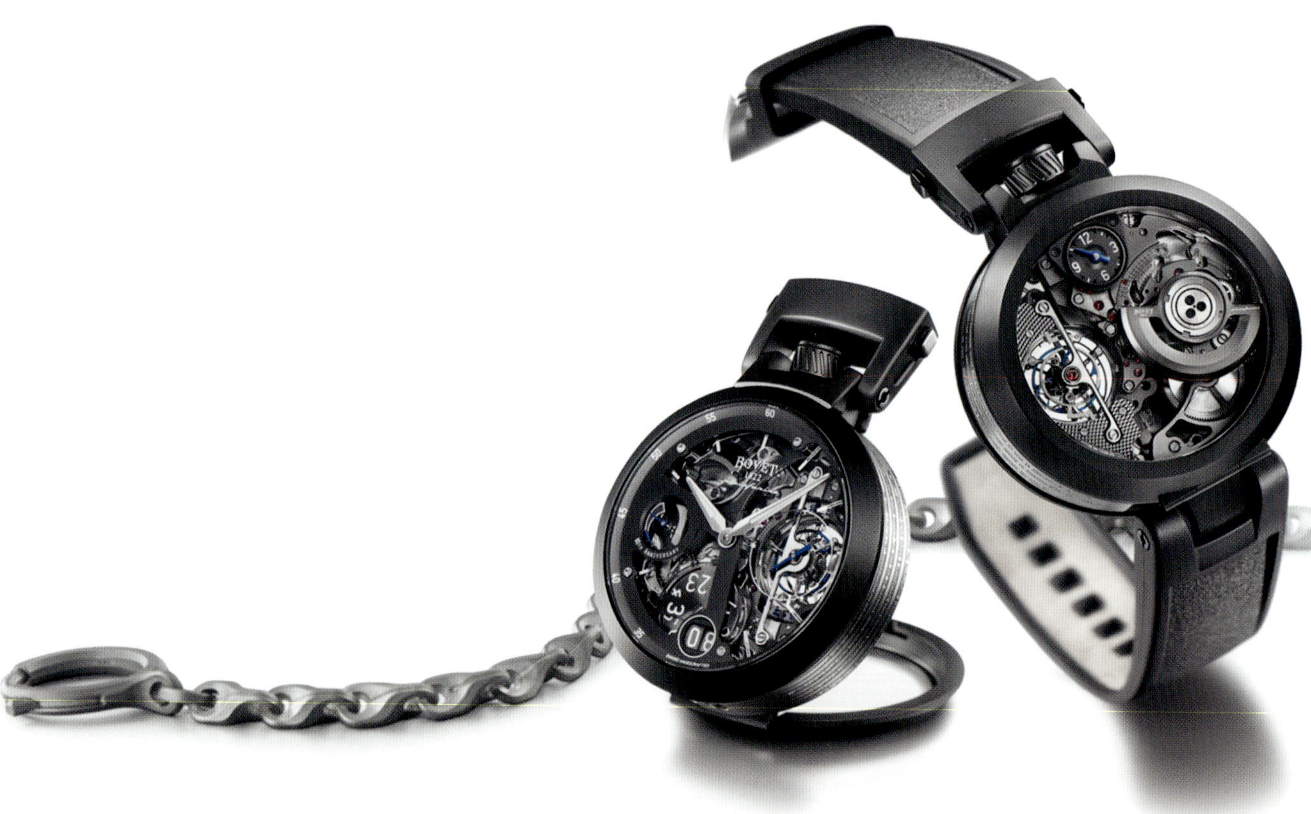

Italian automotive design house Pininfarina is most famous for the many Ferrari cars it is credited with having designed. Unlike most designers, Pininfarina's name appears on all the cars it has produced with its principal, Ferrari.

Pininfarina has also designed watches. The company has participated in a unique relationship with exclusive Swiss watchmaker Bovet in producing a range of interesting timepieces. Perhaps the most impressive Pininfarina watch by Bovet is the Tourbillon Ottanta, which Pininfarina designed to celebrate its 80th anniversary in 2010. The watch is named "Ottanta", or "80", to honour this anniversary, and only 80 pieces were produced.

Unlike many of Bovet's more classical timepieces, the Tourbillon Ottanta is extremely modern in design. It exists in three versions, mixing materials such as diamond-like carbon (DLC) coated steel, titanium, and 18k white or rose gold, to create different styles.

Common with many Bovet watches, is the "convertible" nature of the case, which allows the watch either to be worn on the wrist or to be removed and used as a pocket watch or small table clock. The Tourbillon Ottanta also allows the wearer to flip the case over so that either side may serve as the front.

Pininfarina designed the main dial to indicate the time, and to offer a big date display, a power reserve indicator, and a subsidiary seconds dial. Twist the case around and one can wear it while seeing the automatic winding rotor and spinning tourbillon, as well as a small hand that indicates only the hour. Very few timepieces offer such a variety of uses.

A close inspection of the side of the Tourbillon Ottanta's case reveals eight distinct messages engraved into the metal. Each of these messages refers to one of the eight decades of Pininfarina's history, and is written in Italian. For example, the phrase to celebrate the 1950s – "La vita di un uomo è troppo corta per condurre a buon fine un'impresa", which roughly translates as "the life of a man is too short to bring to fruition a company." Bovet and Pininfarina later continued their relationship, releasing subsequent watch models.

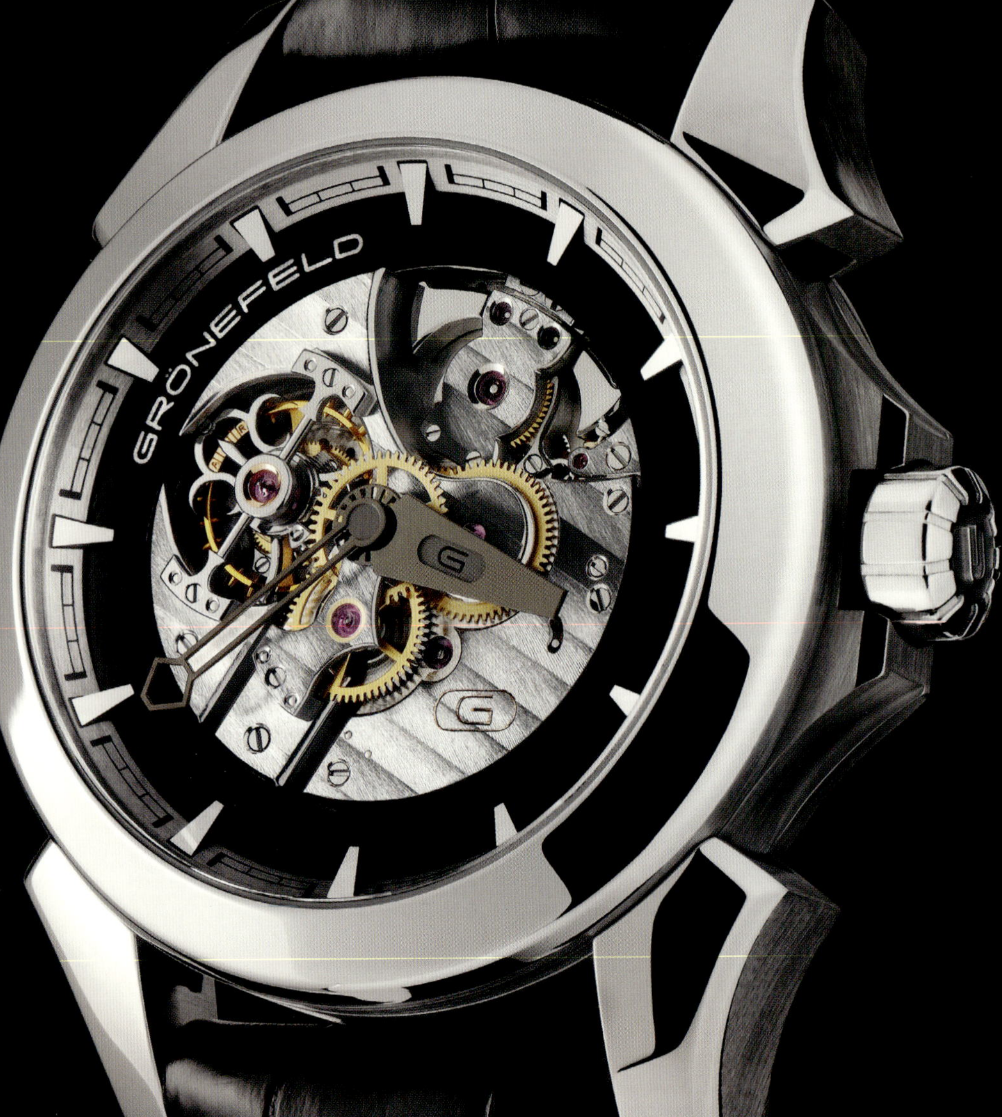
GRÖNEFELD

GRÖNEFELD — GTM-06 TOURBILLON MINUTE REPEATER

$ 374 500*

A HEALTHY AMOUNT OF DUTCH EXTROVERSION IS CONSPICUOUSLY NOTABLE IN THE DESIGN OF THE CASE AND DIAL.

Watch enthusiasts enjoy recognising the differences between timepieces made by different people across the world. An English timepiece will differ from a Swiss one, and the same goes for a German or French watch. These differences can take the form of how movements are constructed, particular decorative techniques, or the entire philosophy behind the design. Of course, it is the available variety of timepieces that keeps collectors so interested.

Brothers Bart and Tim Grönefeld, third generation watchmakers, are Dutch but studied in Switzerland. After working for a series of high-end Swiss brands, they decided to begin their own eponymous collection of watches from the Netherlands in 2008. Their first and, as of 2013, still most exclusive timepiece is the GTM-06 Tourbillon Minute Repeater.

A healthy amount of Dutch extroversion is conspicuously notable in the design of the case and dial. Wanting to make a name for themselves quickly, the dial of the GTM-06 displays its namesake complications without any hesitation, showing off the tourbillon as well as hammers for the minute repeater complication. For watch collectors, a tourbillon as well as a minute repeater are both highly prized features, and Grönefeld wanted to produce a traditional watch with a modern twist. They also wanted the musical notes of the minute repeater to sound as full as possible.

According to Grönefeld, considerable effort went into designing the case, so that the minute repeater chimes could be heard even by the elderly. This effort should be totally understandable to those who are familiar with the frequently minimal sound of most minute repeaters. The flamboyant lugs on the case aren't merely decorative, even though they are somewhat exaggerated versions of flared lugs seen on some vintage watches. The lugs are actually hollowed, and connected as minimally as possible to the rest of the watch, in order to maintain a better resonance-chamber effect in the case.

Grönefeld knows that high-end mechanical watches are acquired for pleasure more than utility, the presentation box of the GTM-06 Tourbillon Minute Repeater mirrors this. Also designed by Grönefeld, the box is designed for cigar smokers. A tray pulls out to reveal a variety of cigar cutters along with a customised black piano lacquered Davidoff lighter. The GTM-06 was only available in 18k red gold or platinum and only 20 were produced.

* Price based on watch in platinum

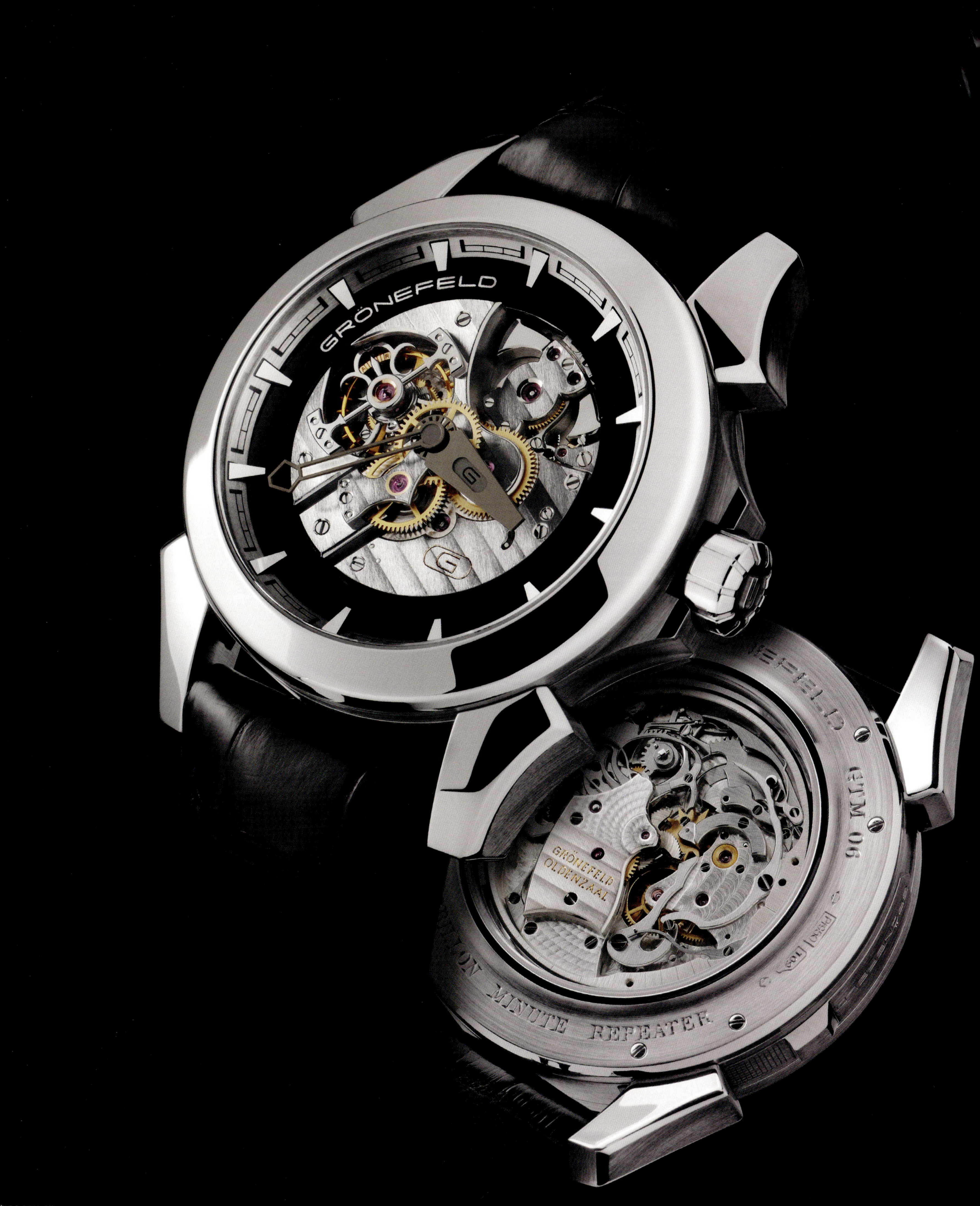
GRÖNEFELD
GRÖNEFELD
OLDENZAAL
GTM 06
MINUTE REPEATER

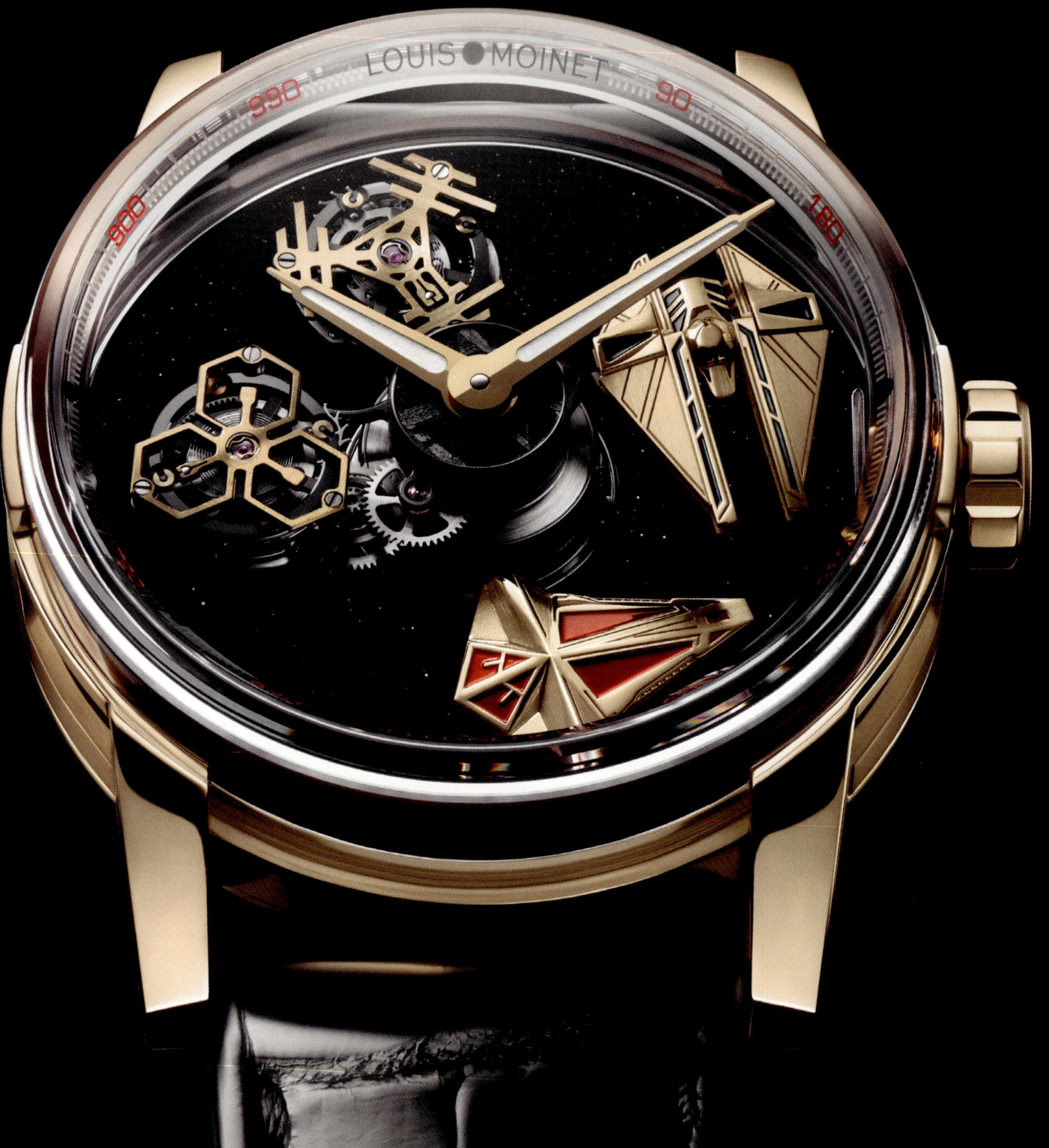

LOUIS MOINET — SPACE REVOLUTION

$ 380 000

Louis Moinet was originally an 18th-century watchmaker who was both an artist and a mechanical genius. He is credited with the invention of the first chronograph-style timepiece, as well as developing an aesthetic style for his work that today is referred to as "Jules Verne-esque". In modern times, the Louis Moinet name was resurrected and is now a richly avant-garde Swiss watchmaker that combines traditional mechanical intrigue with an old-world style showmanship and pizazz. The Louis Moinet Space Revolution is among their most contemporary compositions yet; thoroughly modern in its thematic inspiration, but also thoroughly classic in its decorative and mechanical execution.

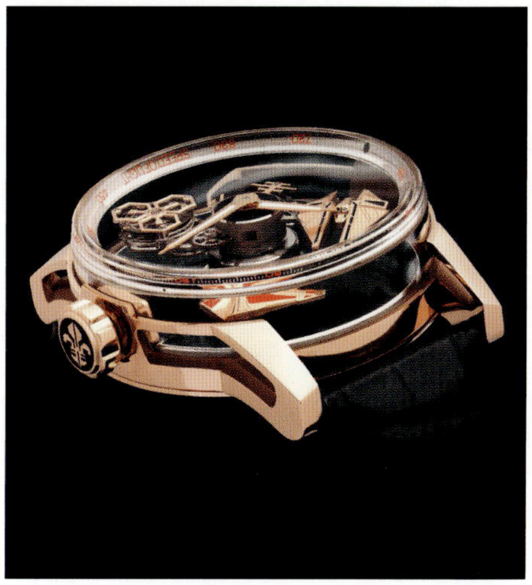

On an extremely basic level, the Space Revolution watch is a luxurious nod to the science-fiction worlds of both Star Wars and Star Trek. Fan enthusiasm is high for both otherwise-unrelated entertainment properties – both of which just so happen to feature imaginative space vehicles and action sequences. As such, the cavernous dial of the Space Revolution watch has a spacey aventurine stone face, above which float two tourbillon-ended arms with spaceships as counterweights, and remarkably sensible hands (given the context) to indicate the time.

From a technical perspective, the Space Revolution watch places dual-tourbillon regulation systems on respective revolving arms (Louis Moinet calls these flying satellite double tourbillons). As these arms move in opposite directions from one another around the central axis of the dial, the spacecraft motifs placed on counterweights appear to fly to and from one another, "battling it out" in this high horological space drama. Carefully decorated by hand, the miniature space vessels echo those in the Star Wars and Star Trek universes. The tourbillon cages are further designed to match the particular science-fiction theme aesthetic.

The Space Revolution watch itself is about 44mm wide and topped with a tall box-style sapphire crystal that allows for an expansive view of the dial inside where all the action is. Powering the watch is a manually wound mechanical movement which, despite the high torque requirements of the mechanism, still offers 48 hours of power reserve while running at an operational frequency of 3Hz. Louis Moinet developed a lever system on the rear of the case which allows the crown to be switched from winding the mainspring to setting the time.

Louis Moinet is by no means the first (or last) traditional-style watchmaker to produce a vividly detailed and equally ambitious timepiece-homage to the science-fiction enthusiast. Watchmakers are often also artistic engineers – a personality that tends to go hand-in-hand with sci-fi fandom.

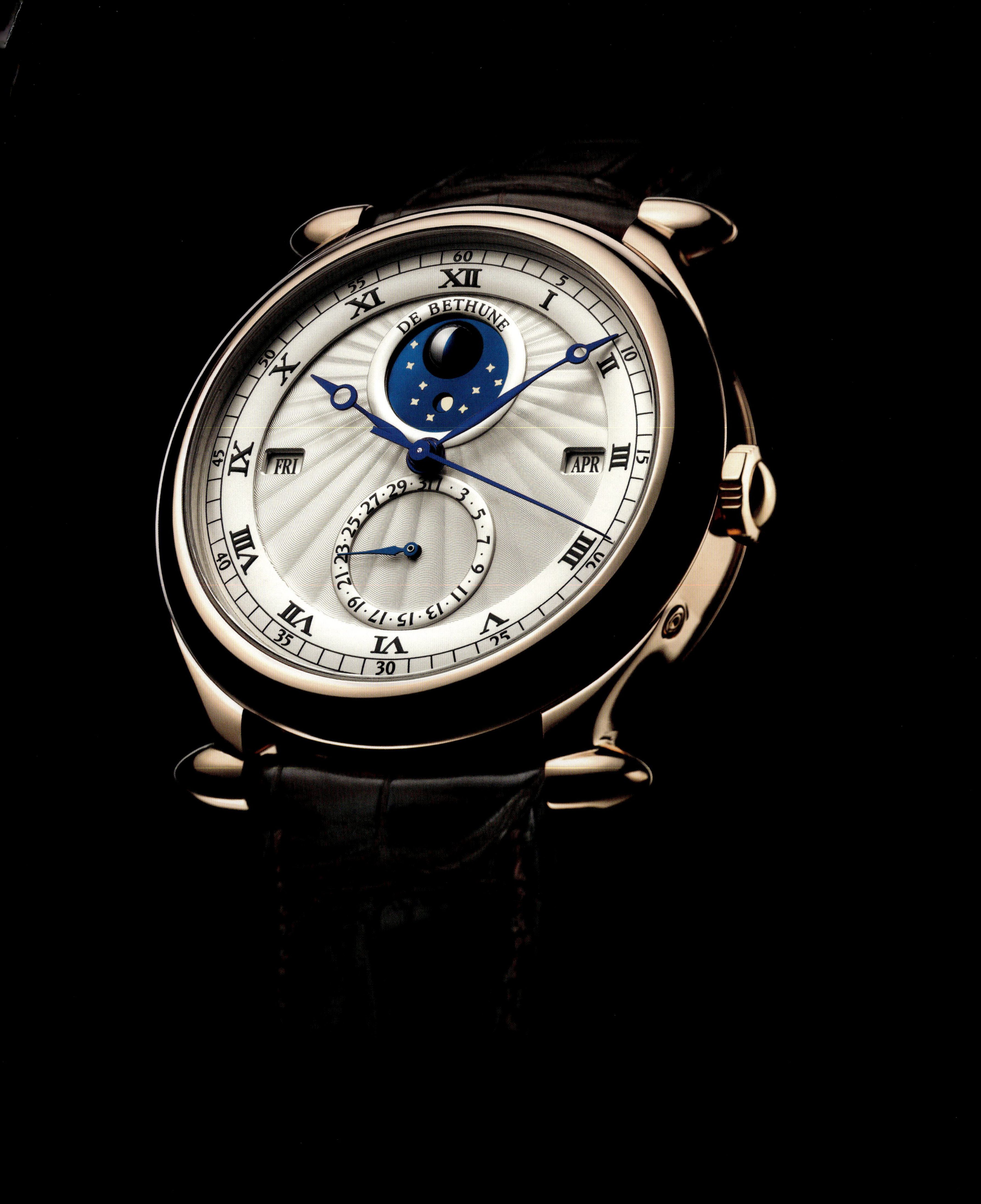
DE BETHUNE
FRI
APR

DE BETHUNE — DB16 TOURBILLON REGULATOR

$ 388 000

IT IS TRULY A WATCH LOVER'S WATCH, BECAUSE IT BLENDS SO MANY ELEMENTS TOGETHER SO BEAUTIFULLY AND HARMONIOUSLY.

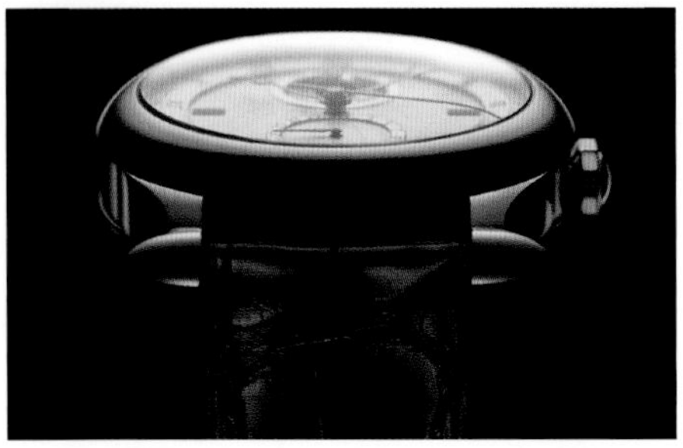

A detail difficult to miss, in this and many other De Bethune watches, is the Star Trek Federation logo integrated into the design of the movement. This is no accident, as De Bethune represents a newer breed of prestigious mechanical watchmakers, that seamlessly combine today's culture and that of historic, traditional watchmaking.

Those familiar with De Bethune, quickly realize that the DB16 Tourbillon Regulator is actually one of their most classically designed timepieces. It fully incorporates most of the brand's strengths, and appeals to even the most particular of watch collectors.

There is a spacey quality to the design of the watch, as De Bethune designers are highly influenced by the world of science fiction. De Bethune incorporates modern technology in its watches as much as possible. A good example in the DB16 is the balance wheel in the movement, that is almost completely made of silicon. Several high-end watchmakers rely on silicon for its frictionless operation and resistance to temperature and magnetism, but De Bethune is perhaps the only one to use it for the balance wheel itself – which is the main regulating organ of the entire movement. It is one of the lightest balance wheels produced, weighting just 0.18 grams.

Use of silicon allows the balance wheel to operate faster, translating into a more accurate movement. A detail pointing to the past, is the use of a jumping – or "dead" – seconds hand that ticks like a quartz movement-based watch, even though this timepiece is purely mechanical. The movement in the DB16 also contains a perpetual calendar, three-dimensional Moon-phase indicator, power reserve indicator, and tourbillon. The features are elegantly laid out, preserving a pristine sense of balance in the dial.

Blending traditional decorative technique with a modern design, the almost 500-part movement inside the DB16 Tourbillon Regulator features a design unlike anything else in the industry – save for other De Bethune calibers. It is truly a watch lover's watch, because it blends so many elements together so beautifully and harmoniously.

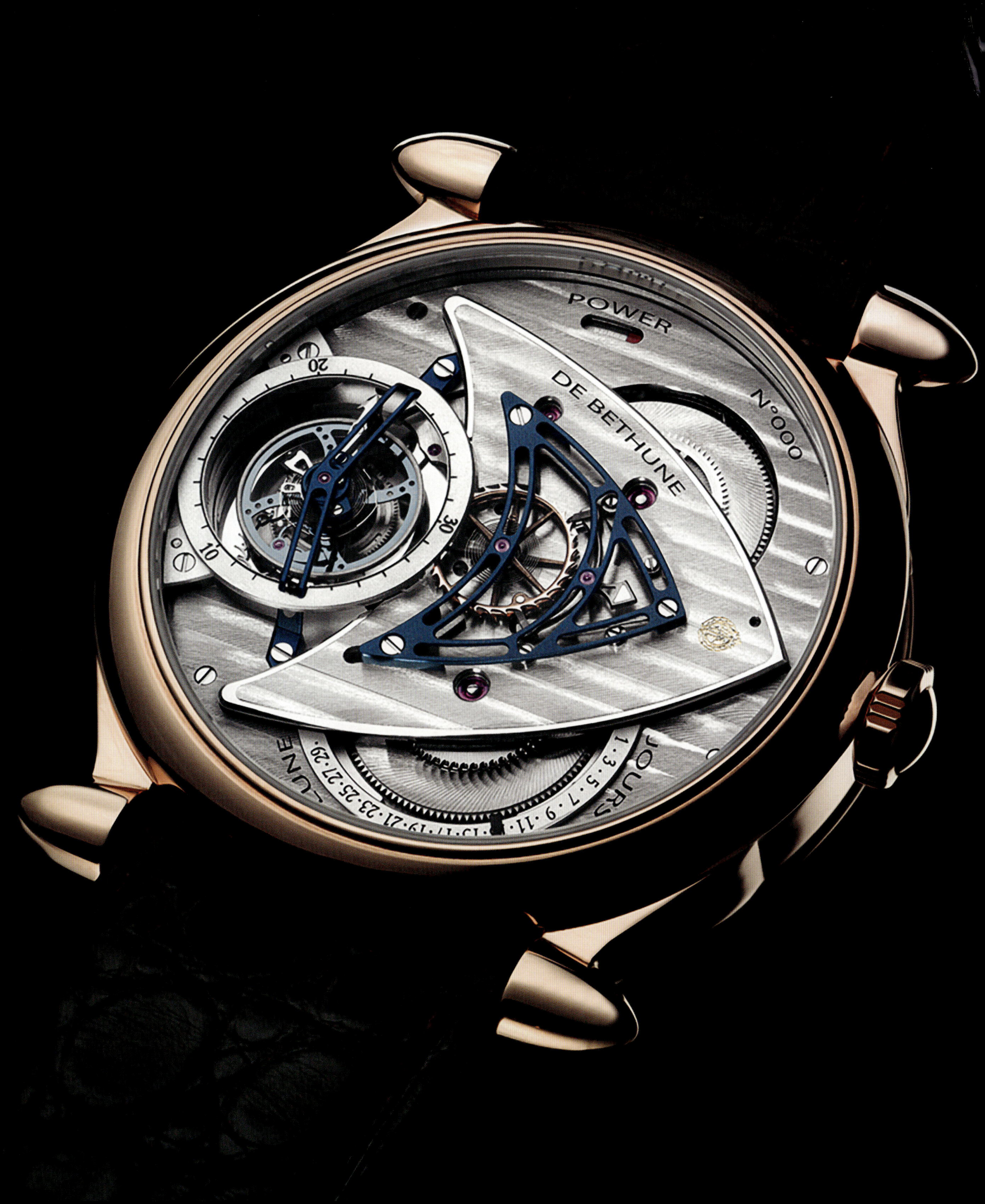
POWER
DE BETHUNE
N°000
JOURS

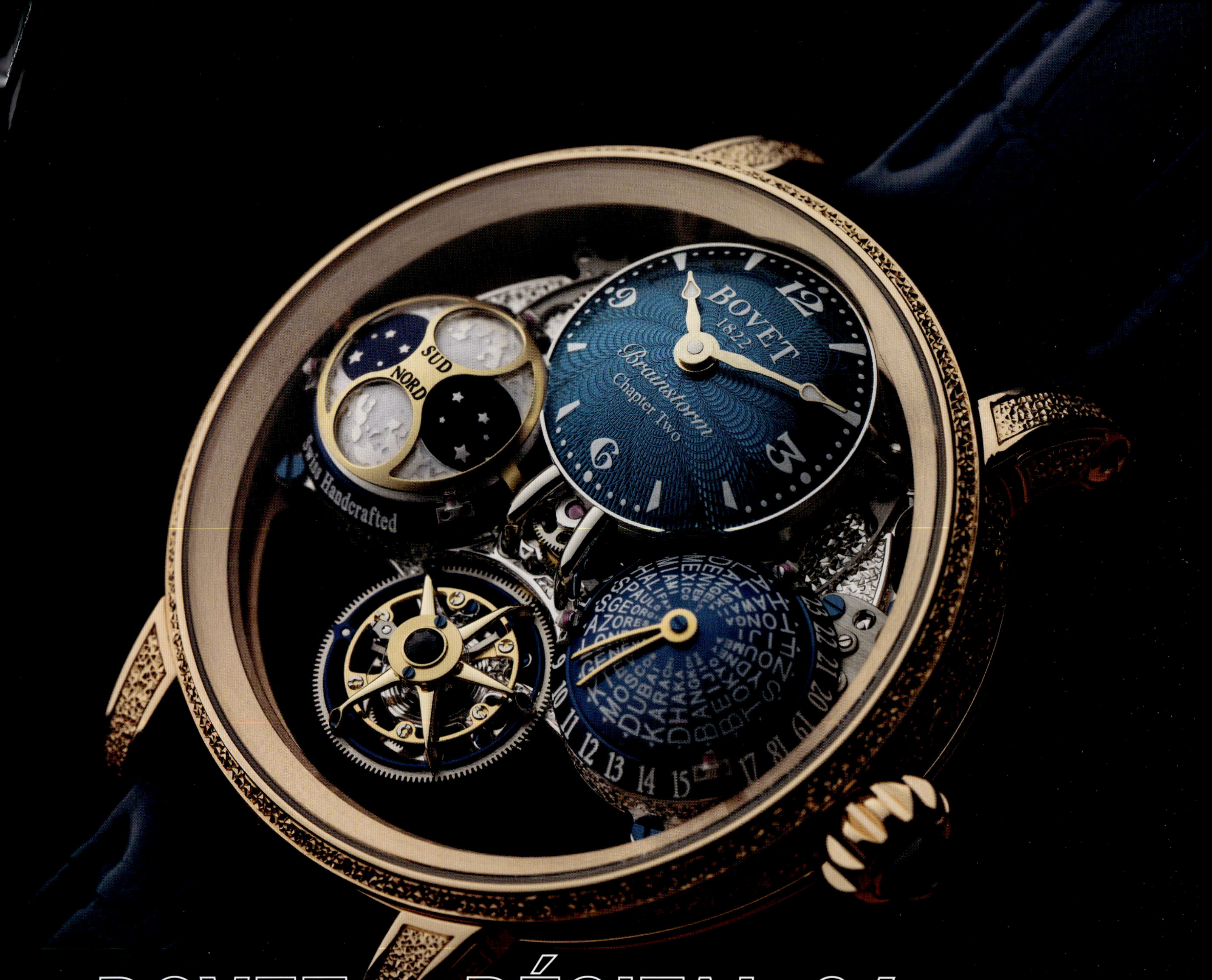

BOVET – RÉCITAL 26 BRAINSTORM® CHAPTER TWO

$ 394 500

The downward-sloping case of the Bovet Récital watch collection was originally inspired by the shape of classic writing desks. This is in part a homage to the notion that many of today's most impressive mechanical watches are still designed and assembled – in large part – by hand. Making these traditional mechanical luxuries contemporary is a secondary artform, which today involves modern materials and, in many instances, bright colours. The Bovet Récital 26 Brainstorm® Chapter Two is an excellent example of classic meeting modern on the wrist.

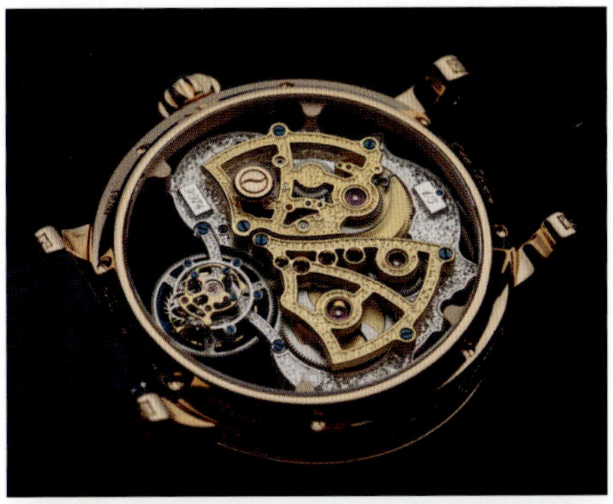

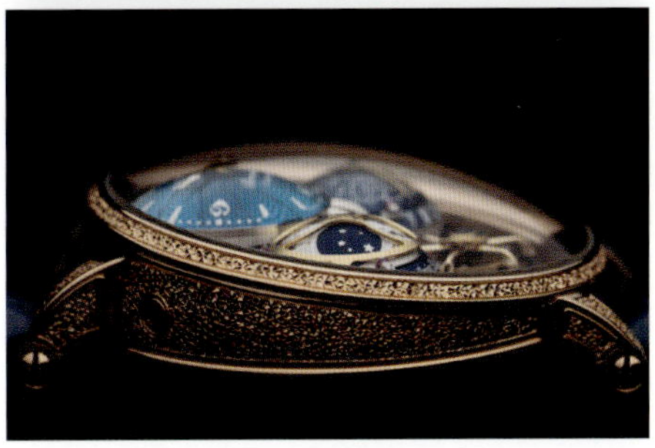

The in-house made mechanical movement was designed from the ground up, with presentation in mind. The watch itself does not have a traditional face, but rather a series of domed dials that indicate the time, a world-time complication, a northern and southern hemisphere Moon-phase indicator, as well as a flying tourbillon – all mounted on carefully decorated and finished metal parts.

The dials are framed by a mostly sapphire-crystal case, which allows for an even more dramatic view of the manually wound movement from all angles – including the sides. Where the Chapter Two really makes changes on the original Récital 26 Brainstorm® watch is precisely in its dramatic display, which in addition to the carefully machined and polished sapphire-crystal 47.8mm-wide case, includes a variety of bespoke colours – as though wearing a timepiece of such monetary value on one's wrist was not peacockery enough.

Another ode to modern tastes in luxury watches is Bovet's liberal use of luminescent material for the Récital 26 Brainstorm® Chapter Two. Many versions feature luminescent dials, including the distinctive Moon-phase indicator. The luminescent material, combined with the ability of the sapphire-crystal case to allow light to charge the surfaces, results in an impressive dial display when viewed in the dark – a rare feat in such high-end horology.

The mostly transparent case offers additional advantages. For instance, a discreet linear power-reserve indicator display on the side of the case lets the wearer know when to wind the watch – which offers five full days of running time when fully wound. Wearers can further admire the hand-decorated surfaces of the movement from all angles, which was designed to be as deep and three-dimensional as possible – an aesthetic somewhat distinctive from most wristwatch movements, which are usually engineered to be flat. Only high notes and steep crescendos at this recital of horological technique.

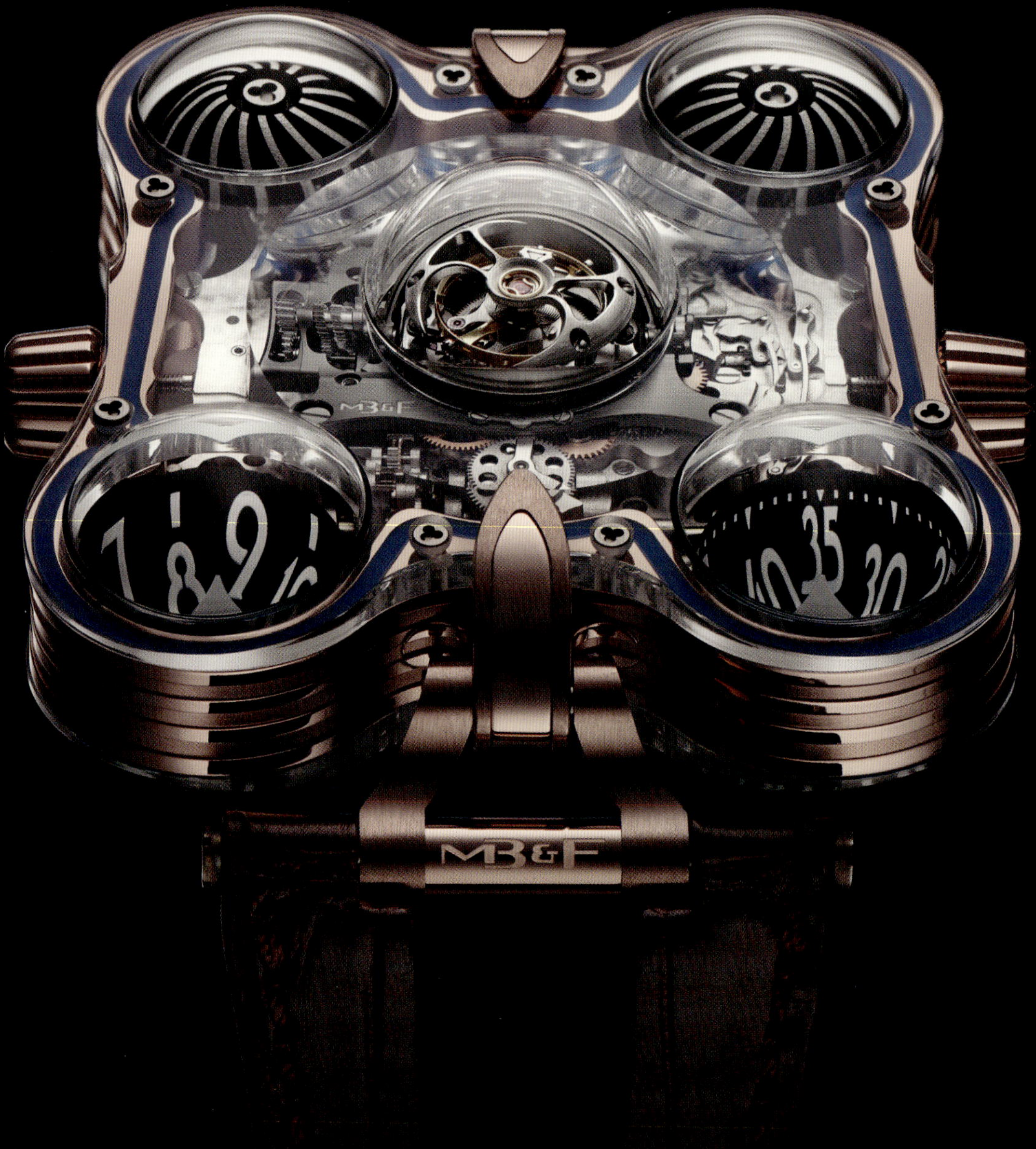

MB&F – HOROLOGICAL MACHINE NO. 6 SAPPHIRE VISION

$ 398 000

When MB&F originally released the sixth member of the Horological Machine wrist-worn mechanical art family, its official nickname was the "HM6 Space Pirate". Swoopy titanium walls with an opening-and-closing shield over the tourbillon were given a biomorphic case design, making for one of the most aesthetically controversial ultra-luxury designs of recent times. Not long after its release, and if only to extend the conversation about the HM6 Space Pirate, MB&F followed-up with the HM6 SV (Sapphire Vision).

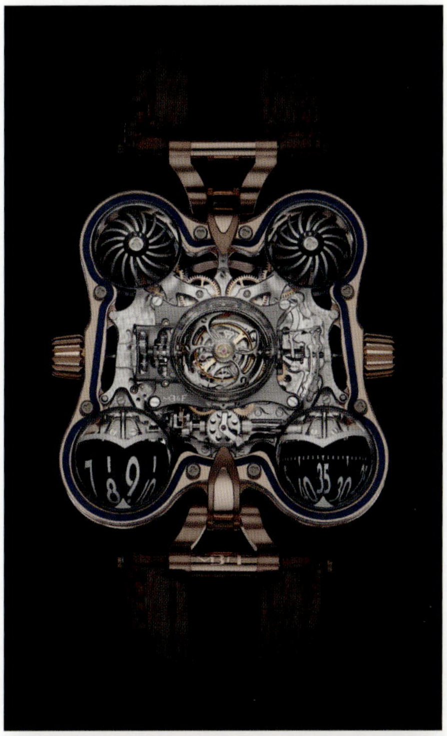

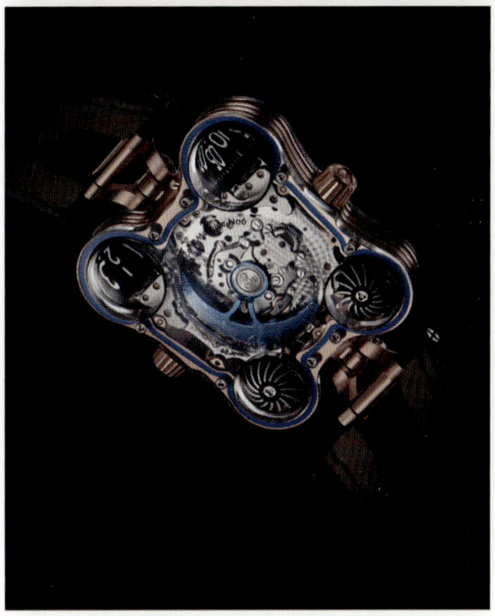

The HM6 Sapphire Vision offers an entirely unique fantasy space-vessel inspired design, whose goal is to show off as much of the in-house engineered movement as possible using large pieces of carefully cut-and-polished synthetic sapphire crystal. MB&F custom-creates each and every family of mechanical movements that it produces, and most agree that the Horological Machine No. 6's flying tourbillon with turbines system is among its most ambitious. Conceived to be almost entirely symmetrical, the 475-part automatic movement uses spherical turbines to regulate the self-winding system, as well as spherical domes in order to indicate the time. Using the ancillary crown, the user can manually crank open or close the titanium shield over the centrally mounted flying tourbillon. This latter detail is mostly for visual amusement, but MB&F is quick to point out that shielding the tourbillon from light does indeed assist in preventing necessary oils from aging too quickly. At MB&F, even all the toys benefit from functional explanations.

On the wrist, the HM6 SV sits less like a wristwatch and more like a ship that has docked on the wearer's arm, being 50mm wide, almost 23mm thick and 51mm long – seemingly capable of taking off for interplanetary travel at a moment's notice. MB&F produced two versions of the Sapphire Vision: one with a base metal case in 950 platinum and another in 18k red gold. Much of the Sapphire Vision's case, however, is sapphire crystal, which together is derived from 11 separate sapphire crystal segments – nine of which are small domes. The case alone is comprised of 78 parts, including the attractively coloured gaskets which are integral for water resistance purposes.

With its hand-decorated and assembled movement patently visible through both sides of the HM6 Sapphire Vision's case, the otherwise complicated timepiece only indicates the time. Hours are displayed on the left rotating dome, while minutes are displayed on the adjacent dome. Pure and not at all simple, this product is all about celebrating the artistry and imagination incumbent in so much of today's best ultra-high-end timepiece designs. MB&F produced just 20 pieces of the HM6 SV in total.

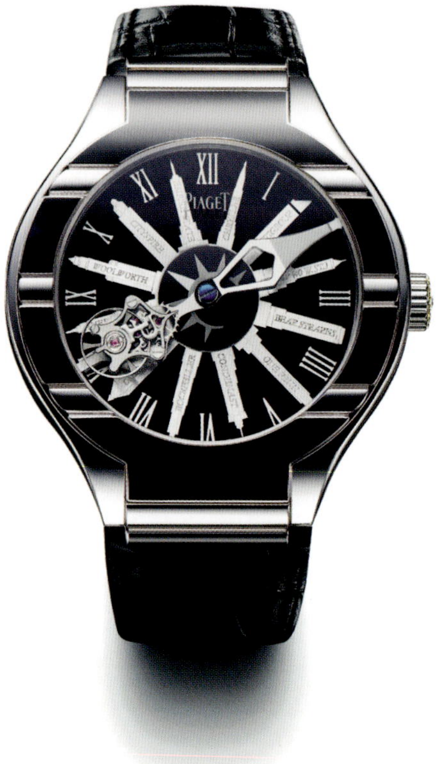

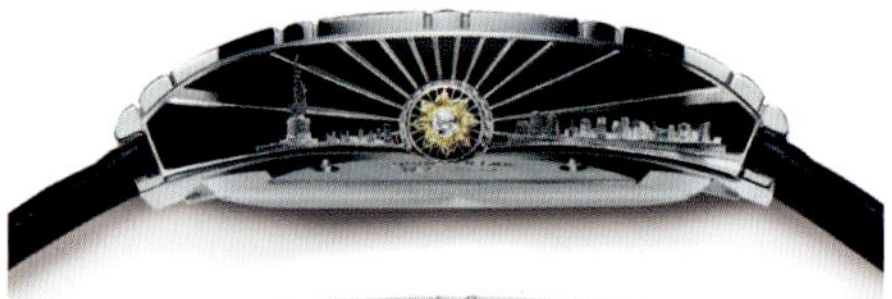

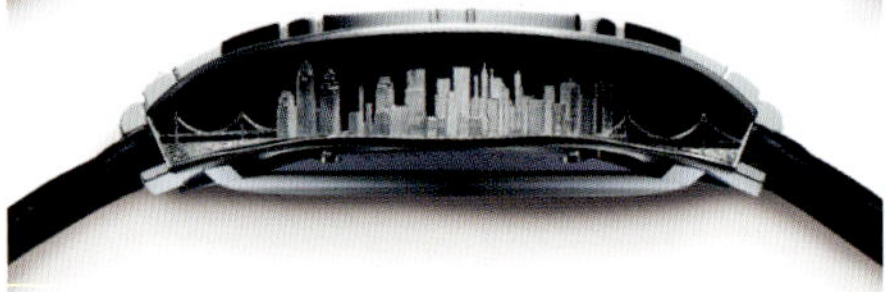

PIAGET — POLO TOURBILLON RELATIF NEW YORK

$400 000

Piaget is sometimes less known for exclusive watchmaking and more for beautifully ornate jewellery and items of diamond-decorated beauty. While the modern Piaget has an elegant veneer well-suited to red carpets, its history lies directly with the production of mechanical watch movements that started in the 1870s.

It was not until 1943 that Piaget produced a timepiece with its own name on it. For much of the 20th century it focused on exclusive luxury watches with a distinct brand focus on producing very thin mechanical movements – something that continues to be prized today.

With a spirit of technical excellence, Piaget continues to conceive unique mechanical movements such as the Relatif Tourbillon found in the Polo Tourbillon Relatif New York. In the centre of the dial is a small disc used to indicate the hours, and above it is a (comparatively speaking) massive structure that serves as both the minute hand and the mount for the flying tourbillon. As the minute hand moves so does the tourbillon as it spins on its own axis each minute, as well as once around the entire dial each hour.

Piaget developed a unique series of limited edition Polo Tourbillon Relatif watches, made to honour various themes – most notably cities. The first of these celebrated Paris, and then other cities such as Venice, as well as New York City. The 18k white gold Polo collection case and dial was decorated with black enamel in order to enhance the contrast of colours. Easily the most impressive element of the watch, aside from the movement, is how Piaget decided to reference Manhattan.

Twelve of New York's tallest buildings (at the time of the watch's release in 2011) serve as hour markers on the art-deco style dial. The sides of the case are even more unique, as Piaget used a precision laser engraver to carefully draw two scenes from the city. The left side features a skyline view of Manhattan, complete with two bridges, while the right side displays a different view and focuses on the Statue of Liberty. Piaget produced just three examples of the Polo Tourbillon Relatif New York watch.

CREDOR – SPRING DRIVE MINUTE REPEATER

$400 000

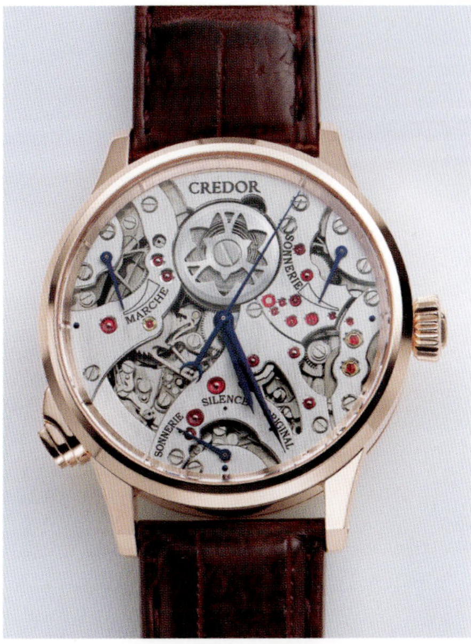

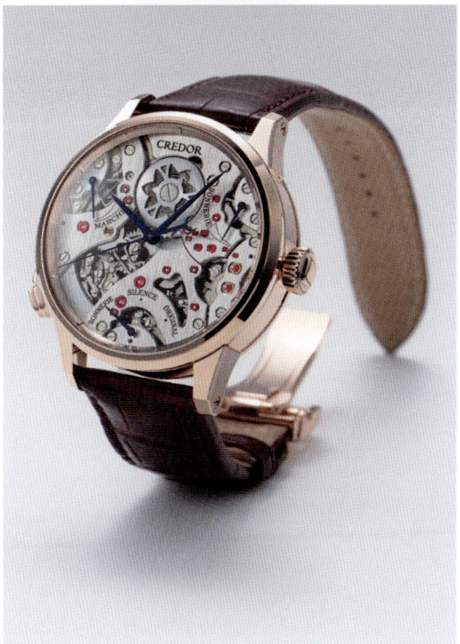

When Toyota wanted to begin selling luxury automobiles in America, they needed to develop an entirely new brand called Lexus, because Americans simply didn't want to spend a lot of money on a brand that also features budget models.

The same is somewhat true for Japanese watchmaker Seiko. While Seiko products can be very accessibly priced, the brand does not limit itself to only mainstream goods. Seiko produces some of the finest made watches in the world under the names Grand Seiko, and the Japan-only brand named Credor. As the Seiko name is often synonymous with high-quality but low-priced timepieces, their most exclusive models are typically reserved for the most knowledgeable of aficionados.

At the apex of the Credor brand is a model known as the Spring Drive Minute Repeater. Highly sophisticated, the watch blends Japanese cultural design, and what is arguably an improvement on a series of traditional mechanical complications. At its heart, the watch contains a system known as Spring Drive, which took Seiko about 30 years to develop.

Spring Drive is a system using a quartz oscillator, inside a mechanical movement, that replaces a traditional balance wheel. Why? Quartz oscillators exist inside today's quartz movements and offer extremely high accuracy, but enthusiasts dismiss them, because they are battery powered versus spring powered, and are rather inexpensive to produce. Seiko wanted to create a hybrid movement that incorporated the allure of a mechanical watch with the accuracy of a quartz watch – Spring Drive is just that.

Built on a Spring Drive base, Seiko's aim was to produce the world's most user-friendly and useful minute repeater. So they produced a decimal repeater that strikes every hour, every 10 minutes, and every minute. Most minute repeaters use 15 minute increments, which are, mathematically, more difficult to decipher.

The Credor Minute Repeater was released in 2011, as a follow-up to the also musically-themed Credor Sonnerie from 2006. In that latter model, to emphasise the most beautiful sound possible, Seiko designed a bowl-shaped bell that, when hit with the hammers, results in a fuller sound than the bar-style gongs used in most Swiss minute repeater watches. The Sonnerie, however, had a closed case back, and with the Minute Repeater, Seiko returned to an open display, offering, an expansive view of the totally hand-made movement.

The piece has subtle Japanese cultural elements. An open section on the dial is meant to resemble a silhouette of a flying hawk, and the motif on the mainspring barrel is of a Japanese bellflower. Only three Credor Minute Repeater are produced per year.

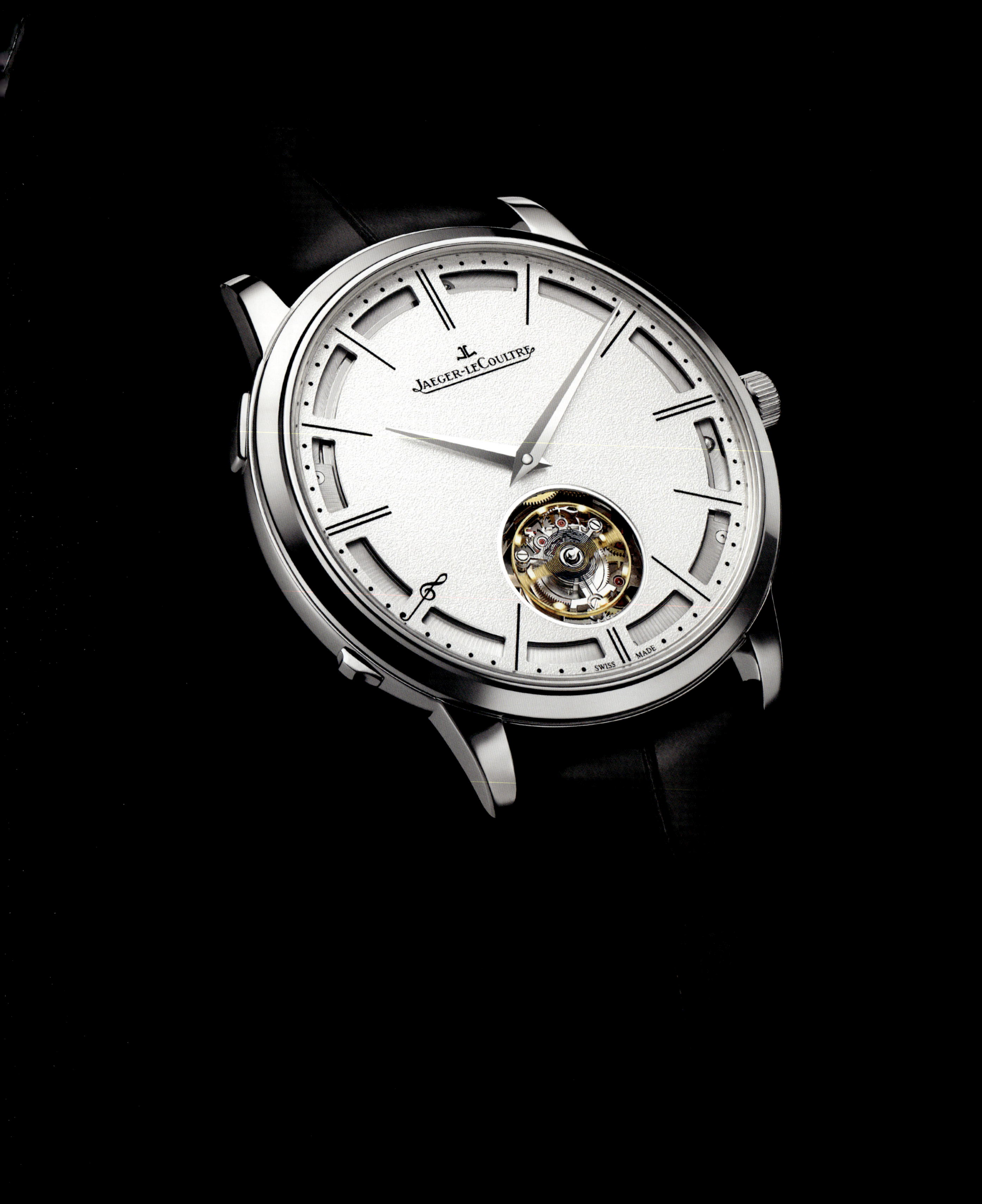
JAEGER-LECOULTRE
SWISS MADE

JAEGER-LECOULTRE — MASTER ULTRA-THIN MINUTE REPEATER FLYING TOURBILLON HYBRIS MECHANICA II

$ 403 000

ULTRA-THIN WATCHES — IN THE PAST, AS TODAY — REMAIN THE DOMAIN OF ONLY THE MOST ACCOMPLISHED OF WATCHMAKERS.

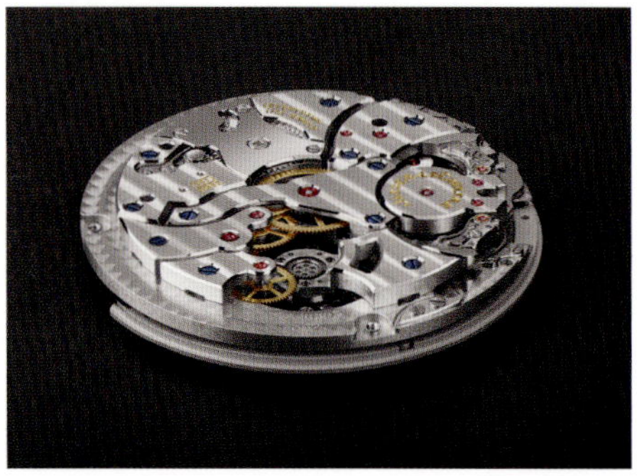

Ask most master watchmakers which timepieces are the most challenging to produce, and many will frown at the thought of assembling "ultra-thin" models. It isn't that all ultra-thin timepieces are vividly complex (even though this Jaeger-LeCoultre certainly is), but rather that dealing with minute tolerances, and the fact that even the most innocent of errors can entirely prevent a watch from working, add to the headache of merely putting these products together. Ultra-thin watches – in the past, as today – remain the domain of only the most accomplished of watchmakers.

There is no specific number that positions a timepiece as "thin" or "ultra-thin"; instead the description is relative to other timepieces. At 7.8mm thick (and 41mm wide), this elegantly simple Jaeger-LeCoultre watch case is thin. What easily makes it "ultra-thin" is the inclusion of a 4.8mm-thick movement, which contains an automatic-winding mechanism, flying tourbillon, and sophisticated minute-repeater system.

Whereas most luxury timepieces in this price category are understandably showy, the Hybris Mechanica 11 (as it is often known among enthusiasts) is understated, with a "stealth-wealth" personality, making it most appealing to experienced aficionados who understand the rarity of such a product. In order to produce such a thin, musical movement, Jaeger-LeCoultre first needed to position the automatic rotor around the periphery of the mechanism as opposed to behind it. Doing so also allows for the wearer to appreciate an unhindered view of the decorated German-Silver movement, which is visible through the rear of the watch.

Minute repeaters are watches that chime on demand to deliver an audio version of the current time using a simple musical code that the listener counts. Minute repeaters must be loud enough – something that always presents an enormous challenge to designers. To increase the volume of the minute repeater, Jaeger-LeCoultre first created perforated holes in the dial of the watch to expand the size of the resonance chamber. Second, they connected the gong system (that the hammers hit in order to create the chimes) to the case itself – as opposed to simply leaving it separate within the 18k white-gold case. A window at 6 o'clock displays the spinning tourbillon-style regulation system which rounds out the high-end package.

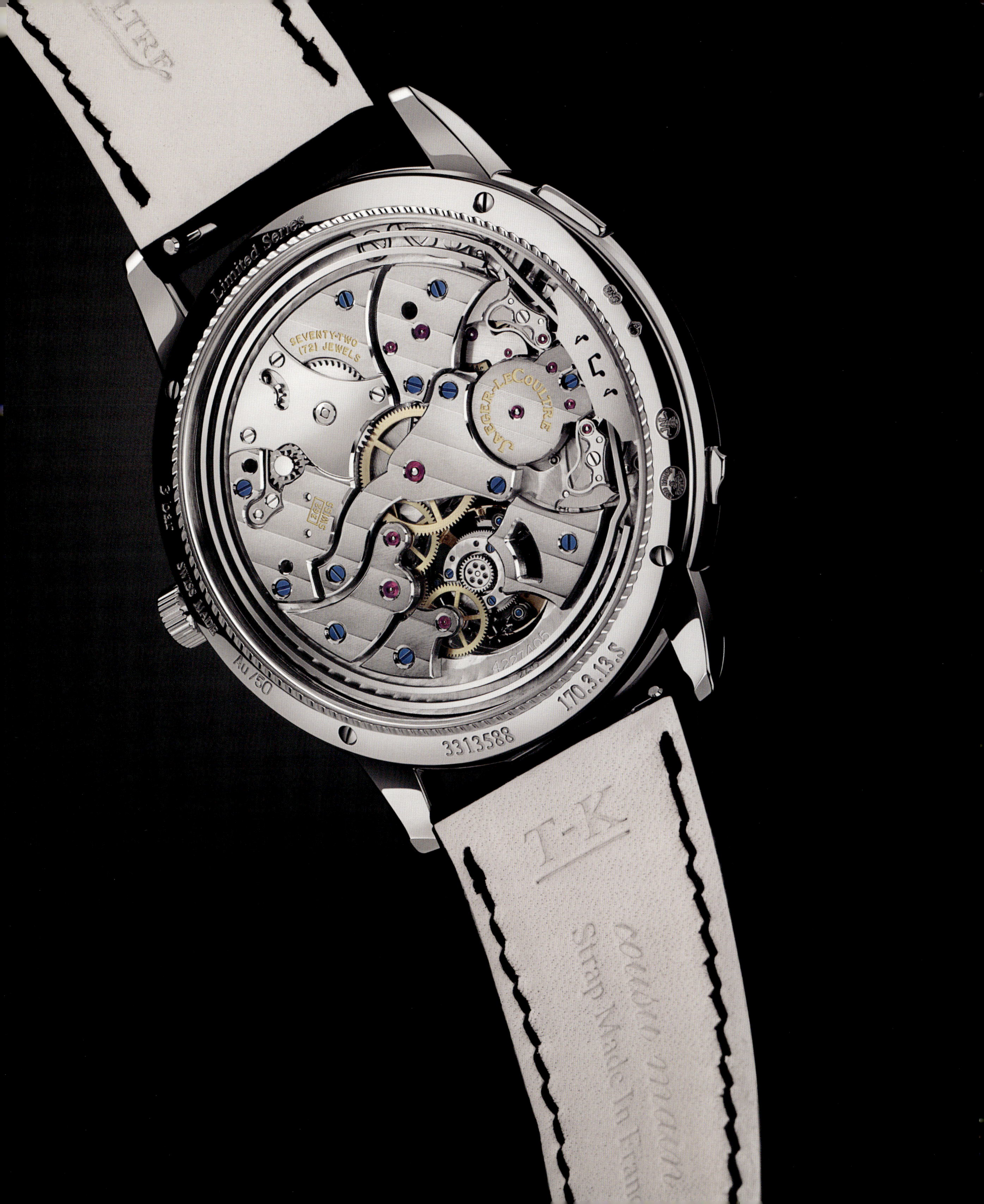
Limited Series
SEVENTY-TWO
(72) JEWELS
JAEGER-LECOULTRE
SWISS MADE
170.3.13.S
3313588
T-K

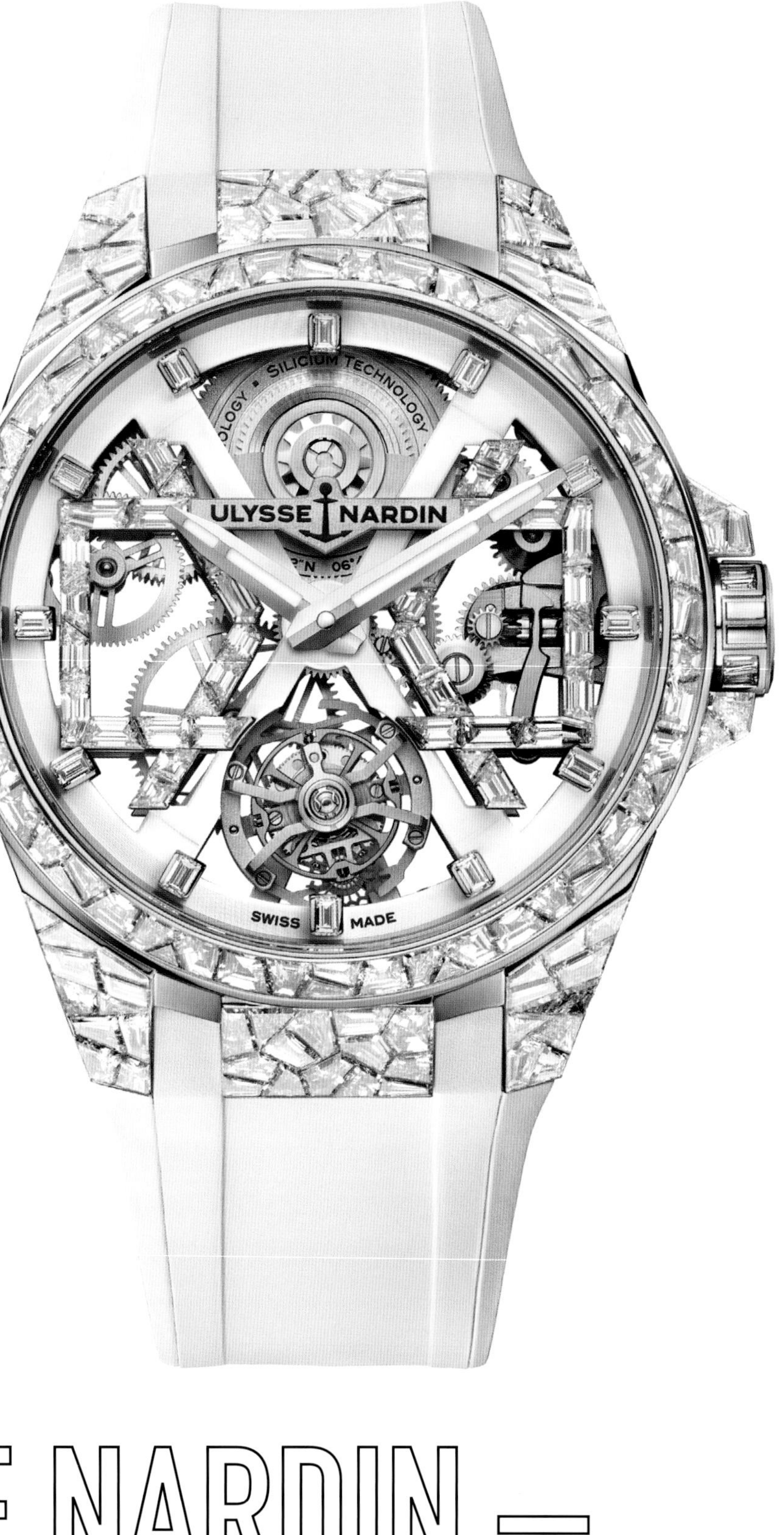

ULYSSE NARDIN — SPARKLING BLAST

$ 410 000

At the centre of the Ulysse Nardin Blast watch is a set of symbols including an "X" that cuts through a superimposed rectangular box. The Swiss brand readily admits that the "X" in the Blast product family is meant to suggest a variety of rebellious themes to the timepiece consumer public, but here specifically, the "X" appears to be cutting through the box itself. This would indicate that, while the watch exists within the lines of what a traditional mechanical timepiece is meant to be, it also defies certain rules and conventions. This is among the more poetic ways that some historic names in old world horology attempt to appeal to younger audiences.

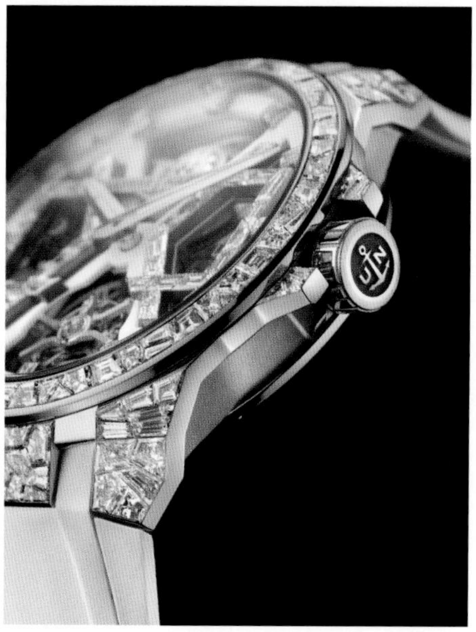

The Blast series itself comes in a 45mm-wide case with a symmetrically designed and skeletonised in-house made automatic mechanical movement that features a contemporary-looking flying tourbillon at the 6 o'clock position on the case. The tourbillon-style regulation system uses silicon technology, which has major benefits over traditional metal components. While silicon components are now more common in the high-luxury space, it was actually Ulysse Nardin who first introduced silicon watch-movement parts in the early 2000s when first debuting the Freak timepiece collection.

Somewhat hidden among the multi-layered and high open-worked watch movement, the solid platinum automatic micro-rotor, that winds the watch as it moves around on the wearer's wrist, is placed on top of the mainspring barrel located just under 12 o'clock on the dial.

Ulysse Nardin's Blast tourbillon watches actually have a relatively reasonable entry-level price of under $50,000 USD. That number increases considerably with the Sparkling Blast version of the timepiece, which is the humble name for a watch covered in diamonds. This high-jewellery version of the Blast adopts the uncommon approach of a more organic stone-setting aesthetic, which positions carefully cut baguette or asymmetric angular diamonds in a patter best described as "shattered crystal".

Gem-setting design goes with the current trendiness of organic textures and materials on otherwise industrially made goods. The perfectly machined lines of the Blast's time-telling engine are contrasted with the seemingly organic effect of the "sparkle-set" diamonds, which total 211 stones (around 13 carats) set into the 18k white-gold case, bezel, crown and dial. The resulting Sparkling Blast timepiece is a fluid combination of highly wearable everyday horology in a highly conspicuous jewellery watch package.

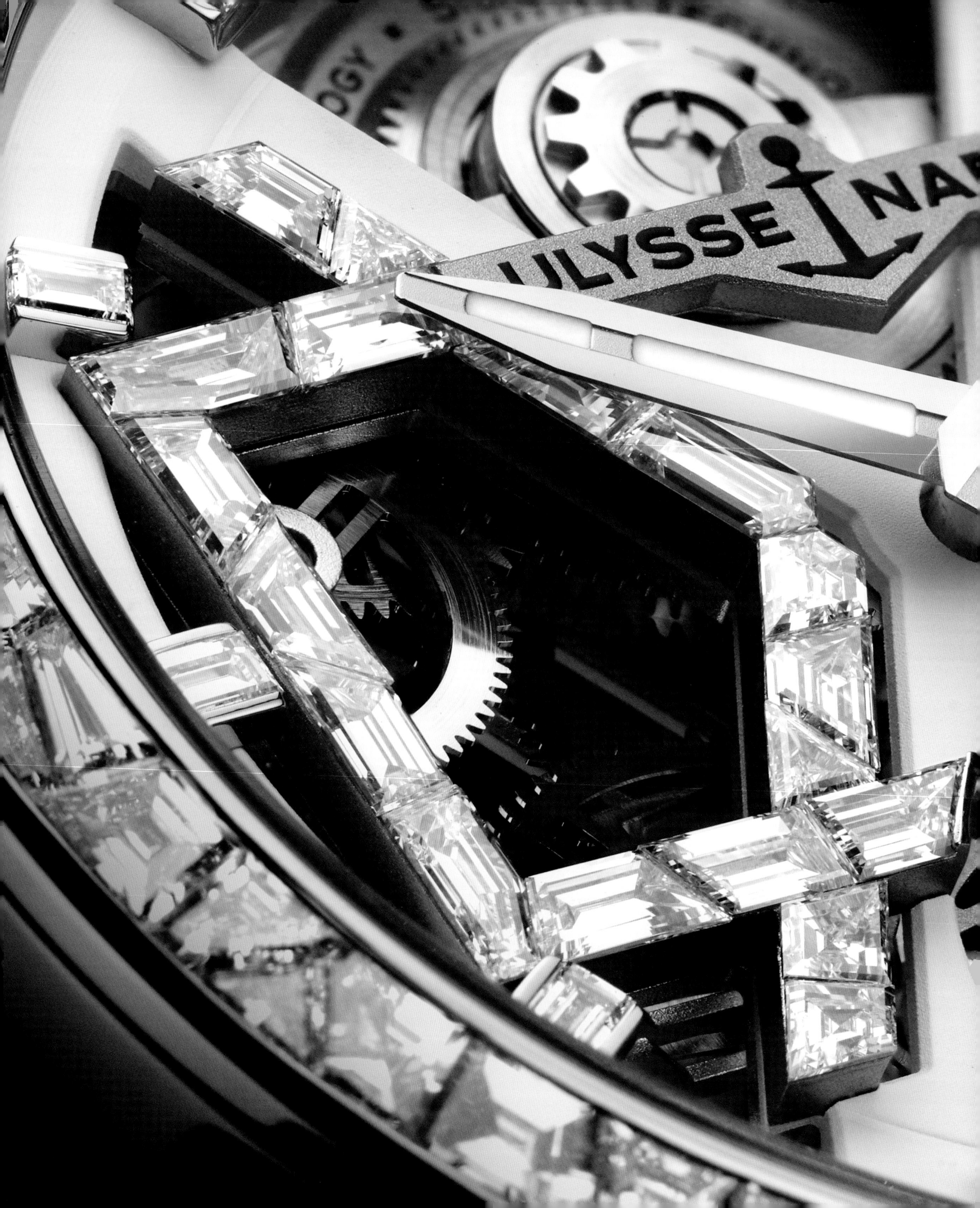
ULYSSE

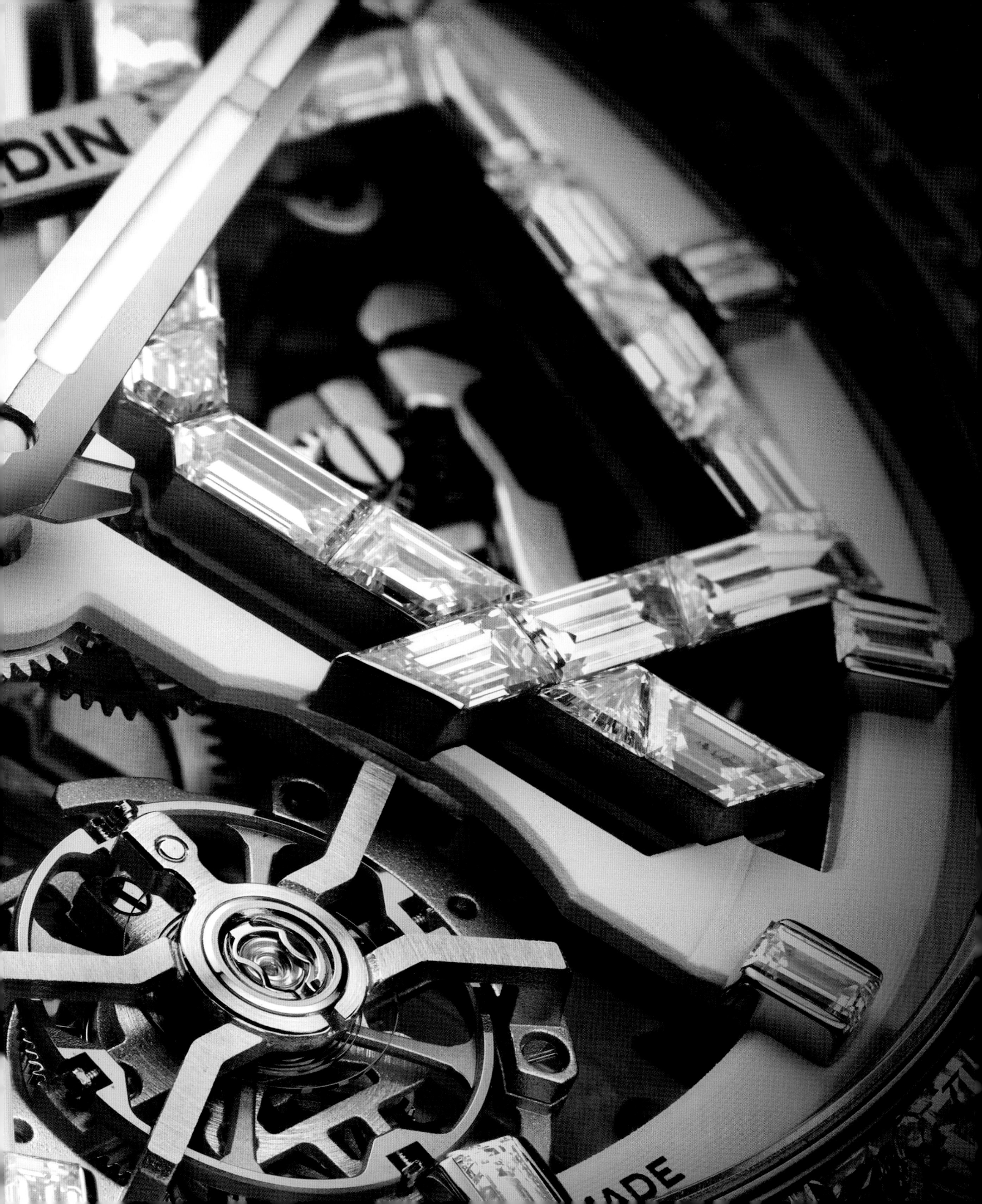

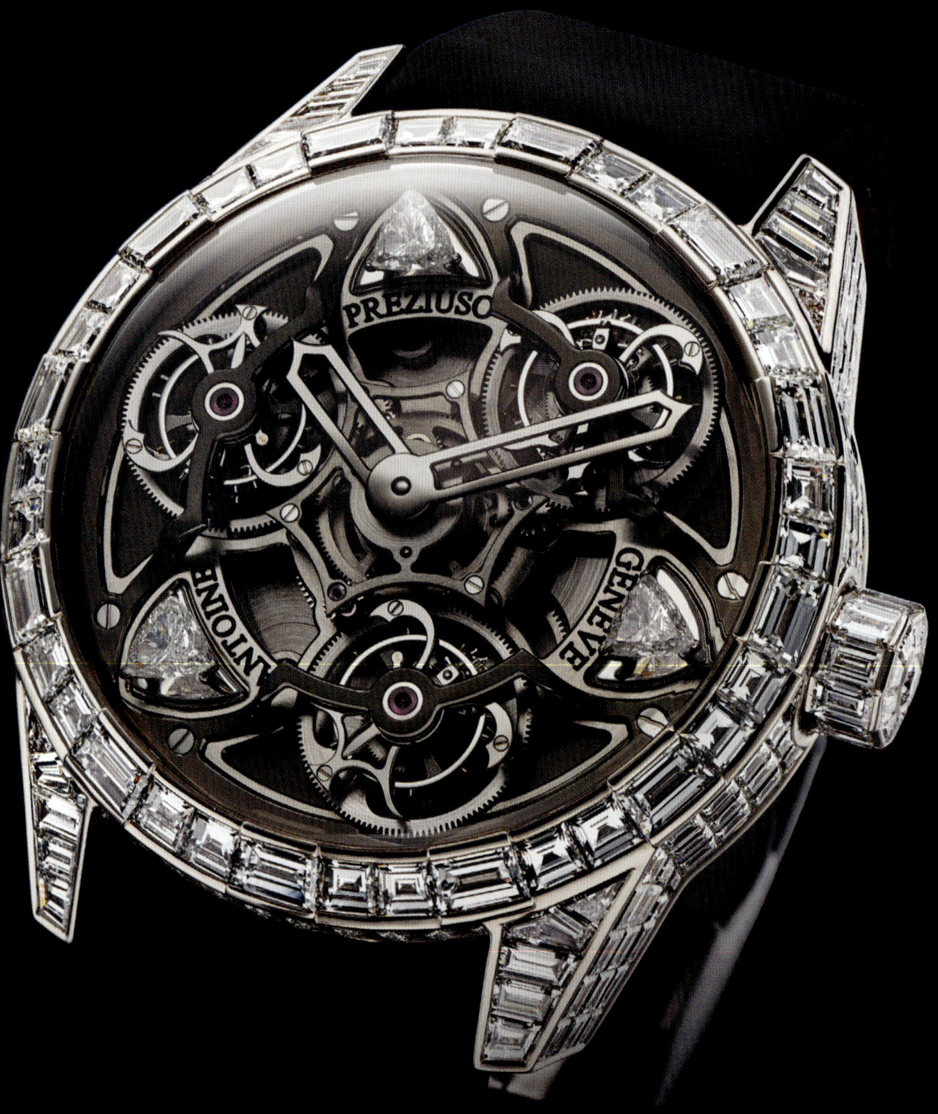

ANTOINE PREZIUSO – CHRONOMETER TOURBILLON OF TOURBILLONS

$ 420 000

Master watchmaker Antoine Preziuso represents a select number of people who helped usher in the modern era of the ultra-luxury watch. Preziuso is one of a few forward-thinking legacy-trained watchmakers who combines his skills producing complicated items of haute horology with his own particular style borne of a larger-than-life imagination. Like many of his contemporaries, Preziuso began by working mostly for other wristwatch brands prior to putting his own name on a watch and thus launching his own brand.

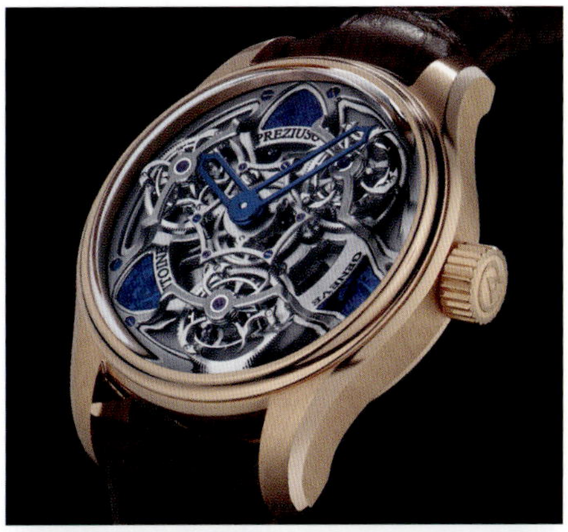

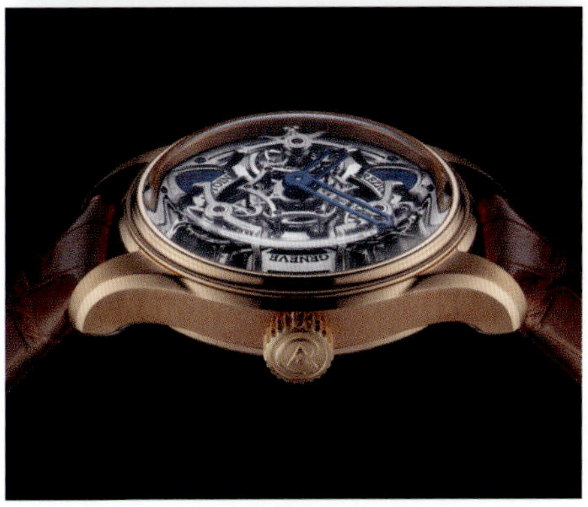

After being relatively quiet for some years, Antoine returned to the scene with his son, Florian, and a product with the non-too-humble name of the "Tourbillon of Tourbillons". The name of the product is less an indicator of the Preziuso family demeanour, and more directly related to marketing practices that help the very wealthy get more excited about one wrist-worn trophy over another.

"Four tourbillons is pretty simple, but three? Now that is where it gets complicated." This statement represents the sentiment of why the Tourbillon of Tourbillons is so impressive mechanically. Not only because the mechanism actually works, but also because at least some versions of the watch have been awarded COSC Chronometer ratings as an indicator of their timing accuracy. Apparently, four tourbillons can share a less complex differential-gear mechanism, whereas three require a more complicated system altogether.

The Tourbillon of Tourbillons has a movement that prominently displays three 60-second spinning tourbillons that are all connected via a differential gear. The trio of tourbillons themselves spin around their own axis every 10 minutes, thanks to the fact that the face of the watch itself also rotates in a "tourbillon-like" manner. The artistic value is not only in the aesthetic construction of the approximately 570-part hand-finished movement, but also in watching its mechanical animation beguile the eyes. For luxury seekers less keen on understanding the patent-protected mechanical movement, the Tourbillon of Tourbillons comes in at least two attention-grabbing styles, which are at least 47mm wide and mostly produced from precious metal such as gold. Antoine Preziuso might be a master of niche horological craft but, as a sharp businessperson, he also knows that at least some of his customers want to enjoy a Tourbillon of Tourbillons timepiece entirely covered with diamonds (which is of course also available for more than double the price) in the brand's Trillion Tourbillon of Tourbillons.

DE GRISOGONO – MECCANICO DG

$429 500

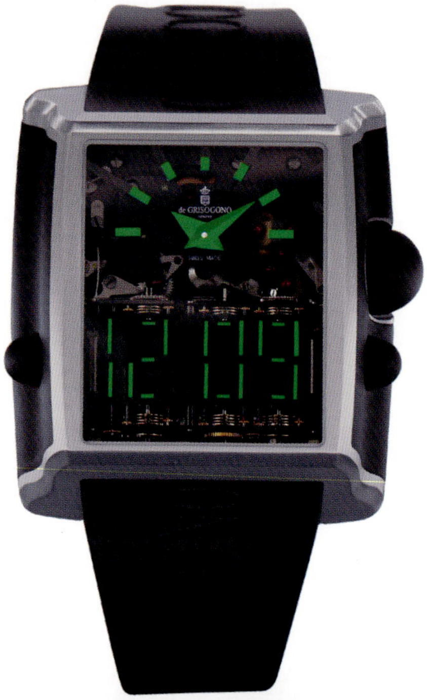

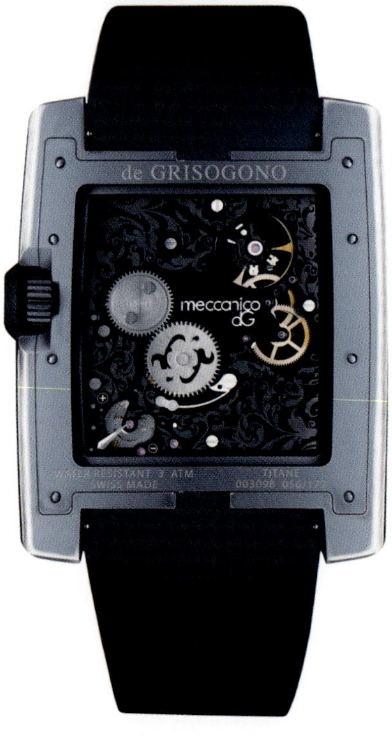

In 2008, the luxury watch industry was still teaming with activity and innovation, thanks in large part to the economic boom – that would soon burst and collapse a large part of the luxury industry. Innovation took the form of truly modern ultra-watches. Timepieces of serious cost began to increasingly eschew the presumption that they would be classic or traditional in design. In the years before, the most expensive watches would often take the form of pieces produced decades, if not centuries, earlier. The "new" luxury watch industry was eager to offer collectors mechanical creations with modern designs.

This backdrop formed a logical foundation for the design of a purely mechanical watch with a digital dial. The irony, of course, being that mechanical watches typically offer analogue dials, while digital displays are hallmarks of electronic innards. De Grisogono wanted to combine the two, which made sense for a generation of new or youthful wealth that was in need of a status watch in a world otherwise surrounded by all things electronic.

Modern computer-aided design was a crucial element behind the successful development of the Meccanico DG, and it took years to complete. The de Grisogono brand is known for a truly avant-garde outlook on luxury, relishing the mixing of traditional elegance with contemporary elements – such as neon colours or digital dials. Other de Grisogono high-end timepieces have included elements such as a dial inspired by a camera shutter and a case that glows in the dark.

The over 650-part movement of the Meccanico DG is a masterful creation that required several years to perfect, even after the watch was originally debuted in 2008. Much of the dial is skeletonised, offering a stylised view of the movement through the front of the watch. The movement features two time displays, each being set separately. Towards the top of the watch is a more traditional analogue dial, and to the bottom is the digital display. Pushers, on the right and left of the case, are used to adjust either minutes or hours, and with each press the digital numbers smoothly transition to the next digit.

Each version of the Meccanico DG was produced as part of a limited edition, and the varieties included models with neon colours or solid gold cases. It remains one of de Grisogono's most noteworthy pieces and an icon of early 21st century watch design.

HARRY WINSTON – OPUS 6

$436 181*

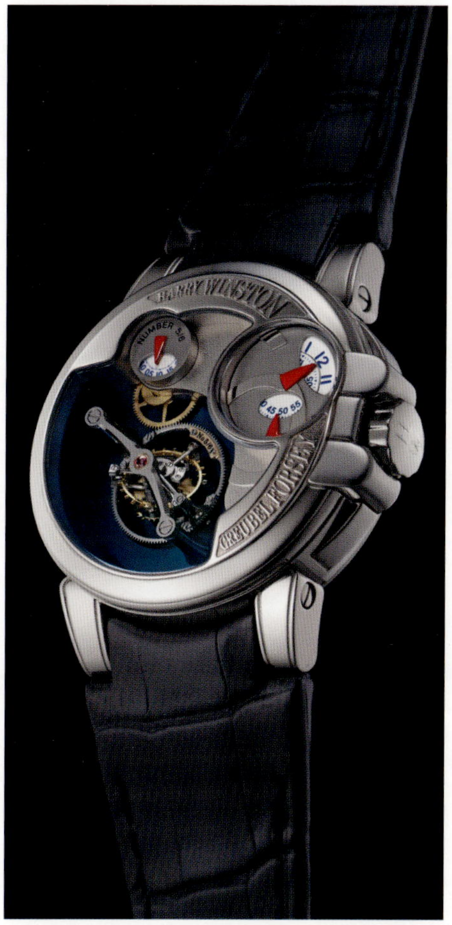

Eleven years after Harry Winston, as a brand, began to produce timepieces, something very unique happened. From the diamond-focused jewellery brand came a timepiece called the Opus 1; less interested in jewels and much more with avant-garde mechanical watchmaking. The then head of watches at Harry Winston was absolutely fascinated by independent watchmakers – people who created unique high-end timepieces on their own without any other motivation than to produce the watches they dreamed to wear.

Completely unprecedented in the watch world, in the year 2000, Harry Winston didn't just release a unique model, but released it as a partnership celebrating both the timepiece and the watchmaker equally. The Opus 1 was made in collaboration with François-Paul Journe (of eponymous watch brand F.P. Journe). The Opus collection was about commissioning a talented watchmaker to design something special, that incorporated his greatest talents as well as the Harry Winston brand DNA. As of 2013 Harry Winston has released a new Opus timepiece each year.

Opus timepieces have become objects of legend. Their unique genesis, and extremely limited production numbers, have led to some interesting occurrences, especially since so much depends on the particular watchmakers whom Harry Winston chooses as partner. For example, the Opus 3 by Vianney Halter was debuted in 2003, but wasn't actually completed and released until around 2010. It simply took that long for the mechanism to be perfected.

In 2006 Harry Winston released the Opus 6 that was produced in collaboration with the up-and-coming watchmaker duo Stephen Forsey and Robert Greubel (of Greubel Forsey). The Opus 6 remains one of the most elegantly designed Greubel Forsey timepieces today, and smoothly combines the appeal of both brands. Known for their highly complicated tourbillons, Greubel Forsey used the Opus 6 to debut a double tourbillon with an inclined inner tourbillon.

Angled at 30 degrees, the inner tourbillon was even less prone to timing errors due to the inclined position. The outer tourbillon turned the entire assembly on its axis. Time was indicated on moving discs in three separate windows for the hours, minutes, and seconds. A large number "6" was also covertly designed on the dial. What is also interesting is that the Opus 6 is a rare example of dual branding on a high-end luxury watch, something that was not common practice, even with the Opus collection. Although all Harry Winston Opus models are only made as limited editions, the Opus 6 was perhaps the most limited, with only six pieces ever being produced.

* Sold at auction for HK$3,380,000 at Christie's, Hong Kong in May 2011.

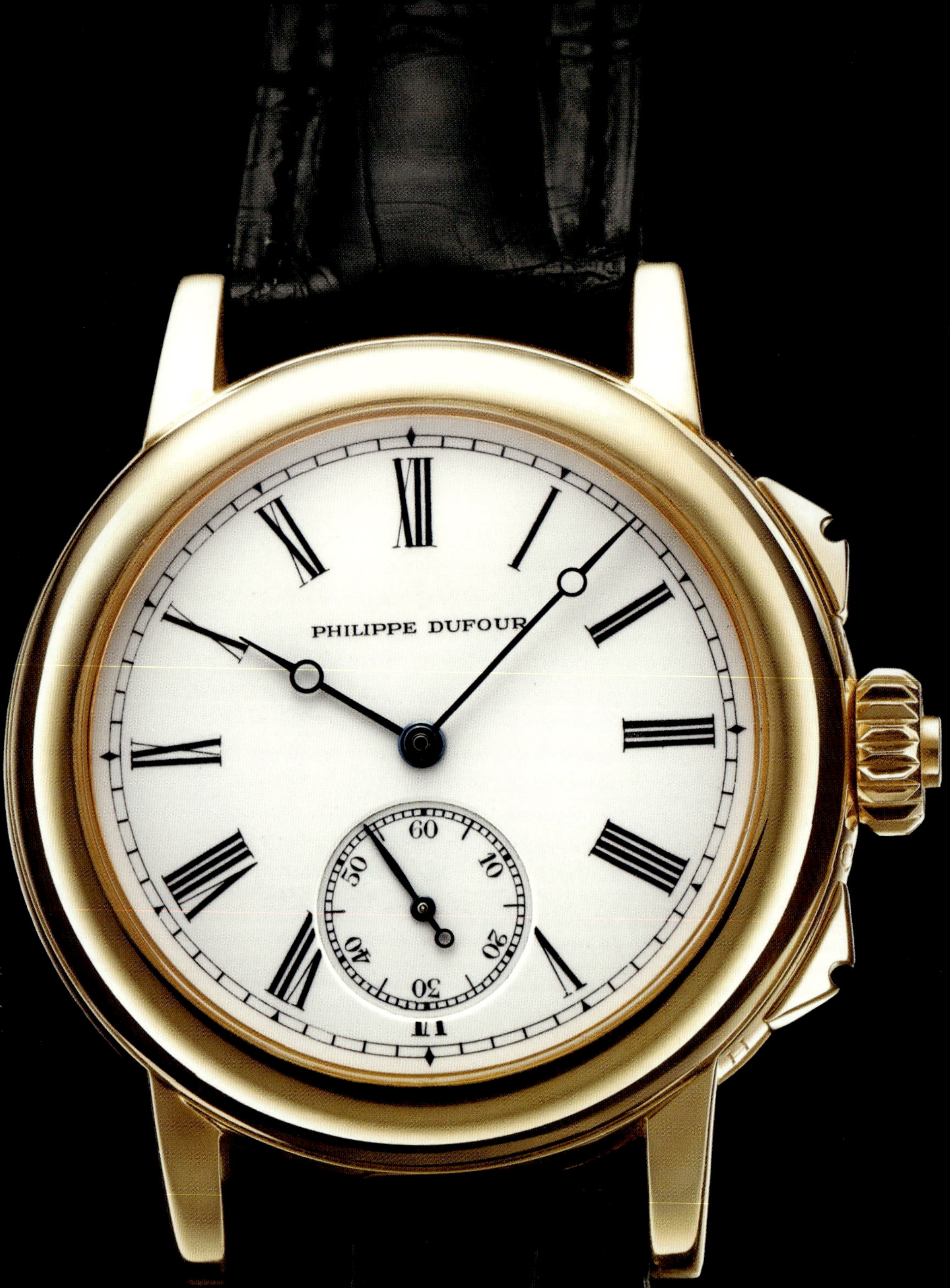

PHILIPPE DUFOUR — GRANDE SONNERIE

$ 437 023*

One of the most respected watchmakers in the world is a humble man who lives simply in the Vallée de Joux, which is part of the "watchmaking region" of Switzerland, near France. In 1989 he began making watches under his own name, and to date only has three models. In fact, his most popular watch is known quite plainly as the "Simplicity".

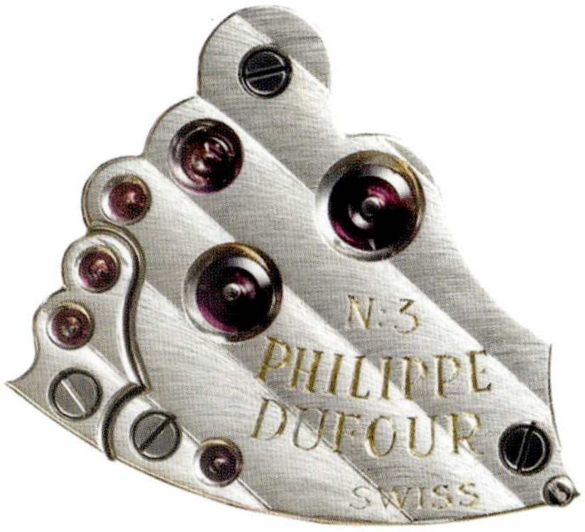

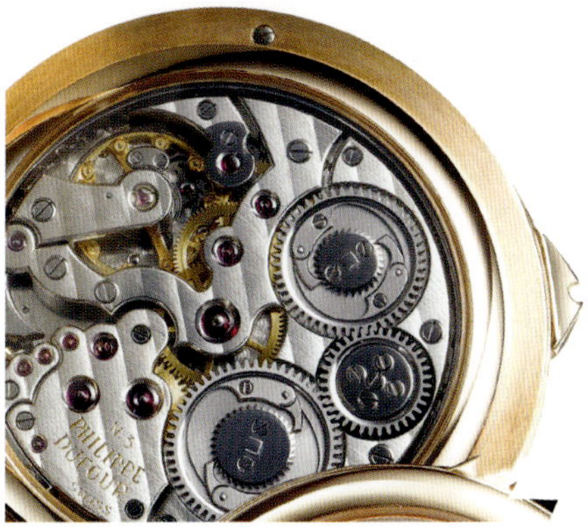

There is nothing outwardly amazing or particularly unique, to most "non watch" people, about his timepieces. They don't seem to exhibit unique designs nor are they made from particularly uncommon materials. In fact, his website is embarrassingly subpar and there is almost no information about him online. So how then, has Philippe Dufour been described with statements such as "genius... most talented watchmaker currently working... and enduring champion of handmade virtues."? In a word, it is about his process. Regularly seen with his tobacco pipe and relaxed smile, Dufour is the type of person who knows how to take his time. Each watch he produces is made by hand, and he only makes about a dozen each year. They also happen to be arguably the finest finished and polished watches on the planet. The reason his watches require so much time to produce is because each component of the movement is lovingly hand polished in a way no-one else has quite achieved.

Collectors pay greatly for the extra 1% of detail that only mastery can provide. Dufour isn't just a wonderful watchmaker, but he understands how to make metal look and sound its best. Before beginning his own brand, he was known for having produced the first ever pocketwatch to contain a grande and petite sonnerie in a single movement, as well as a minute repeater. This trio of ultra-complex musical complications gained him huge prestige, and the relevant watches were sold to the watch brand Audemars Piguet.

Later, Dufour decided to recreate this triple complication piece as a part of his own collection, available to the new eponymous brand's customers. Called the Grande Sonnerie, the piece contains all three of the important chiming features that helped make Dufour famous. Notoriously rare, only a handful of Grande Sonnerie watches are thought to exist. Dufour is known for having a long waiting list for even his more basic Simplicity and Duality models, and the Grande Sonnerie is the product of much more work.

A Grande Sonnerie is a feature that has a timepiece automatically chiming out the hours, quarters, and minutes each 15 minutes. A Petite Sonnerie also strikes each 15 minutes and offers just the hour quarters (15 minute increments) and hours. The watch can be set to either setting. The Grande Sonnerie watch also features a minute repeater, which sounds back the time using a series of chimes on demand.

* Sold at auction for HK$4,820,000 at Sotheby's, Hong Kong in April 2012.

BULGARI – OCTO FINISSIMO ULTRA

$440 000

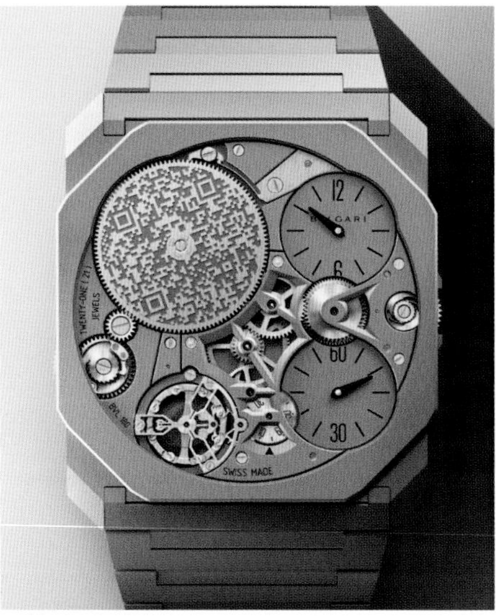

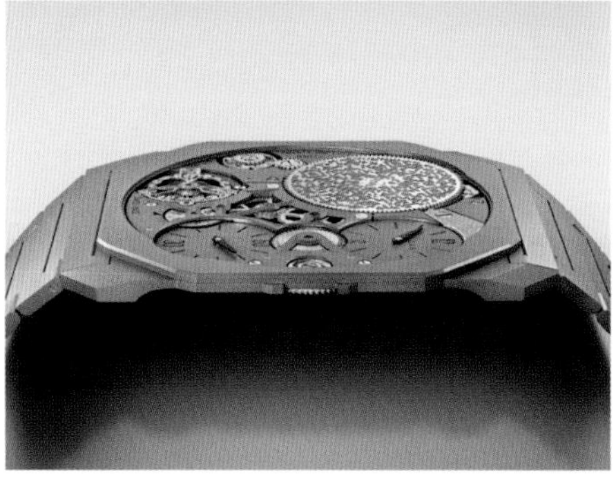

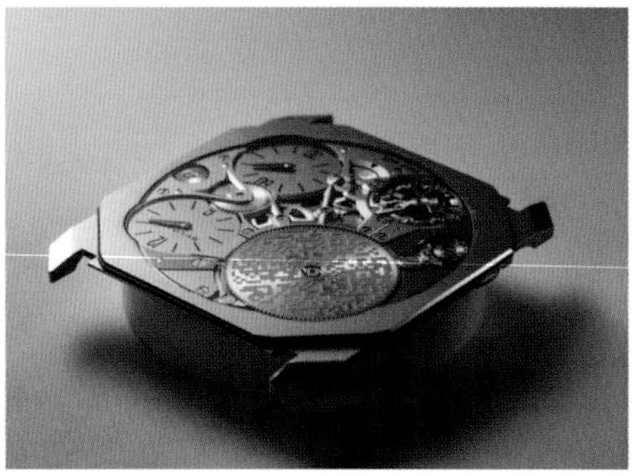

Competition fuels innovation – which is exactly the context within which Bulgari's Octo Finissimo Ultra was born. In the modern era, mechanical wristwatch products don't tend to compete with one another in areas like timing performance or environmental durability. Alternatively, most of the competition in the high-end watch space is related to features such as visual design, materials, weight and dimensions. In this latter category, watch brands have learned that consumers appreciate very thin timepieces. While it isn't solely what they are known for, Italian–Swiss Bulgari is a master of "ultra-thin" watches, and the Octo Finissimo Ultra was – briefly – the thinnest of them all.

For years now, brands like Bulgari and a small number of competitors have battled with one another over who can produce the slimmest watch. Geneva-based Piaget was ahead of the game for a while until Bulgari swooped in with a number of record-setting slim mechanical watches. The fight is now entering new eras of technical complexity with the Bulgari Octo Finissimo having a case thickness of just 1.8mm. That isn't just the movement, but rather the entire case assembly. The watch case is even thinner than the titanium bracelet.

The Octo collection by Bulgari is based on a design owned by the brand that was originally conceived by famed watch designer Gerald Genta. In fact, Bulgari as a company owns the rights to the Gerald Genta name. The Octo Finissimo extended the popular square-case shape of the Octo and introduced a much thinner model, produced with in-house movements. The Octo Finissimo Ultra is a carefully developed halo product that pushes the Finissimo concept even further to its logical extreme – producing a watch so thin, that a thinner mechanism would not be possible using today's available materials.

For example, Bulgari needed to develop a very stiff tungsten carbide material for the Ultra's case, as most metals would easily bend at such slim dimensions. The case back of the watch is actually the baseplate for the movement, which is known as the caliber BVL 180. Surprisingly, even at just 1.5mm thick, the movement operates at a 4Hz frequency and offers a full 50 hours of power reserve with a face that uses separate dials to indicate the hours, minutes and seconds.

The debut version of the Bulgari Octo Finissimo Ultra (a limited edition of just 10 pieces) was made with an etched QR code on the exposed outer surface of the mainspring barrel. The idea is for it to be connected to an NFT – a sign of the larger societal context and luxury product landscape within which the Octo Finissimo Ultra was released. Thinly valued digital assets aside, there is a very real worth to this masterful wafer of high-end horology. Just a few months after the release of this watch, an even thinner machine (slimmer by what seems like a rounding error) was released by Richard Mille coming in at 1.75mm thick and costing nearly three times the price.

GIRARD-PERREGAUX – MINUTE REPEATER TRI-AXIAL TOURBILLON

$441 000

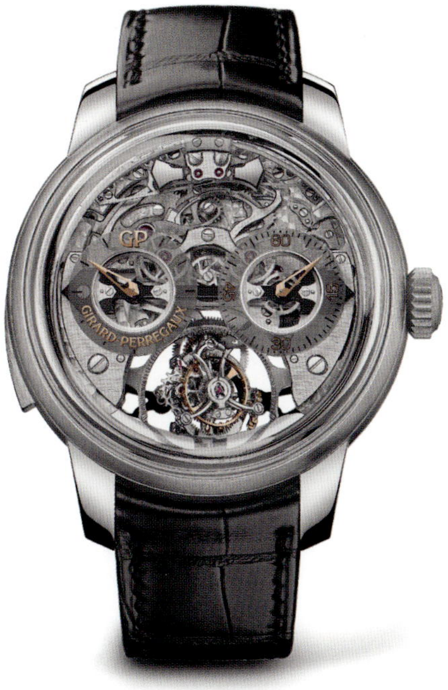

An ultra-complicated wristwatch of this ilk begs the question, "What need is this product a solution for?" When viewed from a practical perspective, the Girard-Perregaux Minute Repeater Tri-Axial Tourbillon might merely be the answer to a collector's question of "How can my next watch be more complicated than my last?" In satisfying the whims of the ultra-well-funded, the goal is to offer them something impressive that they did not expect. Precious few people around the globe even own something as exotic as a triple-axis tourbillon. Among them, vanishingly few have one with an added minute-repeater complication; hence the need to design this especially dramatic and compelling horological creation.

Your "standard" mechanical escapement in a wristwatch (the "regulating organ" that maintains accuracy) uses an oscillating mass in the form of a balance wheel. In a standard tourbillon (already an exclusive item) the balance wheel oscillates while rotating on its own axis by being placed in a spinning "cage". The bi-axial – and the even more exotic tri-axial – tourbillon variants increase that single axis-point of movement to two or three axis points. At that level of complexity, functional considerations have long since been abandoned by the engineers. The three-axis tourbillon mechanisms are therefore all about the artistic technique of producing them, as well as the stunning visual ballet of perpetual spinning motion (on three axis points). Visually, to the wearer, the sphere-like tri-axial tourbillon moves around itself as though on a gimbal. Seeing one on your own wrist happens to be one of the most expensive performances available.

There are 140 parts required to assemble the tri-axial tourbillon itself. Hundreds of additional parts go into assembling the rest of the manually wound movement, which also happens to make up the majority of the timepiece's dial. Time is displayed via a regulator-style layout, which has the hours on a sapphire crystal indicator to the left, with the minutes displayed via a separate indicator to the right. At the top of the watch face, one can view the hammers that create the especially loud chimes in this particular minute-repeater system. In order to enhance the volume of the notes in this musical complication, Girard-Perregaux produced a sound chamber inside of the Minute Repeater Tri-Axial Tourbillon's sizeable 48mm-wide titanium case. The lightweight metal is preferred over a precious metal such as gold or platinum because titanium has better sound-amplification properties, meant to enhance the minute repeater's operation. Somewhat unusual for minute repeaters of this style, the watch case is water resistant to 30 metres.

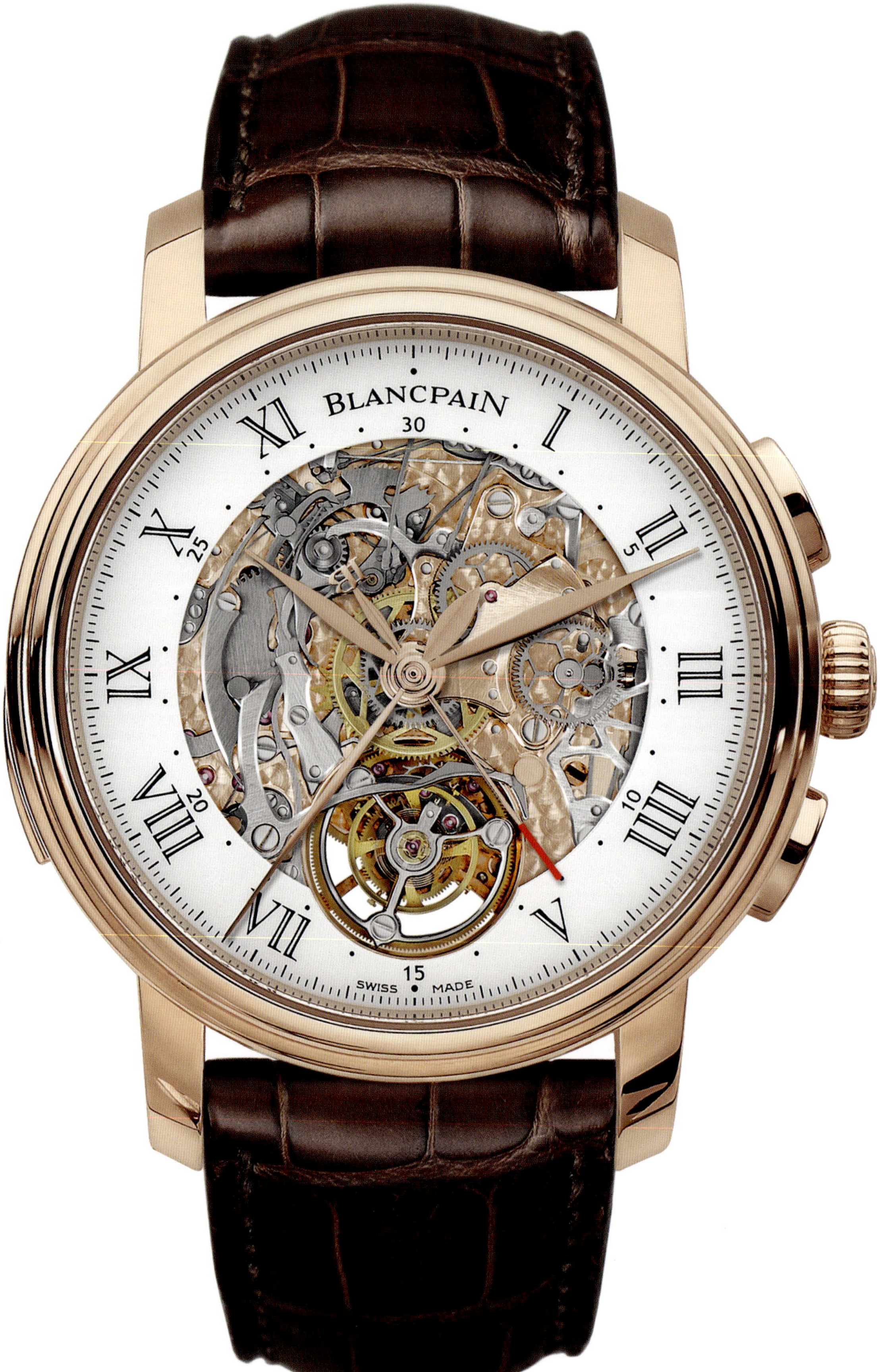

BLANCPAIN
SWISS MADE

BLANCPAIN — CARROUSEL MINUTE REPEATER FLYBACK CHRONOGRAPH

$ 450 000

BLANCPAIN HAS MANAGED TO MAKE THE PIECE LOOK EXTREMELY ATTRACTIVE, EVEN BY CONSERVATIVE STANDARDS.

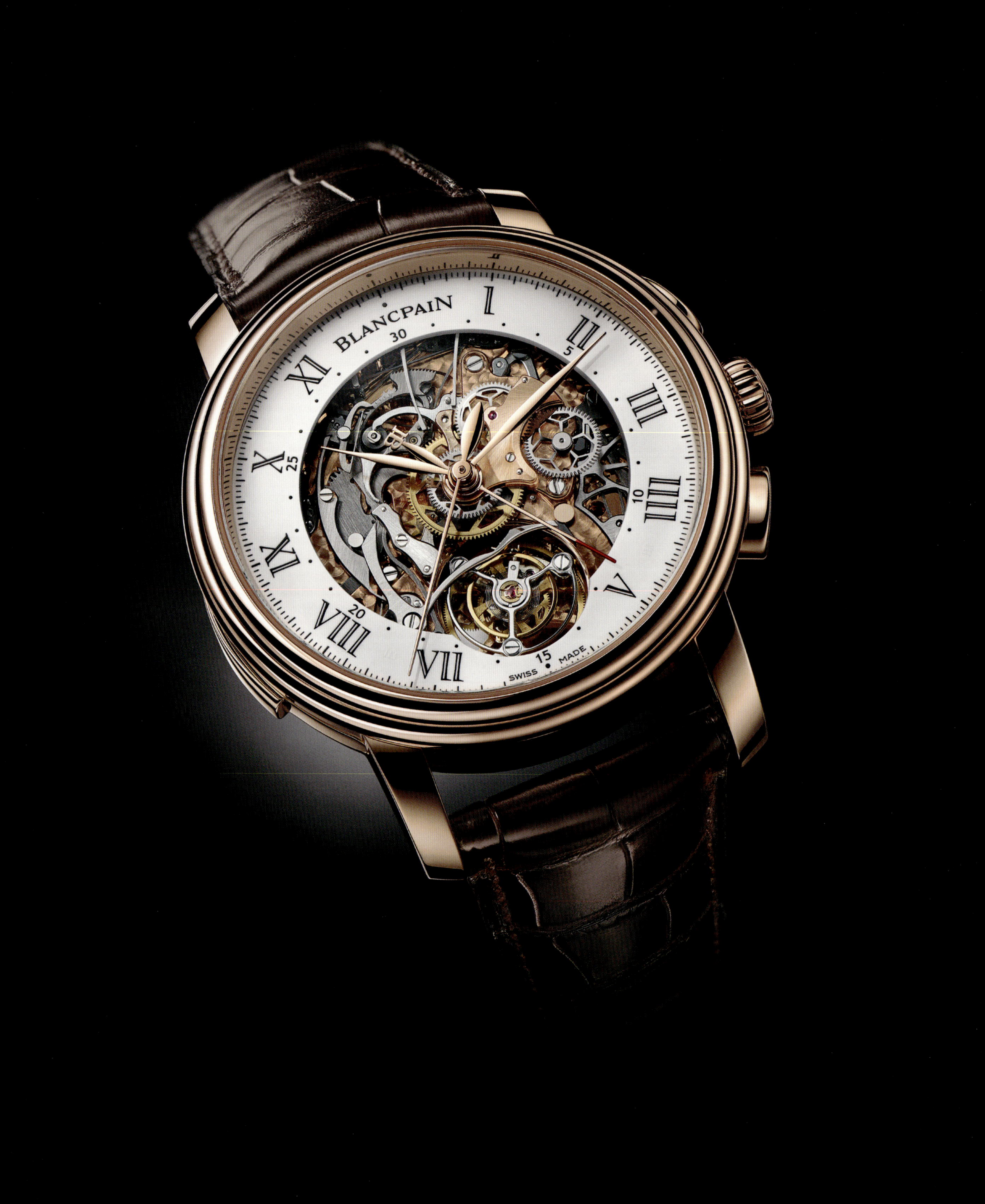
BLANCPAIN
SWISS MADE

As a prestige brand under the larger Swatch Group umbrella, Blancpain is a Swiss watchmaker with the fortunate position of being able to do, almost, whatever it pleases. This relative economic freedom has seen Blancpain time and time again produce record-breaking watches each of which ups the ante for future products.

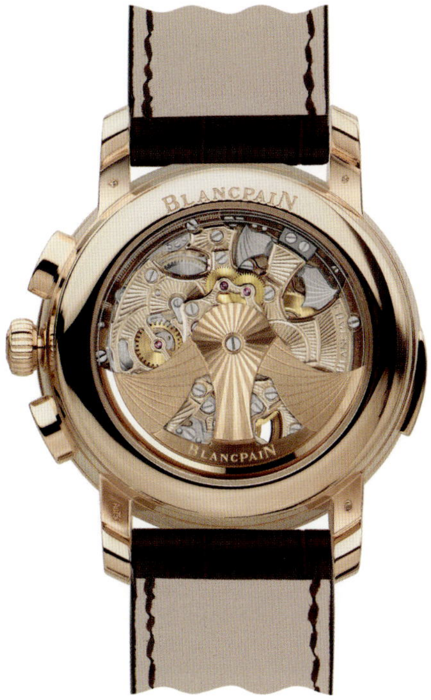

In 2013 Blancpain released the Carrousel Minute Repeater Chronograph. This extremely complicated timepiece is the first in the world to marry together the three complications that form its name. Blancpain has managed to make the piece look extremely attractive, even by conservative standards; and with its wide open skeletonised dial, it has proved a real gem for lovers of mechanical movements.

Conversations about high-end watches do not go very far before someone mentions a tourbillon. This feature frequently serves as a status symbol, distinguishing many particularly expensive and difficult-to-assemble timepieces. Tourbillons are expensive, but they are not nearly as rare as they once were. In 2008, Blancpain deemed that tourbillon watches were becoming too common, so they adopted a similar technology – also invented around the turn of the 19th century – for use in many of their watches. This was the carrousel.

Functionally, a carrousel and tourbillon perform the same task, offering the view of a balance wheel spinning on its own axis. The two mechanisms differ only in the placement of some key components. Blancpain has adopted the exotic complication for use in several of its watches, and in this timepiece it exists with a minute repeater as well as chronograph.

Dial simplicity is intentionally retained in the watch, and the open section of the dial is bordered by a white grand feu enamelled dial. The chronograph feature has no subdials, instead using a rare central minute hand that counts up to 30 minutes. Blancpain ensured that little would distract from a view of the movement, which also contains a chiming minute repeater.

The minute repeater complication is unique, in that it is automatically wound. Blancpain hand-engraves and decorates the automatic rotor and rear of the movement. Decorating and finishing is a large facet of Swiss high-end watchmaking tradition, which is thoroughly emphasised in the Carrousel Minute Repeater Tourbillon.

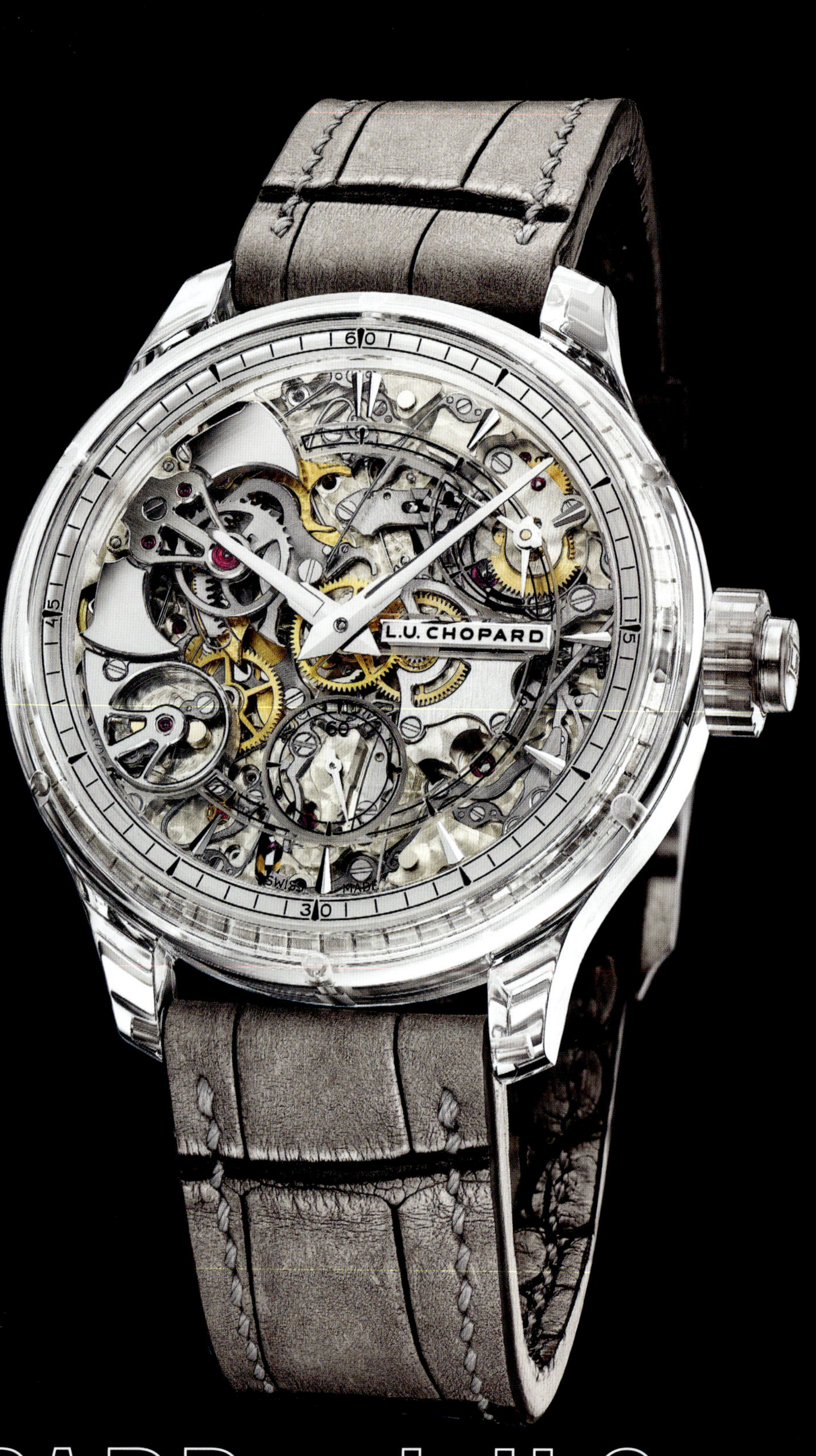

CHOPARD — L.U.C FULL STRIKE SAPPHIRE

$ 450 000

How do you follow-up a musical chiming watch that uses a novel sapphire-crystal gong system to produce one of the loudest, and clearest, minute-repeater performances available on the market? Of course, you produce the same watch but with an entirely transparent case that is also made from synthetic sapphire crystal. This is the origin story of the very limited (just five pieces) L.U.C Full Strike Sapphire watch that Chopard produced to celebrate the 25th anniversary of the L.U.C portion of their manufacture.

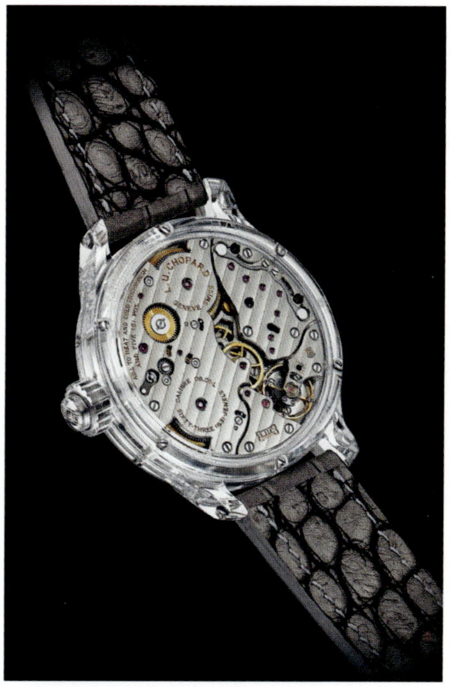

Modern minute-repeater watch cases are typically a tradeoff between durability against water and dust and the robustness of emitted sound. Quality watchmakers carefully try to maximise auditory power while protecting a watch case from daily environmental agents such as moisture (which wreak havoc on metal movements). Often durability wins and many – even fantastically expensive – minute repeaters are weak in volume. That isn't the case with the L.U.C Full Strike, however, and the impressive effect of the hour and minute chiming movement is made even more expressive through the resonant qualities of the sapphire crystal case material.

The 42.5mm-wide case is produced from a few sections of carefully machined sapphire crystal. The top section connects to the minute repeater's gong assembly – upon which polished metal hammers visibly strike via the view through the face of the watch. The result of this technical feature is that the case is technically part of the audio-amplification system – and the concept works well both on and off the wrist.

Impressively framed in transparent scratch-resistant crystal, the in-house made Chopard L.U.C 08.01-L manual movement is an ample example of why enthusiasts appreciate Chopard L.U.C products. The movement features both a COSC Chronometer rating for accuracy (very unusual with minute-repeater watches), and it also bears the Geneva Seal, which is an even more challenging certification. Bearing the seal not only means that a watch movement was produced entirely within the canton of Geneva, but also that the mechanical movement meets particular aesthetic and performance thresholds.

The movement is produced from 533 carefully finished parts and contains two mainspring barrels – one for the time display and another for the minute-repeater complications. Despite the transparent skeletonisation of the dial, Chopard designed the face of the L.U.C Full Strike Sapphire to be legible and it includes full scales for reading the time as well as dual-power reserve indicators.

Musical minute-repeater watches continue to be a favourite horological artform among collectors. For those who value volume and performance, as well as the sheer visual thrill of seeing a watch's movements in operation, few products exist to match the particular appeal of the Chopard L.U.C Full Strike Sapphire.

HUBLOT – MP-07 SAPPHIRE 40 DAYS POWER RESERVE

$474 000

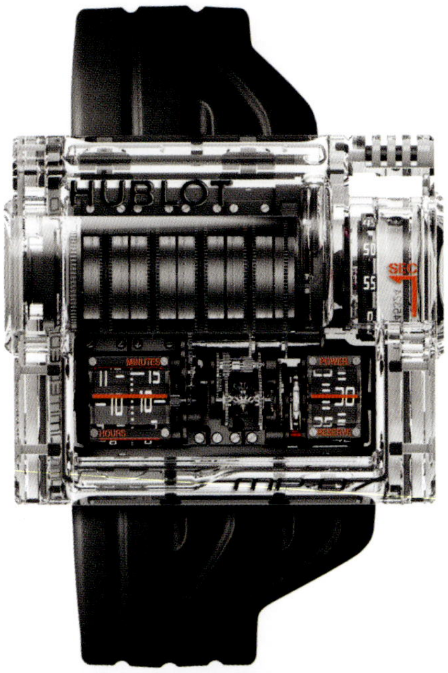

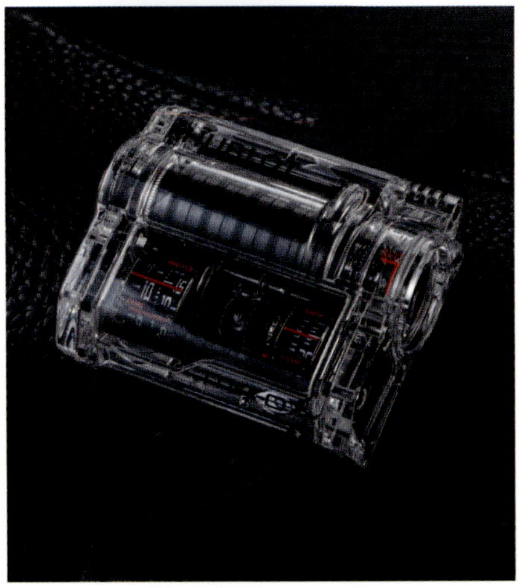

Hublot's "MP" (Masterpiece) collection is where many of the contemporary Swiss watch brand's most avant-garde high-end creations exist. Among the most popular MP watches is the MP-05 "La Ferrari", which has a movement and case inspired by the engine and engine bay of the corresponding Ferrari automobile (of which Hublot is an official timepiece maker). The MP-05 collection contains a similar type of movement found in the MP-07, but of a different style. The more recent MP-07 displays a series of nine horizontally stacked mainspring barrels, which account for the mechanical timepiece's very long power reserve of 40 days.

Time is indicated on rotating drums, which display the hours and minutes, as well as a power-reserve indicator (which is a useful reminder for when to wind the movement, given the long intervals). On the right side of the box-style case is a horizontally mounted tourbillon, which doubles as the seconds indicator.

The most innovative aesthetic feature of the Hublot MP-07 is the case design, which has a rare angular-style architectural box. Hublot faithfully followed the shape of the in-house made movement, which is the real star of the show. To best display the mechanism inside of the case, Hublot produced it from carefully machined pieces of transparent synthetic sapphire. Hublot – more so than most other luxury watch brands – has been charmed by, and thus often uses, the beautiful aesthetic of sapphire as a case material. Once mainly used for the crystal covering watch dials, synthetic sapphire crystal has been adopted as a material for the entire case given its intense scratch-resistant properties. It also helps to showcase the detailed craftsmanship of many of Switzerland's most impressive mechanisms. Hublot's contoured rubber strap does its best to match the watch itself and, while not as transparent, it offers a comparable look.

GIRARD-PERREGAUX – TOURBILLON BI-AXIAL TANTALUM & SAPPHIRE

$478 500

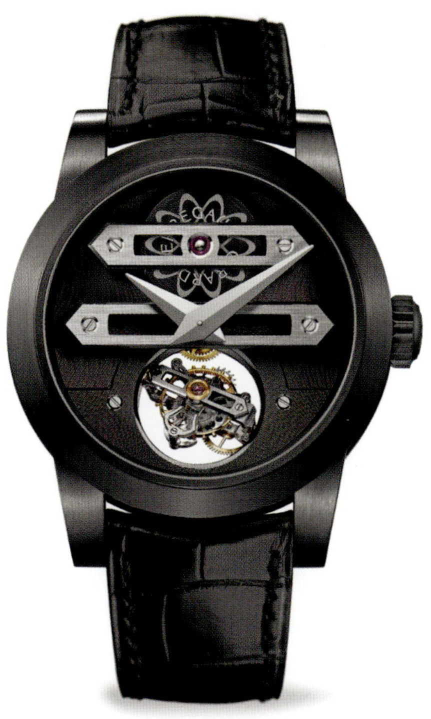

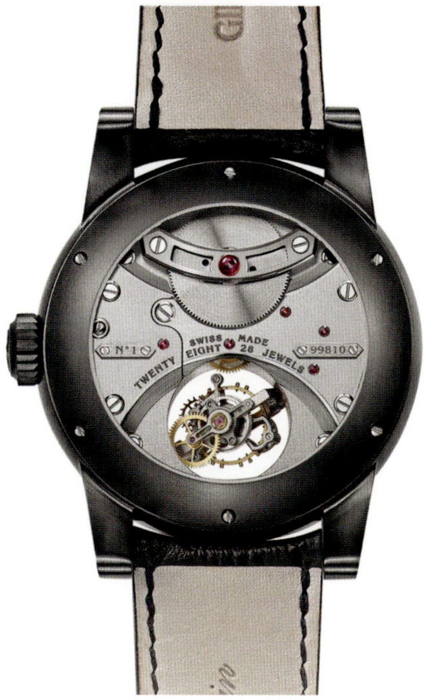

The watch industry has a fetish for materials, which is not surprising, as the overall luxury industry is tied to the idea of producing goods from hard-to-find or complex-to-manufacture components. The rarity of metals such as gold and platinum, as well as precious stones such as diamonds, rubies, sapphires, and emeralds, helped form the foundation for making the ordinary extraordinary, from almost the beginning of civilisation. So it stands to reason that rare materials, which also happen to be aesthetically pleasing, are of great interest to watchmakers.

The wrinkle, of course, is that while gold and diamonds are technically rare and precious materials, they really aren't that hard to come by. One need not venture very far in any major city, when on the hunt for items made from the traditional precious materials. Creative watchmakers thus seek out "new precious materials" to stimulate a more novel sense of exclusivity for their customers.

This particular version of the Tourbillon Bi-Axial, by Swiss company Girard-Perregaux, has a case produced from Tantalum. The engineered alloy is one of many modern metals, and other materials, adopted by the watch industry for use in high-end timepieces. Tantalum, and other materials recently made popular in watches, such as carbon fibre and ceramics, are borrowed from the world of manufacturing, automotive racing, and the aerospace industry.

Tantalum offers the Bi-Axial a deep grey finish, for its admittedly monolithic-style case, which sits tall on the wrist with its stark, bold line. A cool, contemporary sheen, dresses what is, at heart, a very traditionally styled watch, with a lineage going back to the 19th century, when Girard-Perregaux released an ionic pocket watch with "three golden bridges". The design has become a hallmark of certain pieces, and can be seen in this watch, with the bridges being produced in perfectly jet black synthetic sapphire crystal – yet another exotic material adopted by the wristwatch industry.

Two large bridges lie horizontally across the case, while a third bridge is actually integrated in the two-axis tourbillon. Multiple axis tourbillons are perhaps the most exclusive form of the highly desired luxury complication, that rotates an escapement on its own axis. Here the tourbillon, visible through the large opening on the dial, spins around every 45 seconds, while at the same time spinning in another direction, off a different axis point, once every 60 seconds. It makes for a marvellous visual display and adds to the other-worldly feel of the Bi-Axial Tantalum & Sapphire. Released in 2013, Girard-Perregaux produced only 12 pieces.

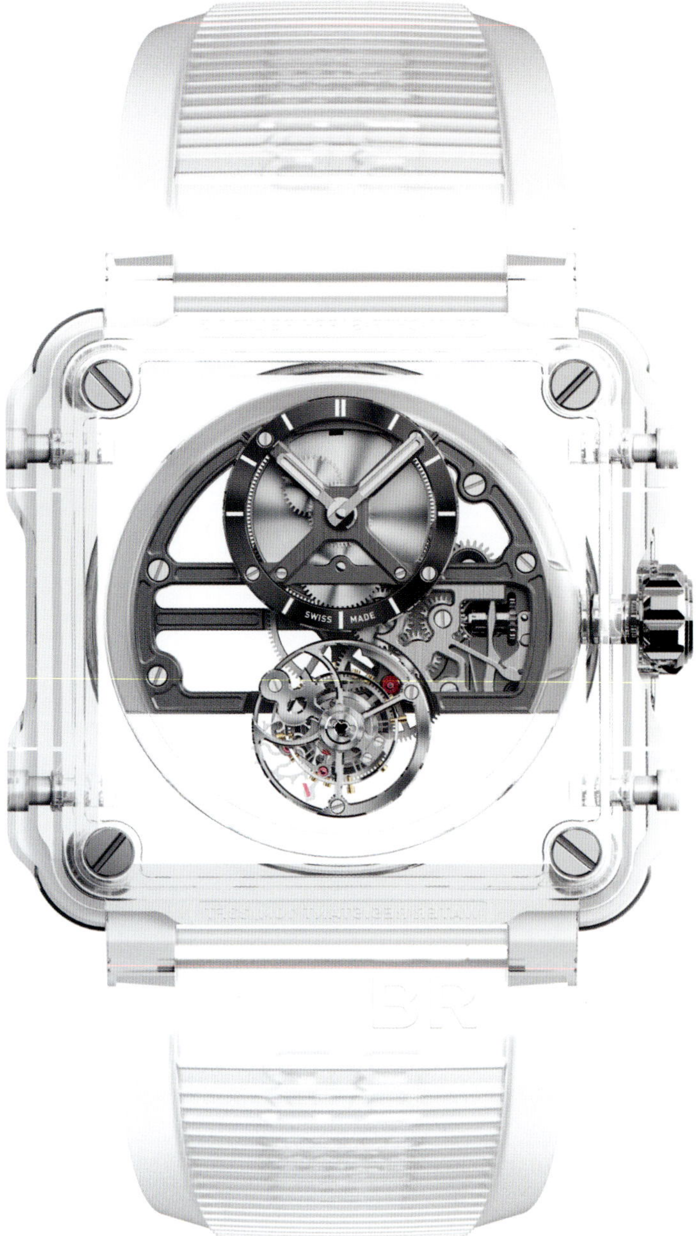

BELL & ROSS — BR-X1 TOURBILLON SKELETON SAPPHIRE BLACK

$ 480 000

When Paris-based Bell & Ross introduced the BR-X1 Tourbillon Sapphire, the blue and the gold-coloured movement versions of the watch (only one of each was produced) were available to purchase exclusively online, eschewing the traditional third-party retailer network. This was a possible first for a watch priced at almost half a million dollars and was a bold move for a brand that historically would not often veer into such high price points. Buyers even got a chance to visit Bell & Ross and meet the team responsible for putting their timepiece together.

The most iconic wristwatch design by Bell & Ross is a 46mm-wide square, known as the BR 01 Instrument, that was inspired by military plane cockpit clocks. The BR-X1 case is a modernised evolution of the BR 01, which – here in tourbillon form – was rendered from synthetic sapphire crystal. Incredibly scratch-resistant, as well as notoriously frustrating to machine, sapphire crystal is quickly becoming one of the hottest materials for modern luxury timepieces. When totally transparent, sapphire-crystal cases offer wear-resistance along with a much more visceral appreciation of the mechanical movement inside of the watch.

Bell & Ross devotees agree that the 45mm-wide BR-X1 case in sapphire crystal offers the most intimate look at the delicate and highly skeletonised, manually wound flying tourbillon movement contained within. Just as fascinating to some onlookers is the view of the screw and gasket systems, which hold the five-part case together and keep unwanted things such as dust and moisture out. In addition to a trendy "ghostly" look on the wrist, sapphire-crystal cases no doubt give mechanically minded watch aficionados an enhanced ability to understand the operation and assembly of their precious horological objects.

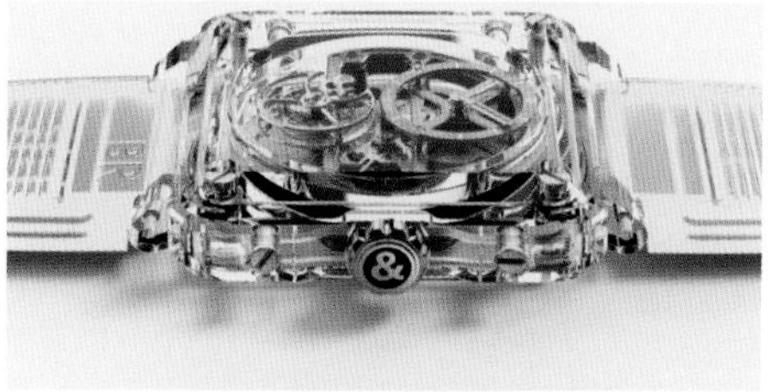

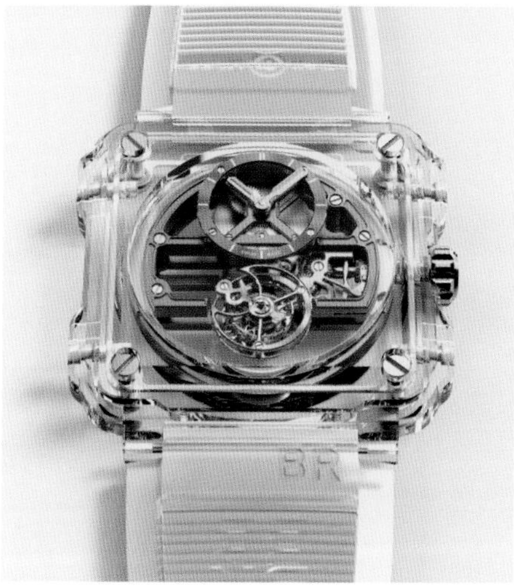

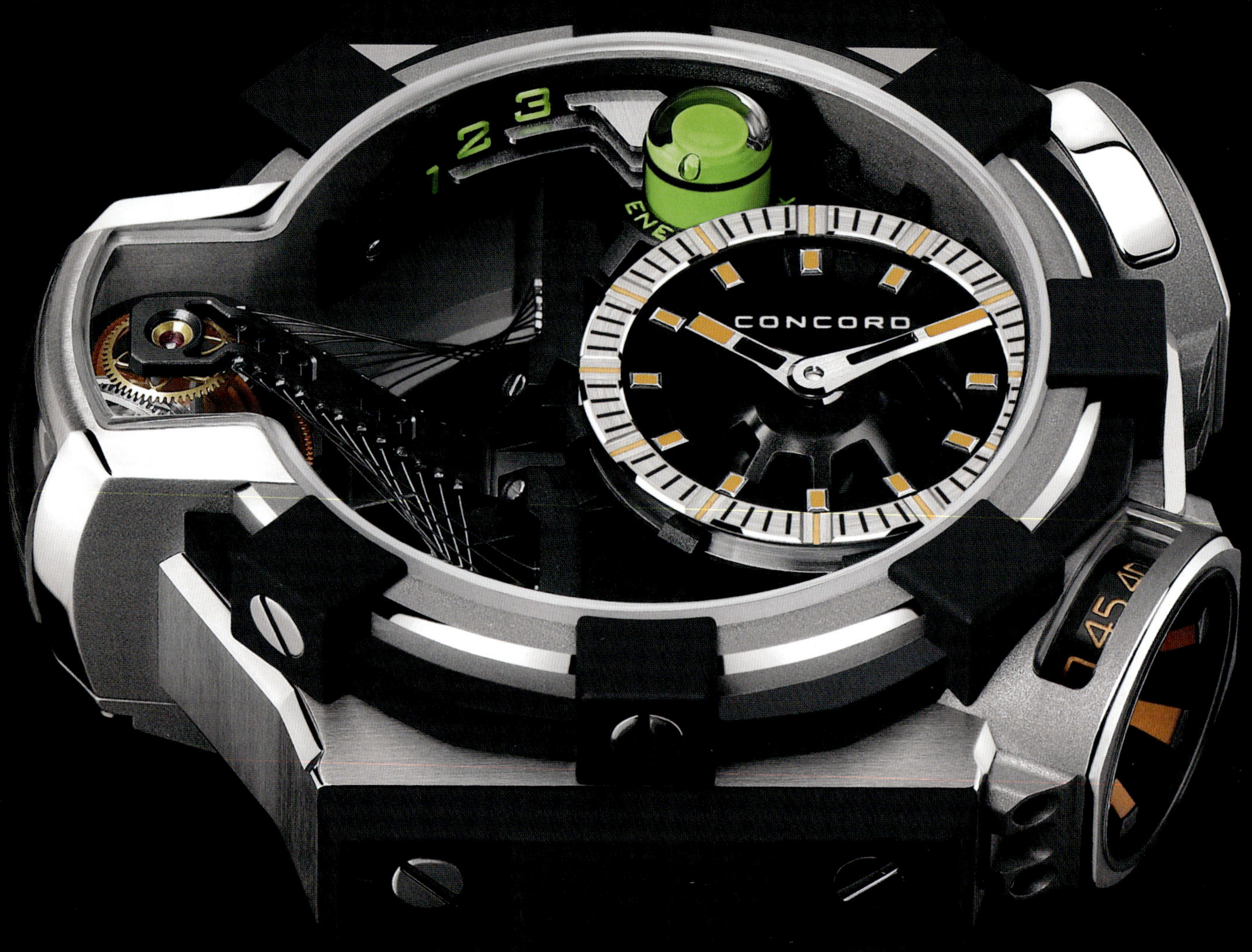

CONCORD – C1 QUANTUM GRAVITY TOURBILLON

$ 480 000

When Concord released the C1 Quantum Gravity Tourbillon in 2008, many people believed it signalled what the future of high-end watchmaking would look like. It was a time of rapid modernisation in the watch industry, in both talent, and perceptions of what high-end collectors wanted to buy. There was less focus on traditionally conservative design, and a great deal of experimentation with what were, in the context of the often staid high-end watch industry, quite radical designs. In many ways the C1 Quantum Gravity Tourbillon helped define an era.

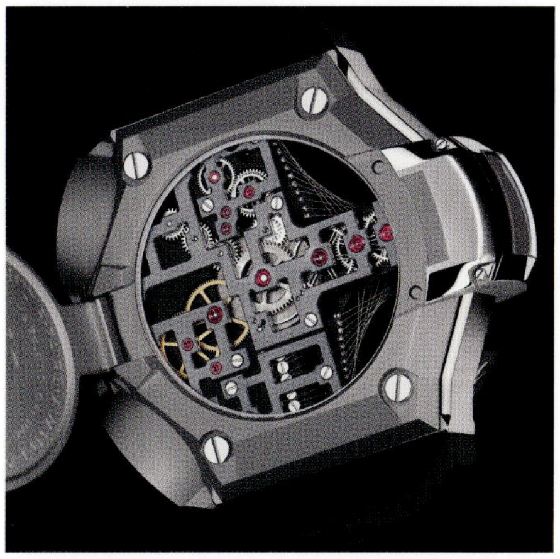

While the "Quantum-inspired" super-watch era never replaced a preference for traditional designs, projects like the C1 Quantum Gravity Tourbillon have had a lasting effect on what modern luxury timepieces strive to be.

Under the Movado group, Concord was "re-launched" only shortly before they released the C1 Quantum Gravity Tourbillon. The brand eschewed much of its traditional DNA, instead opting for a futuristic industrial look, which reached its zenith in this particular timepiece. The movement of the Quantum Gravity is a feat unto itself, in addition to the overall case design. Concord worked with the hottest movement maker of the era, a firm known as BNB Concept, to develop the mechanism inside the watch. Heavy on conceptualisation, the movement features a bi-axial tourbillon (spins on two axis points at once), connected to the rest of the movement with tiny suspension-bridge-style wires. A small cylinder of green liquid is located on the dial, which empties and fills as a means of indicating the power reserve left in the mechanical movement.

The easiest way of understanding the point of the C1 Quantum Gravity Tourbillon is to realise that it helped fully legitimise modern conceptual futuristic design as having a place in the high-end watch industry. Whatever it lacked in elegance, it made up for in inventiveness.

Concord fully acknowledges that the movement was designed separately from the case, something common at the time, when both elements of the watch had distinct appeal to collectors. In mostly titanium and 18k white gold, the C1 Quantum Gravity Tourbillon watch even relied on vulcanised black rubber as a case material and design element. Only 10 pieces were ever produced.

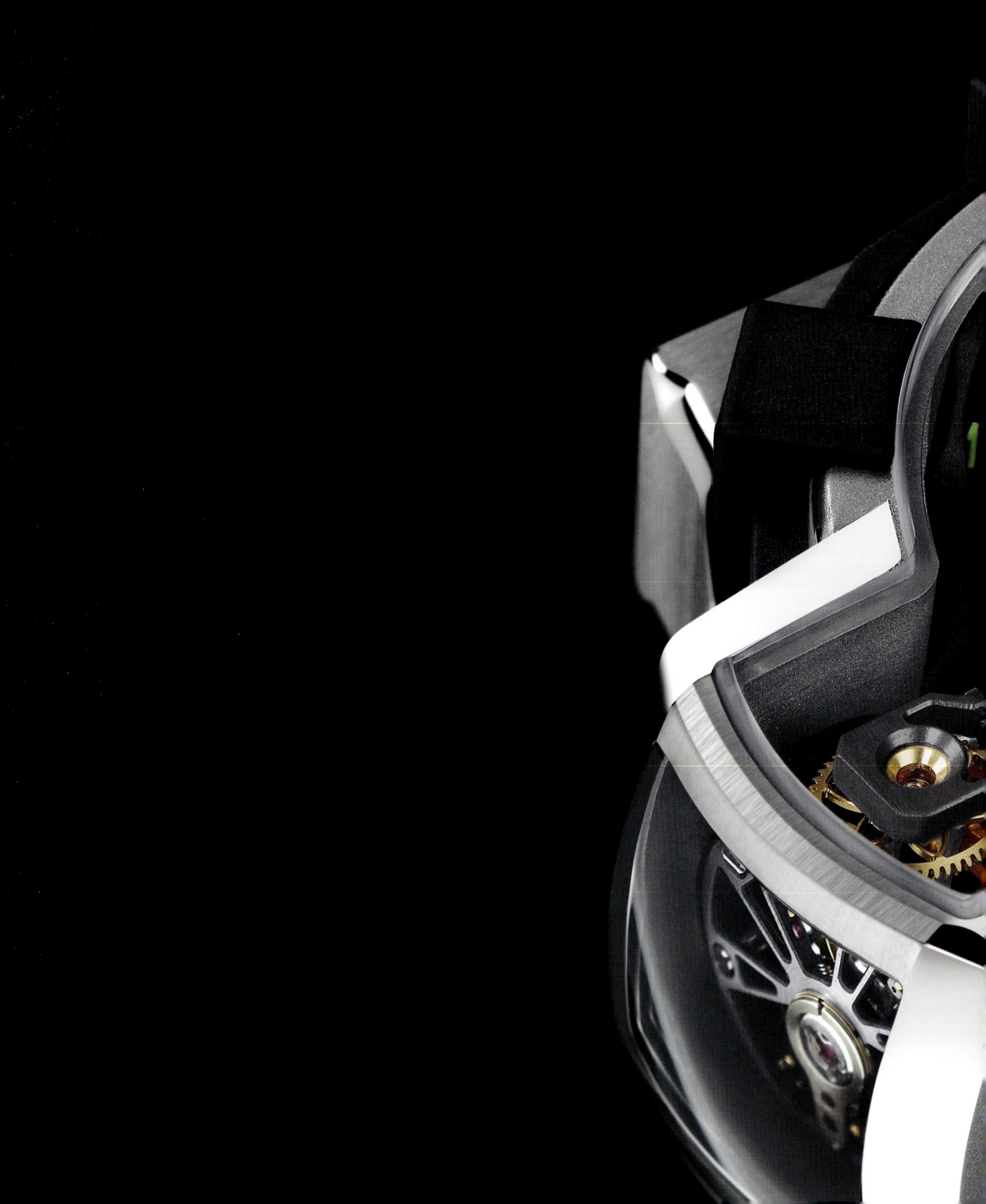

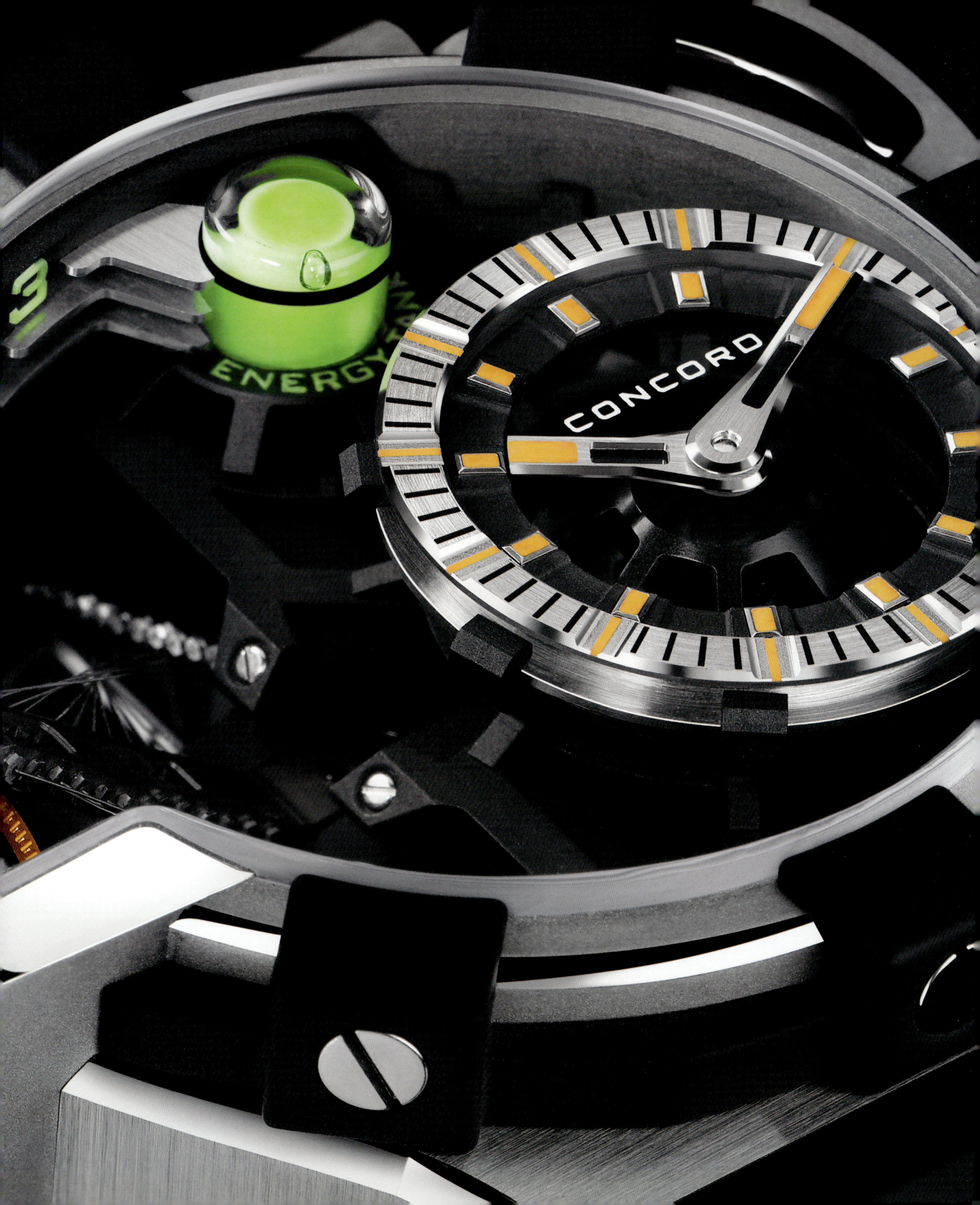
3
ENERGY
CONCORD

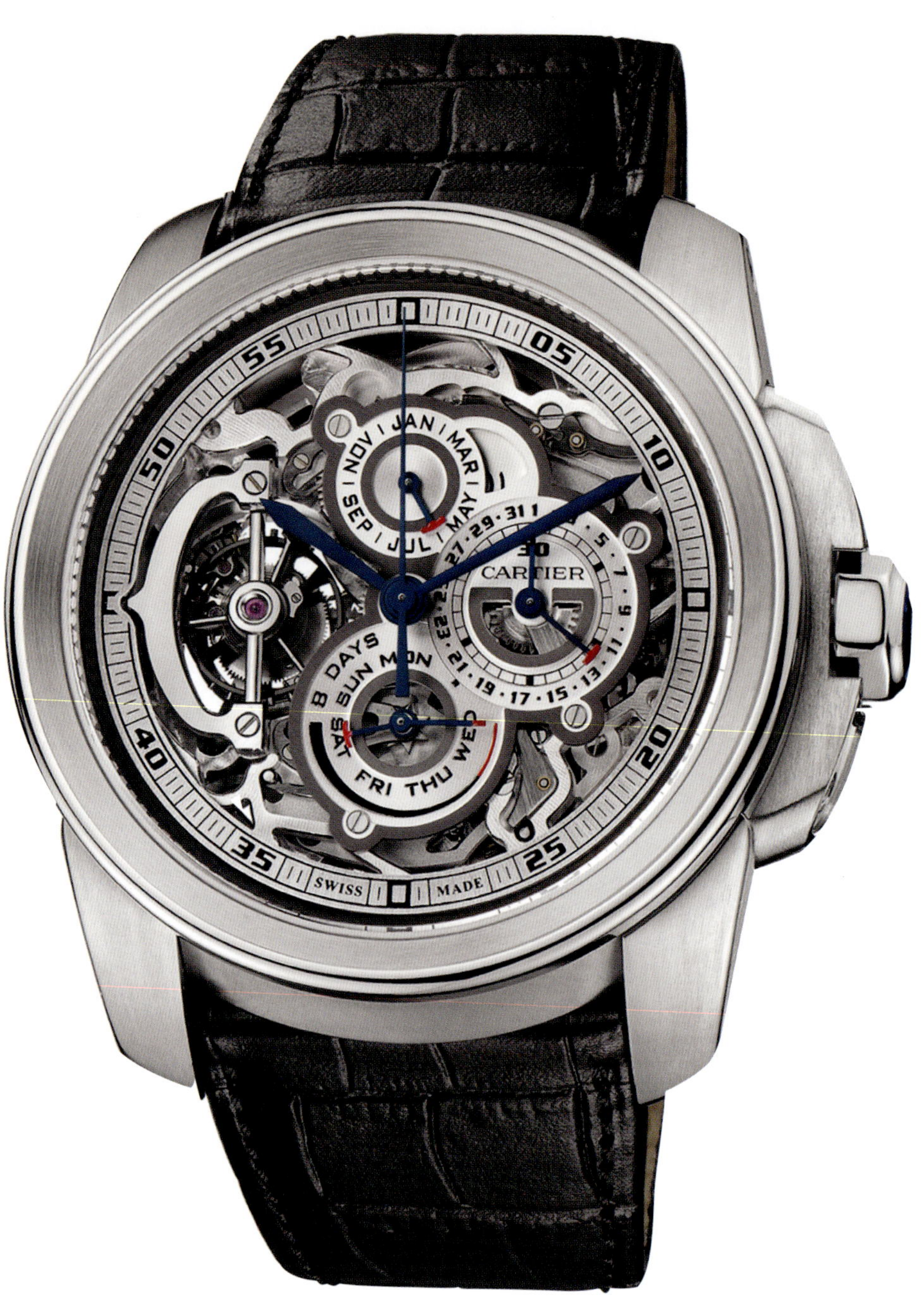

CARTIER — CALIBRE DE CARTIER GRANDE COMPLICATION

$ 483 000

While many top luxury brands thrive on the perception of exclusivity that comes from not being known by the public at large, Cartier enjoys a different sense of notoriety by being a household name. It is not unfathomable for many people to own a Cartier item during their lifetime. Cartier prides itself on offering a range of entry-level luxury goods, but those are merely the start of a long vertical ladder of high-end products and services, which range from bespoke fragrances to royal jewellery.

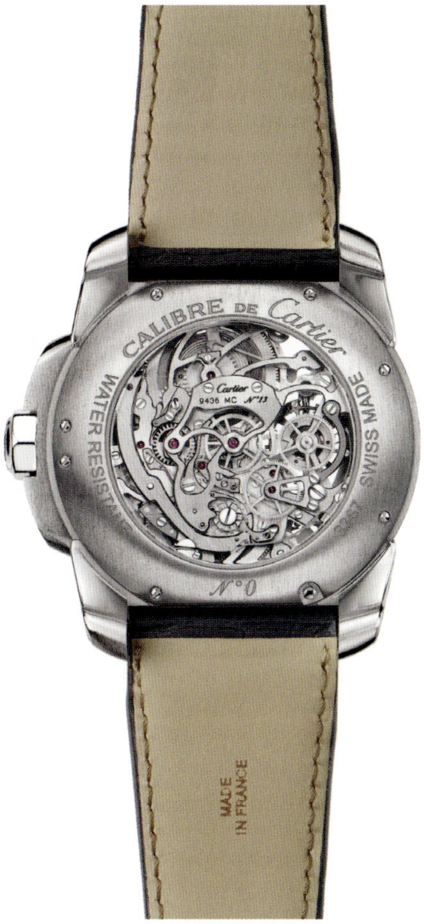

Watches have been an increasingly important element of the brand's product portfolio over the last decade. Cartier has added a wealth of "haute horlogerie" items to its collection of high-end watches, which feature in-house made mechanical movements and some stunning designs and innovations. One of the first ultra-high-end Cartier watches to catch the attention of the watch world was the limited edition Calibre de Cartier Grande Complication.

The name "Grande Complication" is typically bestowed upon watches that combine a series of functions. On their own, each of these mechanical functions should be difficult to produce, but together they make for something much rarer and much more exclusive. This Cartier Grande Complication combines a perpetual calendar (tracking the month, date, day of the week, and leap year), single-pusher 30-minute chronograph, and tourbillon in a manually wound movement with a power reserve of eight days. Note the "C" for Cartier bridge, holding the tourbillon.

Cartier's trump card with the Grande Complication was the ambitiously high price. When it was released, most watch collectors had never heard of an almost half-million dollar Cartier. It began a new phase in the brand's focus on the highest-end regions of the watch market. The Grande Complication's case is a large version of the Calibre de Cartier style design. It is only offered in platinum, and only 25 pieces will ever be made.

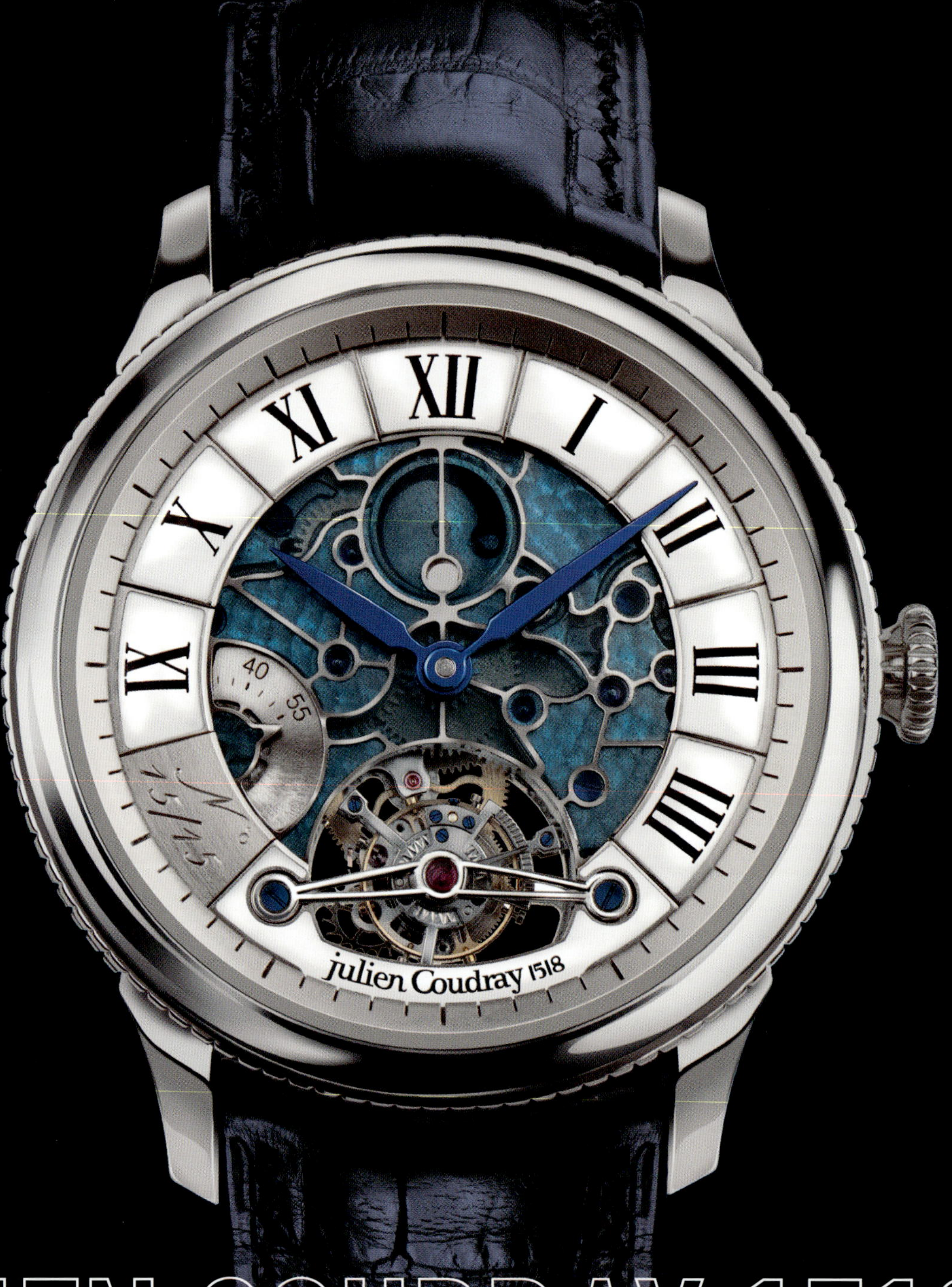

JULIEN COUDRAY 1518 — COMPETENTIA 1515

$ 490 000

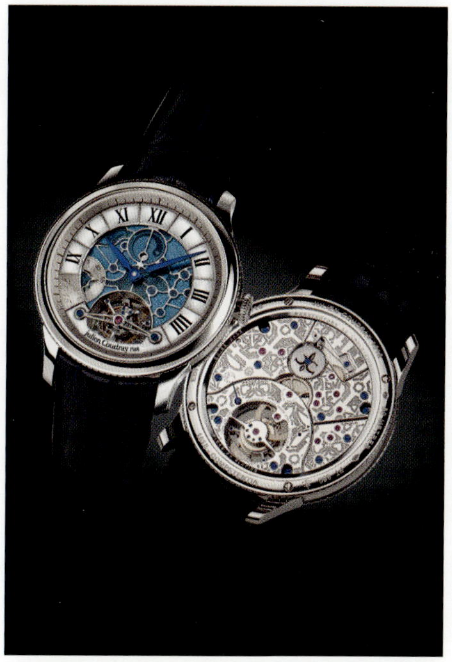

Many watch brands today borrow the names of historical watchmakers. Some of these brands have enjoyed a long history of almost perpetual operation since the heyday of their namesakes, and others have adopted the legacy of a watchmaker whose work is firmly placed in the past. This practice, of building something new based upon something old, is perhaps unique in the luxury industry. The allure of "hand-made" or "ancient technique" has a distinct appeal to luxury consumers. Companies today, producing timepieces that appear to have come from a robust and successful past, are creating pieces that are significantly desirable to collectors.

One of many such brands is julien Coudray, and one thing that makes its pieces different, is how long ago the actual Julien Coudray existed. Rather than being an esteemed watchmaker from the 18th or 19th century, Julien Coudray lived in 16th century France. At that time, clocks and watches were very crude, compared to those of a couple of hundred years later. Nevertheless, Julien Coudray was a master of his time. A clockmaker to kings, Coudray was even said to have had Leonardo Da Vinci in his employ for a few years from 1515.

One of the most interesting facts about Julien Coudray is that some sources credit him with inventing the portable timepiece. Around this time, the spring-driven clock was invented, and still, today, all mechanical watch movements use a tightly wound spring for power.

During the time of Julien Coudray, a timepiece was both a tool and a privilege of the ultra-rich. Difficult to construct, let alone design, timepieces were often imbued with decoration and precious materials, as was the custom of the time with most items used by royalty and the more elite members of society. The julien Coudray watchmaker of today employs much of this philosophy in its modern timepieces. Their Competentia 1515 marries a series of artistic techniques with precious materials in a watch that is unique among today's watchmakers. They begin with both a case and movement produced from gold or platinum.

Precious metal cases aren't rare among high-end watches, but movements made of gold or platinum are highly uncommon. Aside from a few key pieces, almost all the in-house made mechanical movement in the Competentia 1515 watch is in gold or platinum (depending on the model). The movement contains a tourbillon-style escapement, as well as a power reserve indicator, and a day/night indicator on the rear of the movement, which features a small hand pointing either at a smiling representation of the sun or Moon.

The back of the movement (visible through a sapphire crystal exhibition window) is decorated with a unique form of engraving aesthetic known as the Jardin à la Française style. The front – dial side – of the watch features two forms of enamel, which are hand-applied and then baked. The hour markers are produced traditionally from "grand feu" enamel, while the centre of the dial uses a plique-à-jour enamel technique. Quite rare today, plique-à-jour enamelling produces a result that looks like stained glass.

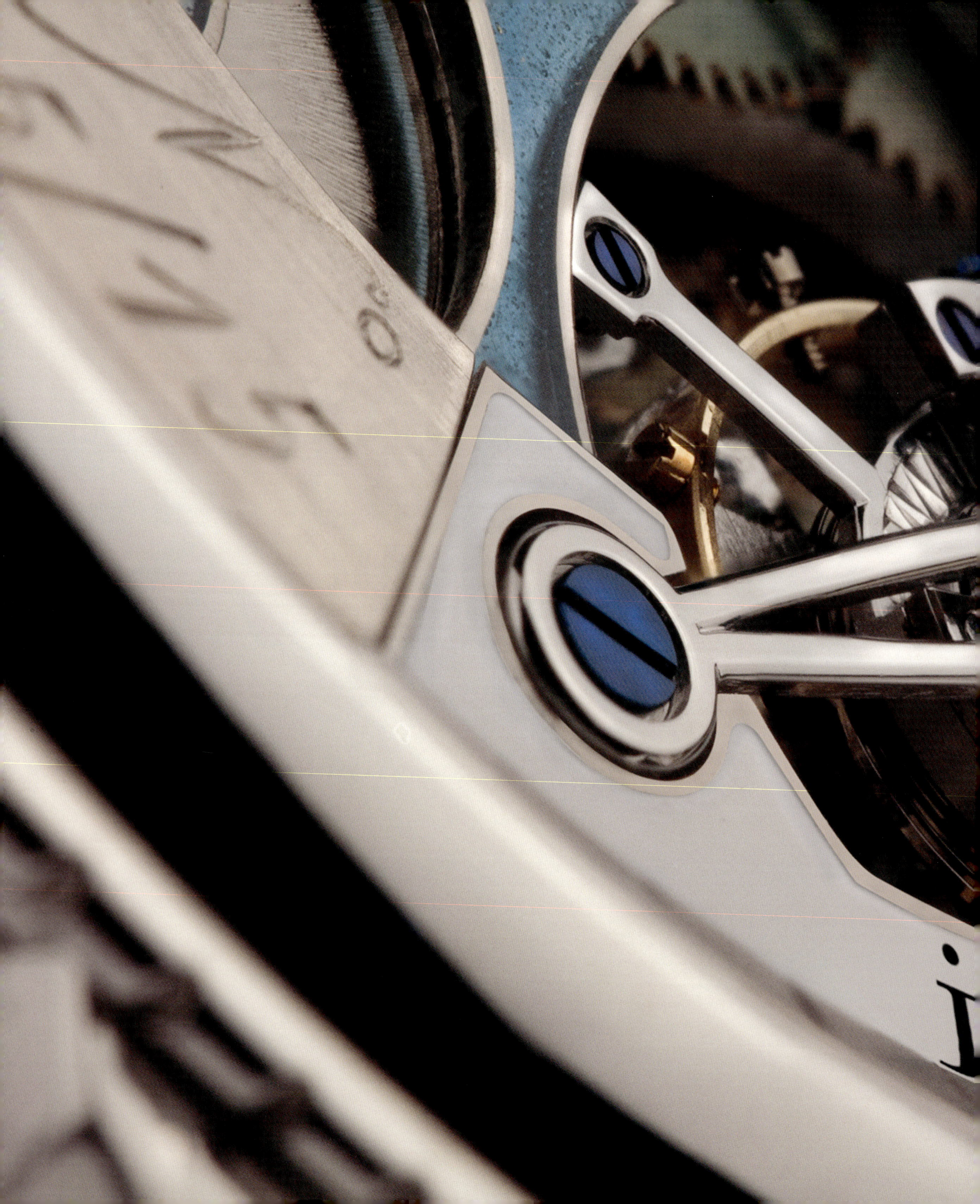

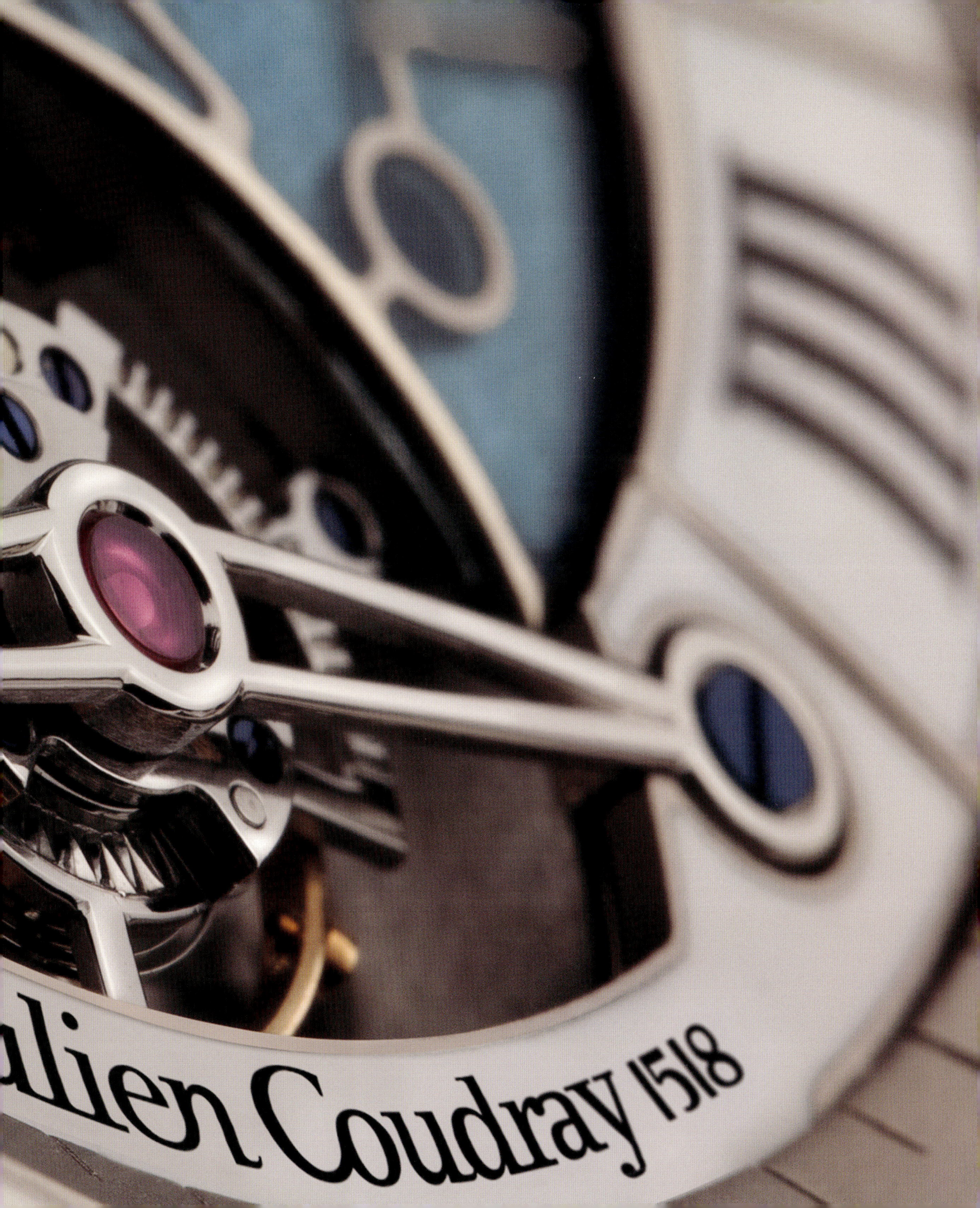
ulien Coudray 1518

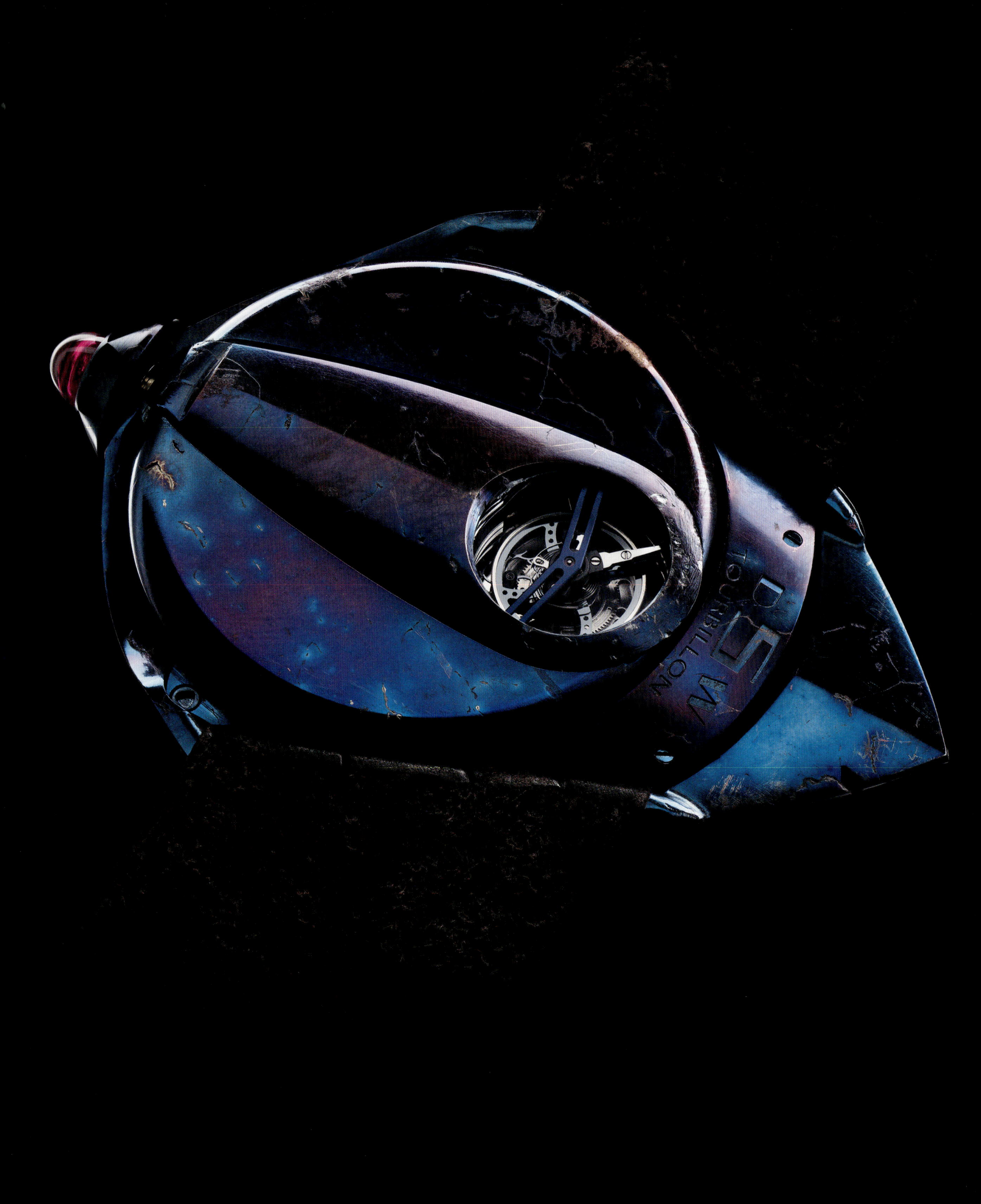
TOURBILLON

DE BETHUNE — DREAM WATCH 5 METEORITE

$495 000

LUXURY IMBUED WITH AUTHENTIC ASTRONOMY FOR FANS OF SCIENCE FICTION IS A FITTING WAY TO DESCRIBE THE OVERALL LOOK OF THE DREAM WATCH METEORITE PIECE-UNIQUE PRODUCT.

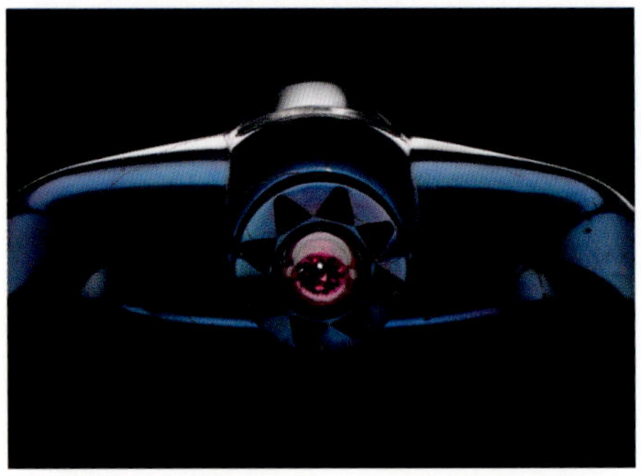

Few ultra-high-end modern watchmakers produce pieces as inspired and as avant-garde as Swiss De Bethune. Run by horological artists and "mad" watchmakers, the boutique company's meteorite-cased watch is a stunning example of De Bethune's peculiarities at their finest. Produced as a one-of-a-kind version of the Dream Watch 5, the Dream Watch (5) Meteorite has (as the name implies) a spaceship-style case produced entirely from actual meteorite. This particular piece of meteorite is mostly iron and is from a rock that landed in Argentina reportedly 4,000 years ago. The first artistic effort in creating this timepiece was to carefully identify which part of the several-kilogram meteorite should be used to create the most interesting and aesthetically pleasing base for the sculpted, organic-looking case.

After being carefully shaped and polished into the surprisingly wearable case shape, De Bethune heat-treated the mostly iron rock, which resulted in its stunning blue colour. The organic imperfections and craters on the case are a central part of the artistic presentation intended by De Bethune. A large natural ruby is used as the cabochon in the crown, which itself contains a large diamond on the inside. Luxury imbued with authentic astronomy for fans of science fiction is a fitting way to describe the overall look of the Dream Watch Meteorite piece-unique product.

Functionally, the in-house made, manually wound mechanical movement displays the time via two turning discs along with an easy-to-overlook spherical Moon-phase indicator (accurate for 1,112 years, assuming the watch remains in continual operation) which is both a common feature in other De Bethune watches and further advances the "space" theme of the Dream Watch 5 Meteorite. On the underside of the case is a window displaying the advanced silicon and 18k white-gold balance wheel set in the unusual 30-second spinning silicon-and-titanium tourbillon regulation system. The movement overall is protected by at least four different De Bethune patents, further ensuring originality and distinction when compared to mechanisms produced by other watch-making companies.

Collector appreciation for De Bethune is often based on the company's unusual designs and intense level of detailing, as well as the sincere effort put into ensuring high chronometric performance for its movement mechanisms. Some might readily say that De Bethune products have both style and substance. Finally, this Meteorite version of the Dream Watch 5 is particularly noteworthy for being able to immediately impress those who are not at all familiar with the world of fine timepieces, just as easily as it can attract the most seasoned horological enthusiasts.

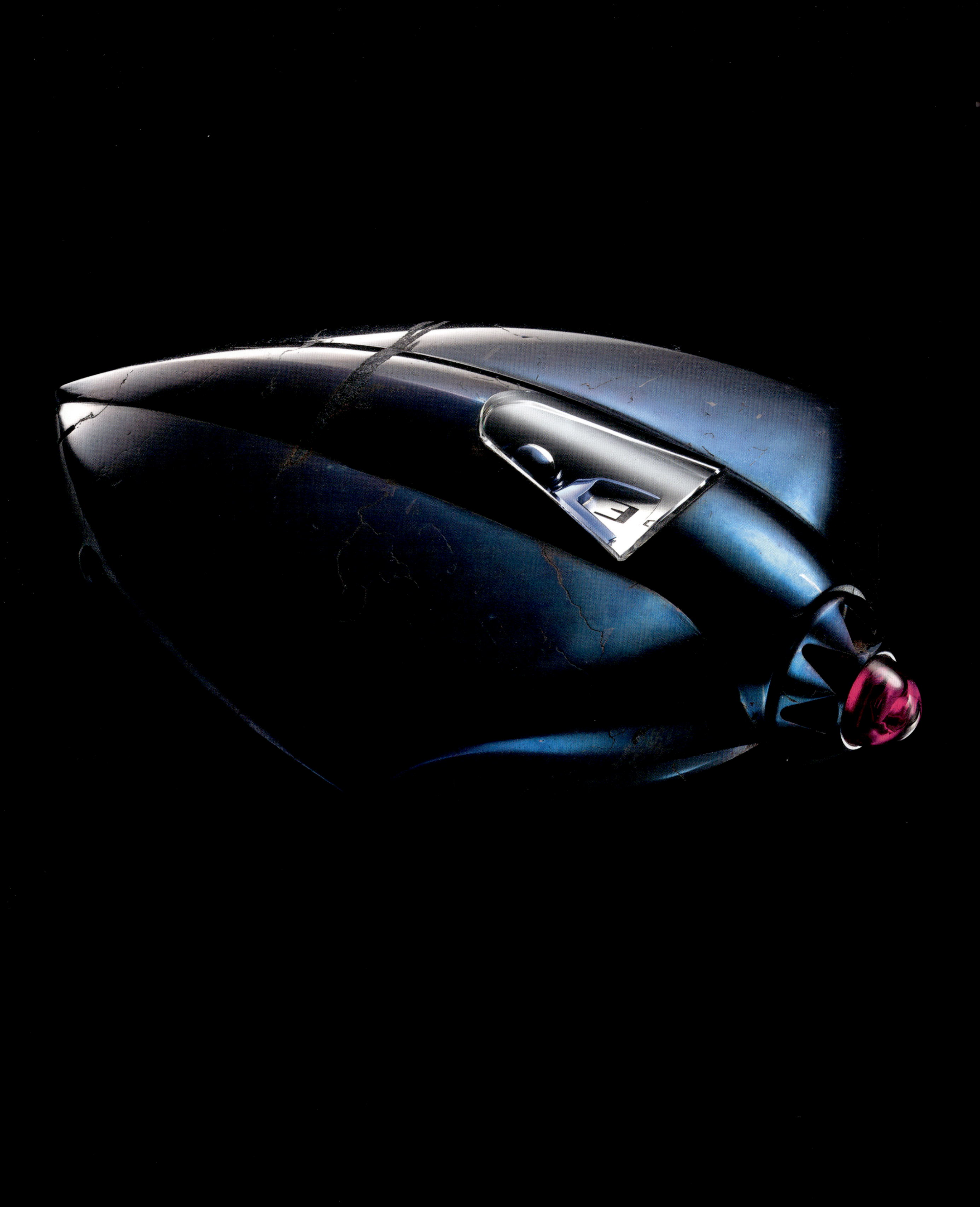

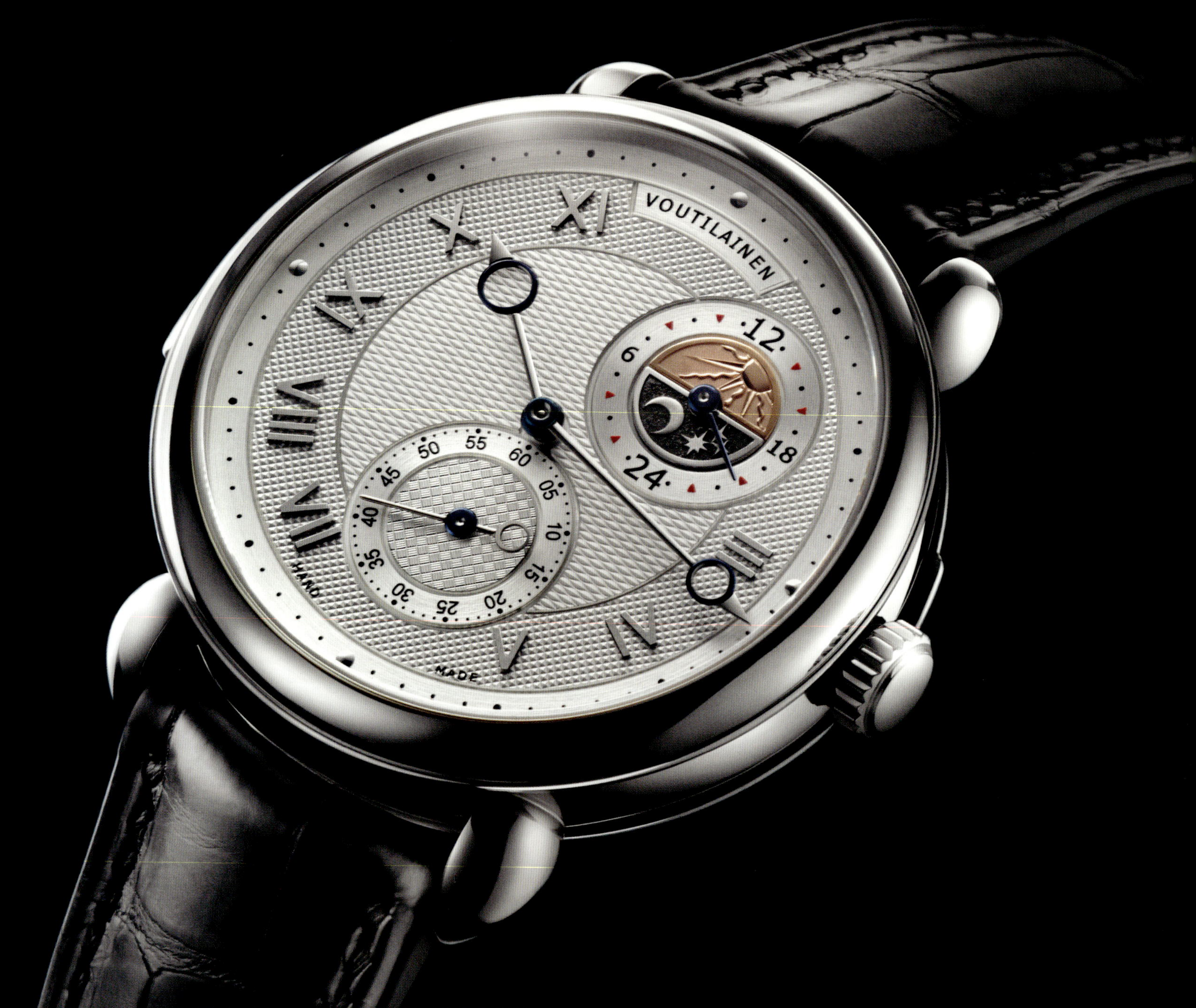

VOUTILAINEN — MINUTE REPEATER GMT

$ 497 000

There is a certain degree of mythos that surrounds the important independent watchmakers of today. Toiling alone or in small teams, two elements make these esteemed members of the watch industry so honoured by collectors. First is the fact that by being independent they can do whatever they like. This typically translates into taking their precious time when making each watch, as well as producing only those watch designs that they truly feel represent who they are and their creative intentions. This means that buyers are purchasing a watchmaker's personality as much as their work.

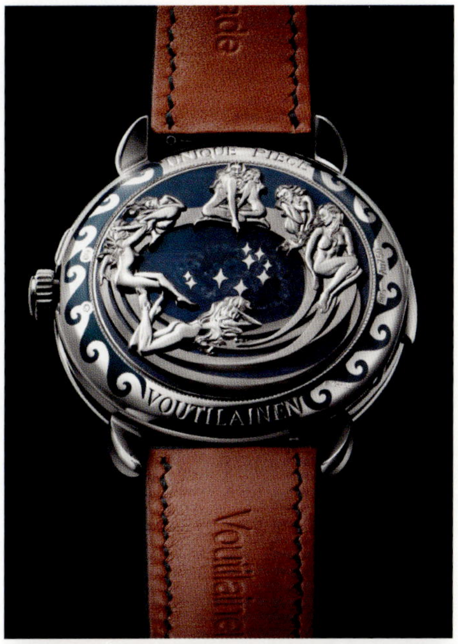

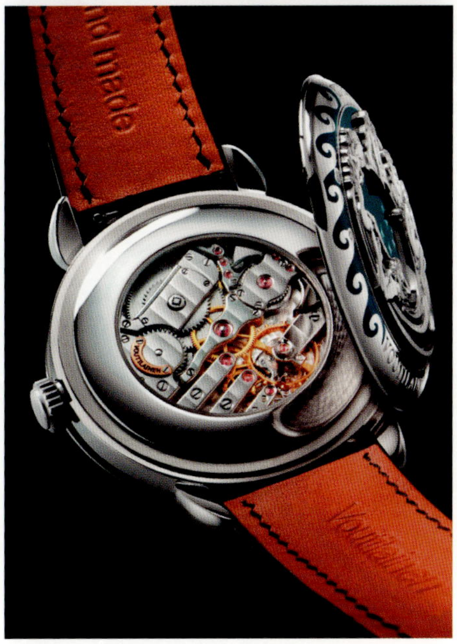

Second is the fact that small, independent watchmakers produce timepieces in more traditional ways. Considered something of great importance to collectors, this is more a function of practicality than it is purely of art. Traditional watchmaking implies that most or all of the movement and case is produced by hand. What this means can vary from watchmaker to watchmaker, but many of them do employ a degree of modern technology to help them produce some of the tiny base parts in the mechanical movements and cases. Having said that, there are highly dedicated watchmakers who produce virtually everything by hand.

Look closely at the dials of many watches by Finnish Kari Voutilainen and you'll see some small text that reads "Hand Made". Such a moniker is relatively rare – even on most other hand-made watches – but it serves as a small testament to why many seasoned watch lovers have a great passion for timepieces of this ilk. A good number of Voutilainen's creations are completely unique. Just one piece is produced and nothing quite the same will ever be made again. Voutilainen watches are perhaps in high-demand because they cleverly mix a honed degree of technical prowess with refined forms of artistic decoration.

A mix of aesthetics and mechanics is perhaps the most important recipe for success in high-end independent watches. The Minute Repeater GMT blends them both successfully. As a unique creation, the watch begins with a mechanical movement that Voutilainen produces, which contains a "decimal minute repeater". This is a rare form of minute repeater that, when sounding out the time using a series of chimes, indicates first the hours, then increments of 10 minutes, followed by individual minutes. The listener then counts them to know the time. Most minute repeaters are a bit simpler and sound out the time in hours, 15-minute increments (quarters) and then single minutes.

On top of the minute repeater Voutilainen has added a GMT indicator for a second time zone. Displayed in a 24-hour format, it occupies a space on the dial with a hand-engraved subdial with a sun and Moon used to indicate AM or PM times. The dial itself is produced in solid sterling silver and completely hand-machine engraved. Three distinct engraved patterns decorate the meticulously detailed dial.

Just as watchmakers can have myth behind them, so can their watches. Voutilainen produced a unique case back for the Minute Repeater GMT watch with a semi-erotic dial featuring Pleiades, from Greek mythology. The seven sisters are carefully hand engraved on a starry display with blue enamel work. The case back is hinged, and opens up to reveal a view of the hand-made and decorated movement.

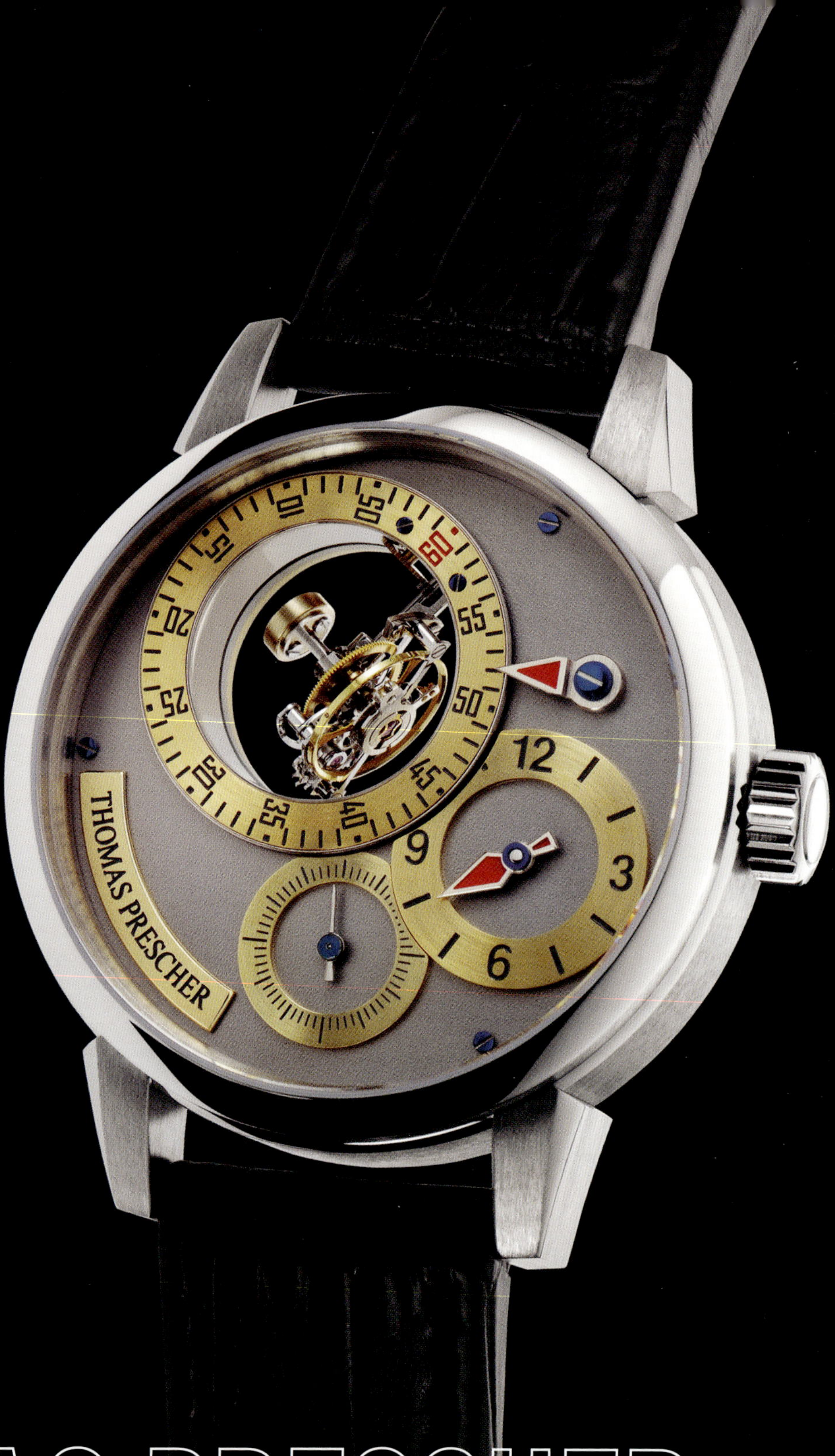

THOMAS PRESCHER — TRIPLE AXIS TOURBILLON

$ 500 000

When once asked why his Triple Axis Tourbillon watch cost half a million dollars, watchmaker and former German Navy soldier Thomas Prescher calmly stated, "because no one else in the world can make one". A true individualist, Thomas Prescher exists as part of a unique breed of ultra-independent watchmakers, who hone their craft in relative secrecy. His customers aren't merely buying a timepiece, but the wearable craftsmanship of a master artisan who can produce something bespoke and totally exclusive.

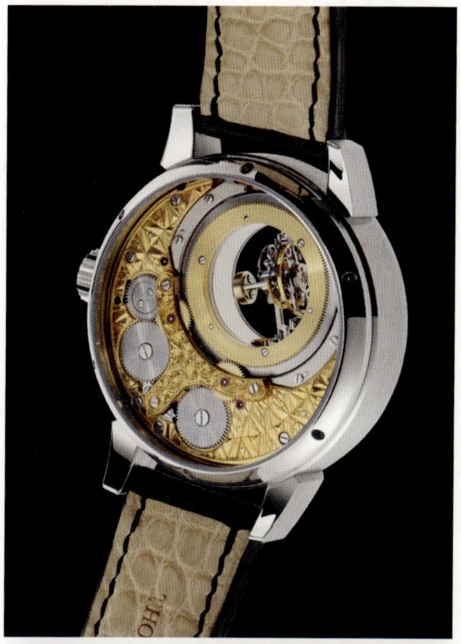

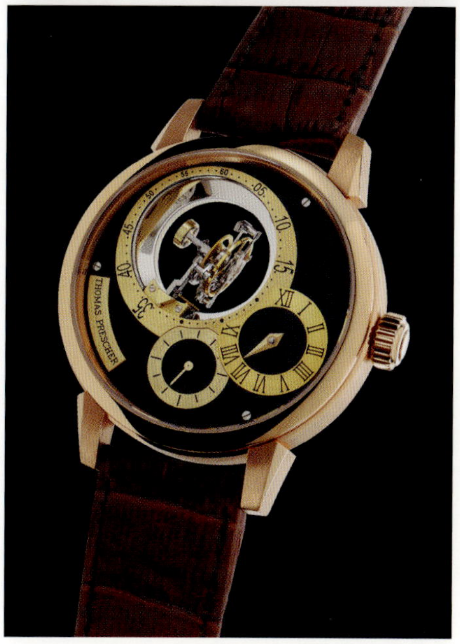

The Triple Axis Tourbillon is perhaps one of Thomas Prescher's most important achievements. He was among the first to create a wristwatch with a triple axis tourbillon, following the lead of clockmaker Richard Good, who created one for a carriage-style clock in the late 1970s. So what is a triple axis tourbillon?

High-end watches with single axis tourbillons are relatively common these days. A tourbillon is a form of mechanical movement escapement that rotates on its own axis. When it was invented at the end of the 18th century, it was designed as a means of making pocket watches and clocks more accurate. Gravity is an enemy to consistency in a timepiece. The regulating organ of the watch mostly consists of a balance wheel that rapidly moves back and forth. The more consistent the movement, the more accurate the watch. Gravity can pull on the balance wheel and create errors that affect accuracy, and purist watchmakers hate that. A tourbillon rotates a balance wheel so that there is no top or bottom. As gravity pulls on each part of it equally, the idea is that the negative effects of gravity are averaged out.

It has never actually been proved that a tourbillon makes a wristwatch (versus a pocket watch) more accurate, but their presence in a piece highly upgrades the decorative value and prestige of any timepiece. So imagine a tourbillon that spins not on one, but on three axis points in three dimensions. That is a triple axis tourbillon. Thomas Prescher's version is quite special and wonderfully interesting to visualise. An open hole in the dial holds the entire tourbillon assembly on an impossibly thin rod. This rod rotates around the window each 60 minutes, and just happens to double as the minute hand. The rod also spins, creating the second axis of rotation.

The tourbillon cage (as it is called) also spins, in the same manner that most single axis tourbillons do, offering the third and final axis point of rotation. Because there are three points of rotation, the watch can safely be referred to as a triple axis tourbillon. Separate dials on the watch offer indicators for the hours and seconds, and each Thomas Prescher Triple Axis Tourbillon is unique and made to order.

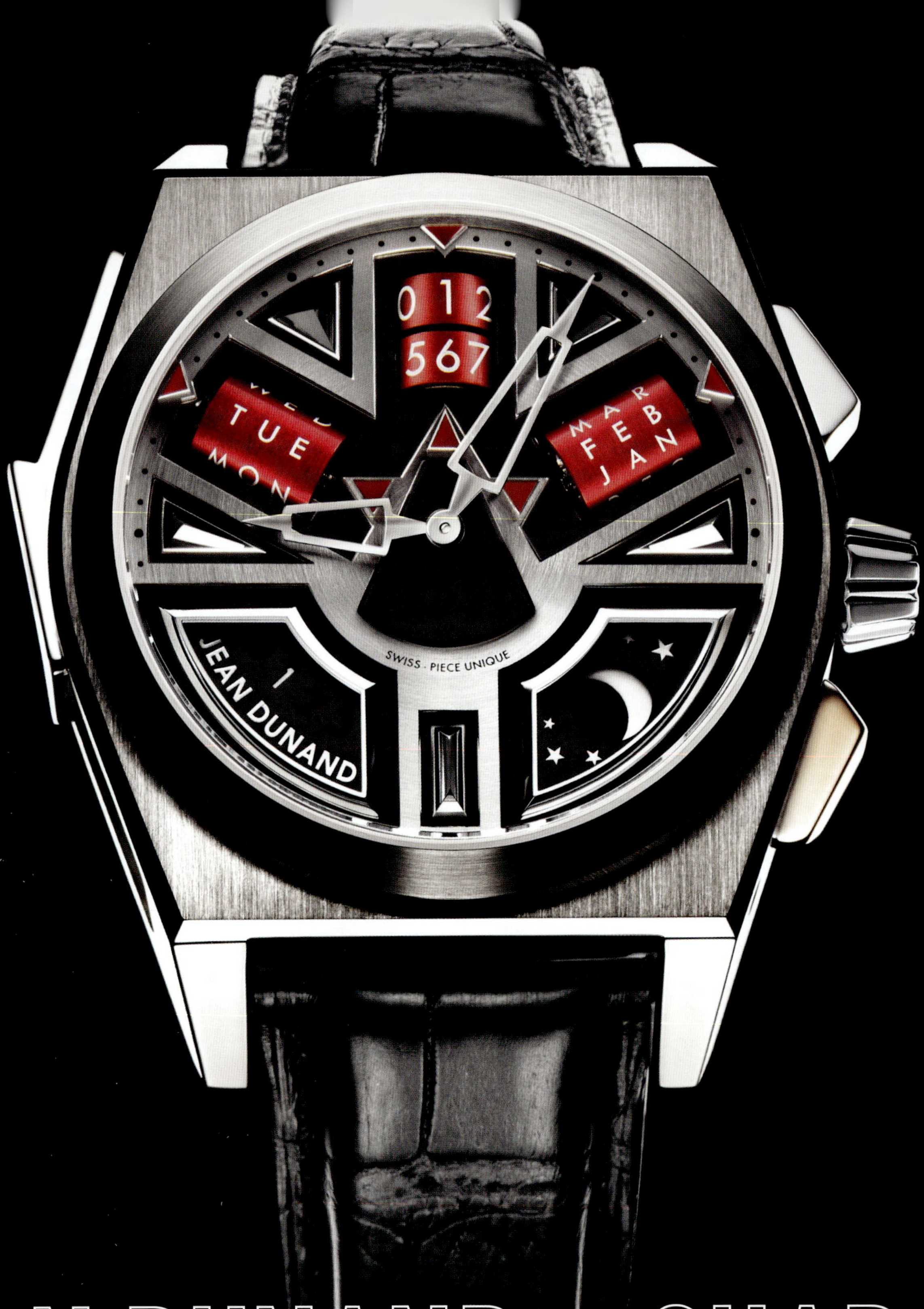

JEAN DUNAND — SHABAKA

$ 500 000

One of the least represented forms of artistic design in modern high-end watches is, surprisingly, art-deco. The art-deco years of the 1920s coincided with the arrival of some of the very first wristwatches, and its theme of combining industrial design with artistic nuance has been seminal in the development of 20th- and early 21st-century design. While some of today's greatest timepieces have art-deco era origins, there are very few new timepieces that properly emulate the famous aesthetic style.

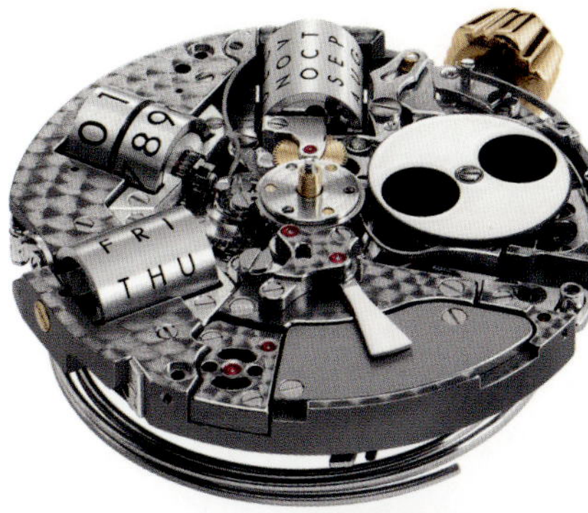

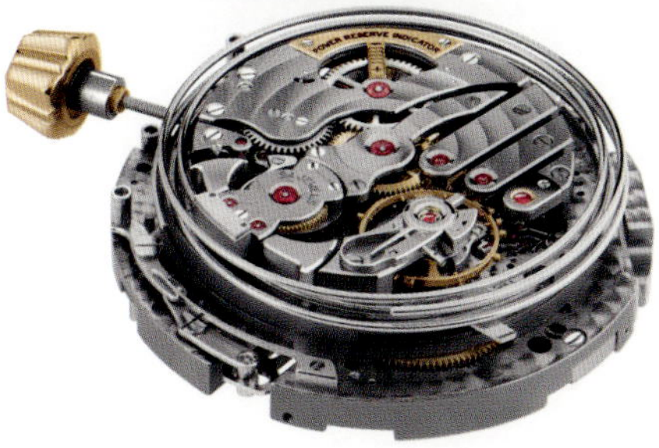

One exception has been the handful of watches produced by Jean Dunand, inspired by a Swiss artist who was often considered the greatest lacquer artist of the art-deco period. One reason that there are so few Jean Dunand watches in existence, is because each piece produced by the brand has been unique. They would never make the same watch twice, and each piece is considered exclusive.

Perhaps Jean Dunand's greatest asset was that its movements were produced by the Swiss workshop of Christophe Claret. One of the "most art-deco" timepieces they produced together was the Shabaka. Combining Egyptian art with art-deco lines, the Shabaka was a monolithic watch housing an extremely complicated mechanism.

At its heart, the wildly designed Shabaka is a grand complication with perpetual calendar and minute repeater. The minute repeater chimes the time musically, and is activated by a sliding lever on the side of the case. The perpetual calendar does not need to be adjusted for over 100 years, because it takes into consideration leap years. Traditional window or dial indicators aren't used on the Shabaka for most of the information. Rather, the watch uses small aluminium rollers that indicate information. The dial also displays the phases of the Moon.

Christophe Claret produced the intensely complicated 721-piece mechanical movement, as well as much of the case. He is among the few high-end watch designers who also considers practicality and ergonomics (no matter how large his timepieces may be in size). Usefully featured on the Shabaka, are little switch-style locks that prevent the pushers around the case from working accidentally. Pressing these pushers adjusts the calendar information, and while locked during wear, they cannot operate.

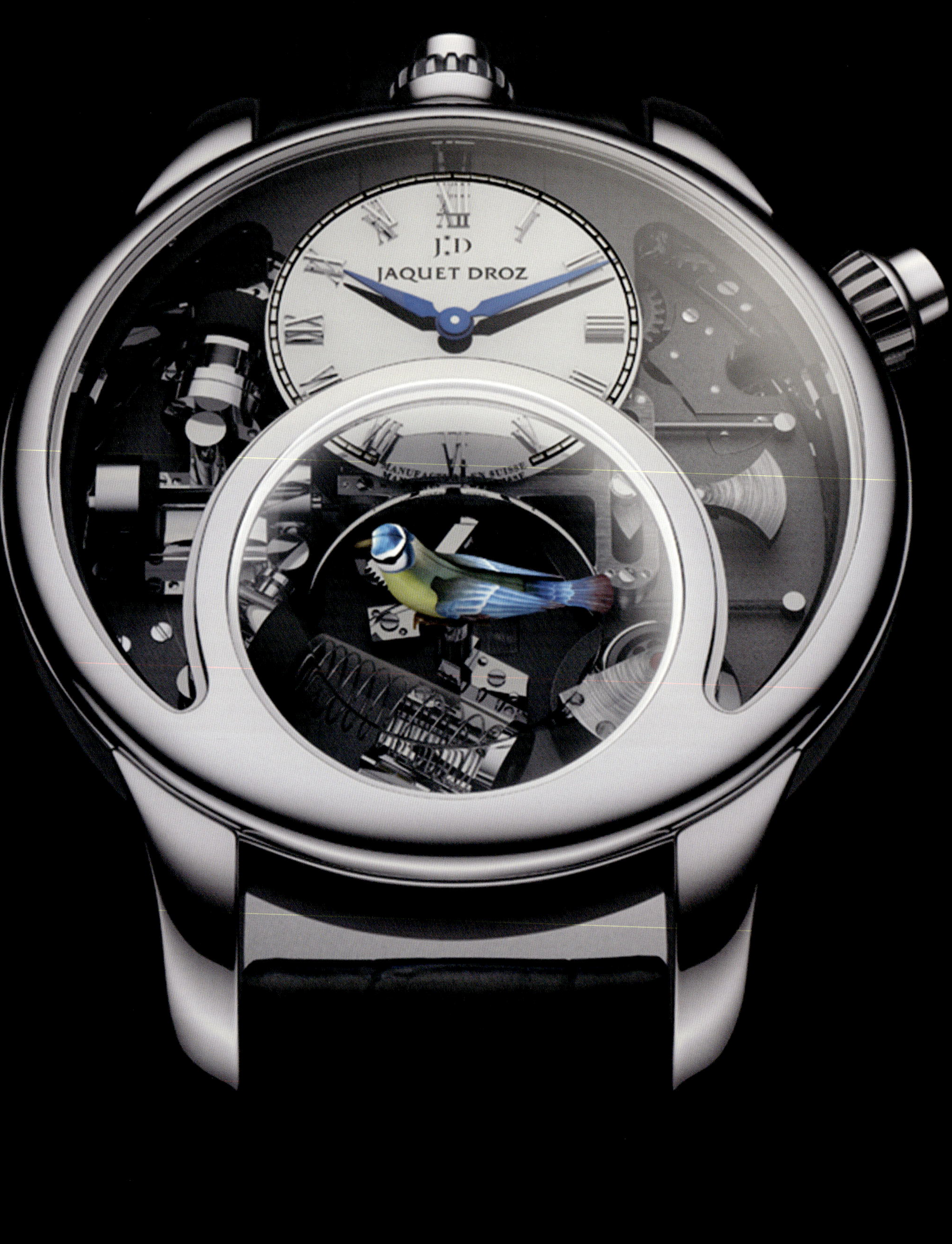
JAQUET DROZ

JAQUET DROZ – THE CHARMING BIRD AUTOMATON

$500 000

TOO LARGE TO FIT UNDER A STANDARD SAPPHIRE CRYSTAL, THE CHARMING BIRD WATCH HAS A BUBBLE IN THE CRYSTAL THAT ACTS LIKE AN OBSERVATION DOME FOR THE BIRD WHILE IT OPERATES.

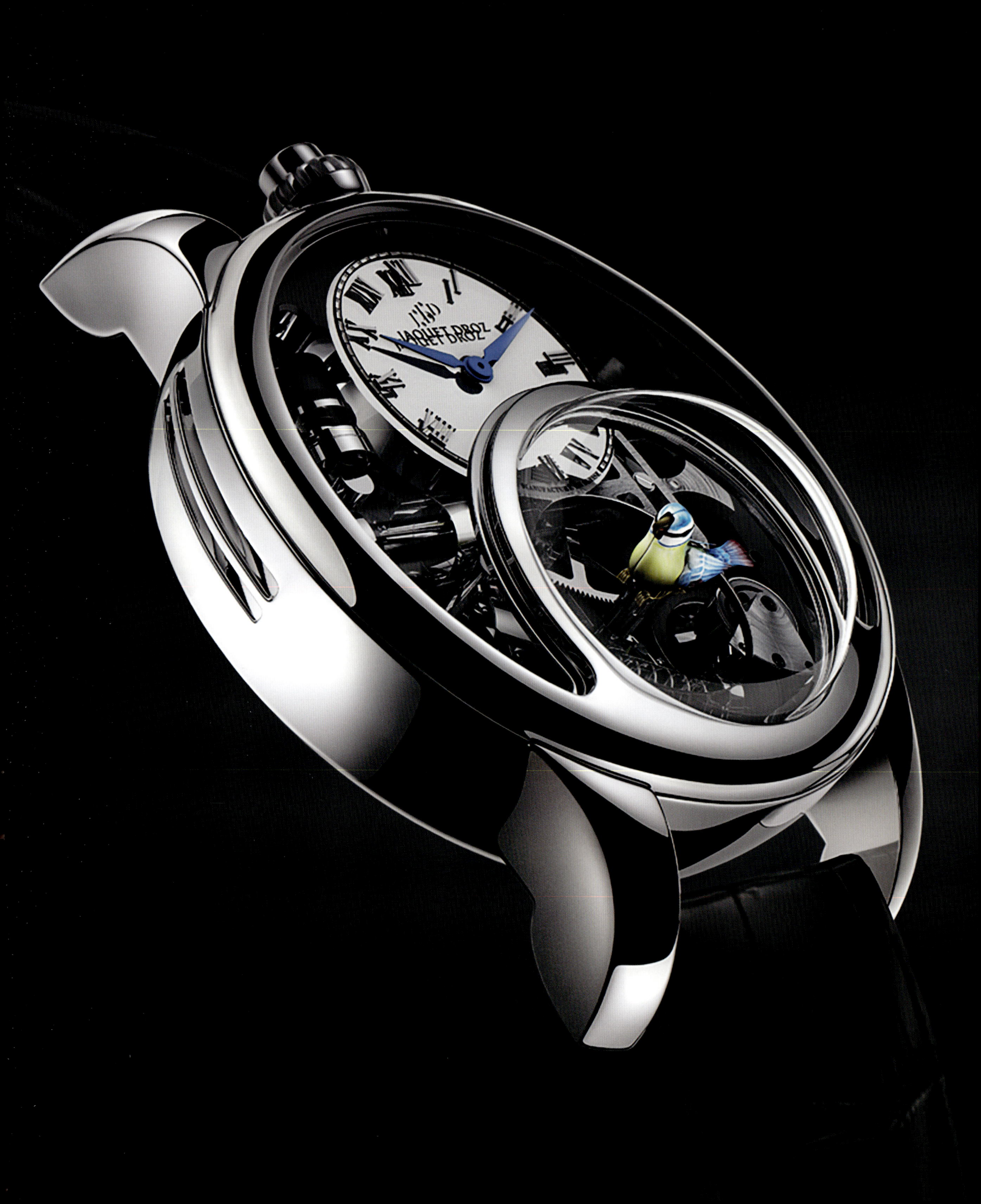
JAQUET DROZ

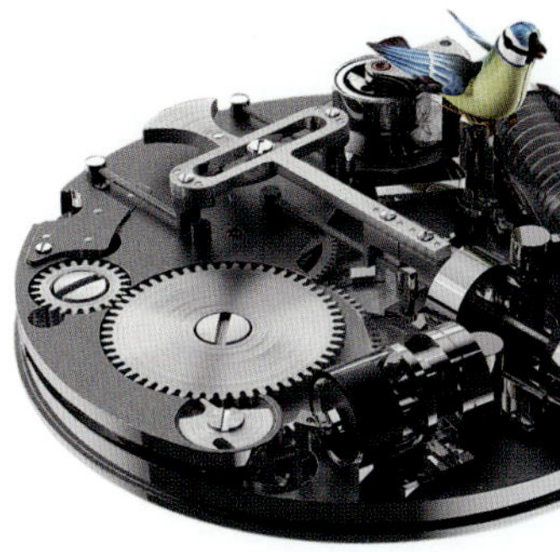

In the mid-18th century, Pierre Jaquet-Droz and his company travelled around Europe and Asia selling timepieces to royalty and aristocracy. While not the only travelling merchant selling timepieces, Jaquet-Droz had a unique asset that made him a favourite invited guest in many important halls in England, France, his native Switzerland, China, India, and even Japan. While the mainstay of his business was the sale of decorated pocket watches, Jaquet-Droz was also an inventor of incredible mechanical automata – even when judged by contemporary standards.

Some of these items he would build for clients on order, while others were strictly for display purposes. One such famous automata with which Jaquet-Droz travelled was known as "The Writer". Designed like a well-dressed child, The Writer was an early form of robot that, when activated, would write out phrases on paper with quill and ink. Jaquet-Droz would create customised program discs that would allow The Writer to create messages, personally greeting a particular king or person of importance in whose presence they were. The Writer automata machine still exists today, and is operated from time to time for audiences in Switzerland. It is also said to have been a major influence behind the 2011 Martin Scorsese movie "Hugo".

In addition to one-of-a-kind wonders like The Writer (and its kin), Jaquet-Droz also produced smaller automata-based devices, such singing birds. A particular favourite of Jaquet-Droz, a mechanical bird puppet would be created and, using a whistle-type device, would engage in a complex and often highly life-like animation.

In around 2000 the legacy of Jaquet-Droz was continued with a new watchmaker brand under the Swatch Group. For over a decade Jaquet Droz was engaged in recapturing the glory of Jaquet-Droz's famous singing automata birds. After several years of development, they released a mechanical wristwatch that contained a fully functioning Jaquet-Droz-style automaton bird inside the dial. Known as the Jaquet Droz Charming Bird, the watch was a true modern feat of mechanical miniaturisation, when it was released in 2013.

Too large to fit under a standard sapphire crystal, the Charming Bird watch has a bubble in the crystal that acts like an observation dome for the bird while it operates. Like the Jaquet-Droz automaton birds of old, the small bird in the Charming Bird timepiece pivots around, flaps its wings, and moves its beak as the piston-style whistle makes realistic bird calls. The only real difference between the Charming Bird and its historic ancestors, is that the older versions had birds dressed in real feathers.

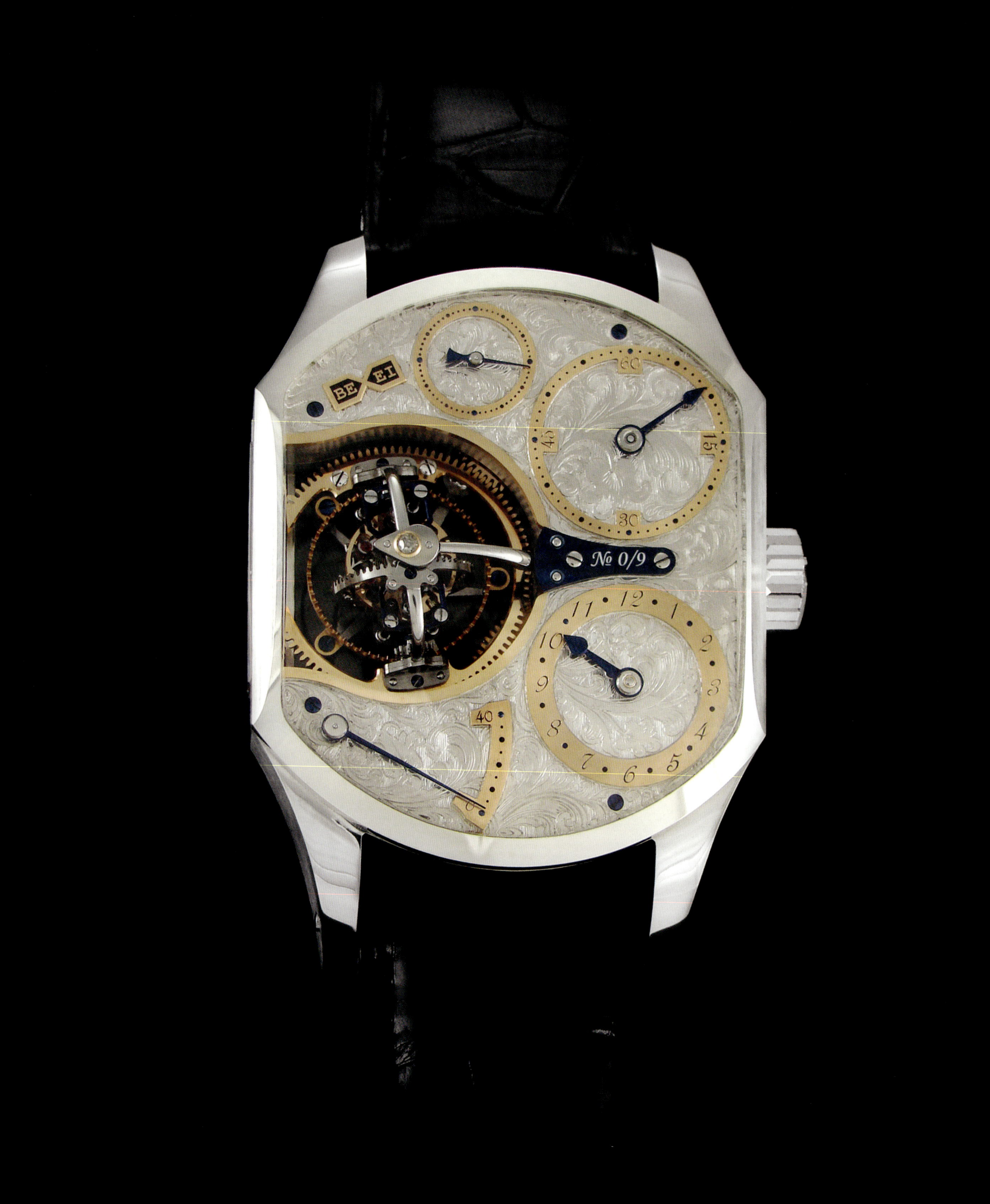
BE EI
№ 0/9

BEXEI — PRIMUS TRIPLE-AXIS TOURBILLON

$ 500 000

BEXEI HAND MAKES AND DECORATES EACH OF THE PIECES IN THE PRIMUS WATCH. EACH EXAMPLE CAN TAKE HUNDREDS OF HOURS TO PRODUCE.

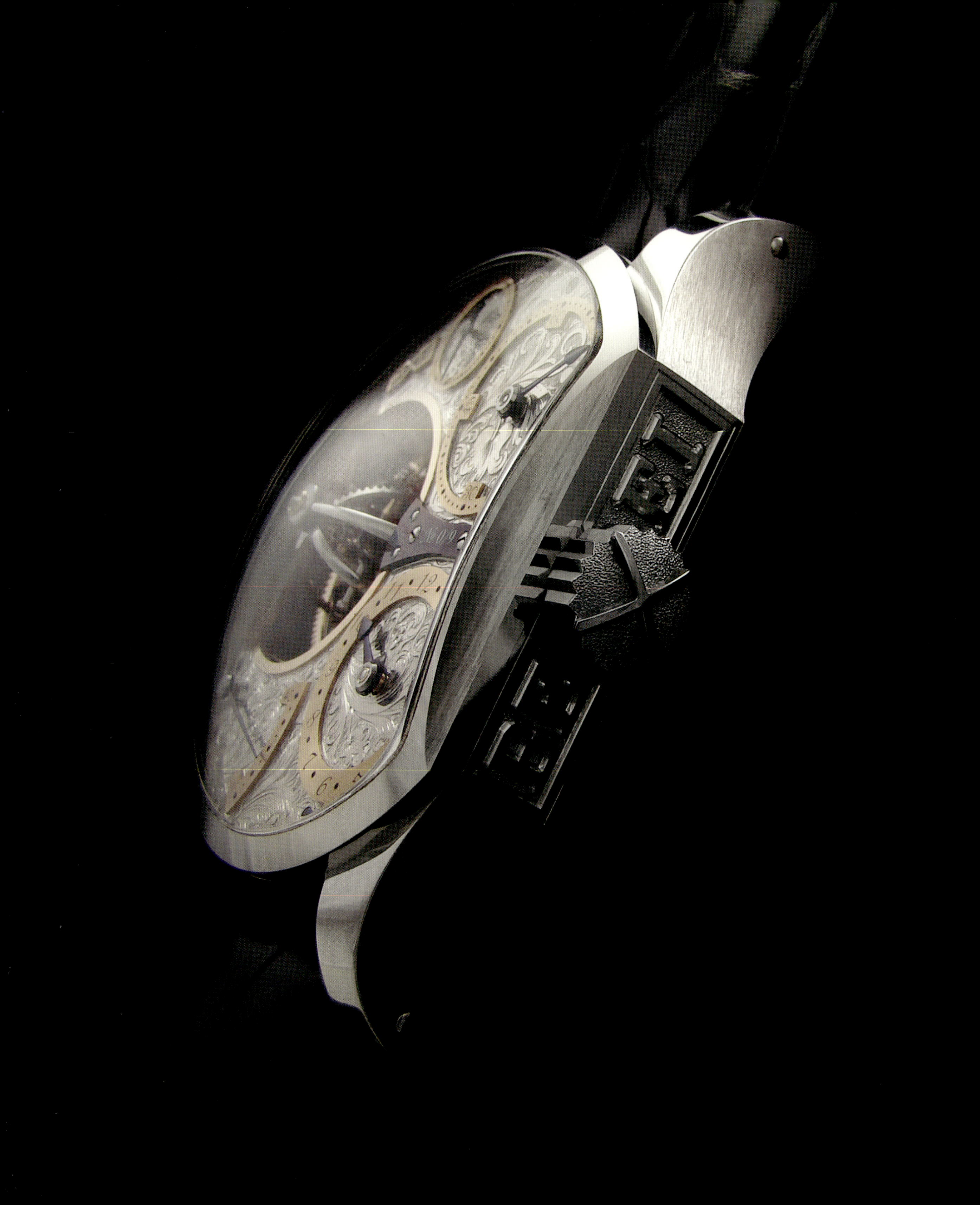

It is often the case that interesting watches come from interesting places. Swiss watches may represent a very large percentage of the ultra-luxury timepiece market, but there are independent watchmakers around the world who offer their own interpretations of high-end horology. One such, is third-generation watchmaker Aaron Becsei, who lives and works in Budapest, Hungary.

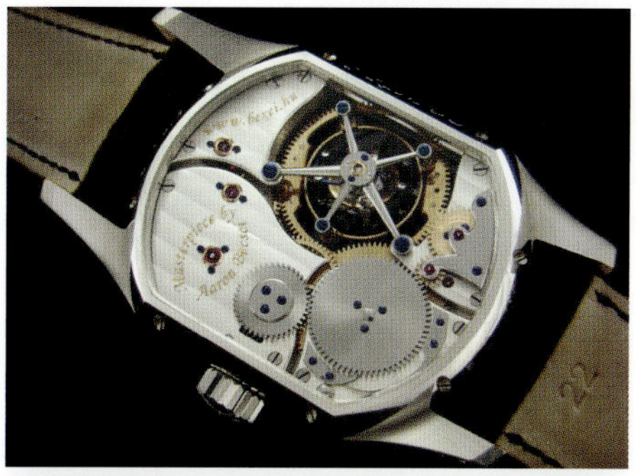

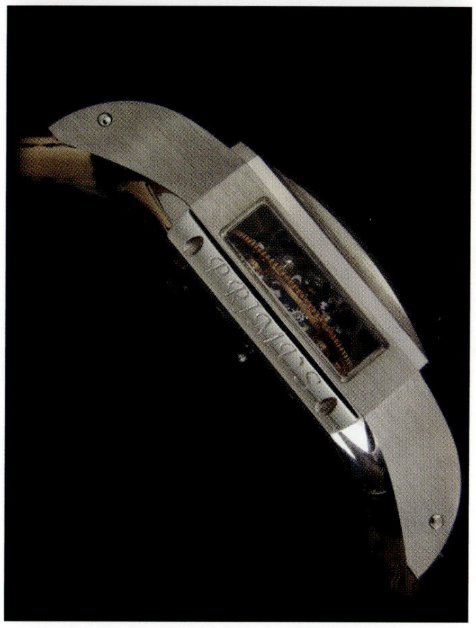

His brand "Bexei" is a play on the spelling of his last name, and he produces just a handful of watches each year, as an addition to his important watch and clock restoration business. In recent history it is often the case that some of the most brilliant contemporary watchmakers have spent time restoring antique timekeeping devices. Many of the techniques that were used to produce the most interesting old clocks, have been lost to time, so it is the role of the restorer to recreate the past.

Bexei's most ambitious creation is a watch known as the Primus Triple-Axis Tourbillon. Many high-end watches feature tourbillon complications that put the balance wheel in a spinning cage that revolves around its own axis. Multi-axis tourbillon watches employ systems that have the balance wheel and escapement rotating on more than one axis.

There is, arguably, no practical benefit for having a dual or triple axis tourbillon. It is an exercise in passion, technique, and inventiveness. All the people in the world capable of producing triple tourbillon movements, could easily have a relatively intimate dinner together.

Featured in a large dial-opening on the Primus, the three tourbillons extend from the small balance wheel in the centre, and each rotates at a different rate. The most inner tourbillon rotates rapidly once each 30 seconds, while the second tourbillon takes a full two and a half minutes to rotate. The outermost tourbillon rotates once in twelve and a half minutes. Bexei uses jewel bearings in the movement, which are a patented feature of the brand.

Bexei hand makes and decorates each of the pieces in the Primus watch. Each example can take hundreds of hours to produce. The 40mm wide 18k white gold case, frames a dial that is hand-engraved with Arabesque designs. Bexei watches are an example of classical almost baroque horological style.

Indications on the watch include the hours, minutes, and seconds, each shown on a different dial – as well as a power reserve indicator. Bexei watches represent a pure, independent, Budapest flavour, each piece being mostly produced by a single person.

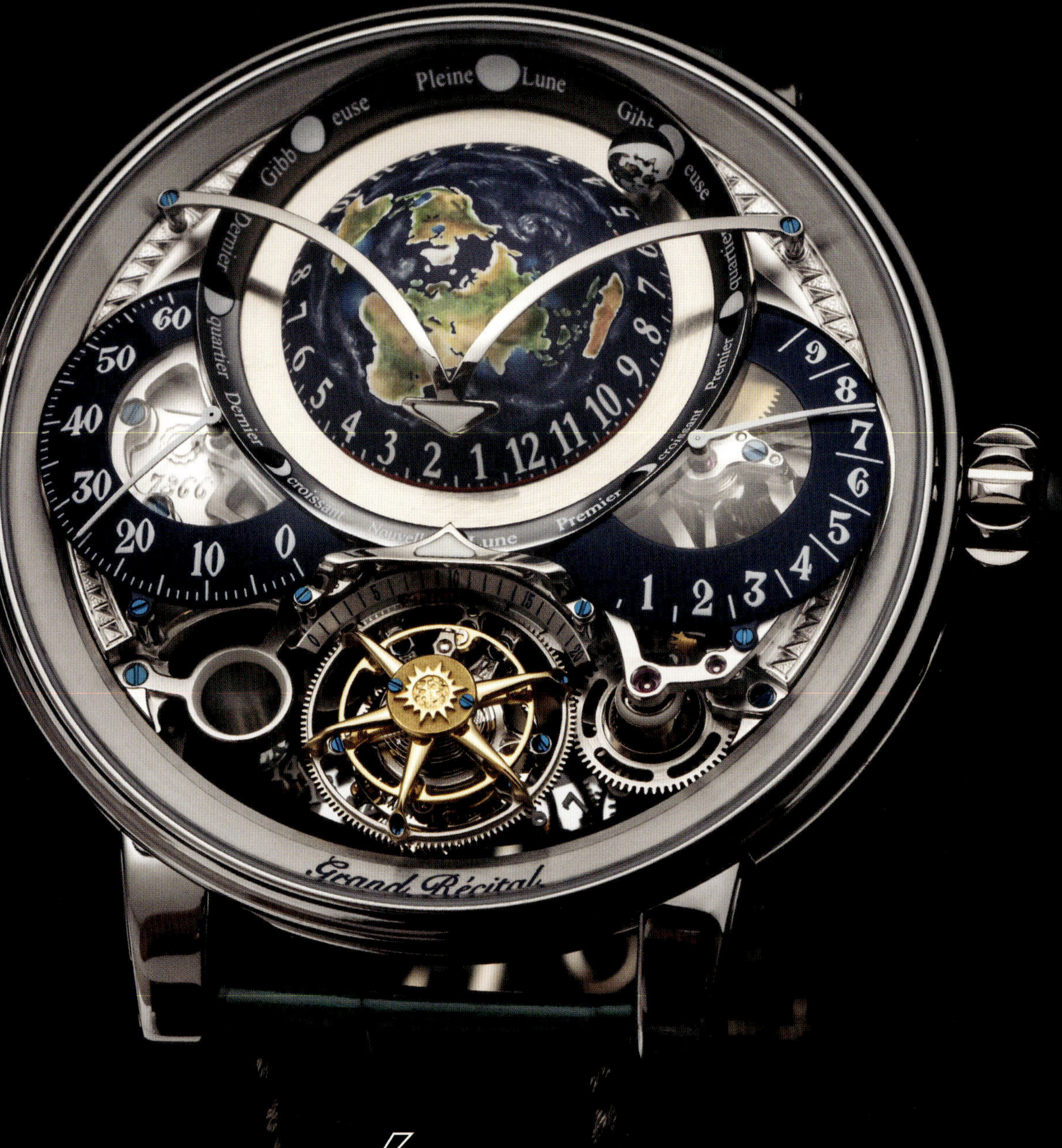

BOVET – RÉCITAL 22 GRAND RÉCITAL

$ 502 200

Built to impress, Swiss watchmaker Bovet's Récital 22 Grand Récital comes in a hefty 46mm-wide gold or platinum case, with a dial that is angled merely to give its wearer a better view. Little visual distinction is made between the carefully hand-assembled (from almost 500 parts) mechanical movement and the watch's many time and calendar indicators. Added features on both the case's stunningly detailed three-dimensional front dial and the rear dial, include Moon phases and perpetual calendar functions.

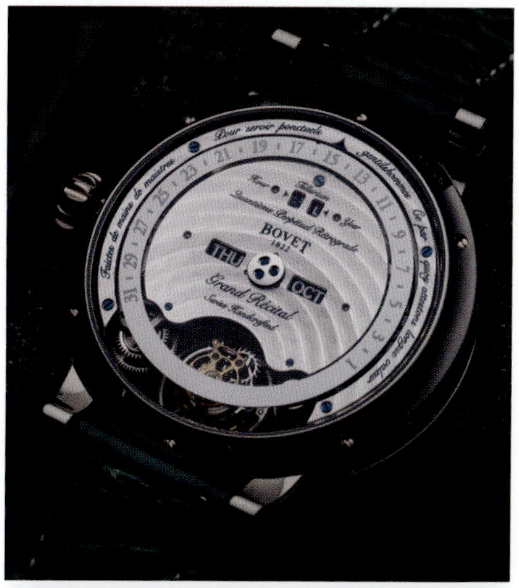

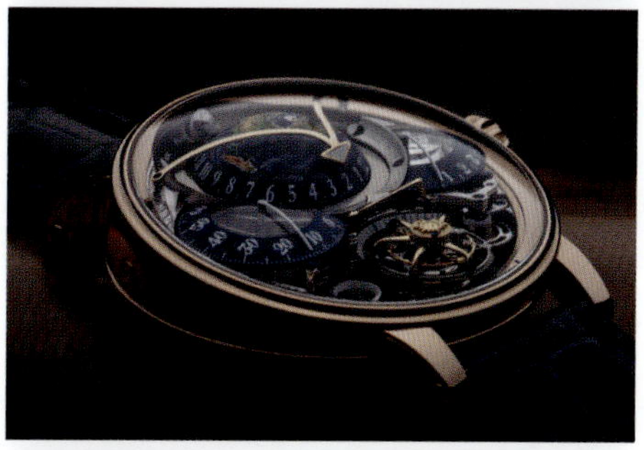

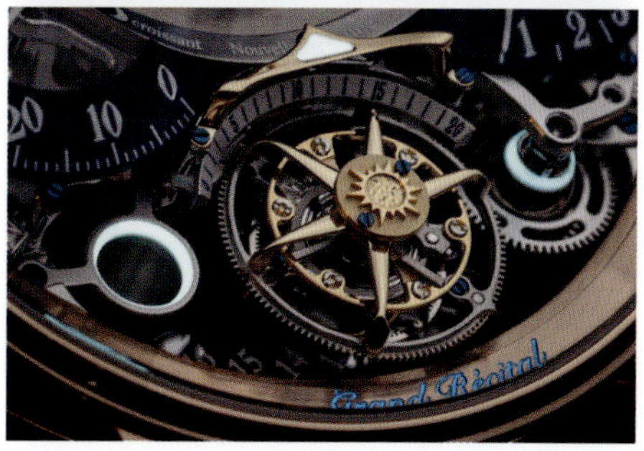

What makes this watch one for collectors is the fact that the main emphasis of the dial isn't on telling the time, but rather on the orrery-style display, which represents the current position and phase of the Moon around our Earth in relationship to the sun. The Earth is represented by the spinning tourbillon positioned at 6 o'clock on the case, while the Moon is a spherical orb that turns from its light to dark side as its phases change naturally across its approximately 29-day cycle. Bovet saved its more intricate efforts for the representation of the Earth, which is hand-painted in miniature. Bovet's artisans even use luminous paint which, after being charged by light, allows the tiny map of our planet to glow in the dark. In addition to its technical and artistic merit, the Récital 22 Grand Récital's concept is intended to make collectors feel on top of the world.

Users tell the time using two domed retrograde hands, positioned at opposite ends of the dial's centrally mounted tellurium-orrery. Windows for the calendar information, such as the leap year, month and day of the week, are elegantly arranged on the rear of the movement. Bovet intentionally designed the mechanism to be asymmetrical and presentable, in contrast to many "watch engines" that were never intended to be prominently displayed. This 22nd iteration in the Récital family of watches is the result of the prolific nature of Bovet's innovation and development department. Bovet regularly ups the ante on its own accomplishments by pushing the complexity of subsequent models as far as it can. The idea is to keep finicky customers wowed (and their buying budgets compelled).

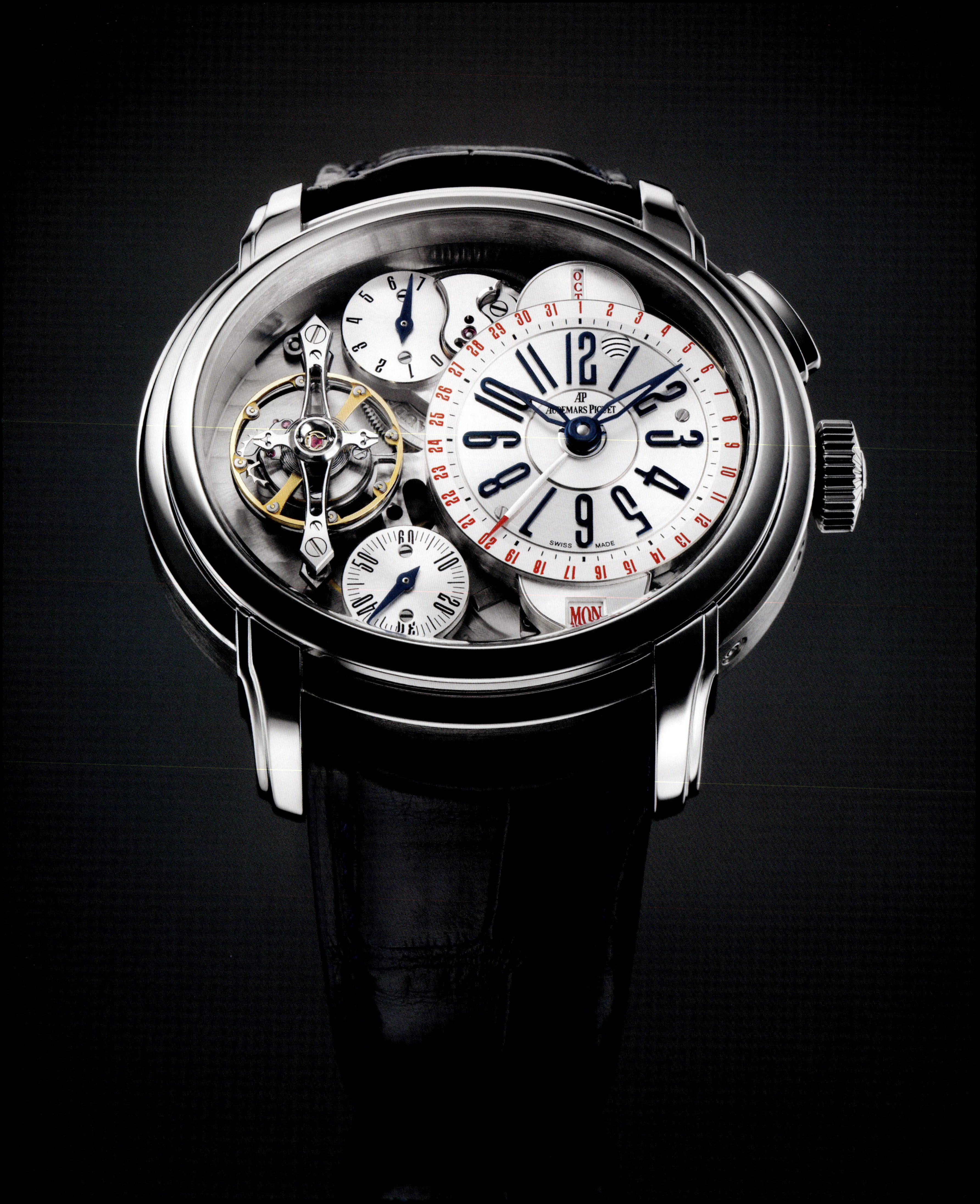
OCT
SWISS MADE
MON

AUDEMARS PIGUET – MILLENARY NO. 5 AP ESCAPEMENT PERPETUAL CALENDAR

$ 503 700

THE APPEAL OF THE AUDEMARS PIGUET MILLENARY BEGINS WITH ITS HORIZONTALLY-LONG OVAL-SHAPED PLATINUM CASE.

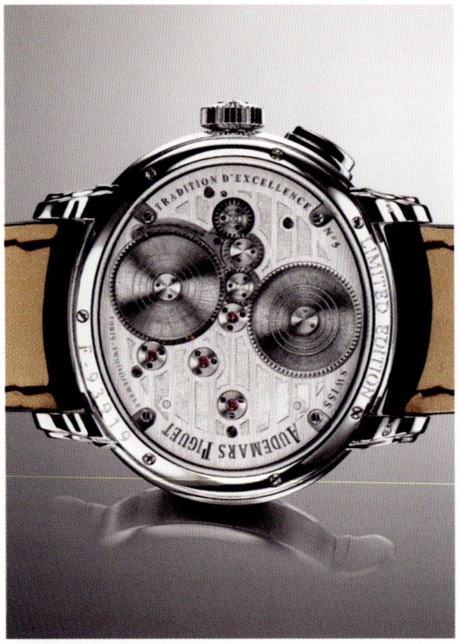

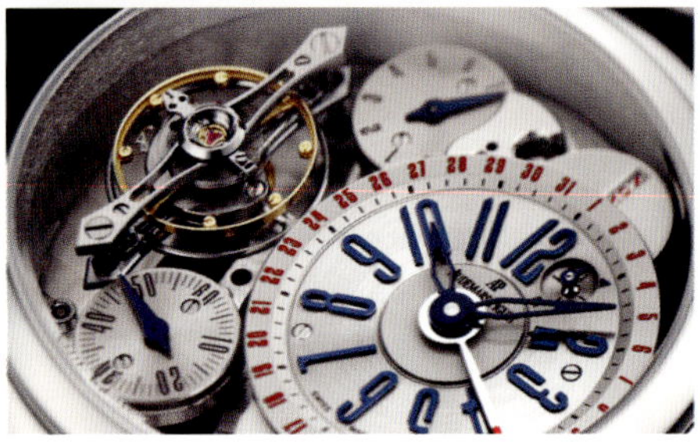

Time is circular, and so are most watches. Nevertheless, despite the logical reasons for watchmakers producing round-dial pieces, uncommon shapes for time-telling machines have been explored for hundreds of years. The appeal of the Audemars Piguet Millenary begins with its horizontally-long oval-shaped platinum case. Still rounded, the almost egg-shaped design begins a journey into a very unconventional piece of high-end horology.

There are no indication features contained in the Millenary No. 5 AP Escapement Perpetual Calendar that don't exist in other watches. What is special about the machine is how its movement is designed, and how some of its unique features help define contemporary watchmaking. A truly laudable element of the watch is that its extra complications are designed to increase both timekeeping performance, and the ability to make adjustments to the time and calendar information.

Displayed on the dial of the watch are the time and full perpetual calendar information. Such a calendar displays the month, date, day of the week, and leap year – meaning that it will never require adjustment during the life of the wearer. The dial also has a power reserve indicator, which is useful since, when fully wound, the Millenary No. 5 watch has enough power to last for a full week.

In 2006, Audemars Piguet chose this watch to debut a technical innovation called the "AP Escapement". All mechanical watches include a regulating system that contains a balance wheel and escapement. In most watches these systems represent technology that was more or less perfected during the 19th century. Audemars Piguet, however, is among the few since then to have innovated and improved upon the escapement. The system helps move power consistently from the mainspring to the movement, meaning it is at the heart of time-keeping accuracy. Through using double hairsprings and a totally new direct impulse escapement design, the AP Escapement system offers a more durable and stable system, which helps the watch to be more accurate and consistent over time. It also happens to have a seconds hands that ticks, versus sweeps.

The movement in the Millenary No. 5 Perpetual Calendar features a rather friendly system when it comes to adjusting the calendar. Unlike most perpetual calendar watches, this one can be set forward or backward in time. Audemars Piguet produced a total of only 20 pieces.

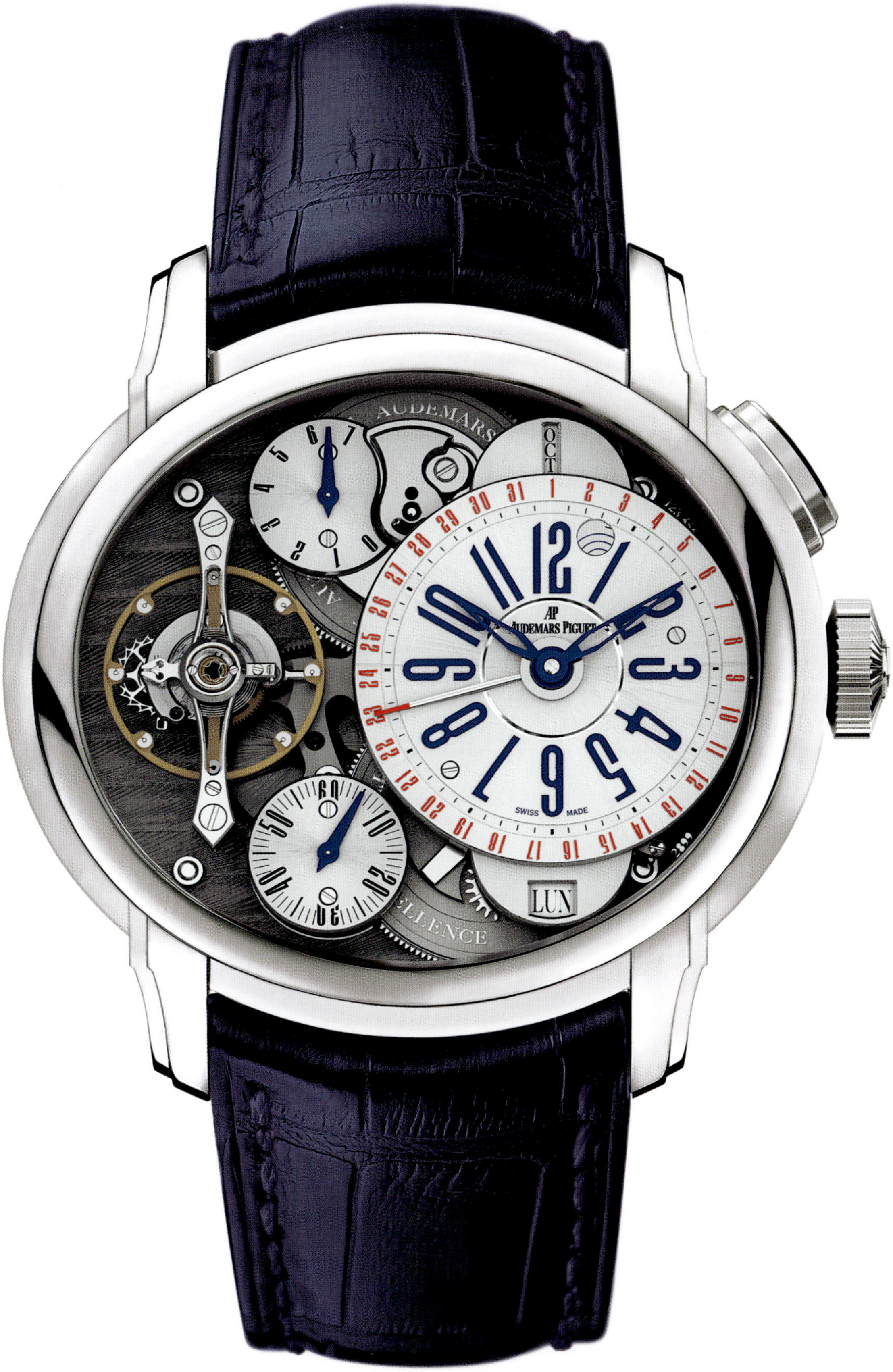
AUDEMARS
OCT
AUDEMARS PIGUET
SWISS MADE
LUN

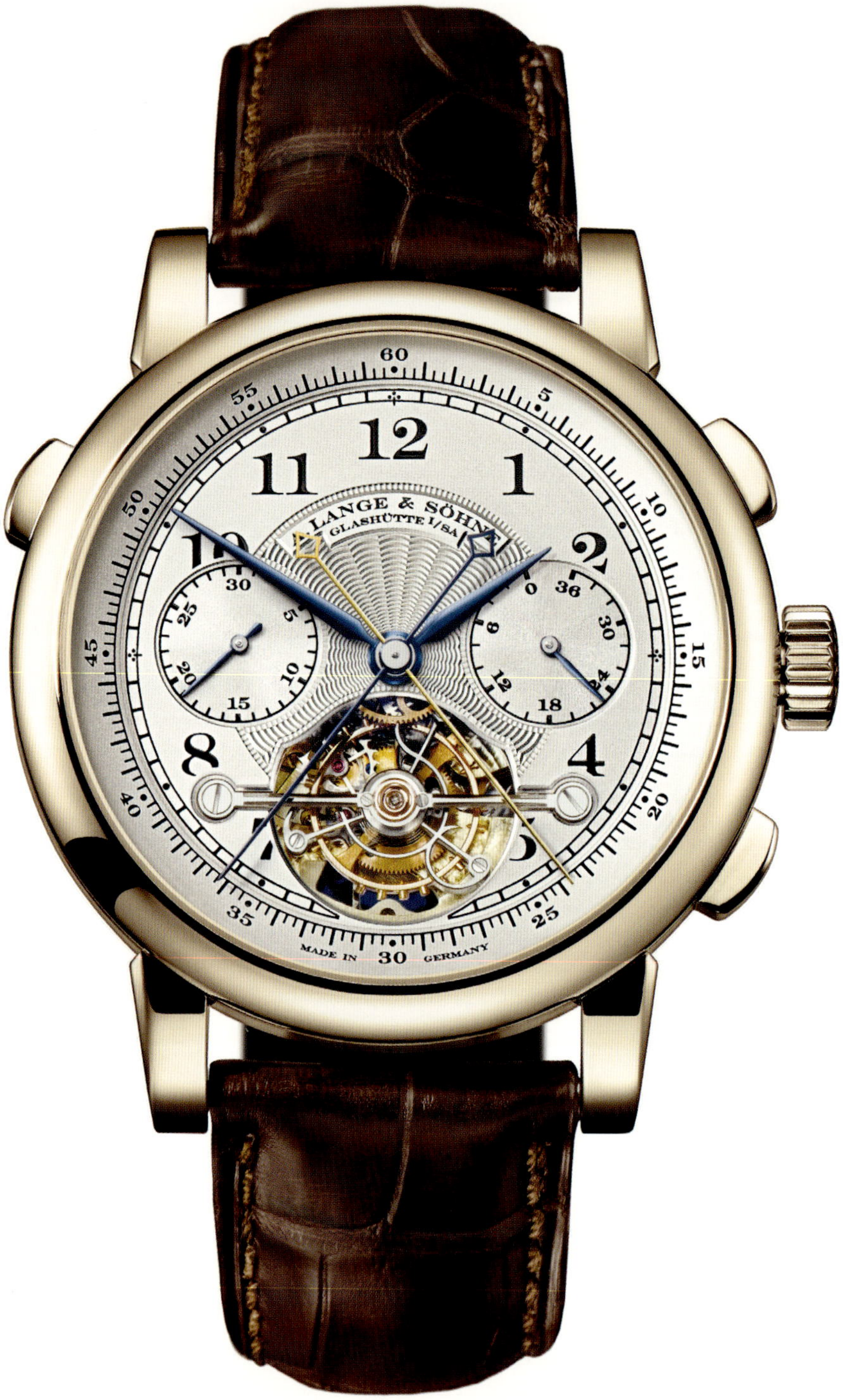

A. LANGE & SÖHNE – TOURBOGRAPH

$ 508 000

Most watch brands come up with original designs, but very few come up with their own metal alloys. Germany's A. Lange & Söhne, a veritable king of Teutonic luxury, can claim to have their own form of gold. In addition to offering common gold alloys, such as 18k rose or white gold, for their watches, A. Lange & Söhne have developed their own gold mixture called honey gold. The name properly describes the warm colour of the alloy, which is intended to be an alternative to the slightly darker and more commonly used 18k rose gold. Honey gold has the added benefit of being about twice as hard as yellow gold, which enhances its scratch resistance qualities.

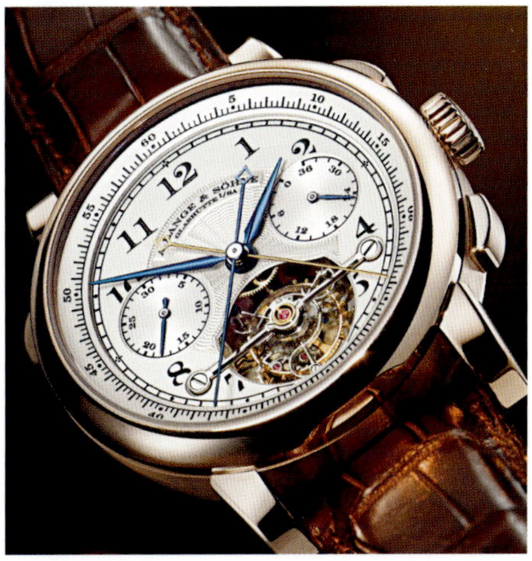

A. Lange & Söhne used their Tourbograph model as one of the first pieces to debut their new precious metal in 2010. They released a trio of timepieces showcasing the beauty of the gold, with the Tourbograph being the star of the bunch. The name is a contraction of "tourbillon" and "chronograph", as the watch contains both features. While this version is from 2010, the Tourbograph was originally released in 2005. It represents a typically beautiful example of German over-engineering, with a movement that contains over 1000 parts.

Watch collectors often consider A. Lange & Söhne to produce the most beautifully designed and decorated mechanical movements that are assembled in any volume. The brand prides itself on hand-finishing each component, as well as on ensuring quality through assembling, disassembling, and then reassembling each movement produced.

From the outside, the Tourbograph appears to feature a tourbillon-style escapement, as well as a chronograph, both of which are visible on the dial. However, the movement hides additional features that help to distinguish a watch of this acclaim and value: the chronograph features a split-second function, which increases its complication; and the movement also contains a fusee & chain transmission, which uses a tiny bicycle-style chain to move power from its mainspring to the rest of the movement.

While conservative in its design, the Tourbograph, like other A. Lange & Söhne watches, blends utilitarian function with a preservation of traditional watchmaking techniques, making it a perennial pick for collectors.

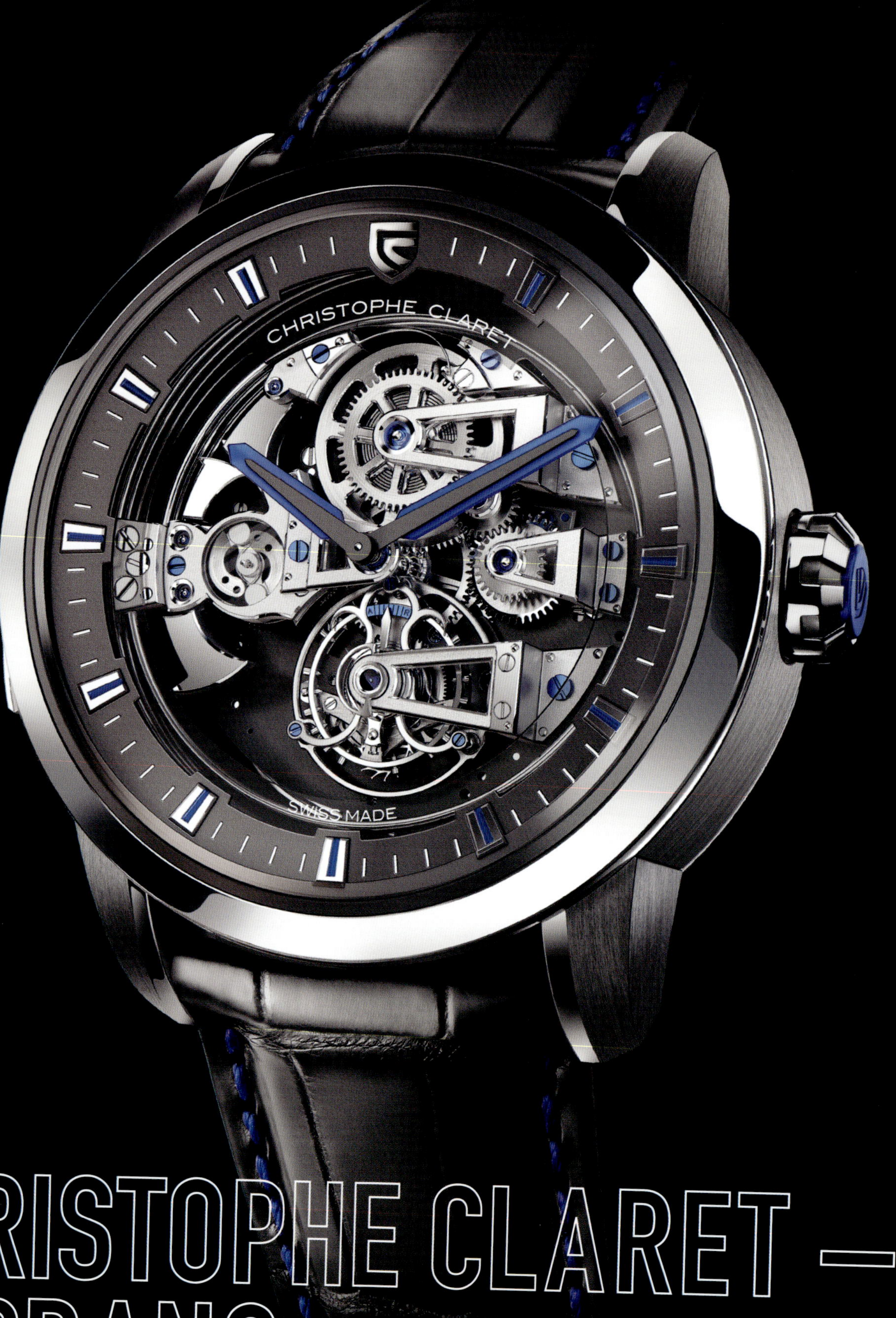

CHRISTOPHE CLARET — SOPRANO

$ 525 000

Musical watches have a great tradition that began with bell towers. It used to be that many cities and villages around the world had a single large clock with bells. Because not everyone could see the clock, bells were used to communicate important moments of the day to the population.

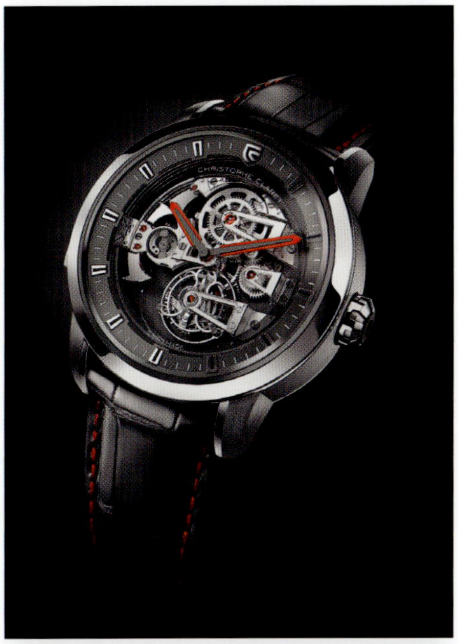

Bell towers later evolved into chiming clocks, that the ultra-wealthy could have in their homes. Such clocks would "strike", for example, "on" the hour and ring enough times to indicate the hour of the day. When pocket watches started to become more popular during the late 18th century, the concept of "chiming the time" was adopted for use in portable time-keeping devices. Thus, the minute repeater and sonnerie were born. Minute repeaters work on demand. A lever on a pocket watch acts to start a series of chimes that indicates the time. Sonnerie watches work more like traditional chiming clocks, striking at set intervals, such as on the hour.

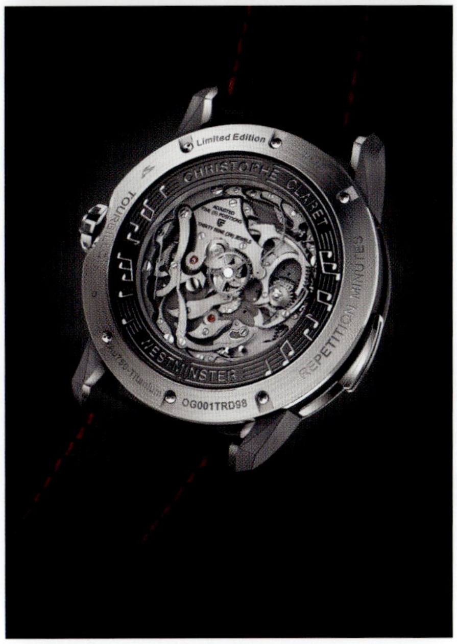

Today, minute repeater complications inside wristwatches, are deemed to be among the most difficult functions both to construct, and to master. Christophe Claret practically began his career working on minute repeater movements, so it is quite fitting that this talented independent watchmaker should seek to produce the best minute repeater watch in the world.

In 2012, Christophe Claret released the Soprano, as a tourbillon-based minute repeater, with perhaps the most impressive series of chimes ever produced in a wristwatch. With a total of four gongs, the Soprano is able to faithfully recreate the holy grail of minute repeater melodies: the full Westminster Chimes, which were composed in 1793.

Most minute repeater movements have two gongs, meaning that the Soprano has double the auditory capabilities of most other minute repeater timepieces. But it doesn't end there. Christophe Claret went deep into the design of the Soprano, to use special software that could assist in helping the watch achieve the most impressive sound possible. Some of the movement components, as well as elements of the case, are produced in titanium, which is both light weight and known to transmit sound very well.

The modern design of the Soprano case shows a totally open dial. Though the piece uses a bridge design from the early 19th century, nevertheless, the Soprano is a very contemporary timepiece. Christophe Claret even uses carefully cut pieces of agate, ruby, or onyx to border the hands. The Soprano is unlike any other available minute repeater watch, and production is limited to 16 pieces.

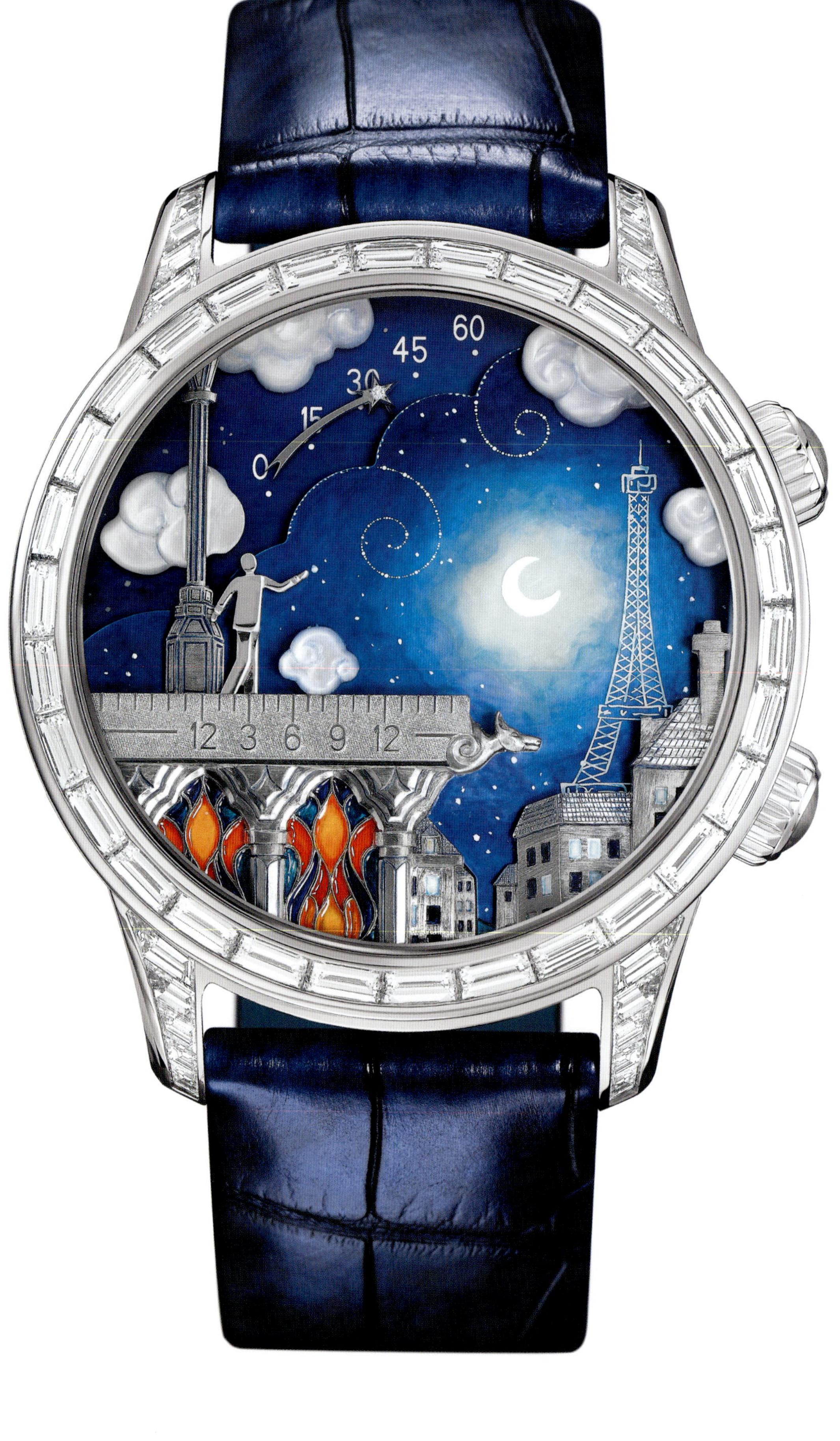
0
15
30
45
60
12 3 6 9 12

VAN CLEEF & ARPELS – POETIC WISH SET

$ 530 000*

WHAT IS STRIKING ABOUT THE POETIC WISH WATCHES IS THAT THEY DO NOT INDICATE THE TIME AT A GLANCE.

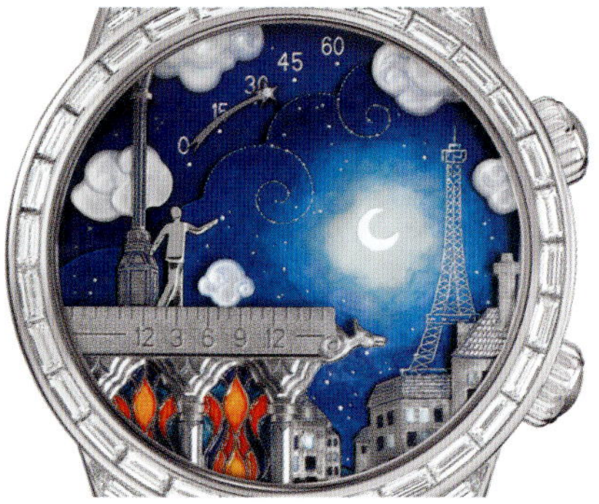

Paris-based high-end watch and jewellery maker Van Cleef & Arpels know how to create an emotionally charged luxury item. In fact, in their own words, many of their timepiece creations contain "poetic complications". Even their engineers are working on making you feel something.

In 2012, Van Cleef & Arpels upped their own ante with a duo of timepieces (for him and her) that embodied the brand's focus on romance, art and precious materials. These Poetic Wish watches take you to Paris for a simple romance between a couple located at two famous landmarks. Each is a watch with an impressively complicated movement and gorgeous hand-made dial.

What is striking about the Poetic Wish watches is that they do not indicate the time at a glance. In fact, to see the time you must activate the minute repeater mechanism contained inside the watch. Once activated, it triggers the movement of two animated elements on the dial, which move into position along the hour and minute scale to indicate the time. This is in addition to the minute repeater chimes that indicate the time to the closest five minute mark.

The ladies' Poetic Wish watch uses a traditional Van Cleef & Arpels case, lined with diamonds, depicting a scene from none other than the Eiffel tower. The female character in the couple stands atop the tower gazing across the river to Notre Dame cathedral. The dial is hand-made, using a combination of techniques including engraved gold, engraved mother-of-pearl, and careful enamel painting. Most of the work is done under a microscope requiring copious amounts of time to complete.

Set in a Van Cleef & Arpels Midnight-style case, the men's version logically takes place with our male character situated atop the Notre Dame. His view, as he longingly gazes at his love, is of the Eiffel Tower. Similar decorative techniques are used to produce a very different design for this dial, which includes a pleasant night sky, again with mother-of-pearl engraved clouds.

The reverses of the watches allow open views of the mechanical movements, which include innovative features designed to improve the sound of the minute repeater. Often, the chimes from such functions are muffled by the case. In order to reduce this effect, the Poetic Wish watches have minute repeater gongs that are attached not to the case, but to the sapphire crystal itself.

* 'Midnight Poetic Wish with diamond bezel' for Men, $530,000
'Lady Arpels Poetic Wish with diamond bezel' for Women, $470,000

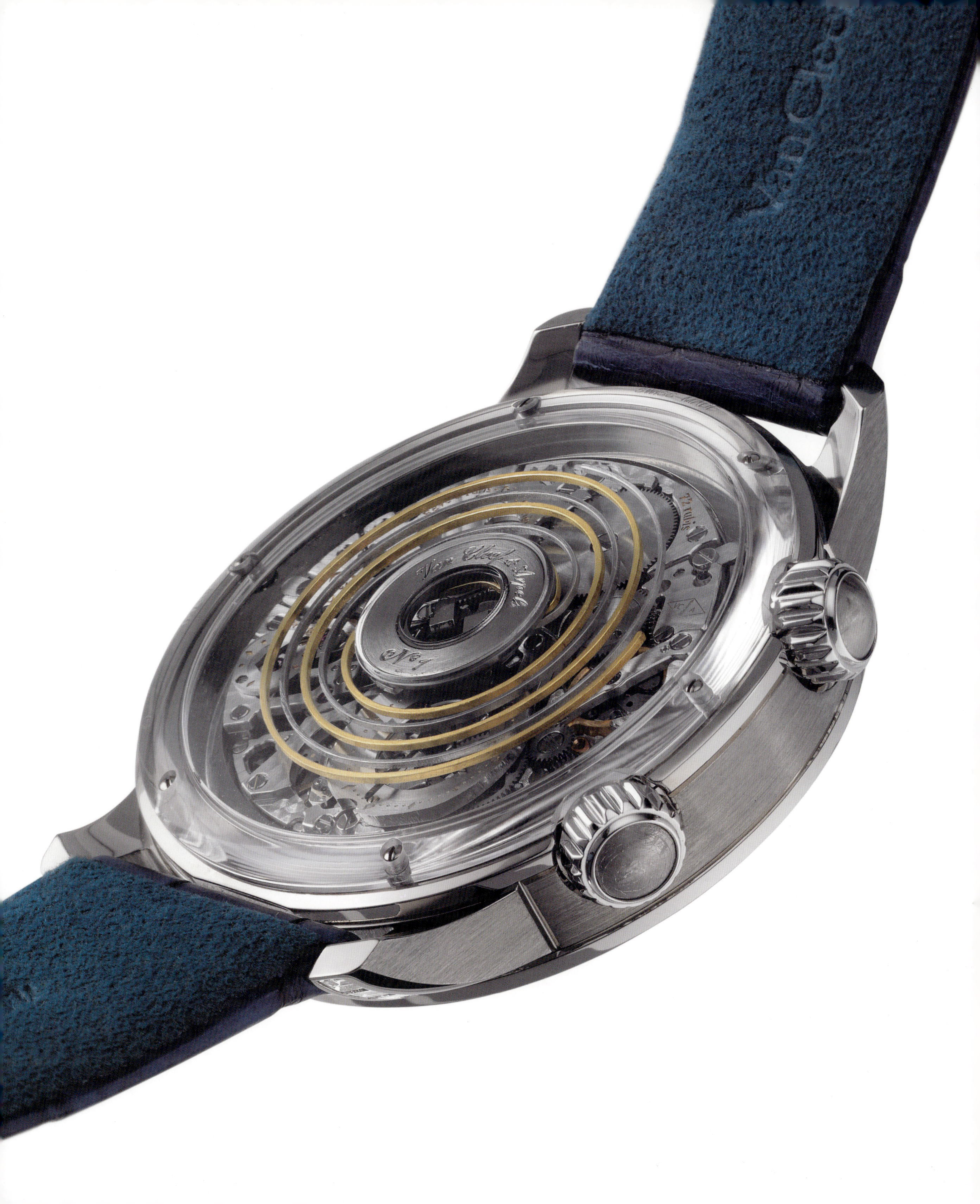

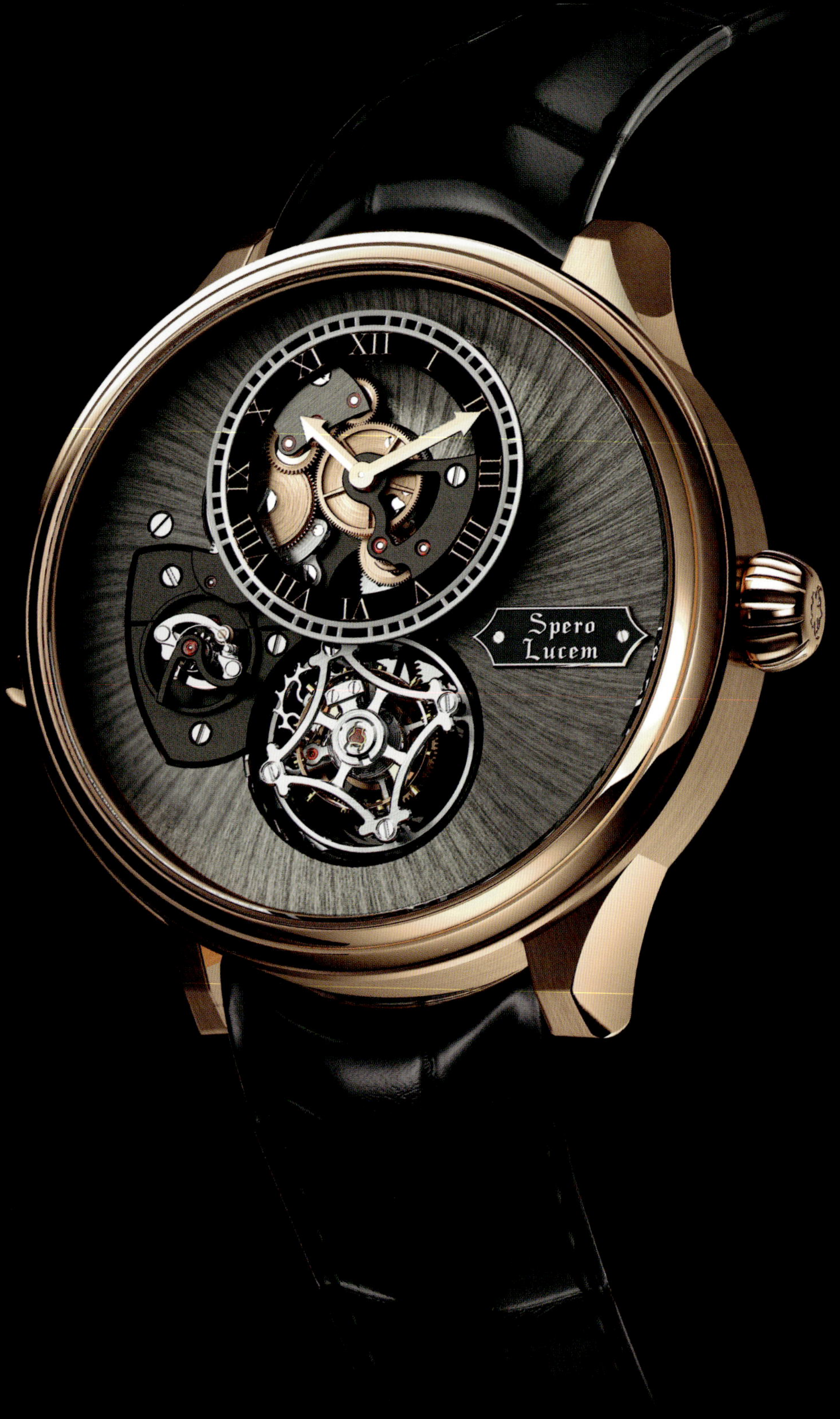
Spero
Lucem

SPERO LUCEM — LA CLÉMENCE TOURBILLON MINUTE REPEATER

$ 532 000

A HIDDEN COMPLICATION IN THE LA CLÉMENCE WATCH IS THE "CRAZY HANDS" COMPLICATION. THE WATCH CONTAINS BOTH A TOURBILLON AS WELL AS A MINUTE REPEATER.

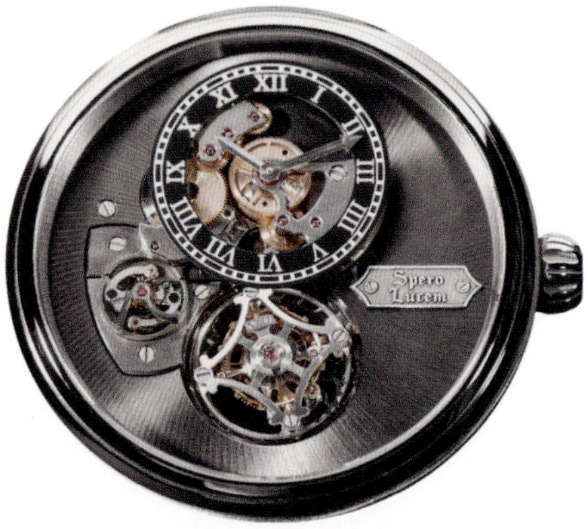

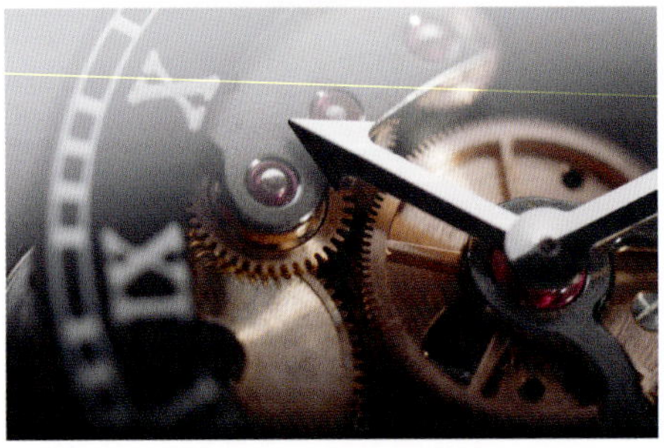

At first glance the La Clémence watch is an almost serene example of traditionally classic watch design that incorporates a set of high-end complications. The simple round case has a mostly austere dial, with a gentle machined polish, that gives way to a series of large openings, offering views of the mechanical movement and inner workings of the mechanism. Collectors might argue that the design nicely integrates both horological charm with a pleasant and conservative wearing experience.

All that is true, but the La Clémence watch released in 2013, by the new brand Spero Lucem, has an additional feature designed to lighten one's mood, which is part of the brand's overall personality. "Spero Lucem" roughly translates into "I hope for light", which is part of the extended Latin phrase "post tenebras spero lucem" (after darkness, I hope for light). The phrase was adopted by religious Calvinists, who would go on to be a prevalent part of the population in Switzerland, especially Geneva.

Calvinists shunned decorative items and luxuries, but there were loopholes. A primarily functional item – such as a watch or clock – could bear decorative markings. The luxury timepiece might be argued to have been born in the 16th century as a product of the Protestant Reformation, when Calvinists and other groups formed new religious Christian groups outside the previously dominant Catholic population. Luxury was thus hidden within what was essentially a tool.

A hidden complication in the La Clémence watch is the "crazy hands" complication. The watch contains both a tourbillon as well as a minute repeater. The latter is a feature that uses a series of chimes to sound back the time to the wearer. When the minute repeater is activated on the La Clémence, the hands on the off-centred time dial spin around randomly without cause or sense. They return to their original positions and continue to indicate the correct time when they are done. According to Spero Lucem the "crazy hands" complication is a "smile inducer", meant to celebrate the long heritage of Geneva, and the less obvious signs of status and wealth that are, nevertheless, a hugely important part of Swiss society.

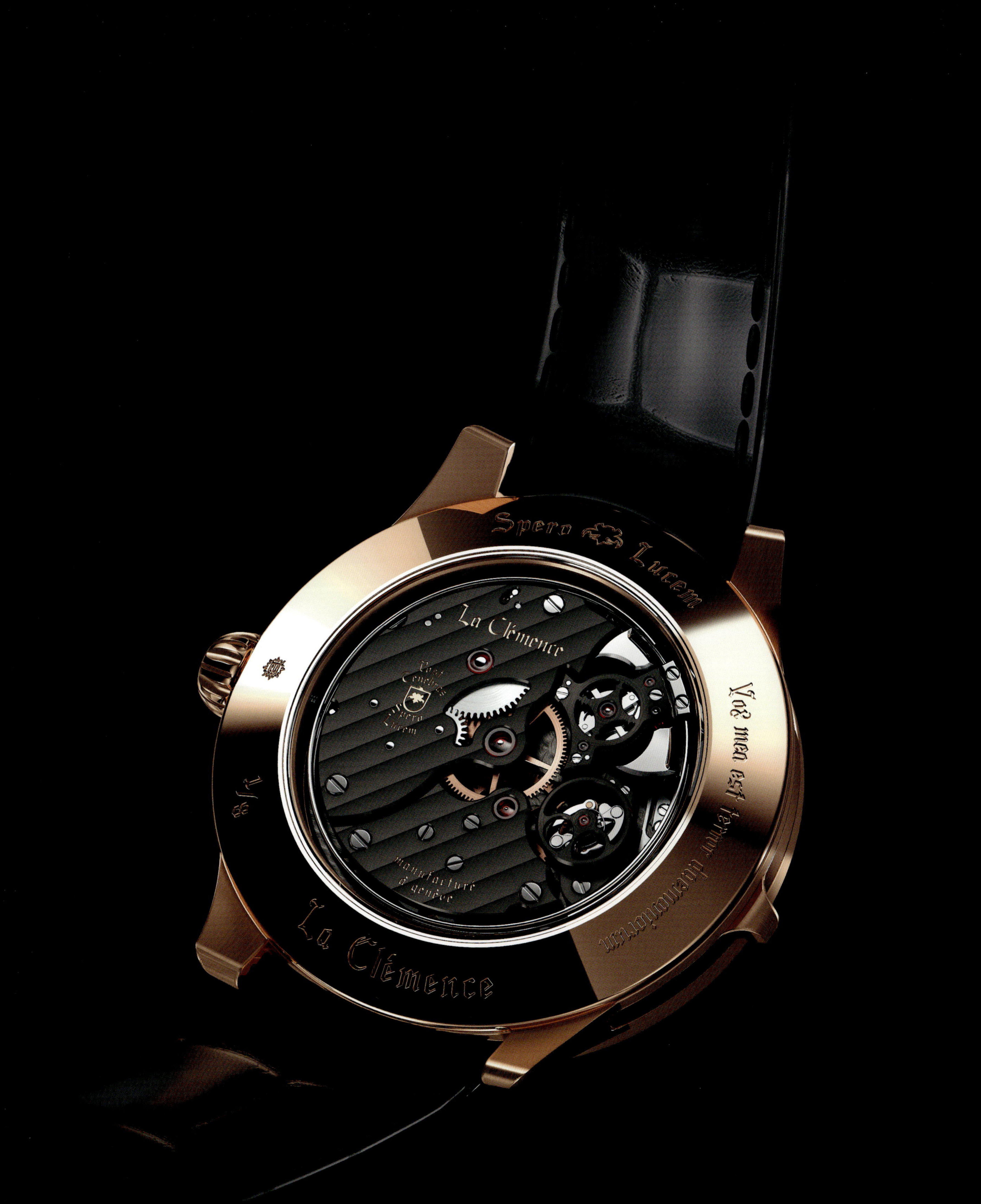
Spero Lucem
La Clémence
1/8
La Clémence

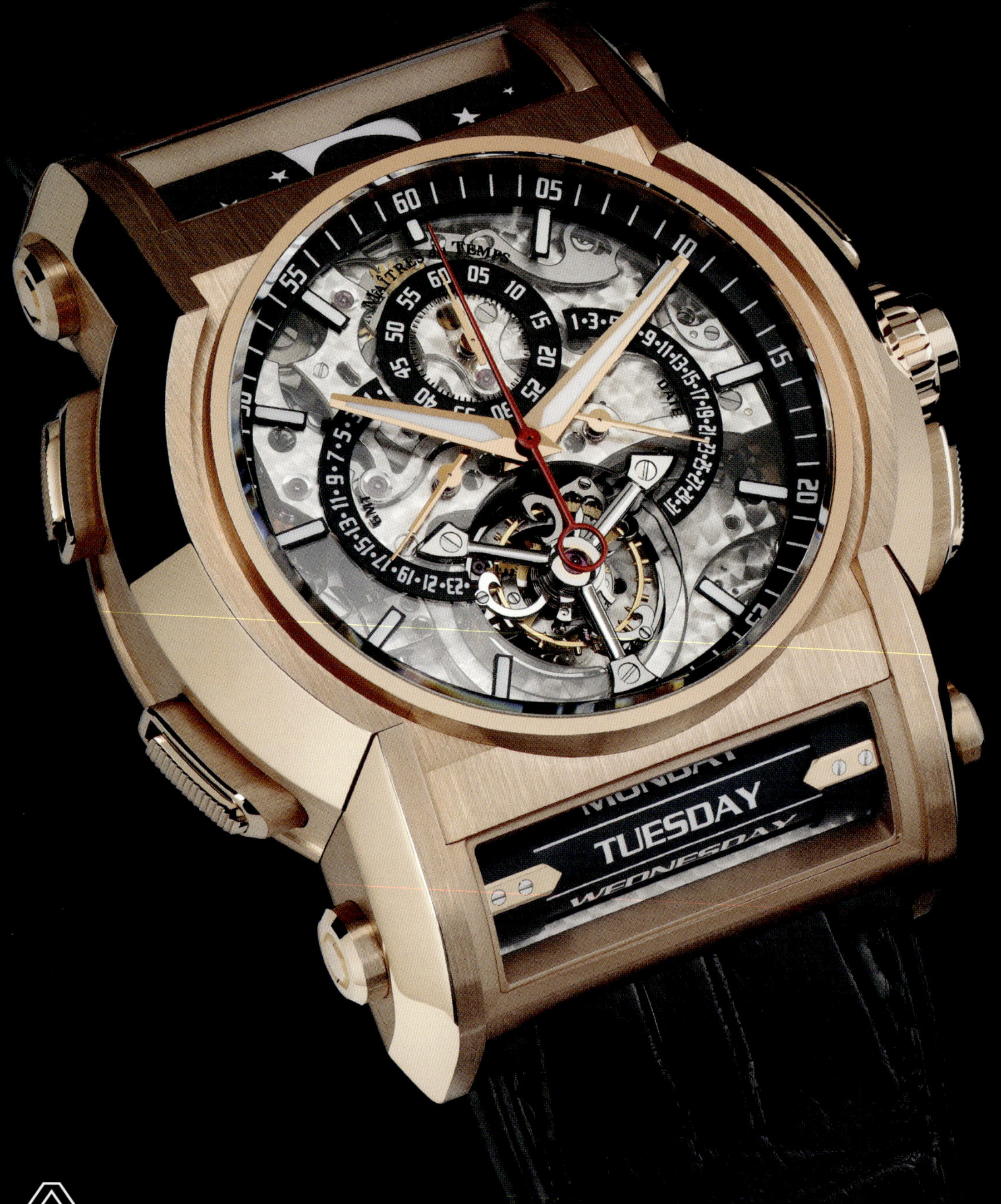

MAÎTRES DU TEMPS – CHAPTER ONE ROUND TRANSPARENCE

$ 540 000

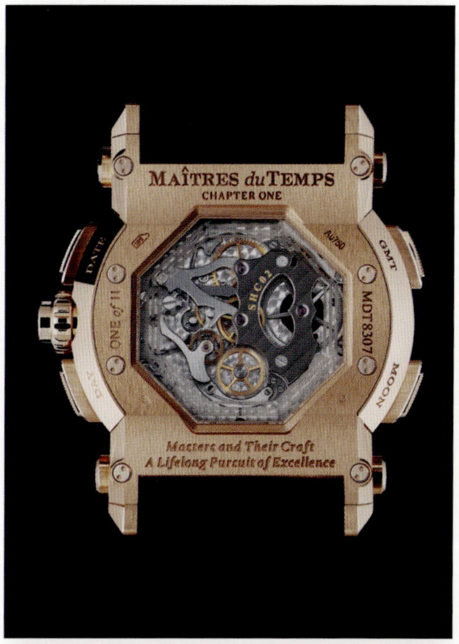

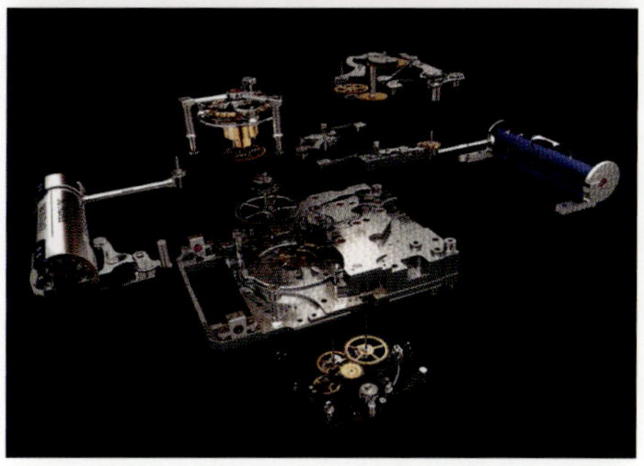

A good watch brand is nothing more than the sum of its good watchmakers. Realising that, when it comes to exclusive high-end timepieces, brand image doesn't convey value as well as personality does, the founders of Maîtres du Temps ("masters of time") established a luxury brand dedicated to openly working with some of the world's finest watchmakers. In 2008, their first watch, known as the Chapter One, was an accumulation of work by master watchmakers Christophe Claret, Roger Dubuis, and Peter Speake-Marin.

The tonneau-shaped (barrel) case of the original Chapter One was so large, that it was barely wearable on most wrist sizes, being over 62mm tall and 45.9mm wide. An artistic tour-de-force of design and technology, it set the stage for what Maîtres du Temps would be in the future, with its next creations. The Chapter One was not only highly complex, but bore a number of never-before-seen features as well as a beautiful design.

While the trio of esteemed watchmakers were involved in the design of the Chapter One, the movement was mostly produced in Switzerland by Christophe Claret in his horological wonder workshop. The movement did two things for the very first time. First, it used rollers placed on the top and bottom of the case, as displays. The upper roller slowly spun and was used as a Moon-phase indicator, while the lower roller indicated the day of the week. The second novel feature was a sliding lever in the case pushers that prevented them from being accidentally pressed. Doing so could cause one of the indicators (such as the date) to change, and this new safety system was considered an extremely clever invention. For such a high-end luxury watch, it was also uncommon to see the pusher functions clearly engraved on the back of the gold case.

The Chapter One watch dial displays the time, chronograph (monopusher-style design, with a single button integrated into the crown to control starting, stopping, and resetting), second time zone, date indicator, and a view of the tourbillon. Complex and attractive as the Chapter One is, nevertheless, Maîtres du Temps was interested in pushing its design potential further.

In 2010, Maîtres du Temps released a modified version of the watch known as the Chapter One Round. Using the same movement, this new design features a completely different case and dial. Rounder in shape, it proved much more wearable than the original barrel-shaped case. Despite its ergonomic improvements, the Chapter One Round was limited to just 11 pieces.

The most impressive Chapter One model was later released in 2013 as the Chapter One Round Transparence. Building on the Chapter One Round, the Transparence includes a skeletonised dial, able to show many of the highly hand-decorated movement's 558 parts. Once again, Maîtres du Temps limited the Chapter One Round Transparence's production, and only 11 pieces were ever made.

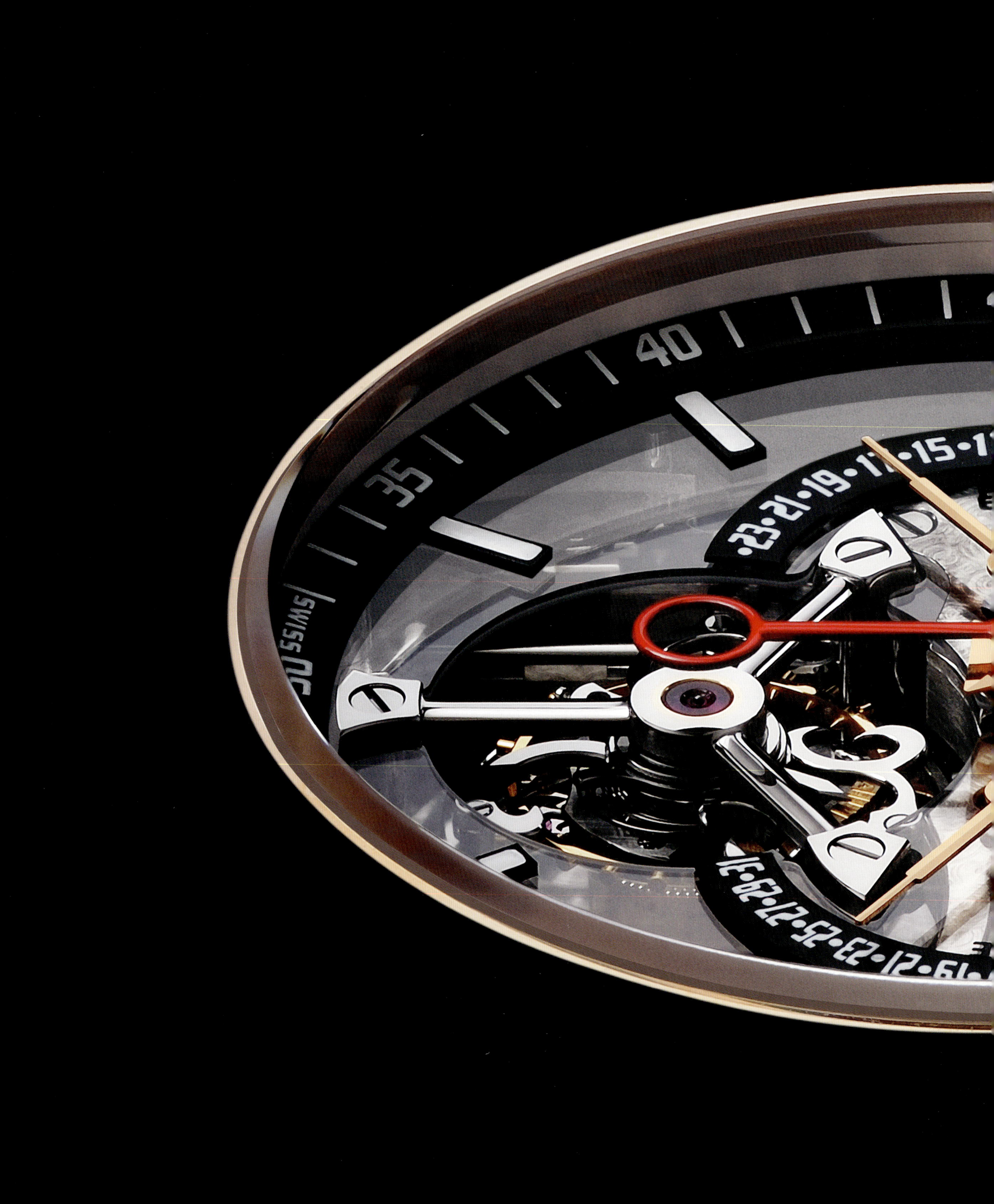
40
35

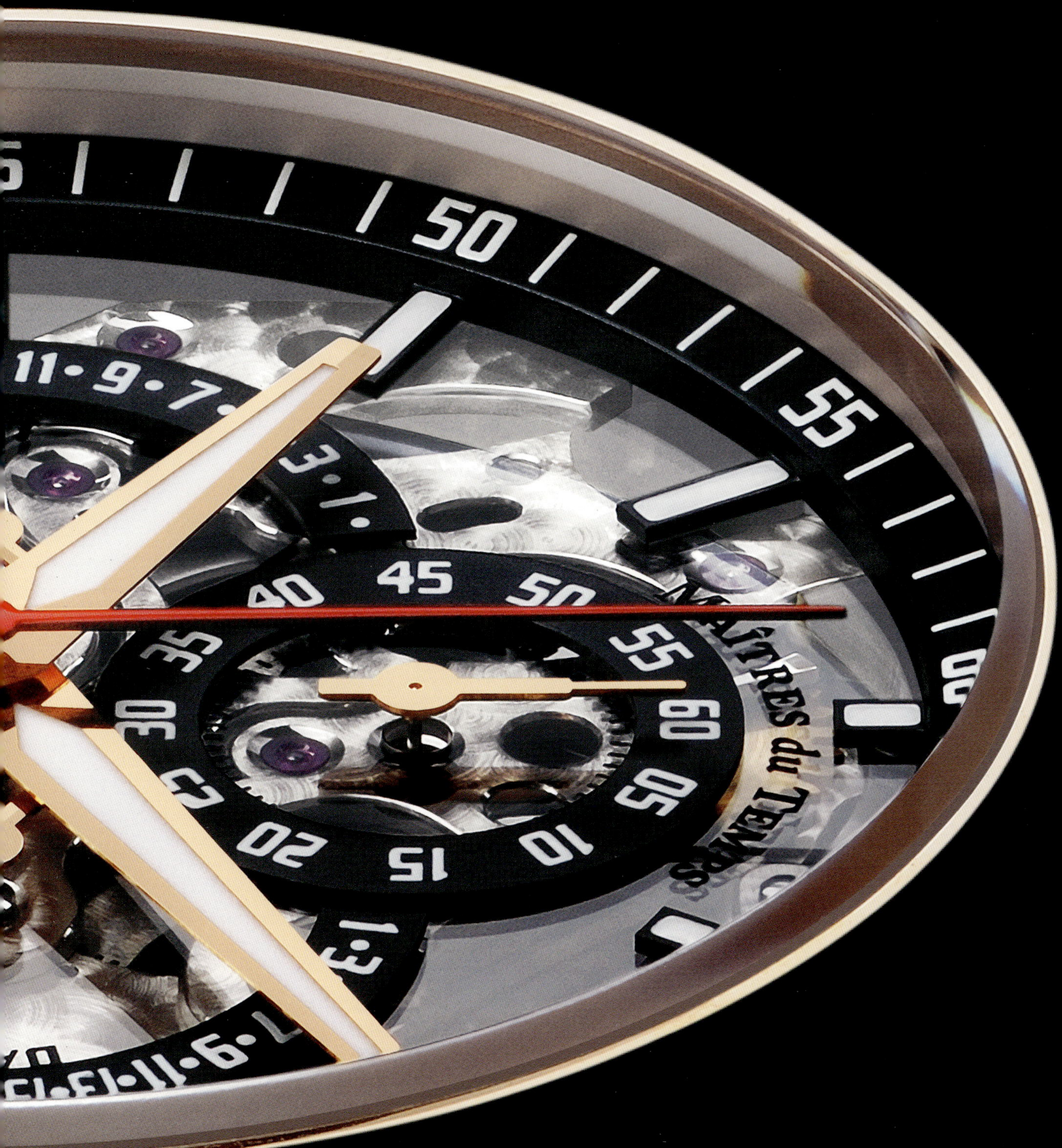

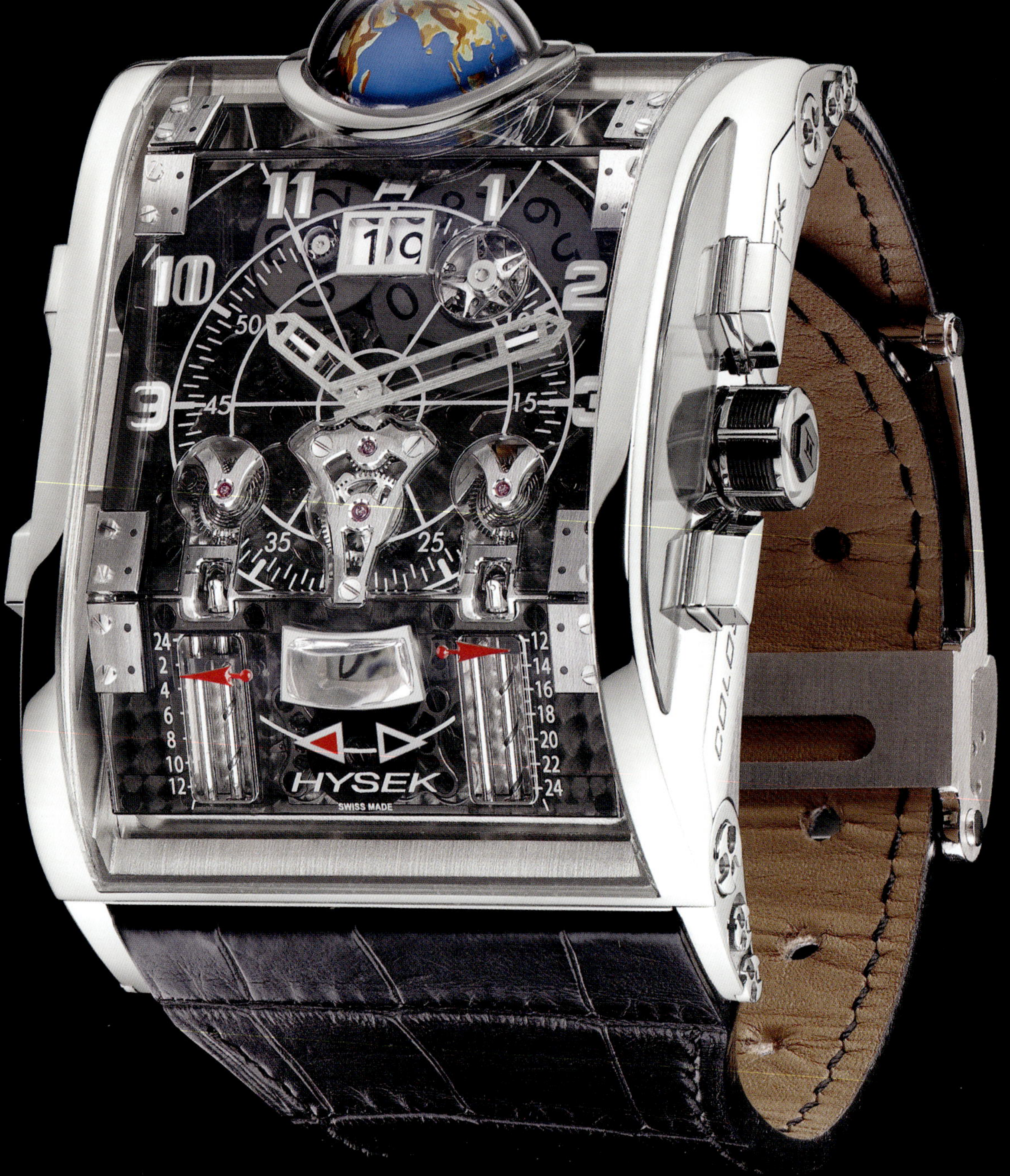

HYSEK — COLOSSO

$ 550 000

During the mid-2000s there was a field of thought in the ultra-high-end world of luxury watches that the more over-engineered something was the better. This was a novel idea, because you had a situation where watchmakers produced products that answered questions no-one asked. The goal during this time was to impress and inspire awe, and to display, to an increasingly finicky group of collectors, that you had produced something no-one else could have imagined. It appealed to the very core of why some people buy high-end watches; to stimulate their need for novelty while showing them a machine that might have previously been thought impossible.

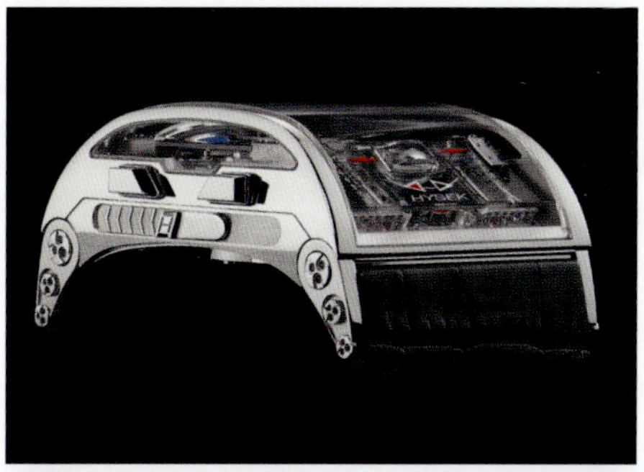

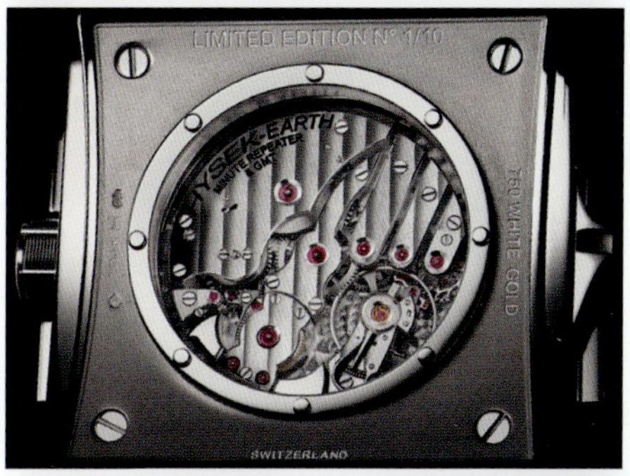

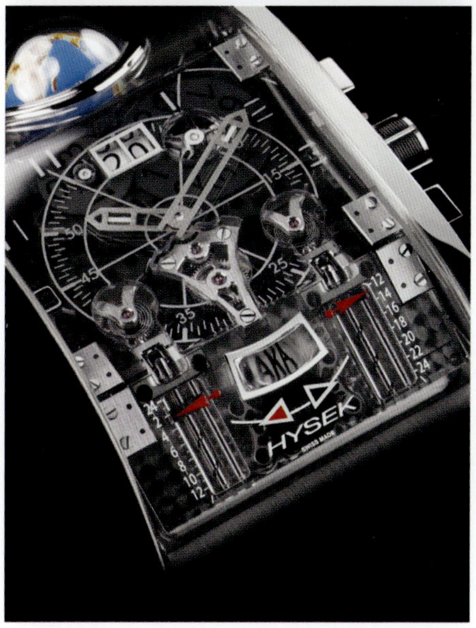

This mentality was quite different to that which motivates most makers of watches, be they large companies or independent workshops. Watches are typically born from a perceived market demand, or often the production of something that a watchmaker or designer personally wants to wear on their own wrist.

Things that stray from the norm are no doubt going to be interesting, especially when they fit in your palm and are priced at over half a million dollars. Toward the end of the last golden age of "shock and awe" watches, came the Colosso by Hysek. The brand was started by the famed watch designer Jorg Hysek, but by the time the Colosso was released, in 2008, he was no longer associated with the brand. His legacy of unique, and highly avant-garde yet functional design, carried into what the brand would continue to produce, as one of the industry's rarer watchmakers.

A large three-dimensional representation of the Earth, in full colour, is perhaps the first thing most people notice about the Colosso. Sitting under a dome of sapphire crystal, the globe turns fully each 24-hour period, coinciding with the time. It makes a bold first impression. In short, the Colosso is a multiple time-zone watch, with a minute repeater, housed in a distinct case, made from sapphire crystal and gold, that offers a view of the movement's inner workings.

Minute repeater travel watches are rare – mostly because of their limited utility. The point of a GMT or multiple time-zone watch, is to be used while travelling, so that the wearer can be aware of their home time as well as local time. In the Colosso the second time zone is represented via two linear displays at the bottom of the case. Pushers move a disc in a reference city window, so that the user knows the relative location of where else in the world they are reading the time from.

Time is indicated on a larger, more traditional display, that has a big date indicator (using two discs to indicate the date). Under everything, is a vivid view into the complex mechanical movement contained within the bulky mass. Inside the watch is a minute repeater mechanism that, when activated, uses a series of chimes to sound out the time musically. These are often fragile complications, so their inclusion, in a watch meant to be worn while travelling, is less than common. A rare creation, the Colosso arrives in a presentation box made from a form of fossilised wood.

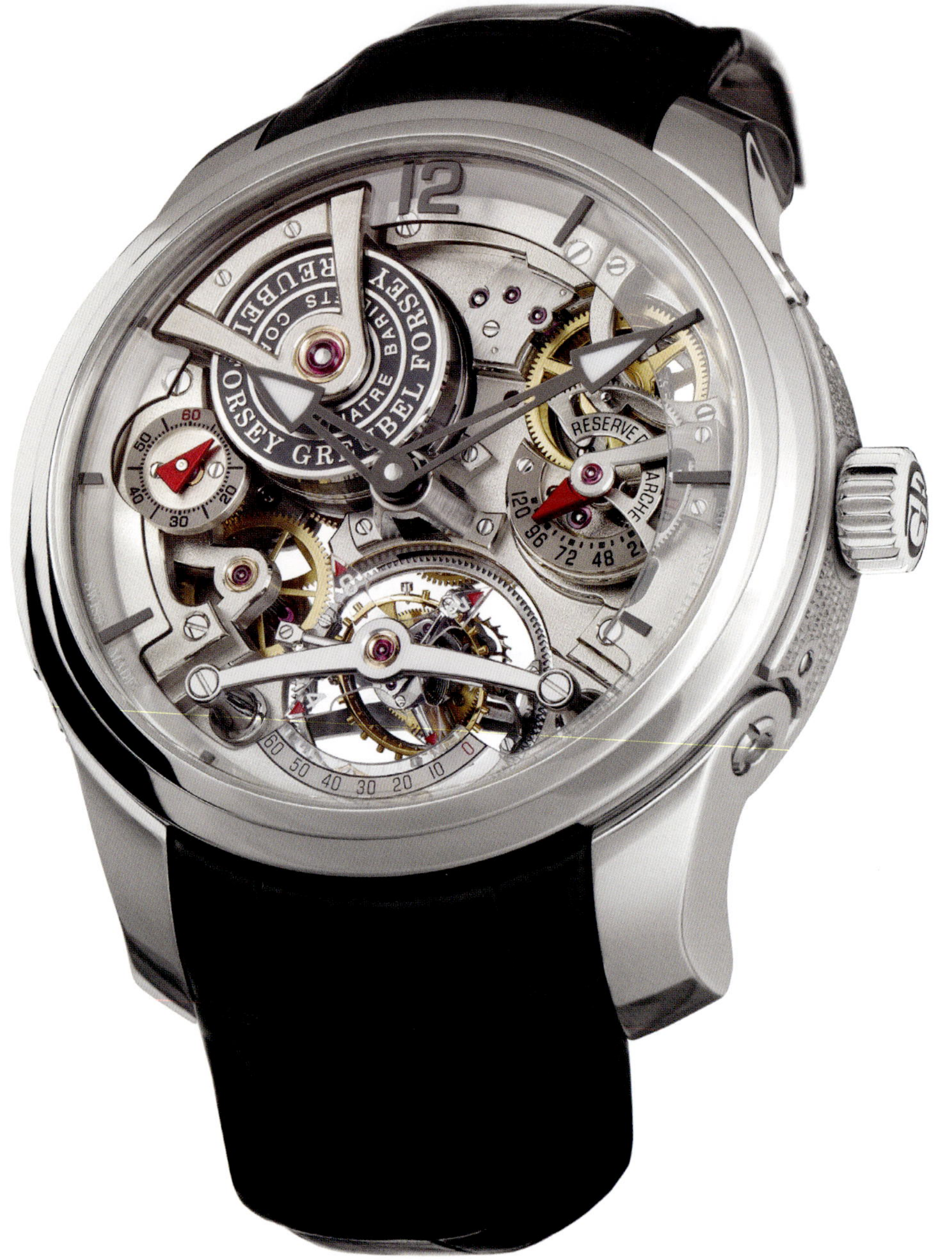

GREUBEL FORSEY — DOUBLE TOURBILLON TECHNIQUE

$ 550 000

Robert Greubel and Stephen Forsey make for an interesting couple, given that the two watchmakers are known for producing some of the world's best "finished" timepieces. Finishing is a major element of what goes into the production of the best luxury watches. It is a general term for the detailed and meticulous work that goes into beautifying tiny elements of a watch's case, dial and, more importantly, the movement.

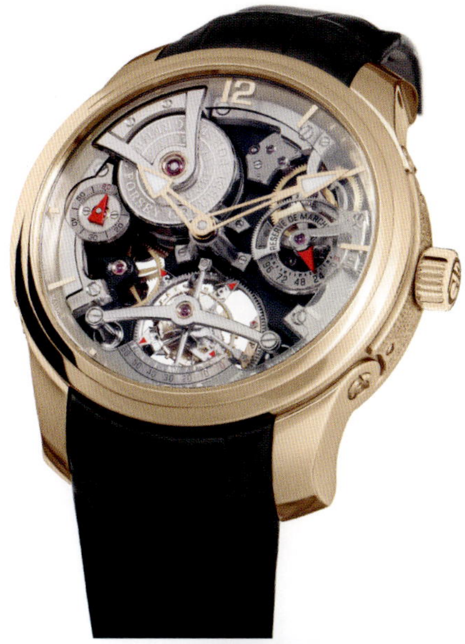

Finishing is related to the concept of "decoration", and in practice reveals itself in the fine polishes and detailed hand-attention that virtually all pieces of Greubel Forsey movements receive. Modern mechanical watch movements typically use parts that are made from precision industrial cutters and mills. It is true that in some extreme cases the parts themselves can be hand-made, but human work is simply not as precise as that of the CNC, laser cutter, and wire erosion machines relied upon in contemporary workshops.

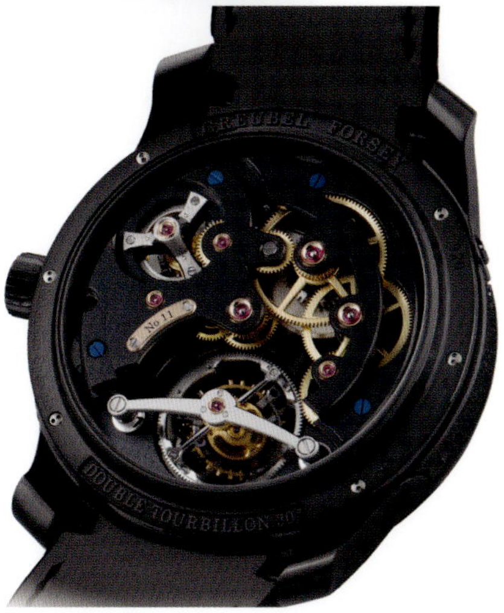

In fine watches, after the pieces of a movement are completed, they are carefully inspected and finished by hand. Typically under a microscope, a watchmaker will polish their surfaces, using techniques that are sometimes centuries old. Everything from special types of wood to unique solutions are used in the finishing process, and almost every component of watches from brands like Greubel Forsey receives this type of attention. It can thus take weeks to finish the parts of a movement that takes just a few hours or days to assemble.

This artisanship is wonderfully expressed in the totally open dial of the Greubel Forsey Double Tourbillon Technique. Assembled from 385 parts, the mechanical movement is totally open for visual inspection, appearing like a microcosm of moving gears, polished surfaces, and carefully angled edges. Greubel Forsey even designed the dial markers to be printed on transparent sapphire crystal around the dial, as well as the seconds indicator over the tourbillon.

The movement contains a double tourbillon, referred to as such because it is designed with an inner 60-second tourbillon that sits inside of an outer four-minute tourbillon. A long power reserve of 120 hours keeps the caliber running for the better part of a week. Greubel Forsey offered the Double Tourbillon Technique in versions and materials ranging from 18k red gold and platinum to titanium. Around the periphery of each case is a secret message to the owner, from the watchmakers, helping to make each of these timepieces among the most exclusive in the world.

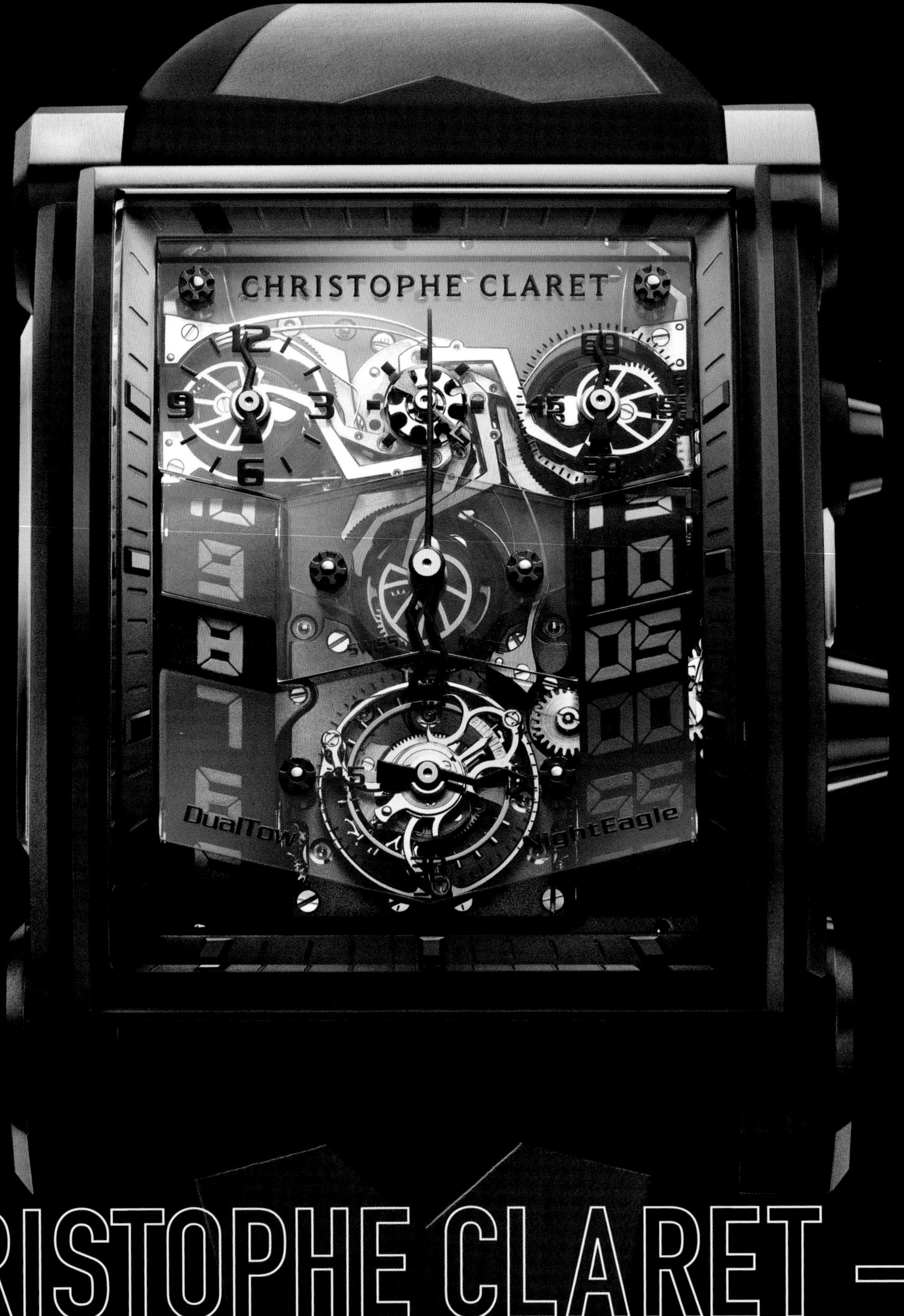

CHRISTOPHE CLARET – DUALTOW NIGHTEAGLE

$ 595 000

For years Christophe Claret and his tightly guarded secret techniques, made mechanical fantasy watches a reality. Brands, both major and niche, relied on Claret's Swiss workshop to design and produce some of their most ambitious pieces. Claret is known as a master of his craft, and frequently wows the watch industry at large with the design and functionality of his newest creations. For most of Christophe Claret's career his name has been largely unknown.

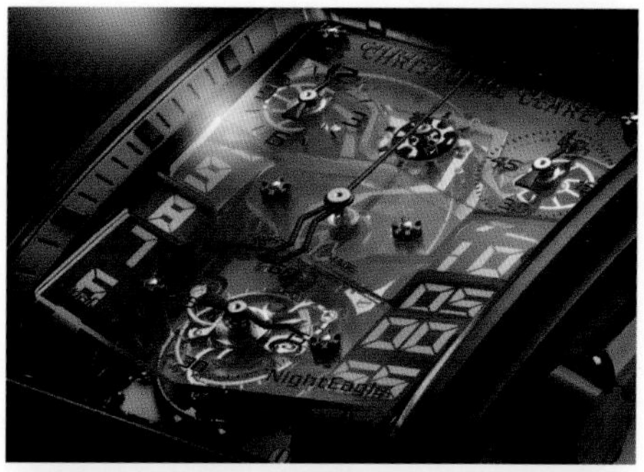

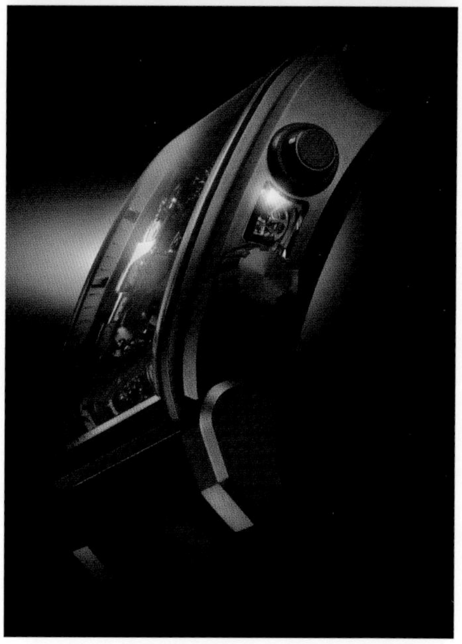

After the 2008 financial crisis, Christophe Claret decided to shift his business model and create a new, eponymous, brand. He would still offer design and production services to others in the industry, but his primary focus would be on the newly formed Christophe Claret watch brand. The mission of the brand is to incorporate and interpret traditional watch making with elements of the modern world. For him, the mechanical watch of today is but a fantastic, emotional toy.

Toys can evoke passion, and that is just what Christophe Claret watches are meant to do. The first timepiece to bear his name was released in 2009 as the DualTow. It unofficially celebrated 20 years of Claret's watch manufacture. The incredible watch came in a fully bespoke rectangular case, that clients could customise online with the "DualTow Configurator." Claret claims that the watch could be rendered in "unlimited colours".

The DualTow watch displayed the time using two tread-like belts, with one for the hours and another for the minutes. The totally exposed movement also featured a 12-hour chronograph that used a marvellous planetary gear system, and a tourbillon. Built to impress, one of the most interesting features of the watch is a minute repeater-style striking system that sounds a chime each time the monopusher chronograph button is pressed. Claret remarked that this feature was inspired by the fact that mobile phones often emit a beep when keys are pressed, or information is entered, and he wanted to connect the watch with modern lifestyles.

In 2010, Christophe Claret released a revised version of the DualTow known as the DualTow NightEagle. Even more impressive than the first model, the NightEagle version of the DualTow has a case and dial design inspired by the sharp looks of modern military stealth aircraft, such as the American F-22 Raptor and the F-117 Night Hawk. The NightEagle was more limited in its colour configurations, as Claret's vision for it was to have a darker look. Finally, the NightEagle offers a more open view of the movement, as the geometric transparent plates on the dial were produced from sapphire crystal. Christophe Claret limited production of the DualTow NightEagle to 68 pieces.

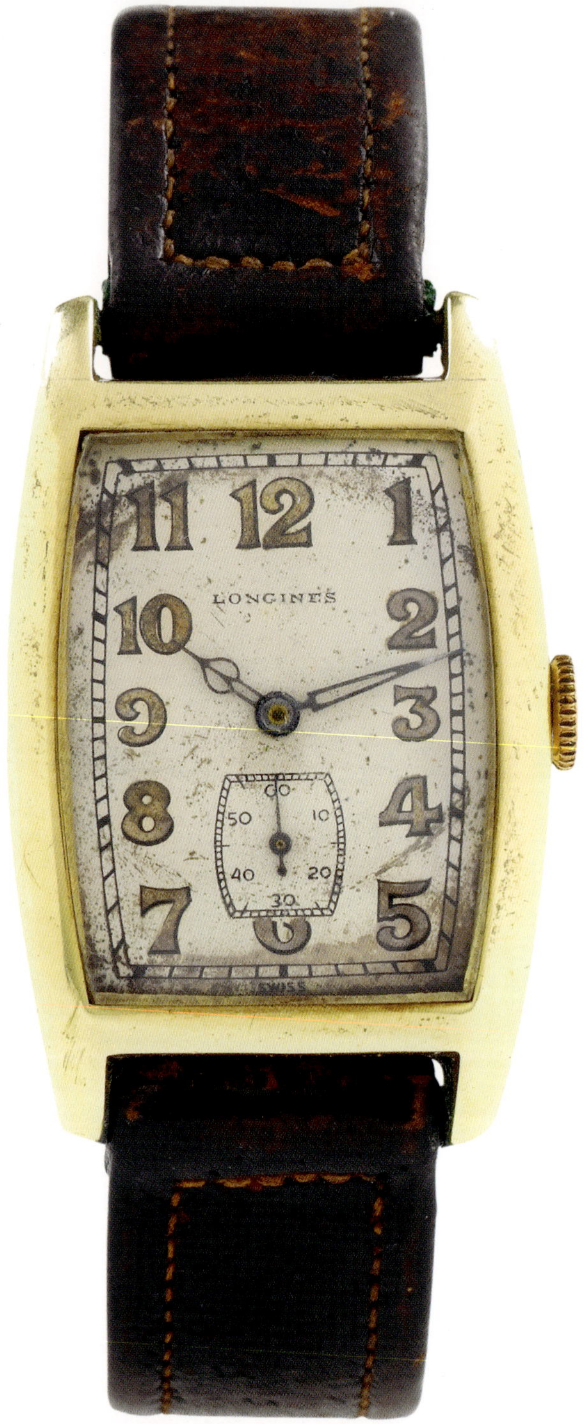

ALBERT EINSTEIN'S PERSONAL LONGINES

$ 596 000*

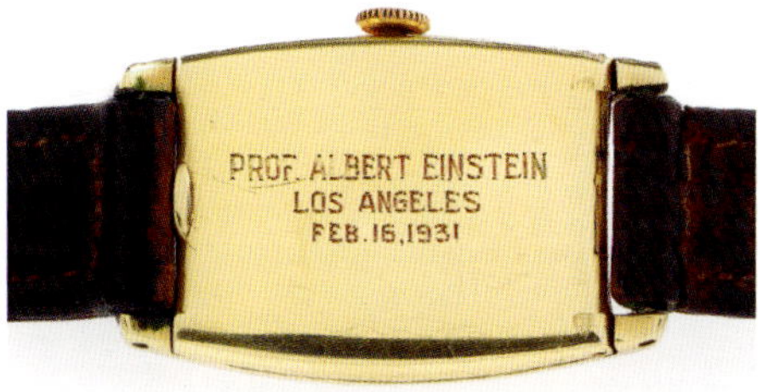

A wristwatch is sometimes valuable not because of its inherent technical merit, or importance to horology, but because of the person who owned and loved it. In 2008, one of Albert Einstein's personal watches sold at auction for over half a million dollars. Produced by the Swiss watchmaker Longines in 1929, aside from being owned by and engraved for Einstein, the piece was a relatively common example of a fine gold watch from that era. One of the greatest allures for collectors is the fact that people of great importance relied upon particular watches during their daily lives, at moments of distinction, and during times of crisis. Perhaps the most valuable feature of an otherwise average collectable, is that it was not only owned by a celebrity or some other important human being, but that it was also loved by them for many years.

The auction house of Antiquorum, which sold the watch in 2008, offered a pre-sale estimated price of no more than $35,000. Yet the final hammer price was many times that. One of the key elements in evaluating the value of a watch owned by someone like Einstein, is the establishment of provenance. While it is true that the watch displays a personal engraving to Einstein on the rear of the case, which reads "Prof. Albert Einstein, Los Angeles, Feb 16, 1931", such a marking alone is not enough to establish that Einstein himself owned it.

Fortunately, history offers numerous proofs that Einstein owned and wore the watch, from testimonies of when he received it, to photographs and news clippings of him wearing it over the years. Such pieces of historical evidence are required if significantly enhanced values are to be attached to the personal effects of those whom society celebrates.

Einstein did not purchase his Longines watches (it is known that he owned a second Longines piece in the form of a pocket watch). While visiting Cal Tech in Pasadena, near Los Angeles, in 1931, Einstein met a well-known Rabbi in Los Angeles named Edgar Magnin, whose tenure at his Wilshire Boulevard temple lasted 69 years. Often known as a "Rabbi to the Stars", Magnin was highly active in local politics and other civil affairs. He invited Einstein to a luncheon in Los Angeles on February 16, 1931 and presented the wristwatch to him, on behalf of the Jewish population in Los Angeles, as being a person they considered an honoured individual in the Jewish community. During the same event, Einstein's wife also received a watch.

* Sold at auction for $596,000 at Antiquorum, New York in October 2008.

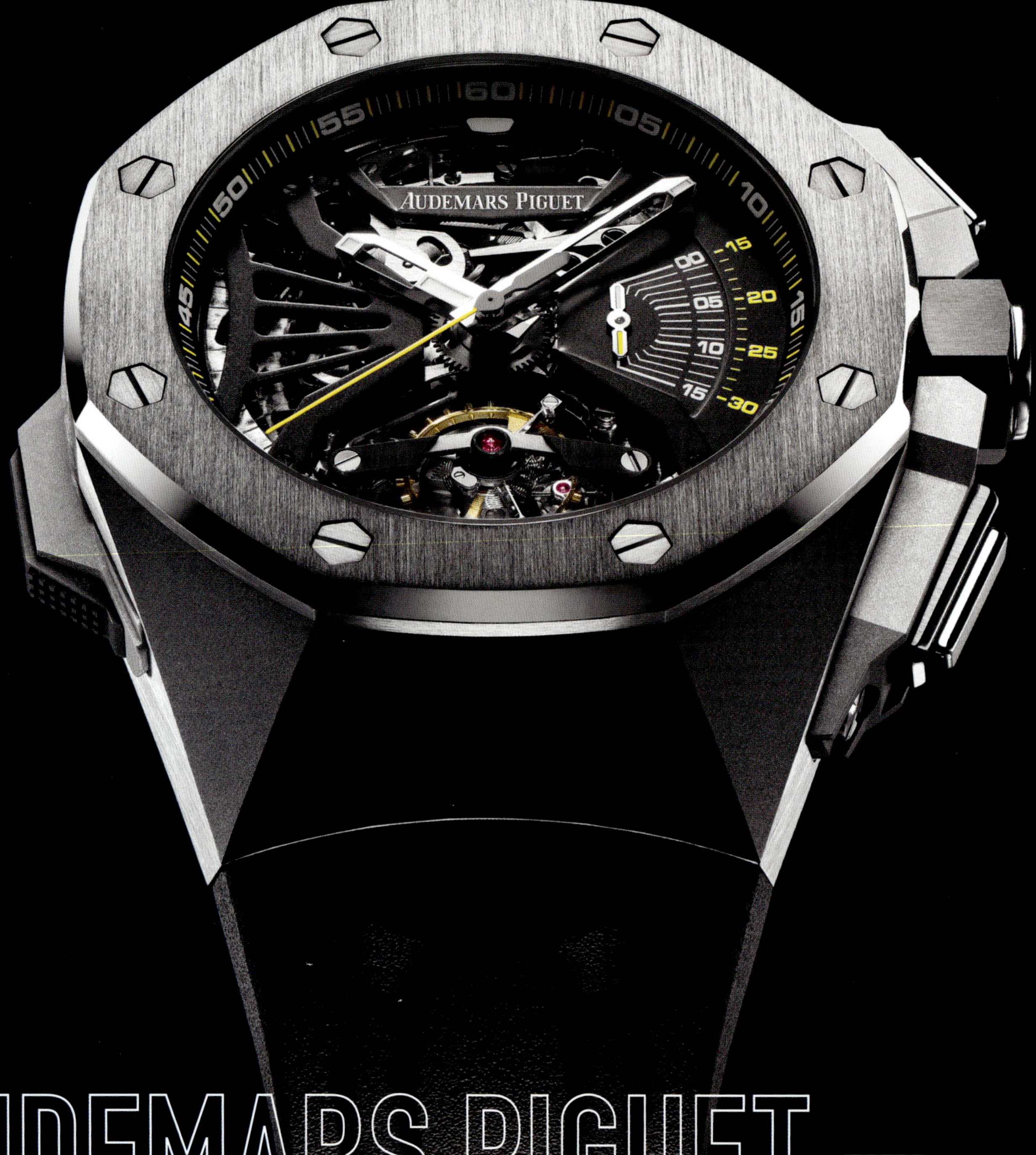

AUDEMARS PIGUET — ROYAL OAK CONCEPT SUPERSONNERIE

$ 597 400

Historic Swiss watchmaker Audemars Piguet has long been a master of the minute repeater. "Repeaters", as they are sometimes known (because they "repeat" the time), are musical watches which have a function that chimes the time using a "code" of musical notes that is easy for the user to interpret. Minute-repeater watches are interesting in that they cannot truly be mass produced, given the individual tweaking and formidable amount of professional attention required for the delicate hammer-and-gong systems inside the case.

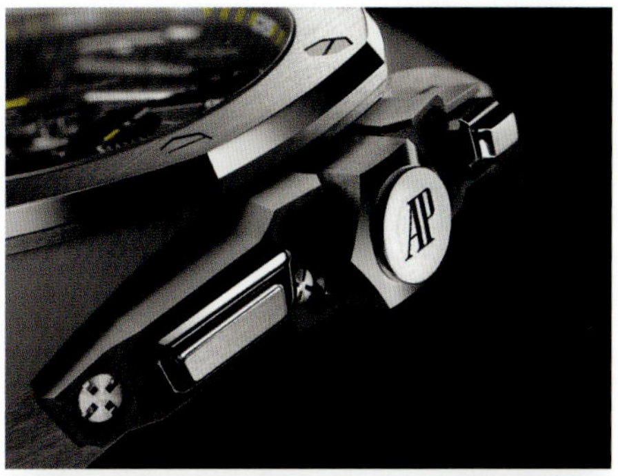

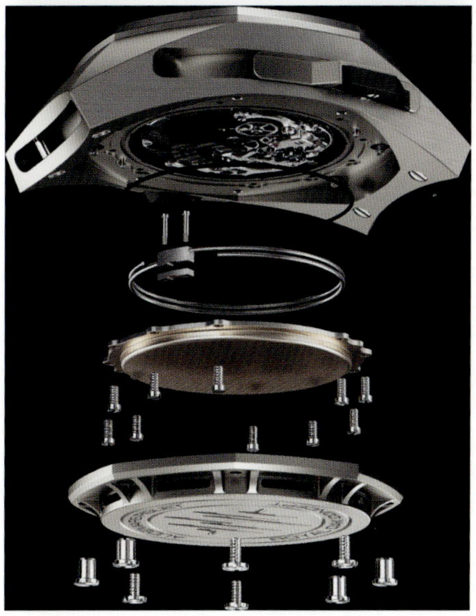

Additional attention is needed anytime a watchmaker seeks to improve upon the age-old technology that powers these devices. Minute repeaters have been in existence for so long that they were originally designed to let their wealthy owners know the time when there was insufficient candlelight by which to read a timepiece dial. More recently, in their "Sound Research" lab, Audemars Piguet employed sensitive advanced instrumentation- and audio-capturing software to study how to make a minute repeater's sound both louder and crisper.

Traditional minute-repeater watches were not water resistant, which allowed their sound to travel a bit farther than is possible with many modern watches. Today, timepiece owners expect durable, water- and dust-resistant products that are, by definition, challenging to design as minute repeaters, given that sound is muffled inside the case. After almost a decade of research and development, Audemars Piguet filed for three patents that apply to various innovations in the movement of the Royal Oak Concept Supersonnerie – the first minute-repeater watch in the esteemed Royal Oak Concept watch collection. Its performance does not disappoint.

The sounds that come from the Royal Oak Concept Supersonnerie is impressive in both clarity and volume. More so, Audemars Piguet developed the mechanism to have a much shorter delay between notes – enhancing the quality of the listening experience for the user. The titanium Royal Oak Concept case is ideal for acoustics, while inside the watch Audemars Piguet have designed a form of resonance chamber that ends with a flat soundboard that sits over the movement. Being an Audemars Piguet watch, the Supersonnerie's movement has other impressive qualities, in addition to the minute repeater, that include both a 30-minute chronograph, as well as a tourbillon-style regulation system.

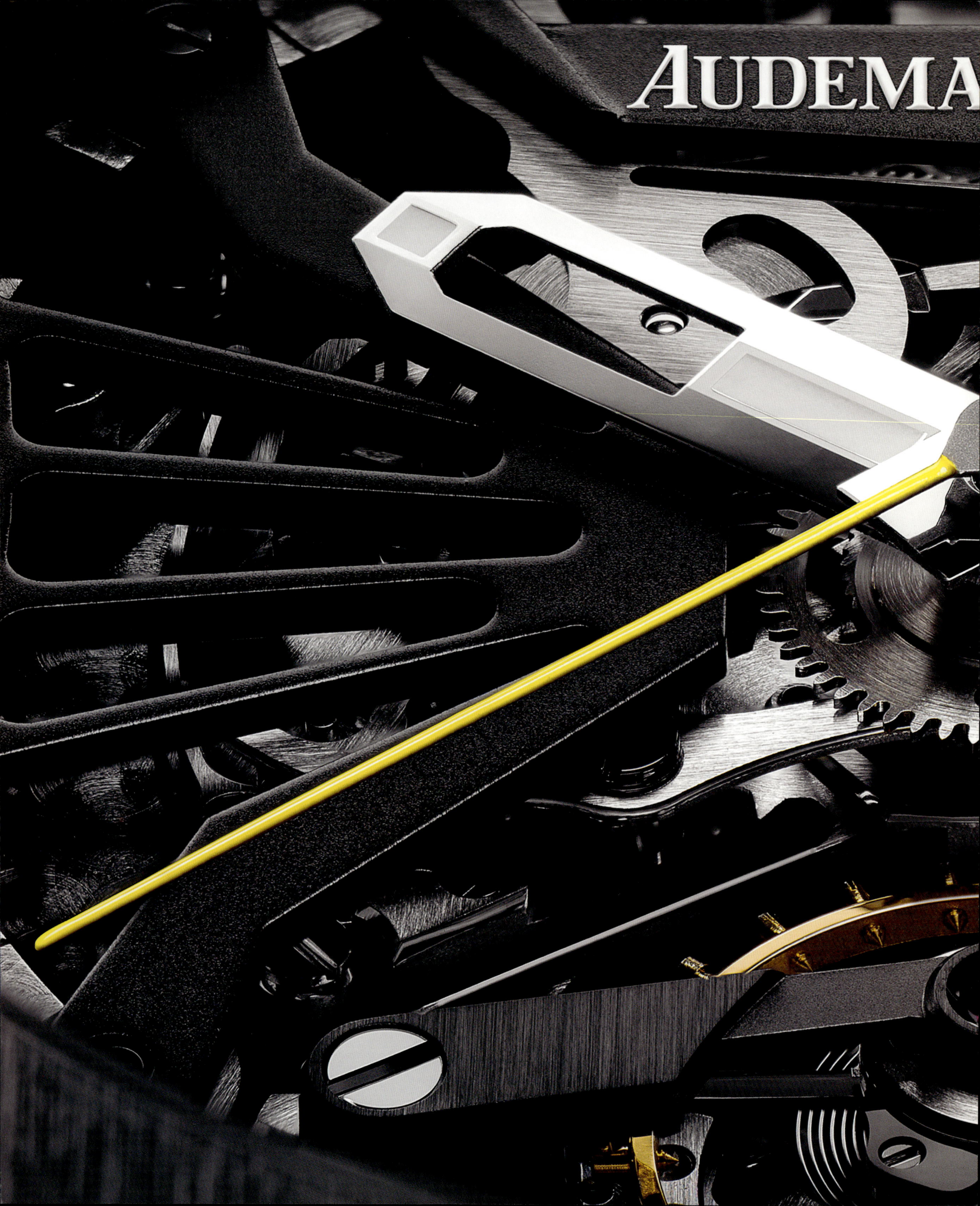
AUDEMA

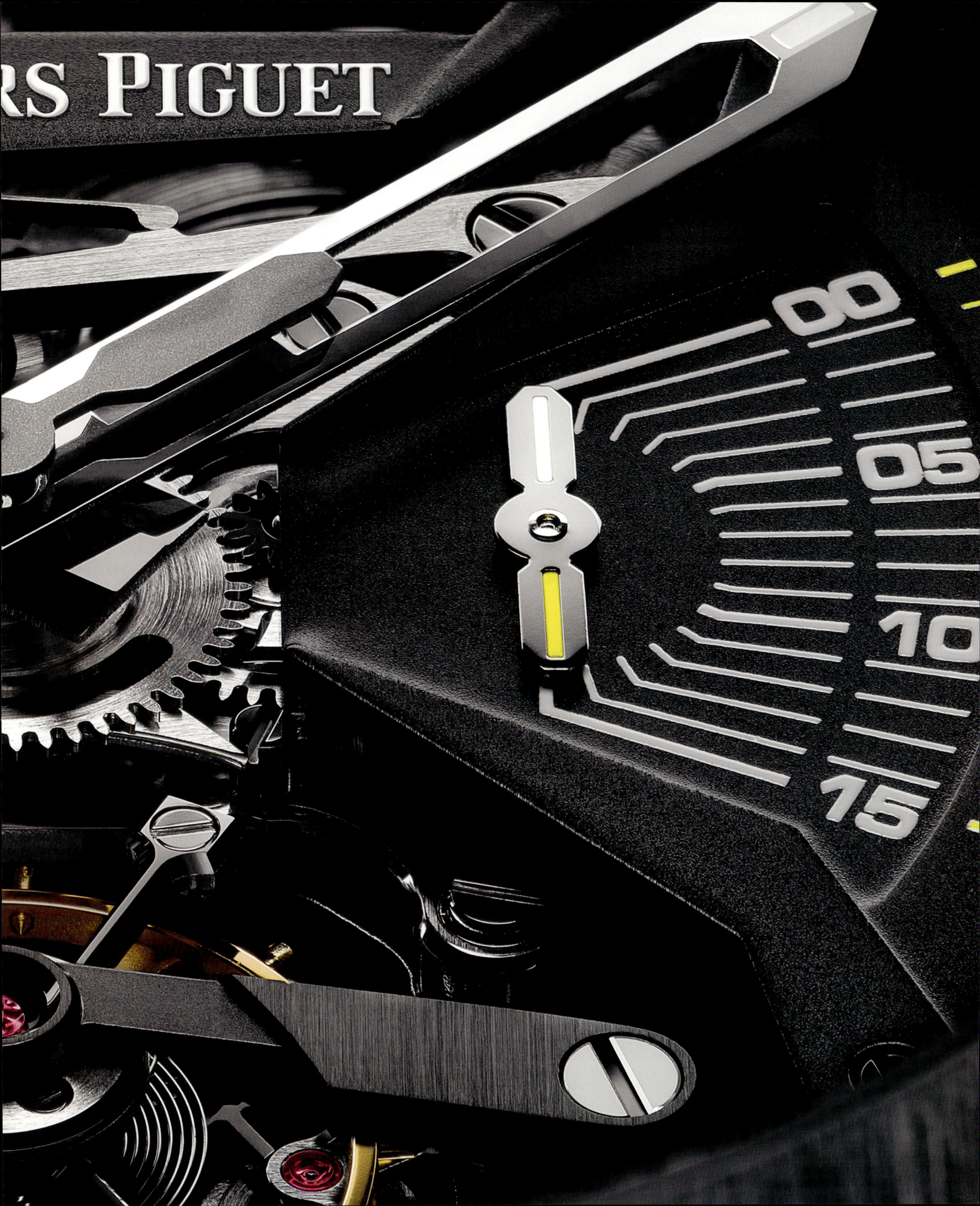
RS PIGUET
00
05
10
15

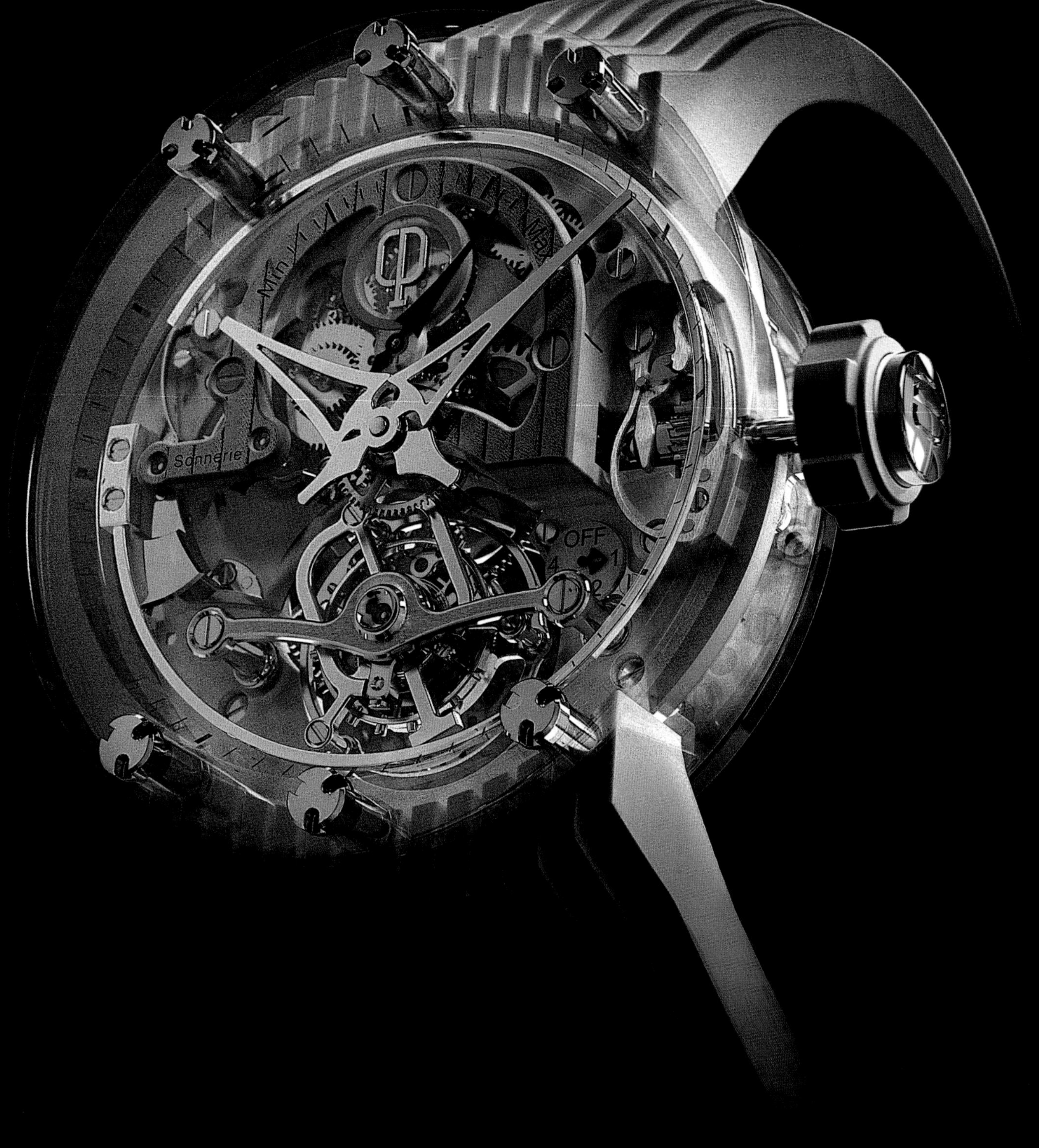

CECIL PURNELL — MIRAGE
$ 601 000

Boutique brands like Cecil Purnell make up much of the diverse landscape of independent watchmakers in and around Switzerland. With limited production as well as limited distribution, customers either have to be at the right store at the right time, or have insider contacts, to even learn about brands such as Cecil Purnell.

Products from small independent watchmakers vary in style as much as the people who buy them. Some take a more classic route, with conservative offerings, but brands like Cecil Purnell are more about wowing wealthy watch collectors who have "seen it all". As a flagship model, the Mirage watch is indeed impressive. Forgoing precious metal for the case material, this watch is produced entirely from pieces of ultra-hard and scratch-resistant synthetic sapphire crystal.

Called the Mirage because you can see right through it, the watch offers an extremely voyeuristic view of the mechanical movement within. The movement starts with a large tourbillon, and includes a power reserve indicator, as well as a sonnerie. At the top of each hour, hammers in the movement strike against a thin coil of metal, which acts as a gong. The message, of course, is that this is a watch meant to be seen and heard.

The Mirage mixes both classic and contemporary styling, for an overall composition that is unique. It sits comfortably in the traditional world of mechanical watches whilst, at the same time, sparking that special appeal of modern design. In some ways it is a watch whose personality is only set by the person wearing it. Cecil Purnell only ever produced five pieces.

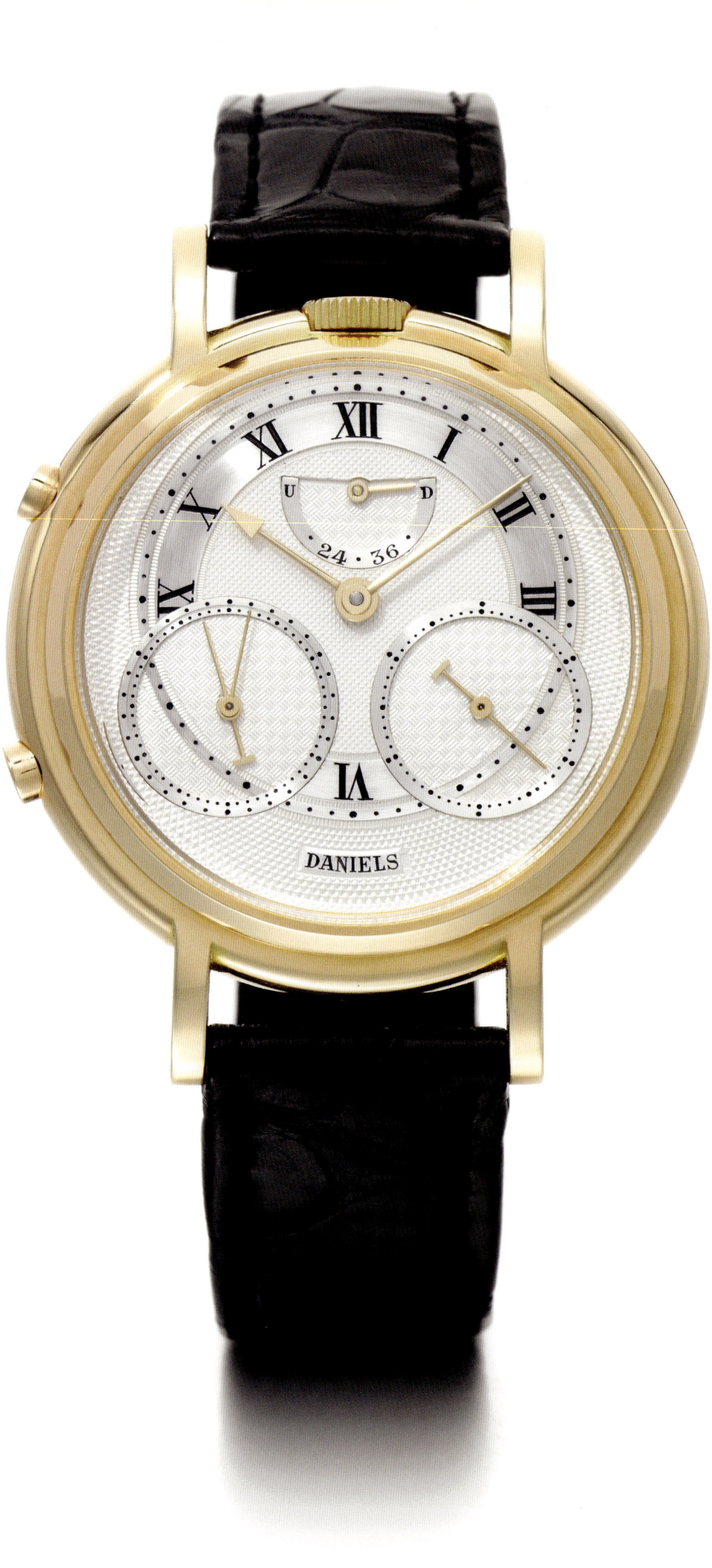

U
D
24
36
DANIELS

GEORGE DANIELS – CO-AXIAL CHRONOGRAPH

$ 619 092*

DESPITE THE WATCH'S HISTORIC APPEARANCE, IT WAS A TECHNOLOGICAL MARVEL, PROVING THE EFFECTIVENESS OF THE CO-AXIAL ESCAPEMENT INVENTION.

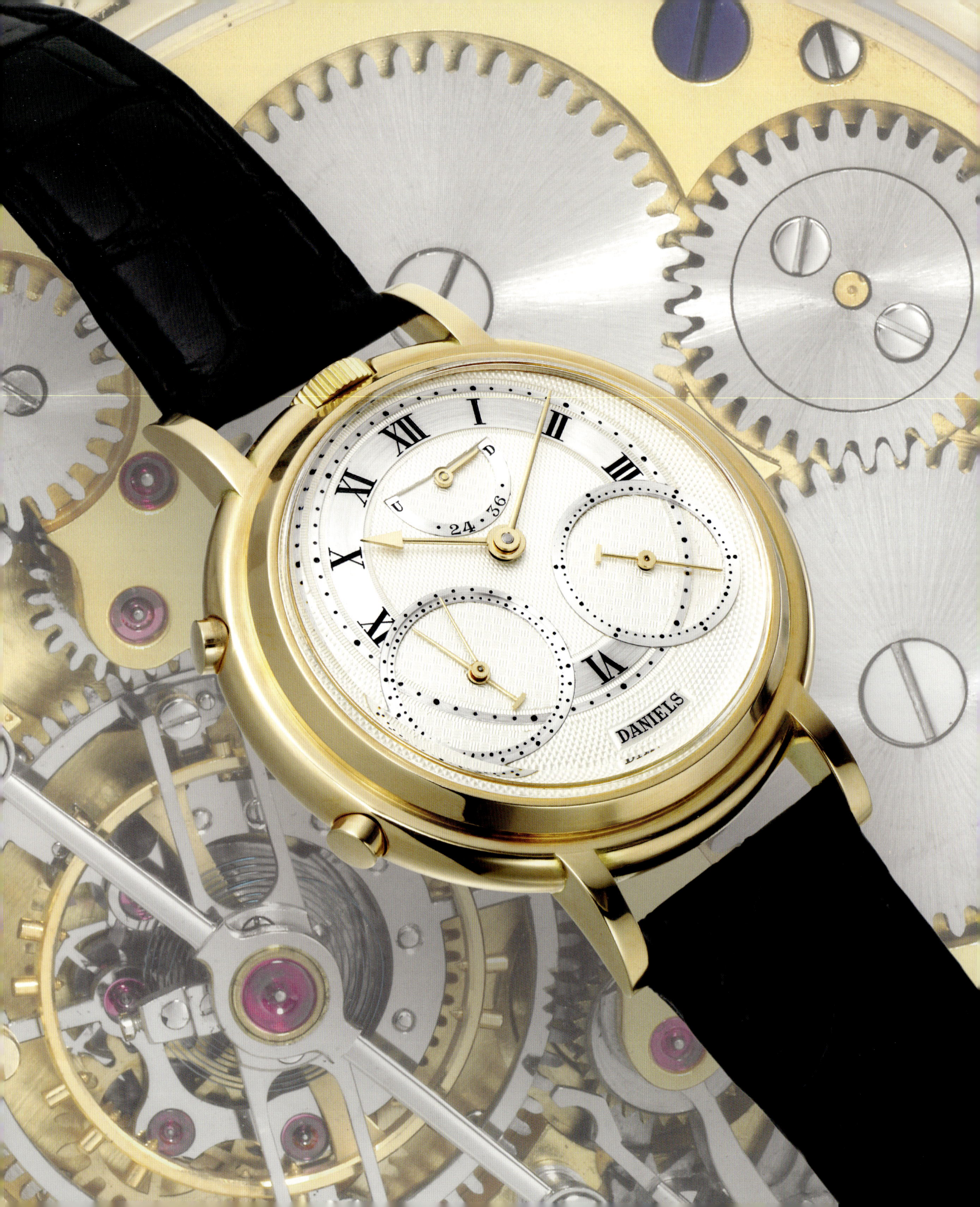
DANIELS

Great watchmakers are rare these days, mostly because they aren't typically needed by society. Great minds often follow the needs of the times, and in our modern era we've more or less mastered timekeeping through electronic means. Those watchmakers who do exist, tend to not follow a childhood dream, but rather fall into watchmaking as a passion they cannot resist. Like many before (and after) him, Britain's George Daniels was an accidental savant. He nevertheless went on to being perhaps the greatest watchmaker of the 20th century, passing away in 2011.

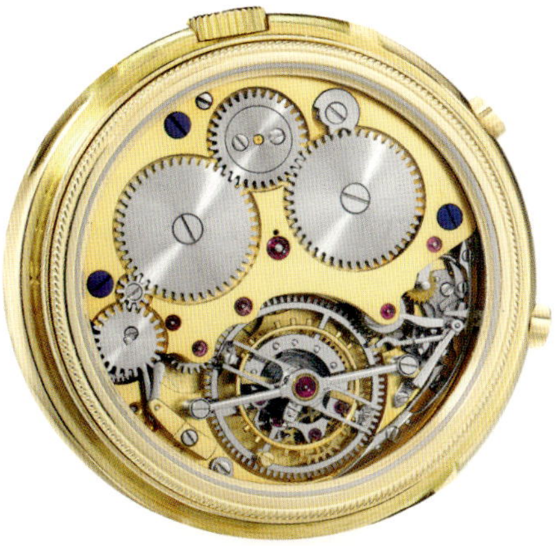

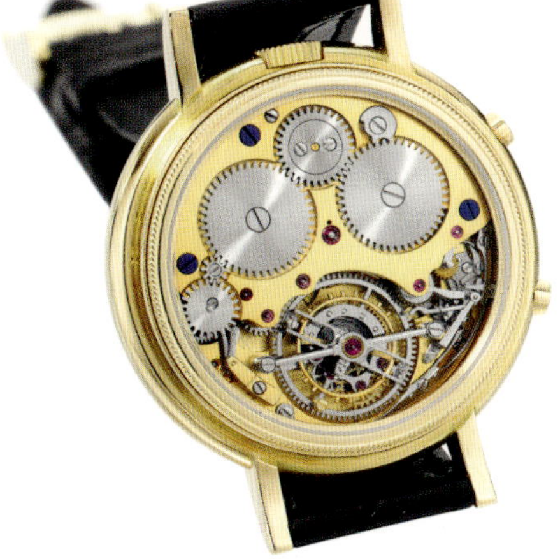

Daniels was eagerly interested in improving an art form that most people considered "set" over 100 years ago. Horology today is often about interpreting and replicating the past, while Daniels wanted to add something new, in order to improve watchmaking. He succeeded in the 1970s upon the invention of the "co-axial escapement", an improvement that would increase the reliability and longevity of a mechanical watch's regulating organ.

Eventually the co-axial escapement would go on to find fame in Omega watches, after Daniels sold them the technology in the 1990s. Today "Co-Axial" is a hallmark of the Omega brand.

It was in 1986 when Daniels' co-axial technology would first make an appearance in a timepiece. Over his lifetime, George Daniels only produced 37 timepieces and the Co-Axial Chronograph is among his finest creations.

The completely hand-made watch and movement contained a four-minute tourbillon with co-axial escapement, chronograph, and power reserve indicator, as well as the time. Typical of Daniels' design ethos, the aesthetic of the Co-Axial Chronograph is based on traditional watchmaking from the 17th and 18th centuries. Despite the watch's historic appearance, it was a technological marvel, proving the effectiveness of the co-axial escapement invention.

When Daniels died, in 2011, a series of items from his estate were auctioned off, including the one-of-a-kind Co-Axial Chronograph watch. At a 2012 Sotheby's auction in London it fetched a price of £385,250.

George Daniels wrote a series of books, including one simply titled Watchmaking. It invited those interested in horology to attempt making a watch, and a few did, taking his advice. One of those people was Roger W. Smith, from Bolton, who ended up being the only person Daniels ever took on as an apprentice. Roger W. Smith is Daniels' protégé and continues the Daniels legacy by making his own timepieces, in the former Daniels workshop on the Isle of Man.

* Sold at auction for £385,250 at Sotheby's, London in November 2012.

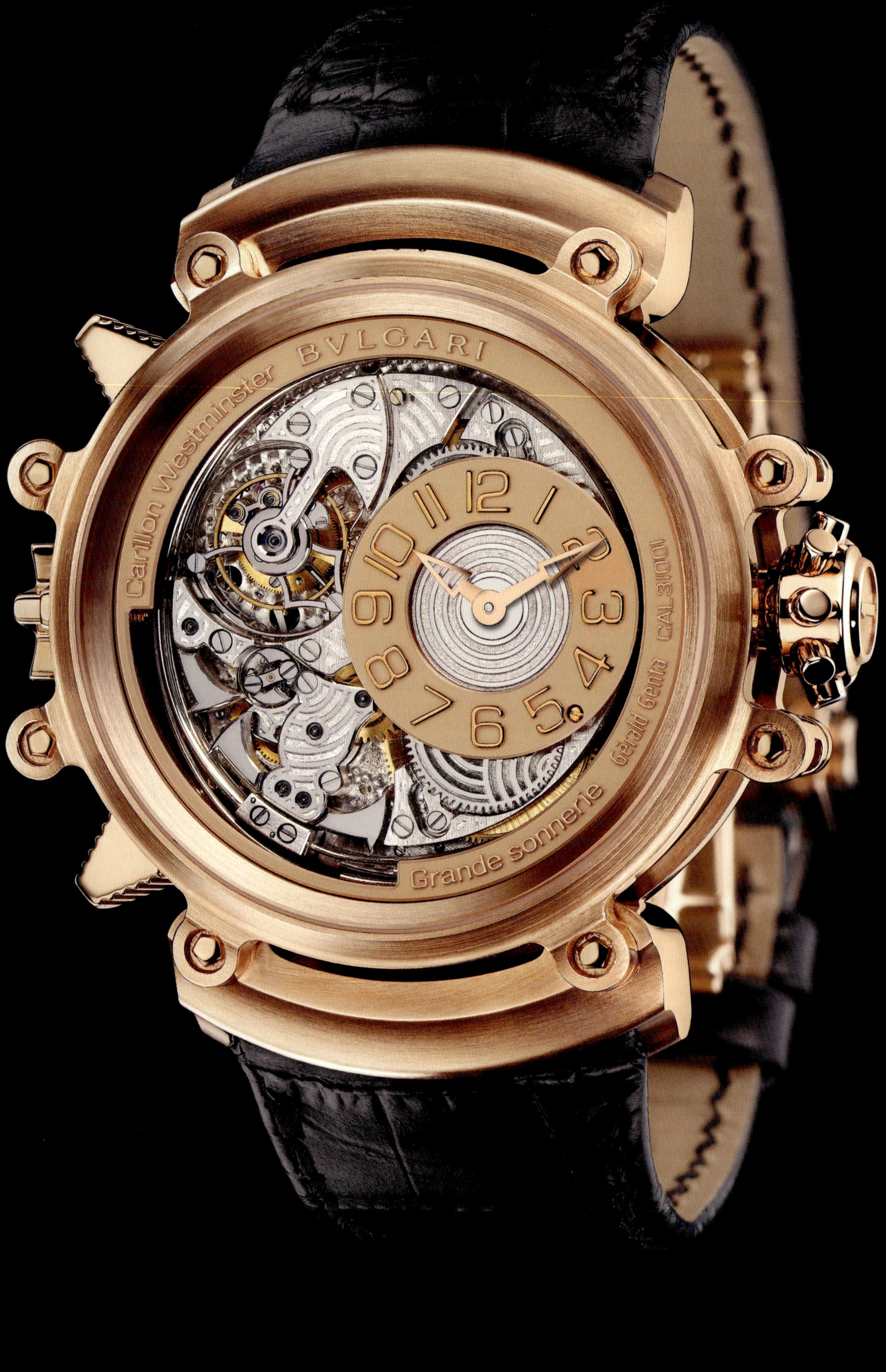
BVLGARI
Carillon Westminster
Grande sonnerie
Gérald Genta
CAL 31001

BULGARI — MAGSONIC SONNERIE TOURBILLON

$ 620 000

AT HEART, THE WATCH IS A MUSICAL TIMEPIECE THAT USES A SERIES OF CHIMES TO INDICATE THE TIME TO THE WEARER IN THE FORM OF A CODED SONG.

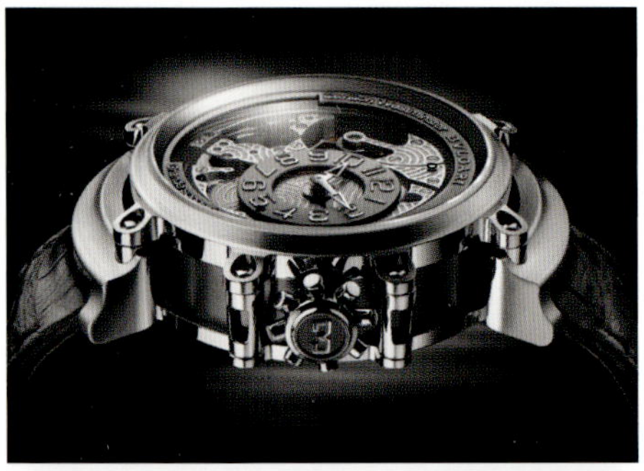

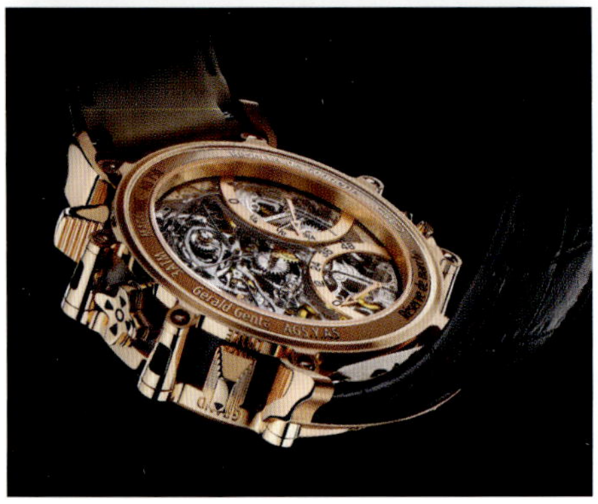

Enough can be said about the Magsonic Sonnerie Tourbillon watch to fill an entire book. It is a traditional mechanical watch of the computer generation, heavy on details, complication, and mysteries, that extend to the ownership experience. Realising the intimidating nature of even explaining the Magsonic Sonnerie Tourbillon, Bulgari even developed a series of apps designed to demonstrate how it works and what it does.

At heart, the watch is a musical timepiece that uses a series of chimes to indicate the time to the wearer in the form of a coded song. Sonnerie watches do this at certain intervals, such as on the hour. What makes this watch more complicated than most sonnerie-style pieces is the level of functionality, and the range of the musical sounds that it can produce. It has the ability of playing what is known as the full Westminster Carillon, which is based on the chimes of the clock at the Palace of Westminster (Houses of Parliament) in London; that is, a long series of notes indicating the time.

The watch began life under another brand, which was named for the late famous 20th-century watch designer Gerald Genta. Owned by Bulgari, Gerald Genta was consolidated during the economic crisis in 2010. Originally known as the Arena Metasonic Sonnerie, the watch was later renamed, employing the name Magsonic. The title isn't just a fancy sounding term, but also a metal alloy developed for the watch. Using computer simulations, Bulgari developed Magsonic to optimise the transmission of sounds from the case. Often a watch case acts to absorb chimes from the movement. The watch is produced mostly from Magsonic and titanium.

Incredibly baroque in appearance, the Magsonic Sonnerie Tourbillon has a case full of pushers and crowns. A complex set of switches allows one to properly use the various functions of the watch. The impressively intricate mechanical movement is made up of almost 900 parts, which only a few master watchmakers can even assemble. The dial of the watch indicates just the time, and displays a tourbillon.

When purchasing a Magsonic Sonnerie Tourbillon, it isn't just the watch that one gets. Certain remarkable watches such as this come with equally remarkable presentation boxes. Bulgari designed a unique transparent box for the Magsonic Sonnerie Tourbillon that electronically opens via a fingerprint scanner. It then reveals the timepiece in a sort of elevator, and the entire box even lights up.

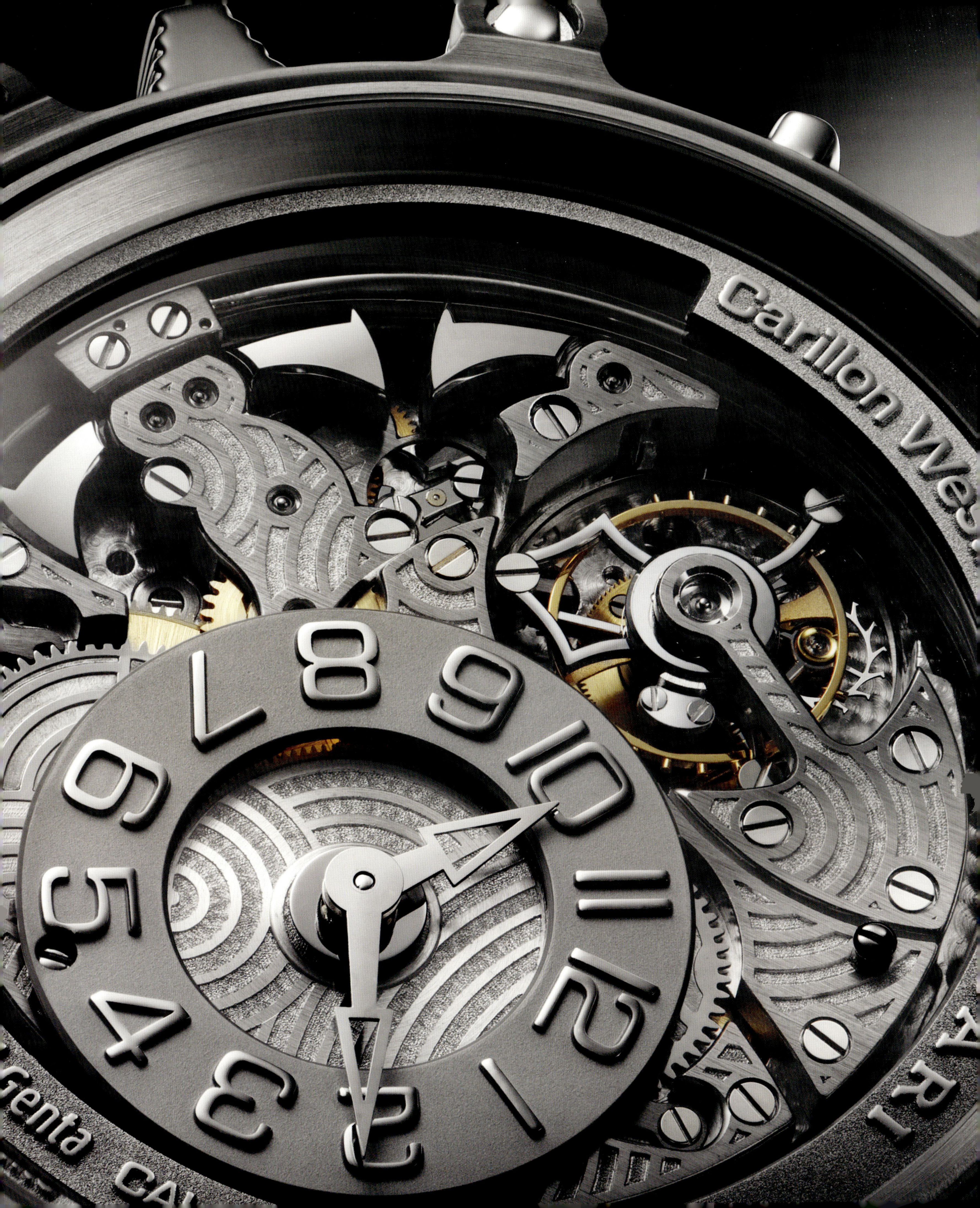
Carillon
Genta

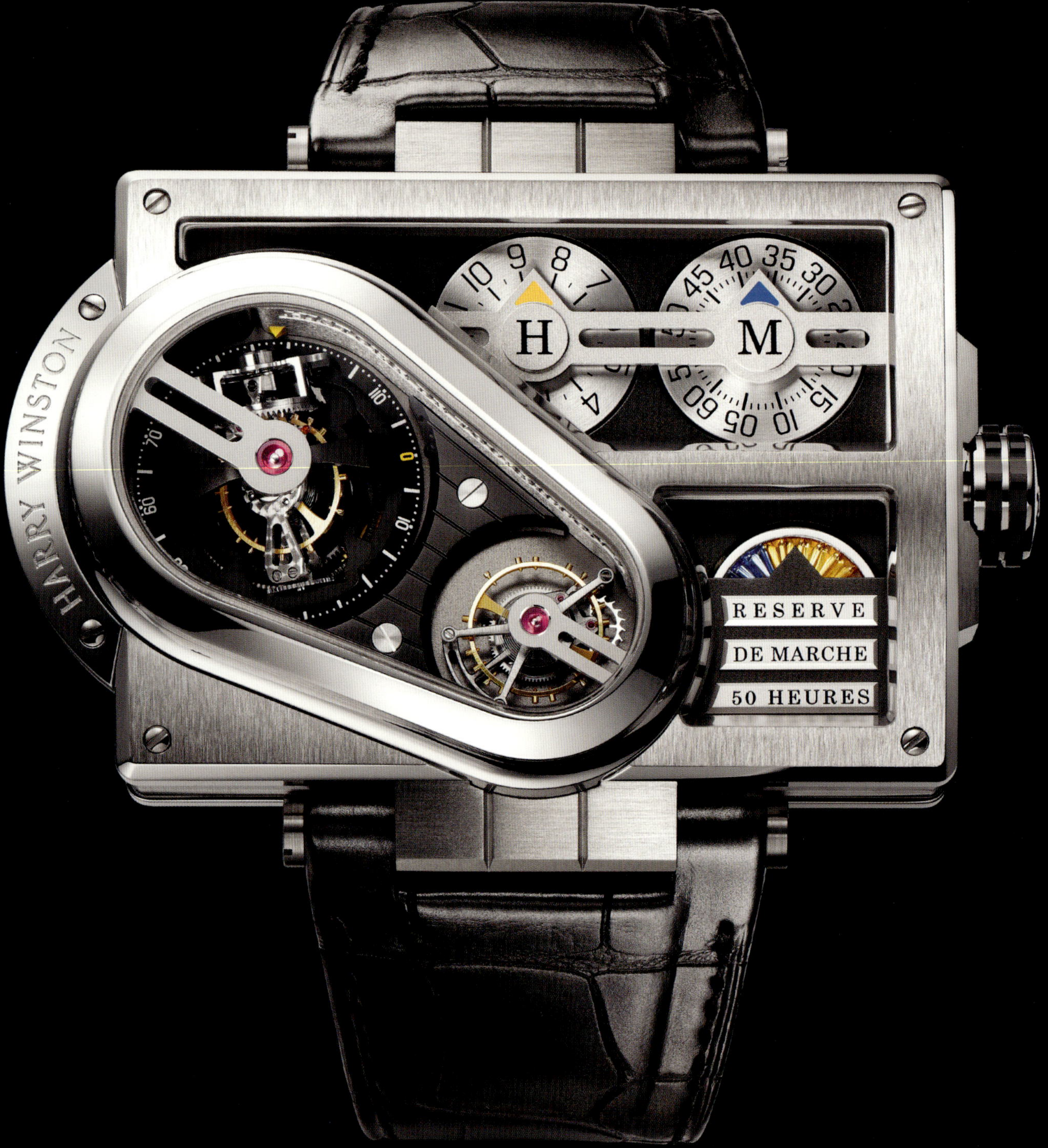

HARRY WINSTON — HISTOIRE DE TOURBILLON 3

$ 622 000

Little known and amazingly creative, the small collection of exclusively limited edition Histoire de Tourbillon watches from Harry Winston are some of the most unique timepieces on the planet. In 2009 Harry Winston surprised the watch world (once again), by releasing the Histoire de Tourbillon1 timepiece. It was a self-proclaimed re-interpretation of the tourbillon and, through what would be five eventual models, the Histoire de Tourbillon family has offered something truly original to the ultra-luxury watch world. As of 2013, the fifth Histoire de Tourbillon has yet to be released.

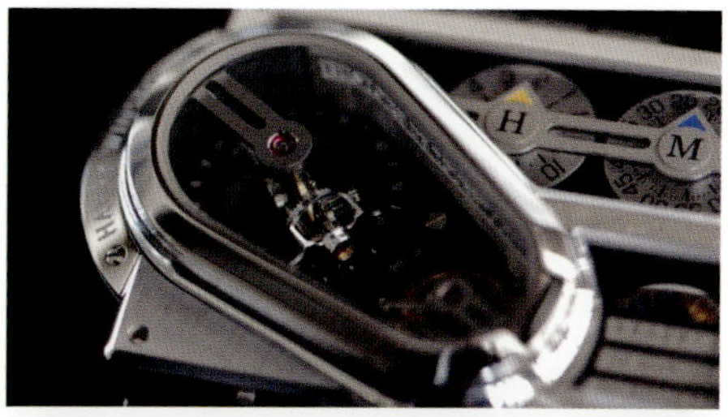

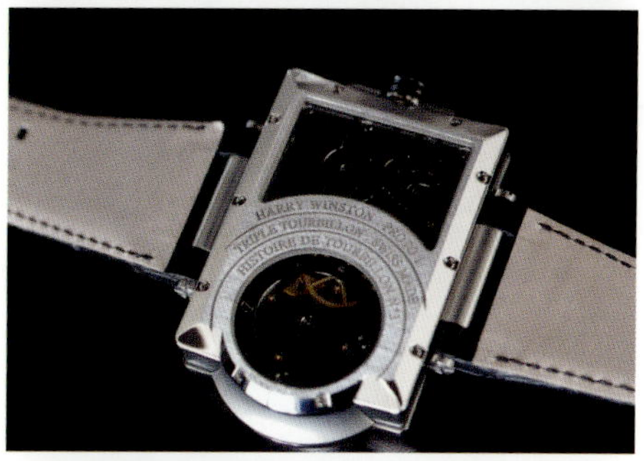

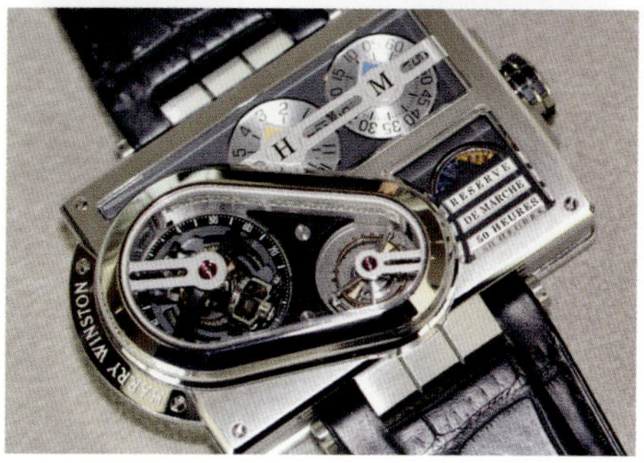

In 2012 Harry Winston released the third instalment of the Histoire de Tourbillon with the 3. It should be noted that none of the Histoire de Tourbillon watches appear anything like one another. Other than each of the models sharing yellow and blue colour accents, and offering the same original take on how to display a tourbillon, the pieces are entirely distinct.

Why a focus on tourbillon-style escapements and then a deconstruction thereof? Tourbillons are traditionally escapements that revolve around their own axis, originally designed for pocket watches in the late 18th century. Meant to enhance accuracy, they serve mostly as decorative features in modern wristwatches. They also serve as status symbols. Having a timepiece with a tourbillon means wealth. Harry Winston – in a pure luxury vein – attempts to play with this concept, not only imagining different forms of tourbillons, but also of timepieces themselves.

The Histoire de Tourbillon 3 begins with a rather large 65mm wide case that is made from 18k white gold as well as Harry Winston's own alloy, known as Zalium. Shaped like a box, time is told via two discs that independently tell the hour and minute. A large open window offers a view of the movement, and a display that is a triple tourbillon.

For this version of the Histoire de Tourbillon, Harry Winston wanted three tourbillons in each timepiece. The largest tourbillon is a bi-axial double tourbillon with an internal 40-second tourbillon and an external 120-second tourbillon. To the right is a third tourbillon that rotates once every 36 seconds. The mastery is in the display, watching the two balance wheel spins on each of the three axis points, in unison.

While not a mainstay of each Histoire de Tourbillon model, the 3 slyly incorporates what Harry Winston is mostly known for: precious stones. A power reserve indicator on the lower right of the case, used to let you know when to wind the mechanical movement, is lined with 11 sapphires and 3 citrines; when the latter pass by the arrow, it is time to wind the piece up. Harry Winston produced just 20 pieces of the Histoire de Tourbillon 3.

GIRARD-PERREGAUX – VINTAGE 1945 JACKPOT TOURBILLON

$ 625 000

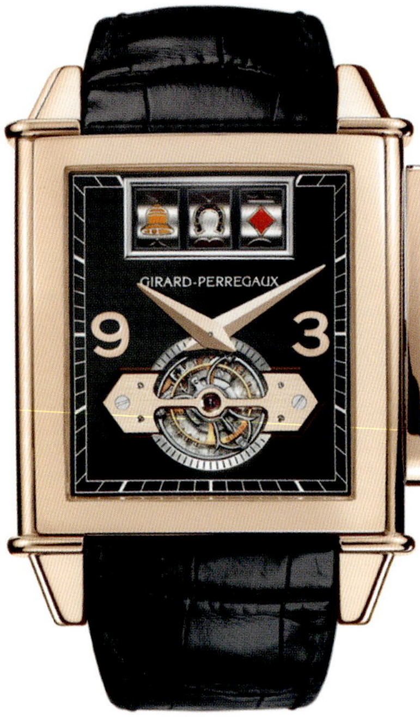

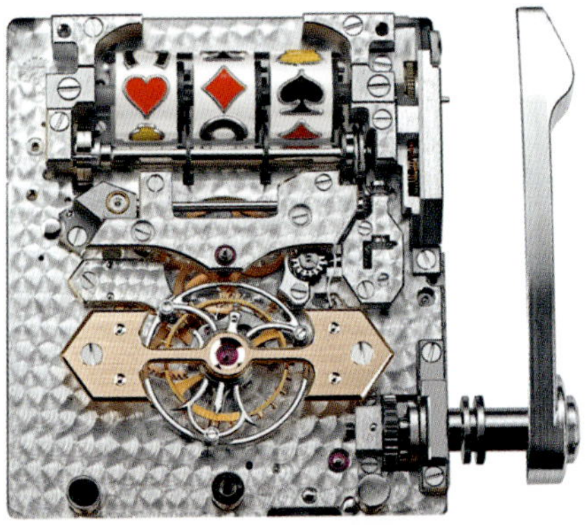

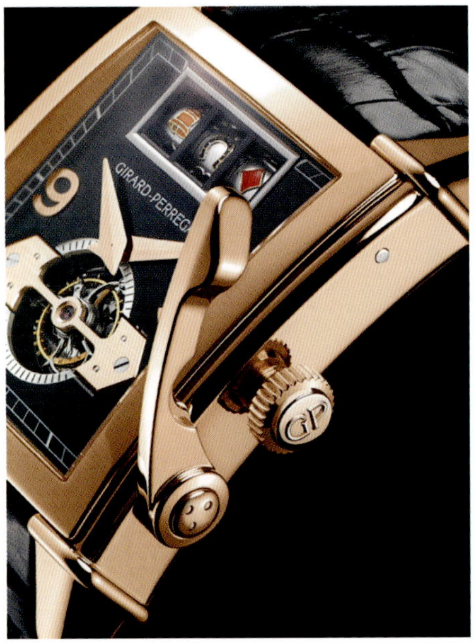

It has been suggested, more than once, that the "difference between men and boys is the price of their toys". A timepiece such as this faithfully illustrates the aforementioned theory. In the mid-2000s there was perhaps no other more talked about watch than the famous Jackpot Tourbillon, a stand-out piece in Girard-Perregaux's Vintage 1945 family of timepieces. To sum the piece up, fantastically priced, it contains both a tourbillon-style escapement as well as an actual, working miniature slot machine game.

A pull-arm on the right of the case, over the crown, is used to start the wheels moving for the slot machine. Lining up the three liberty bells means a jackpot, which the user has a one in 125 chance of getting. Nothing is to be won but the satisfaction of knowing that your highly complicated timepiece can be used for amusement and killing time.

When it was originally released in 2007, the Jackpot Tourbillon was debuted at the brink of the financial crisis, having been planned and produced while many around the world were still making and spending money freely. The timepiece was intentionally lighthearted, and meant to celebrate gambling, which can either be interpreted as actual or metaphoric, in terms of what people do with their money. The watch celebrated the free, and sometimes emotional spending of money, that helps the luxury world go around, all while tantalising the industry with a new era of whimsical complications not based on those expressed by traditional watchmakers.

Girard-Perregaux's squared Vintage 1945 case made a perfect frame for the slot-machine style watch. Girard-Perregaux needed to produce a totally new and integrated mechanical movement for the Jackpot Tourbillon. The mechanism not only contains a tourbillon and 96 hours of power reserve, but the slot machine complication was joined with a hammer and gong that produced a chiming sound each time it was used. Girard-Perregaux designed a truly fitting presentation box for the watch, that hides the timepiece behind a curtain that opens to reveal actual lighting, showcasing the timepiece. Also inside the box are Casio games such as playing cards, dice and poker chips.

BREGUET – 3282

$ 629 515*

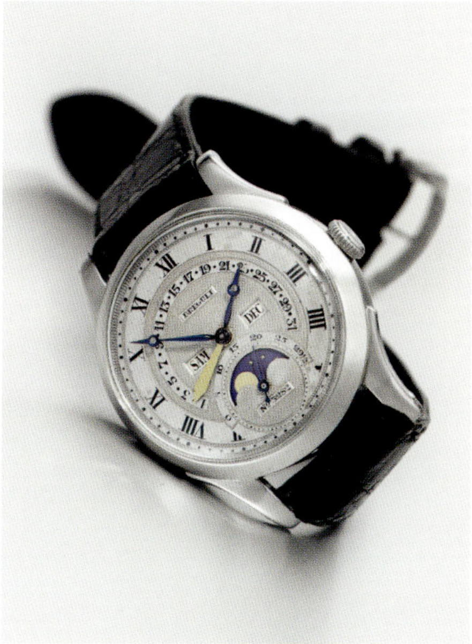

Perhaps the most legendary watchmaker of all time was Abraham-Louis Breguet, from Switzerland. Born in 1747, he eventually moved to France, where most of the leading watchmakers lived during that time. What made Breguet so famous was his ability not only to produce timepieces that look modern even by today's standards, but also his penchant for innovation and for improving the science of chronometry. Today many of the mechanisms found in mechanical watches or on dials still bear his name. For example, the "Breguet over-coil" on many hairsprings, as well as the flagship complication of many luxury timepieces, the aesthetically pleasing animated tourbillon-style escapement. Breguet also lent his name to aesthetic features such as Breguet-style numerals and Breguet pomme-style hands. During his time, he produced inventive timepieces for the Kings of France, Marie-Antoinette, and even Napoléon Bonaparte.

After his death, the Breguet name lived on, continuing up to the 21st century. In 1999, Breguet was acquired by the Swatch Group. Their founder Nicolas Hayek considered Breguet to be a holy grail of luxury watch names; the pinnacle sitting on top of the Swatch Group's pyramid of brands. Modern Breguet timepieces seek to continue the tradition of historic Breguet pieces in terms of their aesthetic qualities and personality. This includes distinctive designs as well as machine guilloché engraved dials. Vintage Breguet wrist or pocket watches are rare to find on the open market. Most are owned by esteemed private collectors or museums, who tend to abstain from selling them.

An uncommon Breguet timepiece from 1935, known as the reference 3282, was auctioned in Geneva in 2007 by the family who originally purchased it. Priced at 10,000 Francs in 1935, the rare 18k white gold men's watch was thought to be unique and was estimated at 150,000–250,000 Swiss Francs. It reached a price of 764,800 Swiss Francs.

The 3282 men's watch is small by today's standards, being 30mm wide. When it was designed, such a diameter was common for a man's timepiece. Surprisingly modern in comparison to today's traditionally designed watches, the 3282 features a distinctive machine-engraved dial, produced in the spirit of original Breguet timepieces. The face displays the time, with a perpetual calendar and Moon-phase indicator. Unique to the watch is the fact that the day and month are displayed in windows, and that the date is indicated on a retrograde scale. The blued pomme-style hands contrast well with the dial, allowing for an impressive level of legibility.

Inside the 3282 sits a movement produced by the famed watchmaker Victorin Piguet, who, during this era, also produced movements for prestigious brands such as Patek Philippe and Vacheron Constantin.

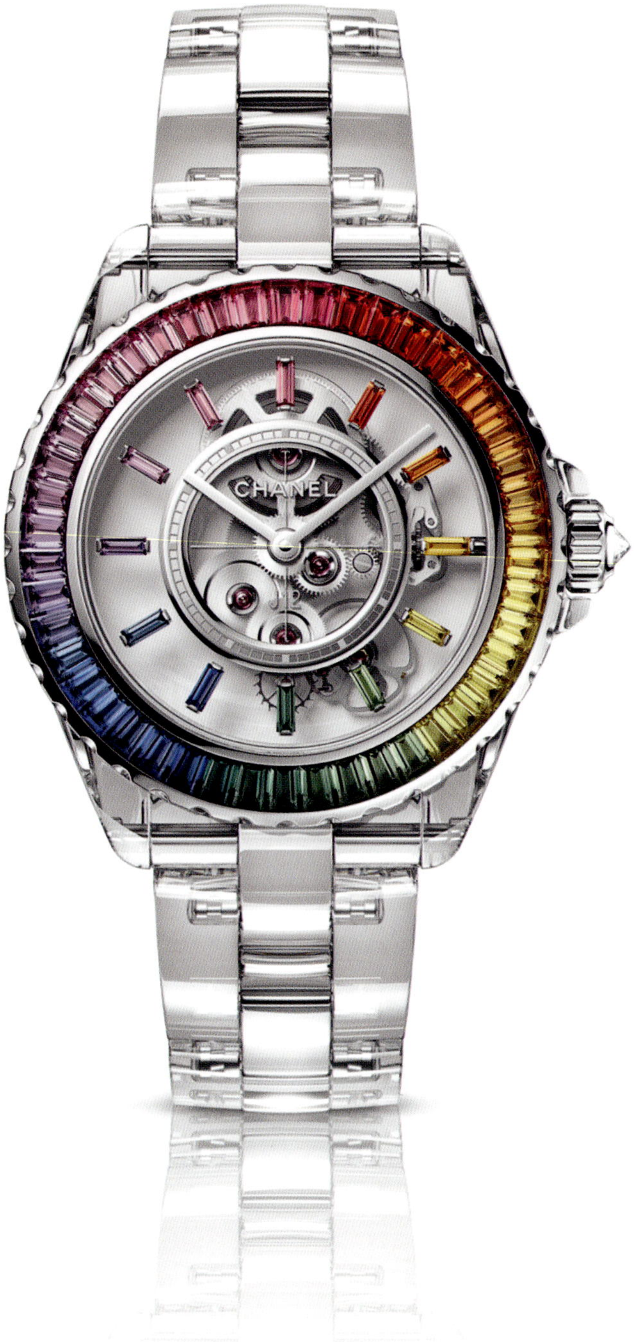

CHANEL — J12 X-RAY ELECTRO CALIBRE 3.1

$ 646 300

Paris-based Chanel is a global fashion powerhouse that also happens to have a robust collection of timepieces – including some at the very high end of the price spectrum. Chanel focuses primarily on women's watches, as well as being an acclaimed innovator of particularly exclusive watches that focus not only on aesthetic trends, but also on high-tech materials and contemporary design. There is no better example to illustrate this point than the Chanel J12 X-Ray Electro Calibre 3.1.

The core design of the watch fits within Chanel's larger and highly prolific J12 collection. Chanel popularised the use of highly scratch-resistant zirconium oxide ceramic as a case and bracelet material in the larger J12 collection. For the J12 X-Ray, Chanel replaces ceramic with an even more durable and scratch-resistant material – synthetic sapphire crystal. Accordingly, the J12 X-Ray has a bracelet and a 38mm-wide case, both almost entirely manufactured from carefully machined and polished pieces of transparent sapphire crystal. The other parts of the case (such as the bezel assembly and crown) are produced from 18k white gold.

Chanel produced two versions of the J12 X-Ray, which were limited to 12 pieces each. One version was the standard X-Ray with a traditional diamond-decoration theme, while the other was the X-Ray Electro with a rainbow theme for the gem-set bezel and matching rainbow hour markers. The X-Ray Electro nevertheless still has some diamonds, such as the large diamond cabochon placed into the crown, as well as diamonds set into the bracelet clasp.

The beautiful rainbow effect created for the dial and hour markers is achieved using a variety of coloured sapphire crystals, which add a vibrancy to the otherwise transparent effect of the X-Ray's clear sapphire case, bracelet and dial. The superlative use of sapphire crystal in many forms makes the J12 X-Ray collection a true testament to the importance of the material in today's luxury watchmaking industry.

Inside the J-12 X-Ray watch is a novel in-house made, manually wound movement known as the Calibre 3.1. The minimalist mechanics use a clear sapphire disc as the baseplate for the seemingly floating movement components. The visual effect allows for a relatively unrestricted view through the entire watch, set against the splendour of the rainbow baguette-cut precious stones. Between the diamonds and sapphires, the J12 X-Ray Electro has nearly 10 carats of gem weight, making this one of the most contemporary high-end women's watches of its era.

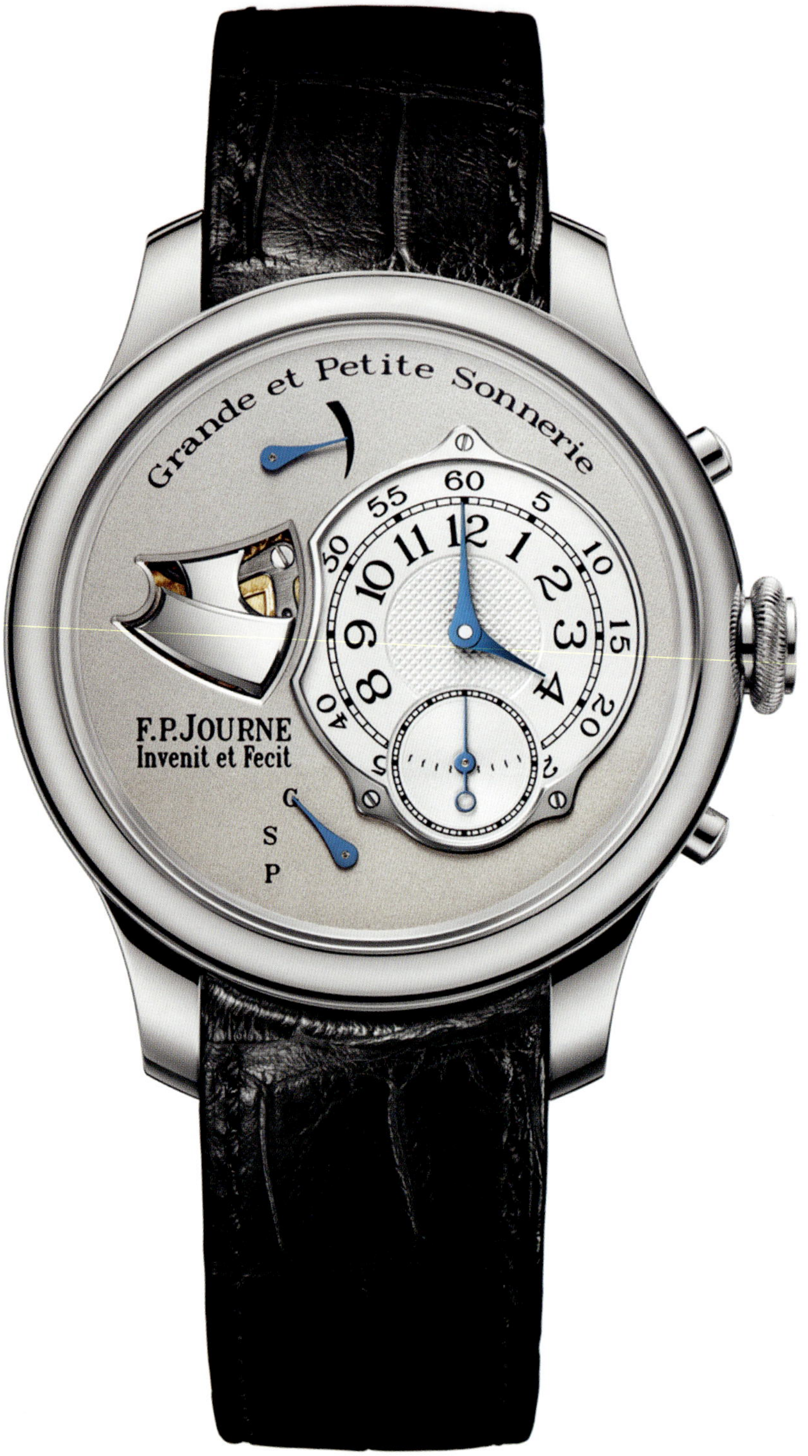

F.P. JOURNE — SONNERIE SOUVERAINE

$ 650 000

It has been said, more than once, that François-Paul Journe is possibly the most talented living watchmaker. Aficionados with the deepest knowledge of horology and mechanics (and the budgets to afford the best) are often seen wearing F.P. Journe timepieces. To answer the question "why?", it is perhaps best to consider the intentions of F.P. Journe himself. His watches are clearly luxury items, but they aren't designed merely to be luxury items in the interests of communicating status or wealth. Journe is dedicated to the pursuit of horological perfection, and creating the best possible timepieces, no matter what the price. He isn't interested in producing status items, and it appears that the most honed minds prefer what he is thinking, when it comes to what they put on their wrists.

The Sonnerie Souveraine is perhaps F.P. Journe's most iconic and descriptive creation, when it comes to the furtherance of his ideals. The goal was to produce a highly functional "idiot proof" version of what is probably among the most delicate types of mechanism ever to exist. Contained in the movement are a series of chiming functions, which include a "grande" and "petit" sonnerie, as well as a minute repeater. Together, these represent the world's most complicated and sought-after chiming features a mechanical watch may have. They are also notoriously easy to break if operated incorrectly. In his own words, F.P. Journe wanted to make the Sonnerie Souveraine "safe in the hands of an eight-year-old child."

F.P. Journe began his horological career as a restorer of antique clocks and watches. He formed his own brand in 1999, and today his firm stands in the middle of Geneva, being one of only a few major watch factories in the city centre. Being independent allows him the freedom to produce whatever he likes, which is partially why this half-million dollar plus timepiece comes in a humble steel case.

Why steel, when even the movement mainplate is produced from 18k gold? The reason is related to the chiming features. Steel is simply a better transmitter of sound than, say, gold or platinum. The quality of the chiming functions, along with their output, is of paramount concern to Journe versus the expression of a luxury product.

Timepieces that combine minute repeaters and sonneries are exceedingly rare. Each is designed to "sound" the time via chimes, but each works a little bit differently. Grand and petite sonnerie functions sound the time at intervals, such as on the hour or each 15 minutes, automatically. Minute repeaters do the same, but on demand, as activated by the user. Combining these functions in a user-friendly watch with a beautifully elegant design is the hallmark of F.P. Journe, and to that extent the watch is a masterpiece.

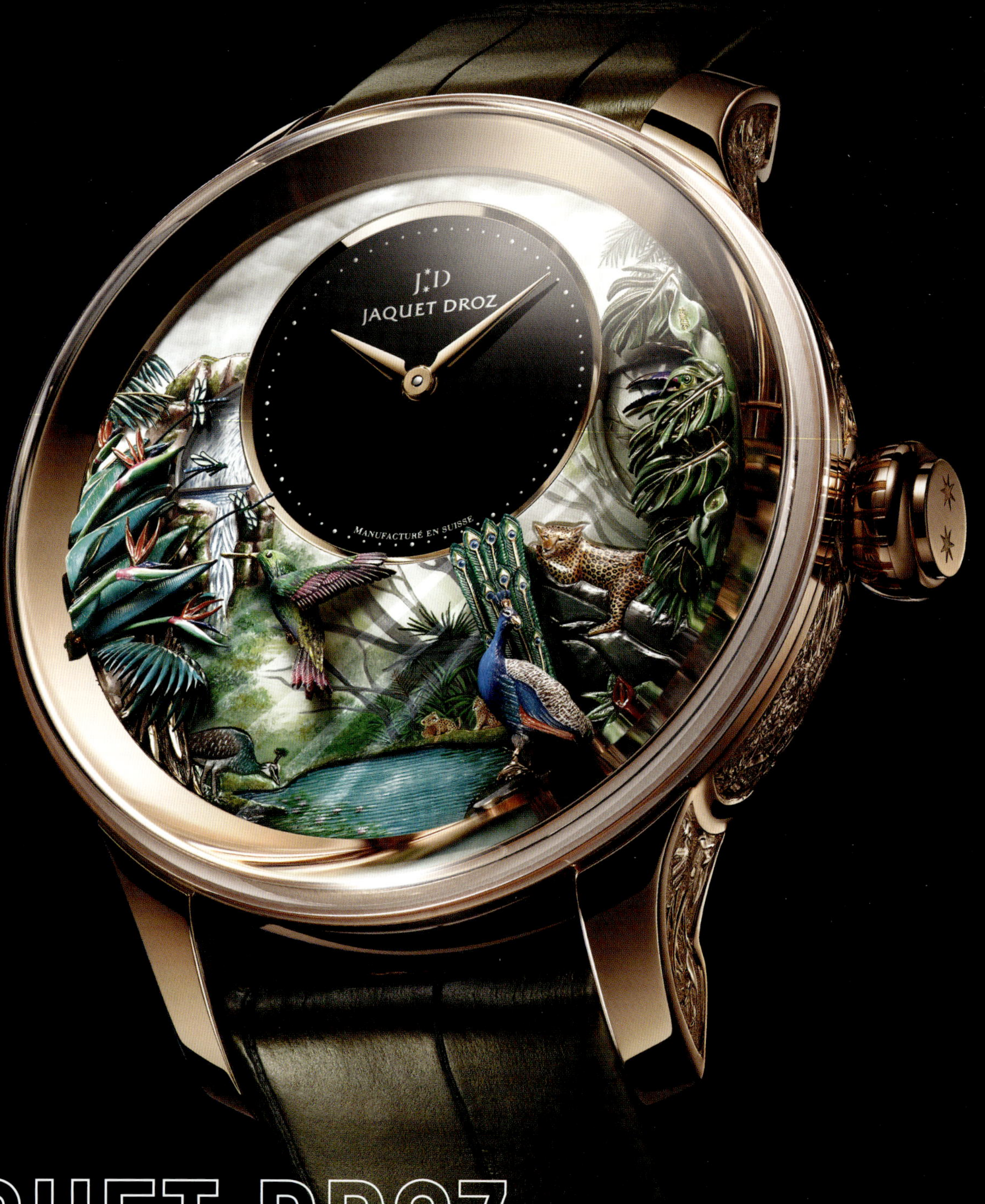

JAQUET DROZ — TROPICAL BIRD REPEATER

$ 661 500

Automatons were robots of the old world. For several hundred years, mechanical creations made to move (even a bit) like living things have delighted onlookers, from children to crowned royalty. Watchmaker Jaquet Droz, in his late 18th-century heyday, was a renowned master of mimicking human and animal beings with intricate mechanical wonders that served as the top-shelf luxury toys of their time. No aristocratic evening event was complete without at least one person pleading for the host to activate his avian automata. In later years, traces of this wealthy household fixture became democratised and most recently kept alive in the form of the humble cuckoo clock.

Less humble is the museum-quality tropical-scene artwork that decorates the dial of the Jaquet Droz Tropical Bird Repeater wristwatch – a timepiece of which there are only eight examples per version in existence. The painstakingly produced three-dimensional scene comes to life as hand-painted and engraved figurines representing the peacock, leaves, hummingbird, toucan, dragonflies and flowing waterfall performing an elegant, scripted mechanical dance. (Note the Tropical Bird Repeater's intentional focus on the flying bird or bird-like species in the face's miniature composition.) What causes the dial to animate is activation of the timepiece's mechanical minute-repeater complication, which is controlled by a sliding lever on the side of the case. Minute-repeater complications often require more than 10–15 seconds to fully chime out the time. During this horological musical performance, the wearer is hearing the result of small hammers striking small gongs, while engaging in the simple pleasure of watching painted gold figurines frolic in a fantasy jungle.

The massive 47mm-wide, 18k red- or white-gold case has but a modest dial for indicating the time – offering just the hours and minutes set against a mother-of-pearl or onyx stone backdrop (depending on the particular model). Completing the package for the Tropical Bird Repeater is the deep green-toned alligator strap. In the world of timepieces there are functional tool watches and then there are artistic statement watches. Among the latter pieces – which includes the Tropical Bird Repeater – are those statement watches whose volume is all the louder thanks to a generous application of artisanal craftsmanship.

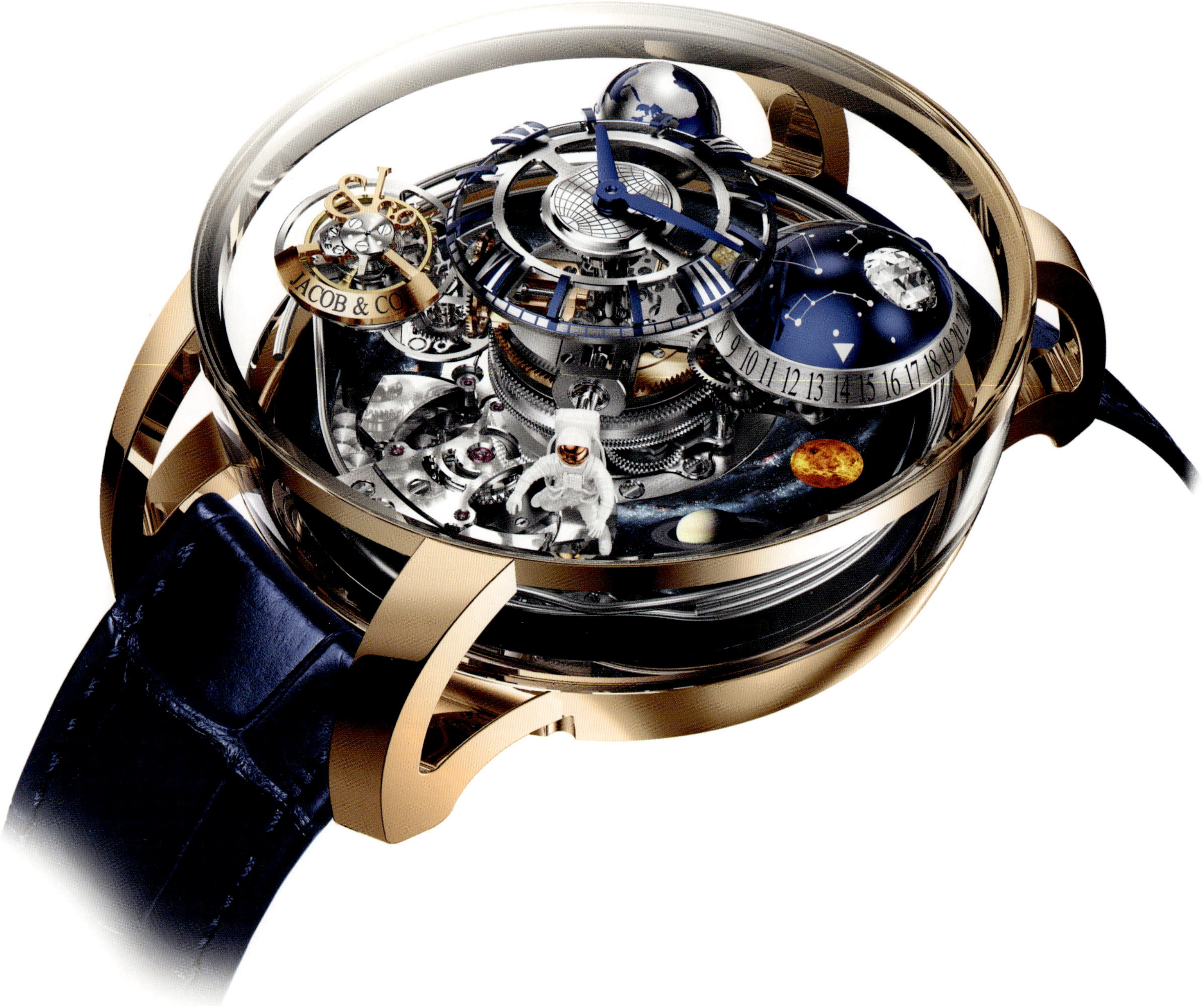

JACOB & CO. — ASTRONOMIA MAESTRO

$ 680 000

Jacob & Co.'s flagship high-complication Astronomia watch collection is immediately noteworthy for its "fish bowl" set-in-metal case. The enclosure follows the space requirements of the mechanical micro-sculpture movement, which features different animated elements on each of the four arms. Most complex among the current Astronomia timepieces is the musical Astronomia Maestro version. This marries the cavernous 18k gold and sapphire-crystal bubble case with a high audio volume Carillon-style time-chiming mechanism, which uses three hammers to strike the intricately coiled gongs.

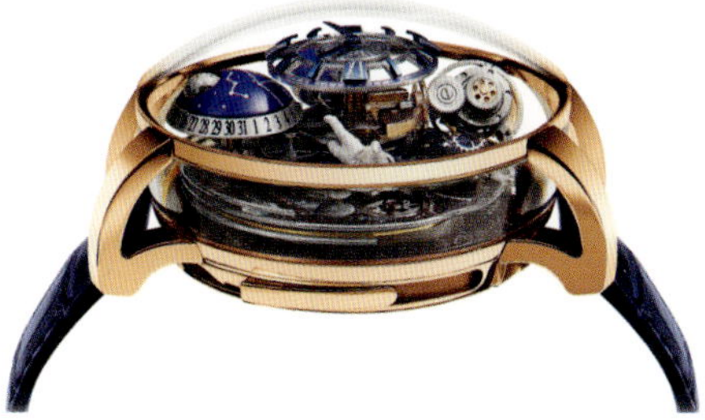

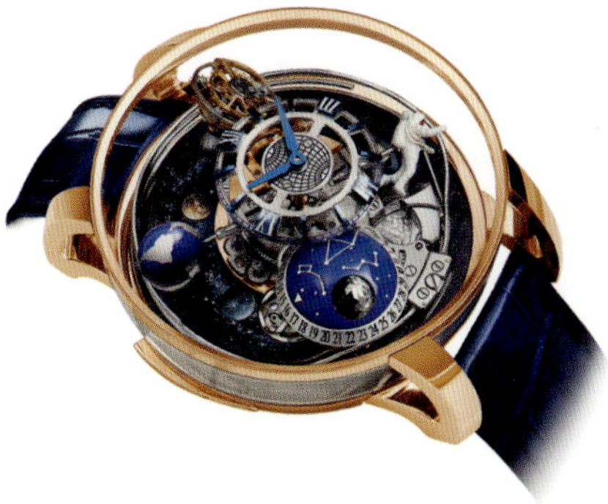

It is the dream of many chiming musical watchmakers to have cases this large at their disposal, given how nicely it can act as a resonance chamber. This Maestro version of the Astronomia literally wraps the minute-repeater complication around the centrally mounted arm, which houses the timepiece's other features. In the middle of the elevated, tower-like mechanical structure is a dial for the time – acting as one of the few functional design cues employed on the Astronomia that is shared by the majority of watches. In most other respects, products like this thrive on eschewing conventional norms.

Surrounding the time dial are an arm with a tourbillon, another with a small globe of the Earth that rotates once every 24 hours, a Moon-phase indicator that uses a spherical diamond as a representation of the Moon, and a constantly spinning hand-engraved astronaut figurine made from magnesium. This latter design element suggests that Jacob & Co. see the design as a way of looking into space and viewing impressive, constantly moving objects.

The Astronomia Maestro's movement (produced mostly from titanium) claims to have a "triple axis" tourbillon given that the tourbillon rotates in two directions, while the set of four arms themselves slowly rotate around the entire dial. The case has no crown, with only the sliding activation lever for the minute repeater visible when the watch is worn. The reverse side of the case has a fold-out crown that is used for winding the 60-hour power-reserve movement, as well as setting the time. Finally, despite the Astronomia Maestro's stately case size of 50mm wide and 26mm tall, it has a reputation for being remarkably comfortable on the wrist.

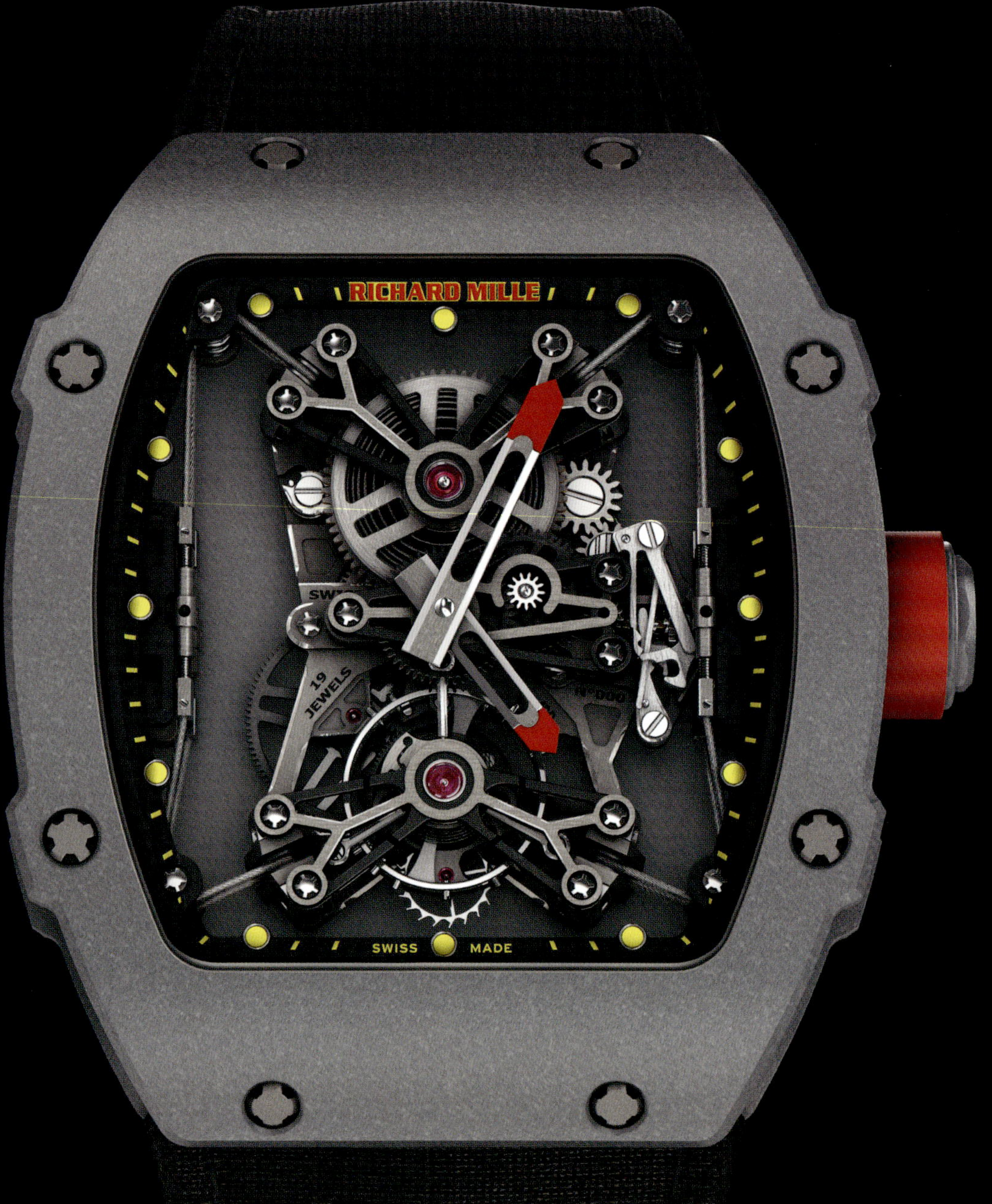

RICHARD MILLE — RM 27-01 TOURBILLON RAFAEL NADAL

$ 690 000

As a luxury brand Richard Mille is a success story. Unable to find a timepiece precisely as he wanted it, Richard Mille decided to develop a new company dedicated to ultra-modern luxury watches inspired by his favourite area of sport and technology – Formula 1 racing. With a series of designs and features found nowhere else, Richard Mille has become proof that contemporary watch collectors enjoy traditional mechanical watches rendered in designs with modern materials.

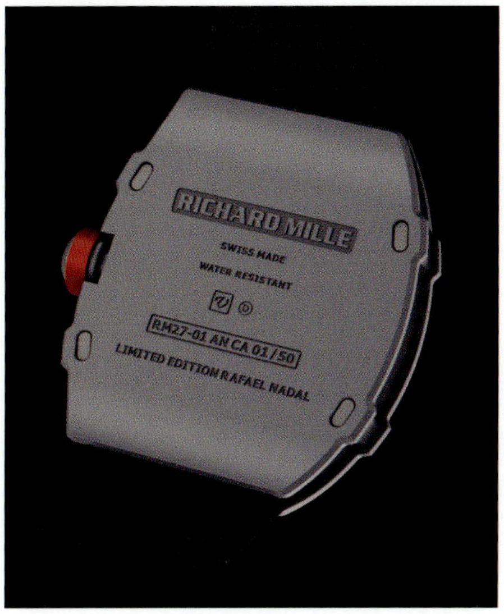

One of Richard Mille's most famous moves was to partner with the Spanish tennis star Rafael Nadal in around 2010. Rather than have Nadal simply as a spokesperson for the brand, he wanted him to actually wear an ultra-expensive watch while playing professional tennis.

The move stunned the media and captured the attention of spectators, because no athlete would want to add weight to their playing arm. Richard Mille used the opportunity to develop the custom RM027 watch, that was to be the lightest tourbillon-based timepiece in the world. To achieve an extreme lightness, the watch relied on a material known as LITAL. Mostly an alloy of lithium and aluminium, it offered a strong, dense material that was highly resistant to shock.

Nadal won the French Open with the half million dollar plus watch on his wrist, and continued to beat his opponents while wearing a Richard Mille. From a marketing perspective it was a brilliant move. Not only was Richard Mille, as a brand, getting a huge amount of attention, but the durability of the watches was being proven. The RM027 watch, and later the RM 27-01 watch that succeeded it, had tourbillon-based mechanical movements that are known to be quite delicate. So for them to exist on Nadal's wrist while he swatted tennis balls was quite a testament.

As a follow-up to the limited edition initial Nadal watch, Richard Mille expanded the collection with the RM 27-01. Not quite as light as the original, the RM 27-01 is a bit larger and more fashionable. It also contains additional durability features. LITAL is still used in the movement, which weighs in at a remarkably light 3.5 grams. The case of the watch is a polymer mixed with "carbon nanotubes". Overall, the watch can withstand acceleration of up to 5,000 g-forces, but it is often pointed out that the polymer case is anything but a luxury material in terms of traditional rarity and value.

A unique feature inside the watch, to increase durability and shock protection, is the fact that the mechanical movement is mounted on a tiny metal suspension cable. Limited to 50 pieces in each version, the charisma and allure of Richard Mille allows a timepiece such as this to be priced quite close to a million dollars.

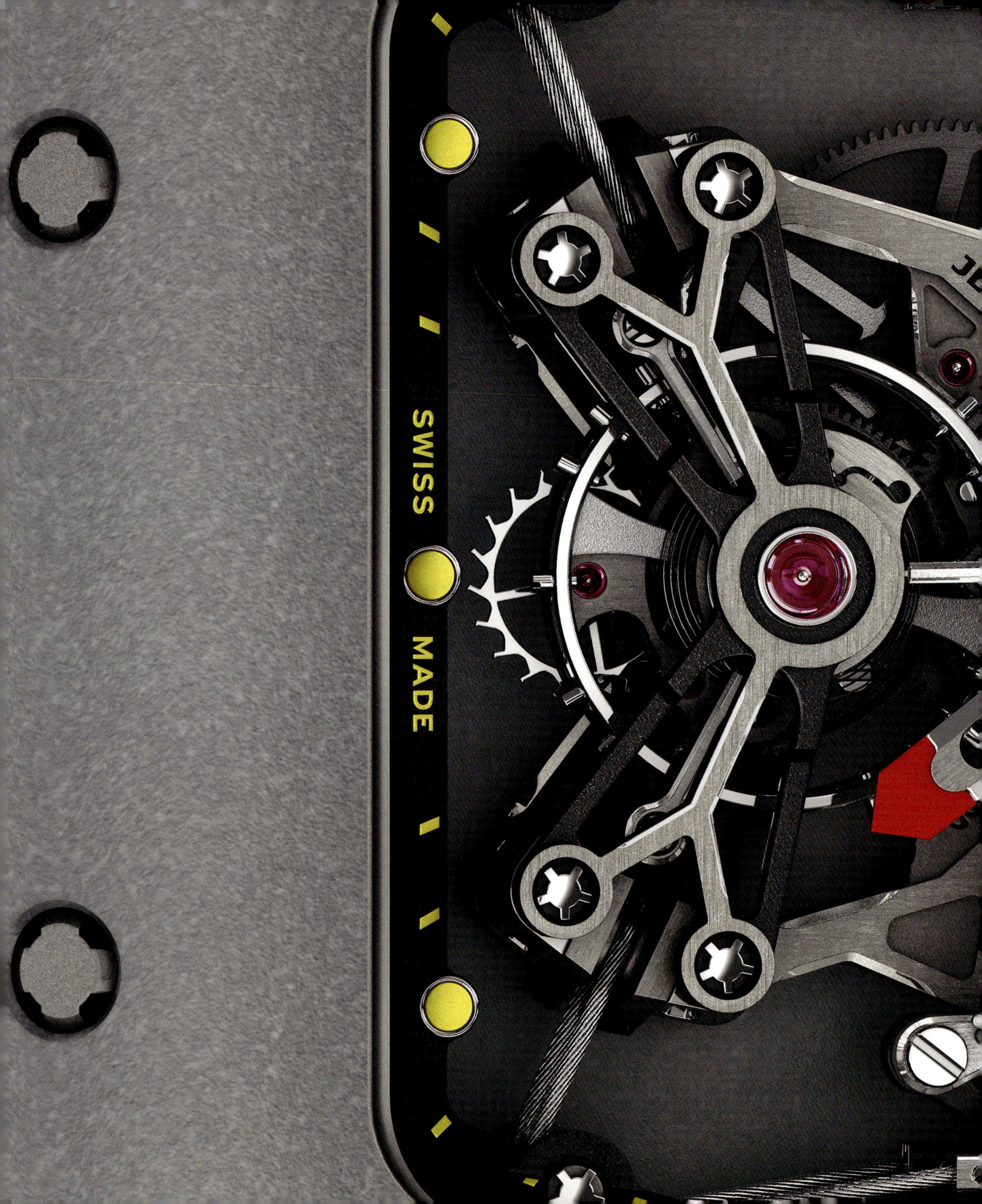
SWISS
MADE

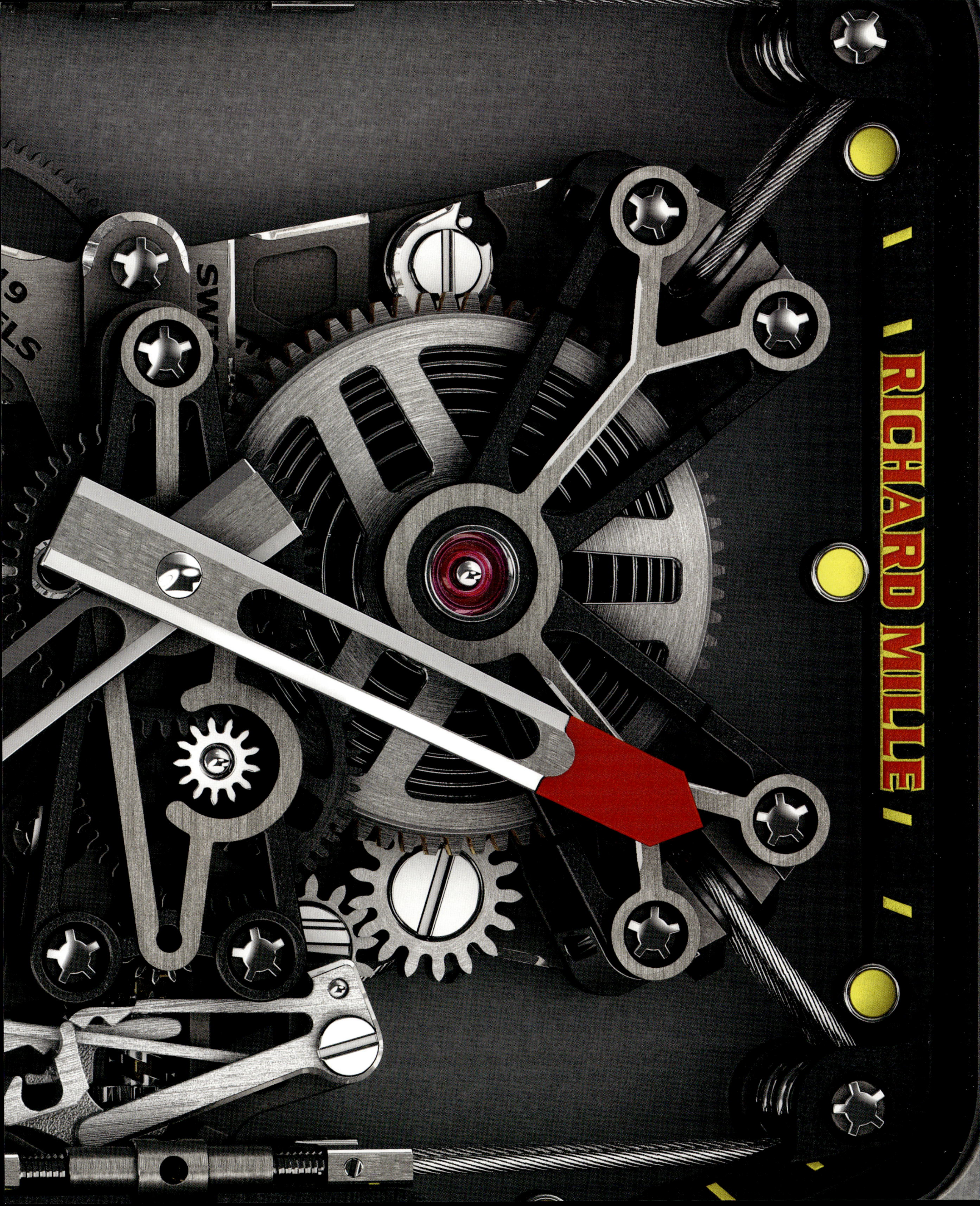
RICHARD MILLE

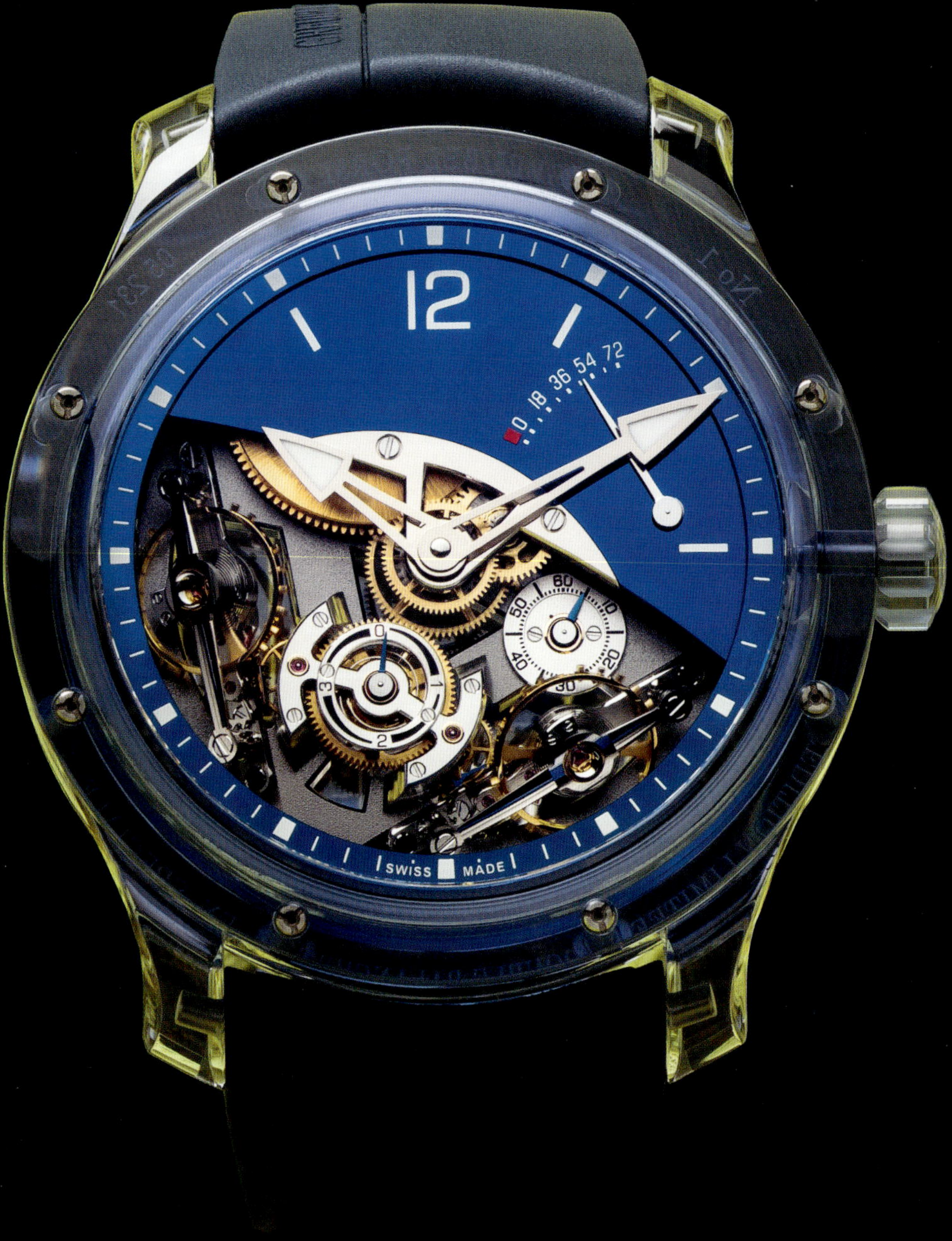

GREUBEL FORSEY – DOUBLE BALANCIER SAPPHIRE

$ 695 000

Mastery of technique is a hallmark at the home of Greubel Forsey in Switzerland, where craftspeople produce some of most highly finished watches in existence. In watch-speak, "finishing" is generally defined as the surface treatment (mostly) metal components are decorated with as part of the construction of the timepiece. At Greubel Forsey, finishing is a lengthy exercise in patience and practice as each individual component is polished under magnification by a trained specialist. At prices like these, collectors demand perfection beyond which the naked eye can even notice.

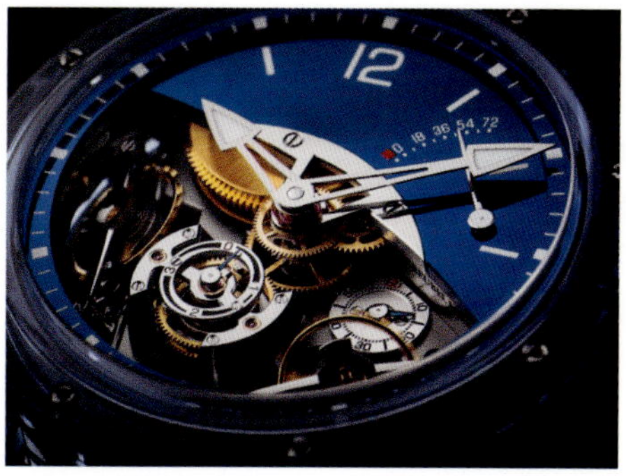

The fervent focus on finishing makes the allure of a transparent sapphire-crystal case obvious for some Greubel Forsey products. Cases slowly machined from pieces of transparent synthetic sapphire crystal (naturally extremely scratch resistant) are all the rage for many ultra-high-end timepieces because it allows the best timepiece makers to show off the beauty of their craft even more. While Greubel Forsey produces the Double Balancier model in traditional metal cases, this limited edition of just 11 Double Balancier Sapphire pieces, produced exclusively for the American market, is the best way to admire the many hours of work that went into producing and decorating the distinctive 284-part manually wound mechanical movement.

What makes the Double Balancier model particularly noteworthy is that it is among the very few Greubel Forsey timepieces produced without a tourbillon mechanism. Instead, as the name of the watch implies, the movement includes two balance wheels mounted at an angle to promote better performance over time. Timepieces only require one balance wheel to operate, so the inclusion of an additional balance wheel is an exercise in promoting better accuracy. Greubel Forsey designed an elegant differential system (with a hand that rotates once every four minutes) that connects the two regulation systems and averages out their results. The operation of the system is as compelling as its aesthetic architecture and which Greubel Forsey make efforts to further display thanks to the semi-open asymmetric dial. Other information on the dial includes the time with a subsidiary seconds dial, as well as a power-reserve indicator for the movement's total capacity to operate for 72 hours until rewinding is necessary.

Blue is the thematic colour for this limited-edition Double Balancier Sapphire, which uses a blue-toned solid-gold dial with matching blue-coloured chapter ring. The blue colours, combined with the fantastic polishing of the movement, results in a bold visual no matter what angle the watch is appreciated from. Greubel Forsey famously touts the durability of this extremely precious luxury item, which comes with either a blue alligator strap or a sportier blue rubber strap.

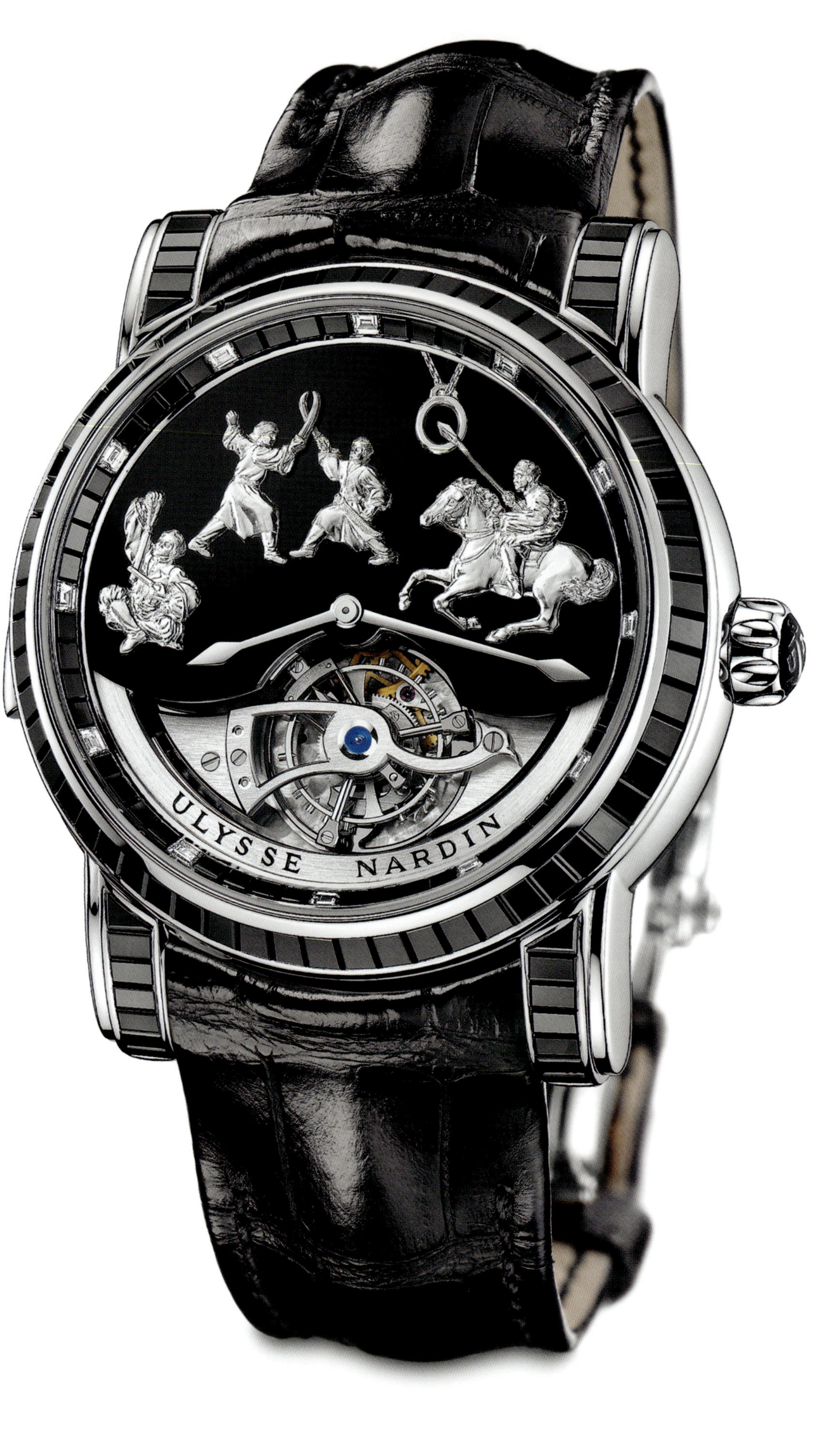
ULYSSE NARDIN

ULYSSE NARDIN — GENGHIS KHAN: WESTMINSTER CARILLON TOURBILLON JAQUEMARTS MINUTE REPEATER

$ 700 000

AS A BRAND ULYSSE NARDIN ENJOYS DANCING BETWEEN USEFUL LUXURY WATCHES FOR DAILY WEAR AND THE ULTRA EXOTIC.

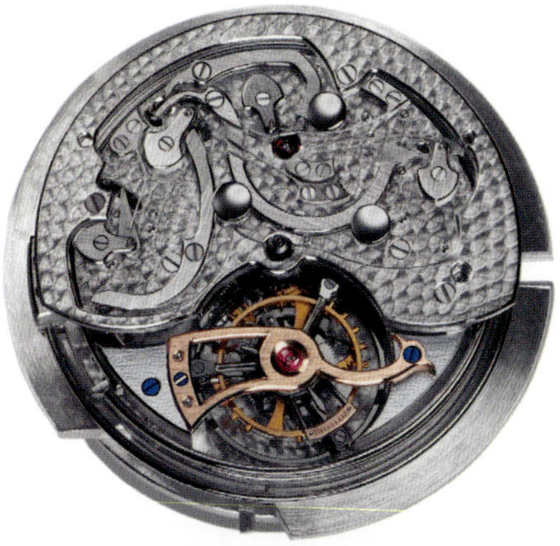

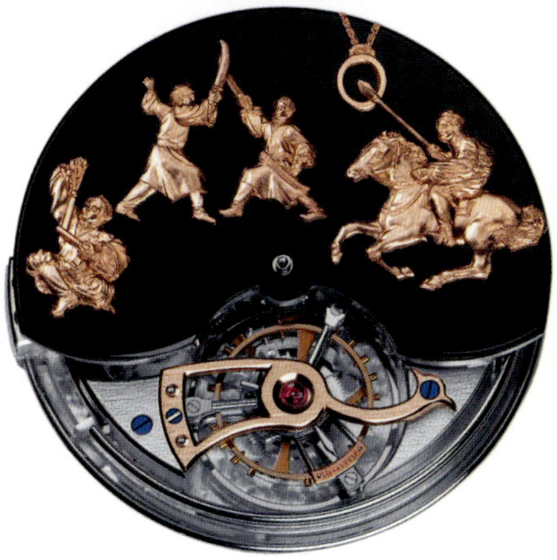

As a brand Ulysse Nardin enjoys dancing between useful luxury watches for daily wear and the ultra exotic. The famed Genghis Khan is among these latter creations and, when it was originally released around 2002, helped spark a newfound interest among collectors for a unique complication known as jaquemarts, which is a form of dial animation.

Jaquemarts were originally more like automaton puppets on certain historic public clocks, and are generally considered to be among the classification of items that predated modern robots. On the dial of the Genghis Khan Jaquemarts watch, the small automatons take the form of Genghis Khan-era soldiers from the 12th century. Their role is to move about in tandem, with the activation of the minute repeater.

When Ulysse Nardin released the Genghis Khan watch it was the first timepiece in the world to combine minute repeater, tourbillon and automaton figure complications. The minute repeater, which when activated sounds the time back in the form of chimes, is further designed to sound the full Westminster Chimes. This offers an improved and highly melodious nature to the sound.

Exposed at the bottom of the watch is a tourbillon, which is a spinning escapement that is part of the mechanical movement emphasised for decorative and historic purpose. It sits under what is a dial made of onyx. Set on the dial are the jaquemart figures, hand-carved entirely in gold. Certain versions of the Genghis Khan watch were produced with highly diamond-decorated cases. Subsequent to the Genghis Khan, Ulysse Nardin presented other similar Tourbillon Jaquemarts Minute Repeater watches with different dial scenes, such as the Alexander the Great Tourbillon Jaquemarts Minute Repeater model. Ulysse Nardin limited production of the Genghis Khan to just 30 pieces.

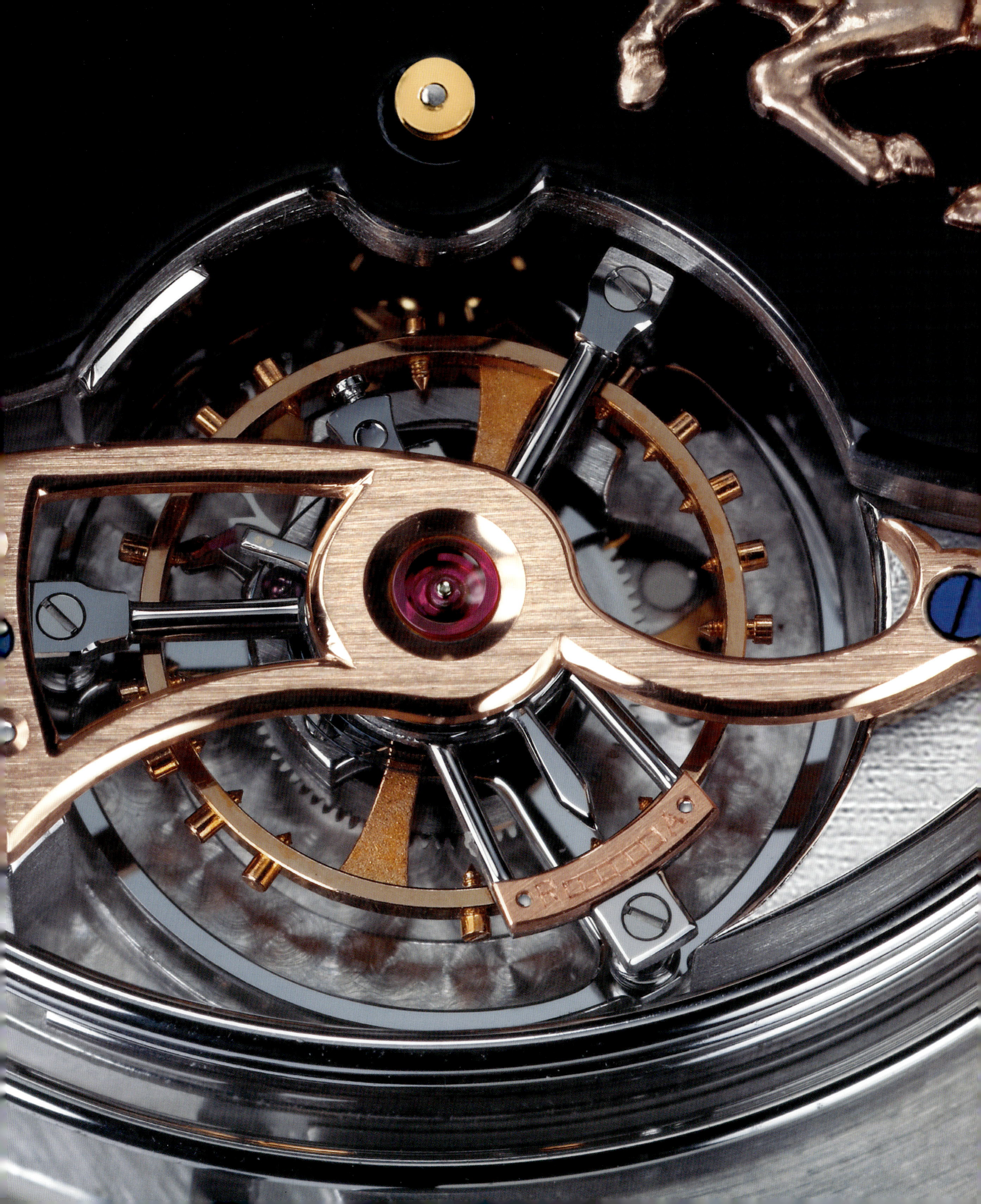

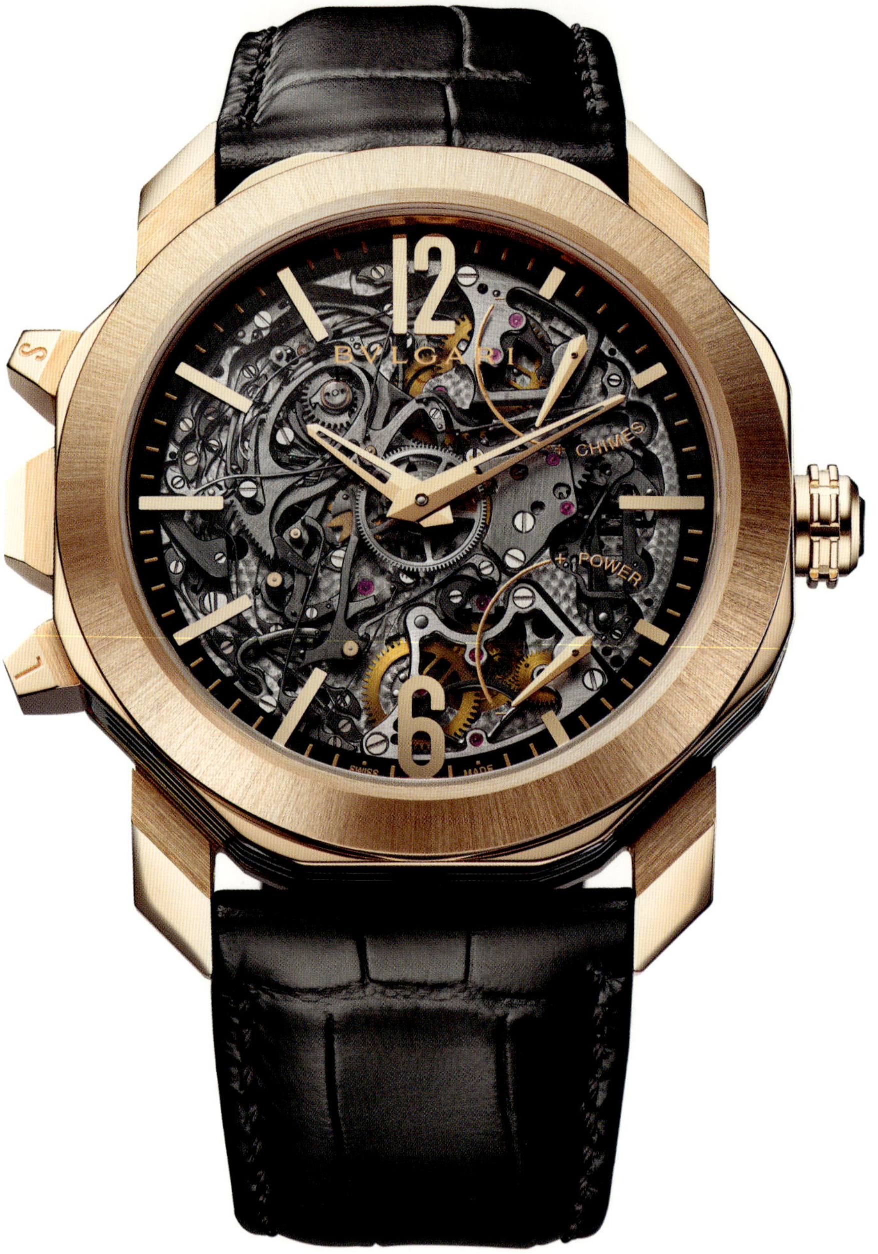

BULGARI — OCTO GRANDE SONNERIE QUANTIÈME PERPÉTUEL

$ 708 000

At Bulgari, the design for their timepieces often comes from Italy, while their prestigious mechanical movements and time-honoured craftsmanship come from Switzerland. The massively complicated Octo Grande Sonnerie Quantième Perpétuel attempts to faithfully merge these two worlds by leveraging the design popularity of Bulgari's Octo case family with a complicated mechanical movement concept that they have been perfecting for over 20 years. At the time of writing, this is the most complicated timepiece ever produced by the renown brand.

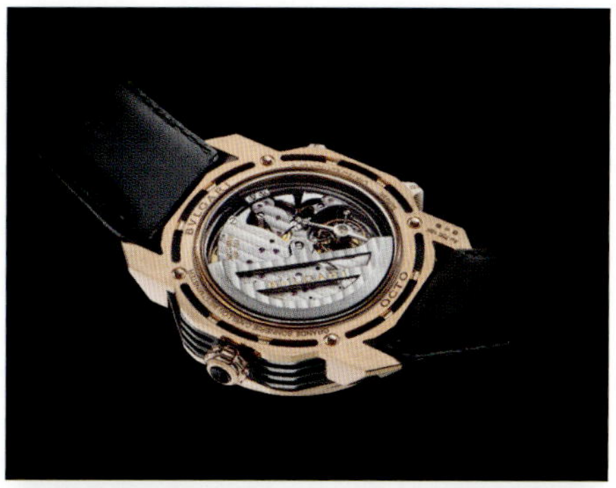

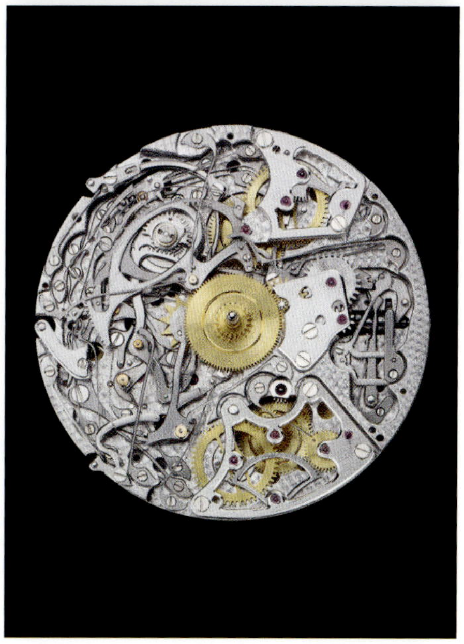

The Octo case family is architecturally inspired and is favoured by watch lovers for its elegant mixture of curved and geometric elements. The entire case is an exercise in contrasts with its eight sides blending with a round dial, accented by a series of angular details on the watch face. This particular Octo Grande Sonnerie Quantième Perpétuel is easily the most complicated (and thickest) Octo watch to date. Its sandwich-style architecture uses a middle-case section that is an integral part of the musical chiming systems in the watch. Most musical timepieces have either sonnerie or minute-repeater complications – but the Octo Grande Sonnerie Quantième Perpétuel has both. The middle of the case acts as an amplifier to increase sound resonance as well as to ensure sufficient water resistance to satisfy modern timepiece-wearer expectations.

The core mechanics inside of the Octo Grande Sonnerie Quantième Perpétuel have been refined over the years by the Bulgari watchmaking team, but this particular caliber 5307 movement adds a few new features which accounts for its superlative complexity. In addition to the time, the watch includes a four-gong chiming system which is responsible for Westminster Carillon-style music chimes that play during the minute repeater and sonnerie functions. Minute repeating is when the watch musically indicates the time on demand, while sonnerie complications do the same thing but at particular intervals (such as on each hour). To the chiming functions Bulgari also added a perpetual calendar with Moon-phase system to the dial. Despite the skeletonised dial showing the incredibly complicated universe of gears, bridges and springs sitting right below it, the Octo Grande Sonnerie Quantième Perpétuel is incredibly legible and elegant given its wealth of details.

At 44mm wide in sand-blasted gold, the watch is relatively small given other existing watches with similar levels of complexity. That means it is uncommonly wearable for a timepiece of this nature. Perhaps most convenient of all is that it has an automatic winding system that is extremely rare in such high complications. At debut, Bulgari announced that the Octo Grand Sonnerie Quantième Perpétuel is a piece unique – meaning that only one example has been produced.

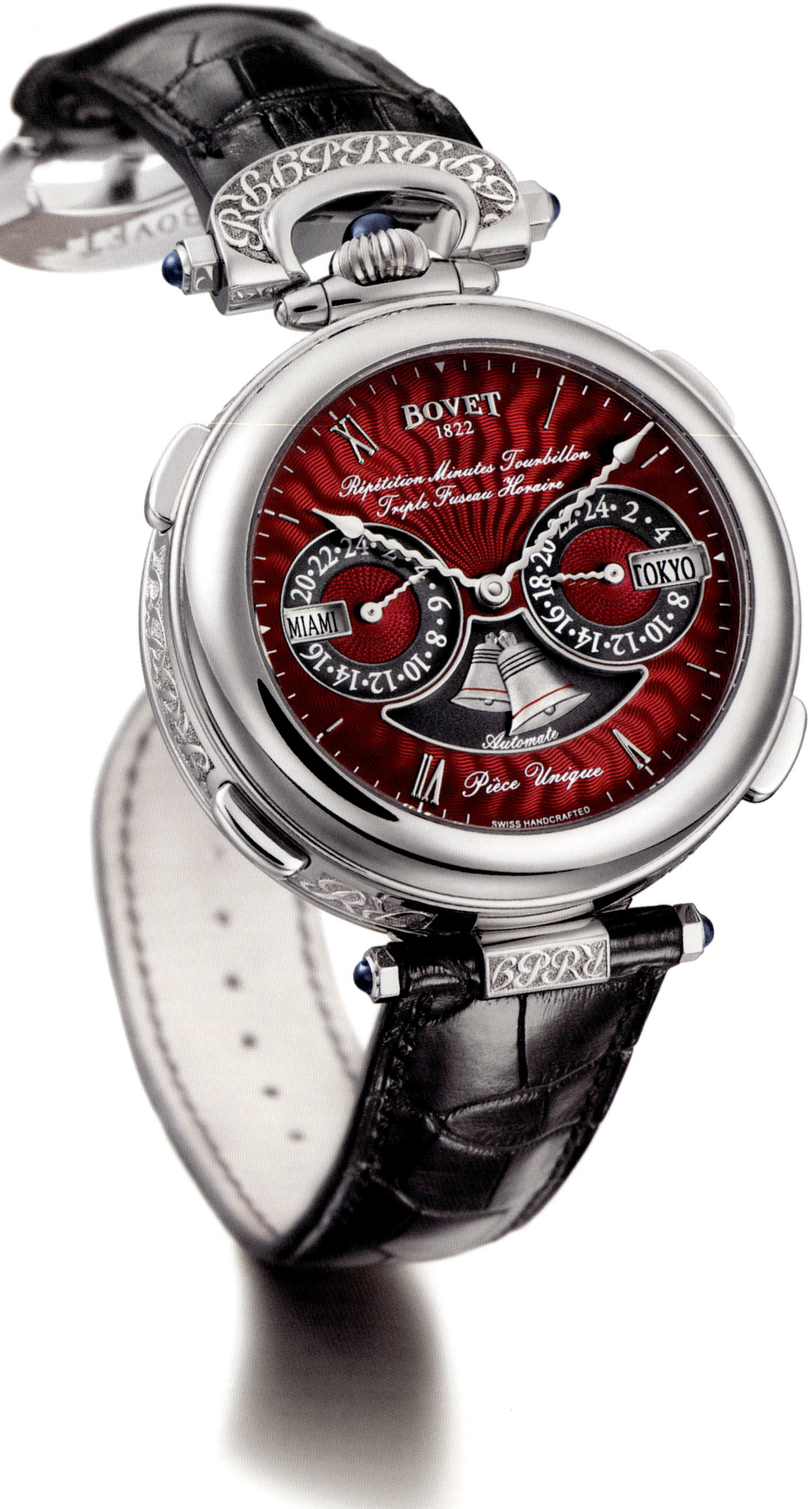
BOVET
1822
Répétition Minutes Tourbillon
Triple Fuseau Horaire
MIAMI
TOKYO
Automate
Pièce Unique
SWISS HANDCRAFTED

BOVET 1822 — AMADEO FLEURIER NOTRE DAME MINUTE REPEATER TOURBILLON

$ 713 000

THE MOST COMPLICATED BOVET AMADEO WATCH IS THE MINUTE REPEATER TOURBILLON NOTRE DAME.

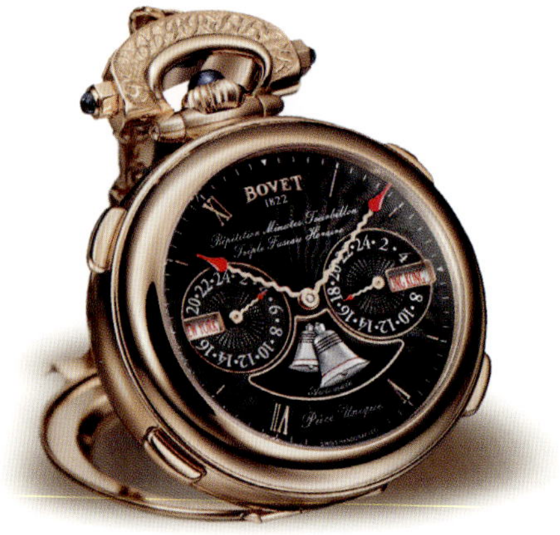

A distinctive element of all Bovet watches is the "ribbon style" protector over the crown, which is located at 12 o'clock. Bovet uses this design feature as a reminder of the brand's history of producing pocket watches for the world's elite, often in Asia.

In fact, many of today's Bovet wristwatches can also be pocket watches. When Bovet introduced the "Amadeo-style" case, they created a new "convertible" system that allows the case to be removed from the straps so it can to be used as a pocket watch, small desk clock, or pendant watch.

The most complicated Bovet Amadeo watch is the Minute Repeater Tourbillon Notre Dame. Like the famous cathedral in Paris, the watch has ringing bells. Inside the Amadeo Notre Dame is a minute repeater function with automatons. Minute repeater complications use a simple code of chimes to sound back the time when the feature is activated. What is unique about the minute repeater in the Amadeo Notre Dame, is that while it is operated, the two bells on the dial of the watch become animated and move.

The Amadeo Notre Dame is also a travel watch, as it contains indications for three separate time zones. The main dial displays the local time, while two smaller dials display the time in other locations. A small window for each of the subsidiary dials shows the name of a key city in the time zone for which its dial is showing the time. Pushers on each side of the 44mm wide case allow for cycling through the various time zones.

The carefully made mechanical movement is manually wound and features a tourbillon style escapement. Each of the Amadeo Minute Repeater Notre Dame watches is produced in an 18k gold case with a machine-engraved and decorated dial.

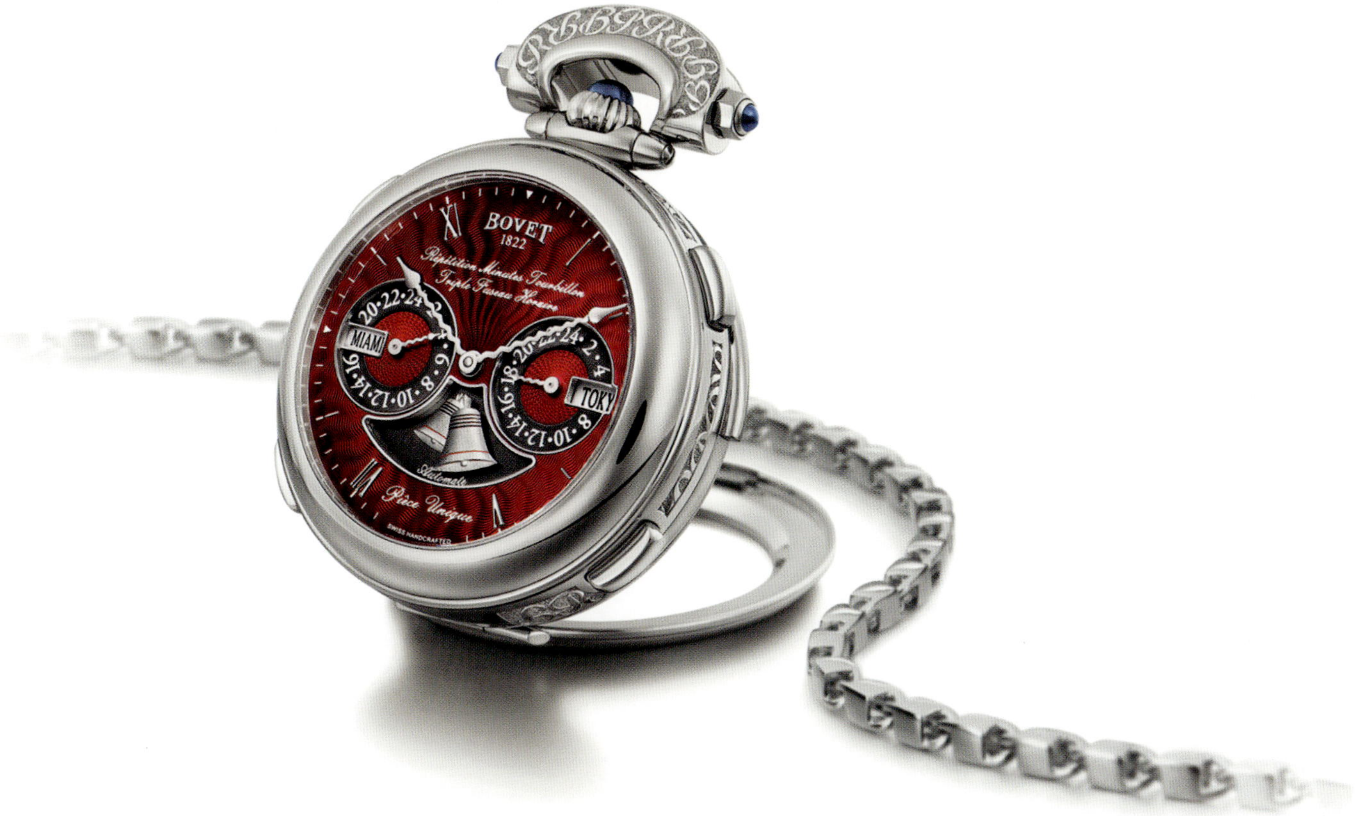
BOVET
1822
Répétition Minutes Tourbillon
Triple Fuseau Horaire
MIAMI
Automate
Pièce Unique

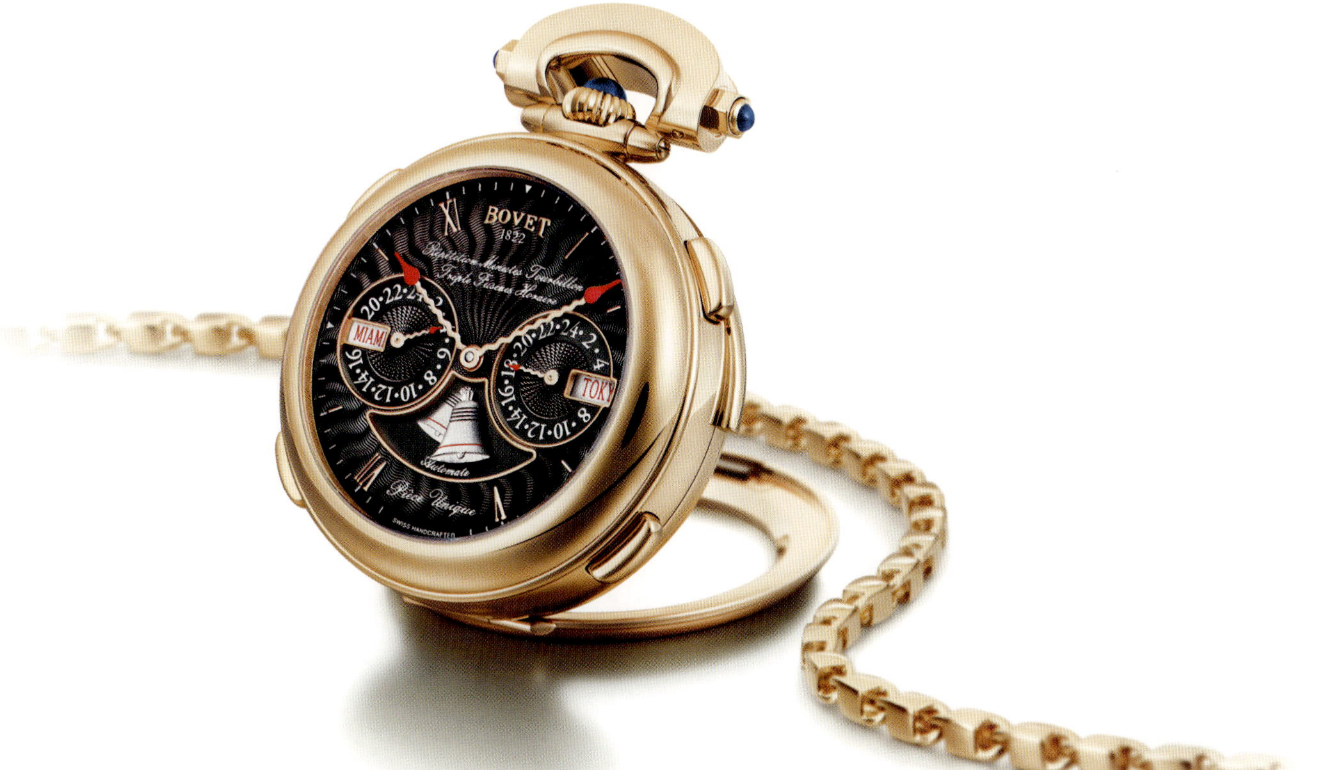
BOVET
1822
Répétition Minutes Tourbillon
Triple Fuseau Horaire
MIAMI
Automate
Pièce Unique

AUDEMARS PIGUET – ROYAL OAK GRANDE COMPLICATION

$741 600

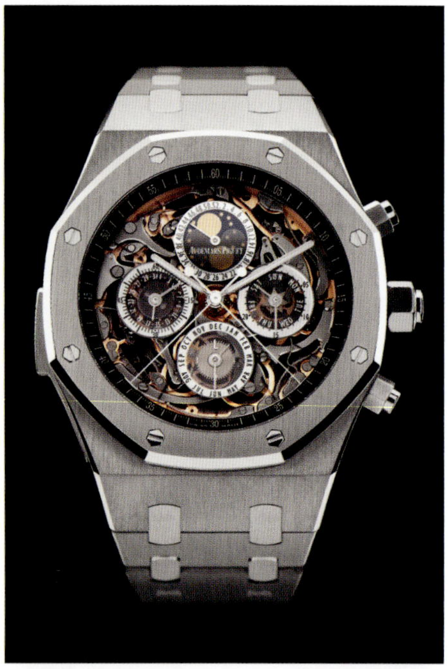

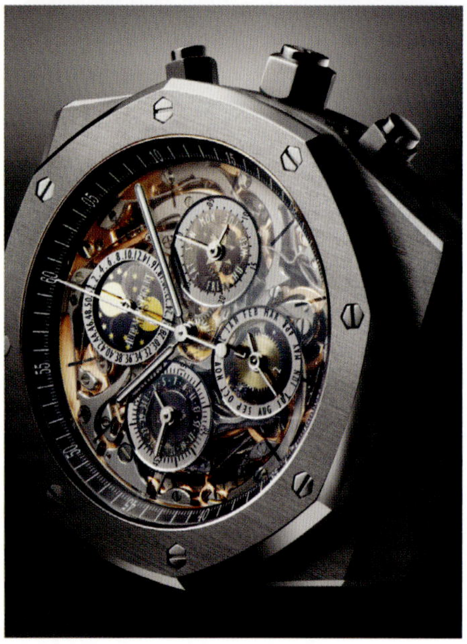

The Royal Oak Grande Complication is the ultimate marriage of a genre-defining sports watch and a world-class "haute horology" mechanical movement. In 1972, Swiss Audemars Piguet released the original Royal Oak as a luxury sports watch, in a steel metal case at a price close to that of an 18k gold watch. It was a gamble in marketing that paid off, as the Royal Oak became an icon of the brand, as it still is today.

Most agree that much of the success of the Royal Oak is due to the design. The watch was conceived by Gerald Genta, a celebrated watch designer, who is credited with many of the late 20th century's most iconic sports watches. The octagonal bezel was a Genta hallmark of the era.

As the Royal Oak continued to be an important part of the Audemars Piguet brand, eventually it received the honour of including their most complicated movement. This version of the Royal Oak contains the caliber 2885 movement, produced entirely by Audemars Piguet. The movement is considered to be not only an extremely complex one, containing 648 parts, but also very useful.

"Grand complication" watches are those that contain a series of complicated features. The 2885 contains a perpetual calendar with a Moon-phase indicator, a split-second chronograph, and a minute repeater that chimes the time using a set of small hammers and gongs. The movement also features automatic winding, and on some pieces such as this, is thoroughly skeletonised for decorative purposes.

GREUBEL FORSEY – INVENTION PIECE 2

$750 000

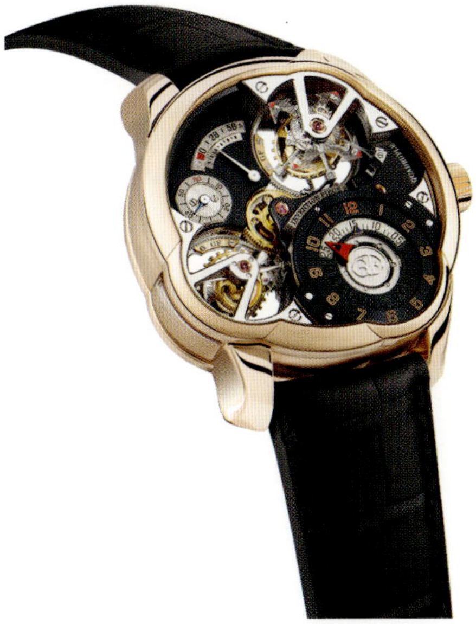

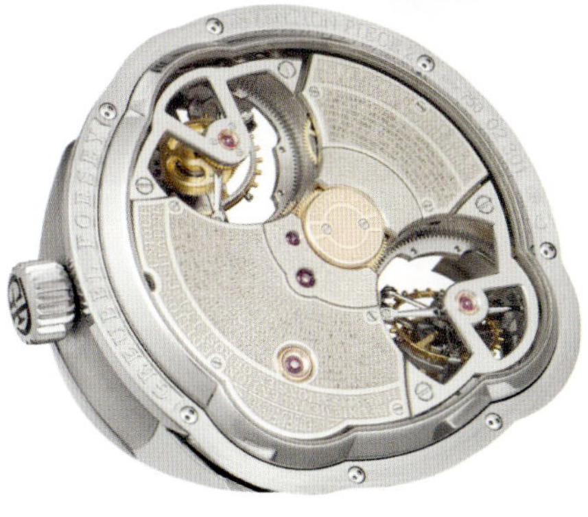

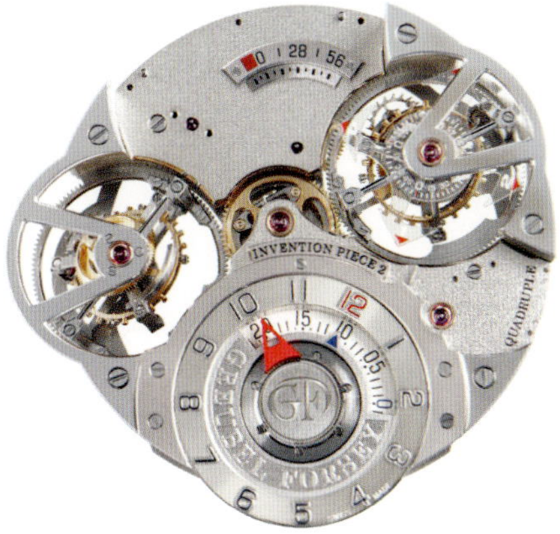

There are very few actual "award winning" watches, but the Invention Piece 2 by Greubel Forsey is one of them. What award did it win? In 2012, Stephen Forsey (of Greubel Forsey) took home an award on behalf of the company for "Best Complicated Watch". The award was given to the Invention Piece 2 by the jury of the Grand Prix d'Hologerie de Geneva (GPHG) – a luxury watch industry award event, for insiders by insiders, that they like to refer to as the "watch Oscars".

Why did the Invention Piece 2 win? Greubel Forsey is a brand with which many high-end watch collectors have a particular fascination because of its extreme attention to detail and innovative take on horological classicism. Extremely expensive, Greubel Forsey products are often defined by an almost obsessive level of finishing and hesitancy to release products until they are ready. A good example is the fact that the Greubel Forsey Invention Piece 3 timepiece was actually released in 2009, a few years before the Invention Piece 2 model was released in 2011.

The Greubel Forsey brand slogan is "Inventors Inventing Inventions". Actual "inventions" are rare in today's world of mechanical watches, because most of what watchmakers produce is based on historic technology. Having said that, the Invention Piece 2 does contain a bona fide novel mechanism, albeit an artistically themed one. The watch contains four tourbillons in a single movement. No-one other than Greubel Forsey has managed to produce a quadruple tourbillon, and the four axis points of oscillator assembly rotating, are divided into two double tourbillons.

In lay terms, the watch contains two tourbillons, each of which contains two points of axis. An outer tourbillon rotates every four minutes while an inner tourbillon (inclined at a 30 degree angle) rotates once every 60 seconds. The net result is less four distinct tourbillons, but really a set of two double tourbillons. For the collector, this mechanical fact is perhaps enough to make the watch award winning, but the design of the Invention Piece 2 was clearly a reason for its prize victory.

Bulging edges in an otherwise round case, and extra sapphire crystal viewing windows, help define the piece as a Greubel Forsey. The dial is a mixture of beautifully hand-decorated surfaces, and a skeletonised view into the movement. Even the indicator dials are inventive: with the dial being displayed with a more or less traditional hour hand, but the minutes showing via an arrow pointing at a moving disc. Even after taking a few extra years to perfect the execution of the watch, the Invention Piece 2 was still highly limited in its production. Greubel Forsey only made 11 pieces in 18k red gold, and another 11 pieces in platinum.

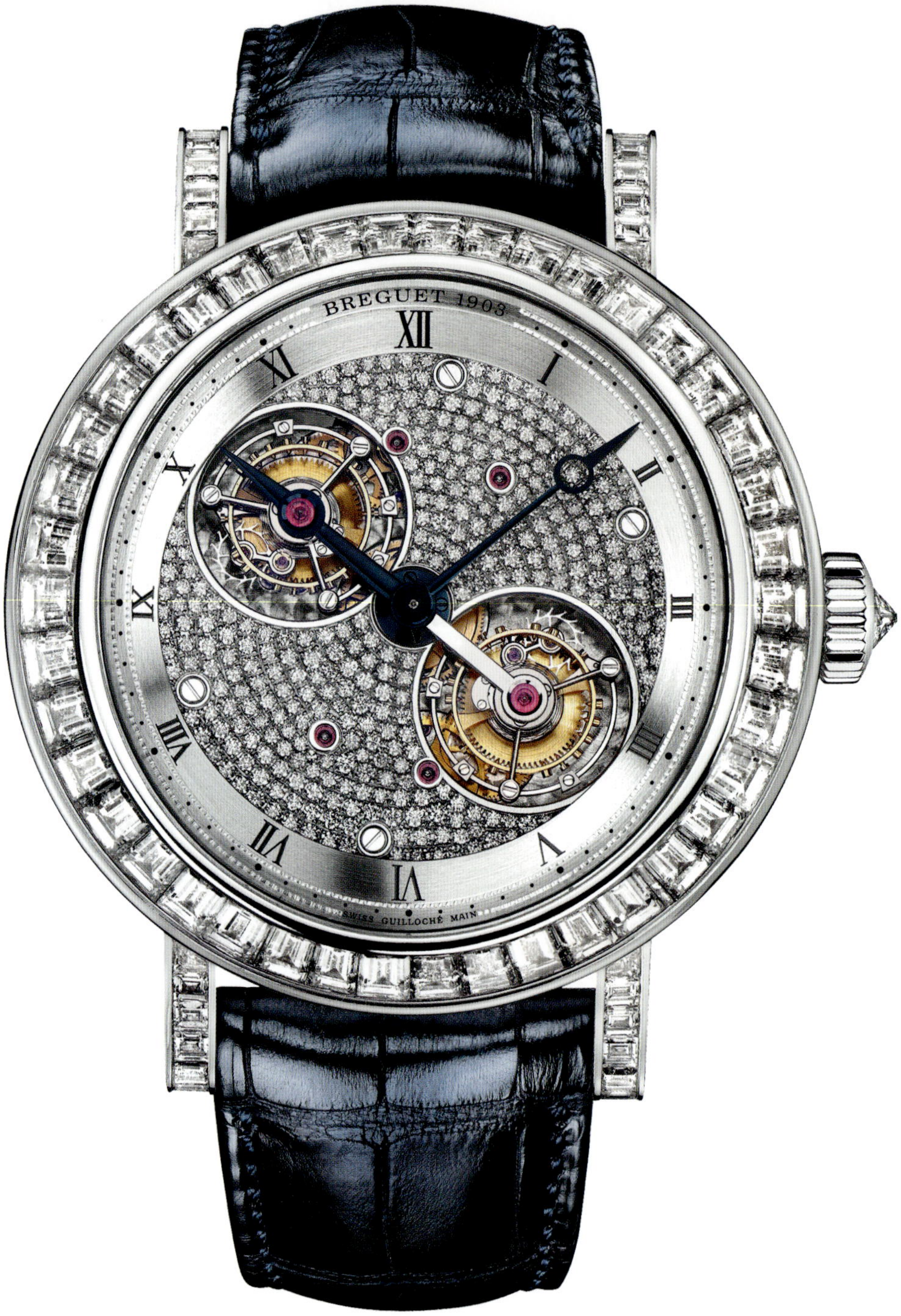

BREGUET — DOUBLE TOURBILLON 5349

$ 781 000

In both size and character, the aptly named "Double Tourbillon" from Breguet stands alone among its sibling products as the historic Swiss timepiece maker. Made of platinum, and almost entirely decorated with diamonds, the case is a massive 50mm wide and almost 19mm thick on the wrist. At the turn of the 18th century, Breguet's namesake and founder, Abraham-Louis Breguet, initially invented the tourbillon regulation system to increase the accuracy and timing reliability of travelling clocks and pocket watches – one of many technical strategies explored at the time by watchmakers. The application of this exotic mechanism would remain mostly dormant until it found new life in luxury wristwatches in the 20th century. Today's Breguet produces a number of tourbillon-equipped timepieces but the Double Tourbillon remains its greatest, and some would say "over-the-top", homage to the tourbillon mechanical concept employed in so many of today's ultra-luxury timepiece products.

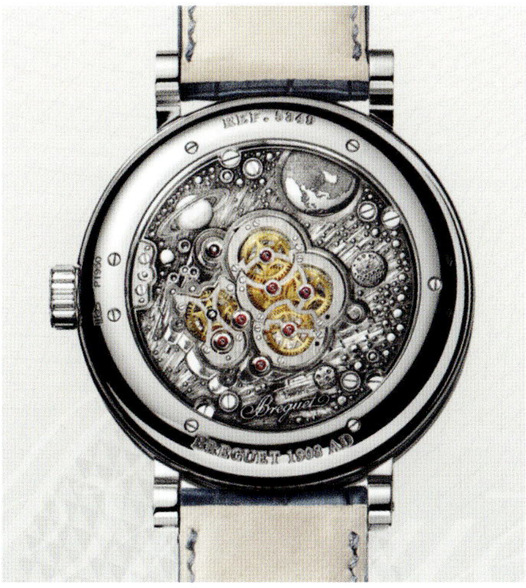

Put simply, Breguet designed the Double Tourbillon watch to contain two independent spinning tourbillon regulation systems which are visible on the dial of the watch. The watch was originally designed to allow its owner to impress (possibly in a case of one-upmanship) anyone else in the room whose timepiece contained just a single tourbillon. Other watchmakers have since been able to include even more tourbillons in a single watch movement – though with an effect often not nearly as elegant as that engineered by Breguet for its Double Tourbillon.

The manually wound 676-part in-house made Breguet movement offers an additional visual trick. The entire inner dial of the watch is connected to the hour hand and thus makes one full revolution every 12 hours. This has the effect of pleasantly altering the visual look of the dial on a regular basis, which is an animation designed to increase the pleasure of viewing the piece. The Double Tourbillon 5349 can be ordered without diamonds, with partial diamond decoration or, as seen here, fully decorated with 107 baguette-cut diamonds on the bezel and lugs, and an additional 310 diamonds on the dial resulting in a total diamond count of 30.30 carats. It is impossible to know what Abraham-Louis himself would have deduced from this evolution of his tourbillon invention – but today's most elite Breguet customers can't help but be seduced by the Double Tourbillon's mechanical ballet display.

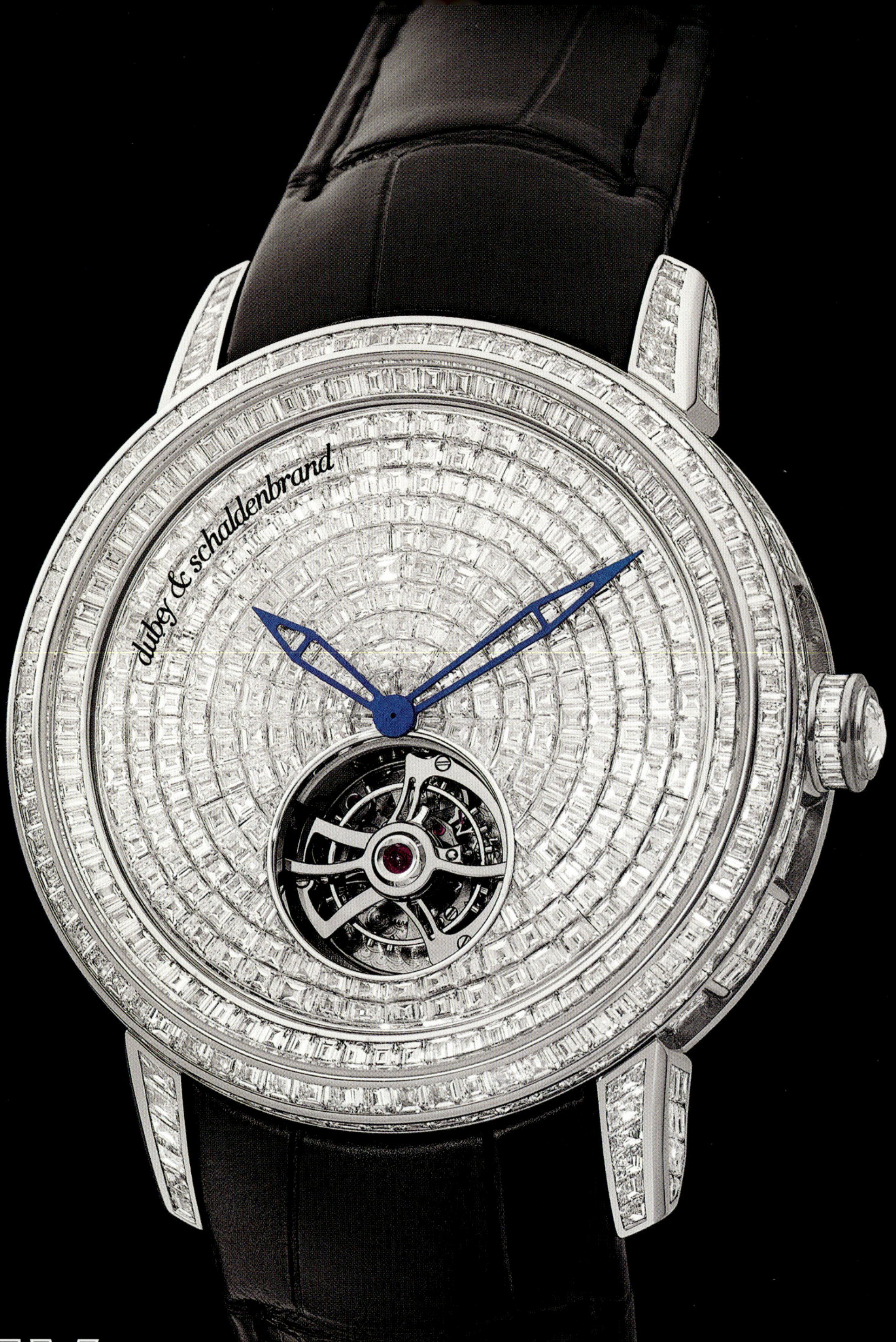

DUBEY & SCHALDENBRAND — CŒUR BLANC

$ 800 000

Even though Swiss firm, Dubey & Schaldenbrand, began producing timepieces in 1946, their products have a distinct art-deco feel in terms of their design. The art-deco era is particularly important to producers of timepieces, since the wristwatch for men was more or less invented during this era. Nevertheless, relatively few decidedly art-deco themed timepieces are produced today – let alone high-jewellery versions for men.

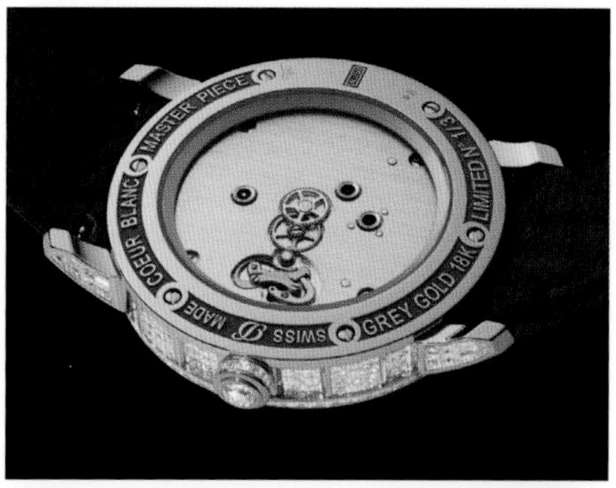

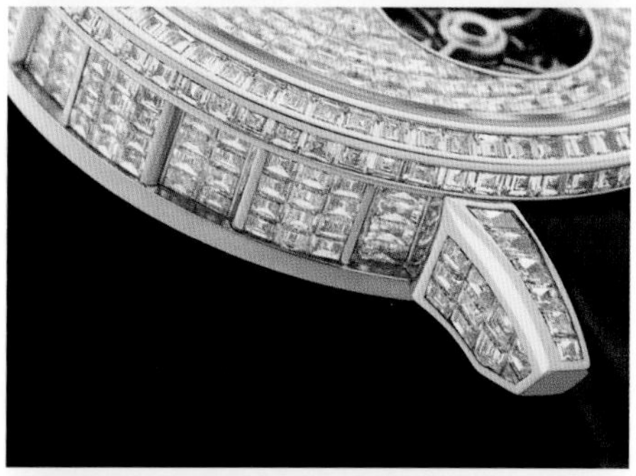

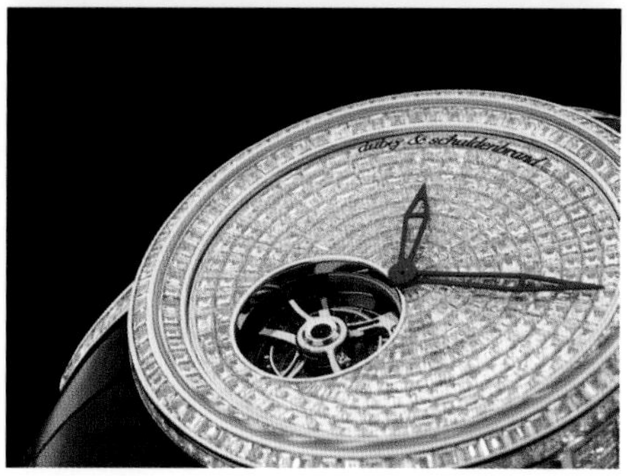

One extravagant piece is the Cœur Blanc, produced by Dubey & Schaldenbrand in 2013. Translating to "White Heart", as a limited edition model, the Cœur Blanc was said to have taken about 500 hours of work to produce, with most of that time being involved in the selection and setting of the diamonds.

Dubey & Schaldenbrand note that 13 individual craftspeople were involved in the production of the Cœur Blanc's case, movement and dial. Few watchmakers make special reference to such details, but it is true that the production of even one timepiece requires team effort and seasoned expertise. Many collectors, primarily interested in watches with highly complicated movements, tend to have less interest in those models with precious stones.

This is perhaps because jewellery watches are often intended for women, or there is a perception that setting a watch with a large number of diamonds, or other precious stones, is a relatively easy task. The truth is that a beautifully gem-set case and dial is as complicated, if not more complicated, than the decoration and assembly of a fine mechanical movement.

The Cœur Blanc begins with a relatively large 45mm wide case, in 18k grey gold, which is set with over 400 diamonds. Each of the diamonds is baguette-cut, and many of them are invisibly set. The complexity is in selecting the properly cut stones (or having them individually cut to fit), as well as in carefully setting the stones. Cases such as this can require weeks to fully set, especially because the invisible setting has diamonds placed immediately next to other diamonds.

Another 255 baguette-cut diamonds are invisibly set on the watch dial in concentric circles. The dial is interrupted by an opening over 6 o'clock that functions as a window into the tourbillon-style escapement as part of the mechanical movement. Blued-steel hands contrast well against the dial, which is intended as a bold display of wealth. Fully baguette-cut diamond-set dials offer the densest collection of valuable stones, while the tourbillon serves as a symbol of technical prestige.

The buckle on the strap of the watch contains another 54 diamonds, which completes a total of 709 baguette-cut stones on the Cœur Blanc watch, weighing a total of 22.55 carats. Dubey & Schaldenbrand will produce just three pieces. Aficionados seeking to use their timepieces as a tool to communicate their status, often choose items such as this.

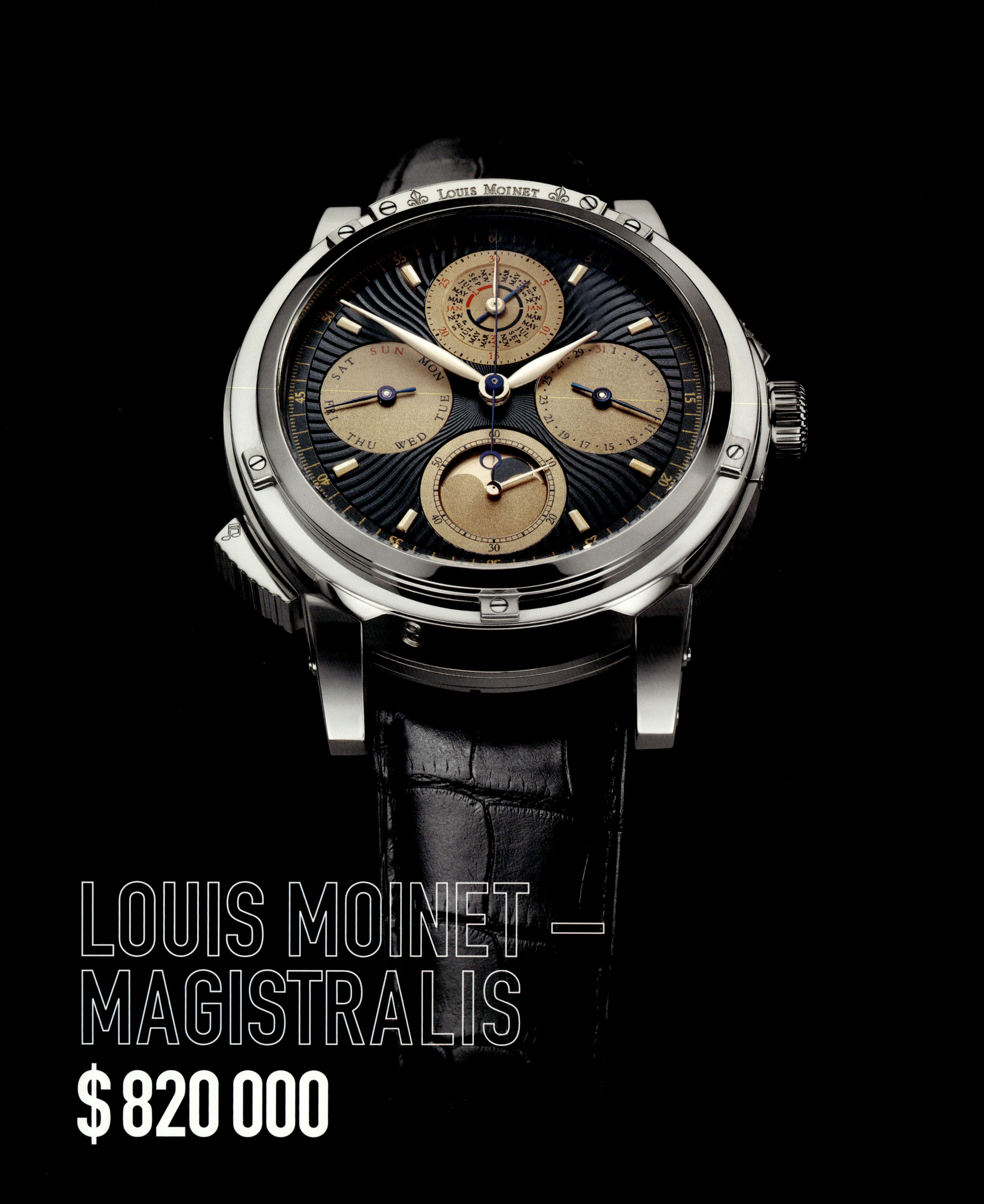

LOUIS MOINET — MAGISTRALIS

$ 820 000

In 2013 it was discovered that the innovative 19th-century watchmaker had Louis Moinet produced the world's first chronograph device. This was interesting news, as his remarkably modern looking pocket watch-style device significantly predated what was previously thought to be the first chronograph (a device to measure an elapsed period of time – also known as a stopwatch). Louis Moinet is considered by most to be one of the godfathers of modern watchmaking.

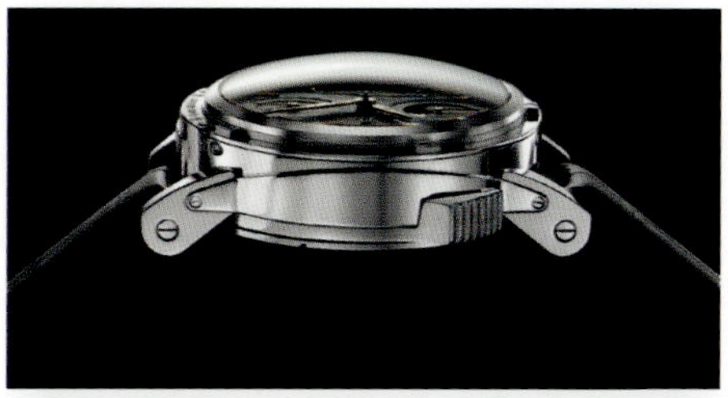

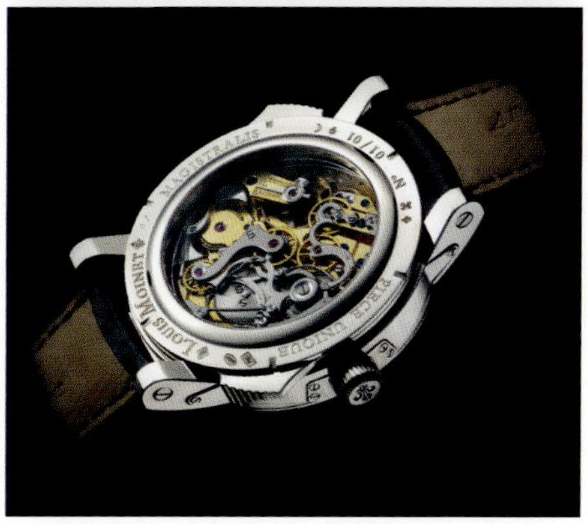

Today, the Louis Moinet watch brand exists as a testament to his legacy, which he partially memorialised in his 1848 book Traité d'Horlogerie (Treatise on Watchmaking). In fact, an original printing of the book, from 1856, was included with this Magistralis timepiece, a unique item that required over a year to create.

Completed in 2008, the Magistralis wasn't so much a new watch, as a modern assembly of things from the past. It is true that the complex 90-piece case and design are novel, and based on the work of Louis Moinet, but inside the watch is a movement that was 100 years old at the time it was placed in the Magistralis.

Produced in the watchmaking Jura region of Switzerland, the movement was probably originally meant to be part of a pocket watch. Wearable, when in a watch sized by today's standard, the complicated mechanism proved too irresistible a project for the Louis Moinet of today. Aged movements require a fair amount of restoration work to operate again. Louis Moinet set out to carefully restore the completely hand-made movement to a fine working order.

The movement is extremely complicated even by today's standards. A true "grand complication", it contains the time, a chronograph, a perpetual calendar, Moon-phase indicator, and a minute repeater. Louis Moinet even restored the movement's original blued-steel hands for use in the watch.

With a fetish for all things celestial, Louis Moinet chose to fit the Moon-phase disc with a unique material – actual rock from the Moon. Using a stone they acquired from a special dealer, the Moon-phase indicator disc has two slivers of Moon rock that fell to the Earth about 2,000 years ago.

Also included with the Magistralis watch is a unique Swiss-Made wooden stand, made from a variety of local maple. Worked by a craftsman who typically produces fine musical instruments, the stand acts as resonance board, allowing the minute repeater mechanism in the watch (that chimes on demand to indicate the time), to sound as loud and beautiful as possible. Louis Moinet produced just one example of the Magistralis timepiece.

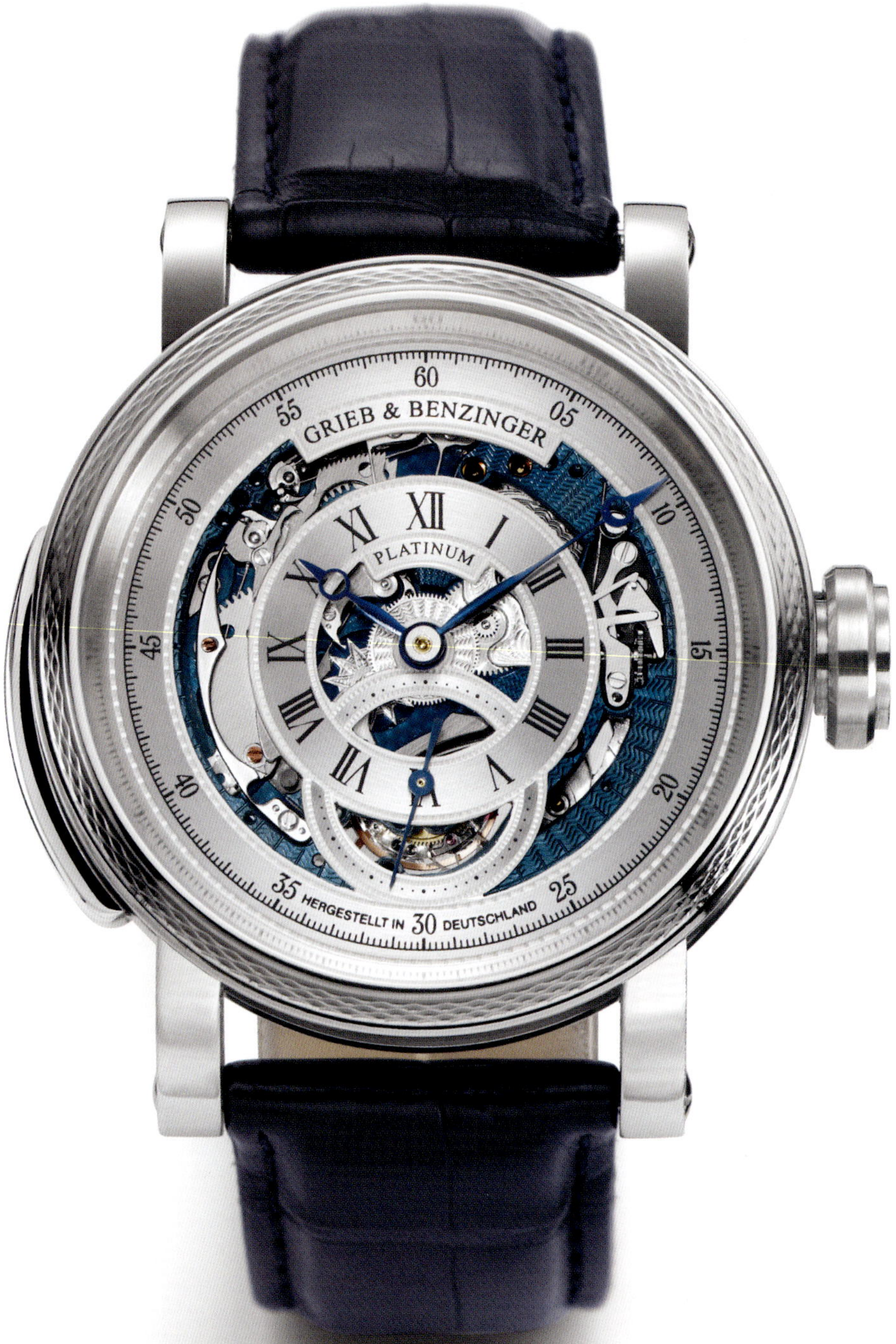

GRIEB & BENZINGER — BLUE WHIRLWIND

$ 880 000

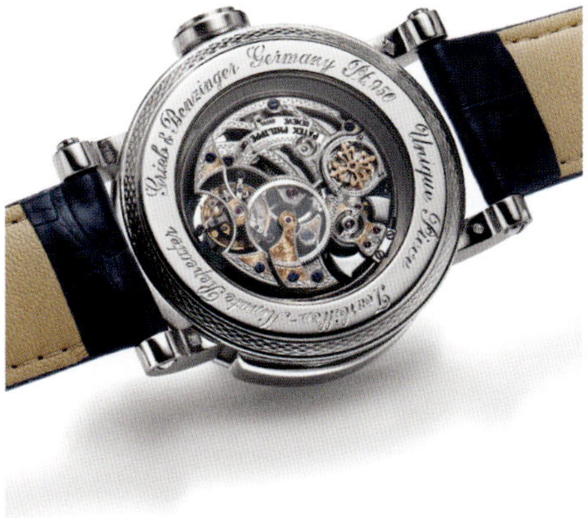

Everything the Grieb & Benzinger team makes is unique. For consumers their services can be somewhat frustrating, because each new watch they "release" is typically already sold. Buying a Grieb & Benzinger watch – just as with a handful of other similar boutique luxury brands – involves a consultative back and forth process with the team to determine what special piece they will make for you, and no-one else produces timepieces quite like them.

Being German rather than Swiss gives the brand a unique personality as well as core of skills. Hermann Grieb is a watchmaker while Jochen Benzinger is a master decorator skilled with using a range of esoteric artistic techniques lost to much of the world. Their workshop contains certain machines, for example guilloché rose engines such as haven't been made for a century. These afford Grieb & Benzinger the ability to create some truly amazing works of horological art.

In 2012, they released one of their most iconic creations, a watch that equally showcased their watchmaking and their decorative skills – it was the "Blue Whirlwind". Completely encased in platinum, the one-of-a-kind creation focused on a movement based on a rare Patek Philippe (an extremely prestigious Swiss watchmaker) mechanism known as the caliber R TO 27 PS from the ref. 3939 watch. The movement contains both a tourbillon and minute repeater mechanism. In 2011, the Patek Philippe 3939 sold at auction for $1.4 million.

Grieb & Benzinger decided to recreate this "collectors' favourite" movement in their own special style. In their customary platinum and flame-blued platinum material choices, the Blue Whirlwind watch slowly took form, as each piece of the movement was hand-made and decorated. A technique used heavily on Grieb & Benzinger watches is guilloché machine engraving, which produces patterns by engraving into the surface as the metal rotates. In total, the movement in the Blue Whirlwind watch took 15 months to skeletonise and decorate, and represents the work of perhaps the most uniquely interesting boutique timepiece producer in Germany.

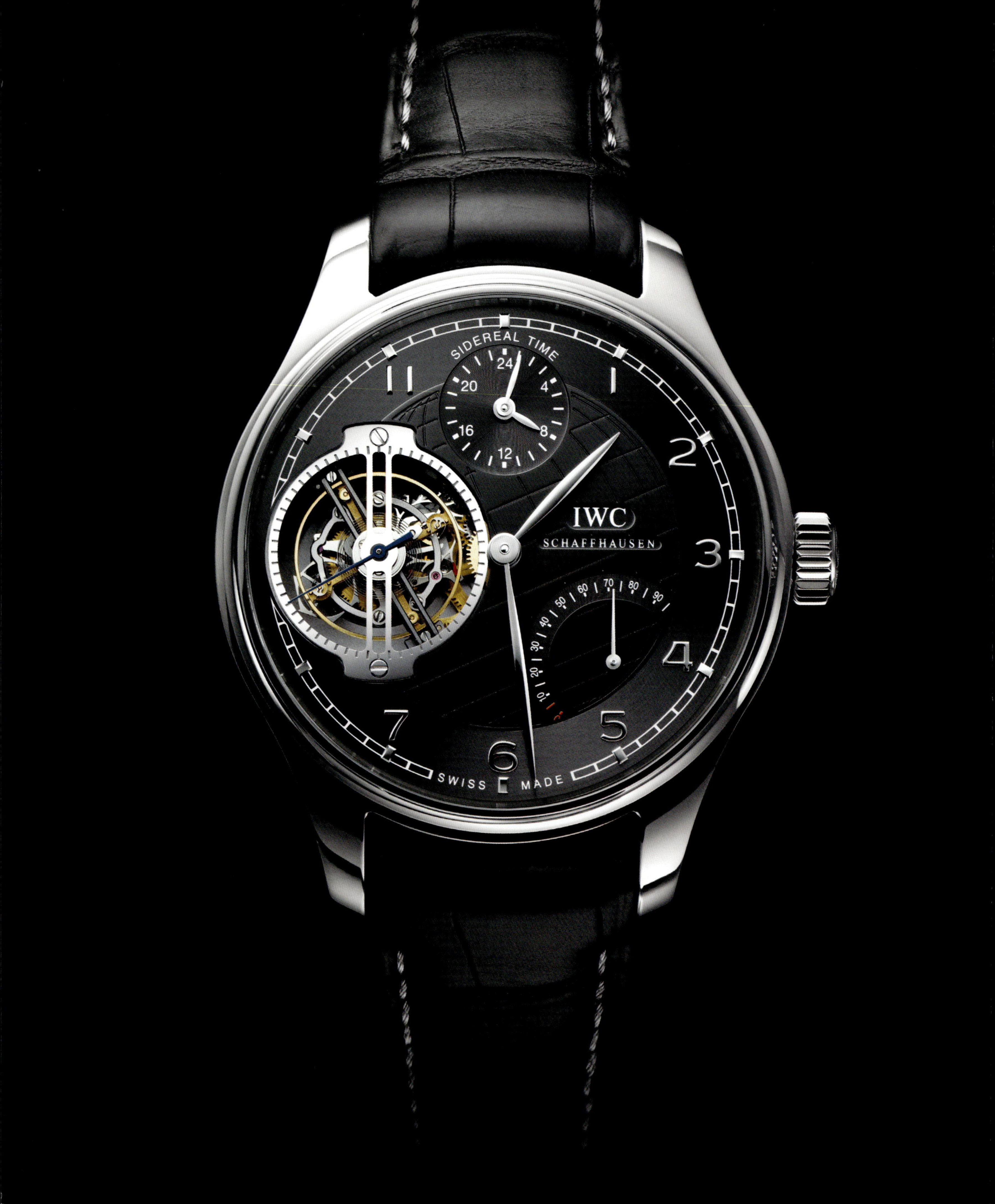
SIDEREAL TIME
IWC
SCHAFFHAUSEN
SWISS MADE

IWC — PORTUGUESE SIDÉRALE SCAFUSIA

$ 900 000

THE PORTUGUESE COLLECTION IS ONE OF THE MOST POPULAR PILLARS OF THE IWC BRAND.

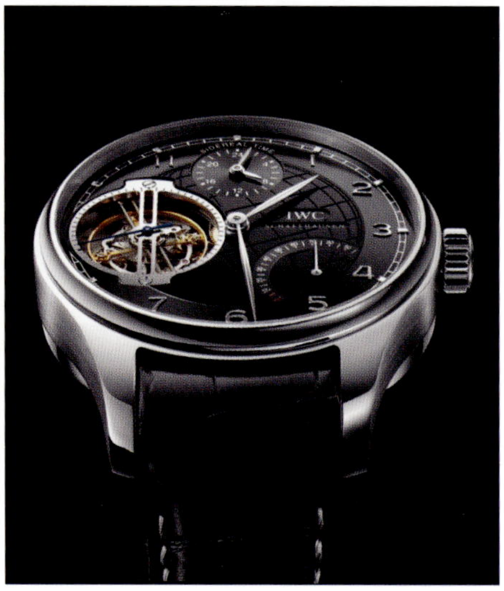

IWC claims that the Portuguese Sidérale Scafusia was a result of 10 years of research; that doesn't sound unreasonable, given the number of its unique complications. The goal of the watch was to sit at the top of IWC as an elusive halo product that would only be produced to order as a custom item.

The Portuguese collection is one of the most popular pillars of the IWC brand. Originally a marine watch designed for Portuguese merchants, the design, today, is a hallmark of classic functionality and elegance, with displays on both the front and rear of the watch, and a unique combination of exotic high-complications. It is, at heart, a timepiece dedicated to astronomical indications.

On the front of the Portuguese Sidérale Scafusia is a tourbillon with a constant force mechanism. This is a special system that ensures consistent power from the movement over time, allowing the watch to be more accurate as the spring inside that powers it winds down. The result is a tourbillon with a ticking seconds hand.

In addition to the power reserve indictor (telling you to wind the watch each four days or so), the dial displays civil (solar-based) time, and sidereal time.

Civil time, the one we all use in our daily lives, is time within a "time zone"; it is based on solar time but, within a particular time zone, will vary from true solar time by up to 15-20 minutes. Solar time is time at a particular location, in relation to the sun.

Sidereal time differs from solar time by up to 4 minutes each day at a particular location. It measures the rotation of the Earth with respect to the stars, rather than to the sun. It is the first hint that the Portuguese Sidérale Scafusia is dedicated to tracking events in the sky.

On the back of the Portuguese Sidérale Scafusia watch is a star chart; and no two are alike. IWC place the coordinates of the view on the chart that are requested by the customer, and each piece is, therefore, individual to that customer. With a series of indications, the chart offers sunrise and sunset times, sidereal time and solar time. Almost hidden, and on the periphery of the star chart, is a perpetual calendar.

Most perpetual calendars display at least the month, day, and cycle of leap years. IWC designed something a bit different for the Portuguese Sidérale Scafusia in that it includes a count of the elapsed days of the year, as well as a leap year indicator.

IWC only produces the Portuguese Sidérale Scafusia on order, and in addition to selecting a custom part of the sky for the star chart, choosing the case material, dial colour and strap are part of the customisation experience.

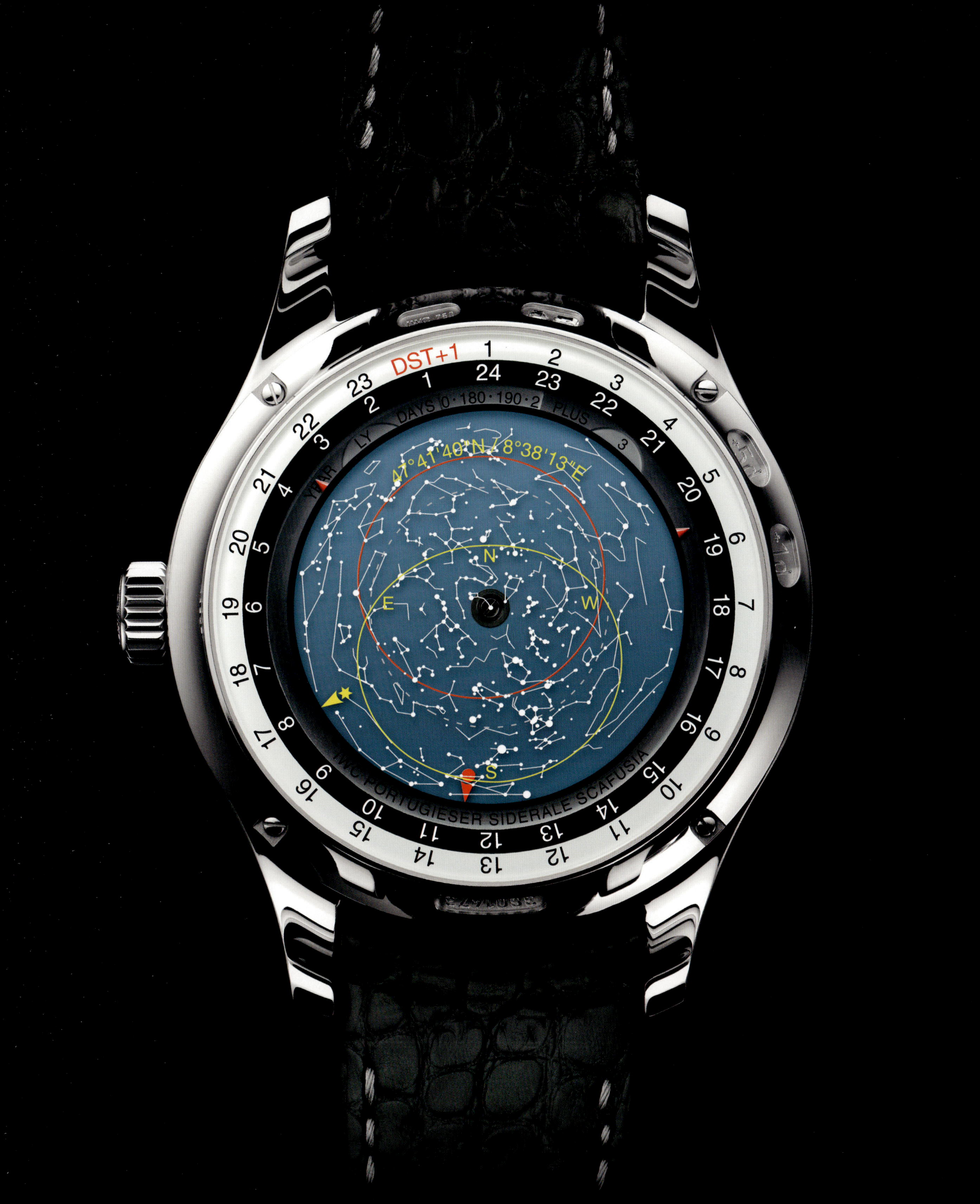

DST+1
47°41'40"N / 8°38'13"E
N
E
W
S
DAYS
PLUS
YEAR
LY
IWC PORTUGIESER SIDERALE SCAFUSIA

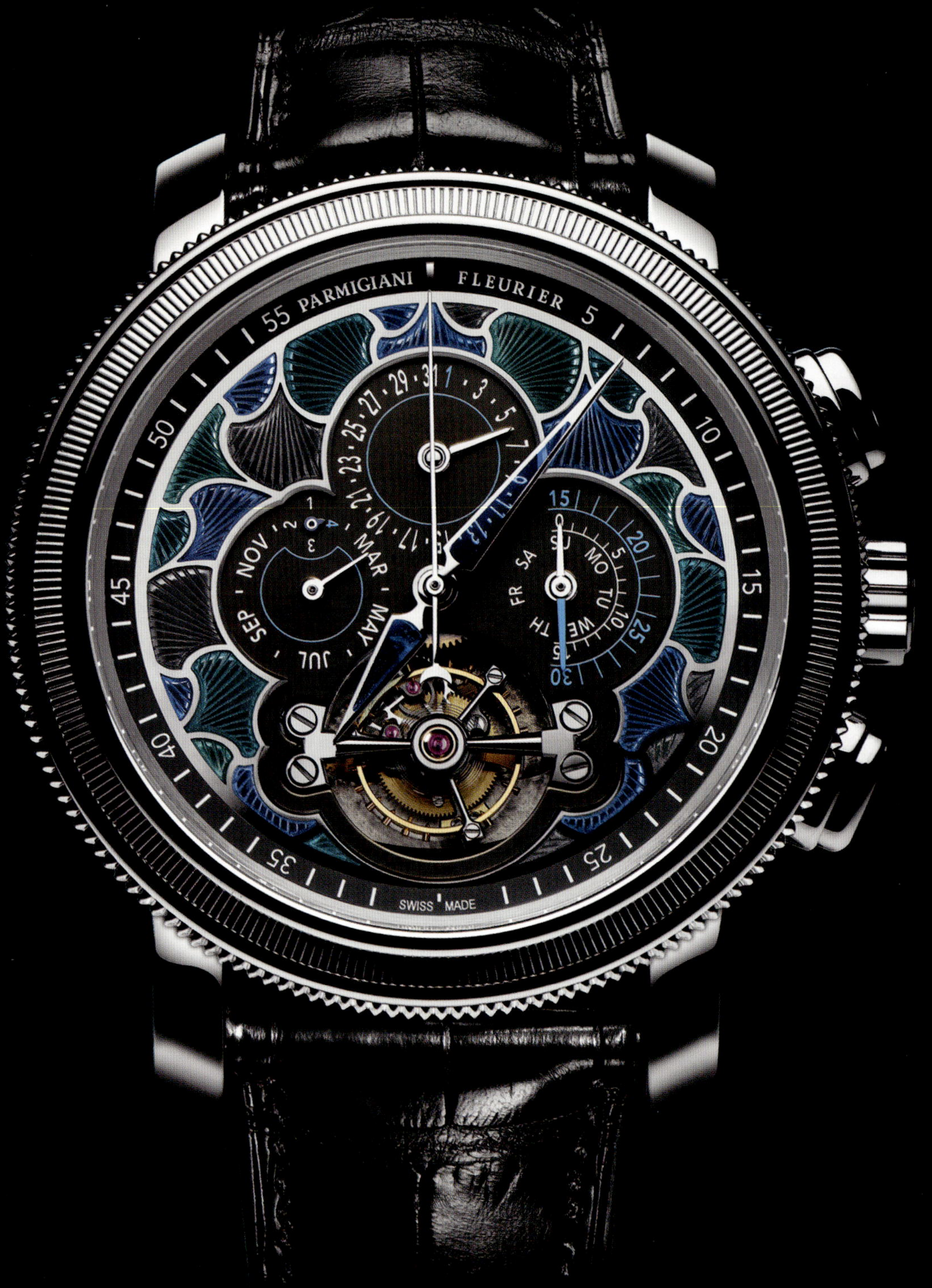

PARMIGIANI FLEURIER — TECNICA PALME

$ 966 000

There are times when a timepiece's decorative attributes are as complex (if not more complex) than the mechanism contained within the case. This highlights one of the major dichotomies of the high-end watch world, insofar that some collectors have a great appreciation for technical achievements, while others have a deep respect for extremely high-effort artistic designs. In other words, some people love the mechanical complexity while others prefer the art – but, often, not both.

This has resulted in a rather slim selection of timepieces that feature both a complex movement and stunning artistic decoration. Though by virtue of their incredible prices, such watches are naturally limited. On top of that, most are one-of-a-kind creations, as many artistic techniques aren't possible to perfectly emulate in multiple pieces.

An exemplary watch fitting this description is the "piece unique" (only one made) Tecnica Palme by Switzerland's Parmigiani Fleurier. A few Tecnica models were produced around 2013, each focusing on a distinct decoration of the Tecnica-style case. One, the Toric Tecnica, was inspired by a labyrinth, and others like the Samba and Palme were inspired by plants. The latter model is among the most persistently beautiful and visually pleasing of Tecnica watches, because it so well presents how a complex movement and artistic technique can join forces to create a stunning result.

Many surfaces of the Tecnica Palme offer a hand-made palm leaf-style repeating pattern, that combines both enamelling and engraving work. Once the pattern design is conceived, an artist uses a microscope, and tools they have often produced themselves, to hand-engrave the palm leaves into the 18k white gold case. The Tecnica Palme watch features the decorative treatment on the dial, case back, movement plate, and strap buckle.

What makes the engravings that much more visually appealing, is the application of an enamel painting technique over the leaf pattern. Mixing their own pigments, a micro-enamelist hand-paints the palm design with various colours and then bakes it for permanence.

The rear of the Tecnica watch case has a "hunter-style" flap that opens with a view to the Parmigiani made movement. The Tecnica collection features four important complication groups. In addition to the time, there is a minute repeater (that sounds out the time on demand using chimes), a chronograph, a tourbillon, and a perpetual calendar. Taking double the effort put into the making of most timepieces – due to the technical complexity of both the movement and case art – a watch like the Parmigiani Fleurier Tecnica Palme requires months to produce, and just one of this type was ever made.

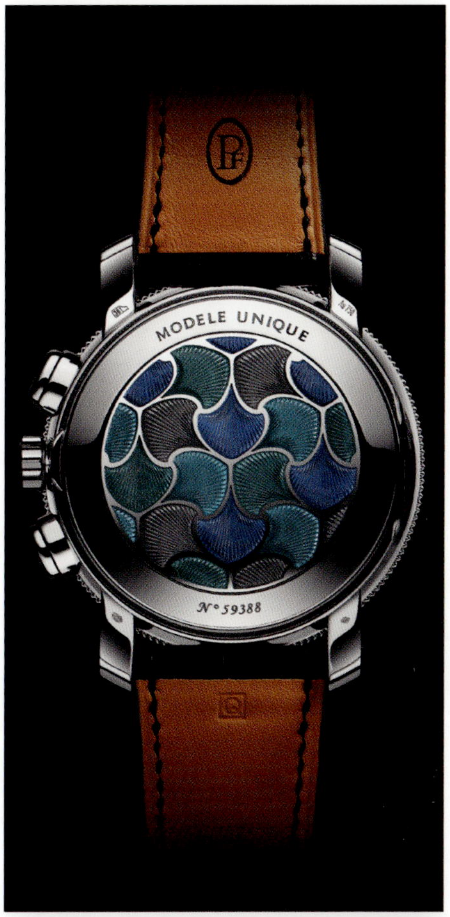

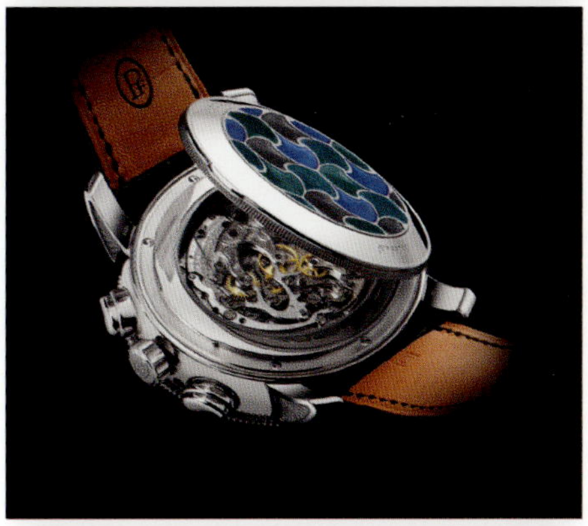

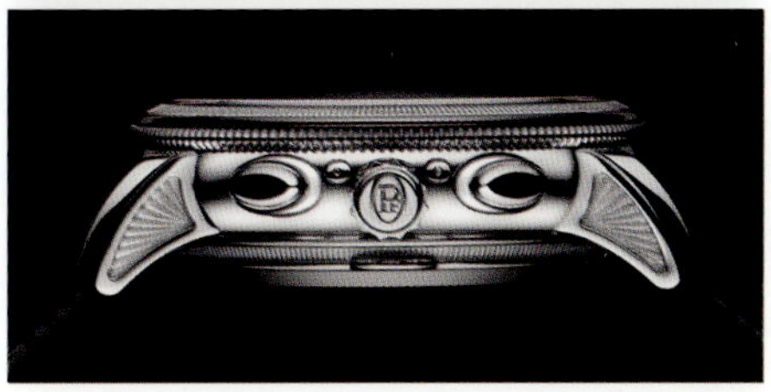

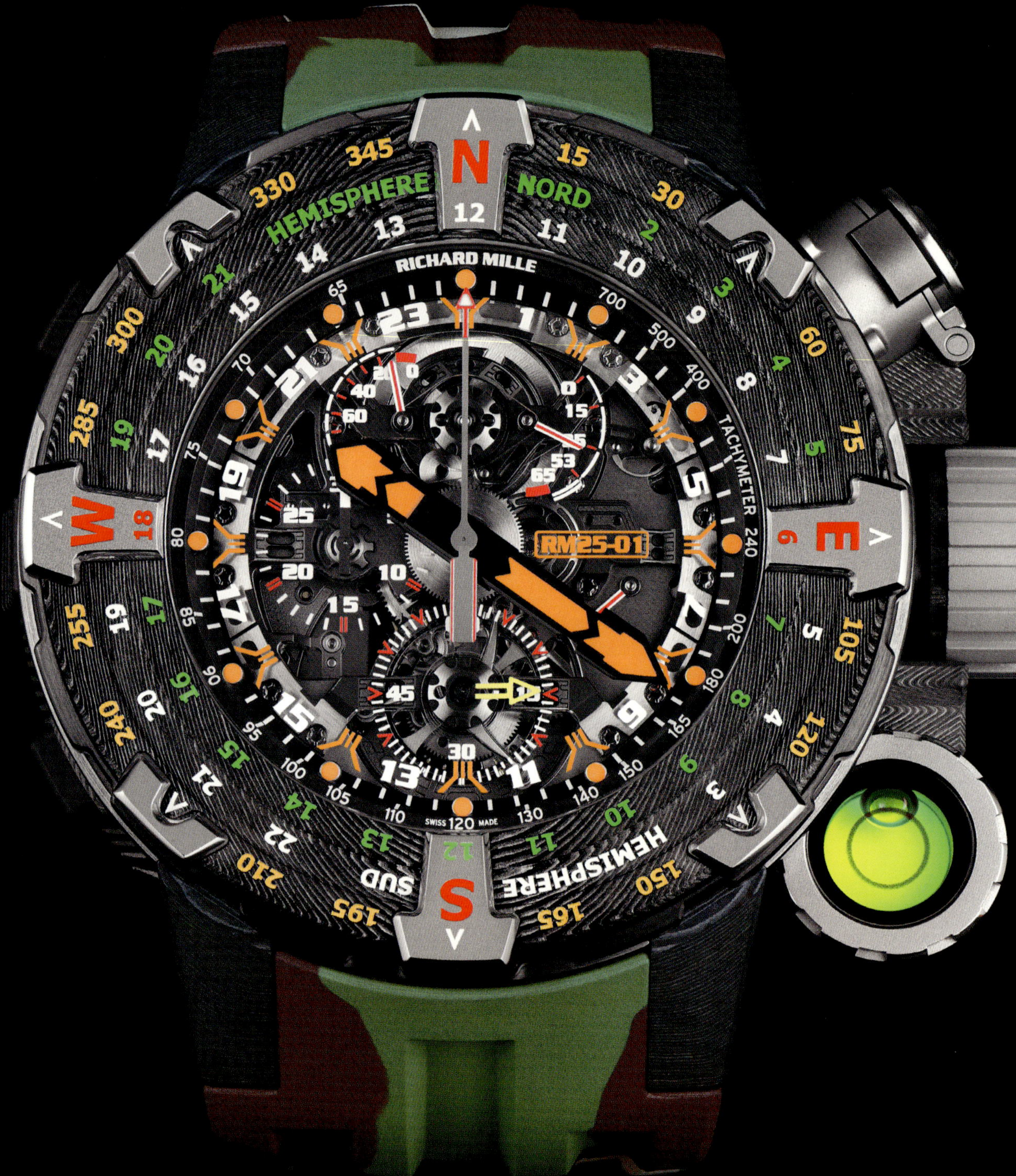

RICHARD MILLE
RM25-01
HEMISPHERE NORD
HEMISPHERE SUD
TACHYMETER
SWISS MADE
N
E
S
W

RICHARD MILLE — RM 25-01 TOURBILLON ADVENTURE SYLVESTER STALLONE

$ 983 000

IN COLLABORATION WITH RICHARD MILLE, STALLONE IMAGINED WHAT RAMBO WOULD HAVE LUSTED FOR IN A TIMEPIECE — AND THE RESULT IS AN INTERESTING COMBINATION OF LUXURY ACCOUTREMENTS AND SURVIVALIST FEATURES.

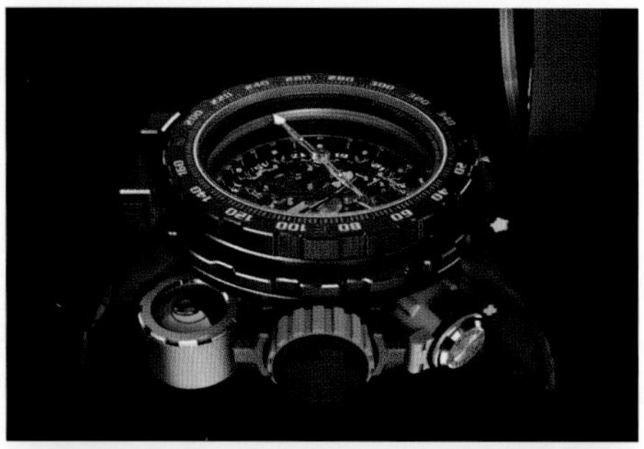

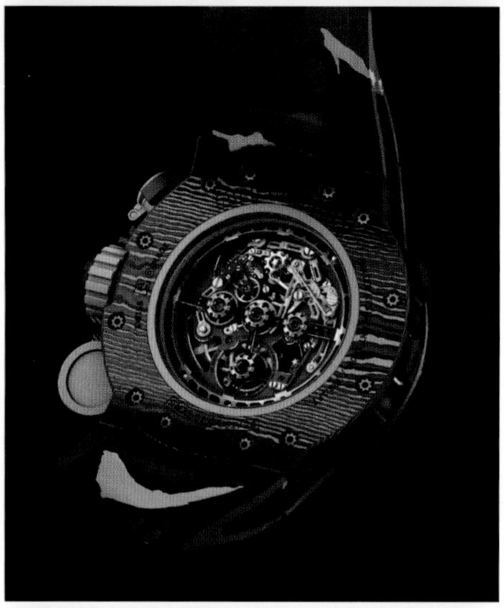

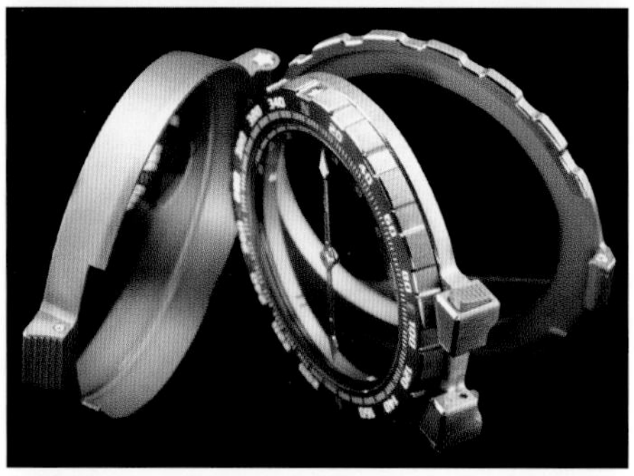

If you are a fan of 1980s action movies, then you will no doubt notice some irony behind the notion of creating an almost million-dollar timepiece inspired by what John Rambo would have worn throughout his survival-style adventure films. Here was a character who preferred a knife and bow and arrows as weapons – rarely even wearing a shirt. To make more sense of the limited edition of 25 Richard Mille RM 25-01 Tourbillon Adventure pieces, you need only understand that its primary inspiration was in fact the actor Sylvester Stallone (who played John Rambo). Stallone is a renown watch collector and tastemaker, whose career in adventure movies has seen him wear increasingly ritzy timepieces – including other Richard Mille watches in later movies. John Rambo may not have worn so fancy a timepiece as the RM 25-01, but Stallone most certainly does.

In collaboration with Richard Mille, Stallone imagined what Rambo would have lusted for in a timepiece – and the result is an interesting combination of luxury accoutrements and survivalist features. No other timepiece to date (and perhaps ever again) has included both a tourbillon-based mechanical movement and capsule containing water purification tablets. Other technical features in the watch include a level, a chronograph and a removable compass. This all comes in a relatively large 50.85mm-wide case produced from hard and lightweight TPT carbon. It would not be complete without a camouflage rubber strap, which itself is complicated to produce at such a high quality given that it requires separate injections of various rubber colours to produce each piece.

Mr Stallone is the first to own a RM 25-01 Tourbillon Adventure Sylvester Stallone timepiece. The honour allows the accomplished personality, actor, writer and director to both celebrate the legacy of his continuing career, and to claim that he is able to play with some of the world's most exclusive toys.

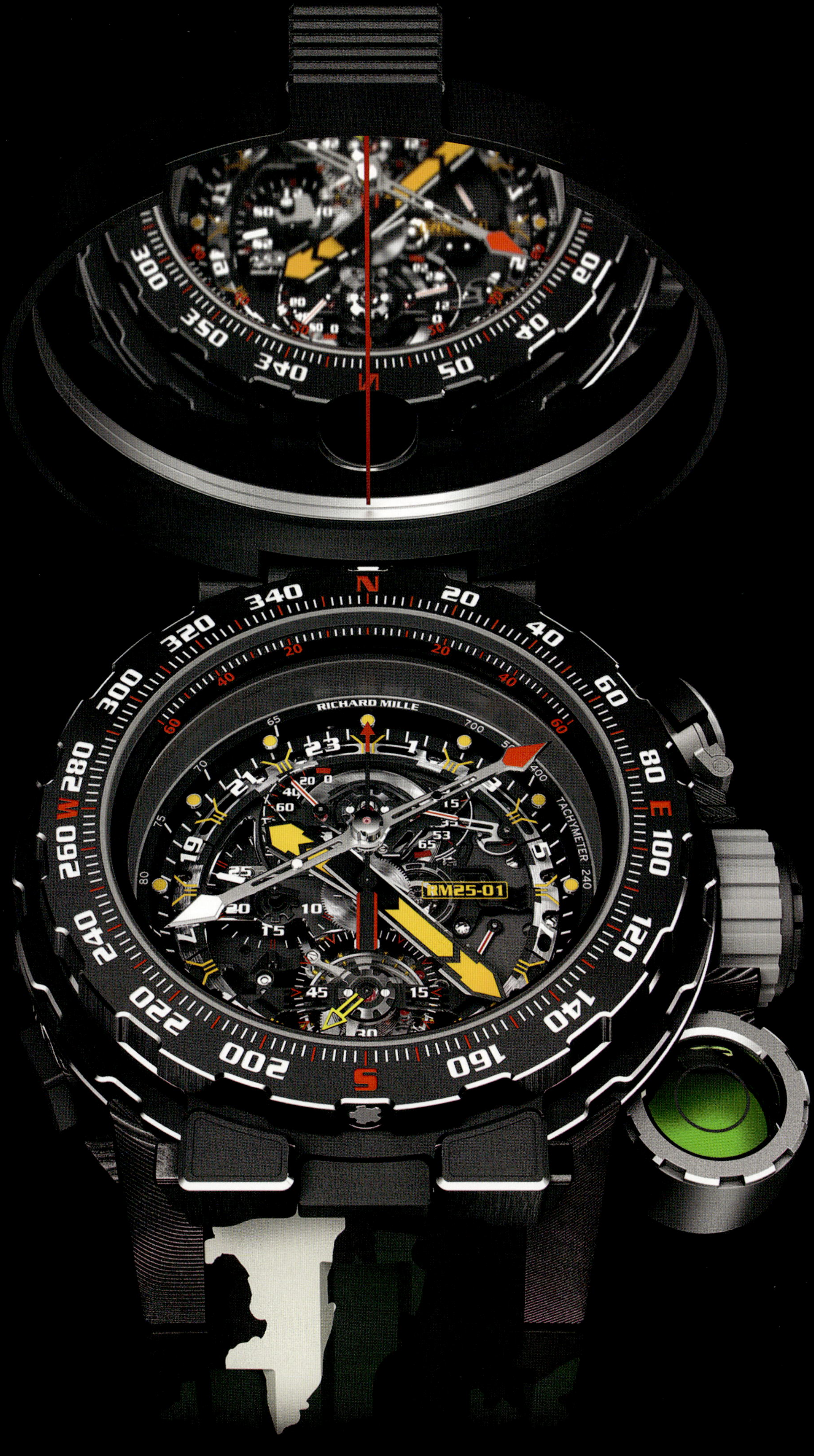
RICHARD MILLE
RM25-01
TACHYMETER
N
E
S
W

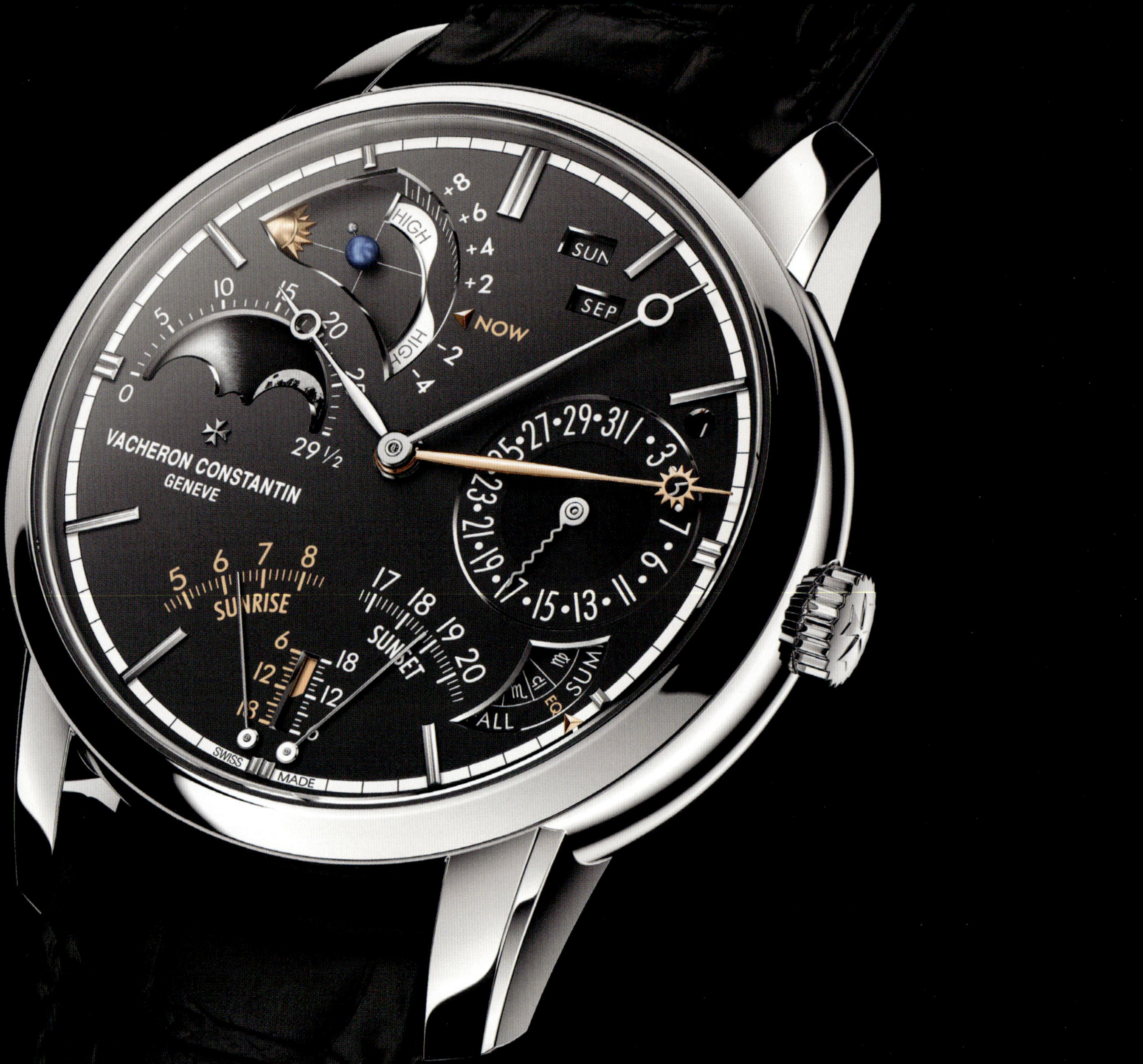

VACHERON CONSTANTIN — LES CABINOTIERS CELESTIA ASTRONOMICAL GRAND COMPLICATION 3600

$ 1 000 000

When it comes to bespoke timepieces, few watchmaker maisons will entertain customers who want not only a unique watch, but one with a unique mechanical movement inside of it. In their Les Cabinotiers department, Geneva-based Vacheron Constantin is among the few major luxury watchmakers to offer bespoke movement creation – for a price. Elite customers must be willing to fund both the research and development of novel "watch engines" and wait the requisite number of years it takes to accomplish the delicate effort of creating, testing and ultimately producing a one-of-a-kind creation that in many instances is worthy of future display in a museum.

One such example of a watch collector's million-dollar-plus zeal for a unique horological creation at Vacheron Constantin is the Les Cabinotier Celestia Astronomical Grand Complication 3600. According to Vacheron Constantin, it required five years of development to produce the fully integrated astronomical "grand complication" tourbillon movement that boasts 23 distinct complications in a lovingly hand-made and decorated mechanism that is comprised of 514 parts. In addition to the sheer complexity of the caliber 3600 mechanism, it is celebrated for its extensive three-week long power reserve and slim size (relatively speaking) at just 8.7mm thick, housed in a 45mm-wide 18k white-gold case.

Indicators for the many complications are placed both on the front and rear side of the watch case. The front of the watch includes a series of astronomical and calendar-related data, including of course the time. The dial side of the Celestia includes various windows and dials for the perpetual calendar display, a Moon-phase indicator, a tide chart, sunrise and sunset times, a season indicator, the relative position of the Moon around the Earth in relation to the sun, and the equation of time. Turn the timepiece over and a printed sapphire-crystal disc over the movement features a turning star chart as well as a power-reserve indicator. Much of the calendar data (such as the sunrise/sunset times) is region specific so the customer of this unique creation would have needed to indicate to Vacheron Constantin in advance what city or part of the world the watch should be linked to in order to offer the accurate information exclusively for that particular area.

A glorious attention to (even the most minute) detail typifies each and every angle of this incredibly exclusive creation. Vacheron Constantin justifies the time and expense of such a project because the research and development required to produce such a difficult-to-engineer movement no doubt assists the creation of the company's future products. The customer of the Vacheron Constantin Celestia benefits by having a product so distinct and elaborate that its future collectability is all but ensured.

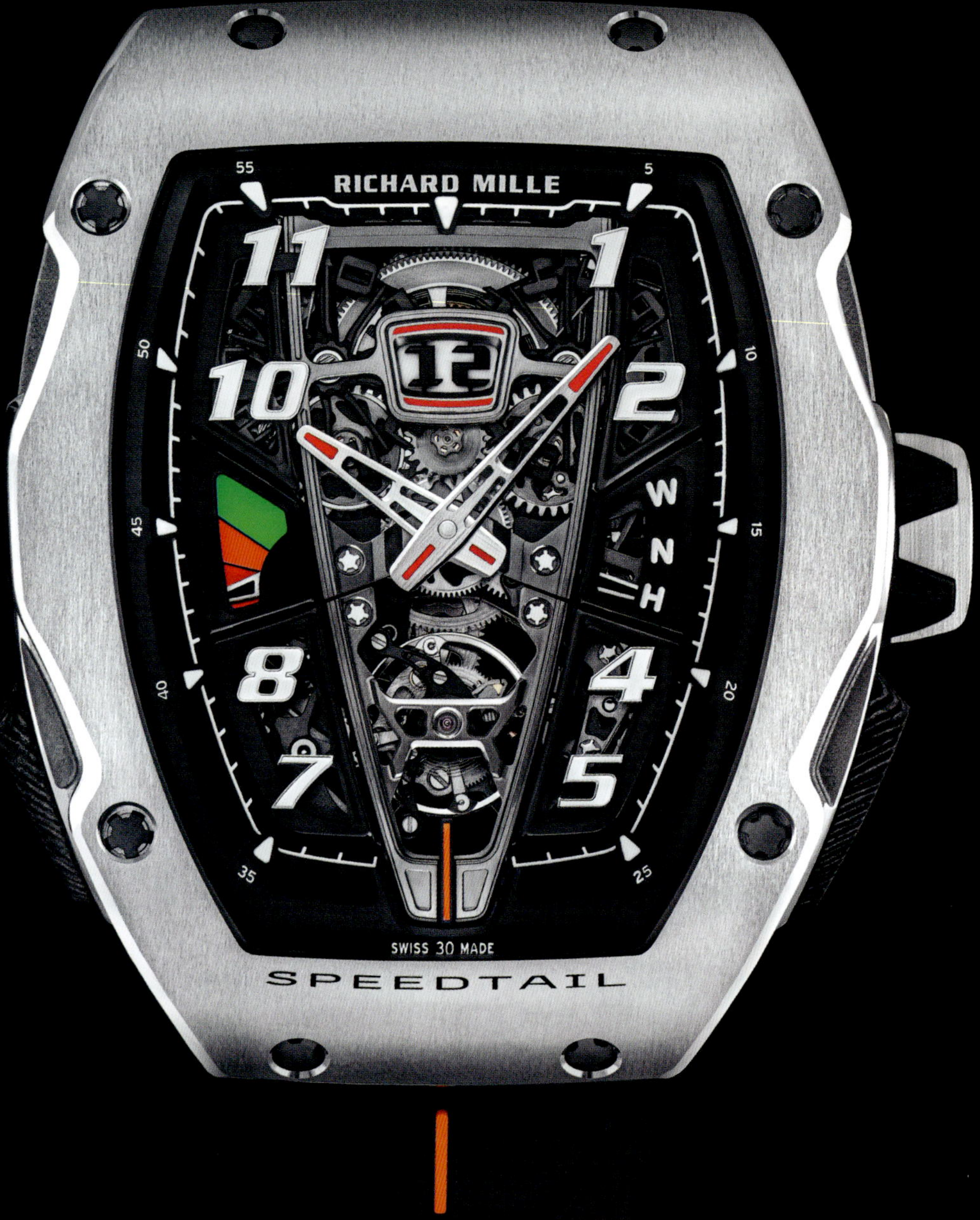
RICHARD MILLE
SWISS 30 MADE
SPEEDTAIL

RICHARD MILLE — RM 40-01 AUTOMATIC WINDING TOURBILLON MCLAREN SPEEDTAIL

$ 1 022 000

THE HIGHLY SKELETONISED MECHANISM DISPLAYS THE TIME AND DATE, ALBEIT WITH FAR MORE COMPONENTS THAN TYPICAL AUTOMATIC WATCHES.

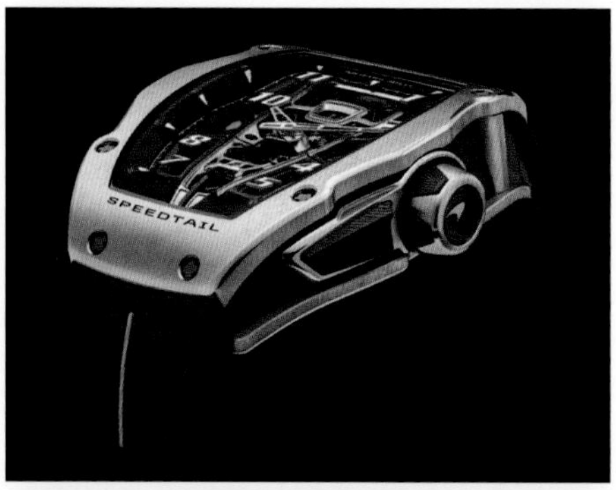

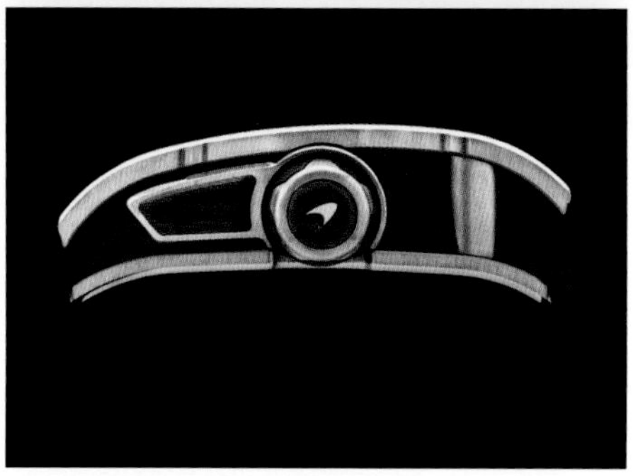

Easily the trendiest timepiece at its high average price point, Swiss luxury watch company, Richard Mille, is also the official watchmaker of British Formula One constructor, McLaren. Supercars and complicated high-end timepieces have always made excellent bedfellows. Richard Mille has a reputation for creating collaboration watches that are heavily inspired by the aesthetic of the partner personality or brand. In the case of the RM 40-01, Richard Mille created a novel case that is inspired by the distinctive rear section of the McLaren Speedtail supercar itself.

This includes a curvaceous case and tapering V-shape on the dial. The 69-part case itself reportedly required thousands of hours of development and is produced from milled sections of titanium as well as exotic carbon TPT material. Richard Mille is often able to create both evocative and elegant watch cases that are also futuristic in design. This is a rare talent and in large part responsible for the popular aesthetic of the brand's mostly tonneau-shaped distinctive watch cases.

Inside the watch is a deceptively simple automatic movement that was newly developed for this particular model. The highly skeletonised mechanism displays the time and date, albeit with far more components than typical automatic watches. The in-house developed Calibre CRMT4 movement is made up of 603 parts, operating at 4Hz with a power reserve of 50 hours. The mostly titanium bridges are hand finished and coated in black. The movement features a tourbillon visibly saddled in the middle of the movement, a power-reserve hand operated by a planetary gear-based transmission system, a skeletonised big-date indicator, and a crown function selector system.

Automatic-winding tourbillons produced by Richard Mille are uncommon. The automatic's rotor – visible through the rear of the watch – is a novel design that mimics the shape of the McLaren Speedtail's...well...tail. The uncommonly complex rotor system is produced from a series of parts in both 18k red gold and 950 platinum.

Richard Mille's success with its car-themed watches, such as the RM 40-01 Automatic Tourbillon McLaren Speedtail, is directly related to the large effort it puts into dreaming up original, partnership-relevant designs. It also happens to be among the rare car-themed timepieces that costs as much as a supercar itself – although the McLaren Speedtail automobile (in this instance) still outprices the impressive timepiece accessory that was imagined to go with it.

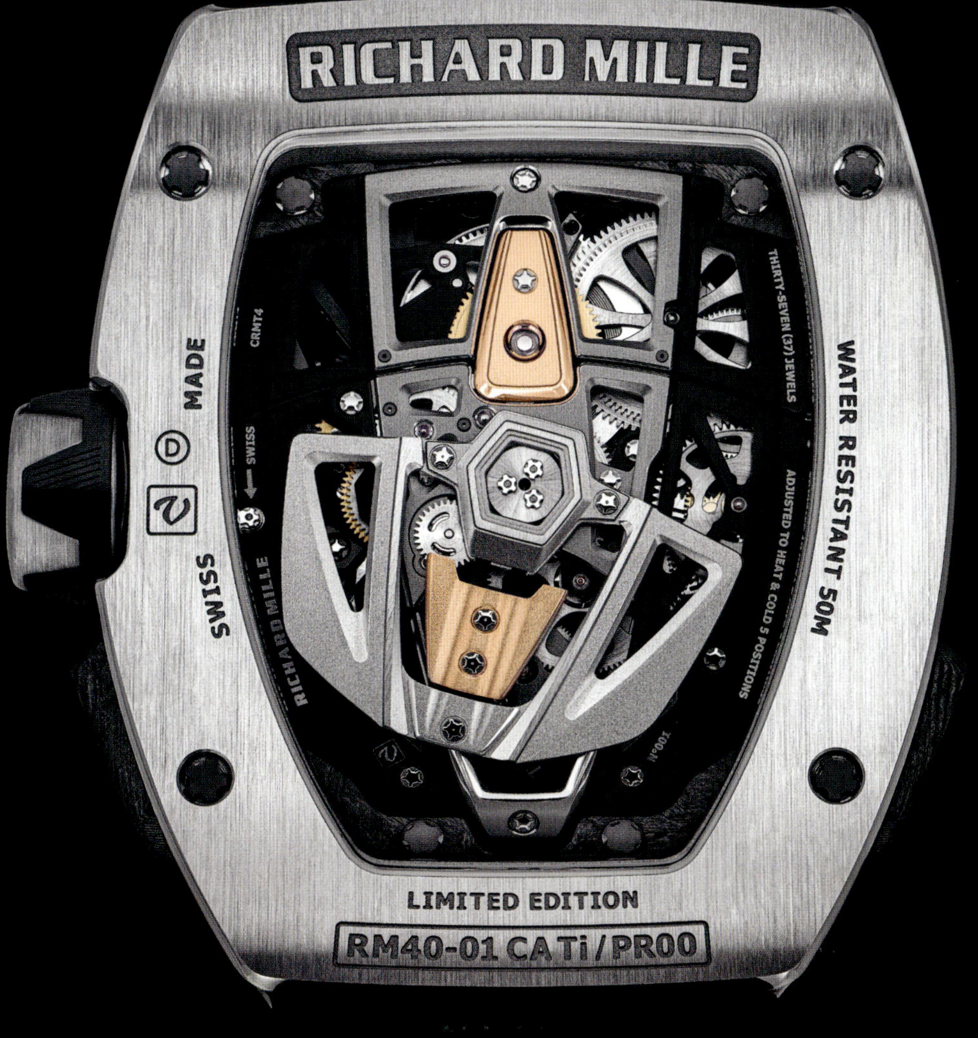
RICHARD MILLE
WATER RESISTANT 50M
MADE
SWISS
LIMITED EDITION
RM40-01 CA Ti / PR00

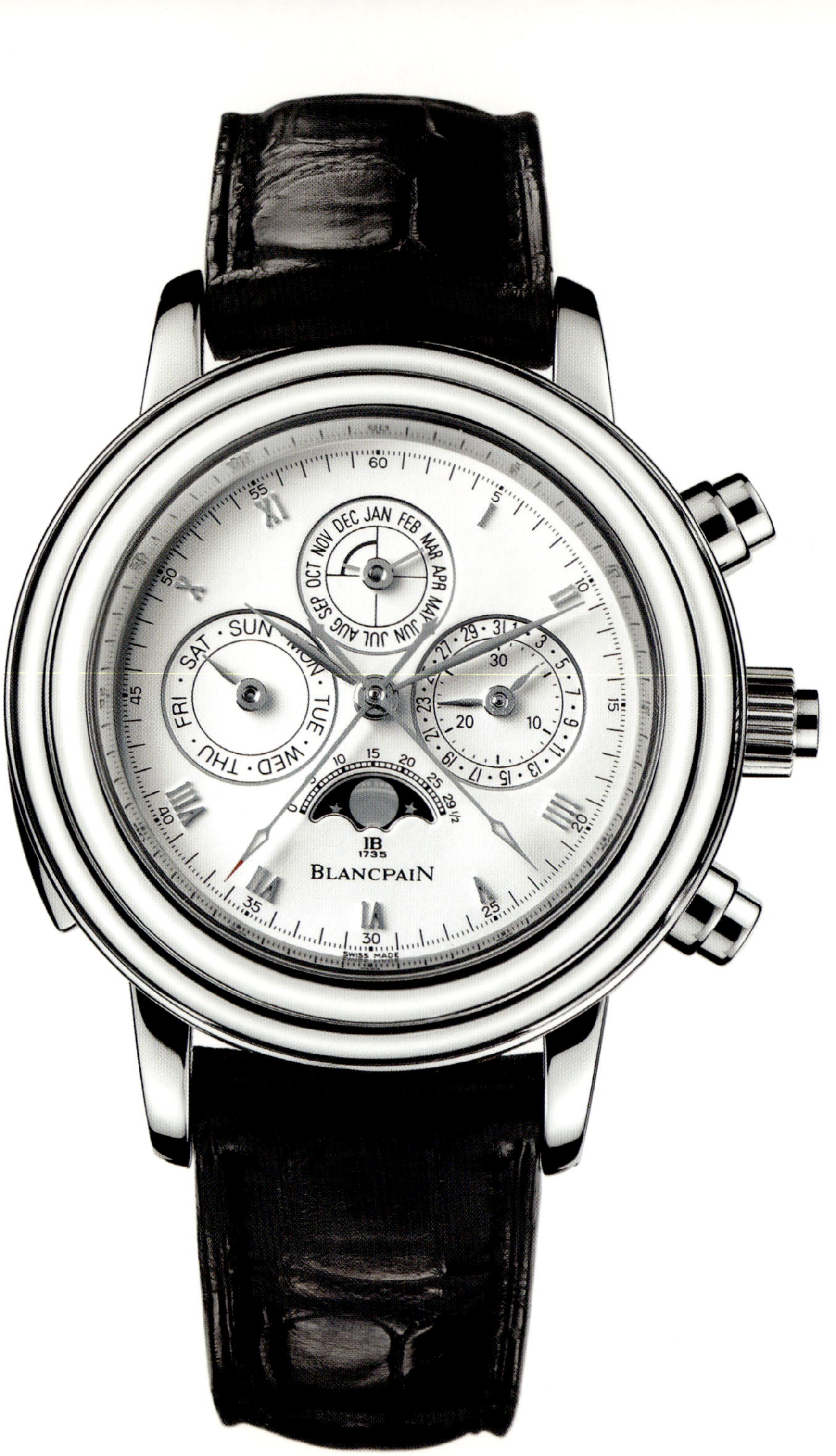

BLANCPAIN — 1735 GRANDE COMPLICATION

$ 1 026 500

One can argue that the story of the modern complicated ultra-luxury watch began with the Blancpain 1735 Grande Complication. The 1980s was an era of despair for much of the mechanical watch industry, as less expensive quartz watches cannibalised the mainstream wristwatch market. Only by going very high-end were watchmakers able to survive, increasing their prices in order to account for less demand.

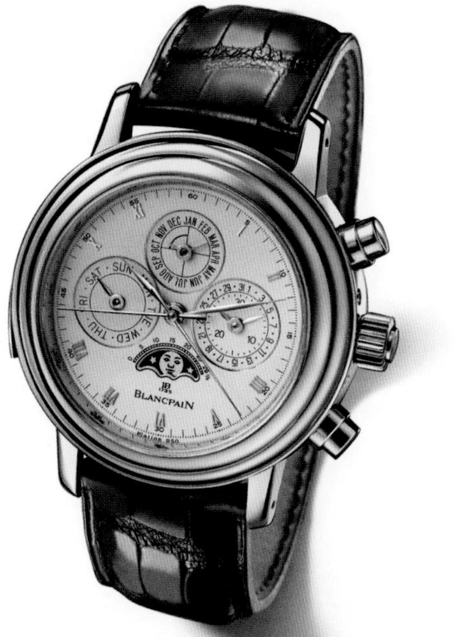

A man named Jean-Claude Biver – who today is a living legend in the watch industry – purchased the historic watchmaker Blancpain for an extremely low price in 1982. His goal was to revitalise the brand and celebrate its status as a maker of traditional mechanical timepieces. Biver hired a watchmaker named Dominique Loiseau to develop an extremely complicated flagship product that would serve as an impressive halo for the reenergised Blancpain brand. It was originally released around 1985.

Using very early forms of computer-aided design, Loiseau and his team at Blancpain set out to create what would end up being, for years to come, the world's most complicated watch. Blancpain designed the 1735 Grande Complication to include a split-second chronograph, perpetual calendar and minute repeater, all based on an automatic tourbillon mechanical movement, housed in a solid platinum case rendered in a very traditional style.

Blancpain promised to make 30 pieces of the 1735 Grande Complication watch in total. The movement of each required an incredible amount of time to make, and each was hand-decorated, tested, and assembled. Even among master watchmakers, so few of them had the skill to assemble the 1735 Grande Complication that it took Blancpain almost 25 years to assemble all of them. The very last of the famed 1735 Grande Complication watches was finally produced in 2009.

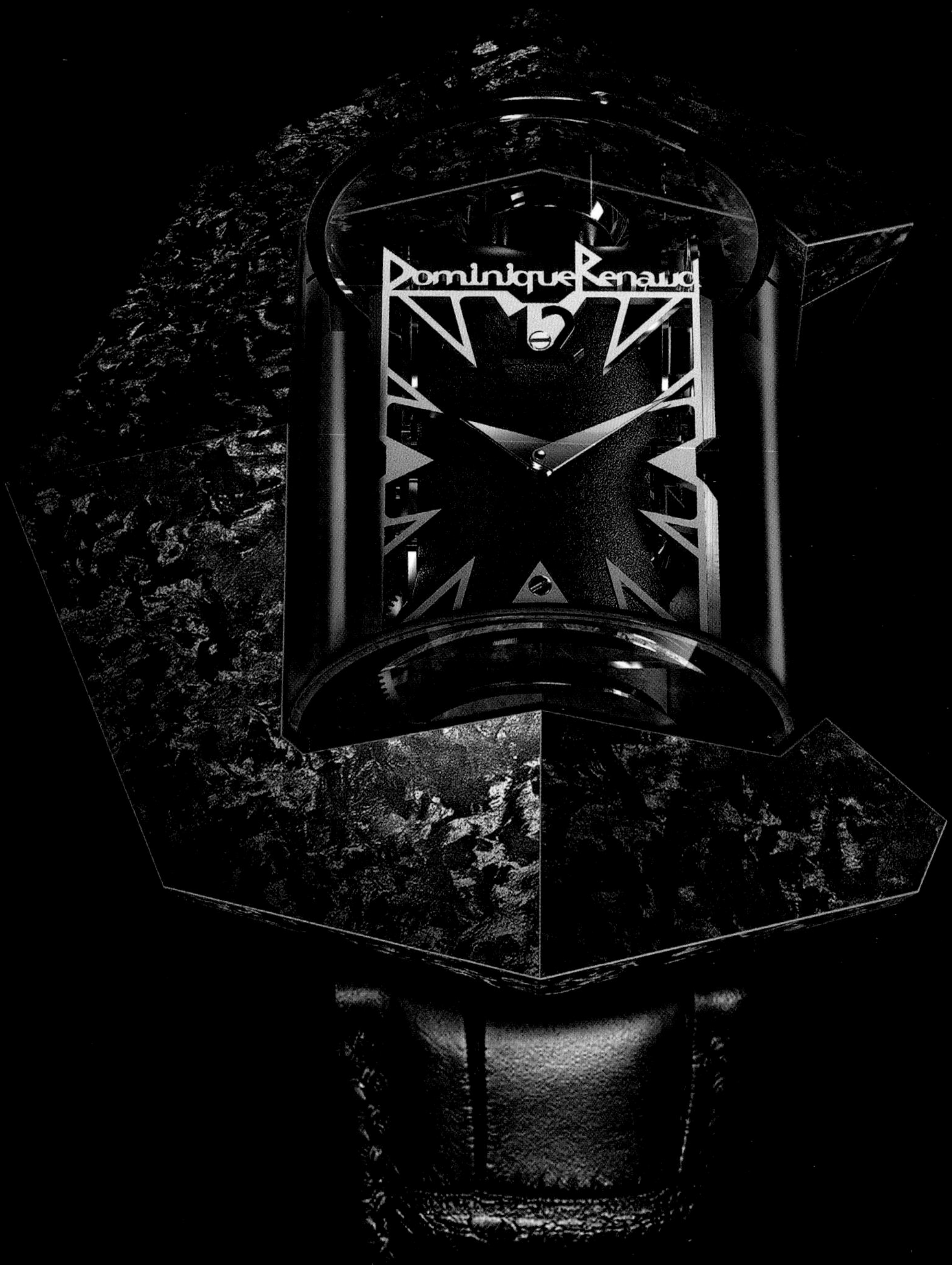

DOMINIQUE RENAUD — DR01

$ 1 050 000

Authentically new technology in the world of mechanical horology is uncommon to say the least. Esteemed Swiss watchmaker and designer, Dominique Renaud, is once again happy to be among the rare few, as the once-retired savant returns to the scene with an incredibly exotic timepiece that finally bears his own name after having spent several years in development.

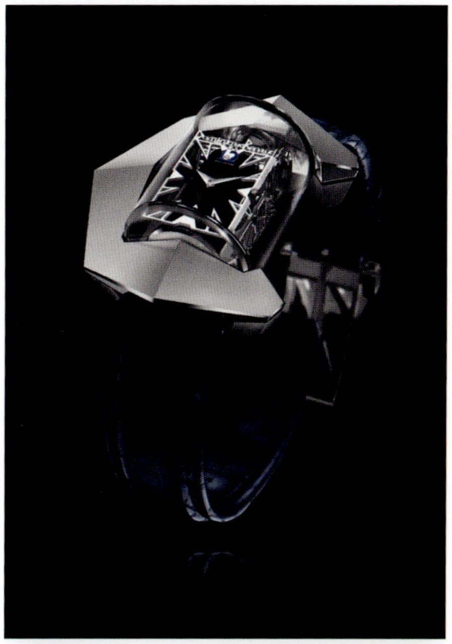

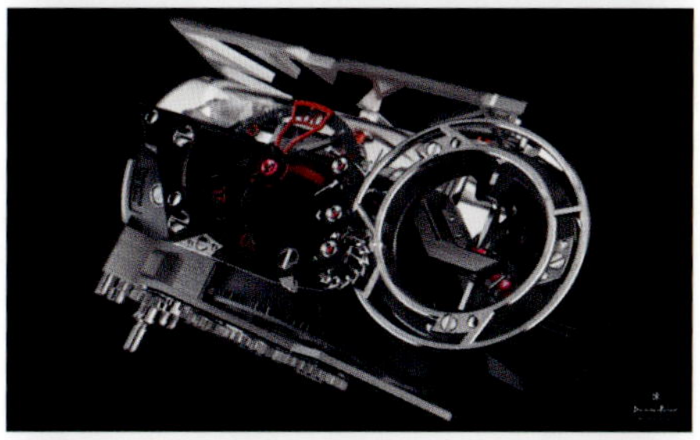

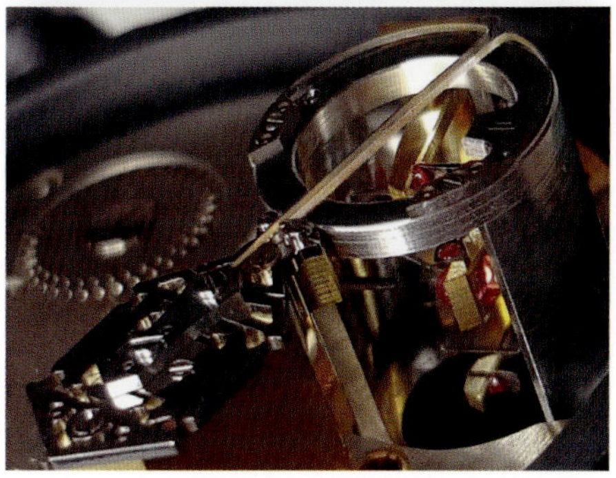

Most timepieces today may be modern made, but they use technology that, in some cases, is hundreds of years old. Much of today's novel technology in the watchmaking space is related to materials and production techniques, not the actual way in which a mechanism operates. Research and development costs are to blame because mechanical watches will never experience the type of production volumes most major companies need to justify years of development. Thus, it makes sense that, when new systems designed to measure time are debuted, it is up to well-funded aficionados to bear the cost of their existence. So is the case with Dominique Renaud's "blade resonator", which he developed to replace the traditional balance wheel and hairspring regulation system at the heart of most wristwatches today.

More accuracy, more stability over time, and less power consumption was Renaud's goal with the DR01. Understanding the mindset of timepiece collectors (after having serviced their needs for years) Dominique Renaud also knows that emotion plays as much a role in capturing the hearts of customers as does technical merit. The DR01 watch case itself is C-shaped and holds a pivoting sapphire-crystal cylinder that can be turned around in various viewing positions. Inside the cylinder is the entirely original movement whose blade-resonator regulation system (named as such because it has what appears to be two thin blades that pivot with a very narrow amplitude) operates at an uncommon 5Hz with a "crossbow spring", and up to three weeks of power when the mainspring is full. One of the major achievements in the DR01 is that it not only replaces traditional mechanical watch-movement technology, but it is designed to be worn on the wrist. This implies that the DR01 remains accurate when the movement is placed in a variety of positions, while offering requisite shock resistance – features that many modern and experimental timekeeping mechanisms cannot claim.

Dominique Renaud calls the DR01 a "lab on the wrist" because the movement he developed inside of the watch can actually be tweaked and adjusted by watchmakers with sufficient understanding of how it works, to experiment with variables such as the operating frequency. Only the most confident of watchmakers would ever proclaim such a promise – though this admittedly niche product will only appeal to the most horologically educated of high-end collectors. Dominique Renaud calls the first of his new watches the DR01 Twelve First (because he only plans to produce 12 of them), with each entirely customised to the tastes of the buyer.

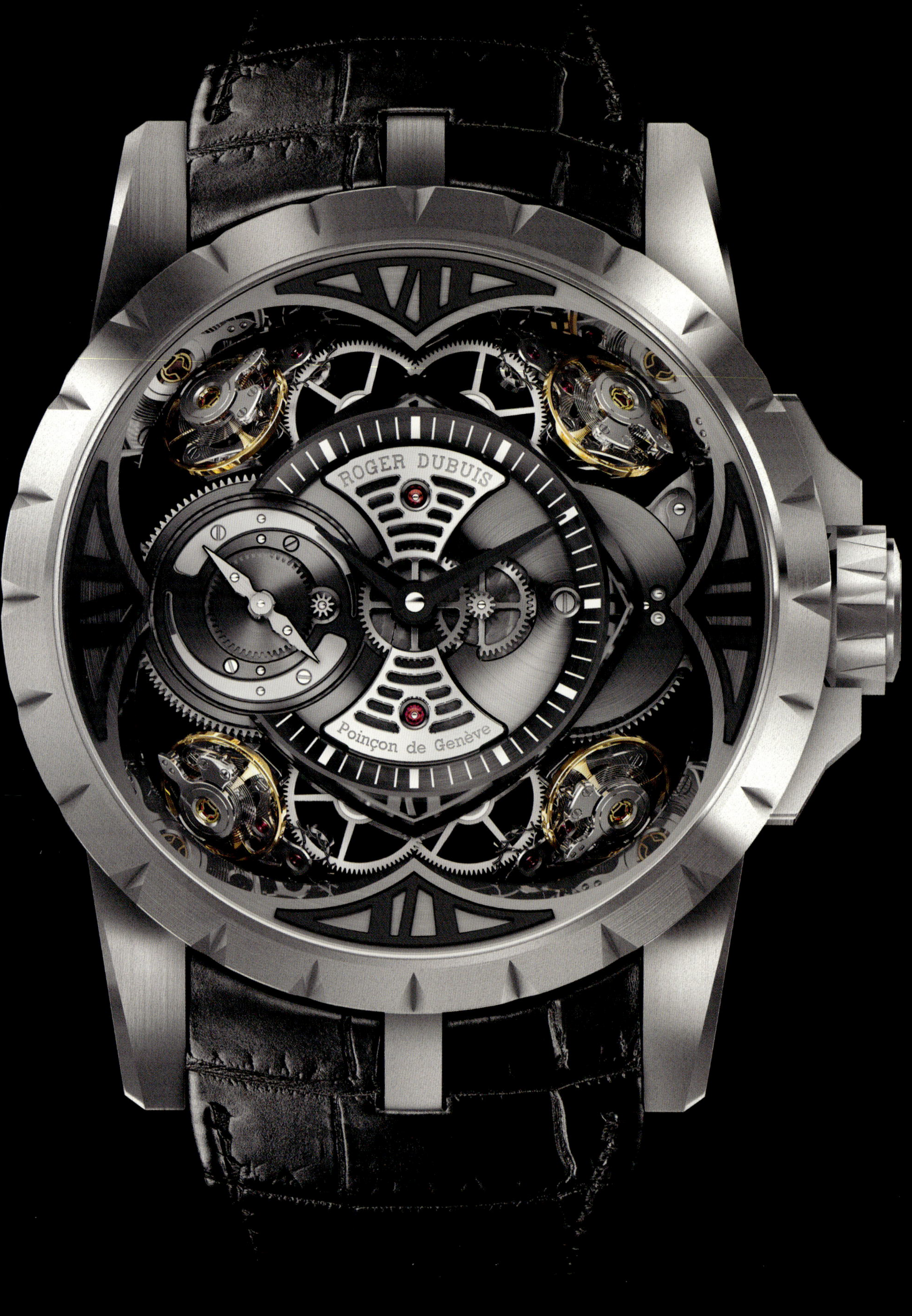
ROGER DUBUIS
Poinçon de Genève

ROGER DUBUIS — EXCALIBUR QUATUOR SILICON

$ 1 080 000

ROGER DUBUIS DESIGNED THE QUATUOR FROM THE GROUND UP, AND THE MOVEMENT IS MADE TO IMPRESS.

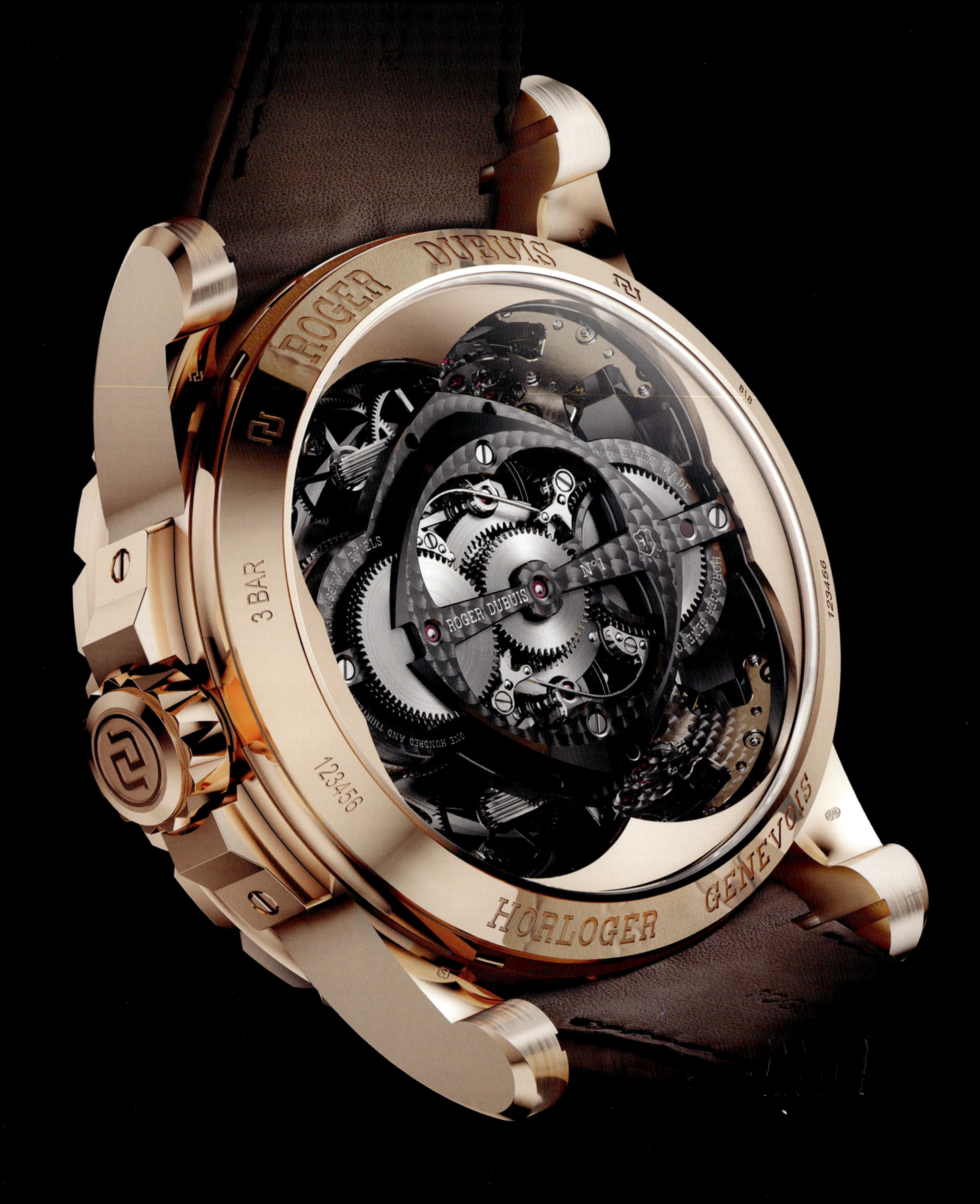
ROGER DUBUIS
HORLOGER GENEVOIS
3 BAR
123456
ROGER DUBUIS
N°1
SWISS MADE
ONE HUNDRED AND THIR
USEFUL JEWELS

The promotional video Roger Dubuis produced upon the release of the Excalibur Quatuor watch in 2013 goes as follows: An eagle in a barren wasteland screams while dodging lightning and speeding towards something unknown. What the eagle has been diving to obtain is a sword stuck in the earth, not unlike Excalibur from the Arthurian legend. Before the eagle reaches his prize, lightning strikes the sword, dislodging it and causing flames to erupt from the earth. The Quatuor watch is then ceremoniously revealed with dazzling video effects.

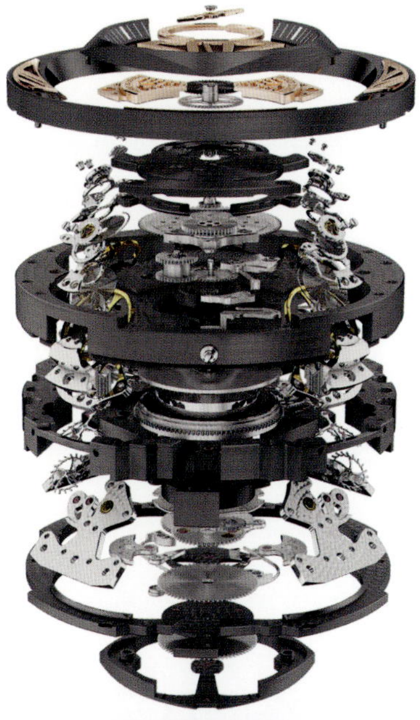

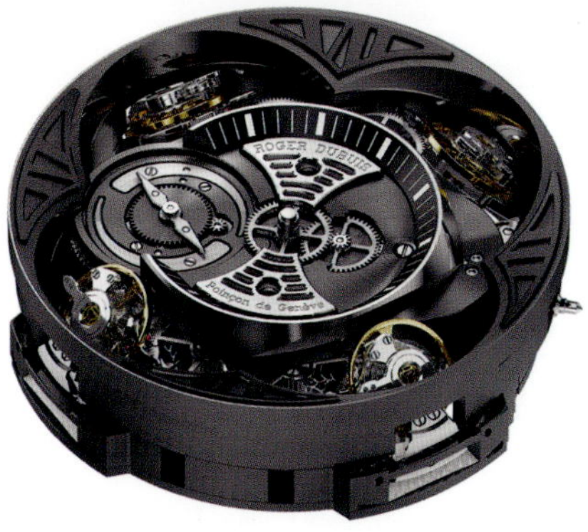

This is modern watch marketing and it has taken the once esoteric concept of mechanical timepiece operation in to a realm of fantasy, intrigue, and no small amount of hyperbole. The result is often just as silly as it is marvellous, and for many collectors their passion for watches is only enlivened upon viewing these cartoons for the rich. Roger Dubuis is among the more avant-garde high-end watchmakers that belong to a large group. When Richemont acquired Roger Dubuis, it was in no small part thanks to the brand's ability to produce highly complicated movements in-house – often tourbillons.

The Excalibur Quatuor contains no tourbillons (often Roger Dubuis timepieces come with more than one). Instead, the novel movement contains four separate balance wheels. Each one is placed at a corner of the watch and uniquely oriented at an angle, as the entire group is connected via a series of differentials. There is absolutely no technical reason for this assortment aside from sheer proof of concept. Roger Dubuis excels in the creation of mechanical circuses, and that is exactly where the Excalibur Quatuor succeeds in both design and presentation.

Roger Dubuis designed the Quatuor from the ground up, and the movement is made to impress. Naturally, mechanical movements aren't typically symmetrical in their design. Movements that are in fact visually symmetrical, are complex feats of engineering, exclusively intended to please the aesthetic sensibilities of the few collectors on Earth willing and able to invest in then for wrist companionship.

Time is displayed towards the centre of the dial, and to the right of the small hour and minute hands is a power reserve indicator that lets one know when to wind the watch. Like everything else on the Quatuor, it is over-engineered the way only a luxury timepiece can be.

Roger Dubuis produced a handful of Excalibur Quatuor versions in materials such as titanium or gold, each as a limited edition. However, by far the most exclusive version was produced from a solid piece of silicon – the first time a watch case was ever cut from the natural material. Reported to be lighter than titanium and harder than steel, the Excalibur Quatuor Silicon watch was produced as a limited edition of just three pieces.

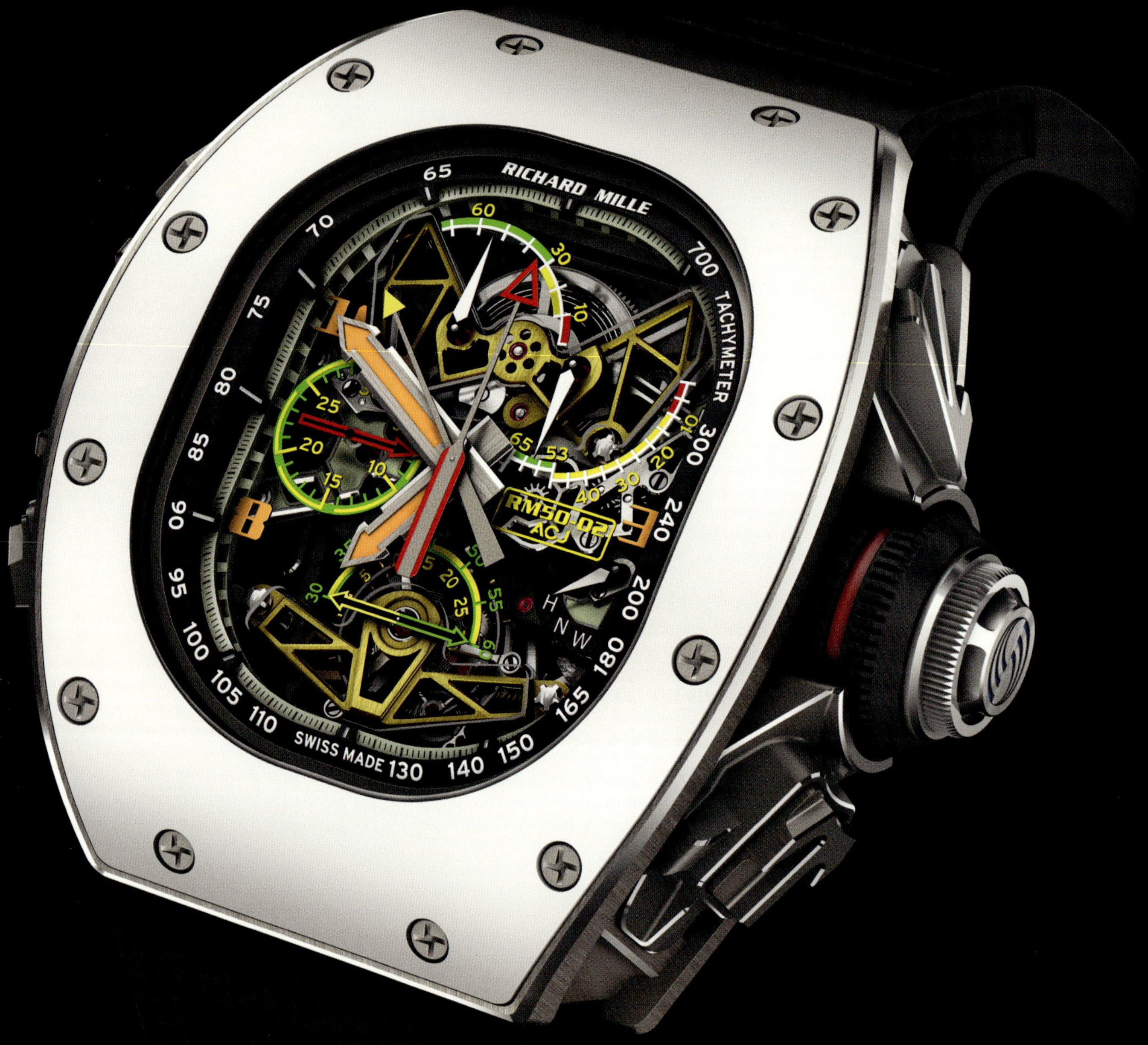
RICHARD MILLE
TACHYMETER
SWISS MADE
RM50-02
ACJ

RICHARD MILLE — RM 50-02 TOURBILLON SPLIT SECONDS CHRONOGRAPH ACJ

$ 1 082 000

RICHARD MILLE CRAFTED A DISTINCTIVE NEW CASE WITH A DIAL AND FUSELAGE SCREWS, INSPIRED BY THE LOOK OF A PASSENGER JET WINDOW.

The RM 50-02 Tourbillon Split Seconds Chronograph ACJ watch is a 30-piece limited-edition collaboration between watchmaker Richard Mille and aircraft manufacturer Airbus, or more specifically for this project, Airbus Corporate Jets (ACJ). Working directly with ACJ's lead designer, Richard Mille crafted a distinctive new case with a dial and fuselage screws, inspired by the look of a passenger jet window. The watch case's white ceramic bezel, paired with an exotic titanium–aluminium alloy for much of the rest of the timepiece body, suggests the light-coloured paint used on plane surfaces.

Aviation-themed watches with design elements inspired by the actual aeroplane itself (as opposed to its cockpit instrumentation) often fall short of their potential. Richard Mille and ACJ managed to accomplish the rather rare goal of imagining a timepiece with design elements that recall parts of a jet plane without the result looking abstemious or kitsch. The precision-machined aerospace-grade metal case is full of modern aircraft design references, including the crown, pushers, and even the gold-toned finishing on some of the movement bridges.

Dazzling bright colours, complex floating indicators, and a richly exposed movement typical of other Richard Mille top-tier creations, also populates the dial of the RM 50-02. The manually wound mechanical movement features a 70-hour power reserve, tourbillon, movement torque indicator, mainspring power-reserve indicator and, finally, a highly sophisticated split-seconds chronograph system. This latter complication is mainly found on select exclusive watches, ranging from the ultra-classic to almost playful contemporary luxury toys such as this Richard Mille model, which is meant to be paired with bespoke custom-made private Airbus jets.

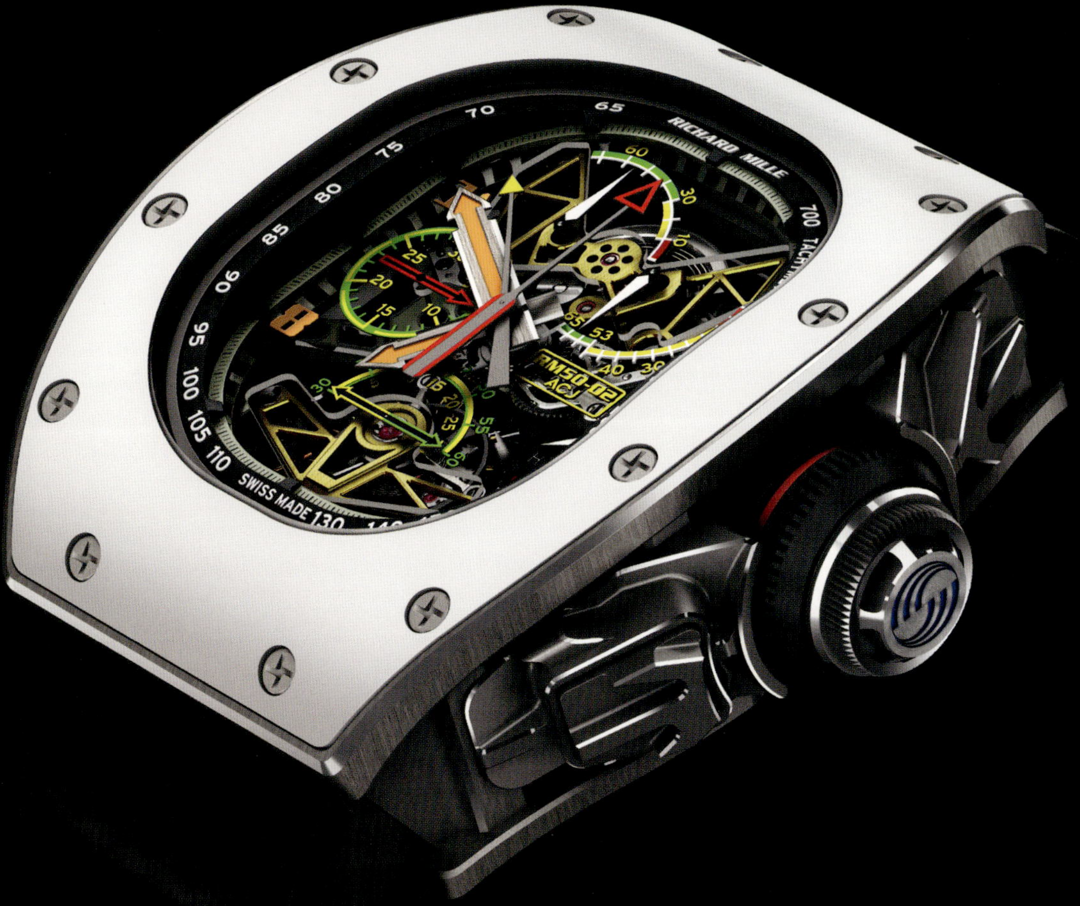
RICHARD MILLE
SWISS MADE
RM50-02
ACJ

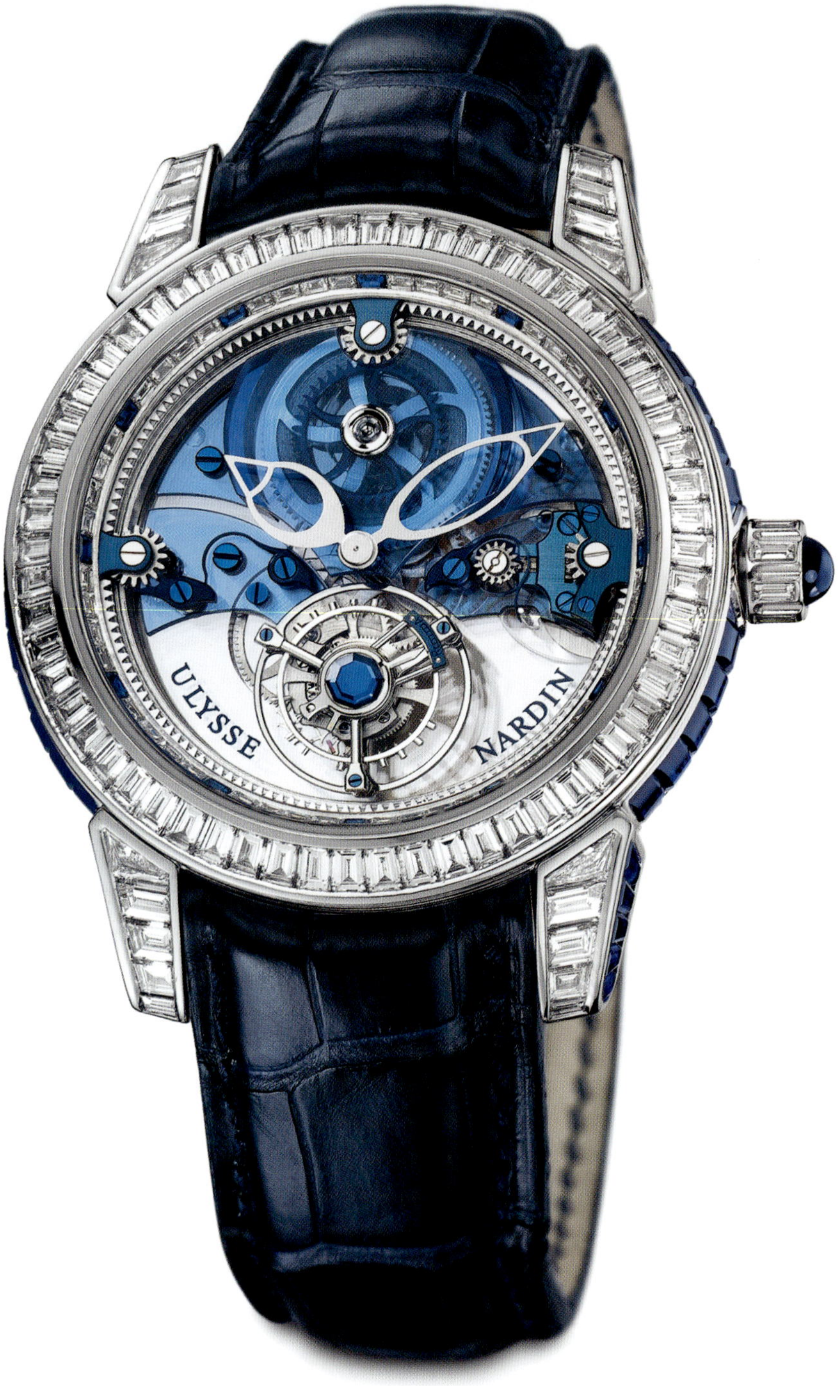

ULYSSE NARDIN — ROYAL BLUE TOURBILLON

$ 1 100 000

It is rare that a timepiece mixes both mechanical complexity and a spectacular array of diamonds. When going ultra-high-end, watchmakers typically choose a jewellery-focused route, or one that is intended to appeal to watch movement lovers. That is because most of the time different types of buyers are interested in these different types of products. Having said that, luxury is also about providing options for everyone, no matter how niche their tastes may be.

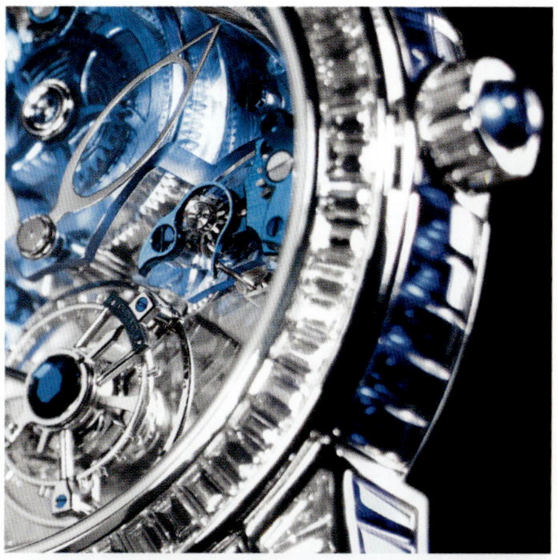

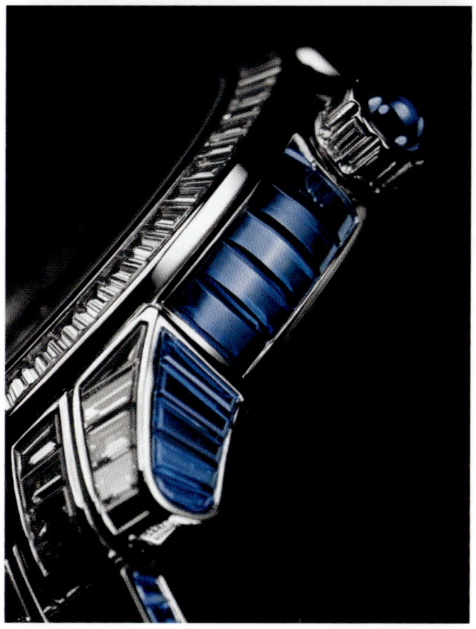

A product that exemplifies this type of niche appeal is Ulysse Nardin's most impressive version of their Royal Blue Tourbillon. Released in 2010, the Royal Blue Tourbillon was available in no less than eight versions, communicating a clear intent by Ulysse Nardin to extend the allure of this exotic timepiece model to as many enthusiasts as possible.

Each of the Royal Blue Tourbillon watches begins with a solid 950 platinum case. Several versions, including this full pavé model are decorated with precious stones. This particular piece is completely covered with baguette-cut diamonds and blue sapphires visible on the case, crown, bracelet and dial periphery. A total of 568 diamonds (almost 34 carats) and 234 blue sapphires (about 17 carats) are used to produce a remarkably decadent frame for the unique mechanical movement.

The integration of the diamonds and sapphires is unique. The sides of the case and bracelet are lined with baguette-cut sapphires giving the watches a "blue edge". Diamonds line the rest of the watch. While there is a less expensive version with round-cut diamonds all over the watch, the larger and more expensive baguette-cut form of the stone is considered to lend itself better to masculine style.

Ulysse Nardin designed the movement to use large pieces of blue and white synthetic sapphire crystal in many places, instead of metal. This gives the movement an almost transparent quality to it. These sapphire pieces are extremely difficult to machine, as there is a high breakage rate. Due to the transparent sapphire crystal at the bottom of the case, the flying tourbillon (set with a large blue sapphire) appears to be almost floating on the dial. The movement has about 100 hours of power reserve.

While typically successful from a design perspective, sapphire crystal plates are rarely used in watch movements because of the inherent fragile nature of assembling them. Though once holes have been drilled and the screws tightened, assuming the plates did not crack during the process, they prove quite durable.

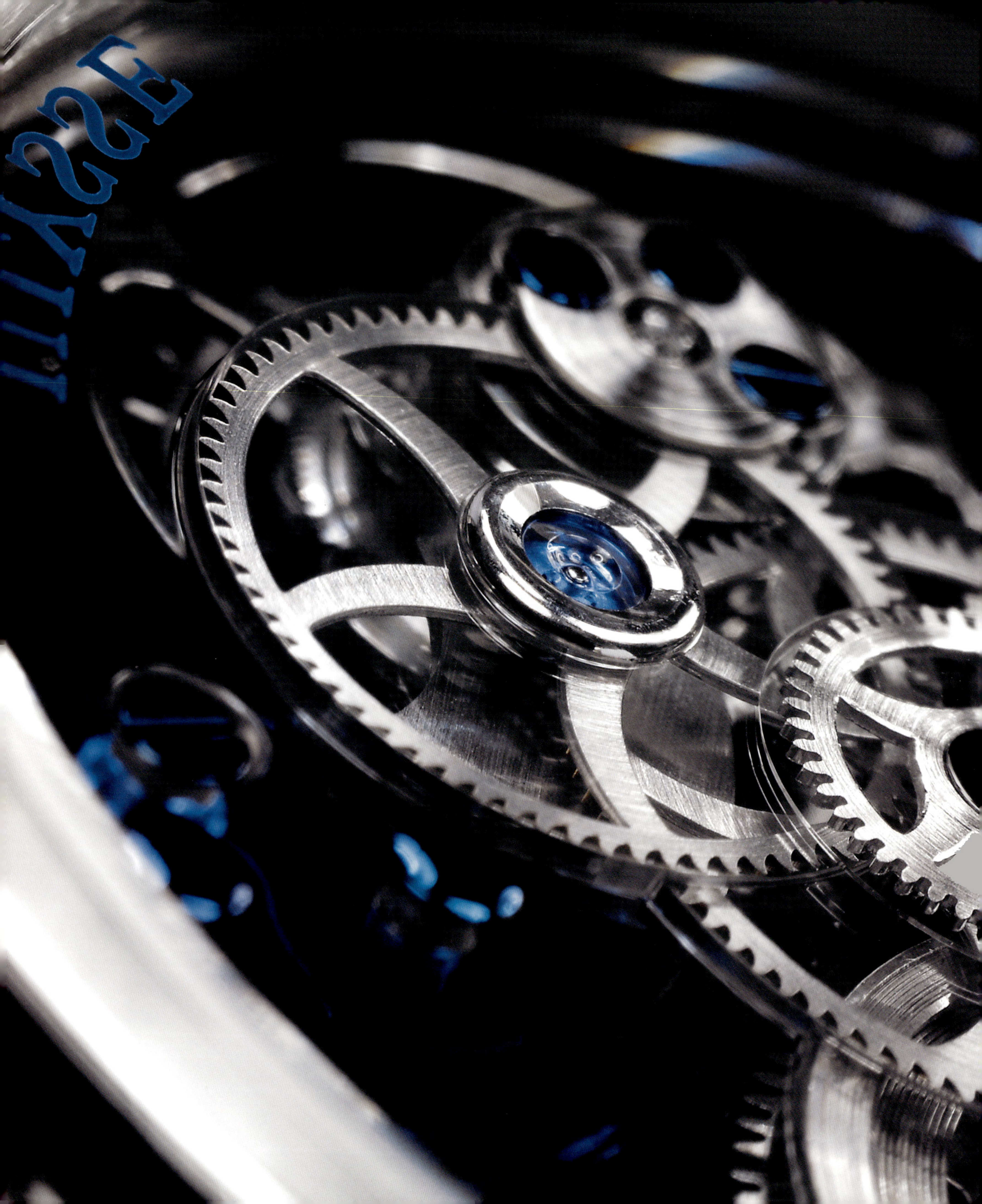

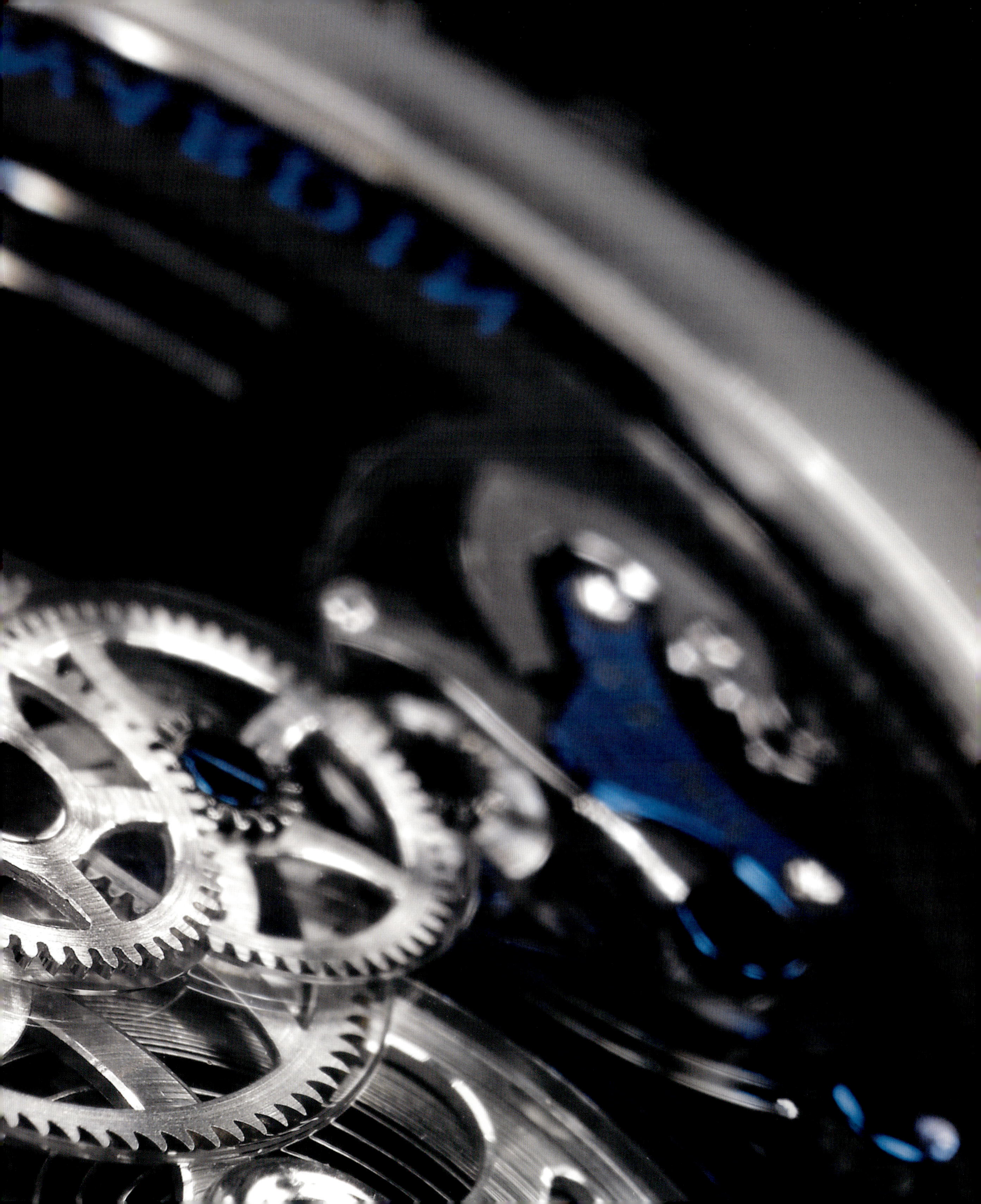

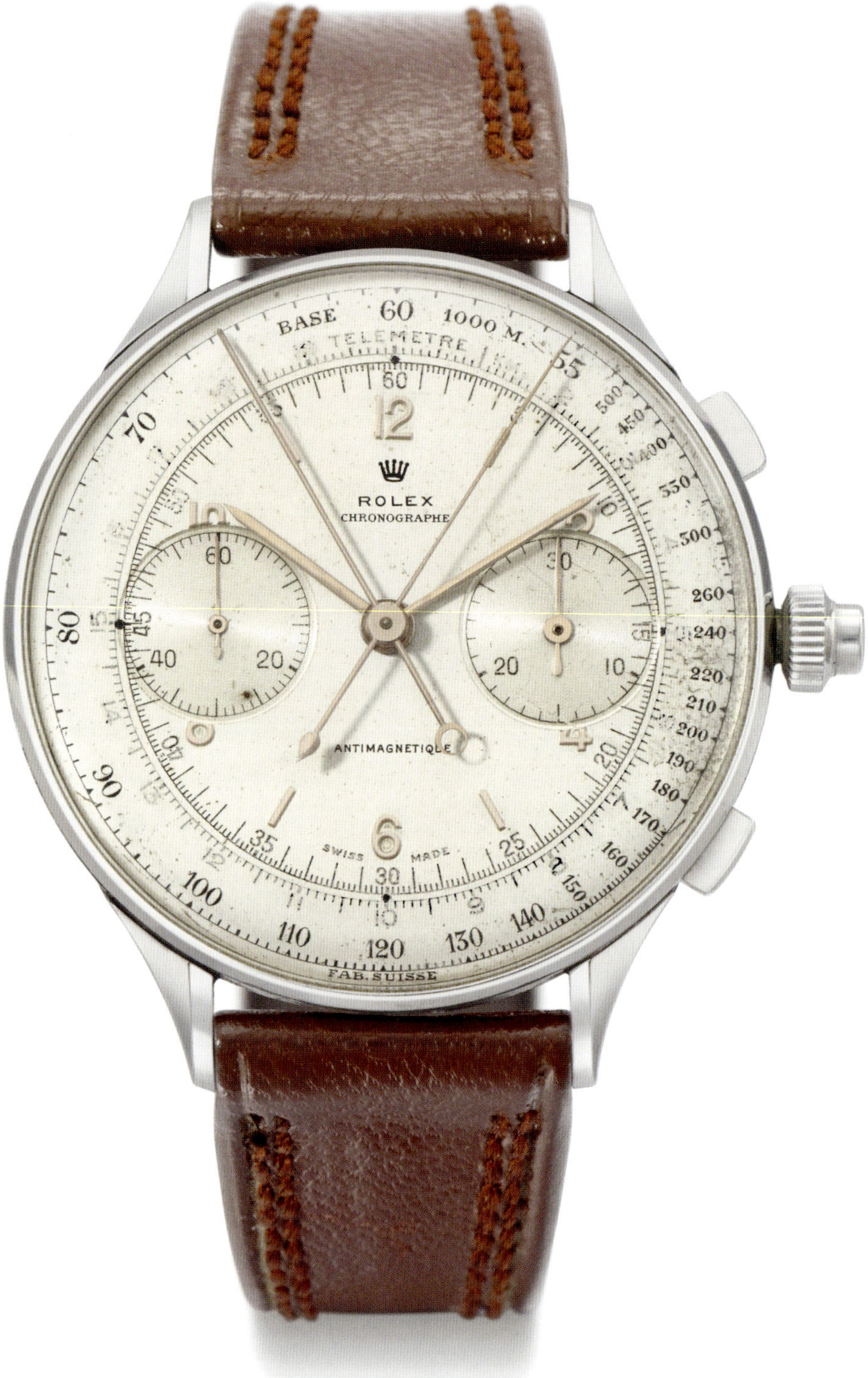

ROLEX — REF. 4113, SPLIT SECONDS CHRONOGRAPH

$ 1 163 746*

Most of the popular and highly successful luxury watch brands are old. The longer a company has been around making watches, the more legitimacy they tend to have with collectors and buyers, who are asked to contribute a hefty sum of money in order to own one of their small wearable luxuries. Consumers often look upon new brands with scepticism, yet the irony is that most seasoned watch collectors are looking for the "next cool thing" and what is "new and innovative".

A new brand, looking to legitimise itself with high-end watch buyers, often finds it difficult to do so if they aren't based on the work of an historic watchmaker or, alternatively, producing something totally wild and attention-grabbing. This latter technique is perhaps the most interesting, but also the most complicated. Watch collectors often like to say that, "whatever can be done with watches has been done with watches". The point being that in their opinion nothing new can be done, because it has all been done before. It is true that finding something genuinely innovative can be a challenge, but a quick survey of products released by new luxury watch brands over the last decade or so reveals impressive levels of ingenuity – regardless of the degree of commercial success.

In 2010, the new brand Manufacture Royale released their debut timepieces called the Opera. Inspired by the past, but firmly planted in today's love of technology, the watch focused on a Steampunk design aesthetic, instead of on something more traditional. According to Manufacture Royale, their inspiration came from the famed writer Voltaire – who actually did have a hand in the Swiss watch industry when he lived in Geneva in the 18th century. Voltaire was a controversial figure who used politics and clever business tactics to disrupt the Swiss watch industry of the time.

The Opera watch was named as such for containing a minute repeater complication that musically sounds the time back to the user. Most minute repeater watches are very difficult to hear, because of their water-resistant cases and the use of precious metals that tend to absorb sound. The Opera watch comes with a case that opens up like an accordion, and a case back that opens completely. In this configuration, Manufacture Royale claims, the sound from the hammers and gongs is much more impressive.

Massively built at 50mm wide, the Opera is a crowning achievement of the attention-grabbing theatrics that have defined so much of the modern luxury watch industry. The totally exposed and skeletonised movement contains a tourbillon-style escapement that is designed to match fittingly with the over-engineered case, being produced entirely from precious metals such as gold or platinum.

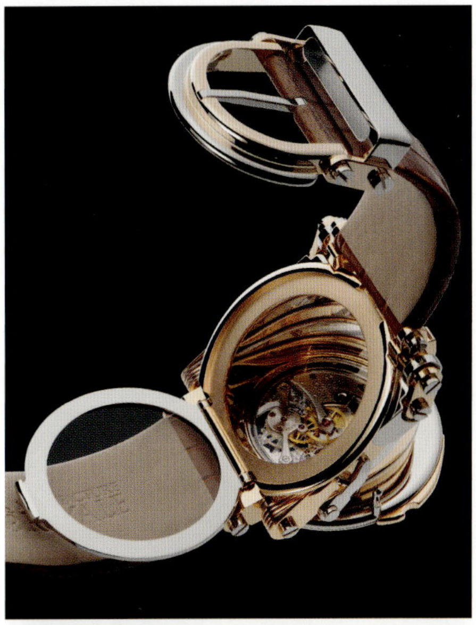

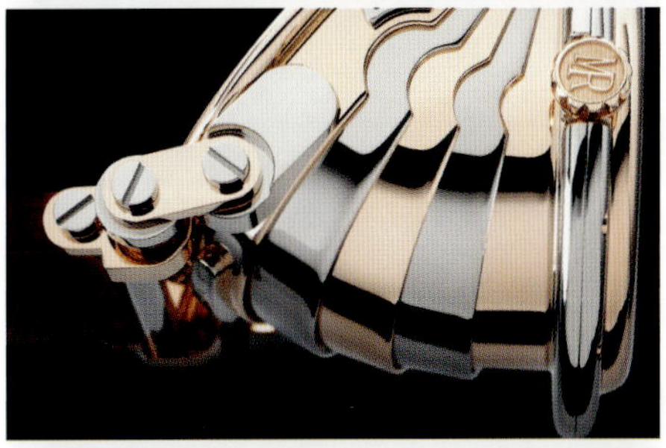

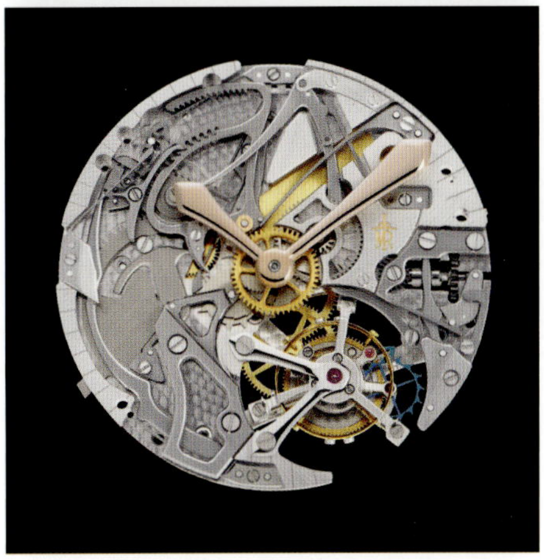

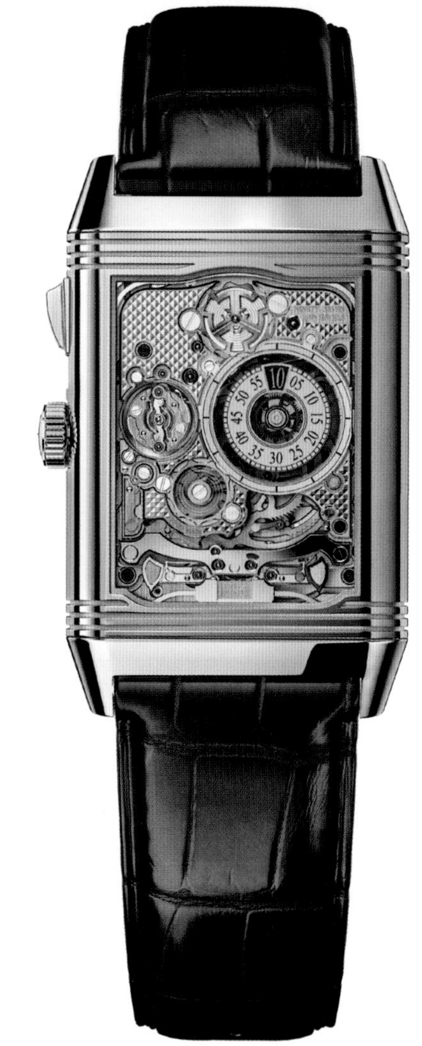

JAEGER-LECOULTRE — REVERSO HYBRIS MECHANICA CALIBRE 185 "QUADRIPTYQUE"

$ 1 350 000

When the "Quadriptyque" debuted from Jaeger-LeCoultre, it was the most ambitious creation released by the storied Swiss watch brand in years, with a simple claim to fame as the "first watch with four functioning faces". Known formally as the Reverso Hybris Mechanica Calibre 185, the mega-luxury timepiece was intended as part of Jaeger-LeCoultre's 90th anniversary celebration of the original Reverso.

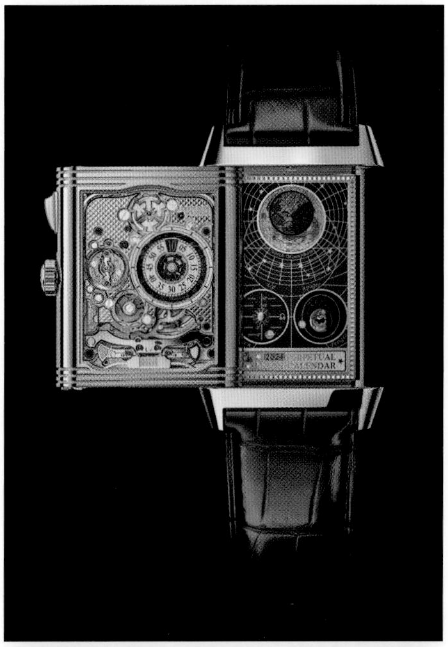

This now iconic art-deco themed rectangular watch was originally intended as a sports watch for British polo players. The reversible case had a traditional dial on one side for the time, and a smooth, protective metal surface on the rear side. The idea being that such a design would protect the fragile (then-glass) crystal from flying debris, mallets and balls.

When Jaeger-LeCoultre expanded the Reverso collection years later, the polo watch became first a dress watch and then a base for some of the company's most impressive complications, including most of the legendary Jaeger-LeCoultre Gyrotourbillon models. With the "Quadriptyque", Jaeger-LeCoultre accomplished something entirely different. The watch has 11 distinct complications (functions) across four different watch faces – three of which can be viewed while the watch is worn on the wrist. Jaeger-LeCoultre proudly claims that the development of the Calibre 185 watch resulted in the Swiss company filing another 12 patents.

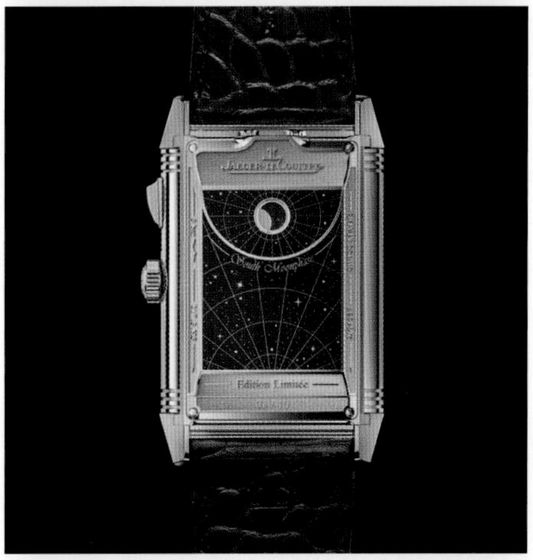

Practically speaking, the most impressive aspect of the Calibre 185 is how elegantly its mechanical systems are designed in conjunction with the case – offering an extremely wearable overall watch thickness of just 15.5mm. The 18k white-gold case is a further 31mm wide by 51.2mm long, making it grand on the wrist, but still wearable overall – as well as attractive.

Complex movement skeletonisation and metal bridge surface decorations frame the Jaeger-LeCoultre Calibre 185's various display functions. The "main" face includes a traditional dial for the time, including a flying tourbillon displayed at the 7 o'clock position. This dial also includes a perpetual calendar display which tracks the month, date, day of the week and leap year. The reserve side of this part of the case offers something entirely different. Here, Jaeger-LeCoultre have designed a distinctive jumping hour time display, as well as a novel minute-repeater system which isn't just compact, but also more efficient in how long it requires to "sound out" the current time using a series of chimes.

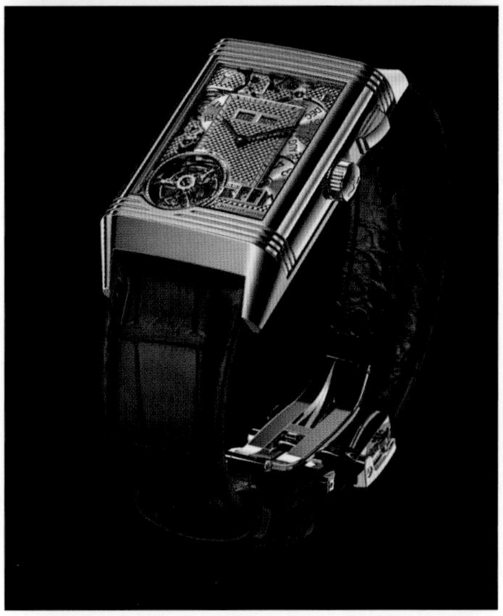

The rear part of the watch case – which would normally just be solid metal – was given its own double set of astronomical complications. The front side includes a beautifully painted and logically designed display for the phase of the Moon, the relative position of the Earth around the sun, as well as the relative position of the Moon around the Earth in hand-painted glory. On the farthest rear section of the case, Jaeger-LeCoultre included a secondary display for the current phase of the Moon (representing the view of the southern versus northern hemisphere), as well as a star map representing a dynamically changing southern night sky. This spectacular Hybris Mechanica Calibre 185 homage to the legendary Reverso was produced as a set of just 10 pieces.

VACHERON CONSTANTIN – TOUR DE I'LLE

$1 400 000*

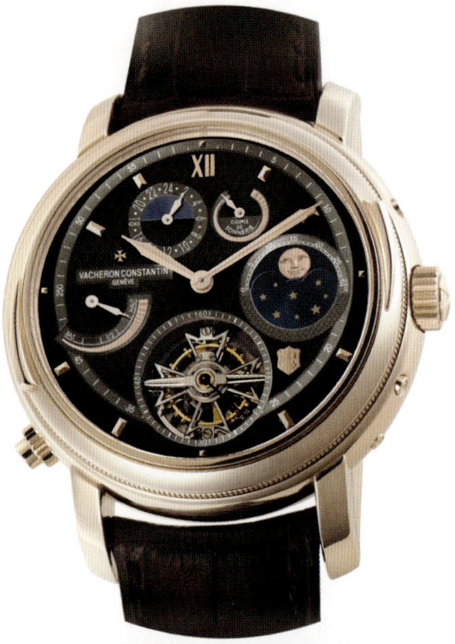

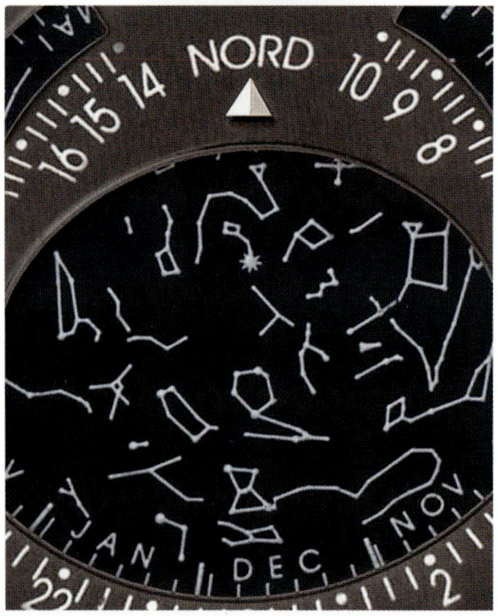

A "secret signature" on the dial of the Tour de l'Ile, at the 12 o'clock hour marker, reads "1755 - 2005". The watch was produced in 2005 to celebrate the 250th anniversary of Vacheron Constantin, and the name of the piece is in reference to a location in Geneva where the brand had its headquarters for almost 200 years.

When it was released, the Tour de l'Ile was the most complicated wristwatch ever produced. In fact, the case of the watch has dials on both sides, as Vacheron Constantin felt there was too much information to display on just one face. Celebrated by the larger watch industry when it debuted, the Tour de l'Ile contains 834 parts and features 16 complications.

Vacheron Constantin claims to have dedicated over 10,000 hours to the research and development of the timepiece, and very few were ever made. Rendered in a classic style, based on an historic Vacheron Constantin timepiece from 1926, the Tour de l'Ile is a perfect example of timeless classicism and extreme mechanical complexity.

The front side of the Tour de l'Ile begins with hour and minutes hands that aren't quite centred, being positioned just north of the centre of the dial, though the hour markers are properly positioned. A large open tourbillon spins on the dial, which also features a smiling Moon-phase indicator, power reserve indicators (for the time and as a torque indicator for the sonnerie functions), and AM/PM indicator.

The bezel of the case is used to start a minute repeater function inside the watch, which, when activated, sounds the time using a series of chimes. The reserve side of the Tour de l'Ile has even more indications that the front side. There, Vacheron Constantin offers a perpetual calendar, sunrise and sunset times, equation of time, and a celestial star map (set to a particular place on Earth just as the sunrise and sun-set times are).

Imminently wearable, the Tour de l'Ile is a masterpiece of watchmaking and proof that Vacheron Constantin knows how to please watch collectors with a timepiece both incredibly challenging and eminently graceful. Vacheron Constantin only produced seven Tour de l'Ile watches. No two were quite alike, with each bearing distinct colours or decorative elements.

* Sold at auction for CHF1,876,250 at Antiquorum, Geneva in April 2005.

LOISEAU – 1F4

$1 400 000

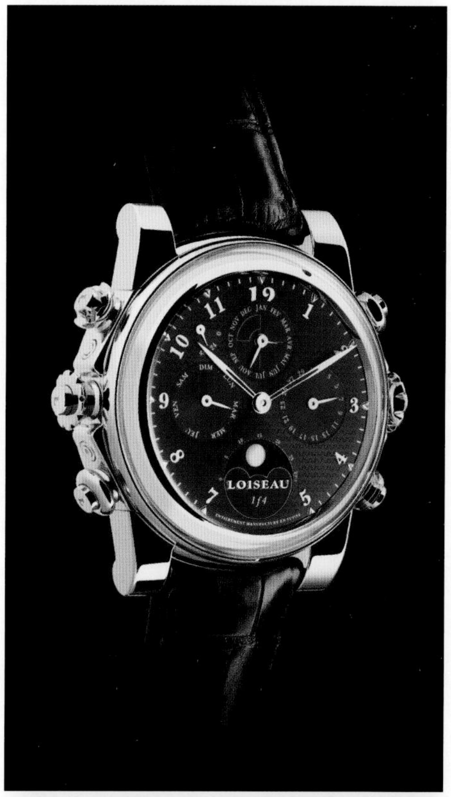

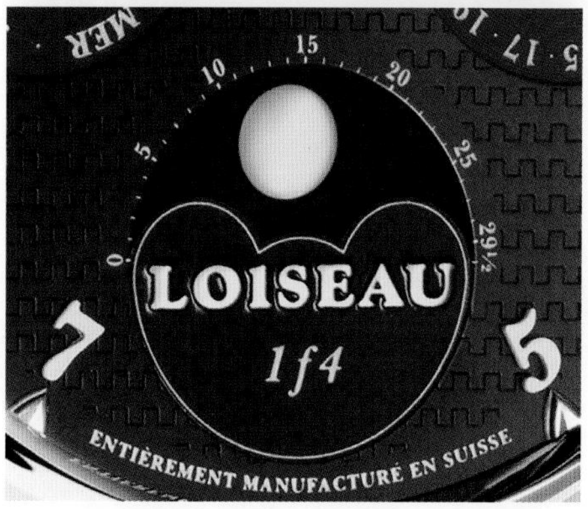

The esteemed watchmaker and pioneer of modern horological advancement – Dominique Loiseau – died in 2013, at what was arguably the apex of his career. People like Dominique are often responsible for the most impressive timepieces released by the "big brands". Unsung heroes who toil, often in secrecy, to produce imaginative luxuries, sold for unimaginable prices; recognition for their work is often only appreciated by a small group of elite fans who are familiar with the breadth of their creations.

For much of his career, Loiseau worked in the background, for brands such as Omega, Blancpain and, towards the end of his life, Girard-Perregaux. In 2012, however, he finally launched an extremely ambitious eponymously named brand that would produce just two watches per year.

While at Blancpain, Loiseau was responsible for the design and release of a timepiece known as the 1735. When it debuted, it was the world's most complicated wristwatch and commanded a price of over $1,000,000. It was so complicated to assemble, with a movement of almost 750 parts, that only a handful of skilled watchmakers could even attempt to produce it. Blancpain originally released the Loiseau-designed 1735 watch in 1989 and only built about 30 of them. It was discontinued in around 2011.

For his own brand, Loiseau wanted to break his own record and once again produce a wristwatch that could be called the "world's most complicated". In 2012 he debuted the 1f4, named after a move in Chess, that contains so many features that it needs to display them on two dials. Thus, both the front and back of the watch have a dial. A unique system in the lugs allow them to pivot, so that the watch can be worn with either side face up.

In total, the 1f4 contains about 32 different complications and has 16 hands across both faces. On the blue-coloured dial, the watch displays the time, perpetual calendar, and Moon-phase display, along with a power reserve for the chiming system. On the other side, you have a display for two time zones, a split second chronograph, and AM/PM indicator, the equation of time, and an exposed flying tourbillon. The movement also contains minute repeater, petite sonnerie, and grande sonnerie chiming functions. It features automatic winding, via a secret peripheral rotor, that can only be seen moving because of a diamond spinning around the bezel.

Loiseau designed the 1f4 as an exercise in efficiently combining more features than anyone else into a wearable, usable watch. With almost 900 parts, only two 1f4 watches a year were made. Upon its release the concept polarised collectors, but many have since embraced the existence of the timepiece and thus, the Loiseau brand lives on.

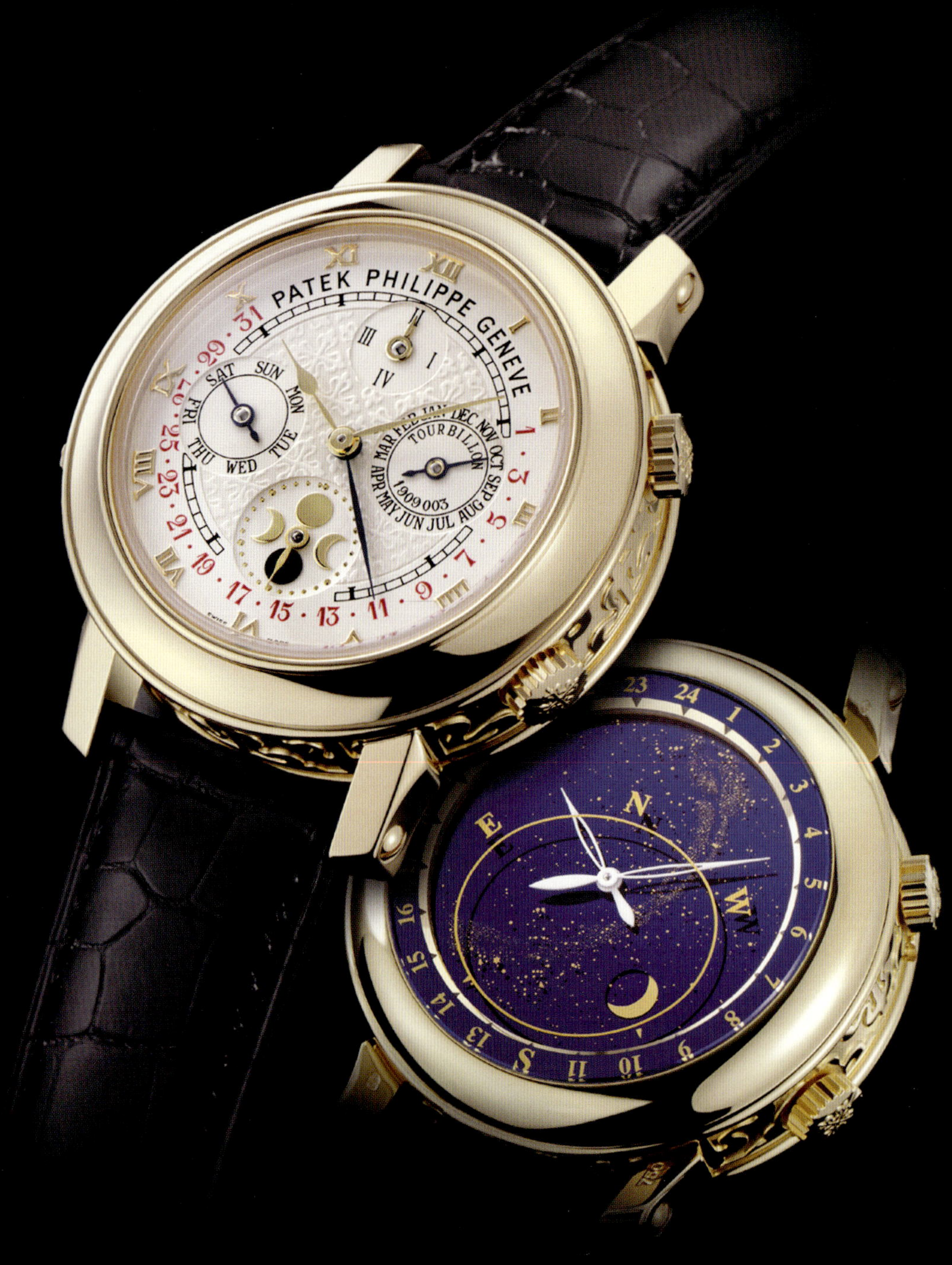

PATEK PHILIPPE – SKY MOON TOURBILLON 5002P

$ 1 450 000*

This is the most complicated wristwatch produced by Patek Philippe. Its high value has been tested at auction, where a Sky Moon Tourbillon sold for almost $1.5 million. Having been produced in a few versions, the original Sky Moon Tourbillon was released in 2001. The watch features a dial on each side of the case, with functions on both sides. Inside, the watch has an extremely complicated and thoroughly decorated movement containing 686 parts.

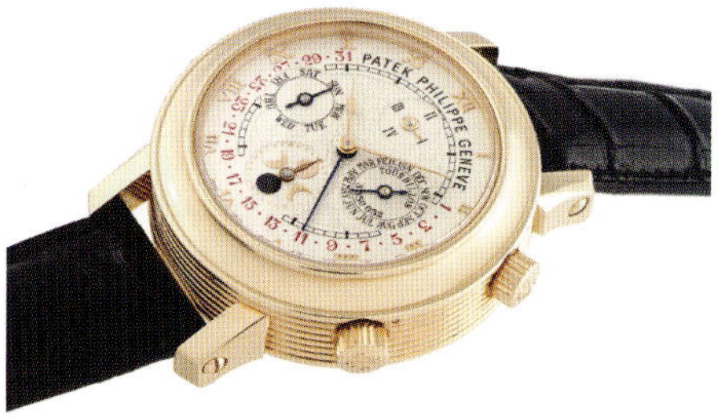

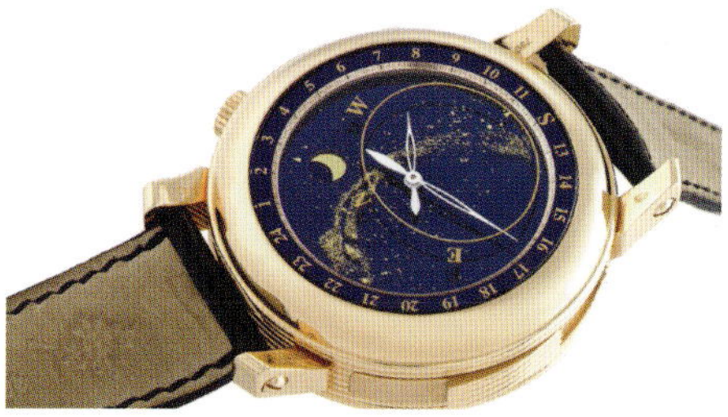

Patek Philippe designed the Sky Moon Tourbillon to incorporate many of the world's most complicated watch functions, all in a single timepiece. The first side of the watch features the time, phase of the Moon, and calendar with day, retrograde date, month, and leap year. On the reverse dial is a map of the night sky, which offers a range of astronomical complications. There the 5002P watch indicates sidereal time on the main dial, the phase of the Moon, and movement of the Moon through the sky. Inside the watch is a tourbillon style escapement in the movement, as well as a minute repeater complication that indicates the time, upon activation, as a series of chimes.

The 5002G is about 43mm wide and has been offered in precious metals such as 18k white, rose, or yellow gold and platinum. In 2013, Patek Philippe developed a new version of the Sky Moon Tourbillon, known as the 6002G, with a hand-painted enamel dial and fully engraved and decorated case.

* Sold at auction for CHF1,202,500 at Antiquorum, Geneva in May 2013.

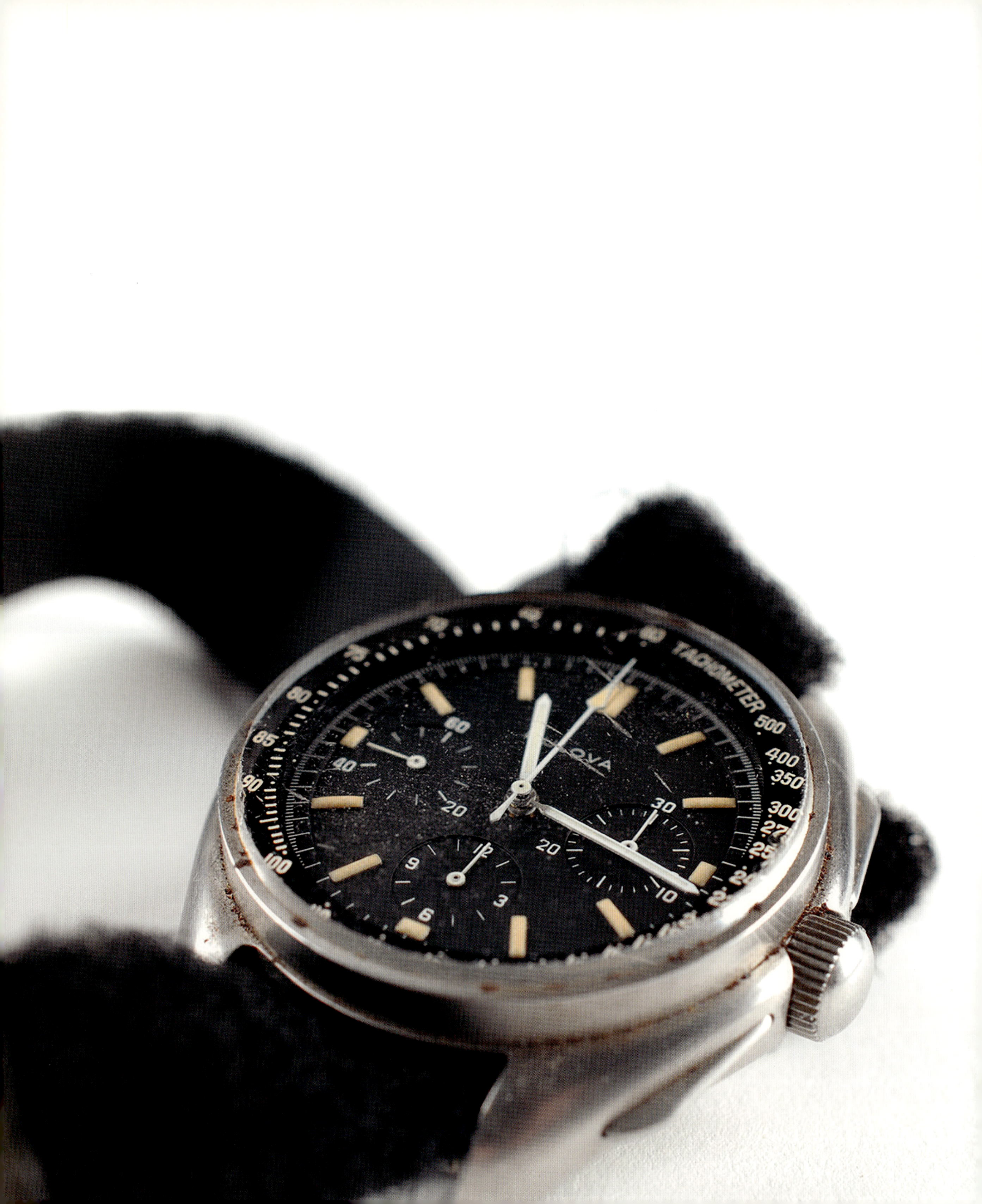
TACHOMETER

BULOVA — CHRONOGRAPH 88510/01 WORN BY APOLLO 15 ASTRONAUT DAVE SCOTT ON THE MOON

$ 1 625 000

ON NUMEROUS OCCASIONS, DAVE SCOTT HIMSELF HAS WAXED POETIC ON THE IMPORTANCE OF TIME FOR ASTRONAUTS.

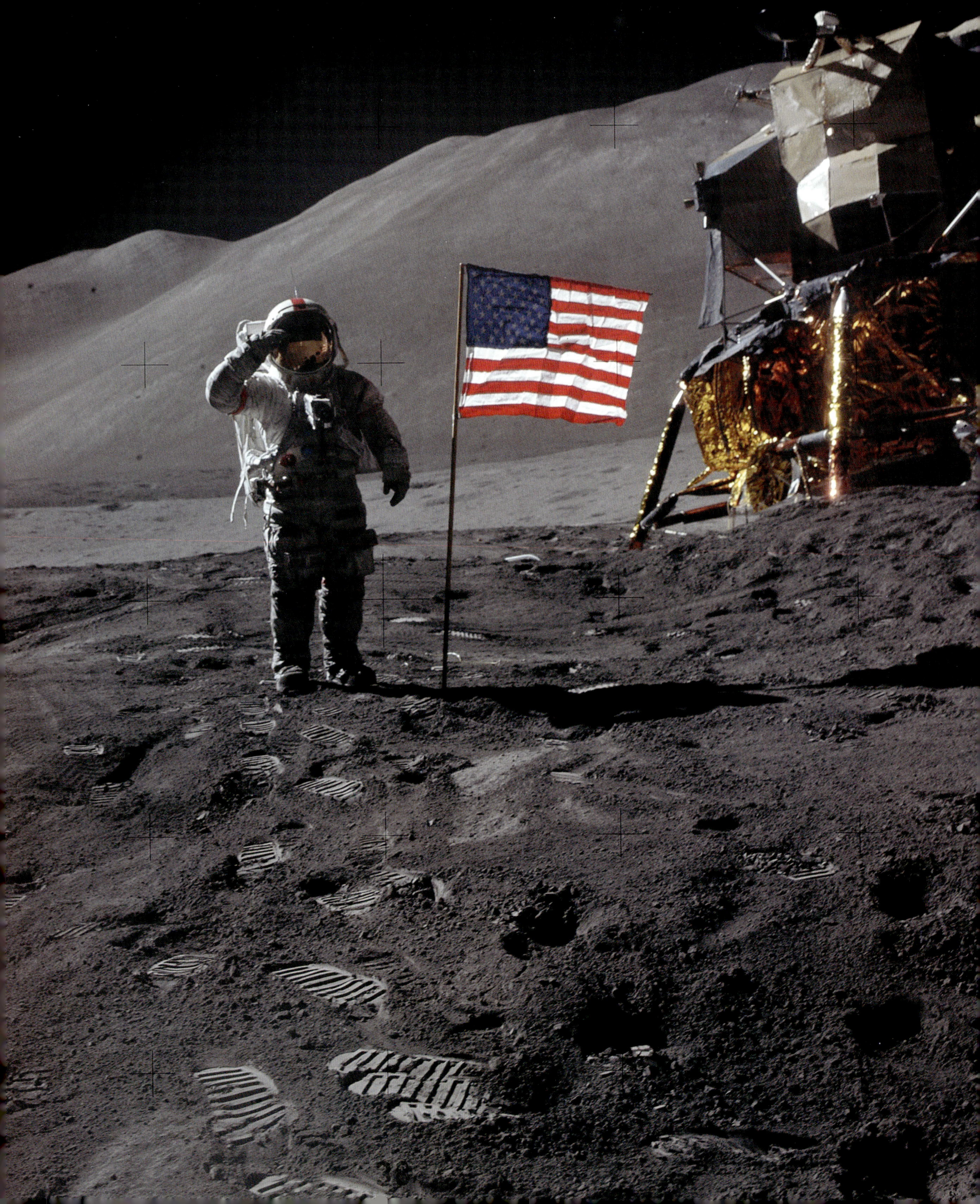

With a starting bid at $50,000, a unique Bulova Chronograph timepiece sold for $1,625,000 at an RR Auction sale in Boston in 2015. What made this watch special was the fact that it was worn by American astronaut Dave Scott during a NASA Apollo mission in 1971, making it the only privately owned timepiece to have travelled to the Moon.

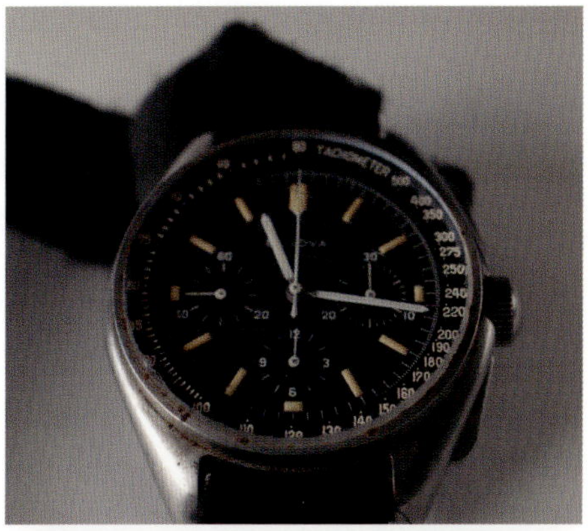

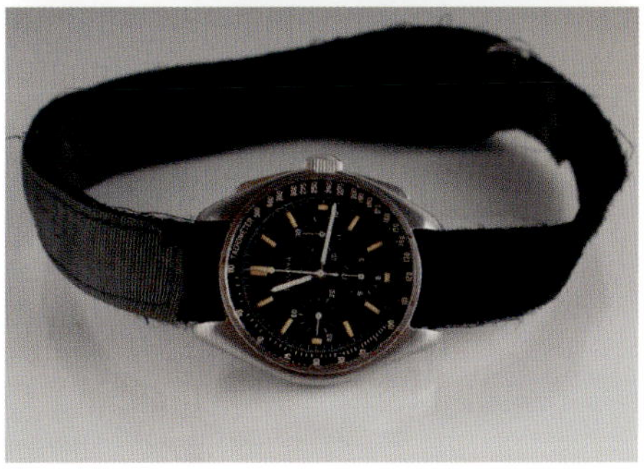

Many timepiece enthusiasts associate Omega watches with those worn by astronauts during the Apollo missions, as the Omega Speedmaster Professional Chronograph won the bid to be the official timepiece for American astronauts (much to the chagrin of Bulova – an American company at the time – who lost the bid). Nevertheless, that didn't stop Bulova from continuing to produce "Moon-worthy" timepieces, and they apparently provided at least one to Dave Scott as a backup timepiece. Keeping track of time was (and continues to be) extremely vital during space missions, so having a properly functioning timepiece when in the spacecraft, and especially on the lunar surface, was absolutely crucial. Without a watch on their wrist – like a diver underwater – astronauts would not be able to track crucial information, such as remaining oxygen levels or remaining mission time. On numerous occasions, Dave Scott himself has waxed poetic on the importance of time for astronauts.

As fate would have it, while walking on the lunar surface, Dave Scott's primary (government-issued) Omega Speedmaster watch sustained damage which caused the crystal to come off, rendering it no longer mission-reliable. Having his privately owned Bulova Chronograph with him, Scott was able to resume his scientific exploration of the Moon's surface with the backup timepiece. Both mission photography, as well as exhaustive notes from Dave Scott himself, proved the authenticity of the watch's inclusion in the mission on the Moon (famously worn on the outside of space suits), as well as its importance to Commander Scott during the mission itself. When sold at auction, the Bulova Chronograph reportedly still contained traces of lunar dust on its surface.

The various Omega timepieces worn on the Moon and during other Apollo missions continue to technically be US Government property – and thus would not be eligible for private sale. This fact meant that Dave Scott's Bulova Chronograph was the only timepiece worn on the Moon that private collectors could feasibly own. Such exclusivity, combined with the incredible scientific and historic importance of the Apollo missions, help explain the timepiece's value to collectors at auction. Not long after the 2015 auction, Bulova released a modern re-creation of the same chronograph-style watch for a much more accessible price of just a few hundred dollars.

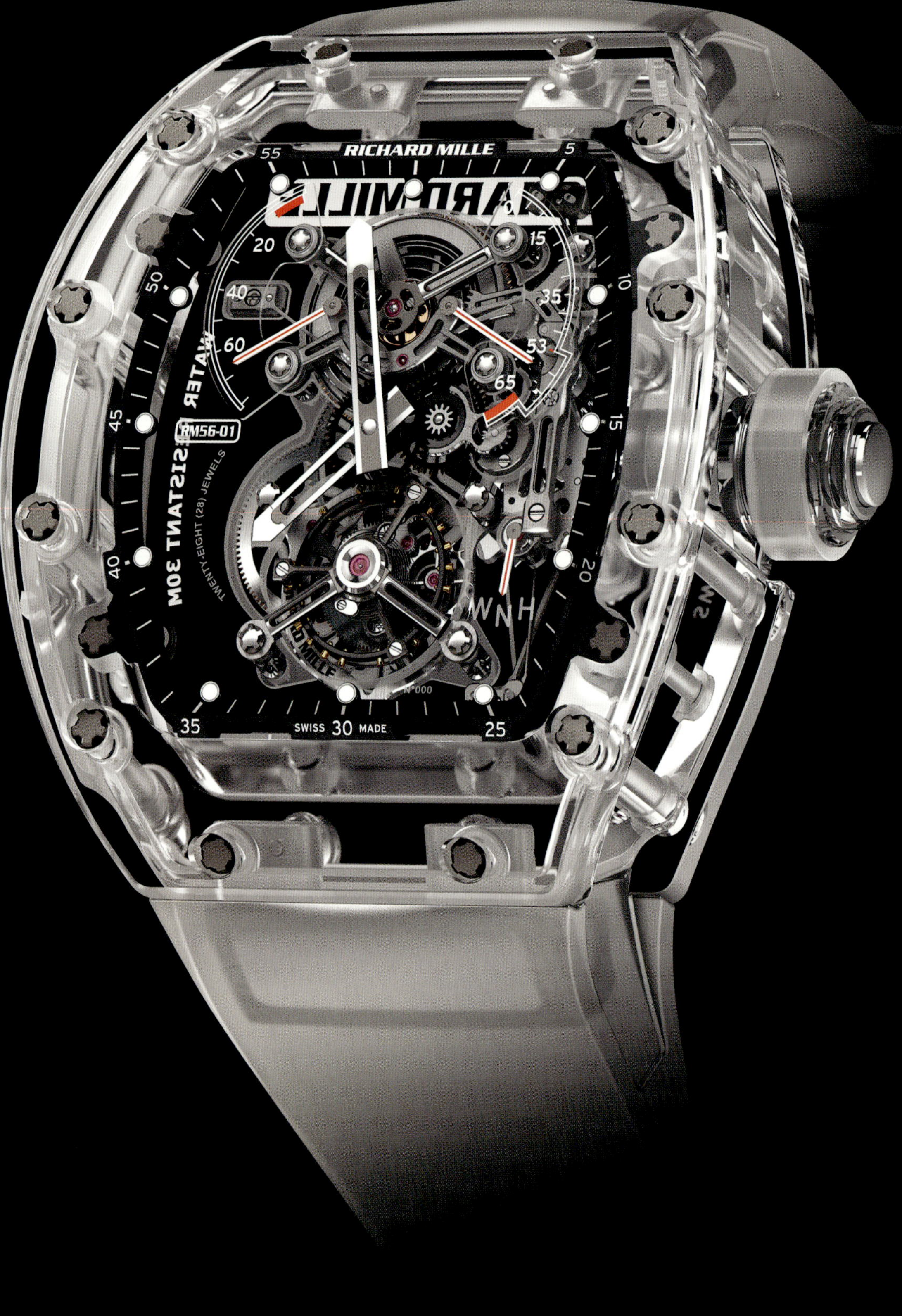
RICHARD MILLE
RM56-01
TWENTY-EIGHT (28) JEWELS
SWISS 30 MADE

RICHARD MILLE — RM 56-01 SAPPHIRE

$ 1 700 000

RICHARD MILLE CLAIMS EACH OF THE RM 56-01 CASES TOOK ABOUT 1,000 HOURS TO PRODUCE.

In the 1980s wristwatches really started to become popular, thanks to the deployment of synthetic sapphire crystal technologies. Traditionally speaking, the most delicate part of a watch (sometimes more so than the movement), was the crystal, and this really became an issue with wrist versus pocket watches. That is because pocket watches could have a closing cover to protect the crystal, which, on wristwatches, was extremely exposed.

Glass was often used as a crystal material, but it could break and shatter with ease. For a large portion of the 20th century, acrylic was relied upon due to its tensile strength, though it was easy to scratch. When synthetic sapphire could be grown and cut into rings to be put over watch dials, it really changed the game when it came to timepiece durability. Sapphire is much more scratch resistant that steel; so much so that watchmakers often claim that it is "virtually scratch proof". Sapphire does, however, require special machines to cut it, which is why most of the time it is simple and round.

A rather important aspect of modern watch design is to allow the watch's insides to be exposed. Mechanical watch movements are often beautiful, and are a major reason why people invest in a mechanical movement-based timepiece. So a watch case that was highly scratch resistant, as well as totally transparent proved to be something ultra-high-end watchmaker Richard Mille could not resist.

In about 2012, Richard Mille released a version of its RM056 watch in a case made of pure sapphire crystal. The RM 56-01 was as controversial as it was expensive. Sapphire crystal is a common material, but the reason for the high price was the time and effort involved in actually making the case. Milling and drilling sapphire crystal often causes it to crack or shatter. The case of this Richard Mille watch involves a range of complex angles and curves as well as necessary holes for the screws that hold it all together. This means that an incredible amount of time and patience was required to produce each case. Richard Mille claims each of the RM 56-01 cases took about 1,000 hours to produce.

Inside the watch is a unique tourbillon-based movement, which includes both a power reserve and a torque indicator. The latter is a relatively obscure feature that refers to the torque of the mainspring. Used with the power reserve indicator, it helps watch movement enthusiasts keep the mechanical movement as accurate as possible. A truly exotic specimen of watchmaking, the RM 56-01 watch was limited to just five pieces.

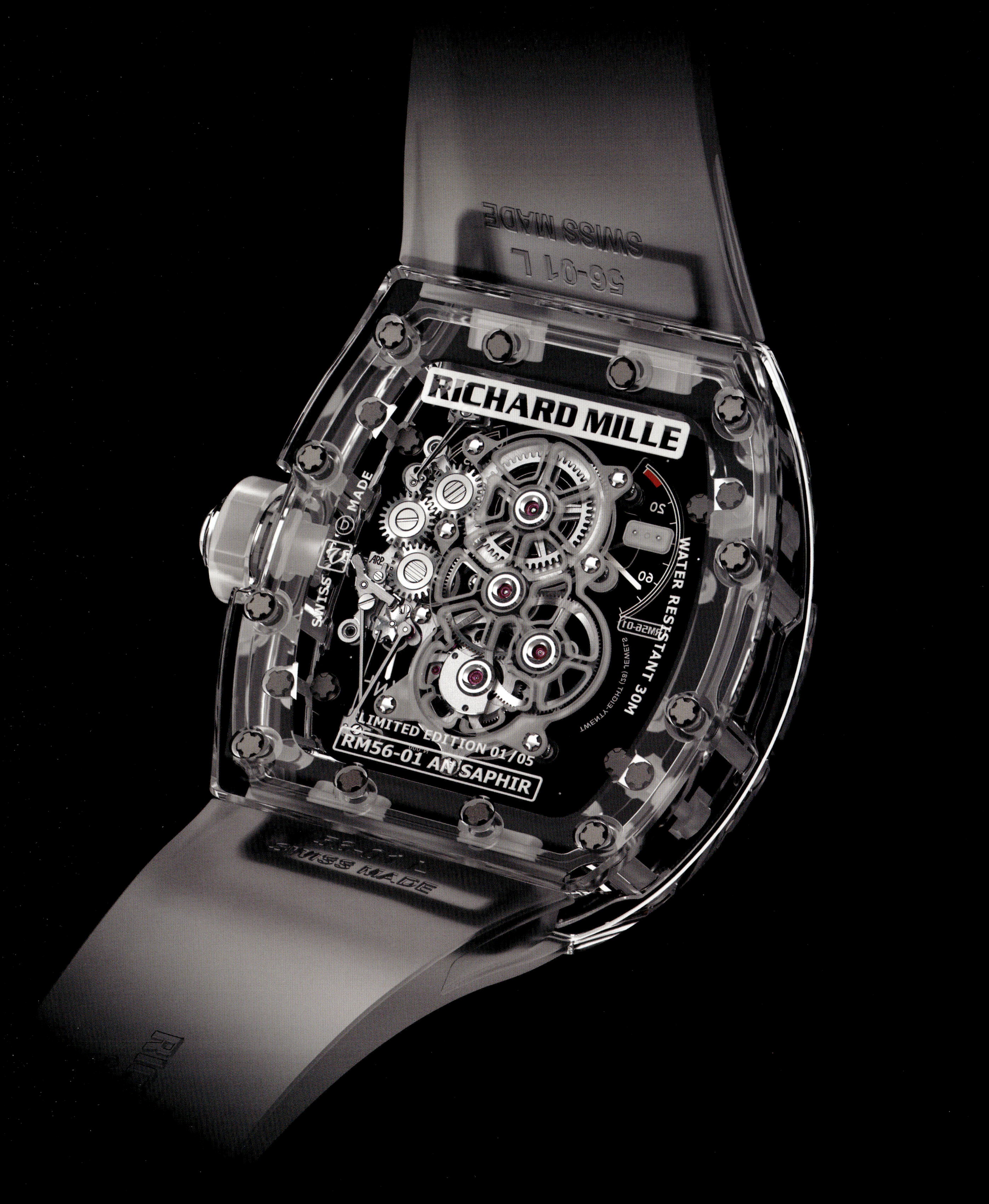
RICHARD MILLE
SWISS MADE
WATER RESISTANT 30M
LIMITED EDITION 01/05
RM56-01 AN SAPHIR

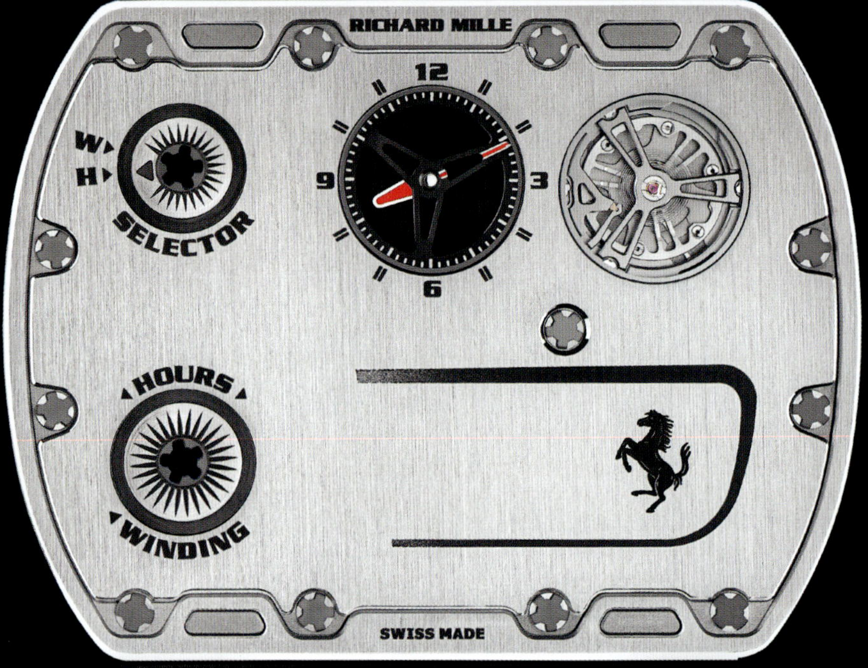

RICHARD MILLE — RM UP-01 FERRARI

$ 1 888 000

Richard Mille was not the timepiece brand that enthusiasts expected to release a watch boasting to be (as of writing in mid-2022) the world's thinnest. Known for typically large and elaborately designed modern ultra-luxury watches, Richard Mille decided to announce their first product collaboration with Ferrari automobiles by releasing a titanium wristwatch that measures just 1.75mm thick. That is 0.05mm thinner than the previous "world's thinnest watch" – the 1.8mm-thick Bulgari Octo Finissimo Ultra; introduced only a few months before the Richard Mille RM UP-01 Ferrari.

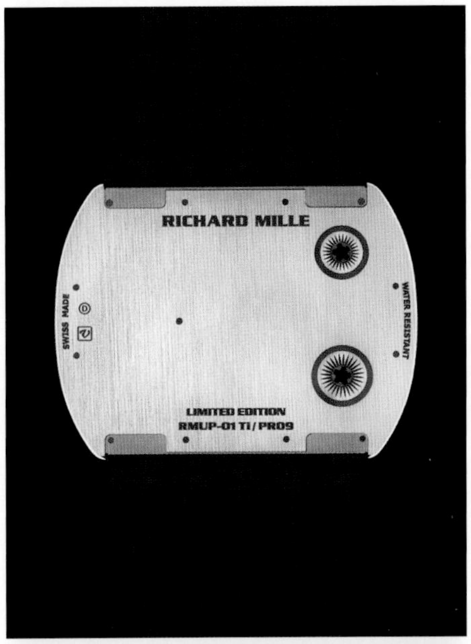

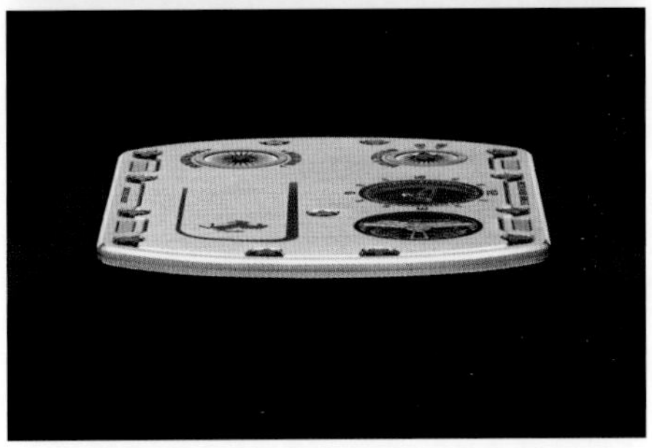

Little about the RM UP-01 Ferrari looks or functions like most other Richard Mille timepieces. The movement used in the watch is a tour-de-force of thin technical prowess, developed with Richard Mille's longtime mechanical-movement collaborator – APRP in Switzerland. While the mechanism and watch case are integrated together to save space, it is claimed that the movement is under 1.2mm in thickness. This required the development of a new, flatter regulation system as well as the total elimination of the crown. Accordingly, in order to set the time or even wind the watch, wearers of the RM UP-01 Ferrari must use a specially provided tool for these tasks.

Reading the time via just the hours and minutes is the exclusive function presented in the watch, displayed via a subsidiary dial on the front of the case adjacent to a view of the slim regulation system. Distinctive Richard Mille screws populate the periphery of the case, which looks vaguely like other Richard Mille product shapes, except that this model is oriented on its side. Fragile when compared to many other timepieces, the RM UP-01 Ferrari nevertheless boasts impressive performance characteristics, including a movement that is able to resist an acceleration of up to 5,000g, as well as an incredibly light overall weight of just 30 grams. Water resistance, however, is a scant 10 metres.

According to Richard Mille, over 6,000 hours of development went into the conception and execution of the RM UP-01 Ferrari, of which only 150 pieces will be produced. Unlike many other products dedicated to Ferrari automobiles, this watch isn't intended as a salute to the Italian maker's famed sports cars. Rather, the watch celebrates mutual values between the two brands, such as a no-compromise approach to engineering as well as always seeking to push performance boundaries further. The only nod to Ferrari on the Richard Mille watch is the placement of the prancing pony logo on the face. As measured by dimensions, the RM UP-01 Ferrari watch costs over $1,000 per micron of thickness.

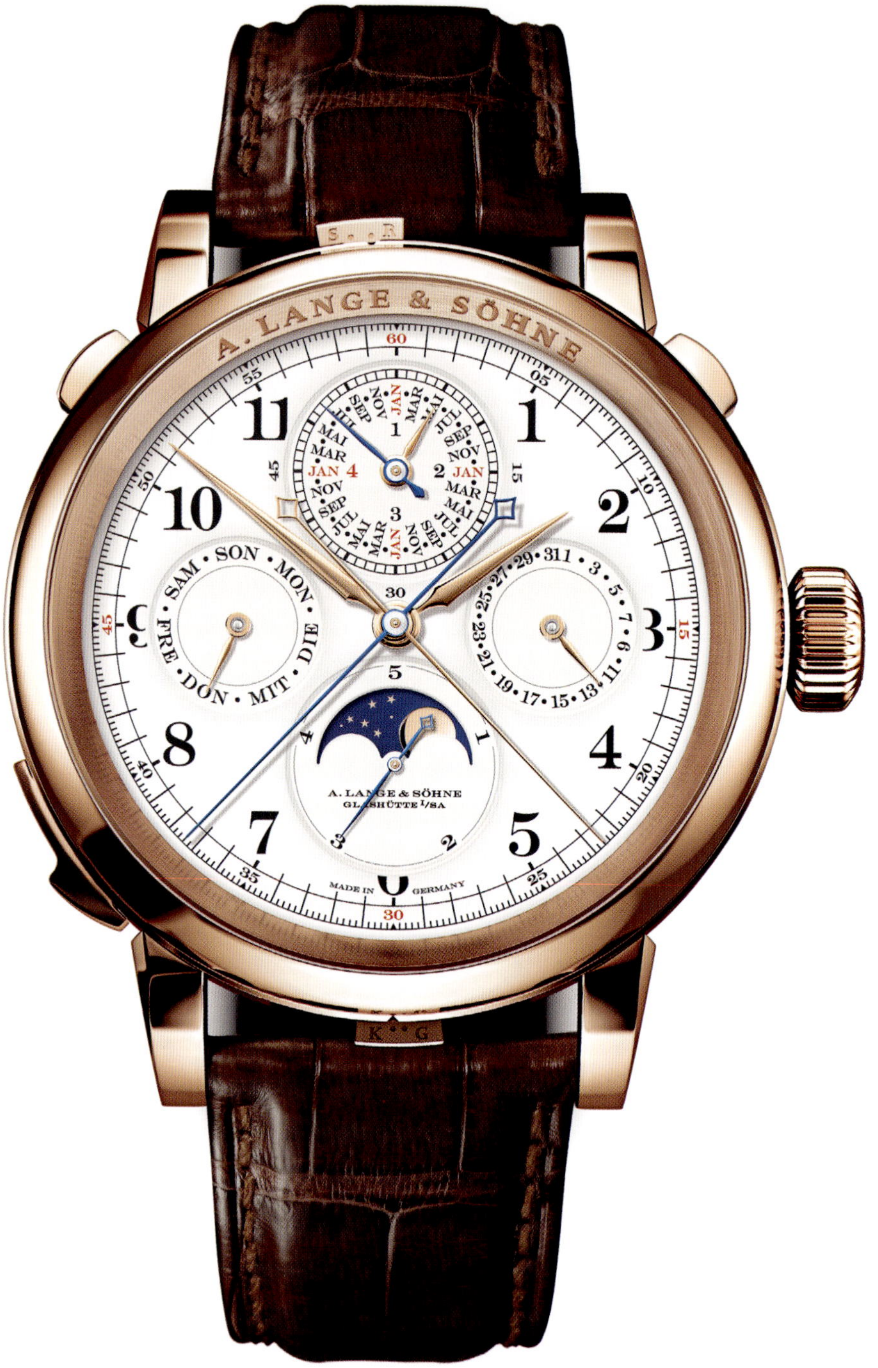

A. LANGE & SÖHNE — GRANDE COMPLICATION

$ 1 900 000

The small town of Glashutte, in Saxony, is home to most of Germany's finest watchmakers. A. Lange & Söhne is considered by many to be the region's finest producer of traditional mechanical timepieces. Classic in style, A. Lange & Söhne takes great pride in the meticulous hand-decoration that each of their movements receives. In 2013, A. Lange & Söhne released their most complicated watch to date, with the simply named "Grand Complication".

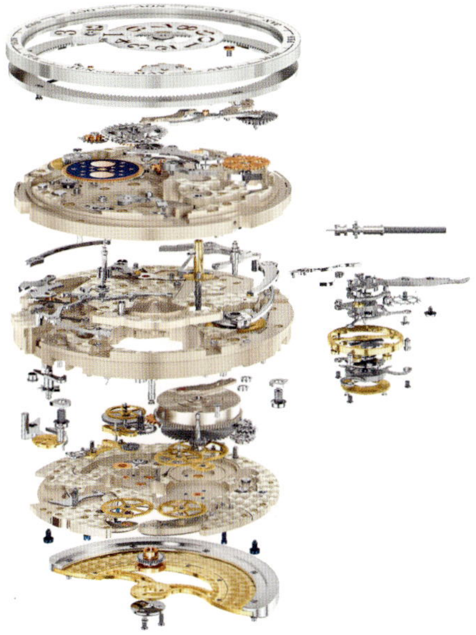

Generally speaking, "Grand Complication" is a term given to certain timepieces that combine, in a single movement, a series of traditionally very complex features. Collectors look for those watches that incorporate as many features as possible, and yet retain elegance in their design. The Grand Complication embodies much of what high-end collectors consider extremely valuable, including, among other features, a full perpetual calendar, chiming functions, a chronograph, and Moon-phase indication.

A perpetual calendar is one that takes into consideration the fact that, in leap years, February has 29 days. This watch displays the date, day of the week, month, and the leap year. The Grand Complication's chronograph is special for two reasons. Firstly, it is a split-second chronograph, which allows for brief timing of a second measurement; and secondly, it has a "flying seconds" hand, used to indicate the measured time down to a precision of 1/5 of a second.

Perhaps the most complex features in the Grand Complication are the chiming functions. The watch combines both grande and petite sonneries and a minute repeater. The minute repeater is a feature that, when activated, causes the watch to sound out the time in a series of chimes. Sonneries, on the other hand, automatically chime at specific intervals (such as on each hour).

The Grand Complication's movement comprises 876 parts, most of which are hand finished by A. Lange & Söhne. It comes in a rather large 50mm wide case and, because it is so complicated, only six pieces will ever be produced.

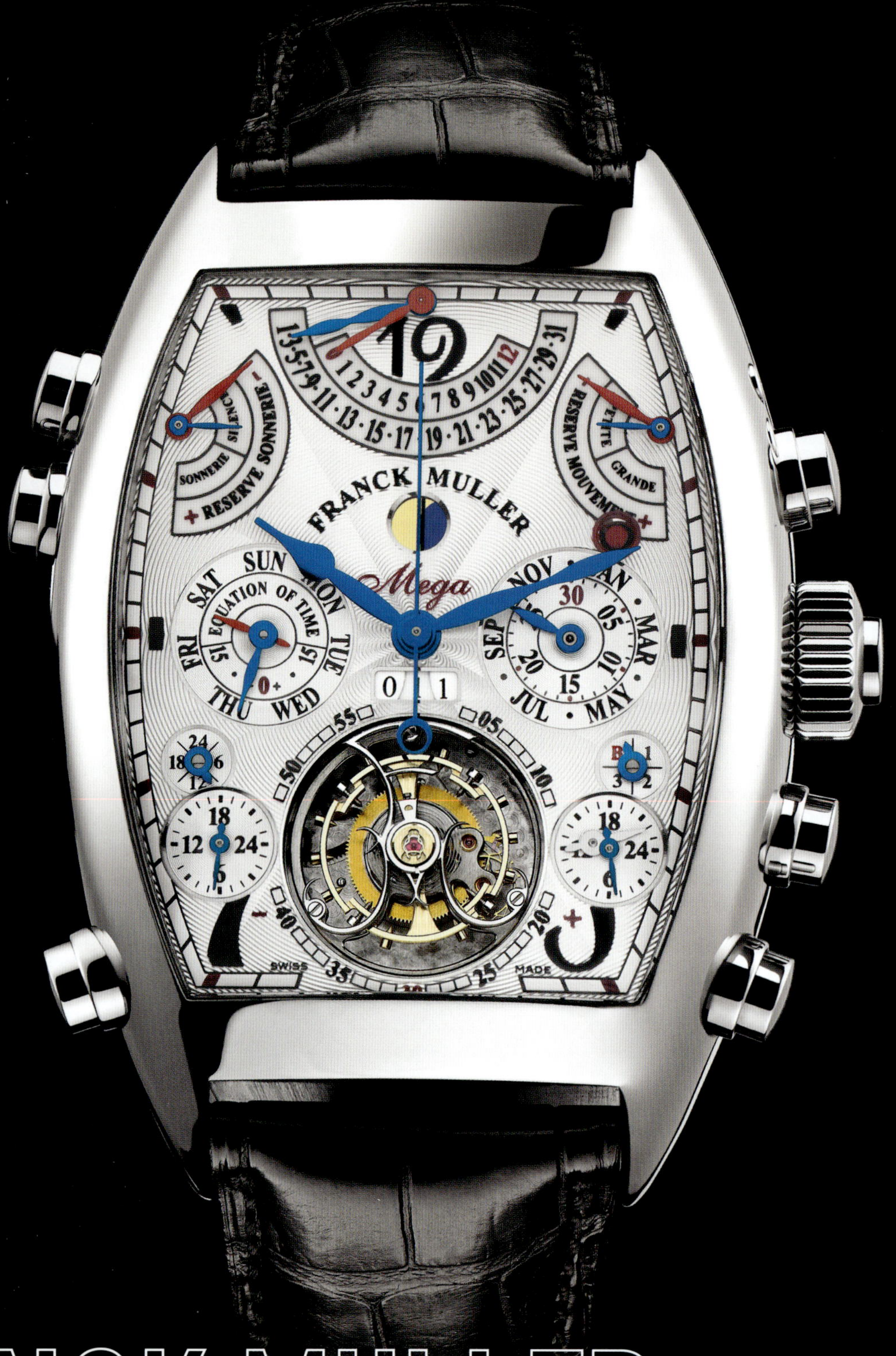

FRANCK MULLER — AETERNITAS MEGA 4

$ 2 400 000

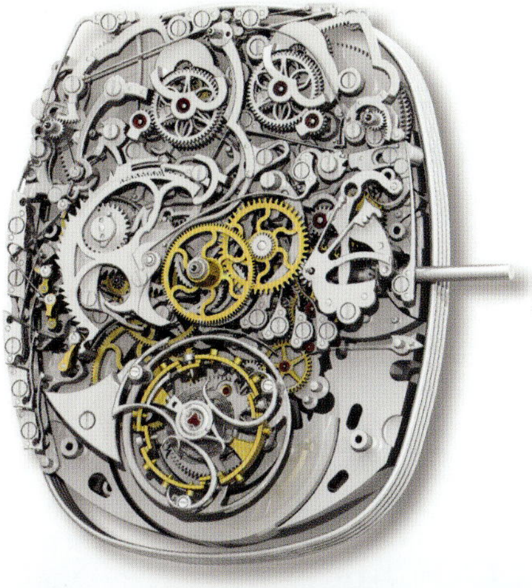

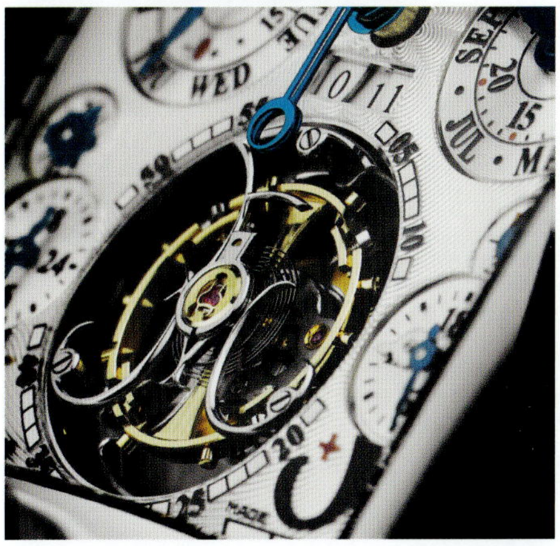

Before the Aeternitas Mega 4 there were the Megas 1,2, and 3. Each represented an extremely respectable achievement in horology; but with the Aeternitas Mega 4, Swiss watchmaker Franck Muller has created something for the history books. Penning something as the "world's most complicated watch" can be interpreted as a subjective description, but when Franck Muller used the term, in relation to the watch when it was finally released in 2010, no-one argued.

A massive platinum tonneau (barrel-shaped) case sits imposingly on the wrist, with its erratically placed seven pushers, and face littered with subdials and hands. Not exactly elegant, the Aeternitas Mega 4 is, nevertheless, glorious; an opus of horology that contains 36 distinct complications as part of a movement that contains a dizzying 1,483 parts.

What makes a timepiece such as this so difficult to design and produce is a basic limitation of space. Even though the case is 20mm thick, the movement of the Aeternitas Mega 4 proved incredibly challenging to arrange, and make room for all the features. A true icon of micro-engineering, the movement must also display information. A different and related challenge presented itself to Franck Muller when trying to design a dial to indicate everything that the watch keeps track of. Masterfully, the Aeternitas Mega 4 not only exists, but it actually works.

Most of the complications in the watch revolve around three distinct features. First there is the perpetual calendar that is accurate for 1000 years. Included, is a year indicator on the dial, as well as a Moon-phase indicator, also accurate for a 1000 years. Related astronomical data further indicates the equation of time (the difference between the civil and true solar time).

The timepiece would not be a grand complication without a chronograph, which is presented as a rattrapante (split-second) version in the mechanism. Franck Muller was, amazingly, also able to include both a minute repeater and related sonnerie functions, which use chimes to sound out the time. The watch also features a display of multiple time zones, and still has room for a window opening to the large-sized tourbillon-style escapement. Franck Muller tops the Aeternitas Mega 4 watch by including an automatic winding micro-rotor.

What is truly spectacular about the watch is that it isn't merely the world's most complicated, but it is actually designed to be wearable, and even useful. Franck Muller never put a specific limitation on production of the Aeternitas Mega 4, and even offers the watch with a range of customisation options, including a case lined with precious stones, and unique dial colours. It is very likely that each piece is produced on order only!

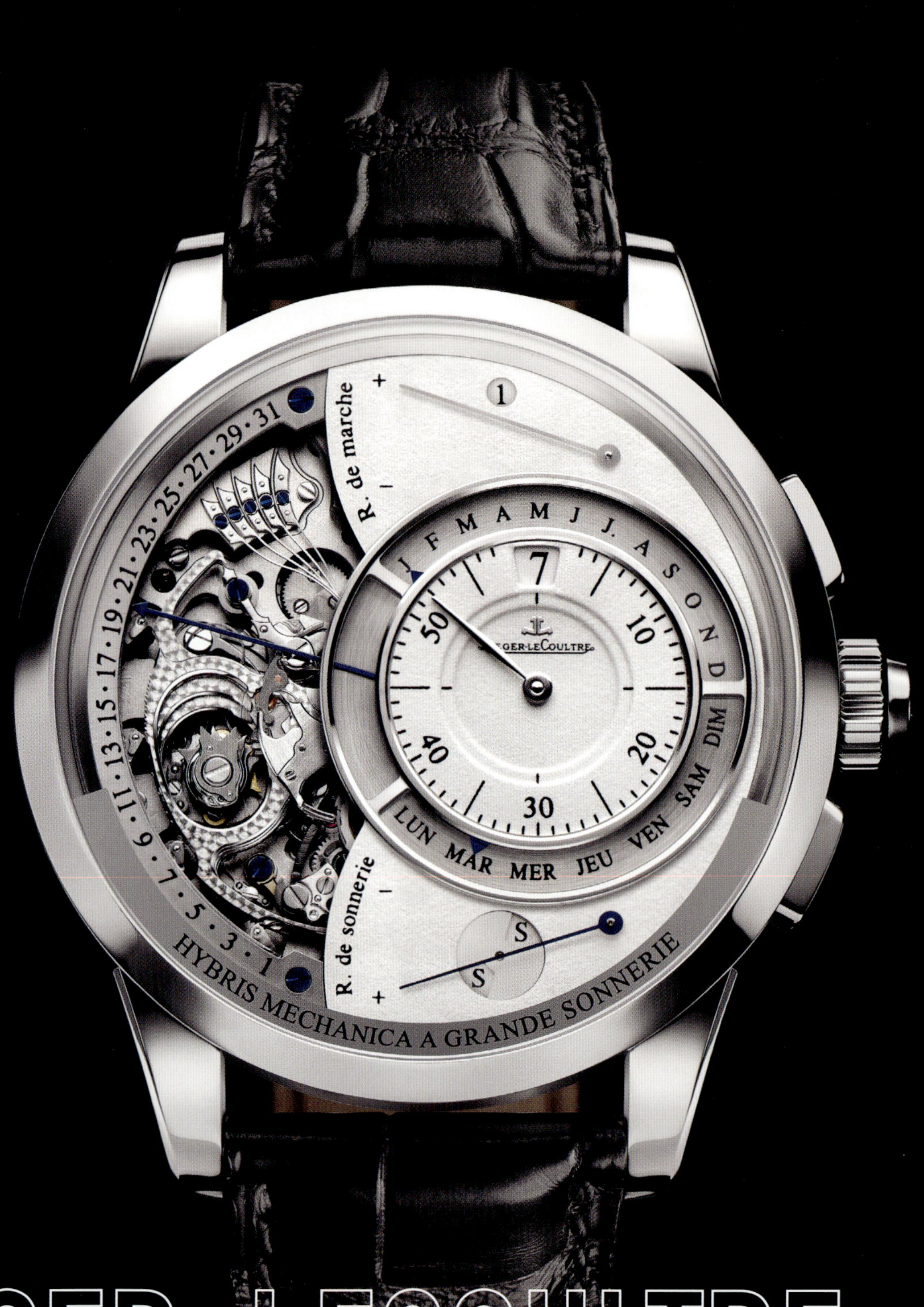

JAEGER-LECOULTRE — HYBRIS MECHANICA À GRANDE SONNERIE

$ 2 500 000

With almost 1,500 parts, and 27 complications, when the Hybris Mechanica à Grande Sonnerie watch was released in 2009, it held the title of "world's most complicated watch". A series of timepieces have held this title over the years and, as time goes on, the world's best watchmakers will claim to be new holders of the "world's most complicated watch" title. Nevertheless, each piece that has worn this crown – no matter for how long – deserves a great deal of praise.

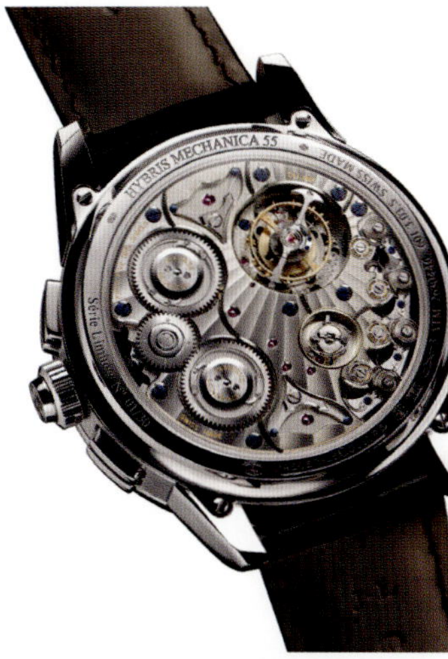

Jaeger-LeCoultre didn't just unseat the previous "world's most complicated watch" by adding one or two extra functions, but designed a completely novel mechanism that performed old tasks in some new ways. In a nutshell, the Hybris Mechanica is a musical watch with a perpetual calendar and a tourbillon, though it has peculiar inventions throughout.

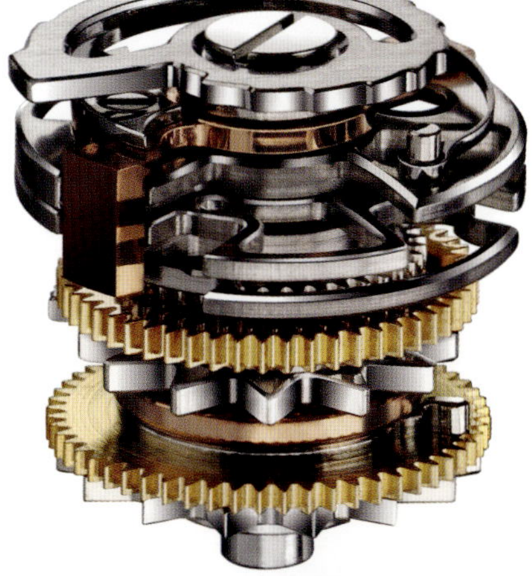

Jaeger-LeCoultre, when they began to design the Hybris Mechanica à Grande Sonnerie, discarded the standard manner of producing a minute repeater and sonnerie watch. These functions are designed, either automatically or on demand, to sound the time back to the wearer, using a series of musical chimes. An established mechanical design is employed by most watchmakers who create watches with these functions.

Jaeger-LeCoultre intended producing the best minute repeater and sonnerie watch ever (in terms of both quality and complexity), so the focuses in the watch were on the quality of the chimes (to be loud and clear), and the duration of the chimes (to perfectly emulate the style of the Westminster Chimes in London's Palace of Westminster). Jaeger-LeCoultre designed a new controlling system for the musical functions, dubbed by watchmakers as the "Infernal Tower" due to its devilishly complex construction. It comprises a three-tiered stack of gears, which when properly made, improves the reliability and precision of the minute repeater and sonnerie.

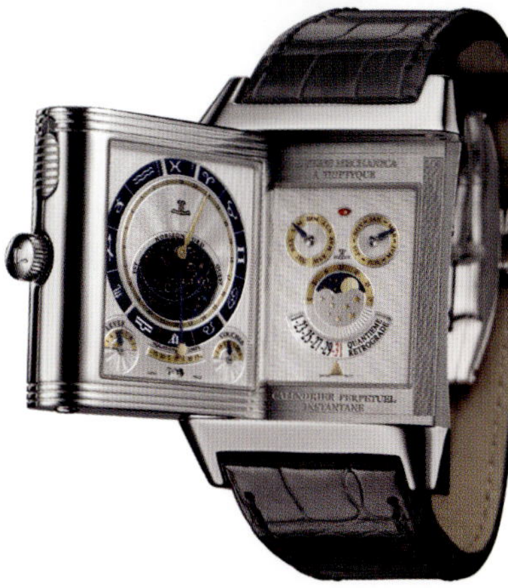

The traditional metal gongs, where small hammers strike in the movement to produce the chimes, are absent from this watch. The Hybris Mechanica à Grande Sonnerie includes a Jaeger-LeCoultre invention they call a "crystal gong". It attaches unique metallic gong structures to the sapphire crystal on the watch, which when matched to the 18k white gold case, yield an extremely bold and clear sound.

Purchasing a Hybris Mechanica à Grande Sonnerie is an experience that one is unlikely to forget. Available by direct order from Jaeger-LeCoultre, the watch comes with two other watches, as well as a very special box. In addition to the Hybris Mechanica à Grande Sonnerie piece, the set also comes with a Jaeger-leCoultre skeletonised Gyrotourbillon and a Reverso Grande Complication à Triptyque. On their own, each of these pieces is an incredibly important watch. The trio of luxury watches comes in a safe. A 1200 kg Jaeger-LeCoultre-branded safe, which incorporates a watch winder cabinet and a special sound system, so that, when it is in storage, the Hybris Mechanica à Grande Sonnerie can be heard striking from outside the safe.

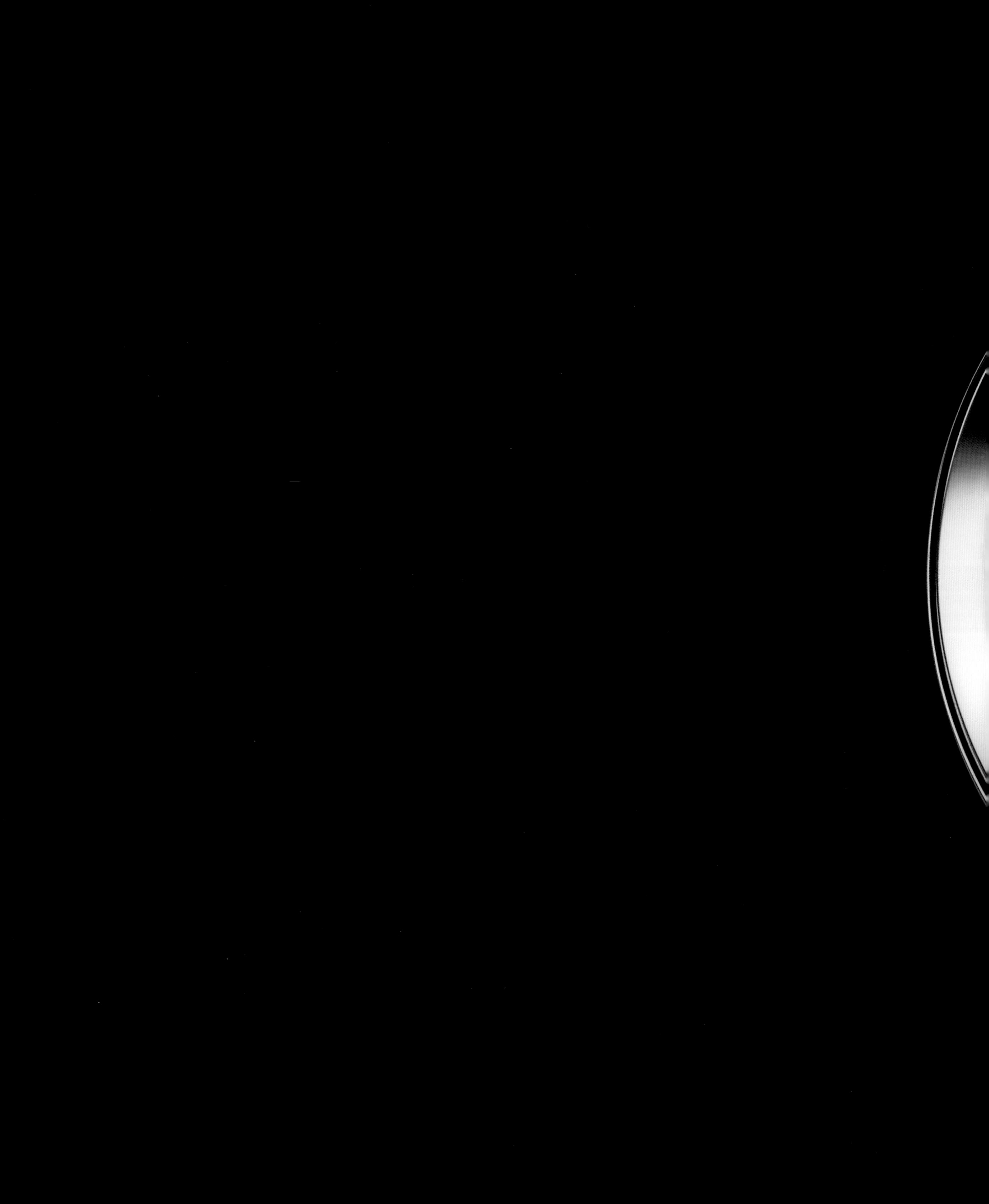

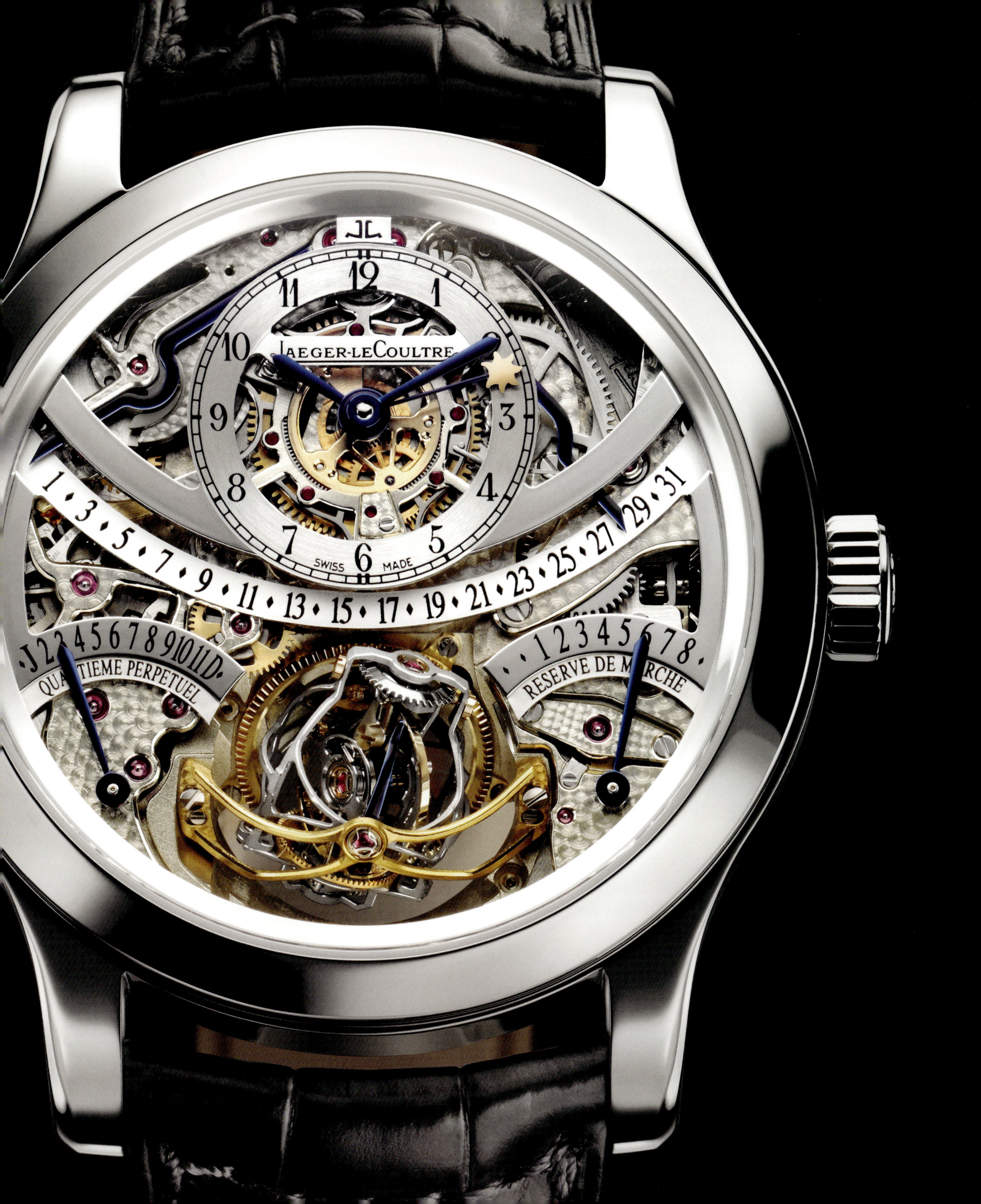

JAEGER-LECOULTRE
SWISS MADE
PERPETUEL
RESERVE DE

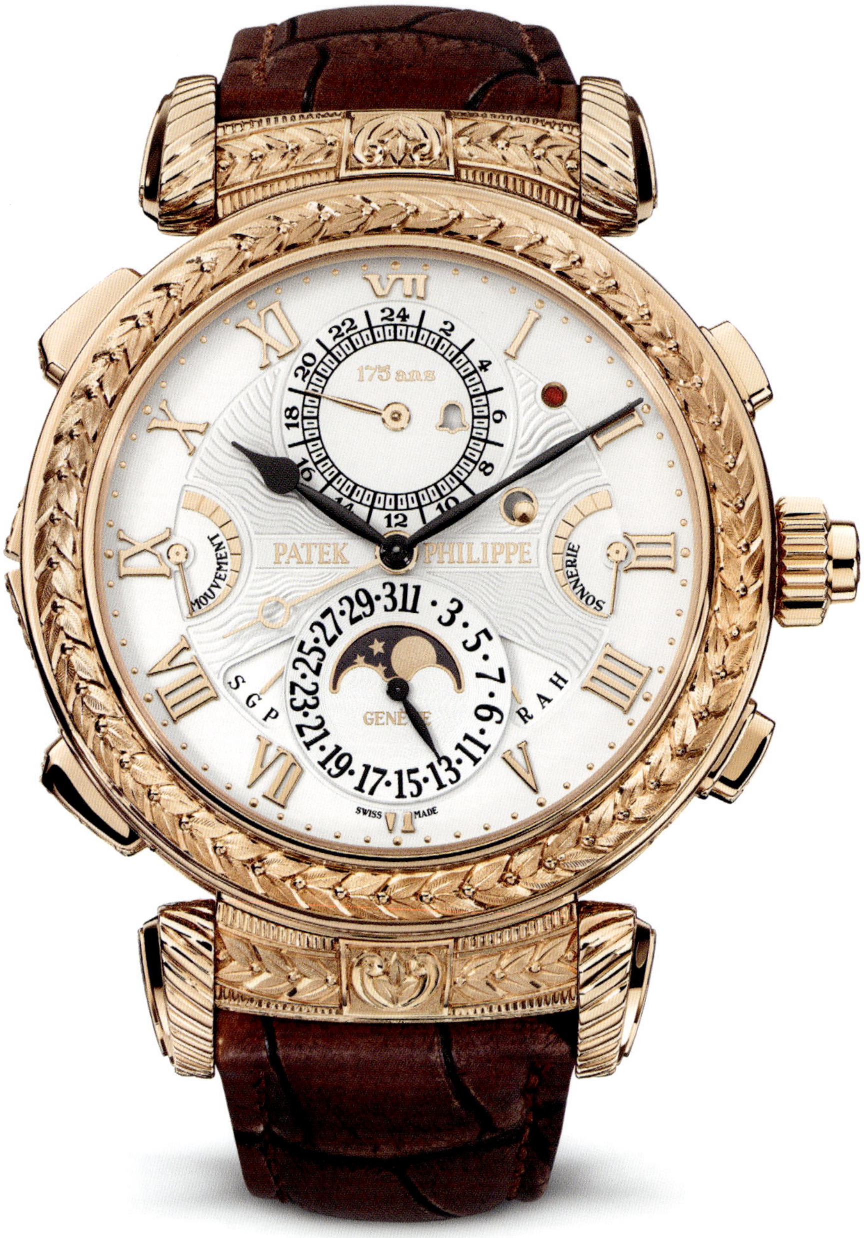

PATEK PHILIPPE – GRANDMASTER CHIME 5175

$ 2 600 000

Swiss Patek Philippe is no stranger to complicated timepieces. The brand's "grand complication" products mostly sold to select, "eligible" clients, and more than a few historic complicated Patek Philippe watches have achieved stunning results at private auctions. For the brand's 175th anniversary in 2014, Patek Philippe introduced their most complicated modern wristwatch to date: the boastfully named Grandmaster Chime (Reference 5175).

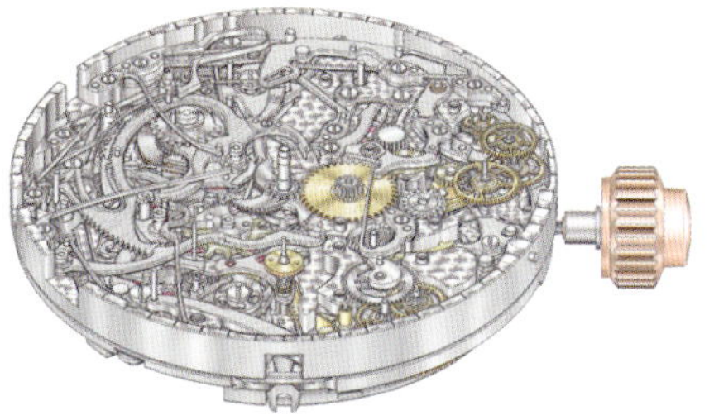

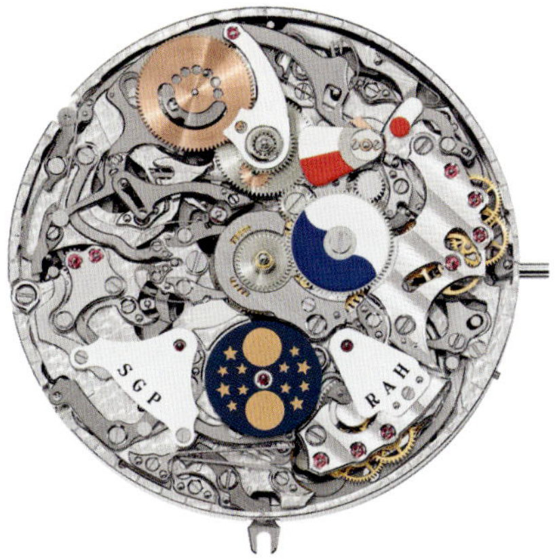

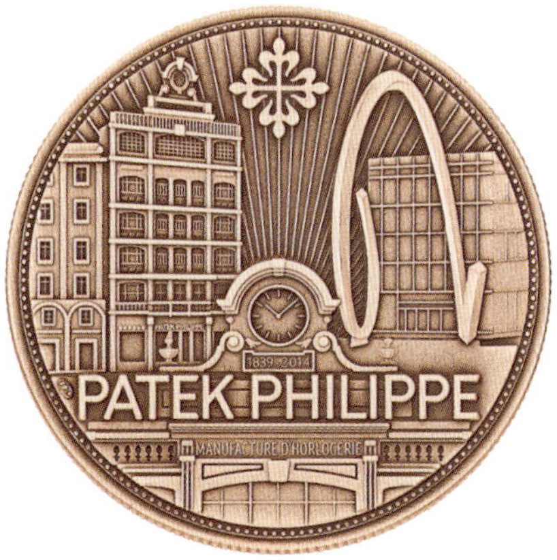

The debut version of the 5175 (Patek Philippe has since released a small assortment of styles) came with a lavishly hand-engraved case full of intricate detail and decoration. Non-engraved cases are also available, but at these prices why not go all the way? The Grandmaster Chime case is uncharacteristically large (for a Patek Philippe) at 47.4mm wide and 16.1 mm thick, in addition to having a system that allows the wearer to pivot the case which can be worn with either side face-up; an appropriate design given that the Grandmaster Chime is full of indicators on both the front and rear side of the timepiece.

The large-sized case (itself made from 214 components) is a necessity given that the in-house made (and amusingly long-titled) caliber 300 GS AL 36-750 QIS FUS IRM is composed of a whopping 1,366 parts, which is more than double or even triple many other "grand complication" watches. The movement contains a total of 20 different complications, and specialises (as the watch name implies) in chiming musical features. Reportedly, Patek Philippe's CEO personally listens to the chimes of the minute repeater in every watch, prior to them being delivered to customers. The Grandmaster Chime goes beyond the classic minute-repeater function of musically indicating the time on demand, with the addition of automated sonnerie chiming functions as well as a chiming system to indicate the date.

Patek Philippe's horological mastery is also displayed in how the information on the two dials is laid out. A focus on legibility helps users to understand the information provided by the many hands, dials and windows that might otherwise create unwanted confusion. Traditional timepiece design elements hide an effective user interface, which is controlled via a series of sliders, pushers and the crown, all of which line the periphery of the case. Those with big wrists and big budgets will best enjoy the endless angles of appreciation available in Patek Philippe's Grandmaster Chime.

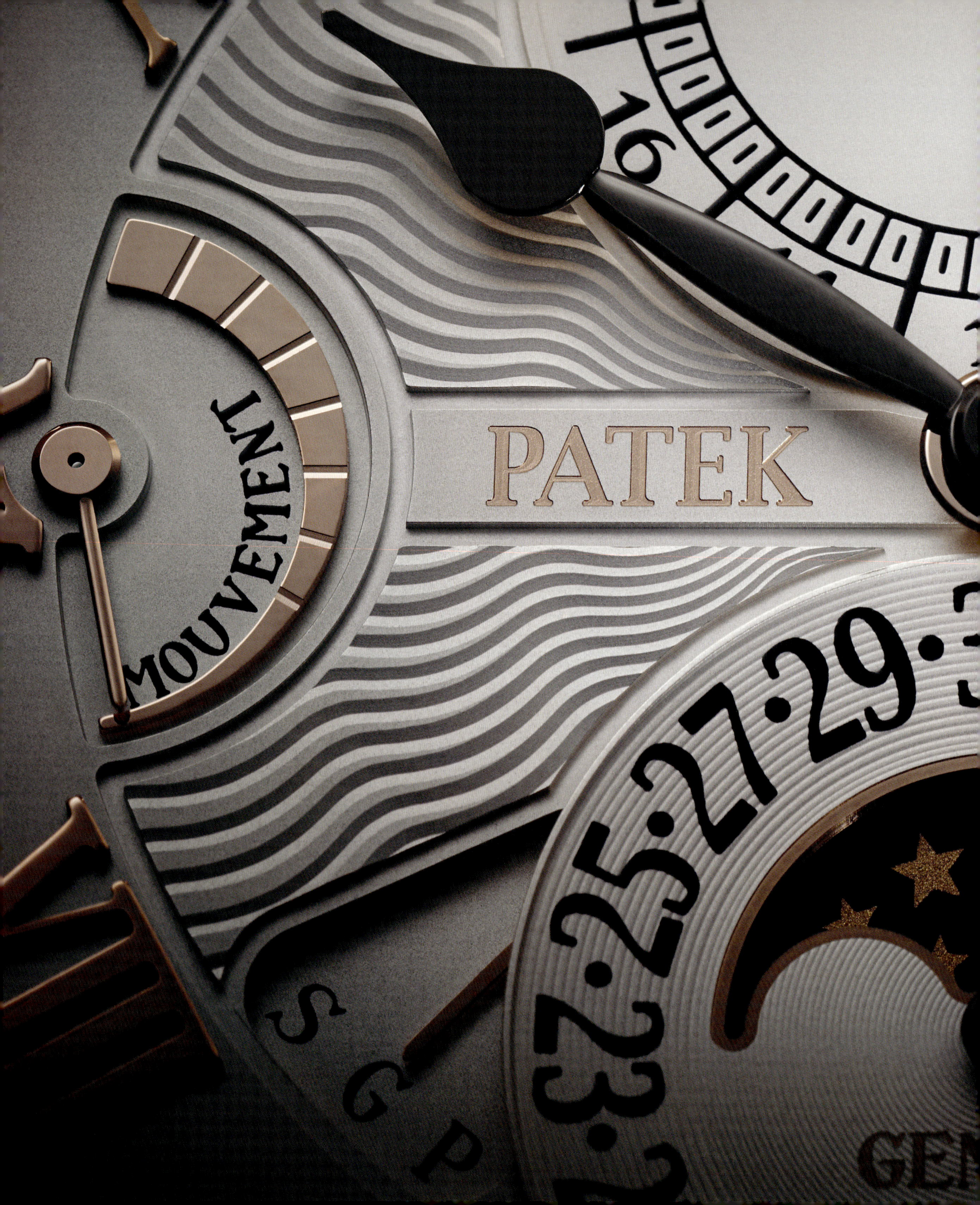
PATEK
MOUVEMENT

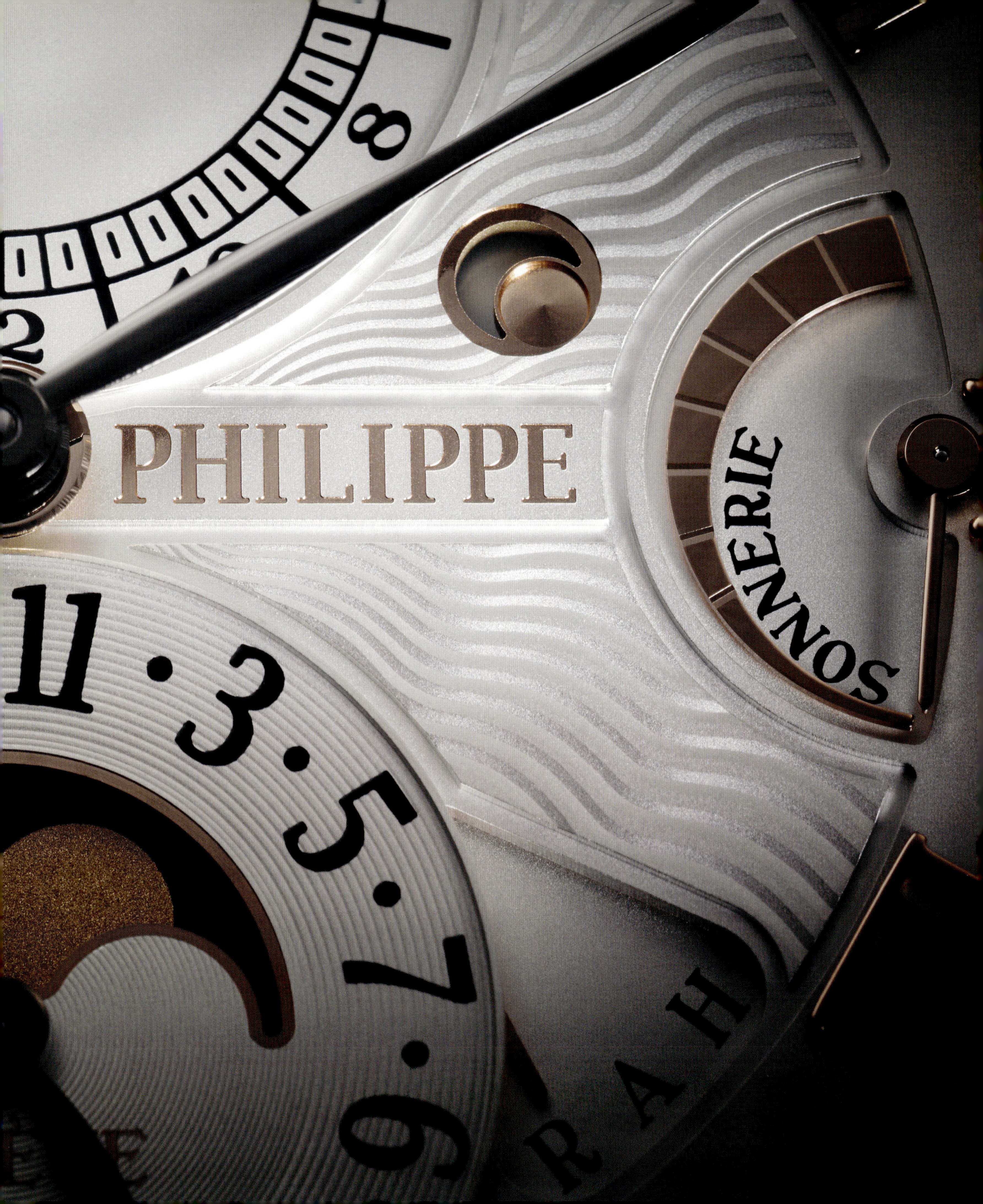
PHILIPPE
SONNERIE

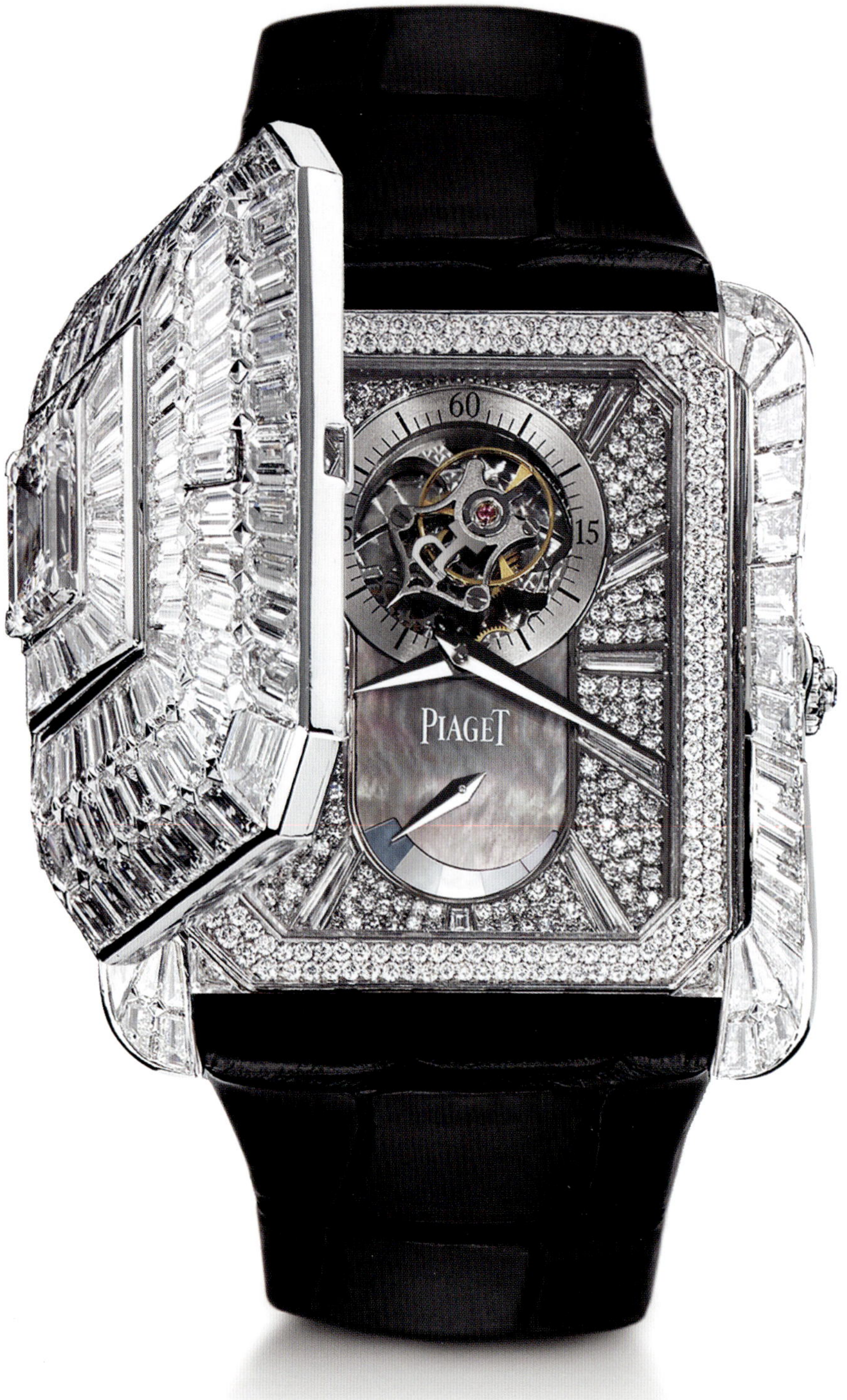

PIAGET — EMPERADOR TEMPLE

$ 3 300 000

Being one of the most expensive timepieces in the world, the Emperador Temple, by Swiss watchmaker Piaget, is truly about the worship of diamonds. The design of the timepiece could be considered an exercise in fitting the largest number of large diamonds into the space of a wristwatch, as diamonds are literally stacked into a pyramid over the dials.

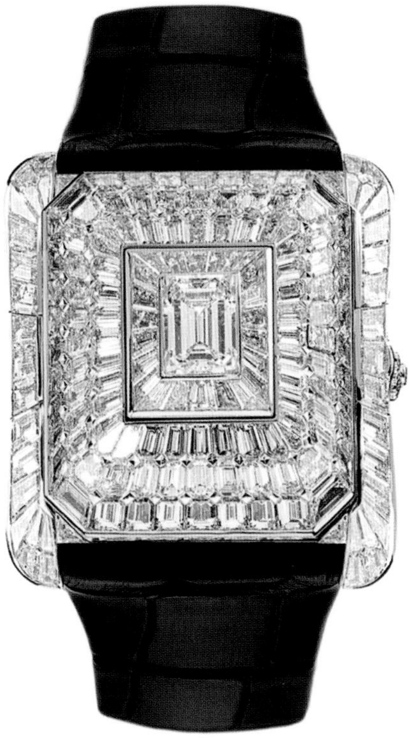

One interpretation of the watch's "Temple" name is the clear architectural connection the design has to ziggurat temples built by the ancient Mesopotamians. The main dial on the watch is covered with a hinged section that produces the pyramid-like structure when closed. The watch has no visible dial whatsoever unless one of the two available sections is opened.

Underneath all the diamonds is Piaget's Emperador watch design. A rectangle with a slight hourglass shape, the Emperador serves as a base on which an intricate array of diamonds are carefully set. Piaget uses a range of cuts on various parts of the Emperador Temple case. Using mostly large invisibly-set baguette-cut stones, the main and peripheral dials are decorated with smaller brilliant-cut stones. Topping the watch off (literally) is the largest diamond on the watch, which is emerald-cut. Tahitian mother-of-pearl is used on the two watch dials.

Watches with closing or hidden dials are often referred to as "secret" watches because only the wearer can see the time. They were originally developed for women, as it was once considered un-ladylike to wear a timepiece at an elegant social function. The Emperador Temple was probably built for a man, making it an exceptionally rare form of secret watch. Even rarer, is the fact that it has two dials. The larger of the two dials displays the time, with visible tourbillon, and power reserve indicator; it uses a Piaget-made ultra-thin mechanical movement.

A smaller and arguably more feminine dial sits atop the diamond stack, revealed behind its own distinct opening. The Emperador Temple watch case contains over 860 diamonds and is matched to a specially designed diamond bracelet that contains another 350 baguette-cut diamonds. The time and expense required to choose and set these diamonds apparently prompted Piaget to produce just one piece, and it was reportedly sold very quickly after its release in 2010.

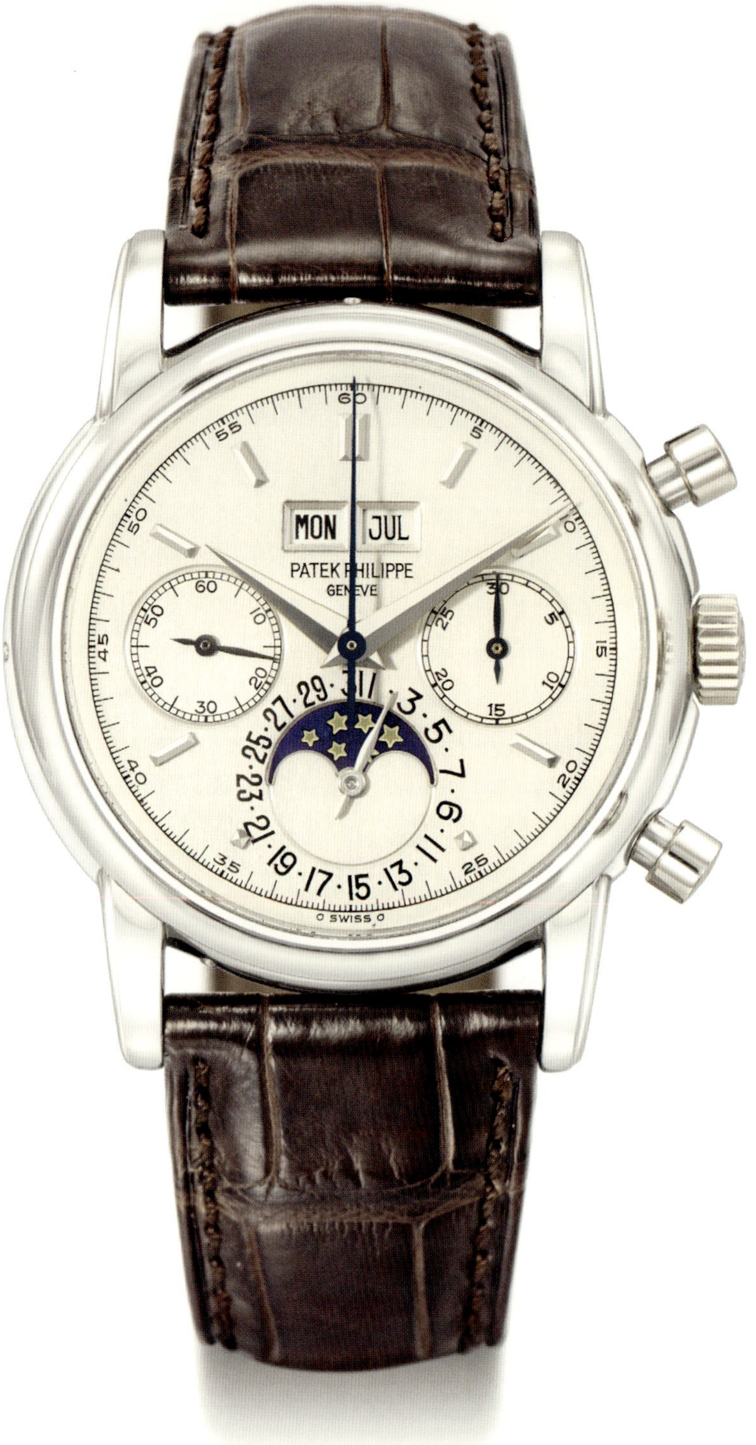

PATEK PHILIPPE – RÉFÉRENCE 2499/100P

$ 3 637 844*

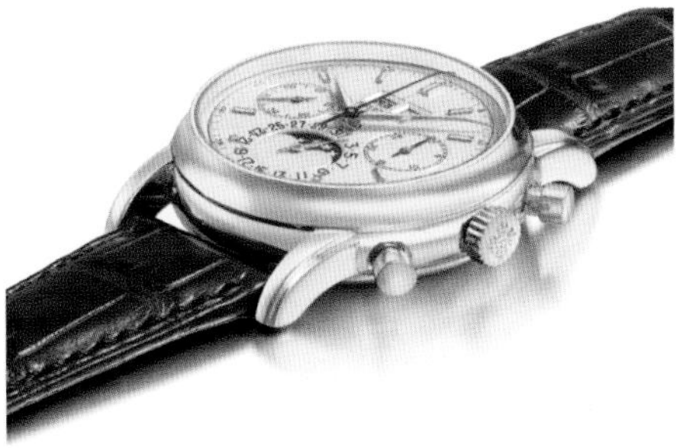

In about 1985, Patek Philippe completed its commercial production of the reference 2499 timepiece collection. A flagship model for the brand, it was considered the pinnacle of style and complication, for a brand that served gentlemen traditional mechanical watches, of high technical esteem. The 2499, more specifically the 2499/100 for this piece, was in official production for an incredibly long time, but relatively few pieces were actually made. Patek Philippe began production of the 2499 in 1951 but less than 350 total watches were made by mid 1980s.

Patek Philippe decided to do something special with the final two 2499 pieces. Watch collectors tend to be extremely interested in case materials, and the 2499 was mostly produced in 18k yellow gold. In fact, historically, Patek Philippe produced most of its high-complication timepieces in "non-white precious metals" such as 18k white gold or platinum. No commercially produced platinum 2499 watches were ever made, but in 1987 Patek Philippe produced two such pieces of the 2499/100, that were, for unknown reasons, intended to remain within the company.

However, soon afterwards, it was decided that one of the two watches should be auctioned off to be in the hands of a serious Patek Philippe collector; the other would remain in a Patek Philippe museum. In 1989, the platinum-cased 2499 watch was sold to a European collector, for just over $250,000. In the 1990s, the watch changed hands again, and in the early 2000s the piece was then bought by musician Eric Clapton, a known watch collector. Based on Clapton's ownership of the watch, it was then generally referred to as the "Patek Philippe 2499 Eric Clapton".

Clapton owned the platinum 2499 watch for about a decade, until it was placed on auction one more time. It was not thought, by the collector community, that the "Eric Clapton watch" would find its way back to the auction block when it was offered once again in 2012 – only the second time since its original purchase. At that point in the watch's history, it was widely considered one of the most valued and important Patek Philippe timepieces of the modern era.

A huge character was attached to the watch, not only for its very rare case material, but also because of its design and complicated movement, which included a perpetual calendar as well as chronograph; yet only seasoned collectors would know of its existence, or of its relative value. To the untrained eye, many Patek Philippe timepieces can look similar; however, minor differences between two watches can result in wide differences in value. Collectors interested in timepieces at this level are looking for incredibly small details that can make a huge difference in value. The 2499/100 watch in platinum sold for 3,443,000 Swiss Francs in Geneva in 2012, which was actually midway between its 2,500,000 - 4,000,000 Swiss Francs estimated price.

* Sold at auction for CHF3,443,000 at Christie's, Geneva in November 2012.

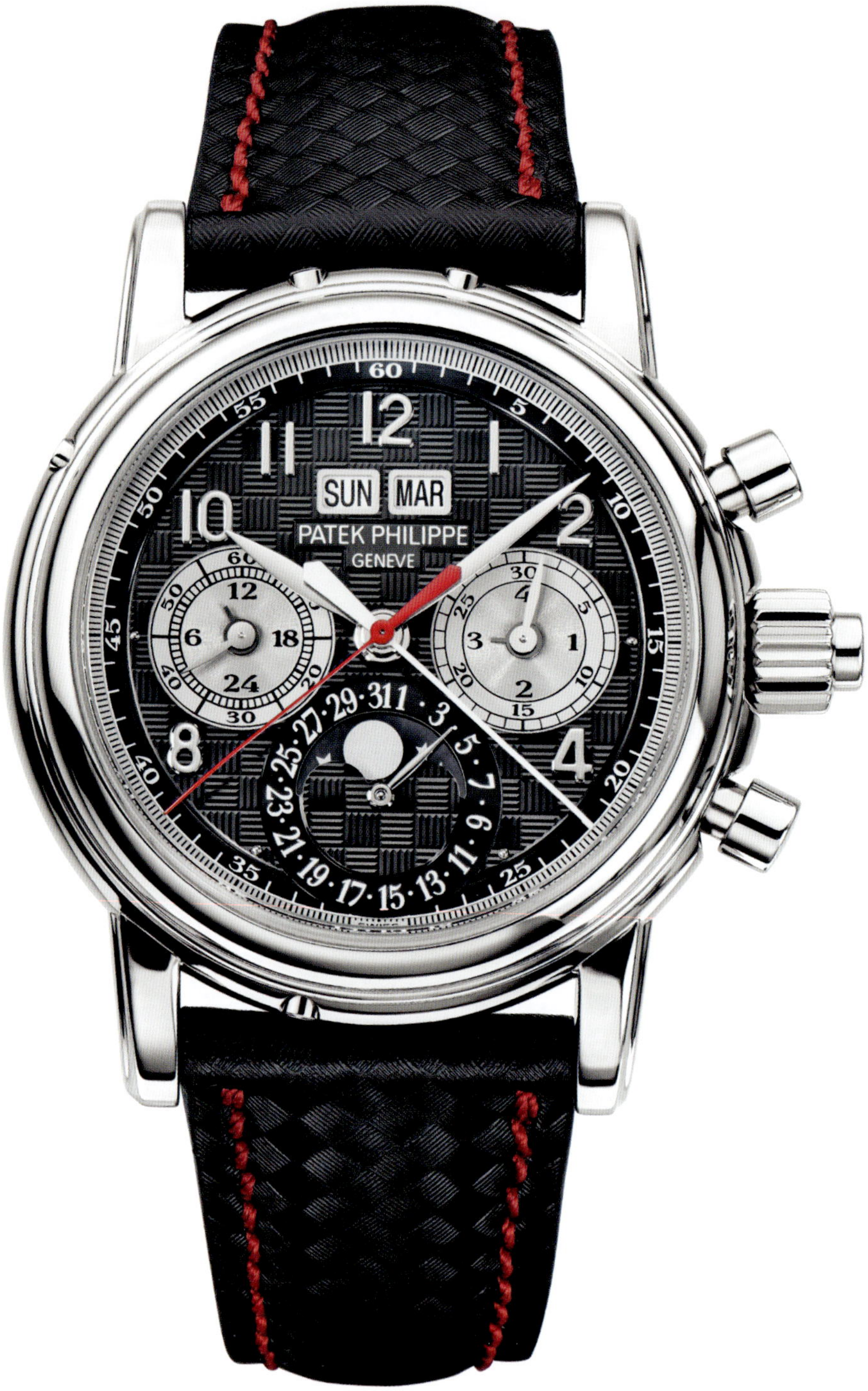

PATEK PHILIPPE — 5004T FOR ONLY WATCH 2013

$ 3985 067*

It has been well-established, at auctions around the world that one-of-a-kind Patek Philippe watches can be extremely valuable. This fact even applies to new Patek Philippe timepieces, in addition to vintage models. In the high-end watch market, as in other luxury markets, vintage goods typically fair better at auction than do brand new ones. One theory for this is that older items have had the benefit of time to prove their value and desirability, whereas new items have not yet been proved to be timeless or of lasting value.

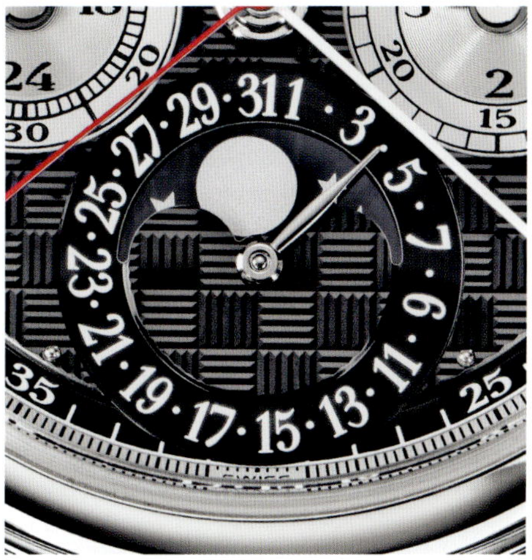

In 2013, a newly made "piece unique" (one-of-a-kind) Patek Philippe watch sold at a charity auction in Monaco for €2,950,000. Known as the Ref. 5004T, the sale of the watch was an almost guaranteed spectacle, while the auction itself was not at all a typical event. Patek Philippe produced the watch especially for the auction series known as "Only Watch". Held every other year, Only Watch requests brands to donate timepieces that will be auctioned for the benefit of a medical charity. Even though the brands must donate the items, Only Watch asks that each piece is either totally unique or the first piece in a limited edition series.

Patek Philippe completed the commercial series of the famed 5004 watches a couple of years before the 2013 Only Watch auction. That meant that no new 5004 watches could be purchased. Unique to this "after series" model was the dial design, strap, and case material. Even the smaller differences on a unique Patek Philippe watch can make it extremely valuable. Typically produced in a precious metal, this 5004T model was produced in a titanium case.

Up to 2013 Patek Philippe has never produced a commercially sold watch in titanium. Only the 5004T, and a handful of other watches destined for auction sale, have been produced in the light-weight strong metal. The 5004T also has a remarkably sporty strap, and distinctive dial that was unlike anything anyone had seen before on a 5004 or any other Patek Philippe watch.

The 5004 was a prime example of a desirable, complicated Patek Philippe grand complication watch. A dream movement for many collectors, the mechanism inside the watch contains a perpetual calendar with Moon-phase indicator, as well as a split second (rattrapante) chronograph – all in a typically clean and legible Patek Philippe style. By modern standards, that 5004T was not even a particularly sizeable watch; at 36.7mm wide, it was smaller than the average men's watch at the time it was sold.

The combination of uniqueness, titanium case material, and distinctive styling, helped convince collectors that this Patek Philippe was not only valuable at the time it was sold, but would also be a valuable watch in the future. Few, if any brands other than Patek Philippe, can command that sense of confidence and demand in a market-untested new watch.

* Sold at auction for €2,950,000 at Only Watch Auction (Antiquorum), Monaco in September 2013.

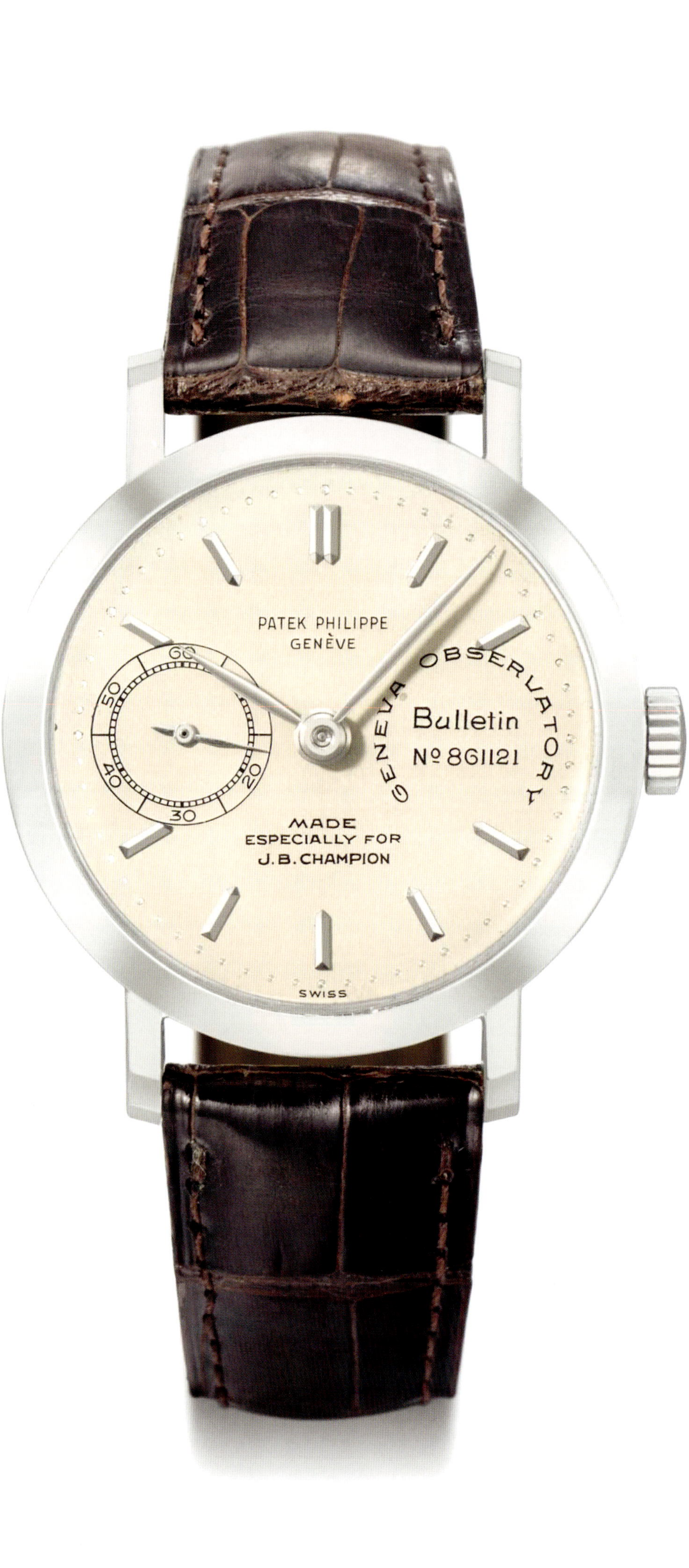
PATEK PHILIPPE
GENÈVE
GENEVA OBSERVATORY
Bulletin
№ 861121
MADE
ESPECIALLY FOR
J.B. CHAMPION
SWISS

PATEK PHILIPPE – J.B. CHAMPION PLATINUM OBSERVATORY CHRONOMETER

$ 3 990 624*

UNLIKE MOST WATCHES, THIS PIECE WAS PRODUCED VIA SPECIAL REQUEST, AS OPPOSED TO FOR A PLANNED COMMERCIAL PRODUCTION.

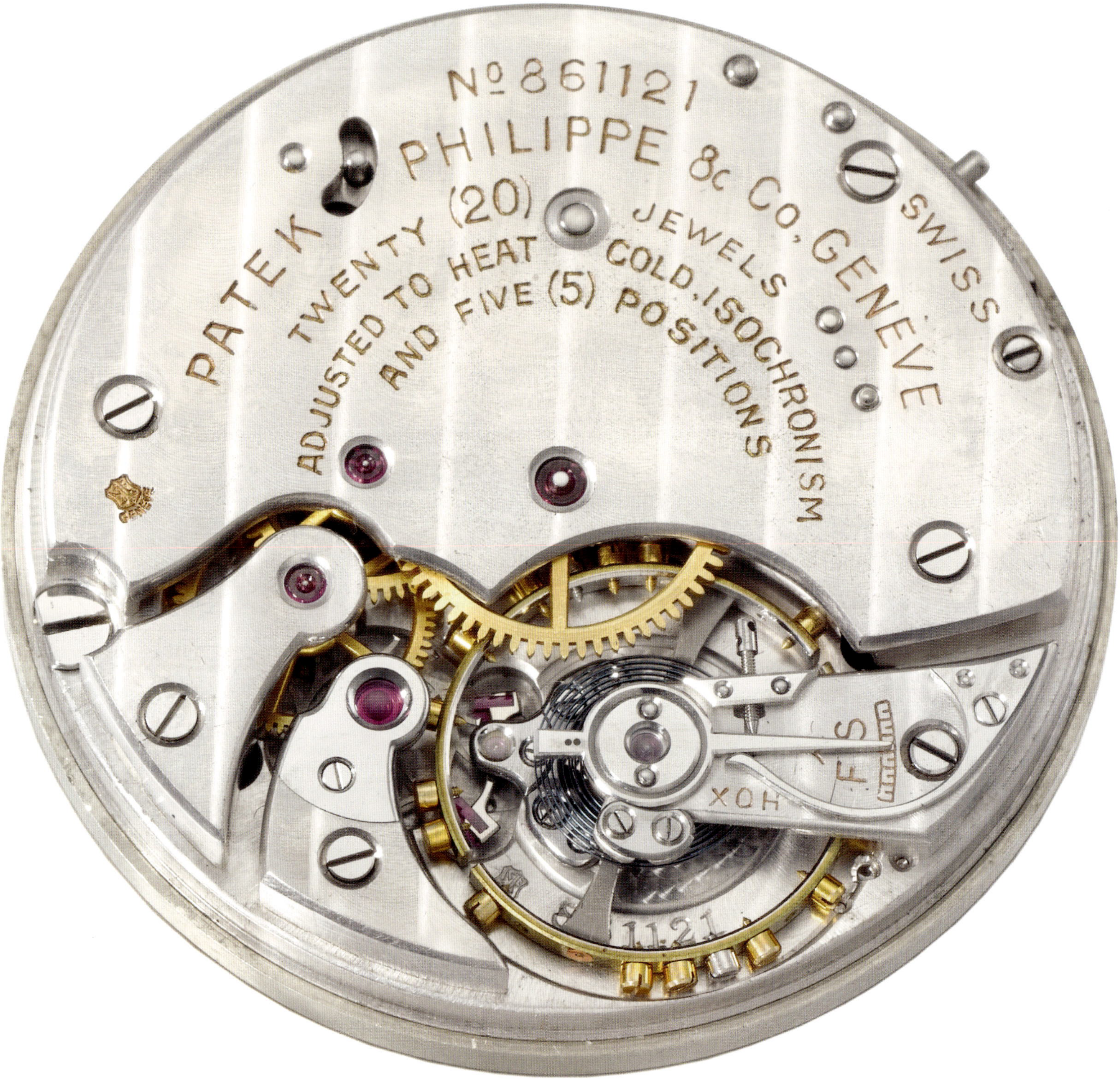
№ 861121
PATEK PHILIPPE & Co, GENEVE
SWISS
TWENTY (20) JEWELS
ADJUSTED TO HEAT COLD, ISOCHRONISM
AND FIVE (5) POSITIONS

The unrivalled champion at achieving high prices at auction for their watches, is Patek Philippe. Their rarest vintage watches fetch not so small fortunes and, as of 2013, their most valuable wristwatch ever sold at auction is a unique piece they originally sold in 1952 to a collector named J.B. Champion.

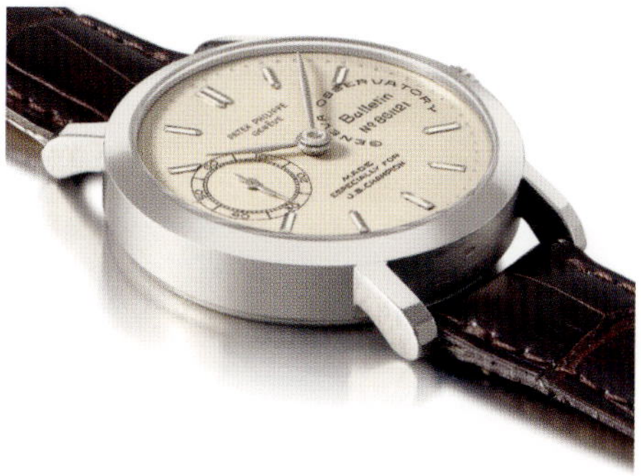

It is easy to consider the almost $4 million sum outstanding, given the simplicity of the watch and its relatively demure nature. For collectors, however, this "Observatory Chronometer" not only represents so many reasons why rare Patek Philippe timepieces are valuable, but also encompasses a range of desirable traits sought-after in rare fine timepieces.

Unlike most watches, this piece was produced via special request, as opposed to for a planned commercial production; it is known to be the second Patek Philippe that American lawyer and watch collection J.B. Champion purchased. A stickler for ultra-precision, he wanted a timepiece that was as accurate as possible. What better movement to use than one Patek Philippe produced specially for an accuracy competition?

The Geneva Observatory held competitions, where watchmakers would submit specially made movements that competed for the most accurate timing results. These "chronometer" movements were rare and given extra design and assembly attention. This particular movement was produced as a series of only 30 pieces, and only two of those were ever actually cased into a wristwatch. This was probably only done after a favoured customer would beckon the brand to do so.

J.B. Champion managed to convince Patek Philippe to produce a wristwatch that was as accurate as possible, and contained a special type of movement never intended for a commercial timepiece. Cased in platinum, the watch arrived with a matching platinum bracelet and unique dial, probably designed to Champion's wishes. No other such Patek Philippe dials are known to exist, adding to the allure and mystique of the piece.

In addition to referencing the Geneva Observatory chronometry competition, the dial also bears the resolute identifying phrase that the watch was "Made Especially For J.B. Champion". Apparently the watch satisfied Mr. Champion's need for accuracy so well that he later ordered a second dial – a more formally-themed face with diamond, as opposed to 18k white gold hour markers – that a watchmaker could swap in as the owner needed.

The timepiece represents a unique experience by one collector, with what is today one of the most desirable watchmakers in the world. Custom or bespoke watches tend to fare better at auction due to their increased rarity, and this watch is even more unique because its owner was known as a passionate and dedicated watch lover. The combination of rare elements and the nature of the collector, in addition to the watch being absolutely unique, resulted in a formula that allowed the J.B. Champion Platinum Observatory Chronometer to be the most valuable Patek Philippe wristwatch ever sold at auction.

* Sold at auction for CHF3,779,000 at Christie's, Geneva in November 2012.

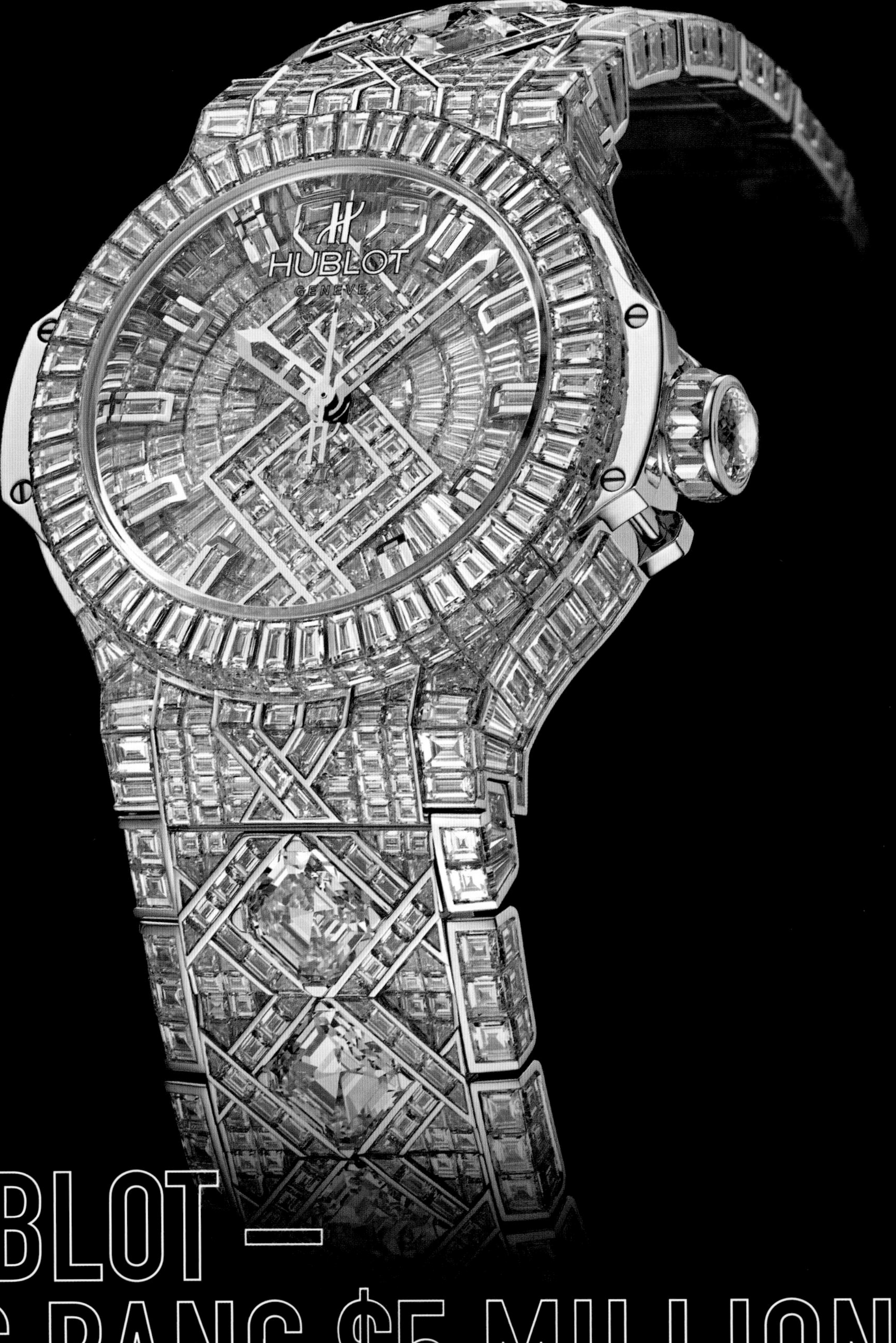

HUBLOT — BIG BANG $5 MILLION

$ 5 000 000

A couple of years before the 2012 release of this $5,000,000 timepiece, CEO of Hublot Jean-Claude Biver wanted to wow the world by producing a watch priced at an even one million US dollars. Based on the brand's ubiquitously known Big Bang watch collection, the $1,000,000 watch was a success during a time when price shock was a valued commodity in luxury watches. Just a single Big Bang $1 Million timepiece was produced, and Hublot later followed up with another version priced around $3,000,000. The trilogy perhaps ends with a timepiece that is hard to beat. It is the Big Bang $5 Million, and it sums up what people either love or hate about fully diamond-decorated luxury items.

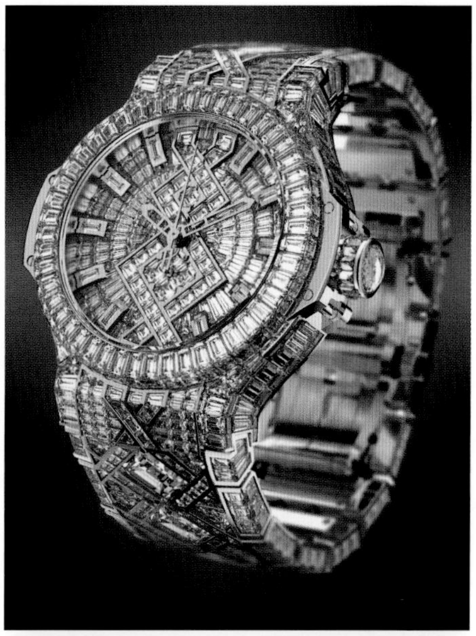

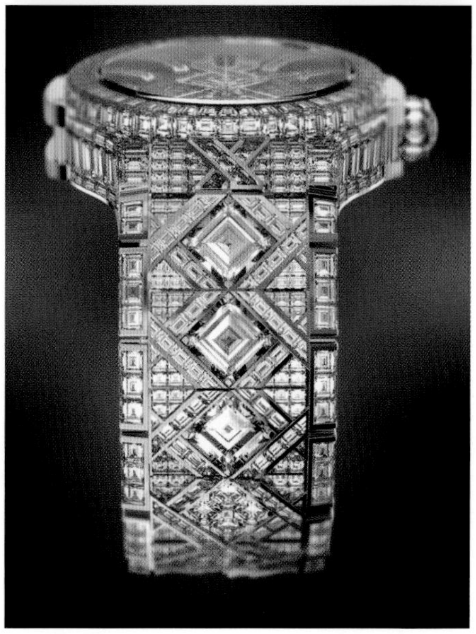

It is easy to dismiss a luxury product covered in shiny precious stones as unsophisticated or simple. Taste aside, the process of producing diamond intensive watches is highly involved. The trick is to arrange the available diamonds in such a way that appears aesthetically pleasing, and symmetrical. With diamonds one is talking about natural objects, so finding those with colour and size similarities is challenging. That was especially true in a watch that uses 1,282 distinct stones.

For the Big Bang $5 Million, Hublot decided to begin with a design, rather than see what diamonds it had available. Often, skilled jewellers will begin, not with the notion of a final design, but by seeing the stones they have available, and working from there. Hublot decided to take the far more difficult route, by designing a version of their Big Bang that would incorporate diamonds all over the case, dial, and bracelet, but in a manner that emphasised a range of unique shapes and patterns. The resulting design was admittedly art-deco and interesting, but ended up requiring a huge variety of stones, some of them quite large.

According to Hublot, it took 14 months to complete the watch, which involved a team of 12 diamond cutters and five diamond setters working full time on the project. Hublot needed to source diamonds from around the world, which included six rare three carat emerald-cut stones. In total, the Hublot Big Bang $5 Million contains over 100 carats of diamonds on the 18k white gold case and bracelet. A totally unique creation, it will be surprising if Hublot (or anyone) attempts to top it.

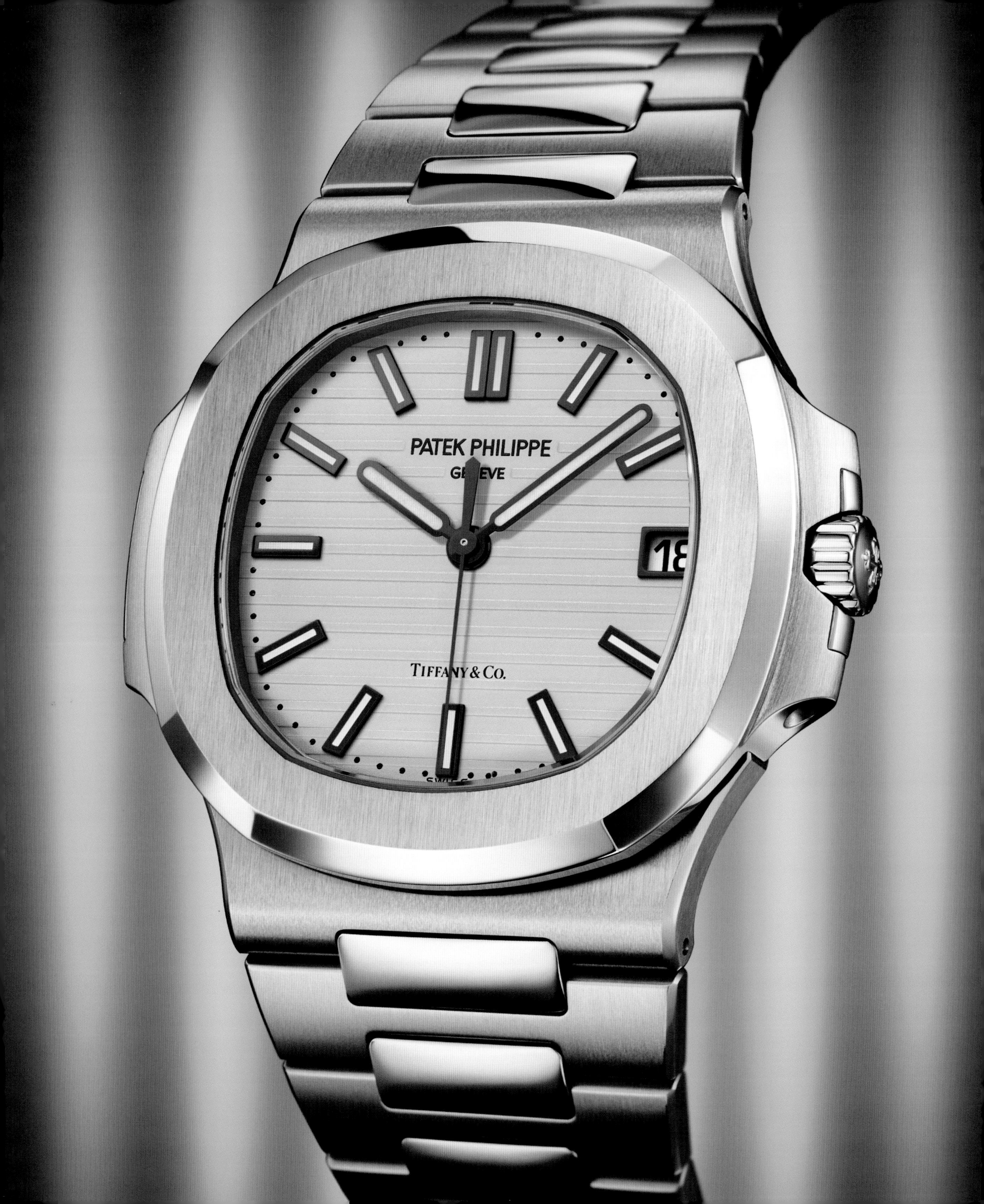
PATEK PHILIPPE
TIFFANY & Co.
18

PATEK PHILIPPE — NAUTILUS REFERENCE 5711/1A-018 "TIFFANY & CO."

$ 6500 000

BY MAKING THE NAUTILUS "TIFFANY & CO." WATCHES AVAILABLE TO ONLY HIGH-PROFILE CELEBRITIES, INTEREST IN THE NAUTILUS COLLECTION OVERALL WAS TRIGGERED, CAUSING BUYER FRENZY.

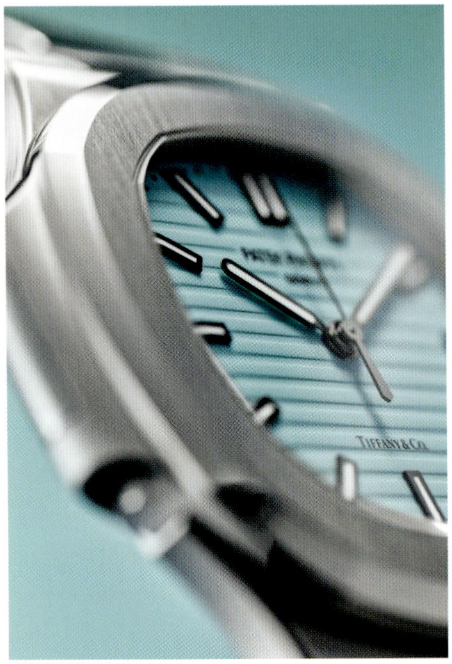

As the production of Patek Philippe's famed Nautilus Reference 5711 watches wound down to a close in the year 2022, the final versions of the product-model generation experienced a level of consumer hype that sent market prices absolutely soaring. The most illustrative example of this phenomenon was the final auction price received for the very first piece of this limited edition 170-piece Patek Philippe Nautilus Reference 5711/1A-018 "Tiffany & Co." set, which was about 125 times its retail price of around $52,000.

What is special about this limited-edition Patek Philippe Nautilus, is that it is one of the rare watches to visually celebrate the historic relationship between watchmaker Patek Philippe and American luxury retailer Tiffany & Co. (since bought out by French multinational LVMH), who has been a Patek Philippe authorised dealer for a number of years. The Nautilus 5711 "Tiffany & Co." watch was produced with the distinctive "Tiffany blue" colour dial, along with the corresponding branding of both companies on the watch face.

Leading up to the Phillips auction of the first piece of the 170 limited-edition watch set, Patek Philippe Nautilus watches were already in such high demand that market costs for most of them vastly exceeded retail prices. By making the Nautilus "Tiffany & Co." watches available to only high-profile celebrities, interest in the Nautilus collection overall was triggered, causing buyer frenzy.

The Nautilus itself is a watch collection that dates back to the early 1970s. At the time, it was designed as a high-end sports watch for well-to-do gentlemen eager for a suitably durable timepiece to wear during activities such as boating or swimming. Patek Philippe commissioned the renowned designer Gérald Genta to conceive the Nautilus for them – the same person who came up with the traditional diving-helmet themed Royal Oak for competitor firm Audemars Piguet.

This version of the Nautilus has a 40mm-wide case and bracelet in steel, and features a time-only automatic movement. Its retail price had already made it one of the most expensive steel watches of its type available, but consumer popularity and low production numbers coalesced with other market forces to raise prices to shocking levels.

Products like this are typically reserved for Patek Philippe's most esteemed clients, who nearly always get first dibs. For this reason, the "public" availability of brand-new pieces such as this model – even at auction – was inevitably going to lead to competition among consumers. The outcome for the buyer? An incredibly decent luxury watch, suitable for daily wear – with a lot of bragging rights to go with it.

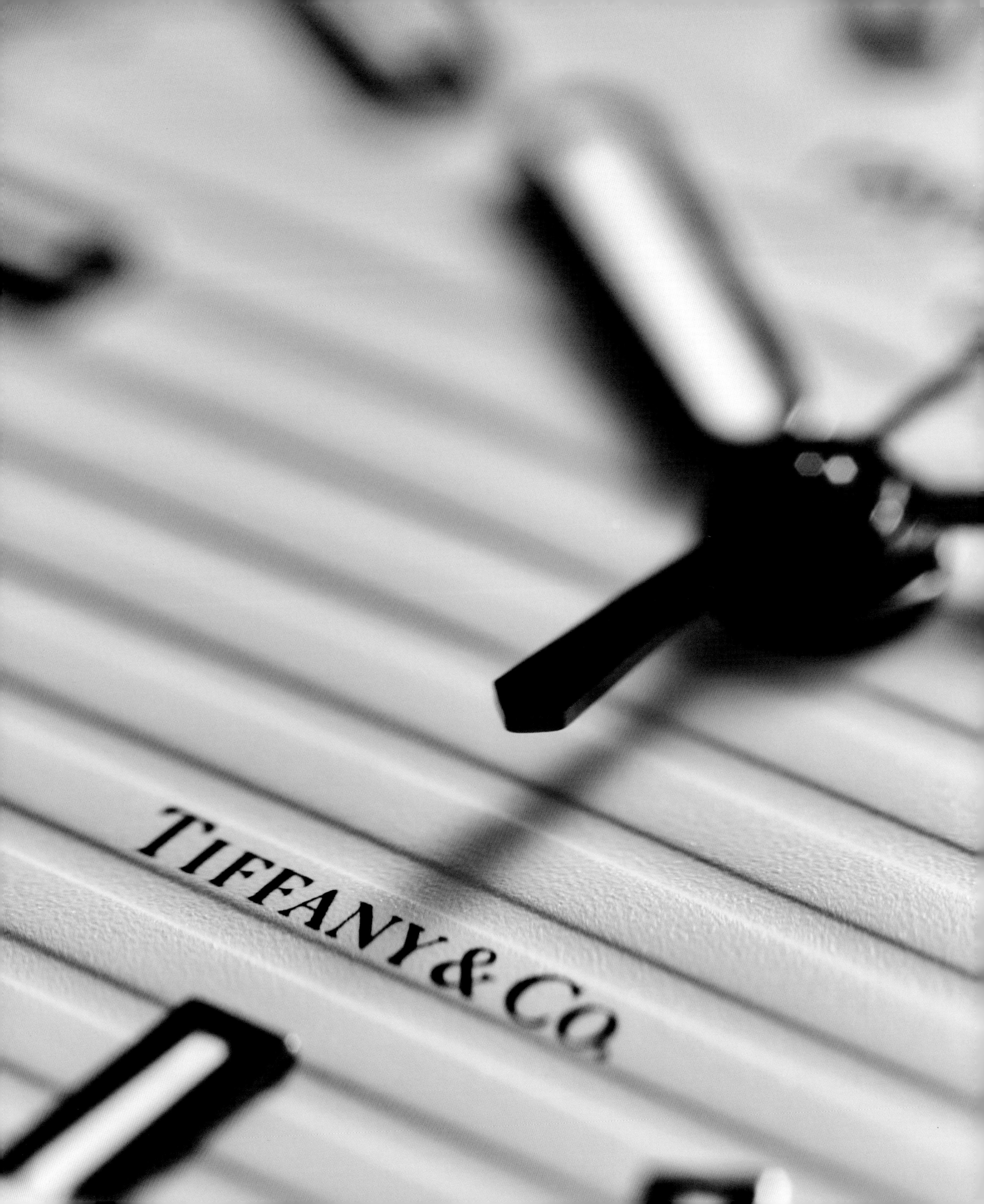
TIFFANY&CO.

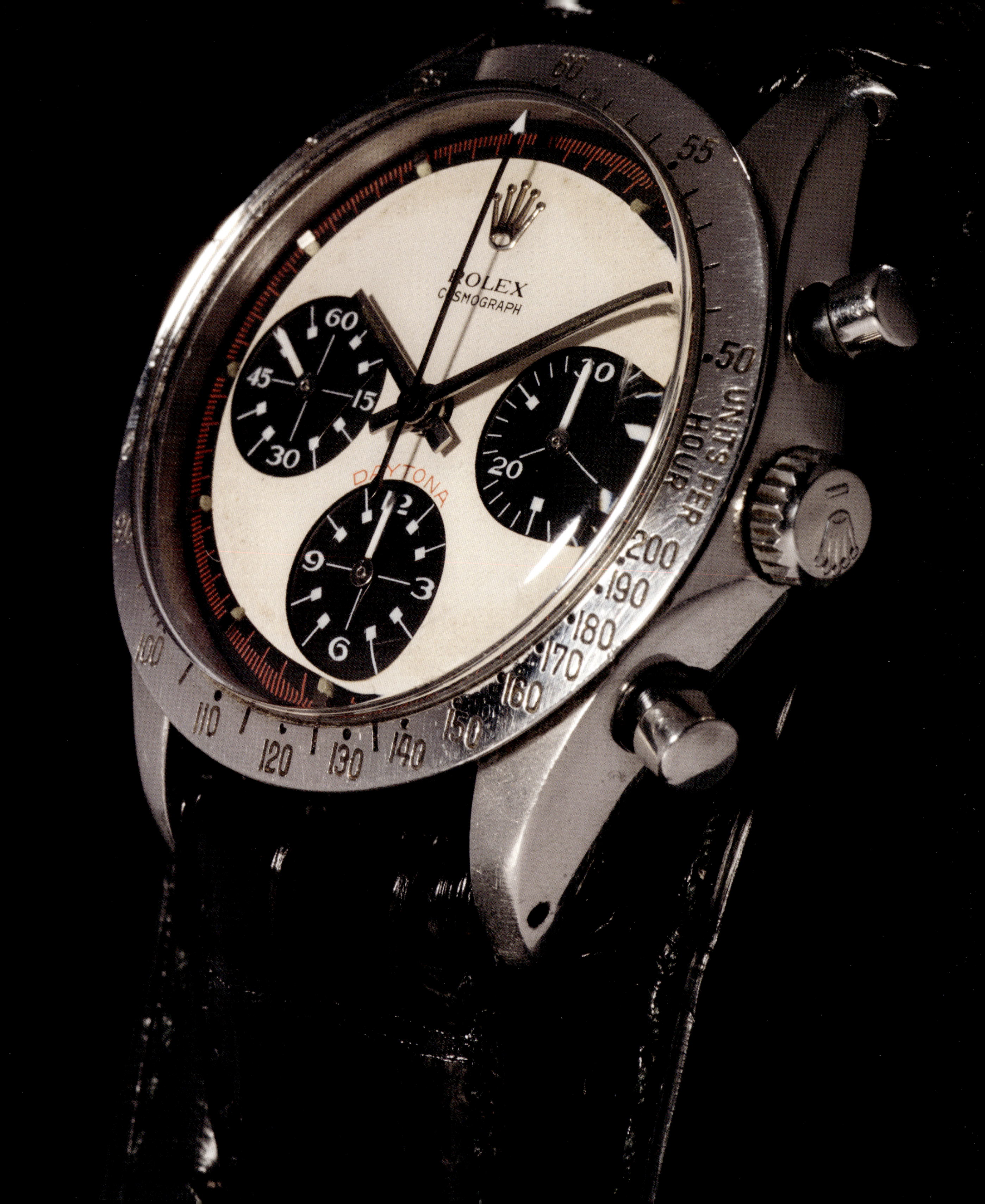
ROLEX
UNITS PER HOUR

ROLEX — DAYTONA REFERENCE 6239 "PAUL NEWMAN"

$ 17 752 500

"DRIVE CAREFULLY ME" WAS THE BESPOKE ENGRAVING REQUESTED BY HIS WIFE, JOANNE WOODWARD, THAT MARKED THE CASE BACK OF THIS PARTICULAR ROLEX MODEL, CLEARLY ADDING TO ITS PROVENANCE AND APPEAL.

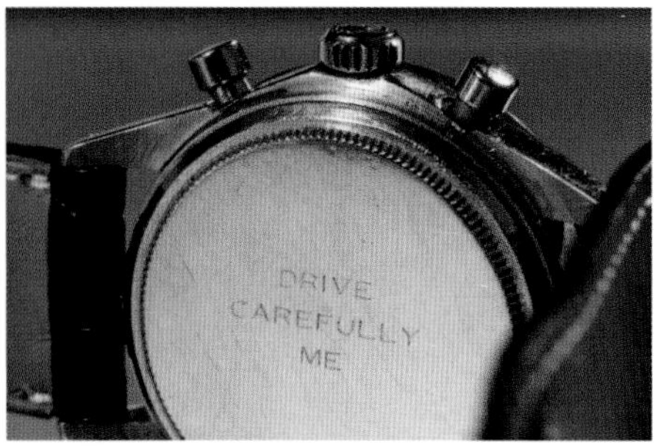

Famous owners have made select vintage Rolex sports watches particular favourites at auction due to both their rarity and provenance. This particular Rolex Daytona Reference 6239 from the late 1960s was owned by late American actor, driver, personality and activist, Paul Newman, and is perhaps the most valuable example to date. In 2017, at a highly publicised auction in New York City, bidder excitement from around the world saw this unique timepiece go from its anticipated roughly one million dollar estimated value to almost 18 million dollars. The astronomical sum is a testament to the interest that collectors have in both Hollywood memorabilia, horological sports-watch history, and the bragging rights that comes with owning a truly famous part of modern wristwatch enthusiast culture.

Created in steel, with an uncommon "exotic dial", this particular watch is said to be pivotal in the later popularity of the Rolex Oyster Perpetual Cosmograph Daytona (the official full name of the Rolex Daytona) collection in general. For enthusiasts, the association between Paul Newman and Rolex is so close that "Paul Newman Daytona" is a term used by collectors to reference a selection of particular historic Rolex Daytona watch dials. Paul Newman owned and wore a number of Rolex Daytona models, having been widely photographed wearing many – including this particular Reference 6239. A famous photoshoot in Italy with Newman boldly presenting the watch on his wrist is often accredited with starting the Rolex Daytona collecting spree among Italian enthusiasts which later spread to other parts of the watch-interested world.

"Drive Carefully Me" was the bespoke engraving requested by his wife, Joanne Woodward, that marked the case back of this particular Rolex model, clearly adding to its provenance and appeal. The official story behind the watch is that Paul Newman gifted the watch to a family member in 1984, where it remained until being consigned for auction years later. No doubt the potential value associated with the watch stimulated motivation to sell it – compounded by the impressive track record that vintage Rolex sports-watches have achieved at auction in the years immediately before the 2017 auction event. In addition, what makes auctions such as this unique is the reliable provenance of this timepiece. Documents and photography supporting Paul Newman's ownership and the condition of the watch had crucial roles to play in assuring buyer confidence. This is especially true in a time when excitement over extremely high prices for vintage timepieces have been known to result in not only the distortion of facts related to the history of a timepiece, but also the cosmetic and technical alternations to watches carried out in secret so as to artificially increase their perceived value. Watches such as this Rolex Daytona, once owned by Paul Newman, come along (as some would say) once in a lifetime.

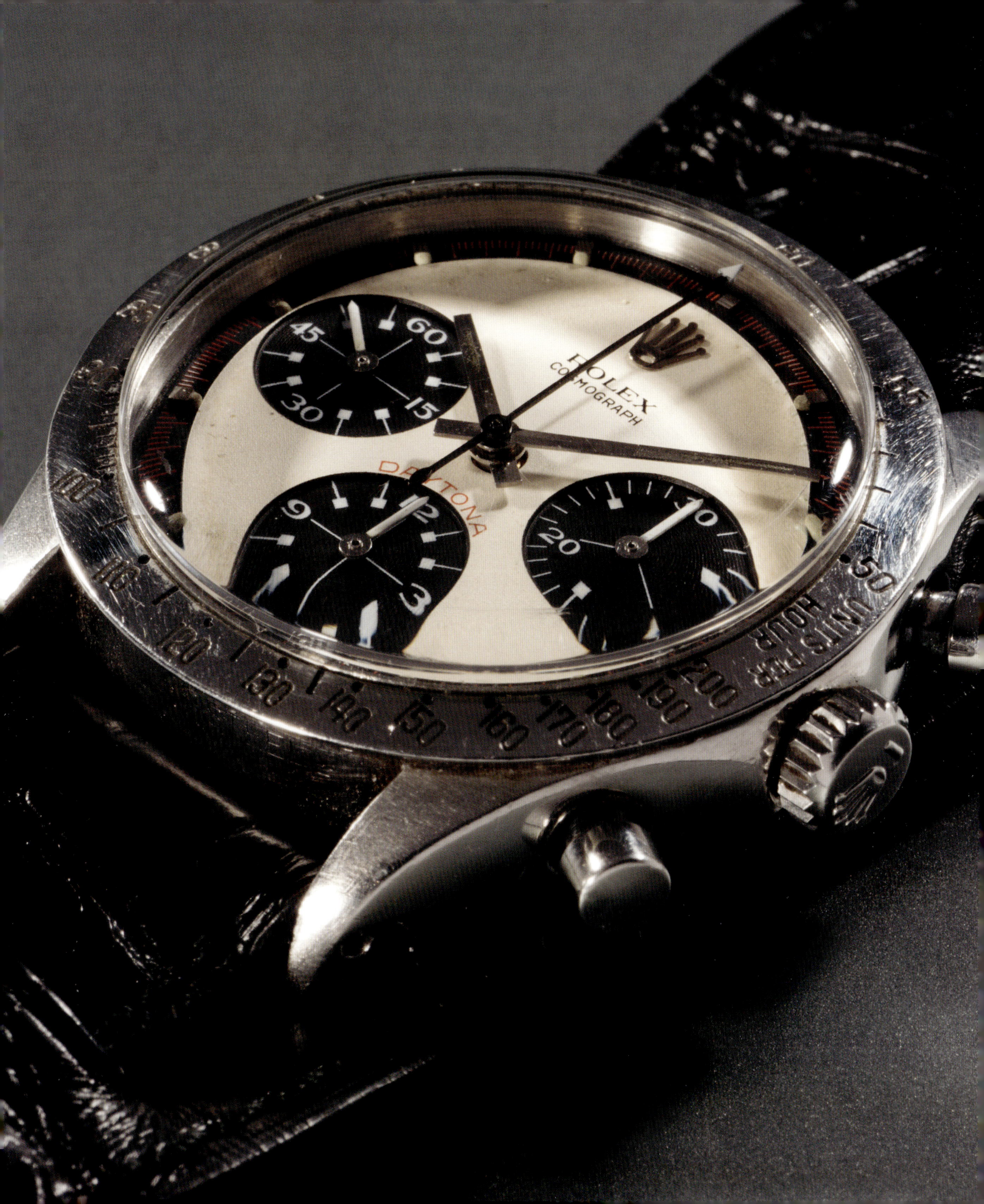
ROLEX
COSMOGRAPH
DAYTONA
UNITS PER HOUR

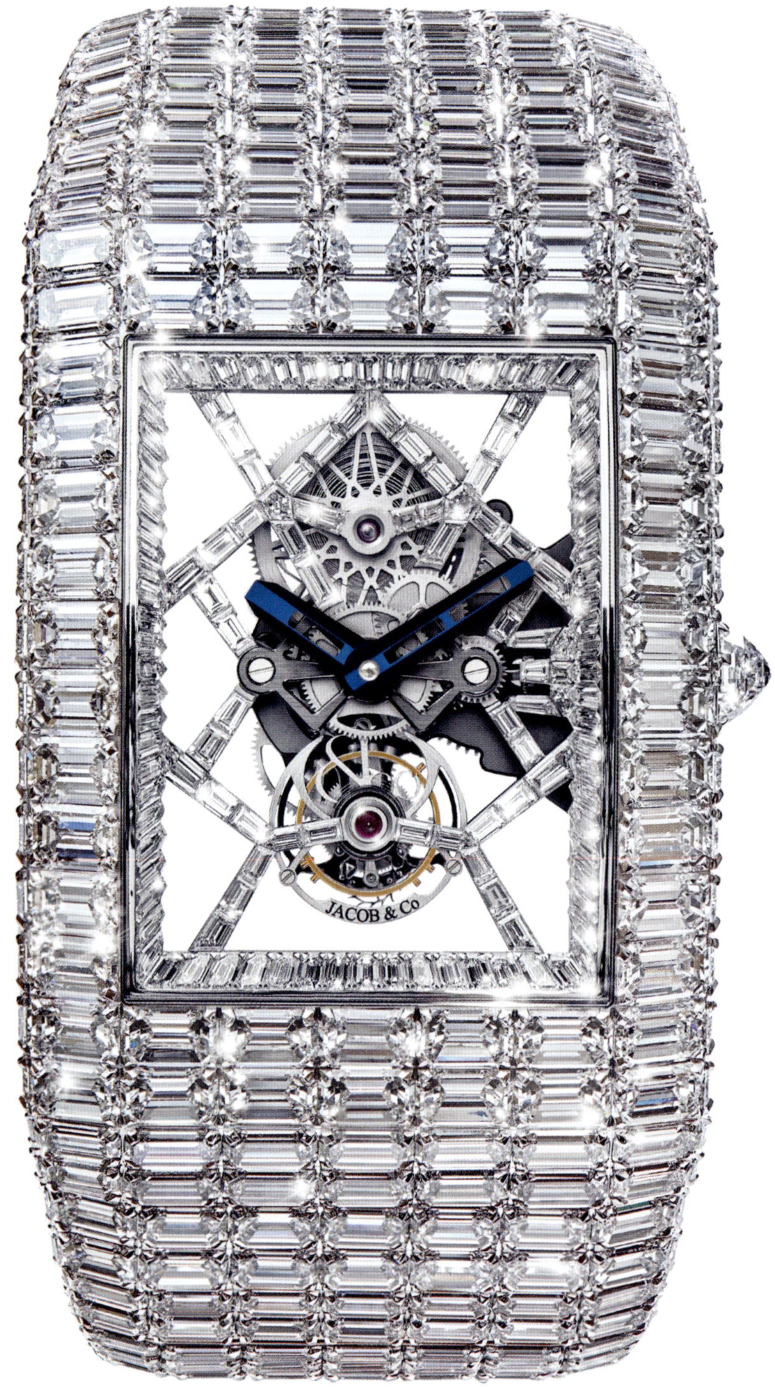

JACOB & CO. — BILLIONAIRE

$ 18 000 000

Jacob Arabo is among the few jewellers in the world who is equally well-known by serious luxury consumers as well as urban culture devotees. The success of his brand, Jacob & Co., can be attributed to not only what it produces, but who it produces items for. From musicians to world politicians, a whole host of the rich and famous have become clients of this characterful brand whose aim is to impress and awe even those who believe they have seen it all.

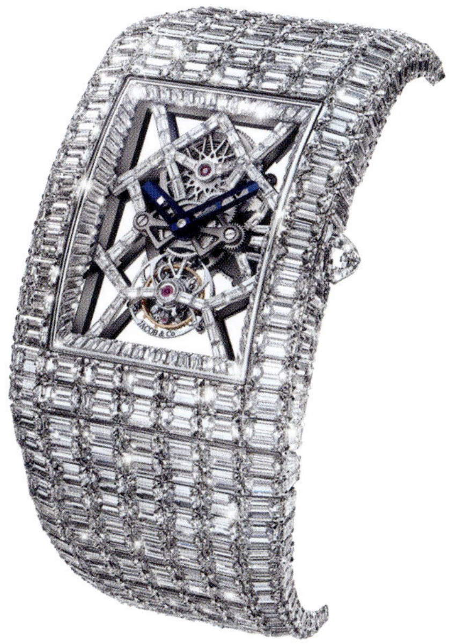

The most exclusive timepiece to date produced by Jacob & Co. is the Billionaire. The name corresponds to the Billionaire Couture fashion label formed by Flavio Briatore, a Formula One racing personality who challenged Jacob & Co. to exceed its own limits. The result is a massive bracelet made up of large carat diamonds that coalesce to house a rectangular-shaped watch dial with a tourbillon-based mechanical movement.

Hundreds of baguette-cut diamonds – sized up to three carats each – are required to produce each of the very few Billionaire watches in existence. With a full-sized bracelet, the Billionaire has approximately 260 carats of total diamond weight set into an 18k white-gold base structure. One can describe the timepiece as holding enough diamonds of engagement-ring quality to woo several dozen of the world's most eligible bachelorettes. A flamboyant and unequivocally status-defining timepiece, the Jacob & Co. Billionaire watch was internationally recognised in the news media when boxing champion Floyd Mayweather acquired one. It certainly isn't every day that a celebrity's luxury purchase makes headlines.

The Billionaire isn't for the "weak of wrist" either. Size-wise, the wide bracelet-style timepiece is a hefty 47.5mm wide and 58mm long, meaning that it will sit off the wrist of many potential wearers. As a watch, the Billionaire is remarkably legible; modern-looking blued-steel hands are prominent on the skeletonised dial that, somewhat uninspiringly, uses diamond hour markers. The manually wound movement is relatively simple save for the spinning tourbillon-style escapement, which is a hallmark feature of many ultra-high-end timepiece products. It also happens to be the shiniest, most lustrous luxury object ever created for a man's wrist.

PHOTOGRAPHIC CREDITS

The author and publisher are grateful to the individual brands for supplying the images used in this book. All images remain the copyright of the individual brand.

The author and publisher are also grateful to the following auction houses for their assistance in supplying the following images -

Pages 256, 350, 352 and 380 - Images are courtesy of Antiquorum Auctioneers
Pages 185, 342, 378 and 382 - Christie's Images Ltd. 2014
Pages 186, 264 and 275 - Images are courtesy of Sotheby's